Gamelan Gong Kebyar

Chicago Studies in Ethnomusicology
A series edited by Philip V. Bohlman and Bruno Nettl

Teruna Jaya (1998 by Ketut Madra, Peliatan, Bali)

*The Art of
Twentieth-Century
Balinese Music*

Gamelan
Gong Kebyar

Michael Tenzer

with a Foreword by Steve Reich

The University of Chicago Press / *Chicago and London*

Michael Tenzer is associate professor of music at the
University of British Columbia.

The University of Chicago Press, Chicago 60637
The University of Chicago Press, Ltd., London
© 2000 by The University of Chicago
All rights reserved. Published 2000
Printed in the United States of America

08 07 06 05 04 03 02 01 00 1 2 3 4 5

ISBN: 0-226-79281-1 (cloth)
ISBN: 0-226-79283-8 (paper)

Library of Congress Cataloging-in-Publication Data

Tenzer, Michael.
    Gamelan gong kebyar : the art of twentieth-century Balinese music / Michael Tenzer ; with a
foreword by Steve Reich.
        p.   cm. — (Chicago studies in ethnomusicology)
    Includes bibliographical references and index.
    ISBN 0-226-79281-1 (Cloth : alk. paper)
    1. Gamelan.   2. Gamelan music—History and criticism.   3. Music—Indonesia—Bali
Island—20th century—History and criticism.   I. Title.   II. Series.
    ML1251.I53T46   2000
    780'.9598'6—dc21   99-34398
                                                                                    CIP

♾ The paper used in this publication meets the minimum requirements of the
American National Standard for Information Sciences—Permanence of Paper for
Printed Library Materials, ANSI Z39.48-1992.

To Pamela Joy

Contents

Part Two: Structure in *Kebyar*

Part Three: *Kebyar* in Bali and Abroad

List of Figures

Foreword

By Steve Reich

BOOKS about non-Western music have played an important role in my life. In 1962 I first became aware of a book of transcriptions and analysis of West African music by A. M. Jones which showed me on paper what I could not understand by just listening to recordings. Music in Ghana is made of repeating patterns of different lengths superimposed so that their downbeats do not coincide. Notation and analysis showed what recordings alone could not reveal. A few years later I encountered *Music in Bali* by the Canadian musicologist and composer Colin McPhee. Though I had again listened to Balinese music on recordings, it was McPhee's book that showed me clearly, in notation and analysis, that Balinese *gamelan* music is in superimposed layers that move at widely differing speeds, from rapid sixteenth notes to long, low gong tones that may come only once every 32 or 64 beats. It is also a music, similar to but also rather different from West African, of interlocking patterns. Of additional interest to me at the time I read the McPhee book was that Balinese *gamelan* players generally do not improvise. They play compositions.

My encounter with these books did not lead me to the library but rather first to Ghana. I went there in 1970, to study the music I had encountered in Jones's book by learning how to play some of it. Later, in the summers of 1973 and 1974, I studied and played Balinese *gamelan semar pegulingan* and *gamelan gambang* at the American Society for Eastern Arts in Seattle and Berkeley. Good books of notation and analysis of non-Western music can not only clarify what one has heard in concert or on recordings but may also inspire the reader to try his or her hand at the music itself. They give a Western composer information about how a particular non-Western music is organized structurally, which may prove to be more fruitful information than just knowing superficially how the music sounds. Imitating the sound of non-Western music often leads to sitars in the rock band and other exotic effects. Knowing how a non-Western music is structured (particularly in terms of rhythm) can lead to a completely new and unforeseen use of one's own Western musical instruments, rhythmic structures, scales, and tunings. This means that books about non-Western music filled with notation and analysis as well as information about cultural context can be enormously useful to Western composers, musicians, and listeners seriously interested in world music. You are holding in your hand just such a book.

Michael Tenzer is a scholar, player, and composer of Balinese *gamelan gong kebyar* music. He says that "the more I performed Balinese compositions and composed my own, the more I was able to intuit theory from personal musical experience." This is indeed how all theory is best learned in Bali or here in the West. Our own academic rules of four-part harmonic writing derive from Bach's chorales, which sprang not from a theory but from Bach's practical composing and performing. Nor is Tenzer creating a theory that has no basis in how the Balinese themselves think about their music. As he says, "Any concepts I have generated myself—whether out of necessity or just for the sake of digging deeper—are grounded in existing Balinese theory."

Tenzer presents a thorough analysis of the rhythmic and melodic structure of the music. Aspects like the interlocking parts called *kotekan* may be of particular interest to composers drawn to working with such materials since they demonstrate centuries of expertise in this musical art. In the latter parts of the book Tenzer analyzes complete compositions in considerable detail. There are recordings on two CDs, made by Tenzer himself, that allow the reader to hear the music notated in the book. The social and religious realities in Bali and the *gamelan's* close association with them are also presented in detail.

Kebyar is twentieth-century music and it sounds that way. It is a relatively new style of music in Bali that was just beginning when McPhee was there in the 1930s and has now become dominant. It reflects the changed Balinese political/social life, which has moved from a court-oriented society to one that is a part of the Indonesian Republic. It also reflects contact that traditional Balinese musicians and composers have had with the West. As Tenzer points out, "In recent music, the composer intentionally distorts or reconfigures inherited norms of style and structure, thereby playing with and against listener expectations. In this restricted sense, *kebyar* has come to resemble the fully notated compositions of Euro-American ensemble music." In contrast to the earlier court music which was composed and performed to be a part of religious or royal occasions, *kebyar* is composed for the audience at a more Western-style secular concert. Radio broadcast and dissemination of recordings have all entered Balinese musical life, moving it closer to the musical realities we live with in the West.

Tenzer goes still further at the end of this book when he compares a recent *kebyar* composition, *gegitaan Wilet Mayura,* with works by Western composers and jazz musicians. Of course the individuality of Western composers, especially in the case of Ives (whom he discusses), is radically different from the essentially shared common practice that all Balinese music is built on. We can marvel at how elastic and open the Balinese are to innovation within their own tradition as well as to much of Western contemporary life style. There is never any doubt, however, after just a few seconds of listening to *kebyar,* that one is hearing music from Bali and nowhere else on earth. Personally, I wish the Balinese continued success in their superb ability to balance between being open to the world and maintaining their own traditions—musically, religiously, and otherwise.

It is interesting for me to write this foreword more than twenty-five years after my initial studies of Balinese music. In the late 1960s and early 1970s non-Western music was perhaps the most attractive path to restoration and innovation for a Western composer. For myself and several other composers and musicians, studying and playing Balinese, Javanese, West African, and Indian music was a way to reconnect with the musical basics—tonal center and rhythmic pulse—that had been lost in the serial and aleatoric music of the time. These musics also suggested new kinds of rhythmic organization that fired the imagination of these same composers and musicians.

Now, more than twenty-five years later, it seems that Balinese music and others have made tremendous inroads into Western musical life and, as a result, have lost their novelty for most Western composers. There are now many dozens of Balinese *gamelan* in North America. Most of these are situated in our most prestigious universities and so thousands of Western students have gained some experience of actually playing in a *gamelan*. In any large record store in America or Europe one will find a large and thriving world music department with CDs not only from Bali, Java, Africa, and India but from all over the globe. At the same time I know only a very few composers who are primarily drawing inspiration from non-Western sources at this time. Music from Bali, Java, West Africa, India, and elsewhere is now just part of the furniture. We have come to accept it as part of the classical music of the world. As composer Michael Gordon remarked, "Almost any composer born after 1950 has some familiarity with *kecak*."[1]

An earlier generation of composers like Henry Cowell, John Cage, and Lou Harrison actively studied non-Western music as something completely new and exotic. Then Terry Riley, La Monte Young, Phillip Glass, and myself studied primarily African, Balinese, and Indian music directly with teachers from those countries with very different results. Beginning with John Adams and continuing on into the younger generation of Michael Gordon, David Lang, and Michael Torke in America this music has become simply another part of the musical universe. In Europe György Ligeti has shown real interest in Central African music via his interest in the excellent work of ethnomusicologist Simha Arom. I get the feeling that for younger European composers non-Western music is also a fact of musical life.

Music in Bali has not stood still, however. Thirty years after McPhee's groundbreaking book, we can now find out from Michael Tenzer about recent musical developments. The richness and complexity of Balinese *kebyar* can be

---

1. *Kecak,* properly known as *cak* and popularly called the Monkey Chant in English, is a Balinese piece for dancers and a chorus of about 200 men singing and chanting interlocking patterns. The text is drawn from the *Ramayana* epic.

judged from the transcriptions and recordings in this book. As for its influence on the West and our influence on Bali, stay tuned.

Tenzer has lived with Balinese *kebyar* and the people who compose and play it for a long time. He knows the music and is also aware of the tensions pulling at *kebyar* and Bali itself from the outside world as well as the influence they continue to have on the West. In this book he has done a remarkable job of setting it all down for us.

Acknowledgments

IT IS auspicious to invoke the turtle's wisdom, so I begin with an epigrammatic fable. Once a young sea turtle surfaced for a breath after its first unaccompanied swim in the depths, and was astonished to discover that its head and neck had passed through a single golden ring afloat on the waters. When I came upon Balinese music at age eighteen, out of all the world's music, I was akin to the turtle. Snug like the ring, *gamelan* fit me, but my encounter with it was as unexpected as the ocean is wide.

Such serendipity is wasted unless harnessed toward pursuit of self-knowledge. One path I followed led to this book. In writing one distills one's self into the pages, and is reciprocally reshaped by them. All told the chapters and figures took about four years to complete, although the ideas germinated for at least twenty-three, and the sensibility traces back farther. But treading the path is something collaborative. It is ritual to thank people and institutions behind the scenes, but one feels strongly impelled to do so and hard-pressed to evoke the sentiment and sincerity attached to the deed.

I am least able to convey this to Pam, my perfect blend of fantasy and reality. Nor can Molly and Maya—whose debuts in 1990 and 1994 put everything in perspective—ever really know.

I was essentially unprepared when I first went to Bali in 1977, had no intellectual distance, and was consumed by the music. The fever brought me sympathetic attention. I thank my first teacher, Nyoman Sumandhi, his wife the memorable dancer Putu Sutiati, and their family, for meeting and holding my gaze. I was also helped then by Madé Bandem and Wayan Gandera. Mantle Hood, Edward Herbst, Andy Toth, and Willie Ruff arranged these contacts. In 1978–79 Madé Lebah, impish humor intact more than four decades after teaching Colin McPhee, showed me drumming of the court *gamelan* and the music of Lotring. In 1982 my mentor Wayan Tembres (*hidup-mati saya*) took me everywhere, got my drumming fingers really moving, laid out a feast of rhythms, and arranged for my first *gamelan* compositions to be played in Bali. Tembres is a *mensch* by any cultural classification. Spending that year with him and his acolytes from Pindha—among them Ketut Kumpul, Ketut Canderi, and the German composer Dieter Mack, then living in Saba—provided a treasured education.

Studying composition at Berkeley I knew no distinction between field and home because of seven halcyon years with Gamelan Sekar Jaya. Wayan Suweca, Rachel Cooper, and I founded the group in 1979, and the fiery Suweca toiled for two years making us into a real *gamelan*. Since then Balinese have been in residence almost continuously. As this goes to press the ensemble has hundreds of performances and three tours to Indonesia behind it, and is celebrating its twentieth anniversary. I thank all the members during that time for building our community, especially Rachel, Rucina Ballinger, Jim and Maddie Hogan, Tom and Bea Deering, Debbie Lloyd and Keith Terry, Wayne Vitale, Lisa Gold, Mudita Nisker, Jeanne Moncrieff, Carla Fabrizio, Steve Johnson, Jim Finck, Nick Robinson, and Eileen Corder. Sekar Jaya brought Bali to the United States in ways that amazed Balinese, and they have said as much repeatedly. The group's many teachers (most are mentioned below) helped pave, as Wayan Dibia put it, "a wider and wider avenue" of exchange.

In Bali older musicians—Wayan Beratha, Madé Demong, Pandé Madé Gableran, Madé Grindem, Gusti Madé Putu Griya, Wayan Jebeg, Wayan Konolan, Wayan Loceng, Anak Agung Gdé Mandera, Gdé Manik, Gusti Ngurah Panji, Wayan Pogog, Nyoman Rembang, Wayan Rintig, Wayan Saplug, Nyoman Senken—some of whom are no longer, taught me the musical wisdom of an earlier time. Ketut Arini Alit, Ketut Gdé Asnawa, Komang Astita, Madé Bandem, Nyoman Catra, Wayan Dibia, Cokorda Alit Hendrawan, Desak Madé Laksmi, Putu Lastini, Pandé Gdé Mustika, Wayan Rai, Madé Rundu, Wayan Sadra, Wayan Sinti, Gusti Ayu Srinatih, Pandé Sukerta, Wayan Suweca, Wayan Wija, Nyoman Windha, Madé Wiratini, and others nearer to my generation have my profound thanks and hopes. It has been a privilege to sustain our friendships, and to work together on *kebyar*. Wayan Gama Astawa, Dewa Putu Berata, Ketut Cater, Ketut Kodi, Komang Sudirga, Wayan Sujana, Gdé Yudana, and musicians younger than I know, as I do, the size of the shoes they must fill. Ketut Madra and his family Wayan Konderi, Madé Berata, and Nyoman Werti were my adoptive kin over twenty-two years of visits, always ready with coffee and conversation after long days of music and research. The inclusion of Ketut's watercolor as cover art for this edition enriches the presentation and stands as sweet testimony to loyal companionship.

Over a decade at Yale University Michael Friedmann was my interlocutor, actual and imagined, for ideas as they developed. Michael was the one who suggested that I not stop at just thinking about writing this book. Martin Bresnick is a model for how to be in music, and opened many doors. Thanks to inspiring theorists and composers Jonathan Berger, Robert Morgan, Jan Radzynski, and Ramon Satyendra. Also in New Haven, two generations of *gamelan*, Sekar Kembar (1986–88) and Jagat Anyar (1993–96), built new communities, always with support from the Yale Department and Friends of Music. Kate Beddall, James Harding, Mary Francis, Chris Burns, Paul Schick, Heather Harwood, Julie Hedges, Steve Brown, Amy Stevens, Tom Burckhardt, and Richard Davis were but a few of the participants.

Eric Oey of Periplus Editions handed me the fine opportunity to write my first book. Early on in this project I received valuable responses from Harry

Haskell, Mantle Hood, and an anonymous reader for Yale University Press, as well as William Austin and Kay Shelemay. Thanks to Richard Wallis for dissecting initial drafts. Other critics at that stage were Rachel Cooper, Wayne Vitale, Sarah Willner, and Kent McLagan. In a galvanizing 1993 phone conversation, Judith Becker brought the goals and limits of my plans into clear focus. She later read most of the chapters and showed me how to improve them. Ben Brinner, Lisa Gold, Ellen Koskoff, José Evangelista, William Benjamin, Alan Thrasher, and Marc Perlman read insightfully at later stages. Thanks to Adrian Vickers for trenchant feedback on an inchoate chapter 3.

As soon as each chapter was done I sent it to Evan Ziporyn, exemplary musical thinker and *gamelan* fellow traveler almost from the first. He repaid me with critique nearly as voluminous as the texts themselves, asking the questions I wished I had asked in the first place, never tolerating facile conclusions, forcing me to hone rigor. Philip Yampolsky, learned and generous, patiently answered my many queries; and when the first draft was done took me to task on the whole. If Philip did not want to be thanked so profusely here, he should not have read and reread my chapters and given me such acute commentary on them. Philip and Evan, despite your best efforts I am still blind to the flaws that remain.

David Brent, Carol Saller, and associates at the University of Chicago Press were superb advocates, making the arduous a pleasure. I thank Steve Reich for his foreword and thoughtful responses to the manuscript. Ketut Gdé Asnawa inspected part 2 in 1998, offered astute observations, and resolved intractable terminological conundrums. Bruno Nettl read the whole and injected inimitable enthusiasm. Martin Ewing drafted the computer plots for chapter 2, and Adriana Dawes refined them later. Ben Reeves's skillful drawings and map add another visual dimension. Gordon Fitzell searched for imperfections in the figures with a fine-toothed comb. Tom Ballinger, Rucina Ballinger, Ketut Prasetya, Rachel Cooper, and Richard Blair contributed photographs. Madé Bandem and Andy Toth permitted me to use materials for illustrations in chapter 2.

Over the years numerous grants and fellowships allowed me to study Balinese music. At Yale College, Bates and Murray Fellowships enabled my initial trips in 1977 and 1978–79. A 1982 Fulbright Fellowship, the Dharma Siswa award of the Indonesian Department of Education and Culture (*P dan K*), and a 1987 grant from the Asian Cultural Council sent me back. Gamelan Sekar Jaya's diverse supporters underwrote our 1985 and 1992 tours to Bali. Yale's Morse Junior Faculty Fellowship, Griswold Fund, and Council for International and Area Studies provided support in 1989 and 1991. Once writing I was lucky to obtain teaching leave both from the Mellon Fellowship of the Whitney Humanities Center at Yale and, for all of 1994, from a National Endowment for the Humanities University Teacher's Fellowship. In my first years at the University of British Columbia, a light course load enabled me to finish.

The UBC Dean of Arts office subsidized the color reproduction of Ketut Madra's cover art. The Hampton Fund at UBC underwrote the compact discs and sundry prepublication costs. At the 1998 recording sessions on Sekolah Tinggi Seni Indonesia's campus, Wayan Dibia arranged necessary local support and permissions, and Nyoman Windha and Pandé Mustika organized musicians, instruments, rehearsals, and everything else. The players and Yong Sagita and his crew from Rick's Records worked with remarkable professionalism. David Simpson did expert mastering in Vancouver.

Three final displays of gratitude: I esteem the work of Simha Arom, William Austin, A. M. Jones, Gerhard Kubik, Colin McPhee, Leonard Ratner, and Lewis Rowell, and aspire to their wisdom. My loving and dearly remembered father Bernard and mother Marion set a tone of commitment, sincerity, and awareness that I hope to sustain. My stepmother Shelley, and sister Toni and brother Peter and their families share that understanding.

This can be taken at face value too: I thank Dadong, Hanuman, and Twalen—monikers for the three generations of Macintosh hard drives (stocked with Finale and Word) that were my unwitting coworkers throughout the book's gestation. They were nearly always kind to it.

Notes on Orthography and Pronunciation

BALINESE and Indonesian terms are italicized throughout, except in the musical examples. I do not suffix English final s for plurals. The English word "gong" is exempt from these particulars, except when part of a Balinese compound noun such as *gamelan gong kebyar*. In recognition of the accepted international usage of the Javanese word *gamelan*, the indigenous Balinese form *gambelan* has not been adopted.

Balinese speaking Balinese or Indonesian usually stress the final syllable in two- and (most) three-syllable words, and the penultimate syllable in longer ones. Regional accents within Bali affect these norms, especially for three-syllable words. Thus either *te* or *kan* is stressed in *kotekan*; and *go* or *gan* in *jegogan*.

The *e* in an initial syllable, as in *kebyar or Peliatan*, is nearly dropped, resulting in *k'byar* and *P'liatan*. Final h, as in *tabuh* or *gambuh*, is sounded. Final r, as in *kebyar* or Denpasar, is briefly rolled.

The following pronunciation guide is pertinent:

Balinese (and Indonesian)	English approximation
a	*o* as in *opera*
ang, eng, ing, ong, ung	*ahng, ung, ing, ong, oong*
c	*ch* as in *choose*
e	as in *bed*
é (Ind. ai)	*ay* as in *bay*
final er	as in *air* (slightly rolled *r*)
g	as in *gold*
i	*ee* as in *bee*
i as the second of two vowels separated by consonant	as in *pick*
o	as in *upon*
u	*oo* as in *loose*

Notes on Notation
and Transcription

STANDARD staff notation is used in this book. The few modifications and special conventions are explained as they arise. The main points are summarized here for convenience:

- For consistency *kebyar*'s five-tone scale is shown throughout as C♯-D-E-G♯-A-(C♯) on the Western staff. This convention is a carryover from McPhee's *Music in Bali* (see 1966:64–65). In Balinese practice there is variation from *gamelan to gamelan* and presumably none are tuned precisely thus. It is important to remember that melodic motion from E to G♯ or A to C♯ (which appear to be Western major thirds, and indeed are acoustically large intervals) is *stepwise*. This may be confusing, since motion from C♯ to E (an apparent minor third, bridging over the D in-between) constitutes a *leap*.
- Melodic instruments often play interlocking parts. I beam the two parts separately on the same staff with stems going in opposite directions. The two interlocking drums are treated differently. Their individual parts are shown separately and beamed together across the staves.
- When a melodic interlocking part is momentarily silent, its complementary part fills in the corresponding rhythmic value (usually a sixteenth note) with a sounding tone. To reduce clutter, I hide sixteenth-note rests in most of these cases, but parts retain their proper vertical alignment. In other cases where the texture and rhythm are dense, some rests are similarly omitted, but only where an adjacent staff explicitly shows the missing value as a sounding note.
- In many analytical figures, especially in chapter 6, some notes are stemless. Blackened noteheads may be used in combination with open ones that mainly come every fourth or eighth tone. The latter receive greater metric stress.
- Notation and *solfège* equivalents:

Staff notation equivalents	C♯	D	E	G♯	A
Javanese cipher equivalents					
(*pélog pathet lima*)	1	2	3	5	6
Balinese *solfège* syllable names	*ding*	*dong*	*deng*	*dung*	*dang*
(vowel abbreviations)	i	o	e	u	a
Balinese notational script	᭟	᭞	᭝	᭟	᭠
Balinese alphabet					
(*Aksara Bali*) names	*ulu*	*tedong*	*taleng*	*suku*	*cecek* (or *carik*)

- The Balinese *solfège* vowel abbreviations are placed below the noteheads of at least one staff in each transcription. For instruments with two-octave ranges—*trompong* and the *gangsa* group (*ugal, pemadé, kantilan*), or the *neliti* part in its two-octave realization (*neliti* order)—the abbreviations are capitalized in the bottom octave. For the higher-octave and single-octave instruments or parts, lowercase abbreviations are used. See figures 7.3 and 7.4 for a summary of drum stroke abbreviations.
- In some figures, large, bracket-shaped repeat signs are used to indicate sectional repeats. Within these, ordinary repeat barlines denote smaller internal repeats.

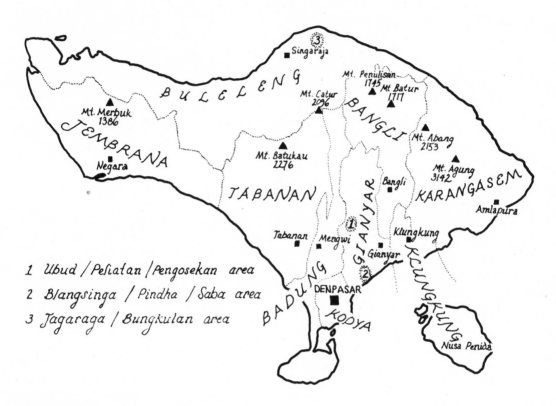

1 Ubud / Peliatan / Pengosekan area
2 Blangsinga / Pindha / Saba area
3 Jagaraga / Bungkulan area

Map of Bali

Gamelan Gong Kebyar

1 Introduction: Encountering *Kebyar*

Making offerings to the gong before a performance, Singapadu, 1992. Photo: Tom Ballinger.

And so, hardly had the delicious sensation, which Swann had experienced, died away, before his memory had furnished him with an immediate transcript, summary, it is true, and provisional, but one on which he had kept his eyes fixed while the playing continued, so effectively that, when the same impression suddenly returned, it was no longer uncapturable. He was able to picture to himself its extent, its symmetrical arrangement, its notation, the strength of its expression; he had before him that definite object which was no longer pure music, but rather design, architecture, thought, and which allowed the actual music to be recalled. This time he had distinguished, quite clearly, a phrase which emerged for a few moments from the waves of sound. It had at once held out to him an invitation to partake of intimate pleasures, of whose existence, before hearing it, he had never dreamed, into which he felt that nothing but this phrase could initiate him; and he had been filled with love for it, as with a new and strange desire.

Marcel Proust, *Swann's Way*

THIS book is a comprehensive study of the music of the *gamelan gong kebyar,* the most popular and influential genre of twentieth-century music developed on the Indonesian island of Bali. Played on a large ensemble of *gamelan* instruments, *gong kebyar* is significant both for Bali and in more worldly musical and social ways. It is a singular product of the island's recent culture displaying exacting standards of artistic achievement, and it has attracted international recognition for these qualities. *Gong kebyar* music is inherently orchestral, hence creatively ambitious, owing to its orchestral *conception:* omitting any of numerous parts in the texture sacrifices musical identity and integrity. It is twentieth-century music in the genuine sense that many of its features, though naturally girded by time-tested, inherited musical practices, were invented and developed after 1900. Like many other musics innovated elsewhere in the world during the past century, *gong kebyar* adopts an assertive and self-aware stance of independence from prior musical categories and functions, an attitude that is clearly audible in the music's gestures and rhythm, even at first encounter. But unlike most, *gong kebyar* crystallizes the vital spirit of its age without recourse to the dominant Western (classical, military, church, or popular) musical idioms and instrument technologies of the period, deftly transforming it into something expressive and lucid. Few musics fit this range of descriptions, making *gong kebyar* a notable part of the past century's global cultural legacy.

My approach is to explore, reflect, and expand upon what the ingenuity of *gong kebyar*'s creators has produced, and to investigate the many forces which have affected their lives and music. These include other Balinese music genres, vocal and instrumental, as well as broader cultural shifts wrought by political and social transformation in Bali during the decades prior to and since the advent of the Indonesian nation in 1945. My aim is to provide musicians and engaged audiences with a range of detailed information concerning this music, and to come as close as possible to furnishing a blueprint and tools for analyzing and perhaps even composing it in a stylistically credible way. In doing so I have tried to distill the essence of many years' interaction with Balinese musicians. I also both update and complement Colin McPhee's still-authoritative *Music in Bali* (1966), which was based on research done in the 1930s, and take the published thought of more recent Indonesian and Western scholars into account. By evoking the music in sufficient detail for people with varying degrees of connection to it, I hope to provide a resource that will encourage its study, cultivation, and reproduction in new contexts. For those involved with *gamelan,* the descriptions should resonate with the music as it is already understood. As a complement to performances and recorded sound, those newly drawn to the subject may wish to use the presentation as an aid to imagining the music in its fullest dimensions.

Like all reports from the field, this one is personal, and I stress from the outset that the book reflects my interests as a creative musician and musical interpreter. There are two primary aspects to this emphasis, each of which is shaped in a particular way by the history of interaction between Bali and the West. The first has to do with the fact that for over a century, Bali has been a magnet for travelers and scholars of all kinds, accumulating a reputation for hospitality and an image of accessibility and allure. Unlike other small, relatively self-contained musical cultures that have received their first substantial ethnomusicological attention comparatively recently (the isolated Kaluli of Papua Nugini, as represented in Steven Feld's *Sound and Sentiment,* are the most celebrated example), Balinese music and musicians have already had considerable and prolonged contact with their counterparts from abroad. Bearing this in mind, I claim no special authority or inclination to speak exclusively on behalf of my Balinese colleagues, for they do not need a spokesperson. Some of them are representing themselves as writers, teachers, and performers both within Indonesia and without. The Balinese government schools of music and dance (SMKI and STSI) and some villages are currently lively arenas for exchange of views about *gamelan* and related cultural concerns. Because of the many foreigners regularly coming to Bali, among them *gamelan* students, such exchange often includes cross-cultural dialogue or collaboration. Beyond Bali, the growing number of *gamelan* performances, study and performing groups, recordings and broadcasts, course offerings, and discussions both off- and on-line all expand *gamelan*'s international status. In these kinds of settings my most valuable contribution can be to augment the range of discourse about Balinese music by including some ideas that are not necessarily implicit in what I have learned from my Balinese teachers. Some of the concepts that I advance would be unlikely to emanate from the primary bearers of the tradition, though I have relied on my teachers for guidance and feedback. As an experienced participant in this music, I have imagined it as if it were my own (which, for my purposes, it surely is), thinking creatively "in" it as well as about it, and offering the conclusions that result when they seem potentially enriching.

The other main circumstance that justifies the personal nature of the report has to do with the general awareness and reception of Balinese music in the West. Few non-Western musics are proportionally as well represented in Europe and North America on commercial recordings and by touring troupes as is Balinese *gamelan,* and it seems to me that the many interested non-Balinese comprise a different kind of group than those commonly designated "outsiders" with respect to a foreign musical culture. The Western romance with Bali has conferred considerable renown on the island, and well before "world music" became an important part of Western musical life Balinese *gamelan* was already something of an icon of musical exotica, familiar to many in name if not in sound. With its highly rhythmic, layered textures and sharply defined compositional structures, Balinese *gamelan* presents its new Western audiences with an intriguingly close analog to the through-composed music of the European orchestra. For Western composers in particular the music offers a compelling alternative perspective on problems of large-scale, multipart musical organization. Starting with McPhee, many of the music's foreign admirers have been attracted to *gamelan* because of how it sounds and are comparatively less concerned with its context. I remark on this now not to prescribe a remedy for the condition (though this book attempts a partial one), but just to note that the sound and structure of the music are chief among the facets of it that for many decades have made a strong impression on musicians internationally. Balinese *gamelan* travels well because it says so much in terms that are not irreducibly Balinese, because it succeeds so beautifully even when abstracted from its context. This supracultural durability is surely one of the most important by-products of Bali's musical achievements, and one which has played a role in increasing the island's fame and prosperity while enriching the rest of the world too.

Learning *Kebyar*

Gamelan gong kebyar, often referred to by Balinese simply as *gong, gong kebyar,* or *kebyar,* is actively learned, performed, and composed in Bali today. Its repertoire is a large and growing body of instrumental compositions and accompaniments for dance and theatrical forms. Like most *gamelan* genres, it has an easily recognizable sonic character, attributable to the nature of its instrumentation and tuning and to the character of its music. Although a relatively new style, it has a number of signature features that set it clearly apart from older Balinese *gamelan*. Unlike other *gamelan,* in which the orchestral disposition of instruments is usually fixed throughout each piece in the repertoire, compositions in *kebyar* are characterized by abrupt juxtapositions of musical materials and discontinuities in tempo, dynamic, metric periods, and orchestration. Melodic and rhythmic patterns, often comprising complementary interlocking parts, are developed to a remarkable degree of intricacy. Cadenza-like passages in swift nonmetric rhythms are played in precise coordination by the entire *gamelan*. The refined ensemble virtuosity required for the music's proper execution is acquired through lengthy, rehearsal-intensive training, usually undertaken in the communal setting of a Balinese community meeting hall. Music is memorized and played almost entirely without notation and, in most cases, without any freedom to improvise.

To say that *kebyar* ensembles are *gamelan* means that they are members of the family of Balinese and Javanese, largely percussive collections of musical instruments designed and constructed to be played together as an inseparable unit. *Kebyar*'s instrumentation and tuning are closely related to that of many other *gamelan* types of the region. They comprise a collection of bronze gongs and metallophones, plus a pair of two-headed drums, and including bamboo flutes and the *rebab* (bowed spike lute), all tuned to a five-tone subset of the seven-tone scale system commonly described by the Javanese term *pélog. Pélog* is not a standardized system, but may be interpreted anew for each *gamelan*. About twenty-five performers are needed to fill all of the places in a typical *kebyar* ensemble.

Like other *gamelan* as well as much music throughout mainland and archipelagic Southeast Asia, *kebyar* is *colotomic* (a term coined by Dutch musicologist Jaap Kunst), meaning that gongs of different sizes are used to mark off circular segments, or cycles, of musical time known as *gongan*. I use the terms "cycle" and *gongan* interchangeably. In conjunction with other instruments, gongs create rhythmic patterns of stress that support melodies. These patterns are analogous to meter as it is commonly understood in Western music, in that both utilize a fixed number of pulsations overlaid with a hierarchic pattern of accents. (Two important differences need noting: first, some *gamelan* meters may be hundreds of beats long, far broader than any conventional Western designation; and second, stresses in Western meter are not necessarily stated explicitly.) Strokes of the largest gong provide accent at the ends of *gongan* and sometimes at important points within them. Melodies are often—though hardly universally—quadripartite, and hierarchically subdivided into duple rhythmic units. The music is also orchestrally stratified, using several layers of simultaneously presented musical material that vary in density and complexity. These stratified, timbrally distinct layers of sound are closely interrelated variants of one another, but they are mainly thought of as emanating from a single, core melodic line, stated as one of the strata. Unlike many other *gamelan* genres, however, *kebyar* music may at times ignore these conventions.

I first heard *kebyar* in the spring of 1976 during my sophomore year at Yale. I was a music major, had already decided to become a composer, and my first compositions had been played. The performance I heard was by the famous *Gunung Sari* group from the south-central Balinese village of Peliatan, on the Nonesuch LP *Golden Rain*. The complexity of the rhythms, the rapid and unprepared shifts in texture and materials, the extremes of tempo and dynamic, the acoustic power of the gongs (David Lewiston, the recording engineer, had placed a microphone very close to them), the unmistakable high spirit and virtuoso discipline of the musicians, and—as in Proust's conception of Swann—the sure impression of a compelling architectural basis, all had a phenomenal effect on me. The album's liner notes provided only the sketchiest information. I had never heard of Bali, yet even before checking a book on the place out of the library I could envision myself going there to study. There was no ethnomusicology taught at Yale then, but the following year Mantle Hood was engaged to give a seminar during the second semester. He helped me to design a research plan, and I departed for the first of many trips to Indonesia in May 1977.

A first hearing is a far from adequate basis for musical analysis, but with hindsight I can aver that my initial responses to *kebyar* proved to accurately predict where my long-term interests would lead. These interests have changed over time only in degrees of emphasis, collectively providing the focus for my investigations and experiences. I divide them into a pair of mutually reinforcing areas: the social aspects of rehearsal and performance, and the technical-analytical aspects of music theory. The latter is the predominant focus in this book, for reasons to be elucidated presently. Involvement in the former reflects my attraction to the particular satisfaction of mastering complex music in an inherently communal setting such as that often encountered in Bali. The fulfillment that Balinese musicians get from playing is evident in the verve and conviction that good *gamelan* bring to performance. Discipline and a controlled, athletic coordination among parts in memorized music such as *kebyar* can be obtained only in a milieu where players learn to cooperate with one another over a long period of time and defer individual concerns to those of the group. This is, of course, an idealized depiction, and there are a complex of reasons why the ideal is usually not fully realized, especially in recent decades. But the communal aspirations for the music are upheld as a model as much as ever, despite the recent changes in economics and lifestyle that have influenced the kinds of interactions Balinese have with one another, and drastically reduced the amount of time most Balinese can allot to music.

It is not only that *kebyar* is rewarding to perform, or that Balinese practices of transmission, learning, and rehearsal are central to the experience of their music. In Bali music-process aesthetics, concepts, and behavior form a particularly well-defined conceptual juncture between the structure of the sounds (which they reflect in many ways) and higher levels of social meaning. By weighting issues surrounding performance and rehearsal, particularly in chapter 3, I ground the subsequent analysis in musical experience, but also carve out a good vantage point from which to arrive at more general conclusions about the music's place in Balinese culture, in both an everyday sense and a broader, more semiotic one.

Theory has been both a way for me to understand structure and an intellectual foundation for my *gamelan* compositions. I have been composing for *kebyar* since 1979, both in Bali with village and conservatory groups and in California with Gamelan Sekar Jaya, the community ensemble I cofounded that same year with Rachel Cooper and Wayan Suweca, using instruments I had purchased in Bali from the *gamelan* maker Madé Gableran. At first I conscientiously emulated Balinese models, but later was deliberately unconventional. I tried to create music acceptable to my Balinese peers by bouncing ideas off my teachers for feedback, making adjustments, and then teaching and performing the music from the lead drummer's position at the center of the *gamelan*. It was impossible to begin hearing and composing in the style without articulating theoretical concepts for myself in some way, and the more I performed Balinese compositions and composed my own, the more I was able to intuit theory from personal experience.

On a deeper level, though, I was also figuring out how to bridge the distance between two of my musical selves: composer trained in the Western academic milieu of the 1970s and 1980s, and performer trained in Balinese villages of the same era. There seemed to me no convincing reason to approach the two traditions dissimilarly; rather it was most satisfying to bring what was valuable in each to bear on the other. It was also counterintuitive to think of pursuing Balinese music in any depth with less than the unselfconscious commitment that only prolonged and intensive experience can supply, and neither I nor my teachers thought that there was anything untenable in a foreigner's aspiration to the highest Balinese standards of competence. What *was* remarkable, particularly when viewed against the reports of some ethnomusicologists in less traveled places, was my teachers' practically unanimous conviction that their music is universally learnable, and the seamless transition from student to performer to composer/teacher through which they led me.

As a student of music in Bali, one confronts a long-standing local discourse of theory, a body of thought comprising terminology and concepts developed in the villages and at the shifting centers of courtly power over many centuries. It covers some topics (scale and scale subsets, pre-*kebyar* formal structures, instrumentation, and generalized relationships among musical parts) for which the fundamental elements of the theory are widely articulated and understood, with some regional variation, by musicians in most places. Specialized topics like tuning or instrument construction are the exclusive domain of the *pandé* (smiths) and a small group of instrument merchants. A further group of structural principles (underlying patterns and principles of melodic shape, figuration, and drum pattern design) are nearly as well understood implicitly, but this knowledge tends to be intuitive and is rarely disseminated verbally since musicians have scarce need to think in such abstractions. As a performer, teacher, composer, and, inevitably, drummer, I had to assimilate all of this knowledge and teach the music orally to be a credible practitioner. But while passive knowledge of the last group of principles suffices for the Balinese, it could not have for me. Articulating the full range of theory for myself, then, was part of a socializing process, a way for me to feel comfortable calling the *gamelan* tradition mine so that I could then communicate it to others authoritatively. But any concepts I have generated myself—whether out of necessity or just for the sake of digging deeper—are grounded in existing Balinese theory.

In explaining these rehearsal-performance and theory-composition issues, I offer an answer to the question "What do they do over there?" A preliminary, succinct response would be that the Balinese play challenging, stirring, and intellectually stimulating music in a social context that ideally emphasizes community over individual values, and that the combined effects of the social support system for music and the historical development of the music itself have yielded a repertoire rich in complexity, variety, and nuance that rewards prolonged study and aesthetic contemplation.

Composition, Theory, and Ethnomusicology

This book comes coupled with my hope of meriting a claim to empathy and community with many kinds of musicians and listeners, particularly—in order of decreasing ease of definition—composers, theorists, and ethnomusicologists; and I will be pleased if they embrace what follows as relevant to their interests.[1] Only among the first group does my claim to inclusion not require any preliminary comments, so long as I myself continue to compose. I take writing in these pages as a composer to mean that I am profoundly interested in making sense of what I hear in *kebyar,* articulating a personal response to it, and understanding the technical and imaginative tools Balinese use to create it. Other composers, directly interested in Balinese music or not, will find here an attempt to fully document a significant, well-bounded, non-Western system of compositional practice, which I cannot be too wrong in thinking will arouse curiosity. In these senses there is a generational continuity between this book and McPhee's. He wrote as a composer too, but lived in a different, less methodologically self-aware era, and might today be struck to see me taking care to promote my interests to such a range of constituencies.

Defining theory and reconciling this book's relation to it are also not problematic, but may require some contextualizing. Music theory can be, has been, and is many things, so that ranging within fairly wide limits one can purport to be engaged in doing it.[2] The scope of what can be termed theory includes modal and scale theory, theory of performance style, ornament, or improvisation, as well as the more familiar harmonic, motivic, intervallic, rhythmic, metric, and formal analysis techniques. It can encompass cognitive and perceptual studies, digital synthesis, acoustic and spectral analysis, semiotics, linguistics, and information theory. To Rameau theory was a justification of musical practice in terms of natural law; to Harry Partch it was the envisioning of a new universe of musical organization, from the instruments to the scales to the compositions themselves; and to Sambamoorthy it was an exhaustive classification system for the materials of South Indian music. In ethnomusicology music theory may mean ethnotheory, the explication of the use of indigenous non-Western metaphors and concepts to describe music.

None of these is more a "true" theory than any other. But in its most widespread and influential post-1945 incarnations music theory is centered around taxonomies and structural analytical procedures for common-practice tonal repertoire on the one hand, and modernist post-tonal, atonal, and dodecaphonic repertoire on the other—parallel worlds of which the latter, following Schoenberg's claims, was the inevitable companion-successor to the former. Theory addresses earlier and more diverse Western music, but with a persistent center-periphery distinction between these and the core repertoires. While of decreasing relevance to some, the continuing musical and cognitive uses of tonal theory mostly remain self-evident to its teachers and their ap-

---

1. I would not rule out historical musicologists either, to the extent that the imperatives of understanding twentieth-century Western music already have and will increasingly continue to take them around the world in pursuit of direct insight into traditions that have had an impact on Western composers from Debussy to the present.

2. See also Perlman 1993:25 n. 9 in a discussion of Palisca 1980:741.

prentices. Though atonal repertoire has failed to achieve its once-hoped-for place in concert life, the pedagogy it spawned lives on in most curricula, indispensably shaping students' approaches to, and sense of responsibility toward, Western music of the early and mid-twentieth century. And while defending itself against accusations of elitism and the privileging of decontextualized formalism (Kramer 1993), theory remains second only to performance as a way to demystify the construction of complex music and foster close engagement with musical sound. It is important to distinguish between the prestige and cultural elitism which theory has been said to bolster and its explanatory value for music.

Except in part 3, Western repertoires are not under my purview here, though they remain close to my thoughts and interests. In terms of the approach to music that their theory embodies, however, the affinities should become clear, for I have conceived chapters 2 and 4 through 8 as curriculum content for an imaginary set of *kebyar* theory and history courses replete with model composition assignments, stylistic identification and criticism, graphic and written analyses, musicianship practice, and ear training. The material is not presented as if in a textbook, though with some distillation and the addition of exercises it could be. The notion of a dependable quorum of students regularly enrolling in such a curriculum is fanciful (even in Indonesia: see chapter 4), but that has not stopped me from organizing accordingly based on the conviction that it could help train multifaceted, aurally skilled musicians. Wallace Berry's invocation to "Structural Functions in Music" is no less germane when applied to *kebyar*:

> The complexities of preliminary and derivative questions about the expressive and intellectually provocative properties of music are such that the theorist's quest is assuredly not for final answers, whose unattainability we know enough to know, but rather for deepened channels of understanding consistent with our responses to music as sensitive musicians. (1987:xi)

From an ethnomusicologist's point of view, however, the issues raised by this kind of theory are different. Concerns persist that music theory embracing Western techniques constitutes negative appropriation that further upsets the balance of world music ecology toward the West. In this book extensive transcription in Western notation, now less pervasive than it once was in the ethnomusicology of cultures that do not already use it, may exacerbate such a perception. The shift of focus away from ethnography may strengthen it more. These concerns do not stem from a belief that the audience for this kind of scholarship is any other than the primarily Western-educated ones I have already identified. Rather they reflect a credo that to guard against the ill effects of appropriation a heterogeneous, multirelational balance of local ideas must precede the intervention of Western academic discourse, and that the latter should be restrained from dominating the discussion.

Ethnomusicologists also understand that their long-standing coexplorations with anthropology, sustained in part to enforce this credo, do not alone ensure the desired results; namely, work more reflective of or responsive to the people and cultures we study. Anthropological critiques of the 1980s point out how even—or perhaps especially—the most artful writers have succumbed to lack of sensitivity to the "native from the native's point of view. There is only constructed understanding of the constructed native's constructed point of view" (Crapanzano 1986:74, writing of Clifford Geertz's *Deep Play: Notes on the Balinese Cockfight*). It is moreover something of an embarrassment to be forced to admit that the best efforts to rebuild our approaches to representation still do not guarantee that others will perceive less imposition of Western perspectives, as has been clearly demonstrated when ethnomusicology is put to the test with Chinese students in Hong Kong (Witzleben 1997:237).

These issues are ultimately best resolved not methodologically but as a function of individual respect and sensitivity toward the people and cultures we study. Concern that ethnomusicology's own Western/modernist past is tinged with Eurocentrism often seems part of a confusing desire to recast old-style power relations while denying the ivory tower's ongoing role in the discourse, or at least paradoxically wishing, from within, for its decline. Given that multiplicity is the foundation of postmodern critique, it is ironic to continue to maintain that "traditionally" Western approaches are inherently less effective. In ethnomusicology this multiplicity is the root of vitality, but it is also at once what makes the field so hard to define and the source of the frustration that makes us try repeatedly to define it.

To digress briefly, however, I admit that it is all too easy for me to make this argument as a Balinist. Particularly with regard to social injustice and power relations, ethnomusicologists' perspectives and preoccupations are often geographically determined. Scholars working with music of the African American diaspora and teaching or writing about it in Western academe will quickly be forced to confront the effects of racism in their own milieus (Monson 1996). Those working in the former Soviet bloc cannot avoid facing the consequences of political ideology and the traumas of war and oppression (Levin 1996). In Indonesia the allied machinations of the government and the tourist industry cynically seek to aestheticize the many regional cultures to make them at once more "modern," less inclined to resist the homogenizing tendrils of centralized government, and more marketable to visitors (Yampolsky 1995). The exemplary success of these efforts on Bali has created a powerful symbiosis between government, tourism, and the culture itself. Working there, the researcher becomes implicated in a discourse and production of art that, while robust and rooted in religious belief, is also disturbingly deferential to the concerns of government and the tourist industry. Balinese individuals' aesthetic approaches to music may in some measure be an accommodation to this, but since such approaches are compatible with Western ones, investigators like me have historically elected to accept the situation at face value and work within the system. (It is perhaps unrealistic to suggest that we have any choice.) The music is in fact a kind of cottage industry in which outsiders' patronage is understood as economically and educationally beneficial. Such institutionalized convictions about art for art's sake, in short, are a difficult current to swim against, and it remains for future ethnomusicologists to do so successfully.

I am hardly the first recent ethnomusicologist to apply Western music theory approaches to non-Western repertoire (see Stock 1993), but I do go further than most in developing a comprehensive and systematic model for musical structure and analysis that covers an entire non-Western genre, and a major one at that. Important exceptions to this are studies such as Simha Arom's (1991), only one (albeit especially impressive) entry in a decades-old debate about structural principles of African rhythm. The most immediately obvious choice of academic discourse for a book on *kebyar* to emulate (save for McPhee's) originates not on Bali but on neighboring Java, where emic oral and written theory is more extensive than in Africa and the history of collaboration with Westerners longer (see Sumarsam 1995). In Java it is understood to be more appropriate to hew to local concepts as a matter of faith, since these have already been so extensively developed and critiqued (Tenzer 1997:171).[3] In this regard Bali and Java are not comparable; my reasons for partially parting ways with Javanists are also set forth in chapter 4.

Though Arom's work has been applauded as a "return to analysis" (Nattiez 1993), in ethnomusicology generally it remains taboo to discuss so-called autonomous structural processes in isolation from the context in which the music is learned and performed. But this oft-cited bifurcation (along with Alan Merriam's tripartite model of the discipline, which is an elaboration of it) has been allowed to harden into cliché. One wonders first of all what exactly it would mean to detach sound and context. Ingrid Monson observes in *Saying Something* that we "continue to have rather unproductive debates over whether the cultural contexts or 'the music' should predominate in our scholarship, as if it were actually possible to make some clear separation" (1996:190). The point is that even when context seems absent it is perforce implied. What Western theorists, even the most austere formalists, would not aver assuming the context of Western thought and society when they discuss music, as it were, autonomously? Others might argue that the deepest value of at least some music is located in its ability to lift the perceiver out of his or her (or the music's own) context, but even this elegant notion is meaningless without context as a referent.

In the study of a complex musical tradition tensions between breadth and depth are always in flux. To focus on sound is not to undervalue context but

---

3. This is even more true for Indian musicology.

to conserve extra time and energy for understanding more of what may be in the inner sonic worlds of teachers and colleagues: to hear the music perhaps not *as* they do, but as *intensively* as they do. I consider that this book would suffer without its historical and ethnographic components, but it is also right to conclude that my basic impulse is toward this other direction. If I have overstated the magnitude of this imbalance in subsequent chapters for the sake of the methodological arguments set forth here, it is to confront head-on ethnomusicology's corporate reluctance to acknowledge the value of the metaphor of autonomous sound.

Using Western-derived theory models enables explanation of an esteemed local knowledge system via equally estimable but foreign ways of thinking to yield hybrid knowledge; it is not a scheme to co-opt *gamelan* on Western terms. Nattiez, whose semiotic tripartition ("poietic," "neutral," and "esthetic" domains summing to the "total musical fact") seeks to legitimize all kinds of explicitly justified analysis (described as metalinguistic discourse about music), condones this procedure:

> [I]n no case should presentation of the musical ethnotheory think of substituting itself for analysis of the music. The indigenous discourse cannot cover all aspects of the musical fact; this justifies yet again the *necessity of undertaking an analysis of the neutral level.*
>
> In the near future, the problem will be to determine how we can use knowledge of the ethnotheory in our analysis of structures, how that knowledge will influence those analyses. But we should not think of dispensing with structural analyses. (1990:194; italics in the original)

Just as surely, Western discourses about Western music also do not cover "all aspects of the musical fact." That is why to assuage lingering doubts I muse on the fascination and gratitude I would feel if a Balinese aimed the spotlight of their intelligence at Western music. It seems to me that I would value very much what such a person had to say regardless of the approach taken.

As coda to this discussion I echo the oft-made observation that systematic thinking and the perceptions of interrelated hierarchic patterns—far from being alien to Balinese thought—are actually part and parcel of them; and at the very core of the ancient Hindu entelechy girding the tradition. Finding the mundane and the cosmological mirrored in one another is an essential aspect of the philosophy shaping both Balinese and Indian Hinduism, and hence a Balinese way of relating to the world. The Balinese *Panca Maha Bhuta* doctrine, as described by Ramseyer, is characteristic: "The basic idea . . . is that the human body as a world in miniature *(bhuwana alit)* is a faithful copy of the world itself, the 'great world' *(bhuwana agung)*. This means that the body as the microcosm contains the same five elements [earth, fire, water, wind, atmosphere] that make up the universe, the macrocosm" (1977:106–7). A quotidian manifestation of this, one of many possible ones, is the conventional mapping of the cosmos onto the family compound by placing the household shrine at the corner closest to the sacred Mount Agung and mother temple Besakih on its slopes, while the pigsty and toilets lie at the opposite end, closest to the dark world of the oceans. Musically such correspondences are also abundant and frequently evoked by Balinese, as later explanation will reveal. Seeing the large reflected in the small and vice-versa belongs to Balinese, Western, and indeed virtually all human thought; it is a "bio-psychological universal" (Meyer 1998:6).[4]

Overview

Developing an understanding of the conventions and constraints associated with the composition of *kebyar* music means examining the music as sound patterning and relating it to other sound patterns in some of the historically antecedent music genres on which it is strongly dependent for materials. In the coming chapters subjects such as orchestration, interpart relations, syntax, and relations between music and dance movement are addressed in turn, viewed alone and in comparison to older music. Though *kebyar* repertoire contains much music originating in older *gamelan,* it transforms these and gives them fresh relevance. An abundant sonic conglomeration of referential structures, it thus opens a window onto Balinese history and society.

The explication of these ideas constitutes practically the whole of the book. But I am also launching an implicit secondary narrative that chronicles my inner dialogue with the music, and my integration of the experience of knowing it with other aspects of who I am, musically and otherwise. Before part 3 this narrative lies mostly dormant, surfacing from time to time in personal remarks, though I think of it as reflected consistently in the progression of the book as a whole. For like any scholarly author I aspire to good teaching, and my teaching reflects cherished personal sensibilities. I can go only so far in answering the question "What does this music mean to the Balinese?"; but I can also try to shed light on the problem of "What does this music mean to me (as an outsider)?" and also, "How can hearing this music deeply help me to hear other kinds of music differently?" Raising the latter questions is my way of exploring the issues of ethnographic authority alluded to earlier. In asking them I advocate a broader understanding of what an authentic experience of the music can be. This is the most candid way that I can devise to deal with the question of my legitimacy as a Balinese musician, without distracting from the central focus of the inquiry into *kebyar.*

---

4. But with regard to building music theories based on the perception of hierarchic structure, Meyer cautions that "what is profound is not the deep structure of a flower (or a piece of music), but the experience of a particular work—its power to move us. . . . Works of art are not propositions *about* phenomena, they *are* phenomena—phenomena that are valued for the specific experiences they provide" (1998:13).

In part 1 (Approaches to *Kebyar,* chapters 2–4) I bring three initial concerns together: music sound, music and society, and frameworks for music theory. I developed chapter 2 in response to my memory of the spontaneous sensations aroused and the curiosities piqued by my encounter with the Nonesuch record in 1976. What I was able to grasp initially—what I imagine one ordinarily perceives at first in such cases—was not so much formal structure (at least explicitly) but rather complex and seemingly impenetrable sound and the easier-to-fathom contrasts obtained in the music through changes in texture and timbre. That is why I first introduce orchestral resources—timbre, tuning, instrumentation, and texture; after all, these are what one can comprehend prior to coaching or further training. Sound is taken as an acoustic phenomenon, conceptually enriched by commentary taken from an old Balinese treatise on music. A spatial model for the *kebyar* scale gamut is proposed, based on actual practice and the treatise's cosmological plan. The chapter goes on to introduce interpart relationships and representative orchestration techniques.

Chapter 3 treats *kebyar* ensemble virtuosity as a social phenomenon by discussing the genre's origins and development, and the musical scene in contemporary Bali. Much of this material has been explored in publications about Bali by anthropologists and historians that are less specifically concerned with music, but it is no less essential for current purposes. *Kebyar*'s history also sheds light on ideas about music aesthetics in rehearsal and performance, and makes it possible to assess changes brought about through the rise of the Indonesian state; in particular, the impact of national ideologies, tourism, formal music education, competitions and festivals, and broadcast and recording media.

As a link between the concerns of the previous two chapters and the focus on structure in part 2, chapter 4 establishes contexts for theory and analysis. I first survey the existing literature on Balinese *gamelan* and then summarize current ideas about music theory for Javanese *gamelan*. A comparison of Javanese and Balinese music and music concepts is thus possible. Important issues for music theory in Bali are then defined based on the analysis of the results of the comparison. The issues give rise to further comparison, between *kebyar* and music of the Western classic era.

Part 2 (Structure in *Kebyar,* chapters 5–8) presents a set of theoretical concepts and applications for use in the analysis of *kebyar* repertoire. Chapter 5 opens with a brief essay tracing Balinese history to 1900, including a cursory survey of the entire spectrum of Balinese *gamelan* and vocal styles. Each genre is uniquely associated with a historical period, social circumstance, and certain music-structural norms; and each has contributed in some measure to the body of repertoires, musical structures, and compositional techniques that today form the collective basis for *kebyar*'s eclecticism. This information is then put to use defining basic characteristics of structure in *kebyar*, including referentiality and affect, identity of the musical object, and "quality" (the sense of stasis or motion).

Chapters 6, 7, and 8 refine and apply these concepts to structural components and compositional strategies. Chapter 6 deals with melody and figuration, categorizing and analyzing the many styles of each, and tracing them to their historical roots. Chapter 7 investigates metrics and the drumming patterns that elucidate meter in *kebyar* and the court *gamelan gambuh, gong gdé,* and *pelegongan* (*kebyar*'s primary antecedents for these musical elements), with goals similar to those in the previous chapter. Chapter 8 depicts the range of techniques available to the composer for shaping complete compositions, and suggests strategies for listening to and analyzing them.

The third and final part (*Kebyar* in Bali and Abroad, chapters 9–10) sketches possible paths to the West. To portray the relevance of *kebyar* in present-day Bali I focus, in chapter 9, on a single recent composition: *Wilet Mayura,* composed in 1982 by Wayan Sinti and Nyoman Rembang, both well-known musicians. The piece presents an admixture of historical styles that is particularly dense, even for *kebyar.* By showing how allusions to aspects of Balinese culture are juxtaposed in the music through the use of specific instruments, forms, and compositional devices, I can portray the unmistakably contemporary experience it gives its audience. The discussion relies on ideas about syntax developed in earlier chapters, but here the focus is on innovation, expression, and communication. At the end of the chapter representative samples from Western music and jazz with congruent traits are introduced for comparison.

The conclusion considers Balinese music abroad, partly on its own terms and partly in its role as an icon for non-Western music. What of the music's meaning for non-Balinese? Through the work of anthropologists, composers, music scholars and performers, Balinese music has assumed a niche in Euro-American musical life and contributed to changing musical values and audiences. Balinese composers have also felt the impact of forces changing the international new music community.

Gamelan developed over centuries with complex meanings for Balinese, and *kebyar* is testimony to its prodigious recent growth. These meanings have been and will continue to be elucidated by the Balinese themselves. But it is now a part of world music culture, where it is accumulating new significance through the experiences of other listeners and performers. The importance of this is not to be overlooked. We profit from hearing the music on Balinese terms but should not forfeit the chance to make it our own: reinterpretation is a desirable result of cross-cultural contact. As one fiber in a web of cross-cultural music processes affecting us all, *kebyar* thus also has symbolic potential. On what level can listeners be expected to cope with the amount of cross-cultural information present in new music? Should we bemoan the severance of ties from historically determined meanings that inevitably accompanies cross-cultural process as a regrettable loss, or embrace the potential embodied in music's liberation from culture-specific values?

As a whole the book is my own reinterpretation. In the broadest sense its venture is to follow *gamelan* on an analytical and ethnographical journey that takes it some distance from its roots. The journey traverses the historical settings in which it evolved and the contemporary ones in which it is now heard in Bali and elsewhere. *Gong kebyar* is shown to have developed from a complex of sources, which today expand and interact in a multiplicity of ways.

Approaches to *Kebyar*

1

2 *Kebyar*
Orchestral Resources

Ugal and *kempli* in *gong kebyar*, Kerobokan, 1982.
Photo: Author.

Of course the laws of the natural function of our ear are, as it were, the building stones with which the edifice of our musical system has been erected, and the necessity of accurately understanding the nature of these materials in order to understand the construction of the edifice itself, has been clearly shewn. But just as people with differently directed tastes can erect extremely different kinds of buildings with the same stones, so also the history of music shews us that the same properties of the human ear could serve as the foundation of very different musical systems.

Hermann Helmholtz, *On the Sensations of Tone* (1877)

ENCOUNTERING the pure acoustics of sound is an important part of many musical experiences, but listeners bring their own cultural orientations and levels of expertise to the event. The sonic surface can be the primary focus for beginners, especially in the absence of substantive additional information about the music. At intermediate stages, while learning to hear and identify structural components, the importance of the surface may recede to a degree. During this stage terminology may be applied, and elements of structure labeled. An advanced musician may or may not wish to be consciously attentive to structure, but in any event will strive for a flexibility that enables changing from one kind of listening to another easily. Being able to shift and reshift the foci of one's perceptions is one of the experienced musician's best rewards.

The three individuals cited below voicing their reactions to *kebyar* share a contagious enthusiasm, but beyond that they differ greatly in what they apprehend in the music, their level of musical competence, and the way their perceptions stimulate them. Their remarks trace a path to musical proficiency along which one may travel over time in undertaking a cross-cultural study of any complex and unfamiliar music. The path as I define it here begins with the reactions of an uninitiated foreigner and culminates with the perceptions of an expert Balinese. Between them is a Western composer engaged in observation and study. In moving toward better understanding, it is important to address the concerns and perceptions specific to each stage of the encounter, as issues that had previously demanded conscious attention become internalized. In this chapter I try to preserve the affect of "pre-structural listening" in deference to the perspective of the beginner, describing *kebyar* in terms of the parameters that control the music's exterior. Yet, as the third quotation shows, these same aspects are of no small significance even to the most advanced Balinese musicians.

The sound of *kebyar* is complex but accessible from various angles. The construction of the instruments, their tuning, jarring discontinuities of dynamic and tempo, and the conventions of orchestration can all be grasped without study and extensive exposure. For many, myself among them, an initial and durable response is arrestingly visceral. Here is John Coast, a British entrepreneur who produced the Peliatan village *gamelan*'s successful international tour in 1952, describing the first time he heard their *kebyar* compositions, at a nighttime rehearsal in Bali:

> Madé Lebah gripped his hammer firmly; then he and the Anak Agung exchanged a lightning glance, and drum and metallophone started together on a terrific chord that I shall never forget, and straightaway we were drowned in the music. . . .
>
> This *gamelan* had a percussive attack, an electric virtuosity, a sort of appalling precision, which, as it echoed and rebounded off that long wall, almost pulsated us out of our seats . . .
>
> Where was the melody? I had no idea! But an incessant cascade of sound rushed through us and around us and deep down into us. The two drums thwacked and throbbed, the deep gongs boomed, the cymbals chattered and clacked; but it was the metallophones and a battery of twelve gongs of descending size on a long, low stand played by four men, which swept us away. The metallophones hammered out patterns of such intricacy, such crisscross elusiveness, and with such a dazzling, brilliant zeal, as was most assuredly outside my comprehension, and from that long battery of gongs came a baffling, staccato syncopation which nothing out of Africa could hope to rival. This music broke its way into us, possessed us. (1953:53)

A few years later Benjamin Britten stayed in Bali for a brief period and had some time to record and transcribe the music. He was no less taken than Coast, though he used different concepts and terminology to describe his reactions:

> There are about twenty instruments: metallophones, gongs, drums. The performers play beautiful, complex music without looking at each other; they have the confidence of sleepwalkers, and smoke cigarettes . . . [The music is] *fantastically* rich—melodically, rhythmically, texture (such *orchestration!!*) and above all *formally*. It's a remarkable culture . . . At last I'm beginning to catch on to the technique, but it's about as complicated as Schoenberg.[1] (italics in the original)

A lifetime of study and participation does not dull the effect, as Wayan Suweca, a famous drummer from Kayu Mas, affirms. Here the deeper level of expertise is reflected by minimal conscious attention to musical structure:

> More than anything, I feel excitement and enthusiasm when I play *kebyar* drums. *Kebyar* is basically music to portray youthful exuberance. Though the music is complicated and takes a long time to master, if the *gamelan* is in tune and the musicians skilled and well-rehearsed, I mainly feel enveloped by the fierce and sharp sounds of the music and instruments. And in that situation the group feels pride for the audience to witness the success of our collaborative efforts. The feeling is that together we have made something of value, both for community and religion.[2]

Coast finds the syncopations "baffling" and has "no idea" where the melody lies in the texture, thus coupling a beginner's innate sense of the music's power and foreignness with an undefined inkling that that power is harnessed by structure. Nevertheless he is enticed, asserting, perhaps with undue modesty, that the players' patterns are "most assuredly outside my comprehension." Responding to the coordination of the players and the physical impact of the sound, Coast metaphorizes with terms like "electric," "pulsate," and "appalling precision" that effectively meld the sound of the instruments and the virtuosity of the ensemble into an imagery of technology and superhuman prowess. These words may reasonably be considered to have been partially inspired by the metallic timbres of the ensemble, and they may additionally have been chosen for their vivid modernist connotations, unremarkable for the West in

---

1. Drawn from two letters to Imogen Holst, January 1956, quoted in Cooke 1987:319–20.

2. "Pada pokonya saya merasa semangat dan berbahagia pada waktu saya main kendang kebyar. Pada dasarnya gending-gending kebyar mencerminkan sikap teruna. Walaupun gending-gending kebyar adalah cukup rumit dan memerlukan waktu untuk dikuasainya, bila gamelannya selaras dan sekahanya mantap, saya akan terutama merasa seperti dikelilingi oleh suara dan gending yang asah dan galak. Dan pada saat keadaan begitu, sekahanya juga akan terasa bangga bahwa para penonton sempat menyaksikan keberhasilan gotong royong kami. Sepertinya kami bersama-sama bisa membuat sesuatu yang bermutu baik bagi masyarakat maupun agama juga." (Personal communication, June 1987. All translations in this book are my own unless otherwise specified.)

the 1950s. But his intuitions about pulsation and acoustic unity are also borne out by examinations of tuning and orchestration, as we shall see.

Britten is somewhat farther along the road, bringing special qualifications to the encounter by virtue of his status as an accomplished musician in his own milieu. Unlike Coast, he parses the sound enough to hear the melody and at least glimpse the organization of other parts. While learning, he is undergoing an accelerated intellectualizing process as a way of coming to terms efficiently with what is there to be grasped. He emphasizes complexity and form and is eager to construct a mental topography of how the forms are constructed, presumably in their broadest and most abstract designs. Along the way he also makes comparisons with the known (in this case, Schoenberg), as though asserting that for him the music's structure is a problem to be solved. Britten represents a cognitive and experiential middle of the continuum, a phase that one passes through in order to aim at where Suweca is.

Suweca is a top-rank performer and teacher, fully in command of the music from both practical and theoretical points of view. He blends instinctive response and analytical knowledge to facilitate communication, expression, and ultimately transcendence. These thoughts provide some preliminary insight into the kinds of values and meanings that Balinese attach to their music. For Suweca, performance and musical expertise facilitate a concrete sense of civic usefulness.

Through memorization and rehearsal, Balinese performers strive to put the patterns and forms of the music "on automatic" while playing in order to direct their concentration elsewhere. Of course, Suweca is describing a kind of performance epiphany, and I do not wish to imply that Balinese musicians are not ordinarily engaged in aurally monitoring the progress of the music that they are playing while they are playing it. They are, and—particularly owing to the absence of notation—often with considerable awareness. What his words do suggest is that such experiences are mainly accessible to experts capable of participating at a level high enough to facilitate a kind of internalized structural perception, or, more precisely, a competence enabling the musician to move beyond conscious labeling of structural events as the music unfolds.[3]

Labeling is one way that Britten improves his understanding, but this kind of intellectual distancing mechanism is not a part of Coast's arsenal, and it is something that Suweca enjoys the option of dispensing with. The latter hears everything in the structure, but puts his perceptions in the service of valuing group effort. Coast, ironically, parses almost nothing in the structure but recognizes that same group effort. What Suweca projects—an integrated sonic world—is precisely what Coast hears, though Suweca chooses metaphors of cooperation, work, and religion rather than comparisons with technological

---

3. To be sure, poorly rehearsed *gamelan* and lesser performers than Suweca may feel equally useful at the civic level, but their peers will still judge them by higher standards of musicianship in any comparison with better groups.

precision. What is important for the moment is that the stimuli provoking Suweca's sentiments—the "fierce and sharp sounds"—are acoustic occurrences that have what appears to be a comparable effect on both him and Coast. This connection provides a conceptual link between experiences at both ends of the continuum of expertise. Though Coast and Suweca are miles apart in their perceptions, one of the music's successes is its ability to speak to both of them on the same terms.

Kebyar Timbre and the "Outside" of the Sound

The "terrific chord" that the Peliatan musicians struck up for Coast is a musical and orchestrational convention called by the onomatopoetic term *byar*. It may be heard many times during a composition, and is often used as a beginning sonority (see figs. 2.13 and 8.3A). The word *kebyar,* from which it derives, means to flare up suddenly or to burst open. Though Coast mentions only "drum and metallophone," *byar* is actually a *tutti sforzando* in which all of the bronze-keyed metallophones play the same scale tone, each in its special register, so that together the more than four octaves of the *gamelan*'s tuned gamut is spanned. Additionally, the *reyong,* a set of twelve horizontally mounted knobbed gongs played by four musicians, strikes a set of eight tones spanning over two octaves in the mid-to-upper register. The largest hanging gong, the cymbals, and a deep-pitched drum are sounded too, blending with the *reyong* and metallophones to produce a sonority that can extend for more than five octaves—from the deepest gong to the smallest, highest metallophone, and farther if the prominent upper partials are counted in.

The same eight horizontal gongs are sounded on the *reyong* no matter which scale tone the keyed instruments are playing; they include two of the five scale tones sounded once each and three that occur twice, each in a different register. In this sense what Coast referred to as a chord truly is a vertical aggregate of pitches, but the *reyong* component's invariance throughout the entire repertoire tells us that its part of the *byar* is not functional harmony, but a timbral extension of the particular scale tone prevailing on the metallophones. One good way of hearing the full *gamelan* sound in these cases is to understand the metallophones' scale tone as a kind of "multiregister fundamental sonority." This is given bass coloration and extension by the large gong and the drum, themselves tuned to invariant pitches not necessarily within the scale (though the large gong is often tuned an octave below the scale's first note), and further enriched by the *reyong,* which acts as a ringing set of complex, formant-like "enrichment tones" in the mid and upper ranges.[4]

---

4. Formants are fixed components of an instrument's sound quality, in the form of unvarying bandwidths of pitch and timbre that are emphasized regardless of the fundamental pitch. To some extent, however, when speaking of gongs and metallophones, each gong or key has its own formant structure.

The *byar* sound is concentrated and intense, with a hard, clanging edge to it. It marshals the full resources of the ensemble at its peak dynamic. The high end of the sound is piercing, and the bottom, booming and sustained by the gongs and lower metallophones, is brought into focus with the crisp report of the drum. Between these extremes is a spacious realm of pulsating metallic timbre, which can be finely differentiated in the listener's ear into the various instrumental strata and their individual sounds and musical functions. This is true despite the near ubiquity of vibrating bronze as an oscillating medium. Though in other musical contexts the *gamelan* sound may be rounded at the crest (when a lower dynamic is used or if a bamboo flute is added to the mix), or simplified (if some instruments drop out of the texture), the *byar* is both an acoustic and stylistic signature.

Two main factors contribute to the acoustic identities of the strata: the timbre of each instrument group's keys or gongs (as determined by both their register and the hardness of the mallet used to strike them), and the tuning of the ensemble as a whole. Let us consider the first factor briefly, and the second in some detail.

In *New Images of Musical Sound,* Robert Cogan investigates the spectra of some Balinese instruments' sounds, revealing analogs between orchestrational convention and acoustic actuality. The sound produced by striking a tuned key is shown to vary greatly depending on the material used to strike it and whether or not it is resonated with a bamboo tube (all *kebyar* metallophone keys are so resonated, but gongs are not). In his first illustration Cogan shows that when the object used to strike the key is comparatively soft (for example a human hand), the resultant sound consists largely of fundamental plus odd harmonic partials—a square-wave spectrum. In a second case, the unresonated key is struck with a wooden mallet; here the formant noise produced at the moment of attack enriches the timbre greatly, suffusing it with a dense cluster of harmonic and enharmonic partials stretching upward, beginning at a distance of approximately one octave above the fundamental. In a third case, the same key and mallet are resonated with a bamboo tube tuned to resonate the fundamental. The effect is dramatic. Most of the rich coloration is filtered out, leaving the fundamental and a "spray of spectral elements" in the upper registers (1984:47–48). The resonating power of the tube is impressive: left to decay on its own, a struck key may still be audible after thirty or forty seconds, especially in the lower registers.

The spectral components of the full *byar* sound can be adduced from this information.[5] The lower-register metallophones in *kebyar* are struck with soft mallets, providing a hollow, singing, fundamental-heavy timbre analogous to that described in case 1 above, except that the presence of bamboo resonators

---

5. Cogan's data was obtained using a pair of metallophones from the *gamelan gender wayang,* a small ensemble used to accompany the shadow play. *Kebyar* metallophones are similarly constructed, though the keys are somewhat thicker.

amplifies the fundamental even more. Cogan's second case applies to the little gongs of the *reyong,* the sounds of which resonate within the inverted-bowl shape of the gong itself. They are struck with a hard wooden stick cushioned slightly with a layer of wound string. In a *byar,* the storm of overtones resulting from the combination of eight *reyong* tones blurs the integrity of the component scale tones somewhat.[6] The third case applies to the remainder of the metallophones in the *gamelan.* These come in three ranges spanning four octaves, and are struck with hard wooden mallets. Though they produce strong fundamentals, they also emit, as per case 3, a limited set of upper partials in the same range as those produced by the *reyong.* In its total spectrum, then, a *byar* sound is stratified. At the bottom, the relatively uncomplex sound of the fundamental coming from the low metallophones (plus drum and gong) dominates, juxtaposed with the clangier fundamental played on the lower two types of metallophones struck with hard mallets. In the next layer, the higher-register soundings of the fundamental are ringed by a strongly audible cloud of partials emanating from the lower half of the *reyong* and the clangy fundamental just mentioned. Also in this part of the sound, partially distorted, are the fundamentals of the eight *reyong* tones. Above the apex of the tuned gamut hover the upper resonances of both the higher metallophones and the top end of the *reyong.*

The inherent acoustic properties of the *gamelan* thus consist of the sound of oscillating bronze and the spectral envelope of that sound as shaped by the particular form of the vibrating medium, the hardness of the mallet used, and the shape of the resonating chamber. Because of the nature of these components, the various timbral strata blend yet are acoustically distinct. The seemingly contradictory rapport enabling groups of instruments to behave in this way is not uniquely Balinese, as consideration of other orchestral traditions would reveal. But it is specially enhanced by Balinese tuning procedures, which both grant common identities to sounds across registers by shaping them into the steps of a scale, and reinforce tones' individuality by avoiding the kinds of frequency ratios that produce simple unisons and octaves. This synergy between acoustics and system design affects musical structure and expression in a variety of ways.

Scale (*Saih*) and Tuning (*Laras*)

In the five-tone *kebyar* scale the octave is subdivided into three small and two large intervals, but the size of the intervals and their absolute pitch varies from

---

6. In my composition *Pascima Segara Madu* (1987) for *kebyar,* I had the metallophones play chord-like formations similar to those conventionally used on the *reyong.* I found that because of their relatively simpler timbre, the metallophones used in this way neither projected as well as the *reyong* nor blurred into a spectrum of pure timbre, as the *reyong* does. Instead, the absence of a single multi-register fundamental weakened the sound and created balance problems.

ensemble to ensemble. The constituent scale tones are named, in ascending order, with the solmization syllables *ding, dong, deng, dung,* and *dang.* The full tuned gamut includes twenty-one tones, extending from low *ding* to the high *ding* four registers above, inclusive. The larger gaps in the scale (ranging from 350 to 450 cents) fall between *deng/dung* and between *dang/*next-octave-*ding;* the smaller intervals (80–200 cents) are between the other tones. The absolute pitch for the tone *ding* varies within a range of about 300 cents; it is most often close to Western C or C♯, but may extend up to or beyond D♯. On average, the lowest tuned key lies near standard C3 or C♯3, about 130 Hz, and the highest close to C7 or C♯7, about 2080 Hz. A large gong, considered to be outside the gamut, oscillates near 65 Hz if it matches *ding.*

The term *pélog,* originating from Java, is commonly used to label the scales of *kebyar* and most other Balinese *gamelan* types, though local terms flourish. In earlier forms *pélog* is a seven-tone system referred to in Bali as *saih pitu* (series of seven). The five tones used in *kebyar* are considered to be one of several *patutan* (five-tone subsets or modes) of the full collection, particularly as used in the repertoire of the court *gamelan gambuh* and *semar pegulingan,* historically significant ensembles that are among *kebyar*'s crucial progenitors. The main melodic instruments in *gambuh* are large bamboo flutes, and *saih pitu* is often referred to therein as *tetekep pitu* (seven fingerings); *gamelan se-mar pegulingan* are mainly of bronze, with orchestration and playing tech-niques related to *kebyar*'s. *Pélog gamelan* of all types contrast with those tuned in the other *gamelan* tuning system, called by the Javanese name *slendro,* which is inherently five-tone and characterized by a smoother pentatonic subdivision of the octave into intervals in the 200–300 cent range. *Slendro gamelan* types are comparatively few in Bali, especially when compared to Java, where each full *gamelan* consists of two sets of instruments, one in each of the two sys-tems. Among the Balinese *gamelan* classified as *slendro* are the *gender wayang,* used primarily to accompany the shadow play, and the *angklung,* a village pro-cessional and ritual ensemble.[7]

The various *patutan* of *saih pitu* are called *saih lima* (series of five). To ex-tract *patutan* from the seven-tone collection, one commences from any origin and takes three conjunct steps, skips one, takes two more, and skips the re-maining degree; this creates the characteristic larger interval between the third/fourth and fifth/upper-octave-first tones. *Patutan selisir,* for example, uses tones 123(-)56(-); and *patutan tembung* uses 456(-)12(-). In each *patutan* the first of the three conjunct tones is labeled *ding,* with *dong, deng, dung* and *dang* proceeding from there.[8]

---

7. The hoary subject of the origins of tunings is elusive and will not be addressed here, except to say that many consider *pélog* and *slendro* homologous, with roots in vocal intonation and song (Nyo-man Rembang, personal communication, October 1982; see also Herbst 1997:37).

8. Seven modes thus derived are therefore possible, but according to current understanding in the *gamelan gambuh/semar pegulingan* repertoire only four have been used. In *gambuh* moreover modes are

But in *kebyar* the words "mode" and *patutan* should be eschewed and reserved for seven-tone contexts in which the various *saih lima* can be heard in
relation to one another. Since no other pitch combinations are possible on
kebyar-tuned instruments I opt to retain the word "scale" to describe *kebyar*'s
collection of five tones within the bounds of an octave, and use the term "scale
tone" to reference the five scale degrees *ding, dong, deng, dung,* and *dang.* When
dealing specifically with the two-octave melodic-registral space of the higher
metallophones, as I frequently shall, I designate lower-octave tones with a
capitalized vowel *(dIng)* and upper-octave ones with lower-case *(ding).* Scale

---

extracted from flute fingerings and overblowings, which cause actual pitch to vary from mode to mode
(Richter 1992), but in the bronze *semar pegulingan* they were extracted from a pretuned *saih pitu* set.

Since the late 1980s, revival of *gambuh*-based seven-tone repertoire has been undertaken with a
new *gamelan* type called *semara dana,* which brings *saih pitu* tuning to *kebyar* instrumentation. The
revival also restimulated interest in modal nomenclature and theory. Wayan Beratha, the composer and
gamelan tuner, charts the various modes in relation to the seven tones of the scale as follows. They are
shown compressed into a single octave:

1. *Selisir*   123 56
2. *Slendro Gdé*   234 67
3. *Baro*   1 345 7
4. *Tembung*   12 456
5. *Sunaren*   23 567
6. *Pengenter alit* 1 34 67
7. *Pengenter*   12 45 7
8. *Lebeng*   1234567

Of these, the underlined *selisir, baro, tembung, sunaren* and *lebeng* are the ones that have been used ·
in *gambuh/semar pegulingan* repertoire. *Baro* and *lebeng* appear rarely; the latter in only one piece
(Sumambang Jawa). Lebeng is understood as a seven-tone mode only in *semar pegulingan* but has a
much more elusive character in *gambuh.*

The two *pengenter (alit* means "little") modes are hypothetical, but were identified and named by
the mid-twentieth-century musician Nyoman Kaler. *Slendro gdé* is so called because it resembles *slendro*; in this *patutan* pitch 7 is labelled *ding,* a special arrangement which emphasizes the character of
slendro in other Balinese *gamelan* (such as *gender wayang).* Two further four-tone modes are identified.
Slendro alit (3457), is used in the *gamelan semara dana* to evoke the particular *slendro* intervals and
comparatively high pitch register of the four-tone *gamelan angklung*; and *jegog* (2357) because it evokes
the unique scale of the bamboo *gamelan jegog* of Western Bali.

Other than the *gambuh*-derived modes, however, these designations are not widely known or accepted. They have become somewhat more so in the 1990s as the seven-tone revival has intensified
(Andrew McGraw, personal communication, February 1998). Moreover, Beratha's classification contradicts McPhee's (1966:141).

A further, unrelated terminological complication arises when speaking of the absolute pitch level
of *kebyar* tunings. In the minds of many familiar with it, the *gambuh selisir* mode is higher and brighter
in character than *tembung* (even though the former's *ding* begins on pitch 1 of *saih pitu* and the latter's
on pitch 4). I was told that this is because the characteristic low tunings of the court *gamelan gong gdé*
were based on *tembung* interval qualities. Whatever the reason, *kebyar gamelan* tuned higher (*ding* in
the range of C♯ or above) are said to be *selisir* in quality; those tuned lower (*ding* at C or below) are
said to be *tembung.* This reflects not an actual pitch difference between the modes, which would be a
much larger one were this use of the terms faithful to the *gambuh saih pitu* model, but a difference
between their perceived characters.

In terms of modal *behavior,* Rai (1996, following Hood 1990) has attempted to show the workings
of overarching pitch hierarchies and melodic formulas in the seven-tone *gamelan semar pegulingan*
repertoire. Hood implies that they may be remnants of pre-seventeenth-century Javanese practice.

tone also has the more abstract connotation of pitch-class, in that it may be used to indicate all concurrent appearances of a given scale degree throughout the gamut.

However such definitions of scale, unison, and octave equivalence apply in Bali, they work primarily at a conceptual level. Acoustically speaking all of these notions are, to varying extents, fictions. *Kebyar,* like all *gamelan,* are tuned as a whole—not by matching the intervals or pitches between registers, but by working outward from a central octave and adjusting the surrounding ones in such a way as to achieve a carefully formed environment of pitch identities and relationships. This totality is referred to as *laras.* It is not possible to describe the *laras* of an ensemble accurately with reference to less than the entire collection of intervals across the full range of tuned pitches. Balinese routinely speak of octaves *(ngembat, penangkep,* or *oktaf)* because the five tones of the scale are functionally linked in the music and conventionally referred to by the same set of syllables throughout the gamut, even though scale tones sharing the same syllable may not be in a precise 2:1 frequency ratio (or multiple thereof) with each other. The actual distances in cents between scale tones varies from register to register, and even between pairs of instruments in the same register. As a result *gamelan laras* are complicated affairs, and tuning is a skill mastered by few.[9] These facts have for some decades been recognized by scholars, though publications on the subject are scant.[10] McPhee (1966: 36–55) measured intervals within a single octave for a large selection of *gamelan,* but without reference to any additional aspects of tuning. The following summary is indebted to the research of Andrew Toth, whose writings on the subject have thus far been available only in Indonesian (Toth 1993).

In his investigation of forty-nine sets of *kebyar* instruments, Toth describes two "polarities," known by the terms *begbeg* and *tirus,* and an "in-between" type, *sedeng.* They refer to interval widths and the degree of contrast between intervals within a given octave, and are used to describe the full ensemble's *laras* as well (1993:102). *Begbeg* means straight or lined up, *tirus* means narrow and converged, and *sedeng* means moderate or average. In *gamelan* with *begbeg*-type *laras* the large gaps in the scale are larger (over 400 cents) and the smaller ones smaller (under 130 cents), creating sharply defined intervallic oppositions. In *tirus,* the relative sizes of the intervals approach "convergence": the small gaps may attain nearly 200 cents and the large ones shrink to around

---

9. Wayan Beratha's tuning for the STSI conservatory *gamelan,* considered to be *selisir* because it is relatively high in pitch (see previous note), has become a popular model. *Gamelan* are often brought to him for retuning, and as a merchant his wares are generally considered the best, though he does not cast and forge keys in his own workshop, but rather contracts that work out to others.

McPhee's statement that "many *gamelan* clubs have their own tuners (1966:36)" may have been true in the 1930s, but is no longer so. Keys and gongs are manufactured exclusively by members of the *pandé* (smiths) clan in one of three main centers: Tihingan (Klungkung district), Blahbatuh (Gianyar district), and Sawan (Buleleng district). Most large gongs are imported from Java.

10. The issue was first raised in Hood 1966:31–32.

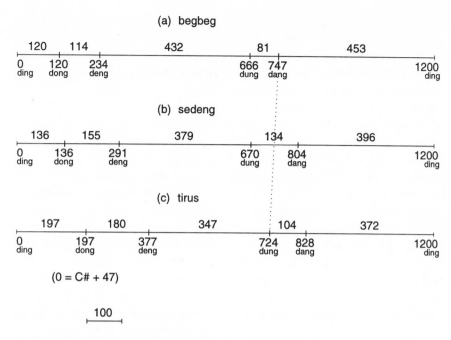

Figure 2.1. *Begbeg, tirus,* and *sedeng* tunings (from Toth 1993)

350. However, the intervals do not lose their *pélog* character or come to resemble the relative sameness of *slendro* intervals. *Tirus* and *begbeg* are associated with different musical and aesthetic preferences: the former is held to be better for old repertoire, and *laras* on the *begbeg* side are preferred for the sharp discontinuities of modern music such as *kebyar*. *Sedeng* tunings attempt to preserve a little bit of the character of each. Specific *laras* are also associated with different regions, villages, or famous groups (1993:105). In figure 2.1 representative *begbeg, tirus,* and *sedeng* interval collections are shown, measured in cents from a common origin tone.

Interacting with the intervallic structure across the full gamut are the properties of scale tones in "unison." Metallophones are tuned in pairs to create shimmering acoustical beats called *ombak* (wave[s]). This phenomenon is audible (it "pulsated" Coast "out of his seat"), and is as much a part of an ensemble's sonic identity as the spectrum or scale. In each pair of tones the lower is called the *pengumbang* ("hummer," from a word for bee) and the higher one the *pengisep* ("sucker," from *isep*, to suck). Gongs are not paired in the *gamelan* and so are not tuned in this way, but all oscillate in pitch to a degree on their own, ideally in concert with the rest of the *gamelan*. (The *reyong* is conventionally matched with the *pengumbang*; a similarly constructed instrument, the *trompong*, is tuned to *pengisep*.) The quick beating in *kebyar* is one mark of the music's intensity; people often vocalize the *byar* sound with an explosively aspirated cry after which the final *r* is rolled so quickly that it practically becomes a buzz, and prolonged in imitation of the instruments. This evokes the proper mood of heightened alertness and excitement.

Toth confirmed that the rate of beating (*penjorog*) is characteristically consistent across the entire range of the instruments within any single ensemble, ranging from a minimum of 6.3 to a maximum of 9.7 Hz, with a mean of 7.8 Hz (1993:102). A constant rate of beating means that there must be a greater difference in cents between pairs of pitches at the low end of the gamut than the high. Consequently, the *pengisep* of lowest-octave *ding* may be as much as 100 cents above its *pengumbang* counterpart—high enough to approach the *pengumbang* of its neighbor *dong*—while the difference in pitch between a pair of keys tuned to the highest-octave *ding* is scarcely perceptible.

The intervals between adjacent tones are slightly different in each register because the multiplicative increase in frequency from octave to octave must be reconciled with the uniform difference in Hz between *pengumbang/pengisep* pairs on which the *penjorog* depends. To achieve this, *gamelan* tuners work outward from a central octave (*petuding*), slightly altering the size of the octave relationships between registers. A simple calculation shows why these alterations are necessary. Suppose that the frequency of a given *pengumbang* tone is 220 Hz. If the *penjorog* rate is 8 cycles per second, the corresponding *pengisep* tone will be tuned to 228 Hz. Precisely one octave above the *pengumbang* note the frequency would be 440, but if the *pengisep* is similarly doubled, to 456, the *penjorog* will also double, to 16 Hz. To avoid this, some or all of the tones are adjusted to preserve the 8 Hz *penjorog*. One solution would be to lower the upper octave *pengisep* to 448 Hz, thus compressing the octave for this half of the pair. Similarly, the *pengisep* could be tuned to a perfect octave and the upper *pengumbang* stretched by nudging it to 448 Hz. Or both could be altered, so long as the difference between their frequencies remains unchanged.[11]

Broadly speaking, if *pengumbang* octaves are tuned exactly 2:1 throughout the entire gamut, the *pengisep* octaves must shrink progressively as they rise. Or if *pengisep* octaves are tuned exactly, *pengumbang* octaves stretch as they rise. But these arrangements are hypothetical. The most common pattern for *laras kebyar* is to widen the *pengumbang* octaves in the low register, bring them close to 1200 cents in the middle, and widen them again in the upper register (1993:106). *Pengisep* octaves are slightly smaller than 1200 cents throughout the range. In this configuration, the extremes of the gamut ring out distinctly. This has the advantageous result of boosting the projection of the lowest register metallophones, which are played with soft mallets and have a muted timbre that might otherwise be hard to perceive.

---

11. Toth provides tuning measurements for an exception, the *gamelan* of *banjar* Sidakarya Tengah, in which the *penjorog* is not steady, but increases gradually from 6.7 Hz at lowest *ding* to 8.8 Hz at highest *ding*.

In the abstract a *kebyar gamelan* may simply be said to encompass four octaves of five tones each, plus the first note of the fifth octave, but it is also accurately described as a set of forty-two independent pitches, half tuned to *pengumbang* and half to *pengisep*. In principle each *laras* is a unique tonal world, unduplicated by any other set of instruments. Well-tuned instruments are suffused with spiritual power (*kasaktian*), making them an attractive medium for entertaining deities or humans. When Suweca spoke of being "enveloped" by the sounds of the instruments, he was responding to the curve of the tuning and the corresponding independence of registers as much as he was to other aspects of the timbre. For him these aspects are of comparable importance.

Cosmology, Aesthetics, and a Spatial Model for Scale Tones

A more esoteric perspective on the independent identities of the five scale tones comes from the *Prakempa,* one of two extant Balinese historical texts dealing exclusively with *gamelan*.[12] *Prakempa* is a *lontar*—a document inscribed on the leaves of the *borassus* palm (*borassus flabellifer*), which has long been the primary medium for writing Balinese literature. Based on the fact that its literary conventions are stylistically similar to the *lontar* genre of court family genealogies called *babad*, the oldest of which appeared around 1750, *Prakempa* is estimated to have been written sometime between the mid-eighteenth and late nineteenth centuries.[13] Like *babad*, it is written in a later version of Kawi, the language of classical Javanese and Balinese literature. The manuscript is not widely known or read, but it has been published and translated into Indonesian by Madé Bandem.[14] At the end of its eighty-four stanzas, one Bhagawan Gottama claims authorship of the text and offers the contents as teachings to his students. The real identity of the writer is obscure, for as Bandem playfully observes, "To think that the author of *Prakempa* is the priest Gottama from the *Ramayana* epic, or Siddharta Gautama, the founder of Buddhism, is to be mistaken indeed" (1986:9).[15] *Prakempa*'s contents, however, point inescapably to the conclusion that this Gottama was a priest of some kind, or at least a court-dweller with access to recondite concepts about the relationship of musical tones to gods and elemental forces. This and

12. The other extant tract is called *Aji Gurnita.* In many details it overlaps with *Prakempa,* but the latter is longer and presents a broader range of ideas and concepts.

13. *Babad* may have been written as early as the seventeenth century (Wallis 1979:17).

14. Bandem's translation from Kawi into Indonesian has been my source for the summary presented here. Bandem's primary source (1986:1), in turn, was a copy of the *lontar* held by Gusti Madé Putu Griya (1906–83), a renowned twentieth-century musician. *Lontar* have for many centuries been the primary medium for disseminating literature in Java and Bali. Calling for a critical edition, Bandem notes that several other versions of the *Prakempa* exist in collections around the island.

15. "Menduga bahwa pengarang lontar Prakempa adalah pendeta Gottama dari wiraceritera Ramayana atau Siddharta Gautama, pemimpin agama Buddha, merupakan sebuah dugaan yang keliru."

other charged and potentially dangerous forms of musical knowledge comprise the bulk of the document's substance.[16] As a synthesis of metaphysical and practical knowledge (albeit on a much smaller scale) *Prakempa* evokes and belongs in a lineage tracing to ancient South Asian Hindu treatises such as the *Natyasastra*.

Right from the outset of *Prakempa*'s exegesis, music is linked to the origins of the universe. After the customary intonation of the sacred invocation syllable *Om* and the obligatory apologies for any mistakes or shortcomings that the author may have brought to bear on the text to follow, *Prakempa* opens with the creation of the world as a consequence of meditations undertaken by Brahma, Wisnu, and Siva, the Hindu trinity of deities, here referred to as a unity called *Sang Hyang Tri Wisesa*.[17] First to appear were three letters, *wisah* (ꦟ), *taleng* (ꦐ) and *cecek* (ꦟ),[18] which emerged from *Sang Hyang Tri Wisesa*'s body. These were followed by the earth, light, weather, the sun, moon, stars, and other celestial bodies, and finally five "dimensions": *Sabda* (thought), *Ganda* (smell), *Rupa* (sight), *Rasa* (hearing/understanding),[19] and *Saparsa* (touch; associated with behavior and self-respect). The five dimensions gave life to "everything that grows and everything that has a mind and thought." [20]

Thereupon the universe was filled with light of many colors, each associated with a cardinal position,[21] a letter, and a tone, as follows:

---

16. Line 53 contains a warning to unqualified or disrespectful music teachers: "after death hell will be your reward, your soul will line the cauldron of Tambragohmuka, you will not be reincarnated as a human, and you will become a termite and everything despised by humans" ("neraka pahalanya hingga sampai saat matinya, rohnya menjadi alasnya kawah Tambragohmuka, tidak bisa menitis menjadi manusia lagi, menjadi kuricak dan segala yang tidak disenangi orang" [1986:77]).

17. *Sang Hyang* is an honorific applied to deities' names. *Tri Wisesa* means "three spiritual powers."

18. The role of written symbols as the ultimate link between cosmological and earthly spheres of existence is emblematic of Balinese reverence for literature and the written word as tools for accessing sacred power. It was the original wave of ninth- and tenth-century immigrating Hindu priests and scribes that helped Balinese rulers of that era accumulate power and legitimacy through the written word, by creating panegyrics linking local princes with deific ancestries.

Additionally, Balinese believe that letters "have not only a practical meaning and value, but a mystical as well. They refer to all parts of the human body and have the power to protect it. That is the reason why the Brahmin priests of Bali, Saiva as well as Bauddha, collect the whole set of *aksara* of this alphabet from the spheres during their daily ritual and in a few *pradaksina* assign them, by the ritual action called *nyasa*, to a place in their immediate neighborhood, as a protection and as a means of enhancing their power" (Hooykaas 1964:37; quoted also in Wallis 1979:103).

As for the notion that letters are the consummate bearers of symbolic meaning, Richter succinctly asserts that "There exists in Bali the concept that all things of the world can be expressed as written signs" (1992:200).

19. *Rasa* in the vernacular means taste, feeling, or sensation, but in *Prakempa* it is used in this way.

20. "Karena ini yang menghidupkan segala yang tumbuh dan yang mempunyai budi serta pikiran" (Bandem 1986:37).

21. The spatial position of Gods, colors, and tones has been noted by Covarrubias (1937:296), McPhee (1946:43), and also Mershon (1970:58).

> In the East, the color was white, the letter *Sang*,
> and the tone was *dang*
> In the Southeast the color was pink, the letter *Nang*
> and the tone was *ndang*
> In the South the color was red, the letter *Bang*
> and the tone was *ding*
> In the Southwest the color was orange, the letter *Mang*,
> and the tone was *nding*
> In the West the color was yellow, the letter *Tang*,
> and the tone was *deng*
> In the Northwest the color was green, the letter *Sing*,
> and the tone was *ndeng*
> In the North the color was black, the letter *Ang*,
> and the tone was *dung*
> In the Northeast the color was blue, the letter *Wang*,
> and the tone was *ndung*
> In the Center Above there were five colors, the letter was *Ing*,
> and the tone was *dong*
> In the Center Below there were five colors, the letter was *Yang*,
> and the tone was *ndong*.[22]

The ten sounds were then ordered into two groups of five. The first array, called *pélog* or *Panca Tirtha* (five holy waters), consisted of *ding, dong, deng, dung,* and *dang.* The second, called *slendro* or *Panca Geni* (five fires) contained *nding, ndong, ndeng, ndung,* and *ndang.*[23] *Panca Tirtha* was manifested in *Semara,* the god of love; and *Panca Geni* in *Ratih,* the goddess of love. From their union, *Semara Ratih,* came the mixture of seven essential tones, *ding, dong, deng, deung, dung, dang,* and *daing.* This series of seven was named *Genta Pinara Pitu* (from *genta,* meaning sound, also a priest's bell; *pinara,* a word whose meaning is obscure; and *pitu,* seven).

The seven syllables of the *Genta Pinara Pitu* series mentioned in *Prakempa* correspond to those used in the *saih pitu* scale of the *gambuh* and *semar pegulingan* ensembles. The etymology of the two extra syllables *deung* and *daing* is not explained in the text, but these terms are in fact used in practice as appellations for the *béro* (nonmodal) tones that fall between *deng-dung* and *dang-ding* in the various *saih lima.* The tones' names are derived from the diphthongs created by fusing the vowel sounds of the tones flanking them.

---

22. Adapted from Bandem 1986:33.

23. In *Prakempa* the initial consonant sound "d" is allied with *pélog* and "nd" with *slendro,* but in contemporary practice both scales may use either initial consonant sound. Because "nd" is a softer sound, it is often used when singing tunes because helps to create a smoothly connected line. Other sounds may be substituted too, such as "j" or "l." The fixed element is the order of vowel sounds: i, o, e, u, a.

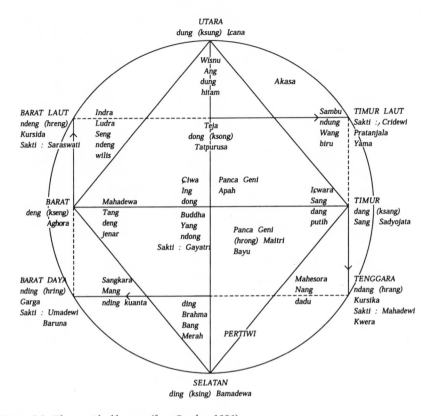

Figure 2.2. The *pangider bhuwana* (from Bandem 1986)

In a mandala-like schema called the *pangider bhuwana* (dispersion of tones around the macrocosmos), shown in figure 2.2, the ten scale tones of *pélog* and *slendro (Panca Tirtha* and *Panca Geni)* are shown deployed at their positions in the cosmos together with their colors and syllables, and linked to one another via deities. The diagram portrays a vibrant macrocosm seen as an interconnected network of spiritual sound, color, and thought, "running," as it were, on powers provided by the gods.

In its specifics, the privileged information represented in the *pangider bhuwana* is not a part of many Balinese musicians' knowledge or awareness. But in the significant sense that tones have unique locations and connotative aspects, there are equivalent principles operative in the domain of ordinary aesthetics. Heard in relation to specific musical contexts, scale tones are felt to have individual character and affect. The acoustic reasons for this are evident from the fact that they are separated by unequal intervals. Beyond this, on the compositional level, the gong tone of a melody (the final scale tone, which coincides with a stroke of the large gong) is an indicator of the music's mood. *Ding* as gong tone is often described as heroic or majestic, *dong* as sensual or demonic, *deng* childish (also supernatural or frightening), *dung* feminine and graceful, and *dang* martial and aggressive. Musicians are not rigid or even in general agreement on these linkages, but most hold opinions on them.

These connotations are merely inchoate when defined solely on the basis of the scale tones' individual acoustic qualities. They are dependent on other factors for their fuller semiotic potential, including the overall tuning of the *gamelan* and the relationship of the gong's pitch to the scale. This is further modified and focused by features such as melodic shape, musical form, and, if the music accompanies dance or drama, the character, locale, and action. Also important are the associations evoked by other gong tones in the repertoire of other compositions that musicians store in their memories, particularly if those compositions have their own theatrical contexts. The scale tone *dong*, for example, may, among many other possibilities, suggest possession and danger because it is the gong tone for *Jauk Keras*, a ubiquitously performed masked dance of a malevolent demon. But the fact that all of these elements play a part in determining individual responses and perspectives does not diminish the tones' essential individuality.[24] The enculturated musician's perception of the uniqueness of tones, the acoustic fact of their independence, and the *Prakempa*'s literary image of their cosmic placement are compatible and mutually reinforcing notions. Their cumulative impact reflects a strong sensation that when *gamelan* melodies move from tone to tone, they proceed not only by either conjunct or disjunct motion along a continuum of pitch relations, but they also—simultaneously and without in any way contradicting this—travel among five independent scale-tone regions, none connected to the others, each with its own sound and associations.

The *pangider bhuwana* is presented less than one-quarter of the way through the *Prakempa*. Gottama thereafter holds forth on a variety of topics. Individual *gamelan* genres are introduced and affiliated with gods, places, and ceremonial functions. Musical instruments and the sounds they produce are mapped to the body above the shoulders and below the nose: gong to the neck, cymbals above the tongue, metallophones at the base of the tongue and open mouth, *trompong* at the tip of the tongue, and *reyong* to the jaw. The pathway of musical sounds through the body—collecting in the head or liver, exiting through the ears, reentering through the nose, and traveling again to the liver, where they merge with the thoughts—is said to be permanently affecting and unendingly pleasurable. The musical elements meter, melody, and rhythm are introduced along with instructions about the proper ratios of rhythmic density

---

24. It hardly needs pointing out that this situation is analogous to the one in Western music prior to the institutionalization of equal temperament.

between the layers of sound in the *gamelan*. The proper way of making religious offerings to *gamelan* is discussed, as are the dos and don'ts of the safeguarding and transmission of musical knowledge (see n. 16).[25]

Bandem observes that *Prakempa*'s value lies in its delineation of four basic aspects of music: philosophy, ethics, aesthetics, and technique (*gagebug*). The first category comprises the cosmological information and origins of tones as described above. Ethics has to do with the role of music, the associations between specific *gamelan* types and prescribed rituals, and the proper respect to be accorded instruments and teachers. Aesthetics encompasses information about scale tones, instruments, and musical structure. Technique, in Bandem's words

> is a central idea in Balinese music. Involving more than the mere skill to properly strike and dampen *gamelan* keys, it has a deeper connotation. *Gagebug* is strongly connected to concepts about orchestration and the fact that, according to *Prakempa,* nearly each instrument has its own special *gagebug* and "physical behavior" aspects. The physical nature of the instruments of the *gamelan* is what transmits their individual qualities to listeners. (1986:27)[26]

Cosmology, practice, and perception are here shown to be connected by their shared dependence on the physical aspects of music.

A Three-Dimensional Model of *Kebyar* Pitch Space

Of the three listeners profiled earlier, only Suweca would associate scale tones with repertoire or extramusical factors like dance or direction. The digression into *Prakempa* was thus a temporary detour away from the acoustic surface intended to enrich the presentation, and to provide culturally relevant background for the model given in figure 2.3. In the model the *pangider bhuwana* is taken as an essentially Cartesian representation of a spatial concept, and is therefore useful as a basis for constructing a three-dimensional drawing of *gamelan* pitch space. Such a model is helpful in portraying the physical dimensions of the sound in all of its timbral and structural variety, in particular the independent character of each tone in the gamut. I feel that this conception is more evocative of the actual sensation of hearing *gamelan* as an acoustical phenomenon than a standard two-dimensional, pitch-against-time axis such as that shown in most music notations. Transcription in this and later chap-

---

25. See Covarrubias 1937:296, McPhee 1946:43, and Mershon 1970:58.

26. "Gagebug merupakan suatu hal yang pokok dalam gambelan Bali. Gagebug atau teknik permainan bukan hanya sekedar ketrampilan memukul dan menutup bilah gambelan, tetapi mempunyai konotasi yang lebih dalam daripada itu. Gagebug mempunyai kaitan erat dengan orkestrasi dan menurut Prakempa bahwa hampir setiap instrumen mempunyai gagebug tersendiri dan mengandung aspek 'physical behavior' dari instrumen tersebut. Sifat fisik dari instrumen-instrumen yang terdapat dalam gambelan Bali memberi keindahan masing-masing pada penikmatnya."

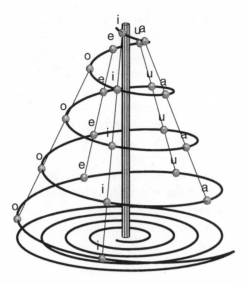

Figure 2.3. A three-dimensional model for the *kebyar* pitch gamut

ters adapts standard Western notation but assumes as a basis this three-dimensional image of the unified but internally diverse sound of the ensemble.

Scale tones' positions in the *pangider bhuwana* are in dialectic contrast with their frequencies, which progress along the continuum from low to high. The tones are illustrated at cardinal points without regard to their relative pitch, registral disposition, or timbre, but these additional parameters are indeed aspects of their characters in musical contexts. There they are perceived not only in such terms, but through their function in the music.

Blending circular and linear representations, the *pangider bhuwana* is here projected into three dimensions as a spiral coil, with the tones of the scale positioned *as if* directionally. (This necessitates some interpretive leeway, for in *Prakempa* one of the five tones *(dong)* is in the center rather than on the rim. The intention is to capture the spirit of the spatial plan and not its precise details, which, as esoterica, do not have specific technical relevance in any case. In the spiral version the pitches lose their affiliations with directions and the center, but they retain individual spatial identities.)

The coil may be thought of as a curved line that accommodates pitch as frequency, progressing up the spectrum. Each solmization syllable for the five scale tones *(ding, dong, deng, dung, dang;* abbreviated here with their distinguishing vowels) is positioned along the same azimuth whenever it occurs, thus preserving the spirit of its invariant "cardinal direction" per the *pangider bhuwana;* but the move up the surface of the cone toward the tip shows the changing registers. Additionally, each tone in the gamut is positioned at a unique point on the surface, such that a series of conical cross-sections, taken at each tone from the lowest one on up, would result in twenty-one circular surfaces of steadily decreasing radii. These aspects represent both the conceptual links between scale tones in different registers and the individual character of each note in the gamut, seen in its acoustic dissimilarity to its counterparts in other octaves.

Moving toward the tip of the spiral, the shrinking distance between adjacent tones depicts the spacious, unencumbered quality of the low register and the compact acoustic and timbral clarity of the high end. The spiral shape is also loosely metaphoric for the characteristic rhythmic features of the music in each register—generally speaking, instruments tuned in the low end of the gamut play sparsely and those at the high end with greater density. This is an aspect of orchestral layering and rhythmic stratification, to be considered in full after the instruments themselves and their classifications have been presented.

Instrumentation

To this point descriptions of *kebyar* sound have been given in the absence of much information about the instruments and the way they are played (the *reyong* chord excepted) in order to facilitate a phenomenological approach to the *byar* and its components. Turning now to instrumentation and orchestration will help to illuminate the constraints and conventions of organizing timbre as it changes with the succession of musical events over time. Timbre in *kebyar* interfaces with musical structure because orchestrational change is used as a tool for setting off formal divisions in the music. Though the range of possible orchestral combinations in *kebyar* is more limited than the size of the ensemble would seem to suggest, it is much broader than in most other kinds of Balinese *gamelan* music where ordinarily all of the instruments play all of the time.

The construction and resources of instruments and instrument groups determine their characteristic playing styles and roles in the musical fabric. Instruments played with soft mallets have ranges at the low end of the gamut, where their slow-speaking tones are confined to relatively slow-moving melodies. These instruments can be featured in the texture only when the dynamic is soft enough for their fundamental-heavy sonorities to cut through. The richer and brighter upper instruments normally dominate the sound. Balance between upper and lower registers can vary depending on the type of music that each of the instrument groups is called upon to play.

Instrumentation in the present-day *gong kebyar* is widespread and fairly standardized, though some regional exceptions persist and musicians' preferences change over the years. It consists of the following, grouped here into three preliminary categories defined by construction and materials: metallophones, gongs, and miscellany. Instrument design and iconography of the usually lavish carvings are explored by DeVale and Dibia (1991); I restrict my comments to basic terms and information relating to performance technique, acoustics, and tuning. The descriptions are keyed to the drawings in figure 2.4 and the chart of instrument ranges in staff notation in figure 2.5.[27] The staff pitches C♯-D-E-G♯-A represent the *kebyar* scale in Western notation throughout the present study for consistency and for the sake of continuity with McPhee, who mainly used the same system. Drum and gong sounds are approximations, since in practice they are not necessarily matched to scale tones.

Metallophones

Gangsa are ten-keyed metallophones usually of the hanging *(gantung)* type, with bronze *(kerawang)* keys *(daun* or *bilah)* suspended on cords strung through holes bored at both ends of each key. The keys hang over bamboo resonators *(bumbung)* that fit in a wooden case *(pelawah; tatak)*. *Gangsa gantung* are also generically known as *gender,* especially those in the upper registers. A few villages, mostly in the north and northeast (such as Tejakula on the north coast east of Singaraja) still prefer the brittle sound of the *jongkok* construction. In *gangsa jongkok* identical keys lie over the resonators cushioned on small rubber pads. They are held in place by posts inserted through the holes and hammered through the rubber and into the case. Metallophone cases are mostly made from jackfruit wood *(nangka* or *ketewel;* Latin *autocarpus heterophyllus)*. The keys are struck with a small wooden hammer *(panggul gangsa)* held in one hand, and the resonance of the keys is damped *(tekep)* by grasping the key just played between the thumb and second knuckle of the index finger of the other hand. A key speaks in three primary ways: it may be allowed to ring until its sound fades (or until the next note is struck), it may be damped prior to the next tone (to facilitate the placement of an interlocking part's tone in between or give *detaché* articulation), or it may be struck and damped simultaneously (a pitched, dry clicking sound results).

All *gangsa* have the scale tone *dOng* as their lowest note and a two-octave, ten-key range ending at high *ding*. The *gangsa* section has nine or ten instruments in three registers, comprising:

1. Four *gangsa kantilan* (called *kantilan* or simply *kantil*), whose high *ding* is at the peak of the gamut. Two each are tuned *pengumbang* and *pengisep*.

2. Four *gangsa pemadé* (called *pemadé*), like the kantilan but an octave lower and with correspondingly larger keys and case.

---

27. Two Indonesian sources may be consulted to augment the information presented here. Additional detailed information about the precise dimensions of instruments and names of their component parts may be found in Aryasa 1984–85:105–27. An excellent primer on the process of manufacturing instruments is Rembang 1984–85b.

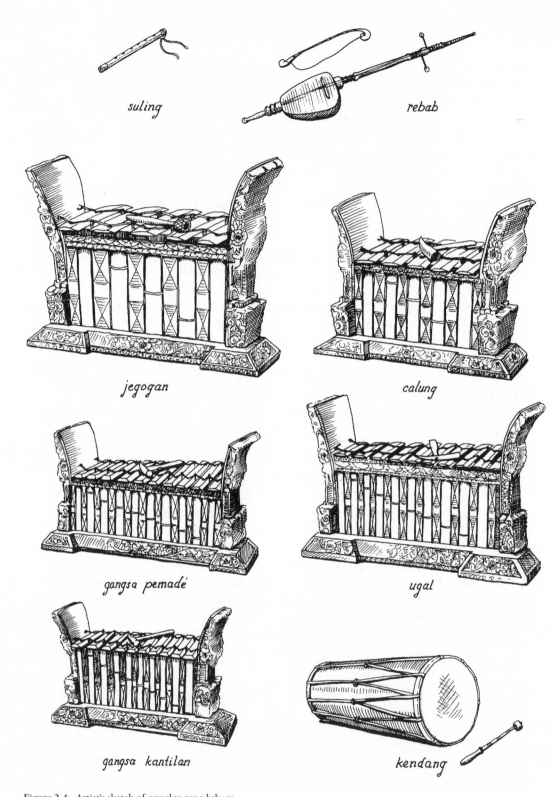

suling

rebab

jegogan

calung

gangsa pemadé

ugal

gangsa kantilan

kendang

Figure 2.4. Artist's sketch of *gamelan gong kebyar*

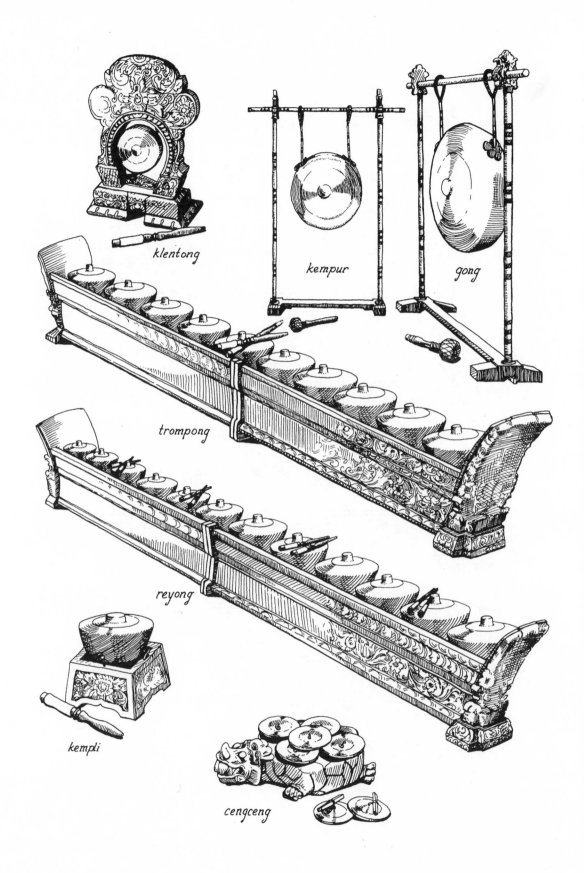

klentong

kempur

gong

trompong

reyong

kempli

cengceng

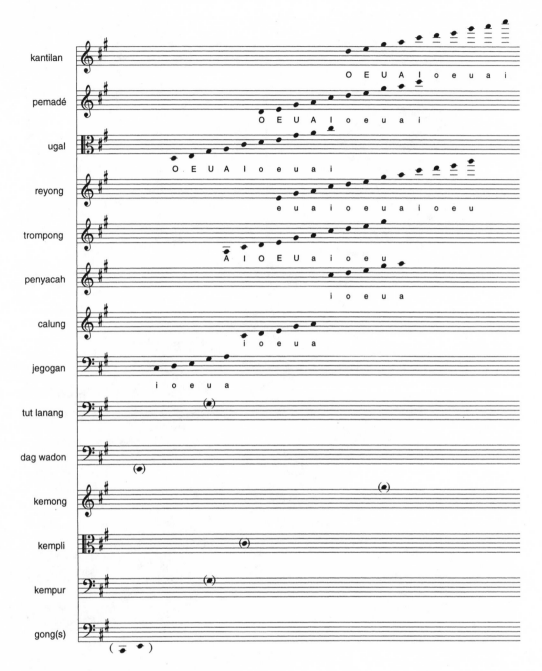

Figure 2.5. *Kebyar* instrument ranges

3. One or occasionally two *gangsa pengugal* or *giying* (most often called *ugal*), an octave lower than the *pemadé,* but also taller, so that its player, who is one of the ensemble's leaders, is more easily seen. If there is one *ugal* only, it is tuned *pengumbang.*

In conventional usage the plural term *gangsa* often excludes the *ugal* even though strictly speaking it is part of the *gangsa* family. This is because the single *ugal* normally plays a musical part different from that of the eight *pemadé* and *kantilan,* and musicians discussing the "*gangsa* part" of a composition may be referring to the latter instruments only. Context indicates which usage is intended.

Supporting the *gangsa* and *ugal* are several kinds of larger metallophones played with softer *panggul,* each a *pengumbang/pengisep* pair. Each instrument type has five keys and a span of one octave, though very occasionally instruments of six or seven keys are used, with the extra keys added on the lower end.

4. The two *calung* (sometimes called *jublag*) are tuned beginning with the *ding* that is the same as the fifth note on the *ugal* and proceeding up the scale to *dang. Panggul calung* are larger than *panggul gangsa* and tipped with rubber.

5. Two *jegogan* one octave lower than the *calung* and considerably larger; these are the largest metallophones and occupy the low end of the gamut. The ends of *panggul jegogan* are small flattened spheres, cloth-coated and padded with rubber.

6. Two *penyacah,* an octave higher than the *calung* (these were once rarely used, but are increasingly seen since the 1980s). *Panggul* are smaller versions of *panggul calung.* More often than the *jegogan* and *calung, penyacah* use seven keys, adding the scale tone *dang* at the low end and *ding* at the upper.

Gongs

Gongs serve colotomic (i.e., cycle-marking or *gongan*-demarcating), melodic, and agogic functions. In the latter two cases they are small, horizontally mounted, and tuned to the gamut. Colotomic gongs, horizontally mounted, are hung in wooden frames or held in the lap. All gongs are played on the boss, save for one special case on the *reyong,* described below.[28] As noted, colotomic gongs are likely to match scale tones, but many *gamelan* groups prefer the extra dimension added by keeping them distinct.

7. The *trompong* is not always present in *kebyar* music, as it is mostly associated with repertoire originating in *gamelan* genres of the courtly past, especially the *gamelan gong gdé.* When used, it fronts the ensemble with a leading melodic line performed by a single musician. In *kebyar* the *trompong* has ten kettles, extending upward from the *dAng* that matches the fourth *ugal* key.

---

28. Two Balinese gongs have a sunken boss; see below.

The soloist plays with two long *panggul* wound with string at the ends to cushion the sound.

8. The *reyong* (also *réong, riong,* and *riyong*) extends across the upper registers of the ensemble with twelve kettles stretching from *deng,* the seventh tone of the *ugal,* to *dung,* the eighth tone of the *kantilan.* The four players are ordinarily confined to a limited number of tones ranging from two to four kettles, but depending on the musical context, players may temporarily overlap into a neighbor's terrain, thereby expanding their range by one or two tones. The positions—*penyorog* (three kettles: *deng, dung, dang*), *pengenter* (three kettles: *ding, dong, deng*), *ponggang* (two kettles: *dung, dang*), and *pemetit* or *petit* (four kettles: *ding, dong, deng, dung*)—are diagrammed in figure 2.6.[29] *Panggul,* two per player, are smaller versions of *panggul trompong.* The *reyong* kettles may be played melodically, on the boss; or agogically, in one of two ways. One is on the lower rim, producing *kecek,* a sound closely resembling that of the *cengceng* (cymbals). The *reyong* component of the *byar* chord is obtained when kettles 1, 3, 4, 6, 7, 9, 10, and 12 are struck simultaneously. Referred to in terms of the *reyong* alone the chord is called *byong* when allowed to ring. When quickly damped it is known as *byot;* when fully damped as *jet.*

The *pemetit* sometimes duplicates the *pengenter* an octave below, but it often has its own part, doubled nowhere else, that rings out brightly across the crest of the texture.

9. The *kempli,* a single small gong held in the lap or horizontally mounted, divides metric periods into beats, or, in some older repertoires, marks melodic subsection endings. *Panggul kempli* are slightly shorter and thicker than *panggul trompong.* The *kempli* is struck on the boss but muted with the other hand near the rim.

10. The *klentong* (or *kemong*), at about 26 cm diameter the smallest hanging gong in the ensemble, marks internal melodic divisions, most often at the midway point. It is often tuned to *dung.* The *klentong* is played with a string-wound stick similar to a *panggul reyong.*

11. The *kempur* (or *kempul*), also often tuned to *dung,* is a mid-size gong, averaging 70 cm in diameter. It is heard in alternation with or in place of the *klentong* as a colotomic marker. The tip of the *panggul* is similar to that used for the *jegogan* but considerably larger.

12. *Gong* marks the beginnings and endings of cyclic melodies and reinforces accents in music without a metric period. *Kebyar gamelan* often use two,

---

29. My informant for these terms was Pande Madé Sukerta, a musician from Tejakula village in North Bali now teaching at the conservatory in Surakarta, Java (personal communication, August 1986). Of them only the last, *pemetit,* is widely known and used.

As for the meanings of the four terms, *penyorog* derives from *sorog* (to push or cause to move). *Pengenter* means leader; this position's player is often relied upon for cueing motions, especially in the characteristic virtuoso passages where *reyong* is heard alone. *Ponggang* refers to an eponymous instrument in the *gamelan gong gdé* consisting of only two kettles, tuned to *dung* and *dang* in the same register. *Pemetit* means "small one."

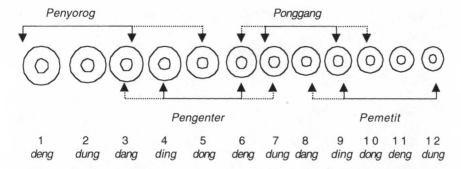

Figure 2.6. *Reyong* players' positions. Kettles aligned with the solid lines comprise the normal span of each position's range; those aligned with the dotted lines are extensions of the range used in special situations.

pitched between 200 and 300 cents apart. The lower, *gong wadon* (female) is used in alternation with the higher *gong lanang* (male), particularly in shorter meters where the frequency of gong strokes makes tonal contrast desirable. In general the *gong wadon* is tuned to *ding,* but some are tuned as much as a whole step below this; the *lanang* often matches *deng.* Most gongs used in Bali are imported from Java, though some are cast at the foundries in Tihingan village. Balinese prefer slightly smaller (ca. 85 cm) large gongs than do the Javanese, because such instruments speak and pulsate more rapidly, melding with the *ombak* tuning. *Panggul* are thickly padded with a combination of rubber, cloth, and string.

The gong *wadon* has the most impact on shaping the overall sound of the *gamelan.* It should be *tangglus* (penetrating) and pulsate at the same rate as the ensemble that it supports. The entire ensemble should be *tangglus* in the same way as the gong, compelling the attention of the listener through sheer sonic power.

13. Other colotomic gongs used from time to time in *kebyar* include the *kempur*-sized *bebendé,* the *kempli*-like *kajar,* and the tiny *kelenang.* All are associated with specific pre-*kebyar* repertoires and used only when those older styles are evoked. *Bebendé* and *kajar* are sunken-bossed and consequently of imprecise pitch. The medium sized *bebendé* is sometimes found in the *gamelan gong gdé,* where it is hung from a stand and provides a mildly syncopated ostinato pattern in conjunction with the *cengceng.* The smaller *kajar,* held in the lap, doubles drum patterns in the *gamelan gambuh* and *gamelan semar pegulingan.* The *kelenang* plays off-beats and is handheld or mounted on a stand.

Other Instruments

Kendang (drums), the melodic instruments *suling* and *rebab,* and *cengceng* (cymbals) comprise the remainder of the ensemble. All but the latter provide timbral contrast in the otherwise all-bronze texture.

14. The two drums *kendang wadon* and *kendang lanang* front the ensemble,

Kendang cedugan, Kerobokan, 1982. Photo: Author.

and in most cases the player of the *wadon* is the ensemble director. *Kendang* for *kebyar* are almost universally made from *nangka* wood cut in the shape of a tapering cylinder about 68 cm long, and with diameters of 30 and 25 cm for the right and left ends respectively. They are laced lengthwise with rawhide strips that control the tension on the two cow-skin drumheads, by means of sliding rings placed over adjacent strips. The skins are stretched over hoops placed over each end of the drum. Inside, the drums are hollowed out in an hourglass shape that allows the larger, right-hand side of the drum to speak with a deep pitch. For the *kendang lanang* the narrowest part of the hourglass is positioned exactly halfway down the drum; this gives it a comparatively higher pitch than the *wadon,* which is narrowed a quarter of the length of the drum from the left head (Rembang 1984–85b:39). Drums are mostly played with a hand technique called *gupekan,* but a mallet tipped with a round piece of hardwood, buffalo horn, or ivory *(panggul kendang)* is sometimes used to strike the right head for *cedugan*-style playing.

Drummers sit cross-legged with the left leg in front and the right foot tucked behind the left knee. The right rim of the *kendang* is balanced just below the left ankle joint and the body of the drum rests along the calf, extending out over the knee.

Dag (rhymes with German *tag*) and *tut* (rhymes with "foot") are the primary pitched sounds of the *wadon* and *lanang* respectively. They are produced by striking close to the edge of the right head, using the base of the palm for *dag* and the area below the fingers for *tut* (see fig. 2.7). The drums are tuned so that the pitch is at least 700 cents higher on the *lanang* than on the

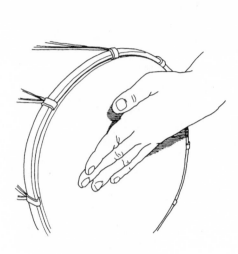

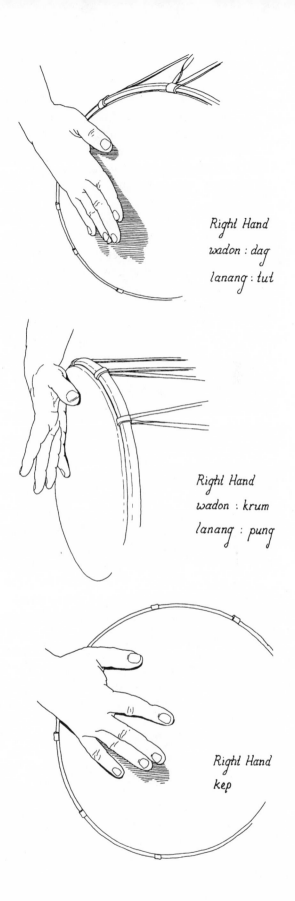

Right Hand
wadon : dag
lanang : tut

Left Hand
wadon : kap
lanang : pek

Right Hand
wadon : krum
lanang : pung

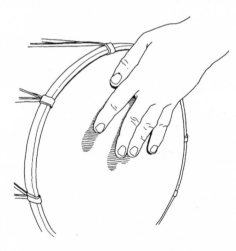

Left Hand
pung

Right Hand
kep

Figure 2.7. Drum stroke hand positions

wadon. Dag is susceptible to a variety of articulations obtained by allowing the sound to resonate, or through stopping it by tilting the palm at one of several angles to dampen the skin. The pitch of *tut* is routinely raised further during performance by pressing the left head to shrink the resonating chamber inside. Played with *panggul, tut* is now called *dug* (rhymes with the "boog" of "boogie"), and the tension on the *lanang*'s heads is slightly loosed so that the interval between *dag* and *dug* is about 300 cents. *Tak* and *tek* (as in "tock" and "tuck"), drier variants of the *cedugan* sounds *dag* and *dug,* are made by muting the left head while playing the right with the mallet.

The higher-pitched and timbrally richer *wadon krum* (or *kum*) and *lanang pung* (rhyming with the "tum" of "tumult" and the "Jung" of Carl), also produced on the right heads, are made by lightly resting the side of the thumb near the upper rim to act as a pivot and slapping against the skin with the length of the little finger about two-thirds of the way down, allowing the other fingers to bounce off the surface. A filling-in stroke, intended mainly to help sustain rhythmic flow, is called *kep* (as in "cup"). To sound it, the thumb remains as it was for *krum* or *pung,* the index finger presses firmly on the surface of the head (thus suppressing all pitch), and the remaining fingers strike lightly.

The primary left-hand stroke is the *kap* (*wadon*) or *pek* (*lanang*); both are usually referred to simply as *pek* (and pronounced, respectively, like "cop" and "puck"). It is produced by slapping the center of the head with the palm while firmly damping the right head. *Pek* cuts immediately through the most intricate textures, and is an important cueing stroke.

Plak (rhymes with "block"), a sparingly used extreme accent, is obtained by forcefully smacking both heads simultaneously with outstretched fingers in the *kep* or *pek* locations. Versions of the right-hand strokes *dag* and *pung* are also obtainable by striking the left head of the drum in a position equivalent to where it is struck on the right to produce the same sound, while maintaining careful damping on the right skin. *Plak* and the left-hand *dag* and *pung* are used mainly in the special context of *kendang tunggal,* solo drumming, discussed in chapter 7.

In standard *kebyar* hand-drumming (*gupekan*), the only three strokes given consistent musical significance are the *wadon dag, krum,* and *kap* and their *lanang* equivalents *tut, pung,* and *pek.*

15. *Suling* (flutes) are made from bamboo, with five or six finger holes bored along the length of the tube. They may be of several sizes and registers. The smallest ones (*suling kantil*) have a biting, whistle-like sound, and a range that parallels that of the *kantilan,* while the *suling calung,* two octaves deeper, have a breathy, full timbre. In between is the slightly less common *suling tengah.* Any of the sizes may be used during a performance, singly or in small choirs if there are enough players available. Because of their penetrating tone, *suling kantil* are rarely doubled, but up to four or five *suling calung* are considered to add a cushioned warmth to the texture. Many *suling* are made so that

when all of the holes are closed they are in tune with the scale tone *deng;* this arrangement is called *tekep deng.* A *suling* tessitura generally comprises about nine tones. Circular breathing *(ngunjal angkihan)* is used for a continuous sound, with a wide vibrato produced by changing the pressure of air stored in the cheeks. Unlike other instruments, which are village-owned, *suling* are often the property of the musicians who play them.

16. *Rebab* are bowed spike lutes used in Bali originally as part of court *gamelan,* but employed in *kebyar* in music derived from those repertoires. They are never used alone, but always to double the *suling.* The two strings are tuned to *ding* and *dung* and played with a loosely strung bow. A *rebab* cannot cut through complex or loud textures like the *suling,* so its only effective use is in soft passages.

17. *Cengceng kecek* (referred to as *cengceng*) is a set of four or six small cymbals, each about 10 cm in diameter, mounted on a flat wooden surface and struck with an additional pair held in the hands. *Cengceng* play as part of an orchestral subgroup with the *reyong* and *kendang,* reinforcing the composite rhythm of their parts. *Cengceng kopyak,* larger crash cymbals 15–25 cm in diameter, are used for *gong gdé* repertoire or processional music *(beleganjur).*

Instrument Classification and Textural Strata

Coast remarked on the "incessant cascade of musical sound" that he heard in Peliatan, and indeed much *kebyar* music sounds at first like a metallic assault of dense, uncontrasted rhythms and a continuous, rapid turnover of notes at various levels in the texture. This presents a difficult perceptual maze for the novice, especially given the typically rapid tempi. Bringing the music into focus requires differentiating between the various unfamiliar components of the full *gamelan* sound and identifying instruments in their standard orchestral combinations and musical roles. Of the several organological schemes that have been devised for *gamelan,* some have attemped to ease these difficulties—especially those designed by or for outsiders.

Kartomi (1990:84–107) surveys the ways in which Javanese *gamelan* instruments have been categorized. She divides the various taxonomies into two groups: the traditional and the literate; that is, those passed down orally for use by Javanese in speaking about their music among themselves, and those that have emerged since the advent of written scholarship about Javanese music in the twentieth century. In the first group are classification systems based on the type of hand motion used to play (shaken, plucked, struck, etc.), tone system *(slendro* or *pélog),* associations with male or female characteristics (e.g., the *wadon* and *lanang* designations for Balinese drums),[30] shape (key as opposed to gong), and the dynamic of the sound produced (soft or loud). The

---

30. The symbolism and significance of musical instruments' gender designations is explored in Becker 1988 and DeVale and Dibia 1991:39–40.

second group contains the systems developed by individual scholars, both Javanese and foreign.[31] These systems are more attentive to the various musical functions that the instruments play, and have the effect of making conscious the divisibility of the total *gamelan* sound into discrete structural elements whose contribution to the whole can be described in abstract, rather than instrument-specific terms. This has been accomplished in many ways, ranging from the five nonoverlapping categories of function posited by Kunst (1949:247) to the interconnected mandala-like presentation of Sumarsam (1984b:112).

Such writers have portrayed *gamelan* music as stratified, or composed of multiple layers of sound interrelated with respect to one another and to the metric period of the music. Much as instruments' spectral qualities form discrete parts of the acoustic whole, their characteristic playing styles may be heard as strata with special roles in the orchestral texture. In Hood's description of Javanese *gamelan,* "different melodic-rhythmic lines form distinct layers or strata of sound, each maintaining its own character in melodic contour, rhythmic idioms, and relative density (the number of musical events occurring within an arbitrary time span)" (1971:52). Useful as such depictions are, however, and notwithstanding their contribution to the conceptualization of musical structure, it is worth noting that the traditional taxonomies are not concerned with the idea of strata.

Javanese *gamelan* organological taxonomies constitute an adequate basis for defining Balinese ones since the instruments themselves and their stratified relationships to one another in practice are, speaking in general terms, alike. All of the traditional schema noted above are used in Bali (though Balinese *gamelan* genres and repertoires are also often classified according to their social and ritual functions), and written ideas about stratification have been adopted as well. McPhee's seven categories of *gamelan* sound organization (1966:27) generally follow those of his contemporary Kunst by depicting colotomic instruments and drumming as separate from the melodic parts, relating to them only in the sense that they punctuate or animate them. No subsequent writer on Balinese music has called for a revision of McPhee's classification.

The taxonomy proposed in figure 2.8 is an attempt to partly remodel McPhee's and bring it into line with the more holistic approach of recent writers about Javanese *gamelan* such as Sumarsam. Like Sumarsam, I view the various layers of sound as lying along a continuum of musical function. I have used a more conventional display than Sumarsam's mandala, with the tuned gamut and other instruments interfaced via the lowest metallophones (the *jegogan*), which provide mediation between the metric and melodic aspects of the music. The five stratum types in the scheme are arched symmet-

---

31. Kartomi summarizes the work of several scholars on this topic, including Kunst, Becker, Martopangrawit, Poerbapangrawit, Gitosaprodjo, and Sumarsam.

Music concept	Stratum type	Balinese terms	Instruments
Elaboration	*Pokok* elaboration (may comprise up to 8 strata)	*Payasan, neliti, ubit-ubitan, kotekan, bunga,* etc.	*Ugal, pemadé, kanti-lan, reyong, penyacah, rebab, suling, trompong*
Abstraction	*Pokok* tones	*Pokok*	*Calung*
Mediation	*Pokok* reinforcement (or colotomic melody)	*Jegogan*	*Jegogan*
Metric structure	Colotomic pattern	*Tabuh, gongan*	*Gong, kempur, klen-tong, kempli, kelenang, bebendé*
Metric elaboration	Colotomic elaboration	*Kendangan* (and other drumming terms), *kecekan, ocak-ocakan*	*Kendang, reyong, cengceng*

Figure 2.8. *Kebyar* instrumental strata (Music concepts column after Sumarsam 1984)

rically around the role of the *jegogan,* with the primary bearers of melody and meter immediately above and below them, and figuration at the upper and lower ends.

Under the "Stratum type" heading, the schema adopts the words "colo-tomic," meaning the use of gongs as metric markers, and *pokok,* a Balinese term meaning root or trunk (what Kunst and McPhee called nuclear melody). *Pokok* refers to the succession of tones played on the *calung,* and is understood to be the "core" melody of the music—the fundament or abstract plan for the derivation of all other melodic parts. Under the designation *pokok elaboration,* the *pokok* is expanded in as many as eight different simultaneous layers above and around it, in myriad possible styles characterized by their greater rhyth-mic density, the timbre and playing style of the instruments, and the structure of the elaboration patterns. Some of the names for these kinds of patterns are given in the "Balinese terms" column; their qualities and those of *pokok* are the sole subject of chapter 6. The most general, all-purpose one is *payasan.*[32]

The *jegogan* play the double role of *pokok* reinforcement and what I have called colotomic melody. They are a linchpin or hinge between the gongs and melodic instruments. As *pokok* reinforcement they stress important *pokok* tones (which mainly occur at metrically important points) in the octave below the *calung.* As colotomic melody they form a layer of slow-shifting tones that fall together with and in between the strokes of the gong and various second-ary gongs, subdividing the music between them into smaller divisions of time. In practice, Balinese musicians refer to *jegogan* tones in both roles: as metric elaboration of the gong pattern, and as a sparser version of the *pokok.*

---

32. *Payasan* means makeup, as on an actor's face. In this usage it refers to any kind of melodic figuration, but musicians tend to use it to refer to a specific kind of figuration played on the *ugal.* This more restricted sense of the term is explored in chapter 6.

The composite *kendang* pattern, formed through the interlocking strokes of the two drummers, is the only musical element in the low register to move at or near the density of the *pokok* elaboration parts. My notion of drumming as colotomic elaboration is based on the standard indifference of drum pattern to details of melodic structure and motion. In much music the drum part is essentially an elaboration of the colotomic frame. For many important older musical forms, drum patterns are composed with internal repetitions that begin and rebegin after the arrivals of gongs or *jegogan* tones. Such forms are classified by the size of their main metric period (*tabuh*) and may have many different melodies composed to fit them, but the drum part is basically the same regardless of the tune. In many *kebyar* compositions this constraint is loosened and there is more explicit coordination between drumming and surface melody and rhythm, but such variants are understood as departures from the normative.

The *cengceng* part moves at a continuous and rapid rate of subdivision without exhibiting the internal variety and relation to the colotomic elements of the music that the drums do. It is nonetheless closely affiliated with the *kendang* in concept, providing a kind of sheen and reinforcement of their rhythms. Though the *reyong* is commonly heard in a melodic role, the *byar* chord is often used in conjunction with drum patterns, as in *ocak-ocakan* texture (see fig. 2.16 below). In *ocak-ocakan*, *byar* chords reinforce *dag* and *tut* strokes and are interspersed with *kecekan*, played on the rim of the kettles, doubling left-hand *kap* and *pek* strokes.

Vertical Relationships between and within Strata

The subject of vertical simultaneity belongs equally to the domain of orchestration and that of melodic and figurational grammar. In keeping with the focus on sound and orchestral color, the issue is introduced here to provide a framework for understanding the relations between strata, not to examine the structure of the patterns and melodies that the strata contain. Though these are hardly separable, for the moment a conceptual distinction between them is of use.

First-order Vertical Relations

All of the *pokok* figuration strata relate to the *pokok* itself according to their individual grammars and stylistic constraints, but adhere to common principles governing verticalities. *First-order vertical relations* are here defined as the interpart simultaneities that occur at metrically or, in the absence of cyclic meter, rhythmically stressed points. At such points, parts are stable with respect to one another if they coincide and are scale-tone equivalent; otherwise they are unstable and invariably en route to coincidence and stability at an upcoming, stronger point of stress.

In full ensemble textures, the most stable points are those marked by *jego-*

gan tones. Allowing for second-order relations (see below), and a few unusual exceptions, any instruments in the ensemble that are tuned in the gamut and coincide with *jegogan* will play on the same scale tone. Any instruments not playing at those points are either syncopated with respect to the *jegogan*, or absent from the texture altogether. The next-most stable are the *calung* arrivals between *jegogan* tones, which normally align with the remaining strata.

In between *jegogan* and *calung* stresses other instruments' vertical alignments may or may not be scale-tone equivalent, but they are in any case melodically (horizontally) directed toward the next important vertical alignments. Certain melodic environments can cause even the *calung* to break rank temporarily. Such motion between instability and stability will be explained in melodic terms in chapters 5 and 6.

In figures 2.9 and 2.10 scale-tone equivalences are mapped between registers for the *jegogan*, *calung*, *ugal*, *pemadé*, *kantilan*, and *reyong* components of the texture. The figures include only instruments tuned within the twenty-one-tone gamut, so *kendang*, *cengceng*, and gongs are not shown. For simplicity *penyacah*, *trompong*, *suling*, and *rebab* have also been excluded from the diagrams, for they each perform in a melodic style roughly characterizable as a paraphrase of the *ugal*, which is sufficient to stand for them here. What remain are five of the most typically differentiated strata. In the diagrams pitch ascends along the vertical axis and instruments' characteristic playing styles

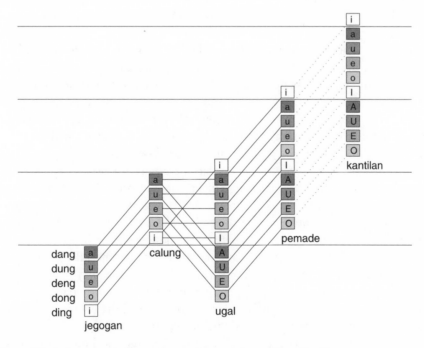

Figure 2.9. Scale-tone equivalences: *jegogan*, *calung*, *ugal*, *pemadé*, and *kantilan*

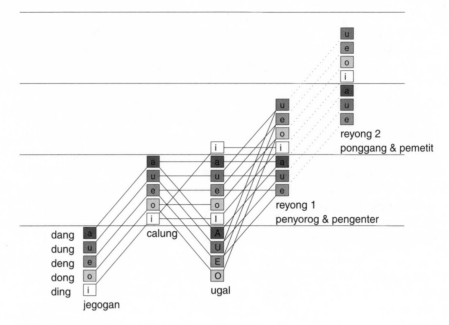

Figure 2.10. Scale-tone equivalences: *jegogan, calung, ugal,* and *reyong*

increase in density along the horizontal. Lines drawn between instruments show how scale tones on one may be positioned, through first-order vertical relations, on the other.

The two diagrams may be interpreted by moving out from the central position of the *ugal* to the left and right extremes. The full two-octave *ugal* realization of the melodic material of a given composition is abstracted into the slower moving, single-octave *pokok* and *pokok* reinforcement on the pairs of *calung* and *jegogan.* The two occurrences of each scale tone on the *ugal* are linked to the single position that they may occupy on the *calung*, which in turn are mapped directly to the *jegogan* an octave below. Moving to the right, the *ugal* tones correspond one-to-one in placement with the *pemadé* parts an octave above, where they are elaborated in a manner characteristic of that instrument's more rapid playing style. In the great majority of cases, the *kantilan* simply double the *pemadé* at the next octave and hence do not comprise a separate stratum; this is indicated here by the dotted lines.

Alternatively, the *calung* part could be used as a referent. Like *jegogan,* the two *calung* always play the same tone. A given *calung* tone may be realized in either octave of the *ugal* part, depending on the direction or register of the melody at a given point in the music; and conversely, the *calung* reduce the melodic ambitus of the *ugal* to a single octave. If, for example, the *ugal* part ascends the scale stepwise from *dAng* to *dong* in its mid-range, the *calung* "wrap around" from their highest note, *dang,* to their lowest two, *ding* and *dong.* In such situations the *pokok* line can be conceived of as having "wrapped around" an imaginary circumference to or beyond its original point. As in the cosmological plan and the three-dimensional model of the gamut, the tones retain their cardinal identities.

It is worth viewing the melody of a *kebyar* composition from the standpoints of both the *calung* and the *ugal,* for neither is subservient to the other. Though it is the full *ugal* melody that is likely to be designated the main, most singable melody of a composition, and it is the *ugal* player, along with the lead drummer, who leads the ensemble in rehearsal and performance, the role of the *calung* in abstracting the music makes it an important locus for perceiving the relationships between strata.

The *reyong* is shown in two overlapping halves farthest to the right in figure 2.10. It plays at the same density as the *pemadé* and *kantilan,* but in its relationship to the *ugal* part brings some asymmetry to an otherwise straightforward plan. The following remarks pertain only to the instrument in its figurational capacity and not to its agogic roles. The full range of the *reyong* is two octaves plus two tones, the "extra" ones being *deng* and *dung* at the peak of the *pemetit* position. Each pair of players together can span seven tones,[33] with the tones *deng* and *dung* in the middle of the instrument (sixth and seventh kettles) shared between them (see fig. 2.6 above). Conceptually speaking, and often literally as well, the upper two players double the parts of the lower two, though deviations often occur as a result of the differences between each of the four positions' individual ranges.[34] Like the *kantilan* in their relationship to the *pemadé,* the upper and lower *reyong* parts do not comprise independent strata—hence the dotted lines that connect them in the figure.

Deng and *dung* are thus seen to be realizable in two positions on the *reyong,* while *dang, ding* and *dong* are found only once each. It is a matter of orchestrational choice as to which register of *deng* and *dung* is used when the *pokok* falls on these scale tones. On the other hand, for *dang, ding,* and *dong,* there is only one possibility. As the web of lines drawn in shows, all scale-tone equivalent mappings of *ugal* to *reyong* are possible in practice.

The constraints of the scale-tone links between the *reyong* and metallophones have a beneficial musical result. Any melodic progression that exceeds the range of the *reyong* on either end will not necessarily do so on the metallophones. This enables, and sometimes requires, the *reyong* part to move in contrary motion with respect to them. Sometimes *reyong* patterns diverge from those of the metallophones altogether, either by necessity or composer's choice. The overall difference in tone color between knobbed gongs and metallophone keys contributes further to the perception of the *reyong* as a separate orchestral layer, especially when its figuration is unduplicated by other

---

33. Occasionally one sees a *kebyar gamelan* with a smaller, seven-kettle version of the *reyong,* played by only two musicians.

34. The greatest deviations occur in *norot* style. See figure 2.14 below.

instruments. Despite the registral overlap and the fact that its functions are often similar to those of the *pemadé* and *kantilan,* the *reyong*'s is a different quality of sound.

Second-order Vertical Relations

Second-order vertical relations are pairs of tones played concurrently within a single instrument or group of instruments. They are measured and classified by the number of scale tones that the interval spans, inclusive of both constituent tones, and not by ratio or affective character. Unlike first-order relations, there is no prerequisite rhythmic or metric alignment that determines when these simultaneities may occur.

Second-order combinations occur only on the *reyong, trompong, pemadé,* and *kantilan.* On the four *pemadé,* the lower and upper tones of the interval are each given to two instruments, one *pengumbang* and one *pengisep.* They are distributed the same way on the four *kantilan* an octave higher. This balanced arrangement ensures that both components of the interval pulsate with *ombak* in both registers.

Of the possible intervals within the range of an octave, those of three, four, and five scale tones are all used. The most common is *kempyung* or *ngempat* (four tones, from *empat,* four), followed at some distance by *nelu* (three tones, from *telu,* three), and five, which is so unusual that no term is in usage for it (*nelima,* from *lima,* five, would be the logical choice). Of these types, only the *kempyung* appears in purely melodic passages, where it may be used in simple parallel motion above a unison line. All three interval types may be heard (with *kempyung* by far still the most common) in interlocking figurational textures, where they alternate with unisons unpredictably, emerging from the motoric continuity of the line as prominent cross-rhythms.

The octave (containing six tones, inclusive) is sounded as a second-order relation only on the *trompong,* where it is called *ngembat.* Compound intervals are not used within a stratum. Adjacent scale tones (intervals of two tones) are rarely played as second-order simultaneities, except as a by-product of "*nelima*" played in two registers, for example between the upper tone of the *pemadé* interval and the lower tone of the *kantilan* interval.[35] This is because any interval sounded across strata is by definition the inversion of the one sounded within them. This same relationship applies as well to *kempyung* and *nelu.* That *nelu* is present whenever *kempyung* is used helps to explain why it is the second most common second-order relation. However, in rough analogy to perfect fifths and fourths in Western tonal music, the two intervals may be understood as differing in level of dissonance: *ngempat* is stable and is used at

35. Adjacent tones may occasionally sound together on the *reyong* in metrically unstressed positions as a chance consequence of the very limited freedom to improvise allowable on that instrument in some textures or forms (such as *norot;* see fig. 2.14), and in a few other specialized kinds of figuration (see the *reyongan* texture in the transcription of *Jaya Semara* in figure 8.3A) Simultaneous adjacent scale tones are less infrequent in the *slendro*-tuned *gamelan gender wayang.*

Kempyung tone pairs	Begbeg size	Sedeng size	Tirus size
dIng-dung	666	670	724
dong-dang	627	668	631
deng-ding	966	909	823
dUng-dong	654	666	673
dAng-deng	687	687	749

Figure 2.11. *Kempyung* sizes, measured in cents

beginnings and endings, whereas *nelu* is unstable and its component tones tend to resolve by folding inward to a scale-tone unison.

The preference for *kempyung* may be attributed to the acoustic fact that the distance between component tones is sufficiently wide to prevent their most concentrated areas of spectral activity from blurring one another. Given the relative sizes of adjacent intervals in the scale, each *kempyung* must bridge at least one of the two large gaps (*deng-dung* and *dang-ding*); the *deng-ding* interval bridges both. This guarantees a breadth of at least half an octave. Using Toth's measurements of *begbeg, sedeng,* and *tirus* tuning types as a basis (see fig. 2.1), a selection of *kempyung* lying between *dUng* and *ding* on the *pemadé* are compared for width in figure 2.11.

Kempyung are here seen to vary significantly in size and corresponding sound. Both the largest (966 cents, from *deng* to *ding*) and the smallest (627 cents, from *dong* to *dang*) *kempyung* are found in *begbeg* tuning, consistent with its characteristic sharp contrasts between interval sizes. This is a disparity of 339 cents; in *tirus* the difference between the extremes of size is only 192 cents, which is less but still considerable.

When a *gangsa* part ascends above the seventh key (*deng*) to where no *ngempat* tone is available, some *gamelan* drop back to unison playing, but others prefer to substitute the tone two steps below, as if moving *kempyung* tones that lie beyond the range of the instrument down an octave. The resultant sound in this case is actually *nelu,* but any first-order relations supporting such an interval would match the upper tone. On the *gangsa* staff in figure 2.12, the three small notes lie beyond the range of the instrument while those in parentheses are their occasional replacements.

A similar arrangement applies on the *reyong,* which employs *kempyung* in most melodic contexts. With each of the four positions controlling only two, three, or four tones, not all players have access to the operative *pokok* note at any given time. In such cases, stylistic convention dictates that the *kempyung* tone be filled in, even if it is lower in pitch (as when the *penyorog* plays *dung* as *kempyung* for *ding*). *Deng, dung,* and *ding* may be realized in more than one way, as seen from the parenthesized pairs of notes above those scale-tone occurrences in the example. Choice of which tone to be used by the player concerned (*pengenter* in the case of *deng, pemetit* for *dung, ponggang* and *pemetit* for *ding*) depends on a range of contextual factors.

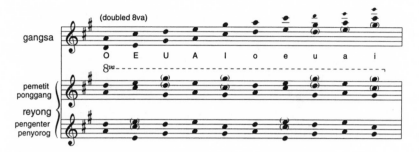

Figure 2.12. *Kempyung* tones for *gangsa* and *reyong*

Orchestration in Practice

An essential aspect of the *kebyar* sound is its variability. In other *gamelan* all instruments play virtually continuously, but in *kebyar* this is not so. Orchestrating for *kebyar* is intrinsic to the process of composition. Though there is broad consensus about specific textures and the appropriate places to use them within a composition, many composers consciously strive for new effects by omitting some instruments on occasion, recombining instruments in novel ways, and by changing configurations often to achieve textural and formal contrast. Indeed, Balinese composers are preoccupied with the issue, as their output and what they have to say about it indicates.[36]

That said, it is equally true that standard *gong kebyar* orchestrational practice holds that too great a disruption of the instruments' normal roles and behaviors will yield an unsuccessful sound. The fixed identities of the textural strata are at the heart of the music's identity and the ensemble will not project if these are sacrificed, for the instruments are tuned and constructed to function only within certain limits. As a concrete example, one would never encounter *kantilan* playing *pokok*-like tones as accompaniment to figuration on the *jegogan*. The latter speak too slowly, have too confined a range, and are too transparent in timbre to project with the sharpness and agility of the *kantilan*. Conversely, *kantilan* are too high and bright to play a supporting role to *jegogan*. It is worthwhile to contrast this circumstance with the more open-ended possibilities of the Western orchestra, where even a flute could play a bass line for the cellos given the right textural conditions.

The following examples present a representative overview of the ensemble's resources in practice. The first three full ensemble textures are presented in order of their increasing degree of differentiation between strata, and

---

36. Composers are wont to raise concerns about orchestration, though usually in imagistic terms. Wayan Beratha spoke of the inspiration for an innovative passage using terraced dynamics in his composition *Palguna Warsa* as a depiction of shifting spectra of light seen through rainfall at sunset. Beratha speaks more generally about the issue in interviews collected for a biography by Wayan Sadra (Sadra 1991:100–107). Another composer, Ketut Gdé Asnawa, was more direct in one conversation, saying that he was actively engaged in a search for new orchestral colors (personal communication, August 1987).

the fourth shows the *reyong* in a nonmelodic capacity (*ocak-ocakan*). The differentiation is defined in terms of level of rhythmic activity and/or independence of musical materials, and not primarily by timbre. Such timbral distinctions are, of course, invariant throughout the repertoire, whereas the intent here is to group instruments according to orchestrational and musical function. To reduce clutter in the transcriptions, here and throughout the book, I often hide sixteenth rests when a different part on the same or an adjacent stave fills in that value with a sounding tone. All parts retain their proper vertical alignment.

Full Ensemble Textures

1. *Kebyar Texture* (CDI/1). The *kebyar* proper is the ensemble's signature playing style, though in most senses it presents an exception to standard *gamelan* practice. There is no cyclic meter and no steady tempo in *kebyar,* but rhythmic activity, only approximate in figure 2.13, might be described as a series of brief, freely connected melodic groupings, played to an extremely elastic and usually rapid underlying pulse. Groupings may consist of as few as one or two tones and as many as ten or twelve. Some may take the form of compact, repeating motives made of irregular, additive chains of tones, while others are more freely formed. The flow may be disrupted with sudden dynamic changes, irregular breaths between phrases, isolated interjected *byar* chords, or local accelerandi on repeated tones.

Kebyar texture is confined to three closely related strata, distinguished by register, degree of rhythmic motion, and component timbres. Compared to other kinds of *gamelan* orchestration, the layers are here the least independent from one another. In the absence of cyclic structure it is imprecise to speak of a *calung pokok* part or the characteristic rhythmic strata which refer to it. Instead, all instruments relate literally to the melodic and rhythmic shape of the *gangsa* melody line, transfiguring it only through simplification and abstraction.

In the most active stratum, the fully developed melody is played in three registers by the *ugal, pemadé,* and *kantilan.* The four *reyong* players divide this melody up by playing only the scale tones that lie within their ranges, and by adding *kempyung* or resting when they do not. The melody is abandoned for *byar* at the most accented spots, shown here at the beginning and end of the excerpt. Other than on the *reyong,* second-order vertical relations are ordinarily absent in *kebyar* texture. Also in this stratum are the *kendang* and *cengceng.* The rhythms of the *gangsa* are reconfigured for the drums' *dag* and *tut,* with *dag* carrying the more accented tones. Reduced to two nonscale pitches the melody becomes a play of irregularly alternating tone colors. The complete rhythm is further reinforced by the *cengceng.*

Comprising a separate stratum are the *calung,* which support select scale tones from the *ugal* part. The lowest layer consists of *jegogan* and gong, always playing together. They emphasize *calung* tones falling just before pauses, in *byar,* and at stressed points in longer melodic segments.

Figure 2.13. *Kebyar* texture: *Oleg Tumulilingan* (CDI/1)

The passage illustrated in figure 2.13 is from the dance composition *Oleg Tumulilingan*, composed in 1951 by Pan Sukra and the famous dancer Ketut Maria, both of the west-central Tabanan region. After the initial *byar*, the opening *gangsa* phrase spans an octave from *dEng* to *deng* but, as abstracted for the *pokok*, it is "wrapped around" and compressed into a unison. The end of the ascent is trumpeted by the ensuing four-tone additive figure *dIng-dong-dIng-deng*, repeated thrice before leaping back to *dUng*. The contour and goal tone of the original ascent are retained in the next group, though the rhythms and actual tones are different. Repetition follows, beginning from the additive figure and continuing until midway through the ascending line, which is interrupted for a *byar* on *dUng*.

In this passage, by reducing the full melodic succession to an alternation between *deng* and *dung*, the *calung* and *jegogan* create an irregular but static line in their timbral and registral bands that set the agitation of the full melody into relief. Put differently, the upper stratum develops a very clearly defined shape by interpolating tones and rhythms in between those of the *calung*. These are segmentable into motives, repeating units, and their transformations. The composite of the three strata may perhaps best be heard as a single entity, with the upper line firmly anchored by the lower levels of *pokok* and gong.

2. *Norot Texture* (CDI/2). *Norot* is a common and elegant orchestral texture used in a variety of musical contexts and tempi. It is also called *nuutin*; both words derive from the verb *tuut*, to follow. *Norot* is considered simple and basic because of the close emulation of the shape of the *pokok* observable in all melodic strata. *Gangsa* and *reyong pokok* figuration in the style always uses the same generic pattern of alternation between adjacent scale-tone figures, though the individual *reyong* parts are actually quite abstract (see also fig. 6.8). Despite the many layers of sound, the overall effect of close alignment between the strata mitigates the sense of their independence from one another. The perception of *norot* as elegant traces to its affective association with court musics, in particular the long melodies and large-scale cyclic meters of the temple repertoire.

In *norot* at least six strata may be discerned, and more if optional melodic instruments such as *suling* or *rebab* are present. Minimally, there are two layers of *pokok elaboration*—that of the *ugal*, which plays a flowing, freely connected version of the *calung* part in the idiomatic rhythms and contours of *payasan* style, and *gangsa* and *reyong*, which perform the adjacent scale-tone figures.

The lower tone of the *gangsa* figure always matches the current *pokok* tone, but the pattern is articulated before each new *pokok* arrival with a three-note anticipation. Though the *gangsa* line can be found embedded in the composite *reyong* part, the sum of the four players' individual parts adds up to much more. Each of the four has a bit of freedom in choosing what to play for each *pokok* tone, though there are only a few standard patterns and ways to link

Figure 2.14. *Norot* texture: *Baris* (CD1/2)

them together. Extra cross-rhythms and melodic patterns can emerge, formed by the spontaneous interlocking of players who often play together and know each others' likely moves. In *norot* texture the *pemetit* part stands out sharply, because it is—at least to a degree, and more so in some contexts than others— unduplicated.

In figure 2.14, taken from the slow middle section of the warrior-dance *Baris*, all of the melodic instruments follow the curve of the *pokok* with characteristic individuality. The *ugal* realization allows for considerable freedom at this tempo. The grace notes and dotted figures used here are typical of *payasan*, giving the line a rhythmic elasticity that sets it apart.

Drum patterns underpinning *norot* vary depending on the character and meter of the music. In this section of *Baris* only a single drummer plays, faced off in an improvisatory duet of movement and rhythmic response with the dancer. The smaller note values match sudden and quick steps, and the accented strokes just before the middle and the end denote abrupt stops. The *cengceng* player follows closely, knowing from experience and by watching the dancer's movements that the density will double during the last quarter of the cycle. Gong, *kempur*, *klentong* and *kempli* (in a time-beating role) provide the colotomic frame.

3. *Gambangan Texture* (CDI/3). In the 1920s, composer Wayan Lotring of Kuta village adapted a composition from the sacred *gamelan gambang* of six instruments for the full-scale *gamelan pelegongan*.[37] In so doing he had to orchestrate for the larger ensemble and invent a drum part, as there is none in the original. Though in Lotring's time this kind of treatment was novel, over the decades of *kebyar*'s growth it has become standard to adapt melodies from outside sources, *gambang* or otherwise, or to compose original music in a style related to these adaptations. In *kebyar* this kind of music is most often only part of a composition rather than, as with Lotring, its entirety, but such passages are commonly called *gambangan* nonetheless.

There is considerable orchestral variety within the *gambangan* style, and often considerable contrast within the presentation of a single melody. What unifies these possibilities is the degree of multipart complexity involved: usually *gangsa* and *reyong* vary the *pokok* in entirely distinct ways, while the *kendang* present a separate rhythm that moves in and out of overt relationship to the melody and figuration. This excerpt (fig. 2.15) is from *Dharma Putra*, a *kebyar* composition of the 1970s played by the *gamelan* from Pindha village. The 13-beat *pokok* (divided 4 + 4 + [2 + 3]), played by *calung* with *jegogan* support, is given three simultaneous but independent realizations. The *gangsa* twice play a 4-beat ostinato with *ngempat* reinforcement, and both the *reyong* and *kendang* play their own set of interlocking parts. Gongs give the metric background with *kempli* providing the beats and *cengceng* giving the surface

---

37. For a full transcription and analysis, see McPhee 1966:309–15.

Figure 2.15. *Gambangan* texture: *Dharma Putra* (CDI/3)

composite rhythm. At the last three beats all instruments but the *calung, jego-gan,* and gongs converge on the melody in a *kebyar*-like rhythmic unison.

4. *Ocak-ocakan Texture* (CDII/4, 6:56, etc.). In *ocak-ocakan* playing the *reyong byar* and *kecekan* are coordinated with *kendang* and *cengceng* to form an agogic layer of changing syncopations. The *reyong* chord may be articulated as either *byong, byot,* or *jet* (open, short, or damped); these sounds and those of the *kecekan* are combined in various ways with drum strokes. The blend of the drums' resonant bass tones with the wide registral span of the *byar* chord gives their combined sound sharpness and bite, raising this purely rhythmic stratum to a level of prominence in the texture equal to that of the *pokok* and *pokok* elaboration. This aggressive forefronting of rhythm is entirely *keb-yar*'s own.

In figure 2.16, from the 1969 composition *Kosalia Arini* by Wayan Beratha, the *gangsa* stratum consists of interlocking figuration while the *ugal* melody, *pokok, jegogan,* and gongs state a rhythmically and metrically regular foundation based on an 8-beat cycle. The *gangsa* figuration creates its own pattern of

Figure 2.16. *Ocak-ocakan* texture: *Kosalia Arini* (CDII/4)

irregular cross-rhythms that sound whenever the two component parts meet in *kempyung,* and this level of syncopation is engaged in complex dialogue with that of the *ocak-ocakan* instruments.

Ocak-ocakan "breaks" can occur in almost any musical context, often with the full ensemble converging on the rhythms in a manner reminiscent of *kebyar* texture. In *norot* or *gambangan* they may serve as emphasis for dance rhythms, as cadential markers of transitions to new sections, or as agents for rhythmic and textural variety.

Partial Ensemble Textures

It is common to feature either *gangsa, reyong,* or *kendang* on their own in *kebyar,* either in unaccompanied presentation or with *pokok* and *colotomic* support only. Such passages are often presented toward the beginning of compositions in the context of rapid and discontinuous shifts in mood, tempo, and orchestration; they may or may not have a cyclic structure. In *genderan texture* (fig. 2.17, also from *Kosalia Arini:* CDII/4, 1:04) *gangsa* interlocking parts are

Figure 2.17. *Genderan* texture: *Kosalia Arini* (CDII/4)

showcased, here combined with *calung and jegogan*. The interlocking parts in this segment give rise to three different second-order simultaneities (*nelu*, *kempyung [ngempat]*, and "*nelima*"). *Nelu* occurs at the very end of the passage with the simultaneity *dong-dung* (resolving to the *deng* between them); *kempyung* occurs primarily as *dIng-dung*, and *nelima* as *dAng-dung*.

Reyongan texture (fig. 2.18, from the same composition at 4:03), may be accompanied but typically is not, serving as it does to showcase players' virtuosity and the instrument's distinctive timbre. *Reyongan* breaks may stretch to a minute or more and are composed of a series of interlocking patterns with changing dynamics, style, rhythmic density, and register. Musicians speak of the implied *pokok* that may be derived from the *reyong* composite by determining which tones would fall in the places where first-order simultaneities might occur, and shaping them into an idiomatic line. Such an imaginary *pokok* is shown in the lower staff.

Kendangan textures (fig. 2.19, also from *Dharma Putra*; CDI/4) are most often found in *kebyar* instrumental pieces. Unlike *genderan* and *reyongan*, *kendangan* textures are nearly always presented in the context of a repeating cycle. A special style of rapid interlocking produces a whirling composite, balancing the measured use of the two drums' six main sounds. *Reyong kecekan* (interrupted for a *byong* chord to reinforce the *klentong*) and *cengceng* double the surface rhythm in undifferentiated rhythmic continuity. Characteristically passages such as this culminate in an *ocak-ocakan* break and are succeeded by *gangsa* or *reyong* interlocking parts, all within the same cyclic frame. Another common procedure is to have the *reyong* and *kendang* play interlocking parts simultaneously, switching to the *gangsa* through the same sort of *ocak-ocakan* link.

ORCHESTRATION has been presented as a preliminary to more restricted studies of compositional elements because it is the direct acoustic correlate to the subjective reactions set forth at the beginning of the chapter, and consequently an appropriate way to "enter" the music. But neither Coast nor Suweca

Figure 2.18. *Reyongan* texture: *Kosalia Arini* (CDII/4)

Figure 2.19. *Kendangan* texture: *Dharma Putra* (CDI/4)

portrayed sound as disembodied. The idea of *kebyar* as a human activity performed by Balinese in large, closely interacting groups hints at a social organization complimentary to the acoustic one. Keeler articulates this connection clearly:

> Balinese music pieces sounds together mosaic-like with each piece distinct but fitting into the cluster of each group within the ensemble: the *gangsa [pemadé* and *kantilan], calung* and *jegogan;* the *reyong;* the gongs; and the drums and *cengceng.* These sections, like the fields of a single color in a mosaic—or the degrees of generality that link together increasingly large and cross-cutting groups in Balinese villages—combine to form an overall design of remarkable unity and clarity . . . common compliance to 'authority' is possible, but that authority lies dispersed among many individuals, and applies only to particular spheres. The unity and total effect depend on the interaction—momentary, single purpose, precise—of the constituent members. In work organizations, this pattern yields vigorous, flexible, and quite remarkably smooth interaction. In music, it yields the electric, mercurial and dazzling sounds of *gong kebyar* (1975:125).

Without this cooperative aspect the music would be seriously diminished in the literal sense that it could not be played well. Understanding that a beginner's impression is shaped by performers' social interactions as well as the music's acoustic qualities leads next to an exploration of *kebyar* in Balinese life.

3 The Social Construction of *Kebyar* Ensemble Virtuosity

Gdé Manik demonstrating *Teruna Jaya,* 1974.
Photo: Rucina Ballinger.

The final result is a candy box of intricately sculpted pieces, with varying degrees of complexity. But how did the candy box arise?

Stephen Jay Gould, "Genesis and Geology"

CONSIDER Coast's, Britten's, and Suweca's remarks once more, isolating their responses to the communication among *kebyar* performers and its impact on the audience. Coast, the novice, was captivated by a "lightning glance" between two leading musicians—one clearly imbued with the accumulated meanings of many years' practice and habit—that triggered the group's "electric virtuosity [and] appalling precision." Britten, the seasoned professional, described the players as having "the confidence of sleepwalkers" despite the demands he understood were being made on their musicianship. The insider Suweca, in a position of responsibility and primarily concerned with the efficacy of the performance, stressed the importance of being "well rehearsed." What mattered was that the group felt "pride for the audience to witness the success of our collaborative efforts," and that the presentation resulted in "something of value, both for community and religion."

All three are reacting to their experience of a highly concentrated energy generated through social interaction but channeled and released through musical performance. For Suweca it must be not only released, but released with the proper control and intention. The intensity of this force connotes something powerful enough to be almost threatening for the first two, given Coast's ominous evocations of sinister technology and Britten's suggestion of subconsciously motivated, eerily precise and entranced players. Though himself a performer, even Suweca cannot claim this power as his own, and must instead distribute it among his co-players and beyond them to society at large. Once more taking a cue from these commentators (plus my own and others' responses), in this chapter I explore the ineffable sources and production of the tight, disciplined energy driving *kebyar* ensemble virtuosity. As a complement to the acoustical and philosophical complexity controlling the surface sound of the *gamelan* detailed in chapter 2, the unified behavior of the performers amid musical intricacy also presents a facade of sorts. While sound is supported by musical structure and compositional logic, the nature of *kebyar* as an activity is strongly shaped by the life and times of Balinese society during the years of its development, as well as by certain culturally conditioned kinds of social action.

Put plainly, what the observers describe is the outcome of a long-term collective effort. This well-honed focus, which every competent *kebyar* ensemble invests time and energy toward, involves memorization of repertoire, mastery of technique, cultivated ensemble agility, sensitivity to the demands of accompanying dance and drama, and administration of sundry pecuniary, promotional, sartorial, and protocol-related aspects of managing a performance organization. To seek the contexts and motivations behind this effort amounts to a quest for the spirit of the music and its makers.

The notion of spirit suggests an unwieldy alchemy of individual interactions. Yet however complex relationships among members of a group are, Suweca's comments suggest that interpersonal dynamics in *kebyar* are considered important only insofar as they coalesce into something of collective utility. This is not meant to minimize the impact of particular musical personalities, but to point out that the cultural practices bringing people together to learn, rehearse, and perform *kebyar* should attract our attention first as determinants of its character. Among these are a strong and ancient capacity for collectivity observable not only throughout Balinese culture but also in agricultural and ritual customs throughout the geocultural region. My initial venture is to set these inclinations in relief against the equally characteristic hierarchic social structures that complement them. I do not presume to offer thereby a tidy explanation for what has led Balinese cultural practice to take its particular forms, but neither can I resist venturing an interpretation of the nourishing effect of some of its most deeply rooted tenets, and perhaps, in this small way, summoning forth something of the music's spirit after all.

While collectivity is a real and powerful force, it is risky to discuss it without reference to the particular cultures and histories shaping individual societies. To approach these aspects of musical life in Bali and underscore their shifting natures, the remainder of the chapter depicts the Balinese milieu that gave rise to *kebyar* in the early years of the twentieth century, the ways in which those conditions differed from earlier ones, and their always turbulent and sometimes devastating transformations in the decades since. Last, issues affecting *gamelan* musicians in the 1990s are illustrated via a narrative of one group's history. The ideological ramifications of historical and social circumstances are included throughout to show why Balinese have identified with *kebyar* so strongly, why it attracts such substantial investments of musical discipline and effort, and how and why it has gathered such a wealth of meanings and possibilities for interpretation.

The Geocultural Roots of Balinese Music

Throughout Southeast Asia people have long valued myriad forms of collective social action even as they have been segregated by systems of caste and status. The natural fertility of the soil and the plenitude of fresh water for irrigation, consumption, and hygiene were resources managed through the coordinated efforts of entire societies. For millennia the majority's staple diet has been rice, grown on terraced fields whose construction, maintenance, and farming call for the ongoing expenditure of significant human resources. Starvation was comparatively rare, and thanks to powerful but navigable currents, trade along the mainland coasts, on inland waterways, and throughout the archipelagoes was prosperous. This bounty had important consequences for ways of life.

> Because their climate was mild and their basic diet of rice, fish and fruits more dependably available than in other parts of the world, Southeast Asians had natural advantages in escaping from the constant struggle for existence . . . [they] were able to employ their evenings in singing, feasting, gaming and entertaining one another . . . participation in festivals, rituals and feasts appears to have been a social obligation as important as work itself. (Reid 1988:173)

The core value of collectivity was shaped in ancient contexts, before the rise of the powerful god-kings in the first millennium A.D. In the organization of early village societies concerted action was the most efficient and effective way to control the natural world and express proper respect for spirits and ancestors. Throughout the region beliefs about the nature of existence admitted no distinction between the powerful, unseen forces inhering in the natural world and the visible, observable characteristics of human behavior or the environment. All matters and events of consequence had a potent spiritual basis; and anything threatening to undermine prosperity, such as disease, famine, or infertility, has characteristically been met with festivals, feasts, sacrifices, and rituals undertaken to reaffirm abundance as a fundamental condition of life. Similarly, elaborate death ceremonies ensure the deceased's safe passage to rejoin other ancestors and the continuation of the necessary dynamic balance between earth and spirit realms. These tenets remained even as Hindu, Buddhist, Christian, and Islamic practices were assimilated as accretions onto local practices over a period of more than a thousand years prior to 1700.

During this time the strength of centralized kingdoms grew to its apex. Monarchic legitimacy was predicated upon a king's putative ability to master and channel the unseen forces of the world. Royal visions of social order engendered the numerous anticollective forces of Southeast Asian vertical social hierarchies, in which the often lethal depredations of slavery, warfare, and elaborate class and status structures segregated social groups and bore down on the oppressed (Reid 1988: 129–36; Geertz 1980:4–10). Court-prescribed ritual was portrayed as parallel in purpose to older practices in order to muster the participation of large segments of the community, but from the peasants' point of view these obligations had a more feudal character. In this encompassing context of beliefs and power structure, all but the most spiritually heightened individuals were effectively impotent to exert control over their situations (Anderson 1972:63).

In the past the texture of day-to-day life and the passage of time were primarily shaped by predetermined successions of communal activities, scheduled according to cyclic calendars. Even since the introduction of the Gregorian calendar and increasing contact with the West, these systems have persisted. Local calendars in Bali, Java, and elsewhere specify the complex scheduling of rituals, as well as auspicious days for commerce, harvest, and other significant activities. The many requirements of ritual preparations demand the mobilization of patterned, dispersed cooperative behaviors. At the same time the calendars, which mark the recurrence of ritually prescribed days without numbering the passing years, foster a sense of permanence through nonprogressive time reckoning. In Bali, ten simultaneous weeks of differing lengths cycle within the 210-day *wuku* calendar; a "wheels-within-wheels" system wherein each day comprises a singular set of confluences and hence spiritual character, making it a unique "kind" of time (Geertz 1973:393).[1] Certain

---

1. For more on the Javanese calendar, see Geertz 1960:77–81. The Balinese calendar is explained in Covarrubias 1937:282–84, as well as in Geertz 1973 and Lansing 1995:28–31. Geertz has been criticized for his essentialized depiction of Balinese temporality, in which Balinese time is described as frozen in a "motionless present, a vectorless now" (1973:404). This is of course engagingly, conveniently, and fundamentally at odds with prevalent and equally essentialized notions of Western progressive time. Later writers have called Geertz's ethnographic authority into question and accused him of oversimplification, notably Maurice Bloch, who wrote that "it is . . . misleading to say that the Balinese have a non-durational notion of time. Sometimes and in some contexts they do, and

days are more spiritually charged than others and require different types and amounts of collective work. The repeating but shifting qualities of elapsing time are thus felt to be interwoven with the ongoing project of maintaining the well-being of the cosmos.

How best can we approach the formidable question as to why and how the generalized cultural forces just described gave rise to Balinese music as well as the many different and diverse musical cultures throughout the region? Perhaps the response is best conceived, as Stephen Jay Gould might do, as stemming from a permanent tension between two fundamental premises of evolutionary development. This is a perspective that, following Gould, ought to shape our understanding of the history of life on earth in all its diversity. One premise is the additive series, in which entities (be they species or cultures) evolve to ever greater complexity and successful adaptation as if according to a linear, prefigured plan. The other is differentiation, through which beings branch out in infinite and essentially random directions, fueled by the potential inherent in their ancestral forms (Gould 1991:412–14).

In Bali, certainly, musical activity is profuse, in part owing to the general conditions in Southeast Asia (as if a result of additive evolution), and equally to the intense and particular cultural conditions that developed there (a form of differentiation). There was proportionately more ritual activity and more temples built, more concentrated royal strength and patronage during the dynastic era, better irrigation and more fertile land, and so on. As an explanation, however, this remains unsatisfying, for we find ourselves locked in at a certain level of analysis, trying to explain cultural manifestations only in terms of one another.

What we do gain by considering these issues is not a conclusion but a poetic metaphor for how music embodies ingrained attitudes and beliefs. With the texture of passing years and the waxing and waning of ritual activity taken as analogies to form and content, we may conceive an imaginary music not to be heard, but to be felt as a sensibility, an abstraction suggested by the intersecting structures of time and human experience. In Southeast Asia the music of voices and instruments, the behaviors associated with it, and the attitudes

---

sometimes and in other contexts they do not, and those where they do not (agriculture, village and national politics, economics) cannot honestly be called unimportant" (1977:284).

I agree with Bloch and wish to limit application of the concept of cyclic time to ritual behavior and its impact on collectivity and music. Bloch says further: "The evidence for static or cyclic time comes from that special type of communication which we can label ritual in the broad sense of the term . . . whether social, religious or state" (1977:284).

Consider moreover the findings of Hobart (1978): "The views of the villagers were summed up succinctly by the priest of the local *pura dalem* [temple of death]. He pointed out that, in his official capacity he used the two above calendars (those cited by Geertz) to estimate ritual dates whereas to the majority of people, as they were farmers, the cycle of seasons was seen as the most immediately relevant. For other matters there was a chronology based on a series of well-remembered events, including wars, earthquakes, and volcanic eruptions, and more recently, the official (Gregorian) calendar."

of the societies supporting it are aspects of systems of values and beliefs that may be discovered in manifold cultural guises. José Maceda submits that the commonalties among Southeast Asian musical systems can be understood by seeking out the hidden elements, metaphysical qualities, and human perspectives that the musics embody. Among these are cooperative work, social order, and temporal cyclicity. He depicts "a life replete with rituals and ceremonies, in constant communication with spirits and deities with whom man corresponded to maintain an equilibrium with nature. In this part of the world, time was recorded less in writing events and more in the erection of stone symbols, shrines, the recounting of oral literature, and the practice of old beliefs and traditions" (1986:11). In Southeast Asia collectivity is a wisdom born of peoples' responses to their environments; a reflection of lives steeped in "mystical experiences quite distant from the patterned dictates of logic and reason" (1979:160). Such knowledge "may be captured in a sound structure or in music, just as an eighteenth-century enlightenment is crystallized in the music of Bach, and the clarity and discipline of Chinese thought are manifest in the music of a South Chinese ensemble" (ibid:167). This kind of knowledge appears in a unique form wherever it is found.

Balinese Collectivity and the *Sekaha*

Balinese prior to the modern era lived daily lives of dense ritual activity organized around the work of rice-farming cycles, their social roles determined by each person's place in the descending rank from king to landless peasant. The intertwining of collective behavior and social stratification was reflected in the many intersecting dimensions of cultural production: craftsmanship and plastic arts, performance and literature, religious belief and practice, court and village polity, agriculture, architecture, and the rest. Each of these was a collective undertaking with broad social and religious benefits, but the organization of people's participation, the sorts of things they did or made together, and the cultural messages their efforts yielded, tended also to reinforce, or serve to legitimize, the divine power of nobles and priests.

As in many other places, one cannot speak of such activities as having belonged to either sacred or secular realms, for the two concepts did not exist as such. The "absence" of the concept of "art" as an medium independent of its function further indicates the devotional nature of expressive forms like music, dance, drama, poetry, painting, sculpture, and weaving, all of which, in Bali, are renowned for their prodigality. As many have noted, Balinese religion—a blending of autochthonous and selected imported Hindu beliefs—permeates daily life even today so thoroughly as to imbue even the most seemingly insignificant personal actions with aspects of religious significance.

Under dynastic steerage for close to half a millennium prior to 1900, Balinese religion and culture responded to a complex mixture of internal developments and accommodations with allies and enemies among the Islamic and Melayu cultures of the region. Starting in the mid-nineteenth century the organizing structure of the kingdoms was gradually supplanted, at first by the Dutch colonial enterprise, and ultimately by the apparatus of the Indonesian nation and the impact of recent global culture. With these supra-Balinese political changes rising classes of civil servants and business entrepreneurs took their places beside the rice farmers and priests. An important link between the disparate eras and circumstances is the enduring institution of the *sekaha* (also *sekehe, sekaa* or *seka;* in all cases pronounced "s'k'ha"). *Sekaha* are nonhierarchic groups or clubs that undertake cooperative work of all kinds, ranging from ritual preparation, irrigation, artistic production, and local governance and extending to contemporary enterprises like import-export collectives, car-rental agencies, and computer workshops.

In considering *sekaha* as functioning institutions I will assess their role in Balinese life as well as view them as a historically evolving phenomenon. The former approach inevitably demands some hypostatization of changing social conventions, but can help explain the particular character of Balinese collective action. Yet such an approach is especially fraught with implications for Bali, or more precisely Bali's image, so it is important to be aware of the genesis of these images. "Packaged" versions of an idealized Balinese culture, in part enabled by generations of so-called authoritative scholarly approaches to the subject (to which the current chapter is clearly heir), have been a basis for the powerful and much critiqued edifice of commodified "cultural tourism" that pervades life on the island today. These images and concepts have been assimilated and put to use by foreigners, other Indonesians, and Balinese alike, and are by now so ingrained that the perspectives of Balinese themselves may seem hardly different from those of their ethnographers (Picard 1990:74). A historical approach to *sekaha* may help counterbalance such essentializations to the extent that it can allow us to see them as imperfect reflections of a truer Bali.

Hildred and Clifford Geertz's overview of *traditional* Balinese social structure is exemplary of the many studies written between the 1930s and the early 1980s (1975:8–31). They use the term "traditional" to portray a twentieth-century Bali essentially unaffected by the confrontation with the outside world seen as originating with the Dutch arrival. (I adopt the word here mindful of its problems.) Their descriptions assume the metaphor of the steady state first applied to Bali by Gregory Bateson, and stress that "values and social organization, especially at the village level, remain but barely changed from what they were in the nineteenth century" (Geertz and Geertz 1975:9).[2] Bali is seen as timeless, fundamentally self-sufficient, and contentedly aloof from what lies

---

2. Bateson influentially applied the term "steady state" to Balinese society. He defines it as "a term borrowed from communications engineering: that ongoing state of a system of interdependent variables

beyond its shores. In this view the many crosscutting levels of society-cum-culture act interdependently to create a remarkably complex and discrete structure that is nonprogressive and at odds with the West. The domains of culture, cited as evidence of the validity of the Geertzes' structural anthropology, are seen as mutually iconic and enriching of the steady state: the many intersecting weeks in the calendrical system exhibit congruences with the overlapping planes of social organization, and so on.

In the Geertzes' model (based on 1957–58 fieldwork in Tabanan and Klungkung) Balinese social structures, while extremely variable and diverse, essentially comprise ten types of groups, with overlapping memberships. Of these I discuss seven below because of their special relevance to *gamelan.* The remaining three—the kin group, the *subak* (irrigation collective) and client-groups of *geria* (residences of *pedanda,* high priests) are omitted. The term *sekaha* may be applied by Balinese to many of these groups, even though only one has that formal designation.[3] Every Balinese is somehow affiliated with each kind, and consequently has a substantive connection to music, whether passive or active. The sum of these relationships gives a picture of music's role in traditional life.

1. The *pura* (temples) are an intricate network of tens of thousands of open-air structures ranging from small shrines for offerings at road intersections or in households to neighborhood and regional temples to the vast central complex at Besakih on the slopes of the island's sacred core, the volcanic mountain Gunung Agung. Each *pura* has its own group of congregants whose affiliation is determined by numerous factors related to the categories in this list. The ubiquity of music at temple rituals underlies the frequent description of Bali as an intensely musical place where "the religious rites of Balinese daily life . . . continue to play a major role in keeping alive a traditional need for dance and music" (McPhee 1966:12).

Gamelan is played in the larger, full-fledged *pura* during *odalan,* anniversary festivals that take place beginning on a specific day in each 210-day cycle.

---

which shows no progressive or irreversible change. The homeostasis of the internal environment of an organism is an example of 'steady state'" (1949:35).

Vickers comments that "One unintended conclusion from Bateson's article, a conclusion which fits into the context of the colonial preservation of Bali, is that the Balinese have no real sense of history or change . . . [he] . . . promotes the idea that Balinese history is a non-event, a stasis not even interrupted by Dutch colonialism . . . Here the ahistorical nature of anthropology relegated non-Europeans to being people without history" (1989:123).

It is also essential to note that the Geertzes' formulations have been revisited and critiqued extensively by subsequent generations of anthroplogists/Balinists, including Mark Hobart, James Boon, and many others. This is in part because more has been learned about Bali, but also because of Bali's pre-eminent role in the development of anthropological thought. Debates about Bali between prominent scholars are in a real sense debates about anthropology itself.

3. The *subak* can be referred to as the *sekaha subak;* the *banjar* council the *sekaha banjar,* and the council of the *desa adat* the *sekaha desa.* This is because all are essentially heterarchic. The obvious exceptions are the clearly hierarchic *negara* and *desa dinas.*

A *gamelan,* or sometimes several different kinds at once in proximate *balé gong* (special music pavilions), may provide instrumental music or accompaniment for ritual dance or theater performances in one of the temple's hallowed inner courtyards, the *jeroan* and *jaba tengah.* In these cases its sounds are directed to the deities who descend to enter their shrines for the occasion, though congregants listen and watch. At other times *gamelan* play in the outer *jaba* courtyard as accompaniment to dance or theater intended equally for the gods and the gathered crowds. *Gamelan* is also needed for other *yadnya* (ceremonies), from *potong gigi* (tooth filing) held in home compounds, to *ngaben* (cremation and death rites), and in processions like the *makiis* to bathe a deity in its shrine at a sacred spring or at the sea.[4] Many larger *pura* permanently house *gamelan* for ceremonial use, especially types with sacred heirloom status or putative deific origins.

Organizing ceremonies is a major collective effort that mobilizes congregations. The ceremonies overflow with *ramé,*

> [or] "copiousness." The Balinese word could also be translated as "plenitude," or as "busy, crowded sociability," or "excitement and fun." From their social life, much of which is organized to maximize the pleasant cooperation of many people, to their religious rituals, which entail preparing great numbers of identical offerings to the swarms of deities and demons that come for them, the Balinese make sure that there is always a constant buzz of activity around them. Their pleasure in being members of a crowd is always apparent. Their pleasure in multiplicity and complexity marks almost every Balinese expressive form. (Geertz 1994:9)

To this may be added their pleasure and encompassing sense of spiritual fulfillment derived from uniting with divine realms and playing a part, musical or otherwise, in safeguarding community well-being.

Balinese view their *pura* as sites for directing a constant effort to balance forces both visible and unseen, malevolent and beneficial. People see *ramé* as the "fundamental energy of the ritual" (Vickers 1991:97), but it is also "given various associations, from positive tumultuous gaiety to dangerous chaotic or immoral behavior" (ibid:94).

2. The *desa adat* (from *desa,* village; and *adat,* customary law), understood as a community with shared devotional obligations, is most commonly organized in relation to three interdependent temple types: the *pura puseh, pura balé agung,* and *pura dalem,* together called the *khayangan tiga.* Deities of origin are worshiped in the *puseh;* cremation rites and offerings to malevolent forces are administered in the *dalem;* and concerns of human welfare, such as the fertility of local lands, are ensured via ritual in the *balé agung.* Each *khayangan tiga* shares a single congregation all living in the same general area, and

---

4. For surveys of Balinese ritual types, see Covarrubias 1937:259–388, or Geriya et al. 1984. For a detailed investigation of a single *odalan,* see Belo 1953.

thus tends to call on the services of *gamelan* that are based in that area when ritual needs arise.

3. The *banjar,* usually glossed as a ward or hamlet, is the preeminent social institution associated with collective action and reciprocal equality among members; it has been the primary and original context for cultivating *kebyar.* The function of the *banjar* is purely civic and fully distinct from the *desa adat's* ritual one, though the population of the former is sometimes a subset of, and sometimes coextensive with, the latter. The *banjar* is steered by a council, the *krama banjar,* consisting of each male head of household within its jurisdiction. At their regular meetings, presided over by a *kelian* (council leader), councils are responsible for all issues relating to social common interest such as property and personal disputes, inheritance claims, and other related *adat* concerns. In addition members are obligated to one another for mutual help in carrying out important life-cycle rituals, such as those associated with death and cremation.

In contemporary *banjar* life numerous terms are invoked to describe the much cited virtues of mutual help: the Indonesian *gotong royong,* which has been part of nationalist ideology; the Balinese *ngayah,* which applied as well to "feudal" obligations to royalty in former times; and the Balinese/Indonesian *suka-duka,* meaning joy-grief, and referring to the unity of the *banjar* work group across the gamut of life-cycle circumstances. They are no lofty precepts, for the terms come up daily and are cited as the proper motivation for everything from personal to institutional behavior. Decisions are taken by deliberation and consensus at regular *sangkepan* (council meetings) and are ideally harmonious, though in practice are replete with intricate power play. In social interaction such tension tends to be sublimated to avoid personal confrontation, but by deemphasizing individuality and dissent in favor of group needs, the *banjar* system fosters an ethos of cooperation.

The *balé banjar* is a centrally located meeting hall, usually a cement or tiled foundation with a pillar-supported roof, open on the sides but often with a wall and one or more small enclosed rooms at one end. Council meetings and other community activities take place in the main area. *Banjar* typically own and maintain one or more kinds of *gamelan;* the most common is *gong kebyar.* Instruments are stored in a secure rear room and brought out to the open floor for rehearsal, where anyone may listen and observe.

4. The term *sekaha* is mainly applied to subgroups affiliated with a *banjar* and comprising membership drawn from within it. What distinguishes this special understanding of *sekaha* from that of the *krama banjar* (which may also be referred to as *sekaha*) is that participation is voluntary. People join *sekaha,* whether devoted to music or one of the many other types, because they wish to. But just as in the obligatory groups, these are formal organizations replete with *awig-awig* (charters and by-laws) mandating regular meetings, financial commitments, fines for absenteeism, and other special obligations for members.

Sekaha treasuries earmark income primarily for internal use, such as instrument maintenance or dance costumes, or for community contributions, such as for temple upkeep or ritual expenses. At the *desa adat* level *gamelan sekaha* members playing in ceremonies expect only portions of the ritual feast as compensation, and performances at temples in other areas are only minimally remunerated. After deducting expenses, any remainder is distributed among members before important holidays. Money earned performing for tourists is passed on as small honoraria to members, but unless one is a well-known teacher, it is impractical to hope for an income from music in the *sekaha* system.

Sekaha members participate to provide music for rituals, to learn in a communal setting, and, should the group achieve status or fame, to acquire prestige. In the common event that the *gamelan* used is a gong *kebyar* the organization is referred to as the *sekaha gong,* and a suitably poetic Old Javanese name for the group is chosen.[5] A *kelian sekaha,* who receives all inquiries and negotiates arrangements on behalf of musicians, may be one of many members who do not perform but see to auxiliary tasks. A local truck owner with no direct interest in *gamelan* may belong to the *sekaha* so that his truck can be made available for transporting instruments, and in so doing feel that he contributes to musical life.

Living in the same *banjar* ensures long-term close social interaction among *sekaha* members. This may lead to friction, disagreement, and even collapse, but many groups are productive over long periods. The *sekaha gong* from *banjar* Geladag, south of Denpasar, has been active since 1925.[6] During this time it has built and sustained a reputation for ensemble precision, the creation of new works, and the preservation of a large body of ritual compositions. At first Geladag's fame was due to word of mouth and the renown of its directors, who were often invited to nearby villages to teach the Geladag style. Over time the group has won Bali-wide *gamelan* competitions (1947, 1957, 1969), toured throughout Indonesia (1949) and to Australia (1969), received medals of recognition from the government (1954, 1969), released cassette recordings of its complete temple repertoire (1985),[7] and been the subject of investigation by a leading Balinese musicologist (Rembang 1984–85a). Some of the century's most celebrated musicians—Wayan Kalé, Gusti Madé Putu Griya, and Wayan Lotring, among others, were closely associated with the group. Through all of this the constant factor has been the *sekaha* members' continuing obligation to perform regularly and on demand for *desa adat* ceremonies. For all of its public

---

5. Some typical examples are *Sekaha Gong Dharma Kusuma (dharma* = sacred duty; *kusuma* = flower) of Pindha village, and *Sekaha Gong Gunung Sari (gunung* = [sacred] mountain; *sari* = essence [of flower]) of Peliatan village.

6. Arthanegara et al. 1980:66.

7. Bali Stereo Cassettes B639, vols. 1–6, contains recordings of the *lelambatan* repertoire (sacred music for temple ceremonies); other releases contain new instrumental compositions and music for dance.

achievements, the Geladag *gamelan*'s connection to its community is what defines it as a *sekaha*.

Circumstances determine a *sekaha*'s level of activity and proficiency over time. Geladag's history is prolific, while other groups are inactive save for when they are called upon to play in temples. Some *banjar* are musically dormant and have their *gamelan* in storage, but in such places the group ideal is still prized. Keeler, echoing Suweca's thoughts, describes *sekaha* participation thus:

> Membership in a *sekaha* implies responsibilities, rights and rewards uniformly distributed. So there is little formal recognition of personal traits, of status, or even of differences in effort. One or two people tend to have the most ideas and take charge of what needs deciding, but since *sekaha* are so single-purposed, this usually does not cause too much tension. For that matter, difference of opinion can be expressed within the confines of meetings, and people may even show a fair degree of anger in the process. But it should be phrased to show that one has the interests of the group at heart, not self-interest. That is, the elasticity and strength of *sekaha* as a social habit—institution sounds absurd applied to something so wonderfully plastic—makes possible the kind of expression close to impossible in other, one to one situations (1975:120)

Sekaha gong rehearsals are rarely subdued or solemn. Particularly when learning a new piece they can be riotously chaotic, as players pair off to work out details of patterns through repetition, starting and stopping, and individual correction. This is an efficient mode of transmission but with a dozen or more twosomes playing independently, all pairs are forced to pound their instruments at full volume just to be able to hear themselves. As the voices and bronze sound intensify, order begins to seem irretrievable, until at some imperceptible signal from *kendang* or *ugal* the commotion stops and the group comes together to play as a unit.

Such transformations from pandemonium to disciplined coordination show a *sekaha* capacity for seamless movement between behaviors that has numerous analogs. One is found in the Balinese cockfight. During betting prior to the match, "the mob scene quality, the sense that sheer chaos is about to break loose, with all those waving, shouting, pushing, clambering men is quite strong, an effect which is only heightened by the intense stillness that falls with instant suddenness, rather as if someone had turned off the current, when the slit gong sounds, the cocks are put down, and the battle begins" (Geertz 1973: 429). Similarly the routines of daily life are periodically interrupted by the arrival of *odalan,* during which *pura* become bustling places, only to empty again as soon as the rituals end. These kinds of abrupt transitions are routinely finessed in *kebyar* too, as twenty-five musicians switch between frenetic rhythms and delicate melody as suddenly and cleanly as locales change in a cinematic montage.

5. Caste and rank in Bali are indicated by title-group name. Those among the minority *triwangsa,* nobles of putative Javanese pedigree and the many hybrids resulting from intermarriage, are distinguished as a set from *sudra,* the commoner majority. Nobles are also called *anak jero* (insiders, referring to their palace abodes) and commoners *anak jaba* (outsiders). *Warga* is a collective term for the various title-group distinctions within the *triwangsa,* as well as the many clan affiliations among commoners. *Triwangsa* population is scattered throughout Bali, densest in the central and eastern regions and sparsest in the west. Some *banjar* may be home only to commoners and a few almost exclusively to nobility, but mainly *anak jero* and *anak jaba* live as neighbors in the same *banjar.* Over 90 percent of Balinese are *anak jaba/sudra;* the remainder are *brahmana* (kings and high priests), *ksatria* (warriors), and *wesia* (civil servants and merchants), or an intercaste combination.[8] Other *warga* groupings like the *pandé* clan of *gamelan* forgers and metalsmiths are nominally *sudra,* but were historically granted special privileges by royalty and retain much of the associated status today. *Warga* groupings also link Balinese with a temple of origin in addition to that in their *desa adat.*

Social hierarchies are defined via title group in Bali according to endlessly subtle and variable expectations about deference and proper vocabulary. Interactions with others of the same or different title are governed by elaborate etiquette and linguistic conventions dictating the proper physical position one must adapt and the level of Balinese language one must speak. Musicians often play *gamelan* at the *balé banjar* as coequals, which can temporarily nullify the ordinary proscriptions about two persons of differing *warga* occupying the same physical level.[9] At rehearsal breaks, when cigarettes, coffee, and sweets are brought over from the nearest roadside stand, all partake together. The temporary erasure of such formal distinctions is not, however, likely to override caste-related tensions that may exist between different status individuals or families in the same *banjar.* And even though the most musically talented members of a *sekaha* are often *anak jaba,* it is frequently *triwangsa* who, because of their unassailable social prestige, are invested with leadership positions. This was true in Peliatan's *sekaha gong Gunung Sari* in the mid-1980s, where the lead drummer and musical director was Wayan Gandera, a commoner, but a nonperforming high-caste member was responsible for negotiations and transactions with outsiders.

6. The former *negara* (kingdoms) and their powerful *puri* (courts) were

---

8. This is a simplified formulation about a much debated subject. The complex mixed levels brought about by intermarriage and the status of numerous family clan associations complicate the system. See further in Geertz and Geertz 1975 and Boon 1977 for extended discussions of *warga,* caste, and marriage in Bali.

9. Sanger (1992:21–24), reporting on research in Sengguan and Intaran, states that *triwangsa* with the high title *cokorda* did not join the *sekaha gong,* and were more often involved as dancers, possibly because of the greater visibility and status that that entailed.

the domains of greatest prestige and influence for centuries, tracing their lineages to the revered Hindu-Javanese Majapahit realm of the ninth to fifteenth centuries. Historically nobility were music patrons (and often musicians themselves), cultivating the performing arts in their *puri* and employing commoners or lower-status *triwangsa* as court musicians and dancers. There is iconographic evidence that in nineteenth-century musical life *sekaha* collectivity was less important than the hierarchies of court culture, for in paintings emanating from both court and village milieus aristocrats and commoners are almost never shown playing together. Representational strategies like this served the interests of each group in its own way. Authoritative *brahmana* court representations showed lower-status aristocrats performing, which reinforced the former's social dominance. Commoners, meanwhile, opted not to paint themselves in a subservient role, which stylistic conventions would have required them to do had both groups been shown together (Vickers 1985:175).

Expressive forms originating in the *puri* are felt to have the highest prestige, most of all those with exclusive ties such as the *gambuh* dance dramas and huge *gong gdé* ceremonial bronze *gamelan,* which were indispensable arms of the court. Areas like Peliatan, Batuan, or Saba, all in Gianyar district, continue to have a high concentration of nobility and a corresponding history of influential patronage and dependence on the support and participation of local *triwangsa.* In Geladag as in other *banjar* situated close to formerly influential and musically active *puri,* the abundance of extant repertoire is felt to be a result of the participation of earlier-era musicians in court ensembles. In West Bali, where few nobility settled, court impact is correspondingly smaller, and less prestigious ensembles made from bamboo (such as the *jegog* and *joged*) enjoy relatively greater popularity. Extended discussion of the significance of court culture for the history of Balinese musical styles is reserved for part 2.

7. In traditional Bali the notion of village as a self-contained territorial jurisdiction was only approximated by the *banjar.* The larger community sharing a *desa adat* was more appropriate in size and became the model for the *desa dinas* (administrative village system; more commonly called simply *desa*) established by the Dutch. The *desa* has been a forum for secular *gamelan* activities at schools and civic functions since the colonial years, comprising the most local such forum in a network of contexts now extending to the highest levels of the Indonesian government.

Adopted essentially intact by Indonesia, *desa* administration closely entwines with the *adat* system centered at the *banjar.* In addition to the *kelian adat,* each *banjar* also has a *perbekel,* an administrator responsible for gathering statistics about population and resources, carrying out government programs such as birth control initiatives and political campaigning, and reporting to the *desa. Desa dinas,* made up of several adjacent *banjar,* have *perbekel* as well with similar but expanded functions. At the next level are the fifty-one

Balinese *kecamatan,* headed by *camat;* further up still are the nine *kabupaten,* or *daerah tingkat II* (second-level administrative regions) under *bupati,* and last the *propinsi,* of which the entire island of Bali is one, headed by a *gubernur.* Indonesia's twenty-seven *propinsi,* or *daerah tingkat I,* answer to the republic's government, seated in Jakarta. From *perbekel* to *gubernur,* all leaders are appointed, not elected.

The Dutch implemented the *dinas* system to enact their hegemony, maintaining that it was needed to protect peasants from the despotic excesses and warring of the late-nineteenth-century kings. Influenced by progressive thought about ethical colonial policy during that era, they saw themselves as intervening to protect traditional culture, which was not viewed as the proper legacy of their adversaries in the nobility but as the province of the less powerful. Their system of indirect rule did not impose European legal mores on commoners but instead subjected them to a new, strictly codified *adat* based on Dutch scholars' interpretations of recondite Hindu texts. It also duplicitously drew aristocrats into mutually lucrative tax-collecting agreements that held them accountable to Dutch law, lessening their power. In so doing the Dutch rigidified previously ambiguous caste strictures, which strengthened society's Hindu character and "ensured that Balinese social and political discourse came to focus heavily on matters of tradition, religion, caste, and culture" (Robinson 1995:32). The "traditional" Bali of twentieth-century ethnographers like the Geertzes is thus partly a Dutch-inspired creation. Their description of Bali as "fundamentally" (that is, not entirely) traditional is an acknowledgment of the *dinas* system's impact on twentieth-century Balinese life, an impact which they nevertheless downplayed, despite its importance.

With the Dutch holding the reins, many nobility became enfeebled middlemen. The legal strengthening of the caste system appeared to boost their power even as the *dinas* system slowly drained it by supplanting the obligation *banjar* members felt to nobility with allegiance to the state. A by-product of the Dutch preservationist policy was its role in encouraging village rather than court music, for the persuasiveness of the *negara*-based cultural forms, with their ability to depict a Bali wholly dependent upon aristocrats and their deific ancestors, slowly began to weaken. Dutch policy could only partly erode this cherished perception, but it did open up previously unimagined possibilities for cultural development. When Indonesia declared independence, such sentiments were officially channeled into the ideology of the republic, giving *gamelan* numerous parts to play in national development that were sanctioned as complementary to its ongoing role in traditional life. Since then the secular role for *gamelan* has mushroomed into an impressive network of government-supported contexts, including study at academic institutions and performances in the public schools, at festivals, and at government offices and events. In virtually all of this activity Balinese *gamelan* is synonymous with the *gong kebyar,* whose rise is synchronous with that of the *dinas* system.

The Changing *Sekaha* I: The Birth of *Kebyar*

In the centuries prior to Dutch rule, people's affiliations and obligations to *pura* and *puri* had grown numerous, complex, and often fractious. This dispersion of power and human resources was straining social cohesion by the time of the 1846–49 Dutch military incursions in North Bali. With the subsequent slow decline of royal power the locus of cultural energy shifted by degrees from the sovereign centers to the previously more peripheral *banjar*. From a perspective favoring nostalgia for Majapahit's former glories these changes were not the final stage of "a relentless progress toward the good society, but a gradual fading from view of a classic model of perfection" (Geertz 1980:15). From commoners' viewpoints they may have felt like the lifting of a yoke. Court life and prestige at the turn of the twentieth century was in any case growing moribund, and it was from these ashes of uncertainty that the phoenix of *kebyar* arose in northern villages to bring a new level of vitality to Balinese arts. It was not that Bali had been previously averse to innovation. If the decline of the *puri* did catalyze the development of a secular art, it is important to remember that for Balinese the concept "secular" was still foreign. *Kebyar* moved *gamelan* into unexplored contexts: it was increasingly unconstrained by the purposes of courts and temples, at odds with the aesthetics and function of court-based performance, and alive to the new century.

The Dutch completed their takeover after the infamous *puputan* ("the end") at Badung (1906) and Klungkung (1908), in which the overwhelmed local kings and their armies were inspired to mass suicide on the battlefield. The north coast town of Singaraja became the colonial capital, growing into a prosperous port in significant contact with wider Southeast Asian and European culture. In tandem with the new awareness of Hindu texts a literary revival was underway throughout the northern *kabupaten* Buleleng in which members of all *warga* were forming *sekaha pepaosan* (reading clubs) to sing, interpret and discuss *kakawin,* Hindu poetry written in Kawi, the Old Javanese literary language (Rubinstein 1992). Reading groups from different *banjar* enjoyed competing before audiences at temple ceremonies and night markets, where they were judged on sung recitation and the skillfulness of a translators' Balinese rendition. Enthusiastic crowds and increasing demand for these literary face-offs stimulated *sekaha* to experiment with new formats. *Kebyar* emerged between 1910 and 1915 as the result of attempts to fuse *pepaosan* competitions with one such innovation, the addition of *gamelan* accompaniment.

The three published accounts of *kebyar*'s inception are quoted below. Origin stories like these conflict but that is to be expected; their significance is in their common depiction of a milieu of heightened creative competition and artistic energy.[10] Simpen's version is the most detailed:

---

10. My conversations with Gusti Ngurah Panji of Bungkulan support Bandem and DeBoer's account, but Rubinstein (1992:92 n. 6) offers confirmation of Simpen's version from the famed

In 1913 approximately, *geria banjar* Tegeha in *kecamatan* Banjar, *kabupaten* Buleleng, held a religious ceremony to ordain a *brahmana* as a priest. Because this was
to be a large affair, followers of the *geria* who owned *gamelan* offered them to en-
liven the ceremony. Those who offered them were the *gamelan* clubs [from] Tegeha
and . . . Seririt. The ceremony was enlivened with these two *gamelan*. As a result a
gamelan competition took place, that is, the *banjar* Tegeha *gamelan* against the Bu-
bunan *gamelan*. Because this was the first occurrence of a *gamelan* competition the
spectators were, accordingly, very numerous. The competition lasted for three days,
day and night. It seems that it was not the *gamelan* melodies that were the focus of
the competition at this time but, rather, the skill of the people at reading and interpreting *kakawin*. Whoever sang more *kakawin* making use of various [poetic]
meters and provided correct translations . . . was considered the victor. The Bubu-
nan *gamelan* executed all sorts of tricks, including sleight of hand.[11] The *banjar*
Tegeha *gamelan* performed a seated dance. The dance commenced in the middle of
the *gamelan* and initially resembled the movements of a person displaying expertise
in performing with the *trompong* mallets with arms extended in front, accompanied
by *kakawin* or *kidung,* while at the same time striking the *trompong* slowly, following the *kakawin* melody. Upon completion of one stanza of the *kakawin,* it was
rejoined for one stanza with a melodic interlude performed by the *gamelan,* that is,
a classical melody. When each side had completed ten rounds, they switched. Thus
the *gamelan* took turns to compete.

From that time on there were *gamelan-pepaosan* competitions and they exerted
a very great influence on the people of Buleleng in the literary sphere. From that
time on many groups of people who performed *pepaosan* appeared. In every village
in Buleleng, including villages in the interior, there were groups of people who
would perform *kakawin*. People usually held *gamelan* competitions during cremations and post-cremation rites or fairs, and they would last for three days. (Simpen
1979:1f.; translation by Rubinstein, 1992:92)

Bandem and DeBoer emphasize music and dance more than the literary
impetus:

In the early years of this century, two villages in north Bali, Bungkulan and
Jagaraga, shared an especially intense rivalry and competed on a regular basis in
creating new music and dance compositions. Bungkulan contributed a new musical
idea—*Palawakia*—in which a virtuoso performer alternately sang, gave textual
interpretations, and played the *trompong,* a musical instrument consisting of a row
of gongs in a carved wooden case, accompanied by a full *gamelan*. Texts were taken
from the *Bharatayuda,* an Old Javanese poem that deals with the final war at the

---

drummer and composer Gdé Manik. Bandem and DeBoer rightly note that "All origin stories have a
mythic aspect, and so it is with *kebyar* . . . Informants have their own agendas and claims for credit
conflict, while the 'true story,' if there ever was one, recedes into the darkness of the irretrievable past"
(1995:85 n. 2).

11. This is clearly a reference to *gaya,* or "flashy" performance style. "Sleight of hand" (*main sulap*)
may refer to a favorite trick of *trompong* players: twirling one *panggul* baton-style in the air before
descending as if to strike a gong, slowly lowering it to the instrument, and then alternately raising and
lowering the *panggul* in both hands in an irregular rhythmic gesture to create suspense over the timing
and placement of the imminent stroke. See also below in the discussion of *gaya* later in this chapter.

end of the *Mahabharata* . . . In 1914, Jagaraga contributed the *Kebyar Legong,* a dance performed by two young women in men's clothing, who interpreted the music of the orchestra in a pure dance medium. (1995:75)

McPhee nearly corroborates Bandem and DeBoer:

> According to the Regent [cf. *Bupati]* of Buleleng, Anak Agung Gedé Gusti Jelantik, who told me in 1937 that he noted the date in his diary at the time, the first *kebyar* music was publicly heard in December 1915, when several north Bali *gamelan* held a *gamelan* competition in Jagaraga, a village still celebrated in Bali for its superb *gamelan* and bold, dramatic music . . . It was some ten years after the date preserved in the Regent's diary that a Balinese audience witnessed the debut of I Maria of Tabanan, who is said to have created the new dance known as *kebyar,* in which the dancer, seated on a mat and surrounded on three sides by the facing musicians of the *gamelan,* interprets in movement the constantly changing moods of the music. (1966:328)

Integrations of dance, music, and drama were already central to Balinese performance, but the discontinuity of juxtaposing discrete genres (in these cases *kakawin* alternating with musical interludes) was something new. In the initial phases it seems that the musical material used was mainly preexisting, but concatenated in such as a way as to create a new aesthetic context and expectation for rapid musical change. One can scarcely imagine the radical and exhilarating effect this early music must have had, particularly in the atmosphere of one-upmanship and daring suffusing competitive *banjar* spirit. Early free-standing *kebyar* compositions fully embrace discontinuity as an aspect of style, as if to forefront Simpen's "tricks and sleight of hand" and show what musical difficulties could be invented and mastered in the twin names of novelty and *sekaha* superiority. Many of the textures described at the end of chapter 2 collide with one another rapidly and unpredictably in instrumental pieces such as *Kebyar Ding,* named, like others of the day, after the scale tone of its opening *byar* sonority.[12] This notably antipoetic title hints at its creators' fascination with the novelty of the musical materials themselves, and their embryonic notions about what sort of genre and repertoire such music would eventually fit into.

An important question to ask about the early stages of *kebyar* musical development concerns the impetus for its revolutionary signature techniques and devices (such as the *byar* chord). Certainly the confrontation with European modernity and the daily proof of the impact it was having on Balinese

---

12. *Kebyar Ding* was recorded by Odeon in *banjar* Belaluan in 1928.

See also fig. 6.18 for *Kempul Ndung,* a similarly titled *gamelan angklung* composition. Generic titles occur in *gamelan angklung* as well, though the motivations for using them are not quite the same. It may have more to do with the nonchalant attitude toward *ankglung* pieces in general, which in any case reflects a similar lack of specific function or poetic association. It is also possible that the occasional use of such titles in *angklung* set a precedent that early *kebyar* composers followed.

life was a general factor in creating an atmosphere of receptivity to the unfamiliar. There must have been an artistically provocative social environment of
uncertainty and instability that fueled compositional experimentation. If seen
mainly as an outgrowth of the smooth narrative continuity, stylized emotions,
and extended time scale of court theatrical and musical forms, the dynamism
and compression of *kebyar* music indeed represent a drastic departure (Seebass 1996:82). Yet vital as this unfamiliar music must have seemed, even its
bolder aspects were not without Balinese precedent. The village *gamelan angklung* popular in the north already used *gangsa gantung* and extended *reyong*
similar to those adapted by *kebyar,* and the *angklung* repertoire is full of irregular rhythms and vocally derived, nonmetric passages that demonstrate
a smoother connection to older music than *kebyar* is usually credited with.
Some unusual northern *gamelan* ensemble types, such as the *gong cenik* of
Jagaraga and Tamblang villages or the *gong druwé* of Godég, employ complex
orchestral textures that may also have been influential.[13] The subsequent rico-
chet impact of *kebyar* back onto these genres throughout this century makes
it difficult, from current perspective, to do more than speculate about what
specific musical form this influence took at its point of origin.

The net effect of this social and musical admixture was to germinate inchoate *kebyar* style, with its hallmark restless intensity. To perform this well
necessitated rehearsing longer for a higher kind of collective musical awareness capable of adjusting to sudden or subtle changes in material, texture,
tempo, and dynamic. This was something unknown in the continuous music
of earlier repertoires, though perhaps less so in village ceremonial music like
angklung. At the same time the extended compositions and complex dance and
drum patterns of the court repertoire provided a foundation of musicianship
and structural sophistication without which *kebyar*'s virtuoso modernisms
might have imploded.

By the 1930s *kebyar* performances had expanded to encompass a kind of
revue including instrumental pieces deriving from diverse repertoires, *kakawin,* and a selection of old and new dances.[14] Parallel developments brought

---

13. A recording of the *gong druwé* is on the 1992 Auvidis CD B 6769 (*Bali: Music from the Northwest*). I recorded *gong cenik* in both Jagaraga and Tamblang in 1982.

14. McPhee describes a program from a 1938 *kebyar* performance at a Singaraja night market.
"Admission was charged to enter the grounds, crowded with food stalls, naive freak shows, novelty
booths, and little gambling tables. Around a large *gamelan* a silent audience sat enthralled for nearly
two hours. Here the performance did not open with the usual crashing *kebyar*. Instead a quiet prelude
by the *gamelan* was followed by unaccompanied chanting by a finely trained male singer of a passage
from the *Mahabharata*. A brief interlude by the *gamelan* introduced a recited passage, and only then
did the customary *kebyar* outburst take place.

1. *kakawin*	unaccompanied chanting of *kawi* text	
2. *palawakia*	unaccompanied recitation in *kawi*, but with line by line translation into Balinese by a second performer	
3. *kebyar*	*gamelan* introduction to the main composition	
4. *condong*	*condong* episode from *legong,* danced by two girls	

about the creation of free-standing instrumental compositions and dances. The *Kebyar Legong* cited by Bandem and DeBoer was later developed into *Teruna Jaya,* a portrayal of a capricious adolescent, by Pan Wandres and Gdé Manik from Jagaraga. It too comprises a varied chain of melodies, tempi, and textures. Maria's significant early contributions were the "sitting" dances *Kebyar Duduk* and *Kebyar Trompong,* in which a dancer, often stooped in a cross-legged squatting posture, interprets the music without recourse to a story or stock theatrical character.

Courts unable to maintain their former financial standard bequeathed or entrusted *gamelan* heirlooms to nearby *banjar.* As *kebyar* instrumentation was refined, groups melted bronze from the large *gong gdé* ceremonial instruments and recast it into the lighter, more agile *kebyar gangsa* and *reyong.* New wooden cases were built and carved to accommodate the suppler keys and longer *reyong,* and smaller mallets adapted from *gamelan angklung* to help musicians play faster and with more control. The development of *kebyar* preoccupied the already competitive *sekaha,* who worked and rehearsed fervently to coin musical innovations and surprises, and to better demonstrate their unity and drive. Increasingly absent at the courts, music thrived at *banjar,* where pieces were practiced to a new standard of excellence distanced in purpose and effect from those in the staid ritual repertoires. Compositional innovation, technological advance, and changing social conditions collaborated to nourish *kebyar*'s early growth.

The Changing *Sekaha* II: *Kebyar* up to Independence

Under Dutch rule the towns of Singaraja and the southern center Denpasar urbanized because they were the seats of the colonial administration and lay close to sea trade and still influential *puri.* Less affected but also growing under *dinas* bureaucracies were the other regional capitals Gianyar, Klungkung, Ban-

---

5. *gabor*	melody from the ritual dance *gabor,* danced by the same	
6. *bapang*	music for a high official, same dancers	
7. *gilakan*	*baris* music, same dancers	
8. *kebyar*	percussive unison passage, same dancers	
9. *gilakan*	similar to no. 7, different choreography	
10. *bapang*	similar to no. 6, different choreography	
11. *pengecet*	*allegretto* in classical style, same dancers	
12. *pengisep*	variation, conclusion of dance	
13. *pengalang*	melodic interlude—*gamelan*	
14. *gambangan*	*gambang* melody with *kakawin* singing	
15. *pengecet*	*allegretto* in classical style—*gamelan*	
16. *pengawak*	slow movement in classical style—*gamelan*	
17. *pengecet*	concluding *allegretto*—*gamelan*	

Here was *kebyar* in a new light, no mere show piece, but a rich and varied presentation, both diverting and serious, in which classical and even sacred elements were interwoven to create a new and popular form of entertainment" (1966:343).

gli, Amlapura, Tabanan, and Negara. Indirect-rule policies caused nearly all Dutch to confine themselves to the two main centers, leaving nobility in putative control elsewhere and bringing about what amounted to an "Indian summer" of court prestige for select royalty shrewd enough to exploit their new figurehead roles. Despite their lack of political power, some acquired great wealth and held sumptuous rituals, which gave the illusion that the *negara* persisted (Vickers 1989:138).

Elsewhere commoners and *banjar* acquired assets as less fortunate nobles were inevitably forced to divest theirs, with the result that the designations rich and poor did not always correlate with social status. High Dutch-imposed land taxes exacerbated economic disparities, and tenant farming and rural poverty increased. Tension both between and within *warga* grew, creating complex new social factions and making Bali fertile ground for nationalist militarism after the Second World War. Increased commerce in the larger towns benefited the small but rising merchant class, and the gap between urban and rural lifestyles widened even as *banjar* and *desa adat* structures remained firm. As the essential link between the *adat* and *dinas* systems, *banjar* became more crucial to social structure than before.

Urban Balinese intellectuals and sympathetic Dutch scholars, mainly in Singaraja, published journals of arts and ideas such as the short-lived *Bhawanegara* (1931–35), creating a print-consciousness of Balinese culture. Among the few Balinese attending Dutch schools in Bali, as well as for other colonial subjects in similar situations throughout the archipelago, Malay slowly gained momentum as a lingua franca. In 1928 a variant of it was formally adopted by nationalist students in Batavia as *Bahasa Indonesia,* the Indonesian language. These parallel developments subtly began to make cultural identity, and hence *gamelan,* seem compatible with Indonesian nationalism.

The 1920 publication of Gregor Krause's photograph-and-text essay *Bali* acted as a magnet to attract early tourists, who came by steamship. In the 1930s a community of foreign artists, scholars, and writers (the painter-musician Walter Spies, anthropologists Margaret Mead, Gregory Bateson, and Jane Belo, the painter-ethnographer Miguel Covarrubias, and composer Colin McPhee foremost among them) initiated a flow of popular and scholarly literature about the island that deepened both local and international perception of Bali as a uniquely rich traditional culture.

Kebyar exploded amid this turbulence in the years prior to 1930, at first spreading from Singaraja east into Karangasem regency and south to Tabanan, home of the dancer and choreographer Maria. One famous *sekaha* in Tabanan was formed circa 1900, according to local sources, when Anak Agung Ngurah, a local prince appointed by the Dutch to oversee culture in the region, donated his *puri's* *gamelan gong gdé* to *banjar* Pangkung. In 1915 these instruments were recast into *kebyar* format, and by 1922 the group had already invited numerous teachers from North Bali to teach them the new style and create new compositions.[15] In the 1920s *kebyar* migrated further south and arrived in the Denpasar area. Among the small first generation of *sekaha* to take shape were those in *banjar* Belaluan (1920), Geladag (mentioned earlier), Sibang (1926), and upland in Peliatan (1926). In all of these places instruments were donated or loaned by nobility, but some *banjar* borrowed money to buy new instruments. A second and larger generation of *kebyar sekaha* grew prior to the Second World War, spreading the style throughout the rest of the island. By then numerous expert teachers were available outside the north, so it was no longer necessary to obtain one by making the long trip over the central mountains. Repertoire and stylistic variants multiplied.

With *kebyar*'s special technical demands, the new empowerment of *banjar*, and an ideological focus on cultural development, some *sekaha* grew beyond their previous functions of meeting *desa adat* ritual needs. Outside Singaraja and environs (where pride of origin and entrenched competitiveness helped *kebyar* to thrive in all circumstances) the new breed of ambitious *sekaha* were at first most likely to emerge in the southern urban areas where tourists would pay for entertainment. The *gamelan* from Belaluan (today called Sadmerta) played throughout the 1930s at the Dutch-run Bali Hotel, right across the road from their *balé banjar* in central Denpasar. They garnered local and international renown through this association with foreigners, and were lauded by Covarrubias (1937:206–10), a distinction still trumpeted there more than fifty years after the fact.[16] The Peliatan *gamelan* likewise set the pace for groups in *kabupaten* Gianyar after they were sent by the Dutch to perform at the 1931 Paris Colonial Exhibition. Entertaining visitors or performing abroad spurred musicians on and made them cognizant of contributing to a growing international perception of the island. Spectators' enthusiasm motivated them to arrange for extra rehearsals, new teachers for new compositions, and more elaborately gilded instruments and dance costumes. Though modest, the income generated from these performances built *sekaha* treasuries and whetted appetites for success. The role of foreigners at this stage in *kebyar*'s growth was to affirm the unfamiliar new sense of the music's intrinsic artistic value, and to impress upon *sekaha* that high performance standards mattered not just for Balinese, but because the world was watching.

The tourist market was yet too limited to involve any but a select group of *sekaha* directly, but the fame such groups garnered was nonetheless alluring. Competition fever spread from the north and both the nobility and the Dutch, delighted to wield the cultural spotlight, sponsored high-profile showdowns between the most famous. Pangkung, Belaluan, Peliatan, and a few other regular winners passed the torch between them, together comprising an elite

---

15. Arthanegara et al. 1980:73–74.

16. Pandji et al. 1978:101. This group history, written for a government documentation project by a local official, quotes Covarrubias at length in English and provides an Indonesian translation.

whose accomplishments inspired envy and emulation. The enthusiasm *kebyar* generated prompted many older music and theater genres to absorb its stylistic traits and urgent pacing, even as cautious Balinese responded negatively to what seemed an overnight transformation and cavalier disregard for older values (Vickers 1986:305). For better and for worse, *kebyar* was the emblem of a rapidly changing way of life.

The Changing *Sekaha* III: *Kebyar* after Independence

Kebyar maintained and widened its early trajectory in the second half of the twentieth century at an uneven rate. Owing to the shortages and hardships of wartime Japanese occupation and the subsequent struggle for independence, secular musical activity slowed temporarily, biding time until the dust cleared and a new cultural sponsor as powerful and influential as the *puri* or the Dutch was able see to the resumption of festivals and competitions. Once this took shape, in the form of the Indonesian government, change occurred at an intensely accelerated pace. During the first years of nationhood, as before, activity was greater in the north, but after Denpasar became capital of Bali in 1949 Singaraja and environs found itself increasingly out of the mainstream. The unconstrained power of Singaraja-style *kebyar* came to be disparaged by southern musicians, who felt that their mandate was to refine the music by consciously integrating materials and stylistic nuances borrowed from the gentler court genres *gambuh, semar pegulingan,* and *pelegongan,* which were rarer in the north.

They did this even as they sought out prominent northern musicians to tap into their latest ideas. Composer-drummers Wayan Beratha and Gdé Manik were two of the most prominent musicians of the era. On separate occasions the two related to me how they had plied each other for musical materials during a 1957 tour to Jakarta to play for president Sukarno. During this time Beratha, son of the Belaluan *gamelan*'s leader of the 1920s and 1930s, was able to master Manik's *Teruna Jaya.* While admiring the music, Beratha could not conceal how strongly he felt that it needed polish for presentation to southern audiences. Similar stories are told about the Peliatan *gamelan*'s reaction to northern-style pieces that they added to their repertoire. Though touted as an aesthetic imperative, the underlying political meaning of these assimilations was that southern musicians were displaying greater allegiance to the courtly past, whereas the north more aggressively rejected it. Mutual musical disrespect simmered.

Indonesia declared independence on August 17, 1945, but fought with guns, intrigue, and diplomacy until independence was recognized at the Round Table Conference at the Hague in 1949. In the 1950s and 1960s the charismatic Sukarno captured public imagination by adopting a leadership style reminiscent of the omniscient *negara* rulers of the romantic past. His enshrine-

Teruna Jaya danced by Madé Wiratini, 1988. Photo: Richard Blair.

ment of collectivity as a centerpiece of nationalist ideology was intended to muster human resources for the task of national development, but as a self-styled modern monarch he was scarcely more attentive than his forebears to the problems of entrenched social inequalities. He also used the glorified, collective image of Balinese culture that was already in place to further promote and symbolize Indonesia to the world, giving the island an enduring sense of national significance that is out of proportion to its size and population.

Half-Balinese himself and a lover of the arts, Sukarno exercised crucial influence on music and dance. He invited prominent *kebyar sekaha* to perform in Jakarta and at his *istana* (presidential palace) near Tampaksiring in Bali. By regularly requesting performances of *kebyar* dances such as *Tari Tenun, Tari Tani,* and *Tari Nelayan* (Weaving, Farming, and Fishing Dances) he promoted artistic social realism, though these pieces were unpopular and have since been virtually dropped. With an eye toward the presumed brief attention span of foreigners encountering Balinese arts anew, he also urged the cutting of some lengthy dances such as *Teruna Jaya,* a trend by now well established.[17] With origins in the revue-style performances of early *kebyar,* by the 1960s tourist performances came to consist of a sequence of *tari lepas* (brief dances unconnected to theatrical presentation) preceded by an instrumental overture.

During Indonesia's first years there was anything but political unity in Bali. At odds were strong factions of anti-Dutch Republican nationalists, underground resistance to them, traditionalists who sought to sustain the cultural approach of the previous decades, others who rejected any return to "feudalism," and Communists promoting pan-Asian awareness. Balinese were torn between the seemingly irreconcilable evils of adhering to the familiar system of oppressive caste strictures, and rallying behind the new Jakartan power base, which many feared would establish a Javanese-style Islamic state and crush Balinese culture.[18] Following consensus, *banjar* (and hence *sekaha*) aligned themselves inflexibly with one or another position. Enmities arose and disturbed musical life, for groups within some *desa adat* were mutually opposed and refused to play at rituals for each other on that basis. Some altogether dissociated themselves from religious life, or disbanded. In areas like Ubud resentments between *banjar* severely threatened social cohesion (Tenzer 1998:118).

The factionalism led to collective behavior in the form of mob violence. In the years leading up to the 1965 aborted Communist coup in Jakarta and subsequent mass killings, in which close to 100,000 were slaughtered in Bali, the nationalists (PNI) and Communists (PKI) emerged as the two strongest parties. One way they vied for support was through *sekaha,* successfully enticing them to declare affiliations and propagandize theatrical performances by inserting partisan dialogue (Hanna 1976:112). After the failed coup, as calls to eradicate Communists were issued and the witch-hunt overwhelmed Bali,

---

17. According to Gdé Manik (personal communication, August 1982), at a command performance in 1952 Sukarno personally asked him to shorten *Teruna Jaya* from 55 minutes to 15. This is the version that Wayan Beratha brought to the south. The original version has been revived only recently.

18. Fear of Islamic domination bolstered support for an officially secular national policy allowing religious freedom. As it turned out, *Pancasila,* the five basic principles adopted by Indonesia in 1945 (see n. 27 below), called for belief in "one god," which meant that religious leaders had to scramble to reorganize the presentation of their beliefs in order for Balinese Hinduism to gain recognition. See further Robinson 1995:183–84, and Vickers 1989 165–66.

sekaha known to be PKI sympathizers such as that in the northern village of Kedis Kaja were killed en masse and their instruments destroyed (Ornstein 1971a:54). Throughout the island the killing was not a disorganized free-for-all, but was carried out by *adat* groups:

> Some village and hamlet authorities exploited the "traditional" institutions of communal responsibility and labor in carrying out the annihilation of the PKI: "One man would stab a victim while another would hit him on the head with a rock. 'I couldn't believe it,' a foreigner who witnessed the blood bath told me. 'One Balinese never killed another alone. It was all community work. The whole village was instructed.'" (Robinson 1995:299, quoting Kirk 1966:42)

This period must be understood as consistent with Balinese societal tendencies rather than as an aberration from a steady-state traditional life, as many have asserted. Far from disestablishing the importance of collectivity, the massacres reinforce it by severing it from Bali's public, apolitical image of unblemished artistic and cultural harmony. They also reemphasize the need to view Balinese society as an entanglement of collective and hierarchic modes of organization.

The *Sekaha* in the New Order

When the killings subsided Bali was left traumatized, shy of internal dissent, and pliantly obedient to Jakarta's policies. After orchestrating internal exile for Sukarno in 1967, the new president, Suharto, established his *orde baru* (new order) with its prominent ideology of *pembangunan* (national development). Between then and Suharto's resignation in May 1998 the long arm of Indonesian government became the most powerful factor shaping life on Bali, bearing heavily on *adat* as well as private enterprise. There remain an insignificant number of Balinese, and in increasingly remote pockets, for whom, as the Geertzes put it not too long ago, life can be described as "but barely changed."

Provincial leaders, operating under Jakartan mandates, do all in their power to promote the conceptual integration of traditional Balinese culture, national development, entrepreneurship, and the tourist industry into a neatly bundled, harmonious framework—an ideology of modern Bali in which art forms like *kebyar* have an explicitly sanctioned secular role. With performing arts at the center of this idyll, the growing number of conservatory-trained, professional musicians have mainly benefited from the attention so long as they hew to the status quo. In part owing to memories of the consequences of dissent in the 1960s, few care to publicly challenge the promotion of culture. In the arts the government-sponsored LISTIBIYA (*Majelis Pertimbangan dan Pembinaan Kebudayaan, Arts* Evaluation and Cultivation Board), founded in 1962 under the auspices of the *Departemen Pendidikan dan Kebudayaan* (or *Depdikbud,* Department of Education and Culture; also known as *P dan K*), has been instrumental in shaping the contemporary forces affecting *kebyar,* issuing certificates of qualification for groups seeking tourist performance opportunities, maintaining close affiliation with the conservatories, and sponsoring yearly festivals and competitions. Below I consider the effects of tourism, conservatories, festivals, and media.

1. *Tourism.* Tourism is now integral to Balinese culture (Picard 1990:74). Music is marketed as authentic artistic expression under the official policy of *Pariwisata Budaya* (Cultural Tourism), which aims to promote Balinese culture as a tourist attraction while using the monetary proceeds to protect it against the negative influences tourism brings. These goals are held to be perfectly reconcilable under careful monitoring and steerage. In an analogous conceptual opposition, traditional culture was also seen as compatible with modernization under the *orde baru.* Bali, like each of the twenty-seven Indonesian *propinsi,* was expected to participate fully in the affairs of the Republic while using the benefits of *pembangunan* to maintain and promote its cultural identity.

To resolve these conundrums and lessen the possibility for clashes of belief, "culture" has become more and more of a staged event. The presentation of Balinese music and dance spectacles to many of the nearly a million foreign and domestic visitors to Bali each year is a major activity generating significant revenue. Some shows take place daily, such as the morning *Barong* and *Kris* performances in Batubulan and Singapadu villages for bussed-in audiences; others are held weekly, and still more are done on special commission. Held at converted *balé banjar,* outside temples, at festivals, in restaurants, in *puri* courtyards, and on stages at the hundreds of hotels, the vast number of performances involve countless musicians and dancers. This has caused the number of active *sekaha* to proliferate, especially in villages relatively close to the southern Sanur, Kuta, or Nusa Dua resort areas, but also to a measurable degree in outlying areas with tourist concentrations like Candi Dasa on the southeast coast.

Kebyar's ability to shift between temple ritual and performances presented for entertainment has long lost its revolutionary luster and is now seen as a normative trait. The genre is a model because it allows for public presentation without any sense of having transgressed the (previously nonexistent) line between religion and life. But for *sekaha* performing older genres with more overtly devotional functions and histories the economic benefits of commercialization were also enticing. As tourism increased, the difficulty of deciding what to present for tourists raised ethical concerns among those arguing that staging sacred forms renders them ritually impure. The debate over this problem led to a 1971 seminar cosponsored by LISTIBIYA and the departments of religion and tourism, to develop a terminology suitable for describing the "relative sacredness" of Balinese performances. Three Balinese terms were proposed (and later formally adopted) to describe very sacred, somewhat sacred, and secular genres respectively. Performances done in the innermost courtyard of the *pura* and indispensable for ceremonies were to be termed *wali* ("ceremonial"); those done in the middle courtyard as optional accompaniment for ceremonies were *bebali* ("offering"); and those done outside primarily for entertainment were *balih-balihan* ("for watching").[19]

Despite the publicity that attended the institutionalization of these terms, few accepted them unblinkingly, and many were confused. No one rejected the notion that some genres are more ritually significant than others; what was unacceptable was the substitution of an artificial trifurcation based on physical space for the instinctively felt continuum along which the unfamiliar concept "secular" had questionable relevance. The dispute pitted the foreign idea of secular, imposed by those wielding the ideological agenda of cultural tourism, against widespread Balinese perception, which did not recognize the concept's validity. *Kebyar* musicians viewed the issue with some bewilderment but went on as usual, playing both in and outside *pura* as the situation demanded, and making offerings to instruments wherever and whenever they played, just as they always had. Moreover when doing sacred or ritually dangerous performances for tourists such as those adapted for the *Barong* and *Kris* dance, care has always been taken to ritually purify costumes and masks just as if the performance was indeed part of a ceremony. This raises purists' hackles but does not trouble most performers, who feel that the consecrated objects are necessary both to protect them and to make the performance *idup,* or come alive (Picard 1990:69). Difficulty in distinguishing between sacred and secular versions of the same theatrical performance exposes the limited utility of the *wali, bebali, balih-balihan* classification, for in the current climate nearly anything can be rendered acceptable for tourist presentation. This results in some transparently bureaucratic reclassifications. For example, the *wali* temple warrior dance *Baris Tumbak* is commonly repackaged as a *balih-balihan* item when *sekaha* perform abroad or for tourists merely by slightly altering the choreography and changing the name to *Wira Yudha.*[20]

By undeniably important international standards, however, tourist performances *do* meet criteria for secular classification. In this light prior Balinese lack of recognition of that concept can be seen as limiting, and its recent official sanctioning helpful. For example, an intransigent problem has been musicians' difficulty adopting different attitudes toward *ngayah* performances,

19. See further Picard 1990:62–71, wherein he shows that the process of categorizing culture derives entirely from Western influence and values. The precedent was set by the Dutch, who differentiated between *agama* (religion) and *adat* as a tactic to consolidate political power.

20. On the other hand, this trend is intrinsic to *kebyar.* Ancient temple-offering dances like the female *rejang* have been reworked in more secular forms throughout the century for presentation outside the temple. Among the most widespread instances are the dance *Gabor,* created by Anak Agung Raka Saba of Saba village, and *Panyembrahma,* with music by Wayan Beratha (discussed in chapter 8). See Picard 1996 for an article-length discussion of this and related issues.

done for community without regard for remuneration, and performances for tourists. Unused to negotiating fair compensation for their services in the latter context, most *sekaha* acquiesce passively and are routinely exploited by guides or hotel management, who pay them for little more than their expenses. Musicians gripe privately but take refuge in dutiful affirmations of traditional culture outwardly, citing "the strength of the *sekaha*" and the "good name of Bali" as reason to accept the status quo. An influential few have tried to raise consciousness, urging *sekaha* to confront the secular reality by limiting their cooperative energies to *banjar* contexts—where they will be appreciated and reciprocated as sacred collective obligations—and demanding more money when *balih-balihan* are taken to hotels. Prominent dancer Wayan Dibia recently wrote: "Performances for tourists are a kind of business, for making money, not *ngayah*. While steadfastly maintaining the quality of their 'artistic wares,' performers must protect their interests" (1994:31).

2. *The Conservatories.* More than any *puri* in any *negara* of the past, the government schools of music, dance, shadow puppetry, and visual arts SMKI (*Sekolah Menengah Karawitan Indonesia,* High School of Indonesian Music) and the higher-level STSI (*Sekolah Tinggi Seni Indonesia,* Academy of Indonesian Arts) set the tone and professional standard for musical life. STSI in particular enjoys deeply entrenched prestige and authority that provokes recurrent spasms of controversy among cultural observers. The academy is an authentic product of the *orde baru,* with prominent allegiance to government programs and ideologies; its degree is virtually the only acceptable goal for young musicians with career aspirations. With few exceptions *sekaha* throughout Bali vest authority in members educated there, and request faculty when seeking a teacher. When STSI artists generate new *kebyar* compositions and choreographies, as they do continuously, they are promptly absorbed into the repertoires of *sekaha* island-wide, only to be dropped for ones that issue the following year. Graduates are employed in hotels, government offices, and schools as teachers and music advisors. Student and faculty ensembles are chosen with disproportionate regularity as official representatives for receiving dignitaries, at festivals and conferences throughout Indonesia, and on a majority of international tours. Music in *banjar* life continues, but the irresistible imprimatur of government and professionalism has elevated everything STSI-made to a previously unimaginable tier of visibility and influence.

SMKI, known first as KOKAR (*Konservatori Karawitan; karawitan* is a recently coined Javanese-derived word connoting *gamelan* that can be glossed as "refined and elegant music") was founded in 1960 at a small campus on Jalan Ratna in Denpasar, which it shared with ASTI (*Akademi Seni Tari Indonesia;* STSI's former name) after the latter opened in 1967. Both were modeled on similar schools in Java.[21] The original teachers were village artists, many of

---

21. See Sutton 1991, chap. 6, for extensive discussion of Javanese conservatories.

whom participated reluctantly and sporadically during the first years (Orn-stein 1971a:40). Gradually the schools gained credibility, attracting large fac-ulties of prominent musicians and dancers to the government payroll and drawing students from everywhere in Bali to apply for increasingly competi-tive entrance. After expansion in the 1970s and 1980s SMKI moved to a larger campus in Batubulan village and STSI to a 5-hectare tract in Denpasar, adja-cent to the museums and stages of Werdhi Budaya (Bali Art Center). With this achieved and growing numbers of faculty with postgraduate training, ASTI was upgraded to STSI in 1988 and authorized to confer higher degrees such as SSKar (*Sarjana Seni Karawitan;* Scholar of *Karawitan* Arts).

The schools' original mandate was *pelestarian, penggalian, pembinaan, dan pengembangan kebudayaan daerah Bali:* preserving, researching, cultivating, and developing Balinese cultural forms. STSI owns at least one *gamelan* of every Balinese genre to facilitate learning and *preserving* their repertoires, and also to display them in an opulent on-campus museum. It sponsors *research* seminars and workshops at which elder artists are asked to teach and have their special knowledge videotaped, recorded, and written about. Student groups fan out to villages where they record tunings and collect *sekaha* oral histories for thesis projects. *Cultivation* is at the core of the heavily practice-oriented approach. Students spend the majority of their degree-earning hours in rehearsal and performance; and the school reaches out to villages by offer-ing community service, consultation, and teaching. Indeed KKN (*Kuliah Kerja Nyata,* Curricular Community Service), which may include cooperative build-ing projects as well as coaching local *sekaha,* is a requirement for graduation.[22] Fueled by public hunger for novelty, SMKI and STSI composers and choreog-raphers monopolize the vanguard of cultural *development* and are able to dic-tate what is acceptable or fashionable in new works. The schools also support self-consciously, radically experimental new music, providing a forum for *mu-sik kontemporer* (contemporary creations), a small but significant body of work so distanced from conventional approaches to composition that it receives little or no attention off-campus.

STSI's inexorable ascendance is closely tied to its director from 1981 to 1997, Madé Bandem, an ethnomusicology Ph.D. born in Singapadu village in 1945 and formally schooled at KOKAR, UCLA, and Wesleyan (Tenzer 1998: 115–17); in December 1997, Wayan Dibia, also from Singapadu and holding a Ph.D. from UCLA, became his successor. Publicly admired and celebrated, Bandem was sometimes criticized for the perceived excesses of his ambitious and highly successful efforts to steer STSI to the center of Balinese culture. Whether or not he merited scapegoating, it is true that when problematized each of the school's achievements can be seen as having had a complementary

---

22. During the initial period of openness and *reformasi* following Suharto's resignation in May 1998, KKN also acquired another meaning: *Korupsi, Kolusi dan Nepotisme* (Corruption, Collusion, and Nepotism).

Wayan Dibia, current director of STSI, 1982. Photo: Author.

deleterious effect. STSI's prominence has contributed to unprecedented international renown for Balinese arts and created new financial rewards for performers and teachers, while consigning all but the most famous *banjar*-based *sekaha* to limited opportunities and lesser status. New compositions and choreographies innovate and convey the vitality of Balinese music and dance to audiences, but the fact that they emanate from the culturally dominant Denpasar campus entices regional groups to capitulate to STSI styles, repertoires, and even *gamelan* tunings. Programs like KKN explicitly target the cultivation of local variants to help counter the tide of homogenization, but it is difficult for the schools to subvert their own authority. Similarly, campus-based revivals of rare genres beneficially promote them but inevitably lead to their standardization. STSI students and faculty work extremely hard to prepare performances for high-profile local or international events, which often causes severe neglect of the curriculum and cancelation of regular class instruction. The school is acknowledged internationally for its success in maintaining the vitality of traditional arts in a modernizing world, and Bandem is sought to consult for fledgling similar schools in Phnom Penh, Fujian (China) and elsewhere in Asia, but STSI is also decried as a propagandistic and excessively powerful adjunct to government cultural showcasing.

Controversies aside, both STSI and SMKI bring together a versatile and hardworking community of musicians and dancers. The current generation of STSI faculty, mainly educated there during the 1970s, is deeply dedicated to the institution and its missions. They maintain this while remaining closely tied to the arts in their *banjar* of origin, which are spread all over Bali. Students and faculty in the *karawitan* division are continuously working at *gamelan*. They comprise a campus community of players with unprecedented breadth of knowledge, remarkable fluency in creating new music and collaborating with dancers, stratospheric standards of ensemble virtuosity and individual technique, and energetic commitment to their peers, their school, and to music as a career. On the ground and away from the political fray, STSI's academic setting fosters intensive *sekaha*-style collectivity.[23]

3. *Competitions and Festivals.* The LISTIBIYA-sponsored *Festival Gong Kebyar* is an important interface between *adat* and *dinas* in contemporary Bali. Held with great fanfare in 1968, 1969, 1978 and yearly since 1982, the festival places one *banjar sekaha* from each *kabupaten* into competition. The groups are selected by regional arts councils sometimes for their reputations, but also to give musically less-known ones a motivating share in the spotlight. Those chosen receive government financial support to prepare a designated assortment of new and existing compositions and choreographies. For this they assemble an array of composers, choreographers, and coaches, mainly (but not exclusively) from their region, and frequently those with conservatory affiliations. Intensive festival rehearsals take place at *banjar* between February and early June, leading to a series of showdowns in which two of the competing *gamelan* perform their selections in alternation from opposite sides of the same stage. The finalists perform at the *Pesta Kesenian Bali* (Bali Arts Festival; hereafter PKB), held between mid-June and mid-July since 1979 at the Werdhi Budaya Art Center complex in Denpasar. Winners are picked by a LISTIBIYA-named jury whose members represent the entire island, but which is inevitably

---

23. I should also mention other educational and preservationist institutions, such as the numerous smaller private *yayasan* (foundations) and *sanggar* (workshop/studio collectives) now dotting the landscape. Some of these play an important role in Denpasar suburbs populated by villagers with city careers. Parents in such families often retain primary allegiance to their *banjar* of origin and faithfully return home for ceremonies and other *ngayah* obligations. Little energy is thus left for *adat* life in their adopted neighborhoods, but a strong desire for their children to play *gamelan* or learn dance in a community setting remains. This results in what are in effect private music and dance schools, some operated in teachers' homes and others in borrowed *balé banjar*. Other kinds of private *yayasan* are found throughout Bali. Some are operated by arts patrons, usually those who acquired wealth from tourism. The Tanjung Sari hotel in Sanur village, for example, has long supported an institute with permanent staff and teachers, a *gamelan*, and a *pura* on hotel grounds. There are many others, some funded from Java or abroad.

dominated by conservatory faculty. Although musical regionalisms are officially encouraged, the jury's academic bias causes some to see the festival as further proof of STSI hegemony.

Musicians old enough to remember consider the tumultuous festivals of 1968, 1969, and 1978 to have been seminal. In the first two, LISTIBIYA inaugurated the festival as a Bali-wide event, ensuring that each *kabupaten* was represented. This egalitarianism solidified the post-1965 resurgence of *kebyar* in the popular imagination and confirmed its new potency as a symbol of Balinese culture's triumphant resilience and allegiance to *orde baru* goals. The impact of the early festivals also helped to disseminate *kebyar* compositional norms, making their general features pervasively pan-Balinese. Wayan Beratha achieved supraregional fame by contributing *Palguna Warsa* in 1968 and *Kosalia Arini* in 1969, both new instrumental works with great popular appeal. In 1969 *kabupaten* Badung's famous Geladag *sekaha* was chosen in the finals over Pindha, equally well known in its Gianyar home, in a controversial decision that still redounds. An elite, much discussed rivalry between Badung and Gianyar has continued since, for in each subsequent festival one or the other area has taken first prize.[24]

In 1978 preservationist factions on the organizing committee argued for greater emphasis on pre-*kebyar* repertoire, calling for *kebyar* arrangements of ritual compositions and fusions of vocal music with *gamelan* to be part of each group's preparations. Since 1982, with few deviations, the requisite list of works has comprised two instrumental pieces, one each in modernized ritual style (*kreasi lelambatan*) and *kebyar* style (*tabuh kreasi*); one using singers (*sandhya gita* or *gegitaan*); one repertoire dance, and one new dance (*kreasi tari*). In 1985 a parallel *Festival Gong Wanita* was introduced for all-female *sekaha,* motivated by the existence of women's groups in Java and the presence of a few female *karawitan* majors and faculty at STSI, and also by the growing number of foreign women who play. Despite virtually no precedent for female *gamelan* musicians in Bali this has been embraced without controversy. Some female groups outlive the festival and continue to perform on secular occasions, but there has been only slight assimilation of women into *adat*-based musical contexts, and to my knowledge there are no mixed-gender groups outside the conservatories.[25]

The PKB features all arts and culture from Bali, and occasionally some from

---

24. Badung was split into Kodya Denpasar and Badung in 1993. Frustrated and demoralized observers in other *kabupaten* cite the monopoly of the southern Gianyar, Badung, and Kodya districts as overt cultural chauvinism. South Balinese point to the geographically diverse jury and speak of the greater refinements and subtleties of their music. In the north and northeast, where musical antagonism with the south is long-standing, periodic independent festivals are held and judged locally.

25. See Tenzer 1998:109–10 for a few further comments on this subject. Bakan 1998 provides an interesting sociological analysis of the recent advent of women playing in the processional *gamelan beleganjur.* See also Vickers 1985 on the role of female musicians in the nineteenth-century courts.

A 1997 tour to Canada and the United States by the Bandana Budaya Duta group from Badung district included five female musicians, the first such I have seen. See further chap. 9, n. 13.

elsewhere in Indonesia or abroad, but its enormous constituency throngs to it for extravagant *kebyar* music and dance productions. Other genres, including evenings of experimental music and dance, revivals of rare genres, shadow plays, and theatrical forms cater to small crowds on peripheral stages. The performances of the *Festival Gong* winners are a central event, as are the Friday and Saturday night *sendratari* (dance-dramas) produced by the conservatories or regional arts councils, typically featuring *kebyar* accompaniment. Both kinds of events play to fanatical audiences normally numbering six thousand and above in the outdoor *Ardha Candra* amphitheater, and are proof of *kebyar*'s immense popularity in mainstream society. For festival finalists these high-profile, intensely pressured situations can elicit superb performances or devastating failures, while the spectacle draws showers of unceremoniously partisan whoops, cheers, and hurled insults from the crowd. Vitale captures the behind-the-scenes mood:

> Perhaps the most absorbing feature of the festival competition is the feeling of electricity in the air as the groups play. In the rehearsals leading up to the festival, there is a steady build-up of intensity. Every manner of precaution is taken to make sure that the members of the *gamelan* retain their unity of ensemble and purity of mind—mostly by making religious offerings, praying for success in the temple, being blessed by the local priests, and so forth. Often at the time a group is chosen . . . the members consult the Balinese calendar and a priest to engage in several important ceremonies. They request from the gods clarity of thought (so that they will learn the pieces easily and fluently), unity of ensemble, *taksu* (charisma and spiritual energy in performance), and freedom from outside disturbance. Some groups even undertake a ceremony known as *masakapan,* in which they are ritually married to their instruments. (1996:23)

In its current form the *Festival Gong* was inspired by the competitive spirit intrinsic to early *kebyar* and the sporadic Dutch and nobility-sponsored competitions of the 1930s and 1940s, but similar festivals are also promoted Indonesia-wide as an important government means for linking arts and culture to *pembangunan.*[26] Though competitions thrive among other Indonesian ethnicities, innate enthusiasm for them comes perhaps especially naturally to Balinese. Officials lose few opportunities to point out the serendipitous harmony of this spirit with government aims and the national ideology of *Pancasila.*[27] With its conceptual union of personal morality, collective behavior, local cultural values, and the national interest, *Pancasila* is often explicitly linked to *gamelan* and depicted as compatible with *adat.* Most Balinese embrace this perceived lack of conflict between traditional and national values, and articu-

---

26. See Sutton 1991:185–91; and Yampolsky 1995:712–23 for discussion of competitions and festivals in Java and elsewhere in Indonesia.

27. *Pancasila,* "five principles," was coined by Sukarno in 1945 and specifies "belief in one God," "nationalism," "humanitarianism," "democracy," and "social justice."

late it with numerous terms and concepts evoking upstanding civic behavior, proper *sekaha* deportment, and the inexorable analogies between them. The words are cited as jury evaluation criteria; and musicians use them to set standards for critiquing themselves, both at rehearsals and in festivals or whenever they are in the public eye. They also have a distinctly contemporary combination of multilingual origins.

Among the most frequently invoked are the English-derived *disiplin,* the Indonesian *penampilan* and *keseragaman,* and the Indonesian-Balinese *gaya. Disiplin* promotes conscious knowledge of what is at stake in rehearsal and performance, connoting not just the discipline of order and obedience to authority but also proper service to community and country. *Penampilan* is presentation, covering stage presence, facial expression, sitting posture, costume color schemes, and all other aspects of performance etiquette useful for assessing group cohesion. *Keseragaman,* uniformity, covers a similar semantic field but also includes specifically musical points such as the precision with which the group follows cues, changes dynamics, speeds or slows; it extends to the evenness with which *panggul* are lifted in anticipation of an upcoming unison stroke. *Keseragaman* is particularly in evidence at the start of a performance, when players wait for a soft *pak* stroke from the *kendang wadon* player. This is a sign to take up *panggul* and hold them slightly above the surface of their instruments. The cue to begin often comes from the *ugal* player, who raises his *panggul* in a gesture indicating dynamics and tempo. When it comes down again the ensemble should be in lockstep.

The ubiquitous *gaya* connotes musical style (including regional style, as in *gaya* Gianyar) as well as a more general spirit, fire, flash, or showmanship. The latter senses are especially central to the festival context, in which mere precision is harshly derided. Current standards of ensemble virtuosity demote such mastery to the realm of basics, valuing instead tightly controlled group expression of musical feeling. *Gaya* suggests a supple charisma, a directed channeling of excess ensemble energy, and a visible manifestation of the "pride for the audience to witness the success of our efforts" that Suweca exulted about. It may take the form of choreographed group movements such as coordinated swaying of the body in the direction of the melody on the *gangsa* or *reyong,* or synchronized twirling of *panggul* between *jegogan* strokes. Lead *kendang* and *ugal* players have measured leeway for individual *gaya* in the use of gestures and facial expressions to convey cues. Crowds enthuse when such histrionics succeed and jeer when they misfire. As depicted through these terms and concepts, the stakes are raised on collectivity in the *Festival Gong* as standards of group behavior are formalized, magnified, exaggerated, and placed on display.

4. *Media and Other Institutions.* Books and articles about *gamelan,* including locally produced scholarship and compilations of pieces in Balinese musical notation, have steadily issued from the conservatories since their

inception. They have a much more modest effect on Bali than comparable publications on Java, for reasons discussed in the next chapter.[28] Far more influential have been government radio and television broadcasts, and the private cassette companies. These promote awareness of regional and stylistic diversity by presenting music from everywhere on the island, while simultaneously facilitating contact that endangers this same diversity.

Though media have contributed to music's commodification and raised the amount of passive consumption that takes place, impact on practice is less evident than in parallel situations elsewhere in Indonesia and Southeast Asia, where traditional music has retreated to special enclaves and popular music rushed to fill the void. There are numerous explanations for Bali's comparative buoyancy: traditional life and tourism sustain a high demand for *gamelan; gamelan*'s central role in the official success story of cultural tourism is undisputed; the burgeoning Balinese pop music milieu (plus the impact of recorded Javanese and Western styles) occupies many people recreationally, but interference with *gamelan* in its ritual contexts is not tolerated; and Bali is small enough that the producers and consumers of *gamelan* overlap to a surprising extent. Although one very occasionally encounters rituals or temple dances accompanied by tape-recorded music, audio and public address systems are mainly used *in addition* to actual *gamelan* at ceremonies, and are considered to enhance the *ramé* atmosphere.[29] Television is more pernicious in creating a passive audience, but overall I see no evidence that media alone have altered the *sekaha* system as a social force.

RRI *(Radio Republik Indonesia)* began broadcasting in 1950 from both Singaraja and Denpasar, but in its initial years had no significant impact (Ornstein 1971a:42). As more Balinese purchased battery-operated radios, and with a fine resident *sekaha* and a commitment to daily broadcasts of *karawitan,* the situation changed in the 1960s.[30] It was RRI's 6:30 A.M. *Acara Karawitan (karawitan* broadcast), avidly followed by listeners all over the island, that popularized Wayan Beratha's compositions after the 1968–69 *Festival Gong.* RRI's role waned in the 1970s as *banjar* were given the first generation of televisions by

---

28. In Bali popular publications on *kakawin* have helped facilitate the post-1970 revival of *sekaha pepaosan.* See Sutton 1991:192–98 for more on print media's impact in Java.

29. *Gamelan* musicians joke about *penabuh Jepang* (musicians from Japan) when speaking of tape-accompanied dances, in reference to the probable origin of the cassette player. Herbst (1997: 134–42) ruminates on the possible deleterious impact of this and other electronic intrusions into the soundscape.

30. Among the formidable musicians in the Denpasar RRI studio group after the 1950s were Gusti Madé Putu Griya, Anak Agung Gdé Raka Sibang, Wayan Konolan, Wayan Pogog, Madé Kuna, and Wayan Senken, all prominent figures on the Denpasar scene whose work together was consistently fine. Their regular broadcasts of instrumental compositions as well as theatrical accompaniments drew a large and faithful following. Griya, the leader, died in 1983. Many of those remaining took their pensions in 1985 and were replaced by a younger group of STSI graduates. These changes, which coincided with a decrease in the number of hours allotted to *gamelan* broadcast, lessened radio's impact.

the government, who monopolized the airwaves with Jakarta-based programming and standard American rerun fare. TVRI-Denpasar began broadcasting from its Renon studios in 1978, and during the 1980s television sales to households soared. The station does not employ its own musicians, but maintains a set of *kebyar* instruments and invites groups into the studio regularly to be filmed for broadcast. Theatrical performances (often with dialogue about social issues, such as the importance of birth control), dance lessons, and STSI productions are among the *karawitan*-based offerings.

Cassettes of traditional music, a major trend here as well as elsewhere in Asia, have been marketed on Bali since the time of the 1968–69 festivals.[31] Recordings and playback equipment were comparatively inexpensive and readily embraced. From current perspective they do not appear to have lessened the amount of music made in *banjar,* but they have affected the nature of transmission. Many musicians I queried now study compositions in detail from cassettes and hence can learn more and faster by listening to recordings during spare or idle time away from rehearsal. A fuller acquaintance with the wide variety of regional styles and techniques accessible on cassettes elevates musicians' sophistication and fluency in general. Cassettes used for dance practice make it more convenient to study, though some dances have flexible movement sequences coordinated with musical cues, and beginners may have difficulty unlearning the order dictated by the recording they practice to. Last, cassettes are now an important medium for documentation and preservation of repertoire, providing reassurance that pieces learned but not in current rotation can be easily accessed in the future.

Currently, Bali Stereo and Maharani are the two most active companies, with a combined catalogue of over two thousand releases. At retail outlets *kebyar* tapes dominate overwhelmingly, including recordings of the latest festival competitions (*kebyar* as well as other competition-prone genres like *beleganjur* or *joged*), compilations of temple repertoire, new and traditional compositions in "definitive" STSI performances, multitape sets of complete *sendra tari,* and collections of dance accompaniments. *Gamelan* throughout the island are represented. The fiscal rewards of recording a commercial cassette can be significant by local standards; in the early 1990s *Festival Gong* winners could demand close to 2 million *rupiah* for a recording, and offer the same repertoire at the same price to competing labels with impunity. This amounts to a one-time boost to treasuries, however, for despite sales predictably in the tens of thousands of units for recordings by *sekaha* in the limelight, further royalties are neither expected nor paid.

Individually, none of these media can be said to have affected the recent history of *kebyar* as fundamentally as tourism, the conservatories, and the *Fes-*

---

31. See Toth 1980 for a list of Balinese recordings available up to that time. See Yampolsky 1987 for a Javanese cassettography, and Manuel 1993 for a study of cassette culture in India.

tival Gong; nonetheless they are, of course, closely connected with these, and consequently with *kebyar* itself. The totality of forces affecting *kebyar* in the post-1960s era forms a wide current of modernizing social and technological change. Balinese musicians' awareness of how changes work to favorably situate *gamelan* on the world stage is a significant aspect of their self-image, comprising a consciousness of transnational relevance that is perceived as an important and necessary adjunct to identities based on traditional culture and the nation-state. Dependent as *kebyar* has been on external contact from the outset, without media to ensure that it can be effectively recorded, packaged, and sent forth into the world, the music might come to seem old-fashioned and parochial to the Balinese themselves.

Changes in the *Sekaha* Today: One Group's Narrative

A recent Balinese government research report maps 2,836 active *gamelan sekaha* (Rendha et al. 1992:19). Among these *gong kebyar* and the smaller ritual *gamelan angklung* overwhelmingly predominate. *Angklung* and other less common ritual ensembles see little recreational or commercial activity, so the demographics of their *sekaha* remain firmly tied to *banjar* and *desa adat*. Owing to academic connections and greater personal mobility, many *sekaha kebyar* today have memberships that are interestingly dissimilar to those of earlier decades. They are still sustained by the *banjar* system but may consist of constellations of players from across village or regional boundaries, and their focus may be almost exclusively tourist, academic, or festival performance. When such groups fulfill ritual functions it is most often by invitation or special arrangement, rather than through an exclusive "ownership" link via the *banjar* to the village temple system. One of the first such groups was the Denpasar-based *Himpunan Seniman Remaja* (Young Artists' Collective) of the late 1970s, which brought together musicians from throughout Badung district for numerous successful performances and cassette recordings. Another, quite typical case, is that of *sekaha gong* Tunas Mekar, based at *banjar* Pengosekan, located just south of the tourist area of Ubud. Its development is described in the following narrative, centered around the *sekaha*'s participation in the 1987 *Festival Gong*. During that time I attended rehearsals and meetings regularly; my account derives from discussions with many group members that year and since.

Prior to 1960 the bamboo *joged* and other, older forms of *gamelan* were played in Pengosekan, but around this time elders pooled a portion of their rice farming income to invest in a *gamelan gong kebyar*. Owing to severe political factionalism in the area virtually no *gamelan sekaha* were functioning amicably (the death toll in 1965 was high in Ubud's environs), and groups available to play at rituals were in demand. The only active one, from neighboring Peliatan, provided the well-known Madé Lebah and his son Wayan Gandera as

Pengosekan's first teachers. The new *sekaha* became proficient and garnered some local renown, most notably in 1969, when they entered a dancer, Desak Suarti, in a Bali-wide *Teruna Jaya* competition.[32] Yet Pengosekan was better known for its *sekaha* of painters than for its musicians, and as music in the Ubud area slowly revived Tunas Mekar kept an increasingly low profile. By the 1980s, after a gradual decline from what was already a fairly low level of activity, the *gamelan* was wholly inactive save for performances at rituals within Pengosekan itself.

Despite this, but in acknowledgment of former strengths and future potential, early in 1987 Tunas Mekar was selected by the Gianyar *kabupaten* offices to represent the region in the *Festival Gong.* This was perceived as a significant honor and taken very seriously as an opportunity for revitalization. At preliminary meetings in February members of the 1960s-generation *sekaha* volunteered to step aside to let the younger people take part, many of whom were their children. In this way, they agreed, the torch of local *gamelan* activity would pass to the next generation. Moreover, it was hoped, a good showing at the festival would augment *banjar* prestige and perhaps enable the group to perform regularly for tourists afterward, thus generating new revenue. A new *sekaha* was formed by drawing upon the Pengosekan *sekaha pemuda-pemudi* (youth association), augmented by a few others from outside the *banjar* (but within *kabupaten* Gianyar) who were needed to dance important roles and, in one case, play drums. By early May rehearsals were being held daily, the *gamelan* had been retuned, new instrument cases had been ordered, and new dancers' and musicians' costumes were measured and in preparation at the tailor's. The new works commissioned were prepared by well-known composers and choreographers from around Gianyar who were picked up in minivans at their homes daily, taken to rehearsal, fawned over, fed, and plied with cigarettes and coffee. A constant buzz of activity around the *balé banjar* profited the local *warung* (drink and snack stands), where benches were always full of players and interested bystanders drinking, eating, and discussing fine points of the new repertoire, the politics of past festivals, the influence of STSI, and the economics of the *kabupaten*'s financial support. For this period the civic life of the entire village came to focus intensively on festival preparations.

Nearing the date of the festival performance in late June the public schools went on break. Many of the musicians were in high school, so at a *sekaha* meeting the opportunity was taken to propose doubling the number of rehearsal hours. A consensus was quickly reached that this was acceptable, for no one held illusions that their competitors were benign. This meant that the *sekaha* not only met each day from 8 to 11 in the evening, but also from 1 to 4 in the afternoon. During the same period numerous other village responsibilities cropped up to place further demands on musicians' time and energy. An

---

32. See Tenzer 1998:8–9 for a photograph of this group.

odalan at the *pura desa* took place for three days around the June full moon, which necessitated moving the *gamelan* back and forth from the *balé banjar* to the temple several times so that rehearsals could continue during the odd hours when ritual music was not needed. Members of Tunas Mekar were of course involved in playing music in the temple (though for this many of the elders rejoined), as well as in other ritual preparations, and they participated in the ceremony itself, asking for extra blessings to ready them spiritually for the festival.

The week after the *odalan* a three-night "bar"—a yearly social and fund-raising event produced by the *sekaha pemuda-pemudi*—was held. It required building a kitchen and setting up a temporary restaurant for food service, festooning the *balé banjar* with decorations, and publicizing, promoting, and staffing the event. As if this were not enough activity to saturate everyone's schedules, unexpectedly, just after the *odalan,* a prominent member of the village painters' collective died, and the officiating priest determined that his body had to be ritually cleansed and cremated without delay. Though the family was poor and preparations for the ceremony were modest by some other Balinese standards, all *banjar* residents had to call on the household of the deceased and offer their help, and many *sekaha* members, bound as well by direct blood ties, were obligated to do a substantial amount of additional work for the family.

Despite all this and many sleepless nights, the *gamelan* hewed to its rehearsal schedule as best it could, for the performance was only ten days away. Over the course of the final week STSI and LISTIBIYA consultants attended rehearsals to evaluate and critique the presentation, and some last-minute changes in composition and choreography were made. Extra hours were spent adjusting dance cues and dynamic changes. In a few cases melodies and drum patterns were actually recomposed at the advisors' suggestions; one of these was a melody the advisors felt dwelled too long in the upper *gangsa* register. With the consent of the original composer it was emended to include some lower octave tones for better structural balance. Particularly indefatigable and admired during this period was the young *ugal* player, Dewa Putu Berata, who had emerged as a splendid musician and leader. Unelectrified until a few years later and suffused with the hissing glare of pressurized gas lamps, his family home across the road from the *banjar* was the site of many postmidnight bull sessions about art and culture, comprising equal amounts of gossip about the festival and solemn affirmations of civic and cultural duty. These further cemented an already intense mood of seriousness and commitment.

Despite a fine performance at the Art Center, Tunas Mekar took second place, losing to the Denpasar group. Following the announcement of the results there was much griping and bitterness over the jury's prejudices and perceived unfair practices, an almost caricatured display given the long-standing rivalry between the two regions. In fact Pengosekan performed stunningly and was cited by the jury only on hairsplitting deficiencies in *penampilan* and *gaya;*

this, however, was enough to cost them the trophy. Wayan Jebeg of Batubulan village, the revered elder composer of their *kreasi lelambatan,* expressed his disappointment self-effacingly, saying that he had now seen it all and was going to retire from music and spend his time at his own *banjar* with the *sekaha tuak* (palm wine drinkers' club). His winsomeness cheered the exhausted Putu Berata and his cohorts. At a loss for ways to spend their reclaimed free time, they soon channeled their frustration by organizing a weekly tourist performance in Pengosekan, as had originally been suggested by the *banjar* elders. This was seen as a way to sustain the level of skill they had worked for, as well as capitalize on what was perceived as underutilized tourism potential in their neighborhood. In the competitive Ubud-area market for tourist dollars this was risky, and the audiences never came in sufficient numbers. No *sekaha* members had contacts in the tight network of tour guides, who were often single-handedly able to guarantee busloads of ticket-buying tourists. Before August ended the project collapsed, and by September Pengosekan was once again silent.

In subsequent years some members of the 1987 festival group joined other *sekaha,* notably one organized independently by a well-known dancer, Anak Agung Anom, from Kutuh, a *banjar* several kilometers to the north. With family resources and income earned performing at home and abroad, Anom had purchased his own *gamelan.* This group, named Semara Ratih, existed exclusively for tourist purposes and had no official *banjar* affiliations, though it contracted the use of the Kutuh *balé banjar* for its regular Tuesday evening performances. During this period also a total of eight Tunas Mekar members entered STSI. The first of these, Berata, enrolled after the 1987 competition and for a time drummed for Semara Ratih. He soon became a locally prominent performer and composer. In 1994 he and his drumming partner from STSI and Semara Ratih, Ketut Cater of Pindha, were asked to coach and compose for a group representing *kecamatan* Ubud in a newly instituted *kabupaten*-wide, pre–*Festival Gong* selection competition. In 1995 their innovative composition *Sunari* was featured in the *Festival Gong* itself. Berata also twice toured internationally under STSI auspices, and thrice taught *gamelan* and dance in the United States.

In 1996 Semara Ratih reorganized after internal disagreements and Berata, one of those who left, formed yet another *sekaha* in Pengosekan in 1997, this time in conjunction with a teaching *sanggar* (workshop/studio) based at his home. Performing members included some from the 1987 group, but also drew heavily upon Berata's now broad network of friends and colleagues, most of whom had gone to STSI with him and still lived within reasonable commuting distance from rehearsals in Pengosekan.

Thus within the period 1960–97, musical activity in Pengosekan waxed and waned repeatedly. With each successive wave, the number of group members from outside Pengosekan increased, in effect forcing a reassessment of the assumption that *gamelan sekaha* are mainly *banjar*-based. Though they still

Members of Pengosekan's *sekaha gong* Tunas Mekar with the author and Dewa Putu Berata playing *kendang* during a 1987 taping at TVRI studios. Photo: Ketut Prasetya.

rehearse in *balé banjar* and exist under *banjar* auspices, memberships may be diverse. This kaleidoscope of shifting activity and membership configurations is typical for many Balinese villages, especially those in proximity to the STSI campus or to tourist centers.[33]

While the motivation behind the original Tunas Mekar was to provide activity for *banjar* members and meet local ritual needs, the existence of the latest incarnation is more the result of an individual's initiative (Berata) and his desire to create a marketable presentation. This, however, does not really pose a risk to Pengosekan's ritual or musical life, since enough trained musicians are still available (intergenerationally) within the *banjar* to provide whatever music is needed for religion. Moreover although the purposes of the new group are mainly commercial, most of the imported players are willing to assist at ceremonies in Pengosekan when they can. This works in all directions: group members retain allegiances to their *banjar* of origin, and often join together in impromptu configurations that cut across *banjar* or even wider regional lines to provide music for each others' ritual needs. Even though the *banjar* and *pura* retain their ongoing local functions as forums for musical

33. This kind of reconfiguration may hinder the formation of strong social bonds, increase the logistical difficulties of planning regular rehearsals, and make long-term commitments more difficult to sustain. But such activity is new only for music, for there have long been "all-star" acting and dancing troupes performing *topeng, arja,* and, more recently, in the *drama gong* genre. Such groups were in part popularized through regular appearances on RRI in the 1960s and 1970s.

presentation, it is characteristic to find that these new layers of supra-*banjar* affiliation have been added on as tourism, educational experience, and individual entrepreneurship combine to bring *gamelan* musicians together in new ways.

Multidimensionality and Collectivity in *Kebyar*

Attuned to paradigm shifts in the humanities and social sciences, recent scholarship about Bali demonstrates that there is "no one significant point of change which encompasses the whole island. There is instead a multiplicity of local struggles and differences" (Vickers 1996:34). It is no more possible to articulate a sleek, coherent Balinese experience of *kebyar* than it is to voice an outsider one or a changing historical one. To stress *kebyar*'s multidimensionality is to elicit the complex contradictions and instability of the associations it carries, including those shaped by the "traditional" world of the Majapahit-based *negara* and the earlier periods of Balinese history from which they grew. To this we must add those engendered by colonialism, nationalism, modernization, media, and tourism, in differing urban and rural contexts, at the academies and in the *banjar*, at the cassette or CD-store counter, in Bali and abroad. In the hotly contested, locally and internationally debated arena of Balinese culture there is no privileged position to take.

Nonetheless, Asnawa, Windha, Tembres and myriad other musicians told me in so many ways that *tanpa perasaan bersamaan megambel tak ada gunanya* (without the feeling of unity there is no point to playing *gamelan*), stressing that for them collectivity is the single most relevant aspect of *kebyar*. It is a different dimension of importance than the changeable symbolisms, uses, and meanings that surround the music; and it is certainly older and more deeply ingrained. Since collectivity is an ancient, hence sacred value, the secular roles *kebyar* plays are secondary in relevance to the part it plays sustaining traditional life. This safe, culturally oriented perspective may itself be a by-product of the deemphasizing of political ideology that the *orde baru* encouraged, as well as an aspect of the current confusion over which elements of culture are important for the Balinese themselves, and which are for "showing" to visitors. But it would be dismissive to conclude that musicians merely reflect government policy and do not value *gamelan* for reasons deeper than those promoted by politicians or dictated by the tourist industry. As Coast and Britten's remarks reveal, the sheer time, work, and discipline that goes into preparing *kebyar* music is simply difficult for outsiders to fathom, and the controlled eruption of energy generated in performance is a force to be reckoned with. In considering this it is well to remember that the power of collectivity is far from utopian: when Balinese endorse it they also profess a way of life that evidently contributed to the tragedies of 1965–66 as much as it has nurtured *kebyar*'s tight musical coordination.

To touch on these issues is to view an evolving society. Yet although musical analysis in subsequent chapters of this book mainly interprets *kebyar*—including its social meaning—by way of sound structure rather than directly via the social context, this is not to be understood as academic devaluation of the practicing musician's experience. It is instead an attempt to circumscribe a domain for scholarship that is complementary to, rather than an inevitably pale reflection of, the satisfactions of playing *kebyar*.

4 Contexts for *Kebyar* Theory

Musicians in *gamelan gambuh*,
Batuan, 1992. Photo:
Tom Ballinger.

HAVING examined acoustic structure and seen *kebyar* in the context of
contemporary Balinese society, the next step is to study the form and
content of specific musical patterns and compositional designs. *Kebyar*'s fusion of its own vocabulary with materials from other genres make it a fertile
site for this kind of exploration. In part 2 I will identify and explain elements
of the music in terms of their structure and their associations with historical
and social aspects of Balinese culture. But my approach to this objective has
been shaped by diverse factors that need to be made explicit as a way of legiti-
mizing the analysis. This chapter explores intellectual context and methodology, leading to an exposition of the boundaries and ambitions of *kebyar*
music theory.

Context for theory locates it in relation to established traditions of thought
and scholarship, and suggests ways in which it may be relevant for future
study on this or related topics, or for those approaching the subject with an
eye for broader concerns. I focus on three kinds of context, conceived
in order of increasing general applicability. The most local concern is to
show how this book can amplify existing scholarship about Balinese music,

particularly the writings of McPhee. The possible wider contextualizations obtained by comparing ideas and concepts of Balinese music with those of the significantly related *gamelan* genres of neighboring Java move the level of relevance up a notch. The third and most general context is a semiotic one, shaped in part by recent scholarship about European music in the classic era. I am concerned with the potential for theory to both encompass and transcend issues of musical structure, and in so doing contribute ideas about the experiences and associations of musicians and audiences in a particular society and time. This is a question prone to generate mere conjecture, but Bali's tiny size and relative cultural uniformity make it a plausible site for proposing circumscribed answers.

Early Balinese *Gamelan* Scholarship: McPhee's Contributions

Save for a few local texts such as *Prakempa* and scattered references in the writings of early Dutch scholars and explorers, Balinese musicology begins with Jaap Kunst and his wife C. J. A. Kunst-van Wely, who together published *De Toonkunst von Bali* in 1925 on the basis of short field trips to the island in 1921 and 1924. Their research is mainly concerned with organology and tuning in court and sacred genres. In the philological and art-historical work *Hindoe-Javaansche Muziek-Instrumenten* (1927), Jaap Kunst (working with the Dutch historian Roelof Goris) included much information on Balinese instruments. But neither book provides a description of what was then a nascent *kebyar*. McPhee's treatment of the subject from the 1930s remains one of two detailed sources for *kebyar* in the literature (the other being Ornstein's 1971 dissertation), though it was still early in the music's development when he was in the field and many of the techniques in use today had not yet coalesced. McPhee was additionally somewhat troubled by *kebyar*'s appeal and felt that it represented a threat to the survival of older genres. His limited data on the music needs updating and, given the influence of his life and work, his dire predictions for the future of Balinese music as a whole call for reinterpretation from the present perspective.

McPhee's articles and books appeared over a span of thirty-one years, beginning in 1935 with a brief field report printed in the American composers' journal *Modern Music* and culminating with the posthumous publication of his voluminous magnum opus *Music in Bali*. Like its predecessor and model, Kunst's *Music in Java*, McPhee's book was conceived as an encyclopedic documentation, an all-encompassing effort of the kind rarely attempted before or since for any complex musical culture. In light of the general narrowing of research specializations that has accompanied the expansion of ethnomusicology since the 1950s, the achievement seems all the more remarkable today. The significance of the book reflects its author's skills and prolonged dedication to the task of completing it, but the breadth and depth of its attainments might not have been possible had Bali been a larger place, less compact or musically dense, and had McPhee's informants been any less willing to collaborate with him fully. Of this he was well aware, as his acknowledgments repeatedly demonstrate.

Music in Bali is "a composer's account of music in Bali . . . as it was practiced in the decade preceding World War II. It is primarily an account of instrumental music and the many different forms of instrumental ensembles, ancient and modern, to be found in Bali at the time" (1966: xiii). The first part of the book is devoted to a succinct account of prewar Balinese musical life. Part 2 begins with chapters surveying instruments, tuning,[1] and notation/ terminology before turning to studies of individual genres. The remainder of the book provides accounts of thirteen different *gamelan,* each examined for its context, instrumentation, tuning, instruments' characteristic playing styles, and formal structures. An extensive glossary and abundant musical examples and photographs are given in the appendixes. McPhee presents concepts and terminology with elegant descriptive prose, but the tone becomes more analytical whenever he wishes to call to the reader's attention some hidden aspect of music structure, such as in the commentary on irregular melodic unit lengths conflicting with the prevailing colotomic meter in a composition of the sacred *gamelan luang* (288–93), or in the relation of drum pattern to meter in *gamelan gong gdé* (99–107). Yet few underlying principles or step-by-step instructions on how to actually put the music together from scratch are provided, as the "composer's account" would seem to warrant. His description of *kotekan* figuration for the *reyong* in *gong gdé* (75–79) and for *gangsa* in the *gamelan pelegongan* (162–66) parse the patterns as surface phenomena, offering no structural grammar or breakdown of what is or is not acceptable in the styles.[2]

---

1. McPhee provided, and apparently took, exclusively single-octave measurements of *pélog* and *slendro* scales. He makes only passing reference (30) to paired tuning.

2. Additionally, the studies of *gong gdé* and *gambuh* drumming (99–107 and 122–32 respectively) conflict with much of what I learned in the 1980s. In a letter to Margaret Mead of 1954 (in the archive of McPhee's papers at the UCLA Ethnomusicology Library) McPhee bemoaned his lack of recordings to work from in preparing the book (he was unable to mount a recording project while in Bali), and said that he was "still struggling with drumming." It is hard to know what this means, but I suspect that his data on drumming was insufficient and, faced with this lack fifteen years after leaving the field, he was compelled to give the subject slightly short shrift. McPhee could not play the drums, and transcribing their patterns through observation alone would be considerably more difficult than transcribing melodies. *Kendang tunggal* (an important type of drumming addressed in the present chapter 7) is never mentioned in *Music in Bali;* nor are many other drumming patterns and principles that are in my view central. My transcriptions of drumming often differ sharply with McPhee's, which may be a function of regional variation or changes that took place in the music during the half-century that separates our research. Yet it is hard to conceive that the old court *gamelan* drum patterns would have changed so much.

To some degree this may be a consequence of the fact that McPhee did not actually play *gamelan* himself,[3] but it more directly corresponds with his view of his work as documentary rather than theoretical. At the time he wrote, few recordings were available and in Bali the academic context or precedent for theory did not yet exist. Instead, he was worried about the very survival of the traditions he studied. Like many Balinese, McPhee viewed the shifting of the loci of musical activity from the courts to the *banjar* taking place during the colonial years as a musically impoverishing process likely to result in the extinction of the court culture's valuable musical heirlooms, though he praised the vitality of *banjar* musical life and the new forms that it fostered. Motivated strongly by his admiration for the balance and symmetry of structure in the repertories of the court genres *gong gdé, gambuh,* and *semar pegulingan,* he saw himself as helping to preserve them by seeking them out and tirelessly transcribing their compositions.[4] In the introduction he notes that at the time

> [t]he imposing *gamelan gong gedé* [sic], the great ceremonial orchestra of the palace and temple, was to be found only in far-off hill villages where the old style of music was still preferred, and was replaced everywhere else by the more modern *gamelan* known as the *gong kebyar.*
>
> To try to preserve in some form of record this period in Balinese music, while older styles and methods survived, became my one desire. (1966:xiv)

By making them the first genres discussed in the book (chapters 9–11), McPhee appropriately recognized the crucial place of court *gamelan* as forerunners to the *banjar*-based music of the *gamelan pelegongan* and the then nascent *kebyar.* At the same time he implicitly sanctioned an account of Balinese history in which post-Majapahit court culture is privileged, while other,

---

3. McPhee's teacher Lebah told me that he did not play; he also mentioned this to Carol Oja (1990:91). McPhee once describes playing *pokok* melodies on *calung* from his own notation (1966: xvi), but this is a simple technical feat and there is no additional indication that he ever practiced or met the technical challenges of more demanding *gamelan* instruments. Nowhere else does he make reference to participating as a player. Like Kunst, who also learned from observation only, he was simply conforming to the social etiquette of the time. Heins wrote the following about Kunst: "Because of the colonial situation it was unthinkable for a European to play in a *gamelan* and thus become one of a group of Javanese musicians. The mutual social barrier (which extended in pre-revolutionary Java also to the high Javanese nobility) was insurmountable; no Dutchman or other foreigner would or could dream of entering the tightly closed unit of a *gamelan*-group in those days" (1976:100). Though the situation may have been somewhat less forbidding in Bali, McPhee was nonetheless similarly constrained.

4. Among McPhee's papers there are thousands of pages of transcriptions and transcription fragments in McPhee's own hand, only a fraction of which were included in *Music in Bali.* These include music from all of the ensembles discussed in the book. Most voluminously, there are transcriptions of the complete repertory of the *gender wayang* ensemble of Kuta village, dozens of *angklung* pieces from East Bali, and incomplete scores for hundreds of *gong gdé* and *semar pegulingan* compositions. There is also a large sheaf of typescript showing the *pokok* tones in cipher notation for *gong gdé* and *semar pegulingan* compositions, some of which comprise *Music in Bali*'s appendix 4.

ostensibly more minor traditions are marginalized. In another forum, McPhee blamed *kebyar* more directly for endangering the court music and called for a renewal of research to "save" the dying genres. He bemoaned the fact that the music of the court *gamelan* had "given way to restless fantasias in which short melodies follow each other in purely arbitrary succession." [5] He also wrote that

> [t]he *kebyar* is, first of all, the negation of all that is classic, all that is controlled in Balinese music, and gave it its clear outline. But a remarkably dynamic energy animates the *kebyar* style, as though to compensate for, or in some way conceal the fundamental weakness of its structure. In this dynamism we find all that is amazing in the Balinese creative spirit; *kebyar* may represent the collapse of tradition, it is indeed a spectacular form of expression for the individual, who gives himself up to the music with feverish intensity. (1938:56)

McPhee's explicit claim is that *kebyar* substituted performance "dynamism" and "intensity" for formal cohesion. But underneath a moralistic tone prevails, as though the music's inevitable and apocalyptic underside is an unchecked hedonism destined to destroy what is of true value in the culture, that is, that which was bequeathed to Bali by the Majapahit courts. This is a manifestation of a typical outsider's fear for the fragility of non-Western cultures that was characteristic of the era and shared by many other visitors to Bali, including McPhee's contemporaries Covarrubias, Mead, Spies, and others. And it was not only their viewpoint, for the belief that local culture owed its very existence to the legacy of Majapahit influence permeated Balinese society. By degrees, and in conjunction with waning aristocratic prestige, this perspective has widened since then to include an acknowledgment of the importance of pre-Majapahit culture as well as Bali's postindependence identity.

McPhee's fear for the legacy of the court *gamelan* sounds shrill today, for although *kebyar* indeed posed a strong challenge to the hegemony of court aesthetic it has also proven to be the vehicle for a musical renewal encompassing the courtly past within its domain. The commingling of old and new musical forms within the genre mitigates concern that past and present are incompatible in contemporary music, or that classical values will fall victim to rampant individualism. *Kebyar* musical structure, it has turned out, is engaged in a profound dialog with its predecessors.

Though McPhee was troubled about the future of the old music, he was attracted, as a composer, to the modern compositions that were all around him, including those of *kebyar*. As mentioned, the sketchiness of *Music in Bali's* chapter on *kebyar* (1966:328–51) can be attributed to the inchoate, only partly established norms of the music during the 1930s, which made the characteristics of the genre difficult to define, and also because of McPhee's

---

5. From a 1961 lecture given at the East-West Music Encounter in Tokyo entitled "Problems of Indonesian Musical Tradition Today (The Music Crisis in Bali)," quoted in Oja 1990:251. The typescript is among McPhee's papers at the UCLA Ethnomusicology Library.

ambivalence about its popularity.[6] Of the village genres, he preferred the music of the *gamelan pelegongan,* still popular in South Bali when he lived there. *Pelegongan's* repertory had a much more refined, courtly affect than did *kebyar's,* and its major practitioners were court-trained. For many years McPhee worked with one such expert, Wayan Lotring, the dancer, musician, and composer from Kuta who was one of the most sought-after exponents of *pelegongan* style, and whose compositional innovations (he was equally known as a drummer and dance teacher), novel for their time, were quickly absorbed and radicalized by *kebyar* composers.

Lotring's music is the sole subject of chapter 18 in *Music in Bali.* (Gdé Manik, the skilled *kebyar* composer from North Bali whom McPhee also knew well, receives no such attention.) Seen from a 1990s perspective, Lotring's importance is manifold. By frequently departing in his compositions from court music's rigid and balanced metrical forms, and by reinterpreting the music of other *gamelan* genres, his approach anticipates that of latter-day composers. And in good measure because of his association with McPhee, Lotring became the first Balinese composer to be celebrated in a Western sort of way for the significance of his individual contributions. More recently, owing to the advent of the Balinese conservatories and the recent dissemination of Indonesian publications about *gamelan,* many of Lotring's contemporaries have been retrospectively canonized, so Lotring's work is understood in the context of what other important musicians of the day were doing. It is notable that the designation "composer," with all of its attendant ideas about inspiration and individual expression, is commonly used today, whereas in the past composers' contributions were not singled out for special acknowledgment.[7] The Western sense of the word is only partially appropriate to the Balinese compositional process, but its adoption to a great extent is attributable to McPhee's relationship with Lotring.

McPhee's books are not available in Indonesian and so are not generally known in Bali, though most foreign-schooled academics at STSI and SMKI have read them, and many students and faculty at those institutions can identify him and cite his accomplishments. He is still well remembered in *banjar*

---

6. Conditioned by the status of new music in the West, he may also have been skeptical of *kebyar's* mass appeal and instinctively disparaged its quality as a way of accounting for its popularity.

7. Often the English word is used, orthographically modified to *komposer,* as is the Dutch-derived *komponis* (from *komponist*). The closest Indonesian equivalent is *pencipta* (creator), but *penyusun* or *penata,* both meaning arranger, are also common. *Karya,* meaning "a work by," is placed before the composer's name in both spoken usage and, significantly, on cassette labels. In the urban context of the conservatories these words are more often heard than the Balinese *karang, acep,* or *ngae* (arrange, create, make), partly because select Indonesian vocabulary is increasingly standard for spoken communication in the cities, and also because concepts of what composers do are undergoing change. In such situations, people are less likely to use the more familiar Balinese words, with their hard-to-dislodge connotations. Because most composition these days, even in villages, is done by people somehow connected to STSI or SMKI, these changes have been embraced there too.

by many elderly people who worked with him directly.[8] His work is clearly influential in Bali, in the sense that it has provided a precedent for scholarship and a model for attitudes toward the preservation and study of existing music. The strands of McPhee's work were picked up in Bali after traveling a somewhat circuitous route via Mantle Hood, who hired him to teach at UCLA near the end of his life and later advised Madé Bandem and Nyoman Sumandhi (the former director of STSI and the current one of SMKI) when they undertook degrees there, and also via Hood's American student Andrew Toth, who taught at STSI in the 1980s. Robert E. Brown, a student of both Hood and McPhee, published an important recording of a *gamelan* McPhee had revived (Brown 1972), established study programs for Western musicians, and arranged for many Balinese to teach and attend university in the United States in the 1970s and 1980s. When students at STSI today do fieldwork in *banjar* and write research papers on their findings, they are furthering a branch of scholarship to which McPhee made the first major contribution. In 1993 the Balinese government posthumously awarded him the *Dharma Kusuma* medal for cultural service, the highest such honor given.

Interest in McPhee resurged in the 1990s with the appearance of Carol Oja's biography *Colin McPhee: A Composer in Two Worlds,* which in turn has prompted critical commentary, performances, and recordings of his works, and a reissue of the memoir *A House in Bali.*[9] In North America particularly, McPhee is seen as a path-breaking precursor of the widespread post-1960s interest in combining Western composition and the close study of non-Western music. Orientalisms aside, the musicological substance of *Music in Bali* assures the lasting value of its author's life and work.

Balinese *Gamelan* Scholarship: 1940 to the Present

During World War II the Swiss chemist and musicologist Ernst Schlager lived in East Bali investigating and transcribing the pre-Majapahit seven-tone *gamelan selunding, saron* (or *caruk*), *gambang,* and *luang* (also called *saron*). These

---

8. Madé Lebah (1912?–96) of Peliatan village was one such notable figure, whose fame among Western students formed a continuity of five decades. Lebah was a prominent musician well known throughout South Bali. He was McPhee's chauffeur, guide, and teacher in the 1930s. He is the thin, black-haired drummer on the left in photographs 86 and 87 at the back of *Music in Bali,* and also plays a prominent role in *A House in Bali.* As a result of his association with McPhee, he gained a broad knowledge of music all over the island. Later, he toured with the ensemble taken abroad by John Coast in 1952. He taught Ruby Ornstein in the 1960s, was my teacher in 1978–79, and provided material for Carol Oja's biography in 1984. He has interacted with many other foreign students as well. See also Harnish 1997.

9. For commentary see, for example, Craft 1991 and Polansky 1993. McPhee's *Tabuh-tabuhan* (1936) was recorded by the American Composers Orchestra (Argo 444 560–2), and his complete orchestral works of the post-Bali period—*Tabuh-tabuhan, Transitions* (1954), *Second Symphony* (1957), *Nocturne* (1958), and *Concerto for Wind Orchestra* (1960)—by Toronto's Esprit Orchestra (CBC SMCD 5181).

were subjects about which McPhee had comparatively little to say.[10] Schlager also collected music notation possessed by his informants, which is preserved on *lontar* leaves beneath Kawi (Old Javanese) language poetry written in *kidung* (*sekar madya*) meters. The notation, called *grantangan,* consists of *pokok* tones only, and was at one time used by sacred *gamelan* musicians as a basis for generating accompaniment for the singing of this poetry (see chapter 9 and also McPhee 1966:56–62 on notation). Some years after Schlager's death in 1960 the musicologist Hans Oesch and ethnologist Alfred Bühler, both of Basel, collaborated to complete his extant writings. This culminated in the 1976 publication of *Rituelle Siebenton-Musik auf Bali,* a concise work notable both for its welcome focus on these sacred genres and for its proposal of theoretical approaches to melody and rhythm in the music.

Like McPhee, Schlager dealt with modal types and the solfège system for pitch names (in the sacred *gamelan* this is slightly different than *kebyar*'s *ding-dong-deng-dung-dang* sequence of changing vowel sounds), but he went further in demonstrating a link between the solfège tones in melodies and the prescribed patterns of vowel endings for lines of text in *kidung* stanzas (1976: 31–36; see also Wallis 1979:197–200). He suggested that the characteristic rhythmic motives used in women's group rice-pounding (*oncang-oncangan*) were the source for the rhythms of melodic figuration patterns, and worked out an elegant framework for realizing their permutations (1976:36–39; 1965:319–32), ideas to which I shall refer again in chapter 6. In offering description and analysis of repertory and playing techniques for the sacred *gamelan* of many East Bali *banjar,* including ten possessing the *selunding* ensemble, Schlager showed that these *gamelan* were more numerous than McPhee had known. He also established, in conjunction with Goris, that the sacred genres' origins predate the post-Majapahit courts of the fourteenth century and later.[11] This opens the question of the degree to which they affected the later Javanese-influenced *gambuh* and *semar pegulingan* and *gong gdé,* and proves that these ancient genres are not isolated anomalies, but played a significant role in shaping the character of the music of the courts. McPhee failed to consider this possibility.[12]

Schlager engendered a tradition of Balinese studies in Basel, almost all of which has remained focused on the East Balinese locations where the original

---

10. McPhee devotes only one chapter to these ensembles (1966:256–93) because his residence in Sayan was some distance away from the villages in which they were maintained and news of upcoming ceremonies was slow to reach him. Such religious rituals were in those years the only times when these sacred *gamelan* and their repertoires could be played, though there has been some relaxation of standards recently.

11. Schlager and Goris developed a close friendship while working together in Bali (Schaareman 1992:7). See also Goris's *Bali: Atlas Kebudajaan* (1952:41).

12. In *Music in Bali,* McPhee's only comment about the age of the sacred *gamelan* is that "in some villages they are believed to be of divine origin, but more often they are considered to have 'come down from Majapahit'" (1966:256). This is a faithful recording of his informants' beliefs, but it contradicts what Goris was able to establish about their origins.

research was carried out. Among the original successors to his work are Oesch, Danker Schaareman, Urs Ramseyer, and Tilman Seebass. Their publications on Balinese music have included Schaareman's study of music in ritual (1986), and Ramseyer's chapter on the *gamelan selunding* of Tenganan village in *The Art and Culture of Bali* (1977). Seebass collaborated with several Indonesian musicians on *The Music of Lombok: A First Survey* (1976), and has written about *kebyar* as well (1986, 1996). In 1992 Schaareman edited an Oesch *festschrift* with thirteen articles containing a diverse international cross-section of recent work, including Richter's analysis of *Prakempa* and *Aji Gurnita* (another *lontar* text about music) and their connections to tuning systems; village- or genre-specific studies (Dibia, Gold, Mack, Nakamura, Ramseyer, Schaareman, Wenten); and articles on social policy (Ramstedt), *kidung* (Vickers), and village music organizations (Sanger, Rubinstein).[13]

Other publications postdating McPhee's fieldwork were also researched and completed in the Bali of postrevolutionary Indonesia, concurrent with a general expansion in Balinese studies that continues to the present. During this period of the founding of the conservatories a call for Indonesian-language publications on *kesenian daerah* (regional arts traditions) was issued from Jakarta. Among those publications about Balinese *gamelan* the most notable are by Nyoman Rembang, born in 1930 in the village of Sesetan, just south of Denpasar, and the aforementioned Madé Bandem. After a career performing and teaching in Bali and Java, Rembang joined the SMKI-Bali faculty at its inception and has since produced monographs brought out by the regional government on *gamelan gambuh* (1973) and *gong gdé* (1984–85a). Each offers a concentrated account of history, instrumentation, and function and provides *pokok* notation for a select repertoire. Additional publications by Rembang include studies of *topeng* (masked dance; 1976, with Bandem), and the construction and tuning of instruments (1984–85b). Like many musicians at the conservatories and in the Denpasar area, Rembang often consulted the elder musician Gusti Madé Putu Griya (1906–83) of Buagan village, a colleague of Lotring and a composer and musicologist who compiled notation for hundreds of compositions and was an oral source for many ideas about music theory and history. His notebooks and teachings, now scattered among his students, deserve to be written up in full.

Bandem's Indonesian publications about music include the *Prakempa* translation and commentary, a survey of figuration patterns based on Griya's classification and terminology (1993), and articles on government policy and the role of traditional arts. He is one of three STSI faculty who have completed Ph.D.'s in the U.S., two of whom took important theatrical genres as their subjects. Bandem's dissertation (1980) examines the eighteenth-century *wayang wong* masked dance theater, which uses *Ramayana* stories, and that of current STSI director Wayan Dibia (1992a) is on the twentieth-century *arja* theater,

---

13. The articles in Schaareman's collection are listed individually in the bibliography.

which uses mainly indigenous Balinese stories and sung poetry. Bandem's focuses on the analysis and interpretation of a full translation of a performance, while Dibia's multidisciplinary survey views *arja* as a case study in cultural change. Their choice of these forms reflects a characteristically Balinese perception of holistic interrelations among the performing arts, for both types combine music, dance, literature, and drama. The third Ph.D., Wayan Rai, wrote about the *semar pegulingan saih pitu gamelan* genre (1996), and Ketut Gdé Asnawa's 1991 M.A. thesis contains close analysis of drumming patterns in the *gamelan gambuh,* the only such work by a Balinese author. Both were written at the University of Maryland under Mantle Hood.

Ruby Ornstein's estimable dissertation (1971a) on *kebyar* was based on research done in 1964–65 in Peliatan and in the northern village of Kedis Kaja, which was burned in the anti-Communist hysteria of 1965. Ornstein carries the subject much further than McPhee. She updates the music's social context by describing the political factionalism of the time as well as the still inchoate roles of government, the conservatories, radio, and tourism. Her catalogue of melodic and figuration patterns and extensive transcriptions of the *tabuh kreasi Hujan Mas* and *Gambang Suling* (both popular at the time) are of great interest. The music Ornstein studied was somewhat more codified than the *kebyar* McPhee knew, but today's music compared with that of the 1960s reflects a development of far greater magnitude.

Richard Wallis's dissertation (1979) and Edward Herbst's book (1997), both on vocal music, survey this "other" half of Balinese musical culture, bypassed by McPhee. They give rich accounts of the major genres of sung texts in Bali, examining them for their vocal qualities, musical organization, prosody, connection to literature, historical evocations and associations, and social and cultural contexts. Writings by Adrian Vickers (1985, 1986, 1989, and others) depict the diachronic course of Balinese history as well as the complexity of synchronic relationships between modes of cultural discourse in Bali, their correspondences with political, social, and religious life, and their literary, musical, iconographic, and theatrical representations. All of these authors appropriately stress the intertextual connections among Balinese expressive media.

The Recent History of Music Theory in Java and Bali

Theory for *kebyar* ought to be shaped by taking the cultural and intellectual backdrop of central Javanese music into account, for the literature on *gamelan* is overwhelmingly dominated by studies in this area.[14] In the period 1973–89

---

14. In the recent past scholarship on Indonesian music has broadened to include regional *gamelan* genres, popular music, and the music of other islands. It has also increasingly forefronted anthropological perspectives, in part because of the powerful influence of Clifford Geertz's work in Indonesia. See Becker 1993 for an overview.

alone over 373 books, dissertations, and articles appeared on the subject (Heins 1990), while articles and dissertations on Balinese music during the same period constituted only a small fraction of that amount.[15] Books and articles on Javanese music are often replete with musical excerpts notated in the *kepatihan* (cipher) system now standardized for use in the conservatories of Yogyakarta and Solo, and widely used by *gamelan* performers and scholars internationally. This has made possible an increasingly powerful and influential discourse, enriched by discussion of specific musical examples, about music terminology, practice, and theory.[16] These writings have had the effect of internationalizing the tradition and building a modern intellectual context congruent with that established for other cultivated musics, though not without generating significant controversy over the attempts to enforce consensus about terminology and practice on a fluid oral tradition. Traditional concepts and the recent writings surveyed above notwithstanding, there is no contemporary Balinese equivalent for this ongoing Javanese conversation.

By acknowledging the substantial body of thought about Javanese music and positioning this book in relation to it I hope to make my work more pertinent to students of that music, and also ascertain whether the issues that have received attention in Java are relevant for Bali. This necessitates viewing the two musics comparatively, an inquiry for which there is surprisingly little precedent. To date such comparisons have been mostly perfunctory and adjectival.[17] Perhaps this is because there are so few musicians sufficiently expert in both traditions, or because there is so much yet for ethnomusicologists to understand within each that the imperative for comparative overviews has not yet attained critical mass. Yet the two areas of study demand consistency of concept and explanation by virtue of their close cultural and musical interrelations, and because of the desirability of seeing them as aspects of a single cultural totality. What I propose to do below, however, is intended first and foremost to clarify *kebyar*'s own identity.

Early indigenous Javanese writing about music, like the *Prakempa* in Bali, dealt with the realms of philosophy and mysticism. Scholarship in the twentieth century emerged from interaction between late nineteenth-century Javanese nobility and Dutch writers like J. Groneman, and later Kunst, who, in *Music in Java,* emphasized the genealogies of scales (applying his teacher Hornbostel's theory of blown fifths), instruments and compositional forms, and the preservation of repertoire through transcription. For these writers mainly the court traditions of central Java were deemed worthy of study; Bali-

---

15. Heins chose to limit his *Music in Java: Current Bibliography* to publications issued since 1973, the year that Kunst's *Music in Java* was reissued. A bibliography covering the years 1920–90 for Balinese music is found in Stuart-Fox 1992:551–61. I made my comparison by eliminating works falling outside the 1973–89 frame.

16. See Becker and Feinstein 1988 for a selection of Javanese writings about music in translation.

17. An extended comparison of Javanese and Balinese musics and their reflection in social hierarchies is Keeler 1975.

nese music was of related interest because it was believed to be a museum of older Javanese practices. (It was McPhee, operating with the same preservationist zeal, who gave the first substantial portrayal of Bali's music as more than a vassal of Java's.) The growing influence of these ideas went hand in hand with the gradual acceptance of notation. These processes had a powerfully transformative effect. Judith Becker wrote,

> Notation is not an object but a technology that implies its own theory. Notation presupposes a linear concept of time, necessitates decisions as to what should be notated, and forces a perceptual bias on the listener. (1980:11)

For literati and court society, Javanese *gamelan* was increasingly thought of as analogous to art music in the West: the central musical achievement of Indonesia's venerable past (Sumarsam 1995:113–29). As a consequence of this plus the introduction of notation, during the first half of the twentieth century cultural prestige became more concentrated at the Solonese and Yogyanese courts. The gradual musical standardization that ensued was difficult for village practices to resist. In search of a cohesive musical identity after independence, some felt that Javanese *gamelan* deserved the status of the "true" Indonesian art music. Though many contested this notion, its impact has nonetheless been strong, and the growth of scholarship was one important factor used to buttress claims for the music's preeminence.

In comparison, Balinese cultural life prior to the ascendance of the conservatories was highly decentralized. Early *kebyar* represented a break from the authority of the courts and a dispersion of the centers of musical innovation and activity among many *banjar*. During the colonial era Balinese nobility was insufficiently influential to encourage recondite scholarly interests, and despite the efforts of McPhee and others to promote the court music in performance, most musical energy in Bali was directed toward nurturing the rapid profusion of the new musical forms of the postmonarchic era.

McPhee's legacy is thus not equivalent in impact with that of the Dutch scholars in Java. Kunst and others helped to reinforce the prestige of courtly patronage, whereas McPhee was helpless in the face of its dissolution and did not remodel his concept of high art to fit the *banjar* contexts where music was thriving. To the extent that SMKI and STSI in Bali now resemble latter-day court centers, attracting musicians from around the island and offering them training stressing greater standardization practice and terminology, conditions were conducive to the growth of a theory discourse congruent to Java's. But other developments affecting the growth of theory in Java have also failed to take root in Bali. Cipher notation has not been adopted, and the indigenous notation, while well known, is used for preservation, introductory teaching in the schools, and sometimes the private jottings of composers, but not for developing theoretical or analytical tools. And although Balinese music's fame has caused it to be seen as a significant national tradition (despite the island's minority status in the greater Indonesian context), there is no Balinese counterpart for the significant presence of thought about Javanese *gamelan* in international music discourse, a presence cultivated through the ongoing efforts of both Javanese and Western scholars.

However they illuminate some of the differences between the social backgrounds for music theory in Java and Bali, these circumstances do not get at the inexorable heart of the issue, which lies in the relationship between musical structure and performance practice in each tradition. The contrasts evident from a comparison of these connections help to explain why what has fueled Javanese music theory constitutes an only partly effective approach for Bali.

Javanese Counterparts for Balinese Music Concepts

The range of ideas that Javanese music theory encompasses has been reshaped by each scholar investigating the subject, and the subtle shades of meaning suggested by crucial terms are regularly recast. To date the discourse has centered around the exploration of a set of instrument-specific rules, concepts, and techniques governing composition and the interpretation of music in performance. Among the many interrelated concepts and terminologies animating the theory, I will discuss five which have been of central concern and juxtapose them with their congruent (though not necessarily equivalent) Balinese counterparts. They are *gendhing,* or musical composition; *pathet,* or mode; *balungan,* or melodic framework; *cengkok,* or melodic pattern; and *garap,* which refers to the application of techniques associated with *pathet* and *cengkok* in the process of realizing a *gendhing.* The Balinese versions of these words are *gending* for *gendhing; patutan* (also *tetekepan* or *saih*) for *pathet; pokok* for *balungan;* and *payasan* (plus the many other terms associated with it; see fig. 2.8) for *cengkok.* The *balungan-cengkok* and *pokok-payasan* pairs comprise a set of inseparable concepts of melody, so I will examine them two by two. *Garap* came to Bali from Java only recently, where it has undergone semantic, but not orthographic, change.

The meaning of *gendhing* is straightforward. The theorist Martopangrawit states flatly that "when *lagu* [melody] is organized into a form, that form is called '*gendhing*'" (1984:17). In both Bali and Java the most common understanding of the term is *gamelan* composition; that is, not a particular performance realization, but only those elements of the composition that give it a fixed identity. These include any style or genre with which it is affiliated, the character of any dance, puppet, or theatrical presentation which it accompanies, and the "aspects of melodic and rhythmic structure that remain constant from one rendition to another" (Sutton 1991:6). *Gend(h)ing* is a generic term often modified by adding the name of a type or genre; thus *gending luang* in Bali refers to compositions from the *gamelan luang* repertoire, and in Java *gendhing ageng* means compositions with long gong cycles (*ageng* means "great," but sometimes the adjective is dropped and the term *gendhing* used alone in this more restricted sense). A Balinese synonym for *gending* is *tabuh;* but *tabuh* also refers specifically to metric classifications in *gamelan gambuh* and *gong gdé* repertoires.[18] Differences between Balinese and Javanese applications of the word arise from the potential for performances of a *gend(h)ing* to vary. This potential is greater in Java for reasons that I will describe. Mainly, however, a *gend(h)ing* is a set of flexible coordinates for creating a performance, not an orchestral score.

Translating *pathet* as "mode" provides an inadequate gloss giving little sense of the specific implications of the term. The elements often used to fix modal identity in other traditions, such as uniqueness of pitch content or prescribed final tone, do not determine it; though in each *pathet* some tones occur relatively more often than others at metrically stressed points. Six Javanese *pathet* are usually distinguished, three in *pélog* and three in *slendro,* each associated with a specific collection of *gendhing.*[19] "A *pathet* is one of a tiny handful of musical categories embodying in the most general kind of way features of hundreds of individual and distinct traditional compositions" (Powers 1980a:437).

Because a central Javanese *gamelan* contains two full sets of instruments—one each in *pélog* and *slendro*—each of the six *pathet* may be heard during the course of a performance, depending on the selection of *gendhing* presented; within *pélog* or *slendro* individual *gendhing* may modulate between *pathet.* In *slendro,* the three *pathet* (*nem, sanga, manyura*) all use the complete five-note collection. Five of the seven *pélog* tones (numbers [1, 2, 3, 5, 6] in *kepatihan* notation) are used in both *pélog pathet lima,* and *nem,* wherein [7] is mainly absent but—especially in *lima*—[3] can be exchanged for [4]. For these five *pathet* there is no distinction on the basis of scale-tone content (within each scale); each is thus subtly defined by myriad factors establishing a hierarchy of tonal importance. *Pélog pathet barang* is more easily distinguished from *lima* and *nem* on the basis of its [2, 3, 5, 6, 7] collection. Here [4] may replace [5], and [1] is omitted.

In the research and writing carried out on *pathet,* among the factors cited as formative are cadential formula (Hood 1954); contour, frequency of occurrence, and strength of placement (Becker 1980); and tessitura and choice of cadential second-order vertical relations (Martopangrawit 1984). The question of *pathet* is also thoroughly linked with each of the other terms and concepts under discussion. In this sense *pathet* is not simply a category, but an aspect of performance practice which musicians must be attentive to as they play lest its essence be somehow diluted through inappropriate application of musical materials. Martopangrawit's invocation to his exploration of the subject

---

18. In Java *tabuh* means mallet, such as one used to play an instrument. This meaning is archaic in Bali.

19. Perlman (1997) provides evidence that there was once a fourth *slendro pathet.*

underscores this point: "What is *pathet?* The question is always on my mind" (1984:45).

In contrast, the subject of *patutan* in *kebyar* contexts is somewhat arcane. Unlike the Javanese, no Balinese *gamelan* has paired *slendro* and *pélog* instrument sets. There exist terms for three *slendro* "*patutan*" (*pudak sategal, sekar kemoning,* and *isep menyan*), but they are obscure and abstract, and known only to a few players and tuners of the *gamelan gender wayang.* There is uncertainty among those I asked as to whether they designate a sort of *slendro* modal practice, akin to the Javanese one and grouped in three categories with those names, or if they merely describe overall pitch level and tuning for the instruments. I have never heard the terms mentioned in relation to actual music. The five-tone *pélog* used in *kebyar* (and also *gong gdé, pelegongan,* and the bamboo *gamelan gandrung*) is already a *patutan* in the sense that it derives from the parent seven-tone scale; but the two tones [4] and [7] are simply not present. Within this [1, 2, 3, 5, 6] collection no further modal subdivisions are said to exist. This does not necessarily mean that they are absent; and it may well be that tonal hierarchies and characteristic modal formulas can be unearthed within *kebyar* melodies, even without the possibility of the extra tone, [4], that can function to refine the distinction between Javanese *pathet lima* and *bem.*

Balinese seven-tone *pélog* (*saih pitu*) is still used in *gamelan gambang, selunding, caruk, luang, gambuh,* and *semar pegulingan,* but these are either archaic or court-originated ensembles, maintained today mostly in their ritual contexts and at the conservatories. As explained above,[20] it is recognized that theoretically, at least, one or more *patutan* can be formed starting on each step of the scale, but only four of these are found with any frequency in seven-tone *gamelan* compositions. Though the 1990s have seen a revival of interest in *saih pitu* ensembles, *pélog* modal theory, and composition, these *gamelan* exerted little creative hold on the musical community during the decades of *kebyar*'s coming of age, except insofar as the structure of their compositions—not their *patutan*—can be adapted for *kebyar*'s five-tone context. Since Balinese *patutan* is not interrelated with performance practice but is instead a component of the fixed *gending* only, it is relevant to music theory in a distinct and less fundamental way than *pathet* is for Java. *Kebyar* musicians need not be preoccupied with it because modal qualities are a composed-in feature of the music. They do not, as in Java, act to constrain decisions performers make in the moment.

According to Sumarsam the Javanese term *balungan* was introduced in 1913 (1995:147) and has slowly come into general use, partly as a by-product of the theoretical disputes it has generated.[21] In his account its impact is a clear case of theory influencing practice. Meaning literally "skeleton," *balungan* is

---

20. See chap. 2, n. 8.

21. Perlman (1993:252–60) disagrees with Sumarsam in some respects and offers a different history of the term and the concept.

usually described as a *gendhing*'s melodic framework and the basis for deriving *cengkok* patterns, as played on the single-octave metallophones *slenthem* and *saron*. When notation was first introduced, the *slenthem* and *saron* parts were chosen from among the many in the texture to be written down. This implied that the *balungan* was somehow more important than or generative of other parts, so that what had previously been a relation of equality was now re-imagined as a network of hierarchies. The institutionalization of this order is a consequence both of notation itself and of the European ideas that engendered its adoption. Kunst, for example, had described the *saron* part as the "cantus firmus" or "nuclear theme," clearly as part of a search for metaphors comprehensible from a Western perspective.[22]

Sumarsam, a theorist who has written extensively about *balungan,* has correctively pointed out that the significance it has been accorded may have served to overstate its generative authority and obfuscate the actual source for other instruments' *cengkok*. For him and others, the *balungan* is best reconceptualized as an "abstraction of the inner melody felt by musicians" (1984a:273). This inner melody is neither a fixed entity nor is it stated explicitly in the texture; rather it is mentally formulated by individual performers according to special constraints in the style and range of the instrument that they play.[23]

Melodic pattern is only one of several senses in which the word *cengkok* is understood, but it is the most common one.[24] *Cengkok* are applied to the realization of *balungan* (or inner melody) phrases on elaborating instruments. There are many *cengkok* appropriate for the *pathet* and *balungan* of each *gendhing* from which musicians may choose as the performance proceeds. "Standard" versions of *cengkok* may be varied by applying *wilet,* or melodic ornament. *Cengkok* and *wilet* on the so-called "soft" elaborating instruments such as *gender,* the xylophone-like *gambang, suling,* or *rebab* tend to have considerably more individual character than the staid *balungan* as a result of their greater range, fluid melodic contours, and varied playing styles and timbres. Moreover, the *rebab* part may not easily submit to segmentation into component *cengkok*. All of the soft instruments may hover for long moments of seeming tonal indifference to one another before converging, as they regularly do, on points of metric stress; but even these arrivals may be blurred by rhythmic idioms that favor delayed or anticipated resolutions. This multipart complexity, sense of studied imprecision, and ensemble "looseness" are all components of a contemplative, inner-directed aesthetic prizing a shared awareness of the *gendhing* but a multiplicity of ways of interpreting it for performance.

---

22. See Becker 1980:11–25; Lindsay 1985:193–216; and Sumarsam 1995 for discussion of these developments. On the subject of the analogy to cantus firmus, see Powers 1980b:40.

23. See also Sumarsam and McDermott 1975 and Perlman 1993:476–79.

24. Sumarsam (1995:230–31) says that it can mean "melodic pattern," "melody," "melodic style," and "melodic formula."

Whether played on *calung* in *gong kebyar* or a comparable instrument in other *gamelan*, Balinese *pokok* are confined, like *balungan*, to a single-octave range. But unlike in Java, the term itself has been widely and unambiguously used in Bali for centuries. Notation on *lontar* has long been a medium for preserving *pokok gending*, and, perhaps because notation has never been used in rehearsal or performance, *pokok*'s generative importance in the musical fabric appears never to have been a subject of dispute. *Pokok* are considered to be the simplified core or "bone" of *payasan*, which may be built from them in any of a number of ways.[25]

Like *cengkok* and *balungan*, *payasan* and *pokok* are structurally linked through first-order verticalities at points of metric stress. For some instruments, such as the *ugal* or *trompong*, the analogy with Java is fairly close: each instrument expands the *pokok* into a wider range (in these cases, two octaves) and embellishes it with *gending*-specific *payasan* and a measure of ornamental spontaneity. Like the various soft instruments in Javanese *gamelan*, there is normally only one *ugal* or *trompong* in the *kebyar* ensemble, so their players are also not required to coordinate precisely with anyone else. But where the Javanese instruments' parts often display disparate contours and connections to the *balungan*, the *ugal* and *trompong* lines have mostly similar contours, and each relates to the *pokok* in much the same way.

Other *payasan*, such as the interlocking parts characteristic of the eight *gangsa* and four *reyong* players, require completely precise note-to-note interaction and coordination, in addition to periodic first-order convergence. These parts are not chosen by the performer but are provided in advance by the composer or arranger. In *kebyar* they tend to dominate the texture far more than any single part ever does in Java, so much so that the overall character of the music is strongly affected. Balinese *pokok* and *payasan* are fused timbrally and conceptually into a single entity, essentially uniform each time it is played; a design that stands in opposition to the polychromatic, relaxed interweaving of the various *cengkok* instruments and *balungan* in Java.

Let me summarize via *garap*, which for both traditions is an umbrella term that covers the application of knowledge about each of the previous concepts. From the foregoing discussion it can be seen that Javanese musicians interpret *gendhing* during performance by applying contextually appropriate selections from a vast repository of *cengkok* and *wilet* to the *gendhing*'s form, *pathet* and *balungan*. Balinese music has very little spontaneity of this sort. Music is memorized and, with few exceptions, fully composed in advance, so interpretation is largely a matter of ensemble cohesion and the replication of effects of tempo, dynamic, and shading that are agreed upon in rehearsal. In Bali *garap* is something that takes place in the mind of the composer or collaboratively

---

25. The metaphor *tulang* (bone) is often used in cases like this to refer to something which retains its essence despite external change.

among musicians during rehearsal, but not during performance. In central Javanese *gamelan* individual musicians contribute to the surface aspects of the texture, which has the potential to differ from performance to performance of the same *gendhing,* whereas in Balinese *gamelan* musicians relinquish their individuality in deference to the full ensemble's goal of producing a nuanced rendition of a set realization of the *gending.* For any given *sekaha,* a Balinese composition is a fixed artifact that has permanence until, by mutual consent, the players or composer(s) decide to change it and to rehearse such changes. One can transcribe it in full and follow the score expecting to hear a fundamentally identical version the next time around.[26]

A second aspect of *garap* is not in the process, but rather in the aesthetic and attitude. Central Javanese *gamelan* values a sense of restraint, which preempts any abrupt changes in tempo or dynamic and assures a musical and temporal environment stable and steady enough to accommodate the continual dialogue between the many interfacing textural strands. In this case Balinese *gamelan,* specifically *kebyar,* may be said to be precisely the opposite: restraint is cast aside in favor of telescoped and dramatic change, as a means for demonstrating the undifferentiated, unanimously directed drive of the full group.

Issues for *Kebyar* Music Theory

A *kepatihan* score for a Javanese *gendhing* gives only the *balungan* and the form. Like a jazz musician's tune and chord changes, it is a road map for performance on which only the major routes have been drawn in. Javanese music theorists' concern with performance practice follows logically from the fact that musicians need a special sort of theoretical knowledge to guide them in realizing *gendhing.* Musicians assimilate theoretical knowledge during their training, study *balungan,* and learn to *garap* "on" them. Theorists work out the rules for *garap* by observing practice, turning unverbalized behavior into active knowledge. Since the specific complexities of the musical surface must always remain a variable, there is scant possibility for theory to deal with the music as a set whole. Indeed, relations between elaborating parts and the *balungan* are usually studied one at a time by theorists, since any fuller score would perforce remain provisional and unlikely to reflect any actual performance.

Theory for *kebyar* calls for the *generative* aspect that has been important for Java. The process of composing melodic materials and drum patterns based on the requirements of *pokok* or form is bounded by formulatable rules. These

---

26. This is particularly true in the purely instrumental, rather than danced, repertoire. There are male dance forms, such as *Baris* and *Jauk Keras,* in which the dancer may exert some control over musical structure. Number of repetitions in some instrumental contexts is also not fixed, and may be tied to external factors such as the progress of a ritual.

rules are naturally essential for Balinese composers to know. When performers master them it also has the positive effect of accelerating the transmission process, since conventional forms and patterns can often be fleshed out from basic information without further explicit instructions. But this type of theory is ultimately less fundamental for practicing Balinese musicians than for Javanese, because, with some exceptions at the smallest level of ornamental detail, the former need not be concerned with shaping these parts themselves. Once the *pokok* and *payasan* parts are composed they may be changed only with deliberate forethought and rehearsal, with such changes initiated only by the composer or an established teacher of the group.

It has been said that with its contemplative personality, Javanese *gamelan* is intended mostly for its performers and select connoisseurs (Lindsay 1977: 40). Balinese *gamelan,* specifically *kebyar,* is more extroverted, and meant for listeners as much as performers. The surface of a *kebyar* piece has a forceful personality, focused and shaped with contrasts in form and content. *Kebyar gending* are expressive and their conventions familiar to Balinese audiences. This quality is particularly measurable when, as is increasingly the case in recent music, the composer intentionally distorts or reconfigures inherited norms of style and structure, thereby playing with and against listener expectations. In this restricted sense, *kebyar* has come to resemble the fully notated compositions of Euro-American ensemble music more than it does the music of Java.

All of this suggests a *reductive* theoretical approach that takes expressive aspects of the fixed composition into account within the context of the conventions of form and interpart relations. The manifest whole is seen as a given and analyzed for its inherent properties, symbols, and meanings, as projected by its listeners and composers. The music can be segmented into units revealed as significant in the light of imported data from domains outside *kebyar* itself, such as other *gamelan* genres, dance, history, ritual, and so on, including meanings it has accrued in contexts outside Bali.

Analytical Approaches to *Kebyar* and the Music of the European Classic Period

A reductive analysis of *kebyar* interprets both the music's structure and discursive power, finding meaning where the two interface. Confronting these issues might be too complex were it not for *kebyar*'s relative uniformity of style and the homogeneity of the Balinese audience it addresses. In this sense (and here is where my methodology reaches the farthest) some of the concepts applied to Western music during the classic period can be used to understand and analyze *kebyar*. My analogy between Vienna in the 1780s and Denpasar in the 1980s is an acknowledgment of the two places' self-containedness and widely accepted aesthetic precepts, and the resulting impact of these factors on the nature of their predominant musical styles. In what follows I set forth three aspects to the congruence between the two musics: the rough analogy between their social and historical positions; the "linguistic" character of their styles and consequent referential capacity; and the flexibility of their structures and syntax. A fourth subtopic contrasts the two cultures' attitudes toward individuality and the notion of compositional materials as intellectual property. The discussion serves as a kind of prelude to part 2, which develops the Balinese side of each comparison in depth.

Historical Context

Both classic music and *kebyar* developed at a time when aristocracy and patronage were on the decline and music, while retaining most of its old religious and state functions, acquired many new secular contexts for composition and performance. In both places and eras the divine privileges of kings (and colonialists) were gradually being replaced by nationalistic communities and new forms of government. In conjunction with these changes the recondite musical styles of the recent past were rejected in favor of a more accessible approach to composition, and a sensitivity to public taste. New music was created not for the pleasure of deities or royalty alone, but rather for audience enjoyment, and was performed at an emerging new forum, the secular public concert. By providing new works for these events, the composer grew in status, and musical style changed rapidly in response to individuals' contributions. Music earned a degree of autonomy through these processes and came to be seen as intrinsically valuable on its own terms. In eighteenth-century Europe the growth of music publishing accelerated and broadened music's dissemination, while in Bali the growth of radio and the cassette industry has had much the same effect.

Referential Capacity

Classic music has often been examined for insight into the significance of its expressive gestures and signs by, among others, Rosen (1971), Ratner (1980), and Agawu (1991), all with related analytical aspirations seeking to portray it as an elegant and communicative language.[27] It is not just the expressivity of eighteenth-century style that has attracted these writers to the music-as-language usage, it is also the generous flexibility of the style in the hands of individual composers, and their ability to bend it, thereby enriching its vo-

---

27. Writers on the classical style have often adopted the metaphor of music-as-language as a way to get at the expressive capacity of the music's syntax and grammar, though this is only one of many possible uses of the analogy. In the metaphor's syntactic aspects, Powers (1980b: 37–54) has also assessed the likeness of improvisation to extemporaneous discourse, as well as the use of generative grammars of musical structure modeled on those developed by linguists (as in Becker and Becker 1979, Lerdahl and Jackendoff 1983, and others). I restrict my view of music-as-language to the intersection between Ratner's notion of expressive topic and the conventions of musical structure.

cabulary, to suit their own artistic needs and reach their audiences. *Kebyar's* discursive plasticity in musical domains and its broad relevance in social ones lead me to adopt the language metaphor for the same reasons.

In discussing classic music, Ratner links the power of the language with the concerns and experiences of people of the time:

> From its contacts with worship, poetry, drama, entertainment, dance, ceremony, the military, the hunt, and the life of the lower classes, music in the early eighteenth century developed a thesaurus of *characteristic figures,* which formed a rich legacy for classic composers. Some of these figures were associated with various feelings and affectations; others had a picturesque flavor. They are designated here as *topics*—subjects for musical discourse. Topics appear as fully worked-out pieces, i.e., *types,* or as figures and progressions within a piece, i.e., *styles.* The distinction between types and styles is flexible; minuets and marches represent complete types of composition, but they also furnish styles for other pieces. (1980:9)

By encompassing materials from all other Balinese *gamelan* genres, *kebyar* also makes use of topics as subjects for musical discourse. One need only remove "the hunt" (to my knowledge there is no Balinese equivalent to the horn fifths of Mozart's time, though there is music with martial associations), read "lower castes" for "lower classes," and substitute any two genres or forms from older Balinese *gamelan* for "minuets and marches" from Ratner's formulation to make this statement fully applicable to *kebyar* and Balinese musical life in our day.

Kebyar topics draw on colotomic meters, drumming, styles of melody or figuration, and instruments that are identified with dance and theater characters, other *gamelan* genres, or with specific well-known compositions. Genre components may be used individually, together as a kind of full-fledged "genre-quotation," or in combination with other topics deriving from different sources. As an example, the sacred *gamelan gambang* (already mentioned in chapter 2 as a source for orchestral textures) is marked by a characteristic kind of *pokok* figuration and a persistent 5 + 3-pulse rhythm in the *pokok.* When either of these appears as part of a *kebyar* composition its origin is unmistakable to practiced listeners. Even though the surrounding musical context may be thoroughly contrasting, the effect at that moment is to suggest the affect of *gambang* and all of its cultural associations. The topic's communicative power is enriched by other factors, such as its location and interaction with the form of the piece and the presence of other topics preceding it, succeeding it, or appearing simultaneously in other strata.

Structural Flexibility

In classic music, topics signify the external world. They in turn are situated within the musical fabric in dialectic accord with structural and syntactic norms. An essentially periodic substrate built from balanced and symmetrical units that extend into large-scale forms provides the music's continuity, while dramatic shifts in melody, texture, and orchestration, and the various types of cadential, progressive, and modulatory functions of harmonic tonality provide contrast. Through the manipulation of these normative elements composers created works that competent listeners perceive as strongly individuated, a perception shaped by the fact that the materials are combined and recombined in recognizably distinct ways.

Structural design in *kebyar*, as in any music, is a defining dimension of its character, and should not be misconstrued as being somehow measurable against a yardstick provided by another tradition. The "quality" of each music's design can be understood only on its own terms. Despite some interesting correlations between the structures of *kebyar* and classic music, I will not bark up the tree of trying to cross-match musical elements (the various gongs with tonic/dominant/subdominant functions, for example). The comparison is more useful at a conceptual level. The pliability of musical elements in the two musics allows for the coexistence of symmetry and asymmetry within a single composition, and in each there can be discontinuities in form and texture where few had existed in historically antecedent genres. While classic composers employed tactics of tonal prolongation, harmonic ambiguity, and phrase extension or elision to build sustained compositions, *kebyar* composers have used an unprecedented variety of figuration patterns, irregular melodic units, unmetered passages, and other musical strategies in theirs. In both cases new forms developed in response to the new potentials. As baroque dances and the explorations of the *empfindsamkeit* contributed to the evolution of the sonata, so have older *gamelan* formal structures and the many experimental compositions of the early years of *kebyar* coalesced into the more or less standard *tabuh kreasi* of recent decades.

Structural elements in *kebyar* that raise analytical issues include scale-tone relations in melodic composition, the technique of constructing melodic elaboration parts and their relation to the *pokok*, the agogic and form-bearing aspects of drumming patterns, the interaction between cyclic and noncyclic segments of the form, and the effect of changes in tempo, density, and texture. Each of these can be approached as purely technical phenomena or, as I have said, in conjunction with the topical discourse they engender.

Individuality

An underlying precept of Ratner's, Rosen's, and Agawu's work, axiomatic in the context of most contemporary scholarship, is that the value of classic works is a function of their individuality, which should transcend (but not overturn) the norms of the style. Though nineteenth-century Western music and its successors are held to be even more individuated, the celebrated core repertoire of classic music is shown to maintain a satisfying and comprehensible balance between personal and stylized expression. The balance is seen as particularly dynamic in the intellectual and cultural context of post-

Enlightenment Europe, with its emphasis on rational thought and empirical knowledge. This deeply embedded cultural viewpoint is reflected in the nearly exclusive reference to the music of Haydn, Beethoven, and Mozart (though Ratner offers abundant examples of the music of lesser composers). Though they stress the commonality of style and affect underlying classic music, the motivation behind the three authors' analyses is to reinforce the prestige of the style by demonstrating the lasting value of its most celebrated composers' individual contributions to Western music.

Yet this viewpoint was hardly that of the eighteenth-century Viennese, who wrote few critical responses to individual works. The reason for this, as Zaslaw underscores, is that

> from the eighteenth century's point of view, the consideration of compositions [is] less as individual "works" than as constituent parts of a complete *oeuvre* or as specimens of a genre, which were dedicated not to the constituting of a repertory but to the carrying on of musical "daily business." If one disregards a few operas, which were already "repertory pieces" in his lifetime, hardly one contemporary text is devoted to a single, unique, completely determined work by Mozart.[28]

It would thus be wrong to adopt Rosen, Ratner and Agawu's stance uncritically and grant any preeminence to the notion of individuality for discussing *kebyar,* for when it comes to critical response, contemporary Balinese society operates much as eighteenth-century Vienna did. Balinese culture today continues to stress collectivity, the necessity of consensus, and the urgency of maintaining the rootedness of religion and culture in the face of rapid change. Like audiences in classic music's time, *kebyar*'s constituency places a much higher value on what is stylized and expressive of something inherently and irreducibly Balinese than on the personal. Though the style as a whole transforms rapidly, established norms of musical structure exert an overwhelmingly strong pull on composers, who tend to draw freely on each other's material or to reuse the same ideas verbatim in more than one composition. Such behavior stems from the particular nature of Bali's oral transmission process, the reluctance of individuals to stray too far from perceived norms, and the sense that new music be should be compatible with the old as a safeguard against the deterioration of cultural values.[29]

That individuality cannot be viewed as a Balinese value is true despite the fact that composers innovate all the time. While I am vitally interested in learning and evaluating such innovations, it is impossible in most cases to trace the genesis of a new musical idea to an ultimate source. Doing so is like tracing the movement of a grain of sand on the ocean floor, an inquiry whose

---

28. W. Kuppelholtz and H. J. Busch, eds., *Musik gedeutet und gewertet: Dokumente zur Rezeptiongeschicte von Musik* (Munich, 1983), 26. Quoted in Zaslaw 1989:510.

29. For a valuable parallel of this musical phenomenon in another domain, see Zurbuchen 1987: 85–86. She explains how literary scribes, editing and copying texts on *lontar* leaves, freely borrow and embellish material from multiple sources.

futility quickly leads to the realization that other processes, such as the nature of the tide itself, are more profitably studied. Even when one can follow the movement of a new musical idea, it does not remain the intellectual property of its composer and is bound to appear in the music of others almost overnight, particularly once the composition is recorded and distributed. It then becomes part of a shared pool of resources. In later analyses I credit individual composers whenever their authorship can be confirmed, but this does not mean that the details of a piece's content are unique. Some portions may be, and likely are, shared by others composed contemporaneously; or they may be quotations or paraphrases from older music.

The same, however, can be said of music in the Western classic repertoire. Though eighteenth-century Viennese did not build an analytical discourse about works of their time, this has not stopped later writers from doing so, much to our enrichment. Similarly, while Balinese do not themselves emphasize musical individuality, we can still profitably experience *kebyar* through an analytical lens that does. Taking care to explicate Balinese concepts first, a refined understanding and appreciation can be gained by seeking insights into individual works.

Elaboration and Style: A Preliminary Analysis

A brief exercise comparing fragments from a pair of recent compositions will serve to inaugurate the application of the concepts sketched above. Figures 4.1A (CDI/5) and B (CDII/7; 7:01) share the same *pokok* but differ in all other respects, including figuration, colotomic underpinning, drumming, formal position, and affect. By virtue of their differences they give a sense of the range of connotative textures and styles that a single sequence of *pokok* tones can support.

On the lowest stave in each system I show an *ugal* realization of the *pokok* done in a rhythmically undifferentiated style called *neliti* (correct, precise). In practice the *ugal* player could have some freedom to make elaborations on a *neliti* melody, but it can also be played exactly as I have written it. *Neliti* is helpful here and in later analyses because it uses the full two-octave range of the *ugal;* consequently the interlocking parts track its precise contour more closely than they do that of the single-octave range of the *pokok. Neliti* is actually *pokok* at double density expanded into two octaves; and the *calung* part consists of every other *neliti* tone, compressed into the *calung's* five-note range. Similarly compressed, *neliti* is also identical to the part of the *penyacah,* the five-key metallophone tuned an octave above the *calung* that many *gamelan* use.[30]

---

30. "[T]he *penyacah* strokes are often called *neliti,* so that the term *paneliti* popularly used with regard to compositional structure has come to mean: the total number of beats in a *gending* or the part of a *gending* measured by the strokes of the *penyacah*" (Aryasa et al. 1984–85:66).

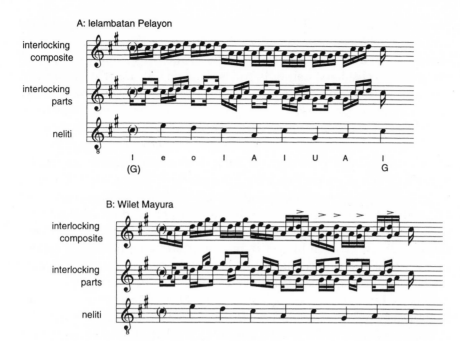

Figure 4.1. Fragments from two compositions with the same *neliti* tones. A. Lelambatan *Pelayon* (CDI/5). B. *Wilet Mayura* (CDII/7).

The first of the two examples is taken from *Pelayon*, a metrically broad and lengthy composition in the *lelambatan* repertoire. It was composed in 1983 for a *Festival Gong* group in Sanur village by Wayan Beratha of Denpasar, in collaboration with several younger colleagues. *Lelambatan* is a genre of stately and formally complex instrumental pieces closely associated with the repertoire of the *gamelan gong gdé*. This segment is heard at the climactic conclusion of the composition, at the peak of dynamics and tempo, after some twenty-five minutes of music. The melody is repeated many times, with a stroke of the large gong at every rebeginning and a pattern of other gongs aligned with the melody through each repetition. There is an interlude of virtuoso drumming just prior to the music in the transcription. The mood, as most any Balinese will attest, is one of extreme turbulence and grandeur. These attributes are partly a function of the *gong gdé* topic and the complexity of the texture, though at performance speed (ca. mm 160) the virtuosity necessary to play the interlocking parts on the *gangsa* and *kendang* with proper expression adds an additional element of panache and grace under pressure. The interlocking parts are in *norot* style, creating regular alternation between pairs of adjacent scale tones, and shifting position to anticipate the arrival of every other *neliti* tone. They follow the melody exactly and are not strongly articulated as an independent stratum.

4.1B is taken from *Wilet Mayura*, a 1982 composition by Wayan Sinti and Nyoman Rembang, performed by the *gamelan* of Angantaka. In this segment the *gangsa* play an interlocking melody in the style of the bamboo *gamelan gandrung*. *Gandrung,* now rarely heard on its original instruments, is often adapted and transformed for *kebyar.* Formerly the ensemble was used to accompany a recreational dance, but musicians now think of it mostly as a source for challenging drum patterns and interlocking parts. Nonetheless, such borrowings retain associations with the eponymous dance, which was flirtatious and exuberant. The pattern shown here is more intricate than that of *Pelayon,* and less firmly tied to the contour of the *neliti,* standing apart from it in a distinctive way. During the second half a cross-rhythm emerges brightly from the texture, formed by the irregular recurrence of a *kempyung.* There are no gongs or drums used, and the phrase is immediately preceded and soon followed by contrasting material. The combination of discontinuity, complexity, and rhythmic independence shifts the locus of interest in the music so that it is shared between the *pokok* and the interlocking parts (in a manner somewhat analogous to counterpoint), whereas in *Pelayon* the *pokok* and position of the excerpt at the climactic conclusion are more important.

Both of these pieces were composed for *Festival Gong* competitions and performed before raucous crowds of thousands for whom ensemble discipline is the main concern. But most listeners are fully aware of certain topical references, such as that of *gong gdé* in *Pelayon.* The *gandrung* topic, while more obscure, still succeeds in communicating its playful affect. To most musicians and their peers, and to the festival juries, the sophistication of a composition's topics is a key aspect of its value. As musicians often told me, "Everything can be used in *kebyar,* and the more the better."

In the foregoing the "neutrality" of the rhythmically undifferentiated *neliti* contrasts with the stylization of the elaborating parts. It is mainly true for *kebyar* that since *neliti* tones are derived from the *pokok* and mapped to other elaboration strata through first-order vertical relations, one may in most cases derive a workable *pokok* or *neliti* by extrapolating from the densest elaborating stratum (though it should be remembered that the unvaried rhythm of *neliti* is only sometimes used in practice). But what we have seen underscores the fact that the reverse process—that of determining the elaboration strata from the *pokok*—requires a style-specific understanding of the referentiality of elaborating patterns, and, by extension, that of other aspects of the music as well. Unlike older *gamelan* styles, in which texture and melodic elaboration are continuous and limited to a few possibilities, in *kebyar* elaborating parts cannot be generated from the *pokok.* The composer's choice and intention are determinate.

Agawu points out in reference to classic music that Heinrich Schenker's *ursatz* "can approach the foreground through systematic diminution, [but] this analytical process cannot generate an explicit, historically specific musical surface" (1991:24). The same phenomenon is illustrated by the comparison of *Pelayon* and *Wilet Mayura:* the shape of the *neliti* (or *pokok*) is necessary but insufficient information. Agawu describes the analytically significant region of "play" as the area where surface topics interact with structure. In the "play" area,

> it is the dialectical interplay between manifest surface and structural background that should guide the analysis. And it is only within such a framework that we can appropriately acknowledge the rich and subtle meanings that underlie the deceptively simple and familiar music of the Classic era. (1991:25)

Omitting "only" and substituting "*kebyar* style" for "Classic era" (given that *kebyar*, like classic music, is "deceptively familiar and simple" to astute insiders only), this formulation is a good summary of the analytical framework that will guide the remainder of the book.

Structure 2
in *Kebyar*

Ritual *baris* dancer, Bunga, 1982.
Photo: Author.

5 History, Repertoire, Topic, and Structure

M EASURED in months or millennia, historical forces work on music to effect change. Emblematically and technically modern though *kebyar* compositions may be, they rest on a continuity of ideas and practices that extend not only deep into Bali's own past, but also well beyond and outside of it. A grasp of what *kebyar* means to its Balinese listeners would be enriched by a study of the philosophical and cultural foundations of both early India, about which we know a considerable amount, and that of Neolithic Southeast Asian and Melanesian societies, about which we know a great deal less, for both of these exerted a formative influence on Balinese society. Though speculative knowledge about origins gradually gives way to a more discrete, documented, and seemingly comprehensible succession of events as we move closer to the present, in the end we have only historiography: the ongoing reinterpretation of society in the form of documents, images, sounds, and ideas that each era bequeaths to its successors. The meanings invested in music of a given time are distilled from a river of history coursing toward and merging with the present.

Though this perspective admits the subjectivity of historical knowledge and is itself more than amply broad, exegesis of Balinese history does not accommodate individual points of view. In their own lives, people experience history not as a force acting from without but as a context, a network of learned ideas, associations, and symbols that conspire to regulate experience. When hearing music, a combination of historical associations and sonic-structural conventions sparks feelings, ideas, and sensations that are both individually and culturally determined. By days and years, an aware listener's perception changes with personal growth and accumulated sophistication. Though an adequate depiction of even a single listener's network of associations exceeds the grasp of any discourse about music, the *idea* of the infinite variability of individual response can at least nourish healthy skepticism toward generalizations that are too sweeping.

Music-structural conventions and the responses they engender owe their particular shape to cultural factors, but they nevertheless exhibit a systematic coherence that transcends cultural determinants. Such coherence is there only to be heard; it is a domain where the music defines itself on its own terms. Unlike the historical and individual perspectives just described, access to this coherence can result only from engagement with the music itself, and is therefore of unique importance. Though Balinese musicians verbally articulate ideas about musical structure to varying degrees, it goes without saying that all of the best and most experienced *kebyar* players have developed sensitive ears. No historically based appreciation for the music can quite substitute for insight into the refined and hard-won perceptions that such people enjoy.

With all of these concerns in mind, part 2 opens with a sweeping grand tour of the outer and inner worlds of musical composition in *kebyar*. This marks the end of the concentration on the musical surface and on the context-setting present and recent past explored in part 1, replacing them with a broader diachronic view of the musical past. Beginning with the macrocosmos of Balinese history and culture, I set forth an overview of music history, noting the kinds of associations that pre-twentieth-century music can carry. Next I move in stages to the progressively focused realms of *kebyar* repertoire, its immediate historical sources, and the subcompositional world of affect and topic. Following this, an "analytical interlude" creates a link to concepts of structure, which leads me to identify structural classes. At the end I start to probe the microcosmos of note-to-note connections in melody for clues about what makes them tick. The ideas developed are applied only to test cases for the time being. Together they form the basis for the exploration of the expressive and technical scope of musical particulars that comes in the next several chapters.

Historical Periods and *Gamelan* Genres

Building a historical framework on which to analyze and interpret contemporary Balinese music immediately raises the questions: whose history, and how shall it be told? One is wary of misrepresenting. Since we know so much more about the history of the ruling classes than we do of those they ruled, how can a balance be struck that does not simply perpetuate these biases? I am mindful of the fact that the complexity of lives and events spanning millennia is scarcely something to be grasped more than a bit at a time, but my purpose here is clearly different in any case. History filtered through music is of another kind of complexity than history itself. It is the special qualities of music-historical complexity that I ultimately seek to reveal, both from the point of view of what is historically verifiable and in terms of the way people understand it.

One Western scholarly view of Balinese history divides it into four eras, partitioned from one another by important discoveries or events.[1] According to this outlook, the earliest postprehistoric stage, that of so-called ancient indigenous Bali, is considered to have begun during the third millennium B.C., when peoples from mainland Southeast Asia migrated south in vast numbers. It came to a close in 882 A.D., when the earliest known copper charters and stone inscriptions were written.[2] The second period, that of older Balinese-Hindu culture, is characterized by the gradual influx both of Hinduism, borne by immigrating priests and scribes from India, and of people and culture from Java. This was not a decisive shift, for Hinduism (and Buddhism, which was also influential for a time during this period) "demanded of adherents the crossing of no boundaries and the renunciation of no previous practices[;] . . . they represented at most an additional set of rituals and deities that could be turned to for certain purposes" (Reid 1993:140). The collapse of the East Javanese Majapahit dynasty in the late fifteenth century sent its leaders fleeing to Bali, which they had claimed as a vassal state since 1343. The cultural development that took place over the next four hundred years under Majapahit descendants comprises the third phase of Balinese history, that of later Hindu-Balinese culture. The final period, already surveyed in chapter 3, includes the colonial and Indonesian years of the twentieth century.

Fundamental principles of social organization that still shape Balinese life

---

1. These categories are those of Goris (1952).
2. See Goris 1954 for transliterations and commentary.

predate the arrival of Hinduism, such as the multiple allegiances that Balinese maintain to their ancestries and local communities. These connections are ritualized through the *khayangan tiga* temple system of the *desa adat,* in which separate temples are maintained for each category, plus one for death rites.[3] During this time Balinese cultivated rice, working the land with simple tools. Villages were clustered together in small groups and are thought to have been ruled by local "big men," as are some Melanesian and Southeast Asian hill tribal societies to the present. Of the material artifacts remaining there are stone sarcophagi (Ramseyer 1977:20), which were likely used in death ceremonies that may have resembled those still practiced in the mountain village of Trunyan.[4] The early documents were in Sanskrit, Old Balinese (which faded from use not long after the 882 inscriptions were written), or both. The use of Sanskrit demonstrates that by 900 A.D. Indian culture was already influential on Bali, coming as part of the great wave of Hinduization that swept Southeast Asia during the preceding half millennium. As a consequence of the durability of the religious and literary traditions introduced by Sanskrit authors, Balinese have since considered the ultimate origins of their culture to be in India. The first such scribes in Bali were priests or literati who had emigrated directly from India, or Hindu emissaries from Java. Sanskrit was then and has remained a liturgical language of the *pedanda,* members of the high priesthood, who intone its chants *(sloka)* seated on raised platforms during temple rituals. The precise meaning of the chants has always been inaccessible to congregants, yet the channel to cosmic forces and Hindu gods that they open provides tacit confirmation of Balinese deific ancestry.[5]

Though the shifts from the second to third and third to fourth periods are marked by important political change, that between the first and second eras is more blurred. After all, the written sources which are the basis for separating ancient from older Hindu Bali may not have been decisively influential in their day, and may have been preceded by many other such documents which have not survived. A tripartition into pre-Majapahit, post-Majapahit, and modern times that takes this into account is thus important too, especially because it reflects the way many Balinese view their own past. These perceptions are in part formed through portrayals of history or myth in Balinese dance, shadow play, theater, and sung literature. Such performances identify characters or events as either in the realm of the mythological (in which case they fall outside the domain of human time) or as pre- or post-Majapahit; but in each case they are linked to the present by means of performance and narrative

---

3. Goris 1960 describes these connections in greater detail.

4. See Dananjaya 1985. Bandem and DeBoer (1995:3–10) describe the *Berutuk* ceremony of Trunyan, stressing its many aspects that link it to ancient Balinese cultural practice.

5. Hooykaas's many publications (1964, 1966, 1971, etc.) investigate the Balinese high priesthood and the body of Sanskrit texts that they use. See Wallis 1979:96–129 for analysis and interpretation of sounded Sanskrit texts in Balinese ritual.

Tua	Madya	Baru
1. *Gambang*	1. *Gambuh*	1. *Arja*
2. *Saron* (aka *caruk*)	2. *Semar pegulingan*	2. *Gong kebyar*
3. *Luang* (aka *saron*)	3. *Pelegongan*	3. *Janger*
4. *Selunding*	4. *Bebarongan*	4. *7-key angklung*
5. *Angklung*	5. *Gong gdé*	5. *Joged bumbung*
6. *Gender wayang*	6. *Beleganjur* (aka *Bebonangan*)	6. *Gamelan suling*
7. *Gong bheri*	7. *Gandrung* (aka *joged*)	7. *Jegog*
8. Vocal genres:	8. Vocal genres:	8. *Kendang mabarung*
Raré (Bal.)	*Kidung* (Kawi & Bal.)	9. Vocal genre:
Sanghyang (Bal.)	*Geguritan* (Bal.)	*Cak* (Kawi & Bal.)
Sloka (Sans.)		
Kakawin (Kawi)		

Figure 5.1. Major Balinese *gamelan* and vocal genres classified by historical period (after Rembang 1973:4). I have added vocal genres and some *gamelan* that he omitted. (Vocal genre languages: Bal. = Balinese; Kawi = Middle and/or Old Javanese; Sans. = Sanskrit)

conventions. In this way the arts may be seen as transmitters and interpreters of historical knowledge, and also as media for insuring its continued relevance to audiences.

The tripartition of history corresponds with Nyoman Rembang's division of Balinese *gamelan* into three groups, *tua* (old), *madya* (middle), and *baru* (new) (1973:4). But Rembang's classification (fig. 5.1) is based mainly on technological considerations. The keyed instruments used in the first six *tua gamelan* are made variously of wood, bronze, or iron. Of these, numbers 1–4 are the sacred seven-tone *pélog* ensembles, and 5 and 6 are *slendro*-tuned. *Gender wayang* is the accompaniment for the shadow play (*wayang kulit*), and *gamelan angklung*—formerly and still occasionally including the eponymous shaken bamboo rattles—is the village-based ceremonial ensemble already mentioned in connection with the early days of *kebyar*. (The drum and gong-based *gong bheri* is an anomaly of uncertain ancestry found only in the village of Renon. Rembang does not explain why he included it in the *tua* group.) Unlike the *tua gamelan*, the *madya* ensembles of the post-Majapahit court feature drums and gongs prominently, strongly suggesting that these changes were Javanese in origin. Even the bamboo *gamelan gandrung* uses ersatz gongs of resonated bamboo. The eclectic group of *baru* ensembles are all inventions of the current century. Some are bamboo, some are bronze, some use drums and gongs and some do not. The percussive vocal chanting of *cak* has origins in ancient *sanghyang* songs and trance ceremonies.[6]

The morphology, style, and function of the *tua* ensembles during the ancient and early Hindu periods remain a matter of speculation, even though iconographic evidence shows that some instruments have traversed the

---

6. See further Dibia 1996.

centuries virtually unchanged (Kunst 1968). Some *tua gamelan,* such as *luang* and *angklung,* were themselves influenced by *madya gamelan* and now use drums and gongs, though in a minimal way. The main point to be made about the music's general associations today, however, is that for most Balinese the pre-Majapahit era is felt to be not so much the actual past as it is suspended in a mythic prehistory that is discontinuous with the origins of the Bali they know.

One minority segment of the population has long held a different perspective. In the Bali Aga ("original Balinese") villages of the mountainous northern and eastern parts of the island, many practices dating from the ancient and early Bali-Hindu periods remain extant. Aga villagers see themselves as caretakers of "real," pre-Majapahit Balinese culture, which they preserved over time with an isolationism that, as in Tenganan village for example, proscribed marriage with outsiders. The persistence of unique time-reckoning systems, ritual practices and attire, village layout, and architecture all add weight to the Aga claims, though in other ways they have been far from unaffected by the trends overwhelming Bali at large.[7] The *tua* seven-tone *pélog* ensembles, largely confined to Aga communities for centuries, are part of this special heritage. For non-Aga Balinese the sacred affect of that music, whether familiar in sound or not, is intensified by the hothouse seclusion in which it is thought to have been cultivated.

During the period of older Bali-Hindu culture Javanization intensified. As the reigns of the Javanese kingdoms of Airlanga (1016–49), Kadiri (1078–1222), and Singhasari (1222–92) waxed and waned, their kings engaged in changing combinations of commerce, warfare, and intermarriage with Balinese rulers.[8] The first Majapahit king, Vijaya, ascended after 1293. During the decades surrounding the 1343 capture of Bali, his kingdom gradually enlarged to include the whole of Java and beyond.

The *madya gamelan* of the fourteenth century and later were associated with court prestige. They were part of a proliferation of literary and expressive art forms that coincided with growing Majapahit power. Kawi (Old [or Middle] Javanese), the language for the literary traditions, is related to Javanese and Balinese, though it is distinct in vocabulary and functions as a language of erudition, art, and learning that has always been, theoretically at least,

---

7. There are numerous extended discussions of Bali Aga traditions in the literature. Korn 1960 is an important early one. Geertz (1957) and Lansing (1983) offer revisionist perspectives. The essence of their arguments is that there is little evidence to support the view that Aga villages were able to protect themselves from Hindu influence to the extent that villagers contend. Like all villages, their relations to the monarchies shifted over time, and their position ranged from influential to peripheral, though the Aga resisted assimilation perhaps to a greater extent than most. Even they absorbed change, however, and share many cultural traits with the rest of Bali.

8. Details of these successions can be found in Coedes's 1944 classic *The Indianized States of Southeast Asia.*

accessible to all. To the present, in Kawi-language performing arts like *kakawin* vocalization, the shadow play, and the *gambuh* theater, reciters, puppets, and actors entertain and transmit the morality and beliefs of that era to the entire society.[9]

Under Majapahit influence the local Balinese culture completed a metamorphosis, already in progress for centuries, into a powerful court-centered culture. An important way that the growing centralized courts accumulated prestige was through cultivating the arts. Music and musical instruments were seen as channels for cosmic forces that conferred status and power upon the kings who tapped into them, thus strengthening the influence of their reigns and philosophies. These doctrines were disseminated through the Kawi recitation of both Javanese and Indic epic poetry, and through newly written dynastic genealogies called *kidung,* along with their dramatizations in the performing arts. In *kidung* verses, which were often in Balinese language, cultural practices outside the courts were marginalized or disregarded, as the history of Bali was written by court scribes to be perceived as the history of its Java-descended royal lineages and their god-like forebears. Through this concerted historiography, the Majapahit rulers and their Balinese successors strengthened the perception of the post-Indic past as Javanese.

In the late fifteenth century, when Majapahit weakened under economic stress and the growing influence of Islam in Java, many of its court permanently withdrew to Bali, where Hinduism prevailed. Consolidation characterized the years 1500–1650, in which all of Bali was governed by the court and expanding empire of king Dalem Baturenggong and his successors at Gelgel, south of the present day city of Semara Pura (formerly Klungkung). In this "golden age," the blend of Majapahit and the antecedent local cultures sank deep roots. Many enduring social institutions were established under Gelgel rule, such as the *banjar* system. During this time the *triwangsa* caste divisions took shape. The Balinese language grew to be structured parallel to *triwangsa* social stratification, with high, middle, and ordinary levels, each with their appropriate contexts for usage. The spiritual and cultural beliefs of the Gelgel court were enshrined as the core values of Balinese life.

An important facet of courtly culture throughout Southeast Asia was the construct of the god-king, whose kingdom was considered to model the cosmos itself. The king was the "exemplary center" of this world, and the rest of it was structured in hierarchical concentric circles around him, with priests, warlords, ministers, and merchants at the interim levels and peasants at the outer circumference.[10] The iconic similarity between this political structure and the stratified structure of colotomic music, as described by Becker and

---

9. The standard work on Kawi literature is Zoetmulder 1974.
10. See Geertz 1980:11 for a fuller description

Becker (1981), provides a powerful explanation for the durability and importance of *gamelan* structure and performance as cultural practice.

From the decline of the Gelgel center to the Dutch takeover two and a half centuries later, Balinese society and its political map were in constant transformation. New kingdoms were formed and dissolved in rapid succession as ambitious princes strove to act as heroically as their poetic counterparts by vanquishing enemies, winning the support of commoners, acquiring riches, and patronizing the arts. Interactions with traders, Islamic rulers, and Dutch adventurers were consistent and ongoing. Villages of this era had a range of economic and social ties to the courts, but their own traditions continued to flourish, both symbiotically with and independently from them. Emerging rulers curried community allegiances by marrying villagers and elevating their status.[11] Some members of the lower castes acquired new power working as taxation ministers or advisors for royalty in certain places. The often contradictory behavior of the kings—on the one hand preserving their claim of divine descent by isolating themselves from commoners, while at the same time integrating with them through personal relations—resulted in complex and variegated alliances with *banjar* and descent groups. As a result, ancestral groups throughout the island maintain connections with distant temples and communities, and localities preserve special traditions based on their singular histories. For the *madya gamelan* of the courts and the *baru gamelan* to emerge later, the effect of these chaotic political networks was to generate musical diversity. The artistic heritage of the Gelgel courts was disseminated throughout much of the island, but it acquired distinct repertoire and style in each area that it took root.

At the time of the first serious Dutch interventions, the map of Balinese kingdoms had begun to resemble that of the nine *kabupaten* of today. In 1856, after a series of battles, the Dutch assumed control of the northern Buleleng and western Jembrana regencies. After the suicidal *puputan* of 1906 and 1908 Dutch control was total. Courts made alliances with the colonizers, but eventually had to contend with reduced power and resources, thereby accelerating a dissolution already begun during the unstable nineteenth century. Assets, including the large bronze *gamelan,* were passed down to the *banjar,* becoming their property and responsibility. With shrinking court prestige and the imposition of a newly rigidified bureaucracy, the *banjar* system acquired new status as primary bearer of tradition, along with the sense that it was incumbent upon ordinary people to maintain what the courts could no longer

---

11. Schaareman (1992:173) mentions this point in connection to Tatulingga, his pseudonym for a village in the northeast. But the results of this kind of union are evident throughout Bali, because of the innumerable mixed caste titles that many bear, which indicate intermarriage at some point in their families' history. The main point for our purposes is that village and state have always had a dynamic interrelationship, so that court music genres were known in the villages, and vice versa.

preserve. Part of this process was the integration of court arts into the traditions of *banjar* life. It was in the context of the early decades of Dutch control and the ongoing destabilization of court-village hierarchy that the *gamelan gong kebyar* emerged.

Scanning the Repertoire

Kebyar repertoire's interface with this history is intricate. This is because—consistent with the kinds of intertextuality observable in other Balinese arts—it absorbs, borrows from, and is engaged in continuing dialog with other *gamelan* repertoires.[12] The boundaries of the genre are thus indistinct. Early *kebyar* repertoire contained innovative works side by side with music taken verbatim from the *madya* court ensembles that were its immediate predecessors. Over the decades, as more composers have come into contact with the full range of their musical past, their ideas have increasingly come to be shaped by the influence of the *tua* ensembles. Today the morphology of *kebyar* comprises distinctly *kebyar* features mixed with a collection of transformations, borrowings, or quotations from antecedent ensembles, sometimes in the form of unadulterated complete compositions, all heard and interpreted in light of both their sources and their new contexts. Categorizing the repertoire is a good place to begin untangling this multigenre web.

Kebyar's growing repertoire can be grouped in several overlapping divisions. One may say, for example, that the repertoire is split between instrumental music and dance or theatrical accompaniment. Or one may choose to distinguish between compositions intended for secular entertainment and those primarily for ritual use. Partly coinciding with this, but distinct from it, one may also speak of *baru* (new) music composed for and specifically performed on *kebyar,* differentiating this from older, more widely known *klasik* (classic) works, possibly deriving from pre-*kebyar* genres, that hold or have earned a permanent place in the repertoire. Another possibility contrasts music that is formally complex with simpler compositions, often for dance, that are built from little more than a repeating melody in a short gong cycle.

Balinese are most likely to explain a composition's place in the repertoire along the lines of some combination of the first three category pairs: instrumental/dance-theatrical, ritual/secular, and *klasik/baru,* combining this with some consideration, if called for, of the music's source in pre-*kebyar* genres. The first pair is the most sharply defined. Instrumental music is never choreographed, nor is dance music played without dancers. There are characteristic

---

12. See Vickers 1986:20–23 for a discussion of the applicability of this concept to Balinese literature and literary texts' representations in painting, theater, and song.

Gamelan pelegongan, Tunjuk, 1977. Photo: Author.

gong cycles associated with instrumental music that are never used for dance, though dance music structures are an important part of most instrumental pieces.

The ritual/secular distinction is tied both to historical aspects of repertoire and to performance occasion and physical setting. From a historical point of view, *kebyar* is dominated by kinds of music originally played on the *gamelan gong gdé* and the more recent *gamelan pelegongan*, reorchestrated and conceived in accordance with the technical capabilities of *kebyar* instruments and musicians. *Pelegongan* traces to the seventeenth-century court *gamelan semar pegulingan*, and both it and *gong gdé* evolved from the still earlier *gamelan gambuh*, the ensemble of long *suling, rebab, kendang,* miscellaneous small metal percussion, and gongs said to be the "oldest form of Balinese dance-drama, [and] considered to be the source of Balinese music and dance" (Bandem 1987:199). The continuity of this lineage does not mean that *gambuh* is actually the sole source, for the *tua* ensembles predate it, though Balinese generally perceive it that way because *gambuh* is the earliest *Majapahit-based* performance genre.[13]

---

13. The view that *gambuh* is *the* source persists and has been sanctioned by the government, which has officially declared it *klasik* and sacred. This was done to encourage its preservation, but is ironic given *gambuh*'s original position as an arm of the state and the highly political discourse of the poetry and theatrical form that it accompanies (Vickers 1986:302).

Most ritual music played on *kebyar* instruments is music originating in or traceable to the court ensembles and associated with their former prestige. As entertainment for visiting deities, this portion of the repertoire plays a direct role in ensuring the efficacy of a temple ceremony or other ritual event. At such events the placement of the instruments in the courtyards of the temple complex affects the music's ritual power and the associations it evokes. In *oda-lan*, ritual music is played inside the temple in the *balé gong* in one of the two enclosed areas, the innermost, sacred *jeroan* or the somewhat less charged *jaba tengah*. In contrast, compositions composed and performed exclusively on *kebyar* function primarily as entertainment and are presented outside the temple in the *jaba* perimeter area, as well as away from the temple at secular events.

The *klasik/baru* separation is partially isomorphic with the ritual/sacred one. *Baru* compositions are of current vintage only, or at most a few years old. Most are created for the *Festival Gong* and subsequently recorded and distributed by cassette companies. In the majority of cases their postfestival life is restricted to the *sekaha* that originally learned and performed them, though owing to the increasing number of outside performers "borrowed" by village *sekaha* for festivals, the ability of a purely local constellation of players to bring off a performance once the event is over is far from guaranteed. Some pieces may become widely disseminated and enjoy a spate of intense popularity before vanishing, a notable example being the dance *Manuk Rawa* in the early 1980s. Others may endure or be revived, occasionally earning the status of *klasik*. *Klasik* is a catchall term that refers to both ritual music and older *kebyar* compositions perceived to be of lasting value, or deserving of special preservation efforts. *Klasik* ritual music comes from court repertoires, and may be taken verbatim or rearranged in contemporary style. Ritual compositions reworked for secular presentation (like fig. 4.1A's *Pelayon*) are considered both *klasik* and *baru*, because they retain the major features of an antecedent composition type but use *kebyar* orchestration, elaborating parts, and performance style. Such music may be acceptably presented in secular performance as well as inside the temple, though in the temple a simpler style is considered preferable.

Composition Types and Theatrical Forms

Applying these initial categories already begins to clarify the effect of musical style and performance context on the associations carried by a composition. The level of composition type and dance or theatrical form is an intermediate step between these general groupings and the specific referentiality of topics. Figure 5.2 forms the basis for the following introductory discussion of the main subgenres of *kebyar* repertoire. Composition types are laid out horizontally

Genre of origin	Instrumental and vocal	Theater and dance
Gong gdé	• *Tabuh lelambatan* • *Beleganjur*	• *Topeng* • *Baris* • *Rejang/gabor/mendet*
Pelegongan, gambuh, and *semar pegulingan*	(Few used by *kebyar* groups)	• *Legong keraton* • *Calonarang* and *barong* • *Jauk* and *telek* • *Rejang/gabor/mendet* • *Arja* and *prembon*
Kebyar	• *Tabuh kreasi baru* • *Kreasi lelambatan* • *Gegitaan* (vocal) • *Sandya gita* (vocal) • *Kreasi beleganjur*	• *Tari lepas* • *Sendra tari* • *Drama gong*

Figure 5.2. *Kebyar* repertoire by subgenre

according to their instrumental/vocal or theater/dance usage, and vertically according to genre of origin. The double line between the two upper rows (pre-*kebyar*) and the lower one (*kebyar*) roughly matches the ritual/secular distinction.[14]

Instrumental Music and Accompanied Singing

The *lelambatan* of *gong gdé* repertoire, musical centerpiece of temple ritual, were once played for state functions at court. As suggested above, they may be played in one of two ways: in the simple, refined style approaching that of the original *gong gdé*, or in a flamboyant *kebyar* reconception. *Lelambatan* are instantly recognizable by their special instrumentation, in which *trompong* and *kendang cedugan* (*kendang* played with *panggul*) front the ensemble. Each composition uses one of a group of extended metric schemes called *tabuh pegongan*, all but one of which are exclusively reserved for instrumental music.[15] *Lelambatan* musical forms and the cyclical meters they are built from comprise a normative minimum of three parts: the *kawitan*, or introduction; *pengawak*, or main body (an extended melody in slow or medium tempo that uses the *tabuh* identified with the piece); and a *pengecet*, a melody or group of melodies in shorter meter and faster tempo than the *pengawak*. Though departed from

---

14. In the case of dance and theatre genres the number of possible avenues of exploration are too numerous to do more than suggest here. A fuller pursuit of the meanings these genres bring to *kebyar* music would call for consideration of the poems and panegyrics underlying them and a study of their performance traditions, histories, and receptions. In what follows I stay close to the music, offering suggestions in the notes for further reading.

15. McPhee distinguishes between composition types *tabuh lelambatan, gending longgor* and *gending gangsaran*. Today the latter two terms are less frequently used and all instrumental music of the *gong gdé* repertoire is routinely grouped under the *lelambatan* heading.

Gamelan beleganjur of Pindha in ritual procession to the sea, 1982. Photo: Author.

in many kinds of music, this tripartite form is an archetype considered as a fundamental model for Balinese composition.

The short, repeating *gongan* of *beleganjur* (also called *bebonangan*) are played by *kendang cedugan, cengceng kopyak, reyong* (eight individual gong kettles, apportioned one to a player), *gong, kempur, bebendé,* and *kempli;* in short, a *kebyar* or *gong gdé* without *trompong* or metallophones. Gongs are strung up on poles, *kendang* are strapped around the neck, and the other instruments are handheld, making the *gamelan* portable. *Beleganjur* was military music at court and is used in the villages for ceremonial processions of all kinds, be they for cremations *(ngaben)* or the ritual transport of small shrines to the sea to bathe the deities inhabiting them *(makiis)*. Owing to its special function, *beleganjur* is classified separately from *gong gdé* in court documents like the *Prakempa,* despite the fact that the former uses only instruments belonging to the latter. Rembang followed this convention too. *Kebyar sekaha* simply remove the instruments that they need from the full set when processions take place.

The music of the *gamelan pelegongan* was dominant in southern and south-central Bali during the early years of *kebyar's* popularity, and most of its dance and theatre repertoire was subsequently absorbed by *kebyar*. *Pelegongan* instrumental music, exemplified by the work of Lotring and others (McPhee 1966:307–27), was an important secular precursor of *kebyar* instrumental music, but it was not absorbed in the same way. Instrumental *semar pegulingan* compositions, composed in the *tabuh pegambuhan* system (related to but distinct from the system of *tabuh pegongan*), are adapted from *gambuh* dance compositions. Like those in the *gong gdé*, the longer *tabuh pegambuhan* are also called *lelambatan*. *Semar* (properly, *Semara*) is the god of love and *pegulingan* means "sleeping chambers": the ensemble was formerly used to enhance the romantic atmosphere in the royal pavilions by providing intoxicating sounds outside. The effectiveness of this body of compositions is said to depend on the high, "sweet" tuning characteristic of the original *gamelan*. Since most *kebyar* are more deeply tuned, few *sekaha* elect to play this music, choosing *gong gdé lelambatan* or other *kebyar* instrumental forms instead. Today instrumental compositions in *pegambuhan* meters are heard only in the few *banjar* with *gambuh, semar pegulingan*, or *pelegongan gamelan*, but their influence is strongly felt in new compositions.

The foremost instrumental music type belonging exclusively to *kebyar* is the *tabuh kreasi baru*, often shortened to *tabuh kreasi*. Unfortunately this terminology is confusing, since the word *tabuh* here does not refer to the *tabuh* meters of *gong gdé* and *gambuh*, but simply denotes *gending*. Remove it, however, and the term *kreasi baru* could also refer to dance or other new artistic creation. I will use *tabuh kreasi* to refer to a specific subgenre of *kebyar* instrumental composition that is exclusively composed and performed for secular presentation and is intended to showcase ensemble virtuosity. *Tabuh kreasi* were rhapsodic and loosely constructed during the early decades of the century but became increasingly codified between the 1960s and 1990s. They are characterized by the use, in no set order, of passages featuring each instrument group in the *gamelan*, either in solo presentation or with accompaniment. These sections and the transitions between them are often abrupt, frequently ametric or at least not marked by gongs, and full of *kebyar*'s hallmark shifts in tempo and texture. Only toward the conclusion of a piece (in the *gambangan* section; see fig. 2.15) does the full *gamelan* predictably play for any substantial time as a unit. Of all *kebyar* subgenres, *tabuh kreasi* demonstrate the most consistently high rate of musical innovation and the most diverse use of topics.

Kebyar instrumental forms also include *kreasi lelambatan*, the elaborated *gong gdé* compositions mentioned above. The analogous *kreasi beleganjur*, currently at what seems to be the end of an intense craze in Bali, first appeared in 1986 and immediately became popular, generating dozens of specialized *sekaha* and festival-style competitive performances. Another *kebyar* trend is the combination of vocal and instrumental music, encouraged by the government to aid in the revitalization of vocal arts. In the *gegitaan*, required for the *Festival Gong* of 1978 and 1982, a trained soloist performs an existing text and melody from the *kidung* genre of old poetic meters, accompanied by *kebyar* and a small chorus. (*Wilet Mayura* is a *gegitaan*.) These were supplanted by the *sandhya gita*, which uses a large mixed chorus and simpler style. *Sandhya gita* are often worked out collaboratively, with one composer responsible for the *gamelan* music, and the other for creating the choral text and tune. The *gamelan* composer assembles an introduction and interludes reminiscent of *tabuh kreasi,* and then fashions a more subdued accompaniment to underpin the sung sections.

Theater and Dance Music

Full *kebyar* instrumentation, with *kendang cedugan,* is used for *gong gdé* theater and dance forms. For those in the *pelegongan* group *reyong* is dropped and either a pair of smaller drums or a single medium-sized drum are used, the latter sometimes played with *panggul.* The presentation and stock character types of all of these forms were modeled on *gambuh* (which, however, has always been exclusively presented with *gamelan gambuh* and never with *kebyar.*) *Gambuh* enacts selections from the *Malat* epic poem, composed in *kidung* meters and depicting the exploits of archetypal Javanese kings of Majapahit. *Gong gdé* forms portray the comparatively more recent Balinese past, and *pelegongan* forms range over a much broader subject matter, but the vocabulary of music and movement in both is indebted to *gambuh. Gong gdé,* emblem of royal political and military power, became the primary forum for male dance. Female dance forms are mainly accompanied by *pelegongan,* which retains *gambuh* and *semar pegulingan*'s strong connotations of sweetness, eroticism, and sensuality, further traceable to themes of romance and sexual conquest in the *Malat.*[16] Much *pelegongan* dance and theater repertoire developed in the villages and courts of South Bali during the late nineteenth and early twentieth centuries, where it also acquired a concern with the control and manipulation of magic and spiritual forces. In one oral rendition of the *Malat,* some of these dances are said to have been brought to Bali from the outside world of Melayu culture (Vickers 1987:35), which could suggest an additional reason for the special powers attributed to them. All of the above forms are strongly associated with ritual, though in this century many have moved outside the temple.

The most familiar *gong gdé* dances use short colotomic meters and include masked *topeng* plays, which dramatize historical chronicles of Balinese royalty (*babad*). Though commonly performed in the *jaba* by a troupe of three to five dancers, *topeng pajegan,* an older and more ritually powerful version for a single dancer wearing a succession of masks, is done in the *jeroan.* The dramatis personae of all *topeng* consists of a number of predominantly male character types, including kings (*dalem*), prime ministers (*patih*), attendants (*penasar*), and clowns (*bondres*). Depending on the story portrayed there are many types, with personalities described as ranging from sweet (*manis*) to strong (*keras*), refined (*halus*) to coarse (*kasar*), funny (*banyol*) to sad (*sedih*), or fierce (*galak*) to timid (*lek*). These general characterizations do not provide much insight into dramatic detail, but as affects they are what is retained by the melodies that accompany specific characters and kinds of dramatic

---

16. Vickers' dissertation (1986) explores this theme in depth.

Ritual *topeng* at the centennial *Eka Dasa Rudra* ceremony, 1979. Photo: Author.

situations. Separate but related to *topeng* are the sacred *baris* warrior dances, performed in groups (*baris gdé,* of which there are several types) or, in a more recent secular distillation, as a solo (referred to simply as *Baris;* see figs. 2.14, 5.4 and 6.3 F, H).[17]

Pelegongan dance and theater repertoire centers on the *legong keraton* female dances, of which there are many versions, and various tales of witchcraft. *Legong keraton* adapts the *gambuh* character of the maidservant (*condong*), who opens the performance with an introductory solo danced to a suite of brief melodies. Her character is sharp and intense, preferably performed by a very young girl. Two dancers (the *legong* proper) enter presently and dance with the *condong* for some time before she exits. The *condong,* not originally a part of the dance when it was created during the nineteenth century, is sometimes dropped now, and multiple pairs of *legong* may be substituted for the standard two. The *legong* next dance the *pengawak* and *pengecet* sections, composed in *pegambuhan* meters, and further melodies specific to each version. Among many subjects presented in *legong keraton* are a fragment of *Malat* (*Lasem*), the *Ramayana* (*Kutir* or *Jobog*), portrayals of animals in natural settings (*Kupukupu Carum* or *Kuntul*) or pure choreography (*Pelayon;* distinct from *lelambatan Pelayon*). All use a similar movement vocabulary, derived partly from *gambuh* and partly from the exorcist *sang hyang dedari* trance dances. *Legong*'s antecedents are thus quite sacred, even if it is characteristically

17. For coverage of *topeng, baris,* and *jauk,* see Dunn 1983, Bandem and DeBoer 1995 and De Zoete & Spies 1938:165–74 and 178–96.

Ritual *pendet* (local version of *gabor*), Peliatan, 1982. Photo: Author.

danced in the *jaba* today.[18] Musically the general vocabulary is likewise uniform, though each version has its own melodies and shares only the meter and drumming of the *pengawak* with other *legong* stories.

An important dance movement thought to originate with *legong* is *angsel,* a sudden break or disruption.[19] Reflected in the dancers' bodies, it may take the form of the sudden striking of a new pose, a quick change of step rate or direction, or a small set of abrupt movements unconnected by the usual smoothness. In brief melodies, *angsel* most often fall prior to gong, though long sequences of them may traverse a *gongan* or series of gongan. Though less characteristic, they may be interpolated into longer melodies at positions fixed with relation to the meter. The rhythm of the *angsel* is anticipated by a set of musical cues and subsequently reinforced by the *gamelan,* minimally by the *kendang* and *cengceng,* and often by the *gangsa* section. *Angsel* patterns spread from *legong keraton* and are now used in nearly all dance. Their characteristic rhythms also permeate *tabuh kreasi* and *kebyar lelambatan,* where the addition of the *reyong byar* increases their disruptive power.

Calonarang and other related stories of witchcraft and exorcism invoke the protector-dragon *barong* and its nemesis the witch *rangda.* Though identical to the *pelegongan,* the *gamelan* that accompanies *barong* and *rangda* stories is

---

18. See Bandem and DeBoer 1995:71–74 for a sketch of *legong*'s history.

19. This was the opinion of many musicians and dancers with whom I discussed the subject, among them Ketut Gdé Asnawa, Wayan Beratha, and Anak Agung Raka Saba. See also McPhee's description of *angsel* (1966:175–76).

sometimes called *bebarongan* (see fig. 5.1). While *legong* was developed mainly in the courts and partakes of their aesthetic of refinement and feminine grace, the intensely charged *barong* and *rangda* are affiliated with exorcist rites and purges, and can potentially send performers and audience members into trance. They appear to have always been a village phenomenon (Vickers 1985: 172). Originally associated with the *pelegongan* repertoire are the plays about the demonic *jauk* characters, danced with masks featuring bulging eyes and white gloves to which long fingernails (symbolizing potent magic) are attached, and the recently revived *telek*, female counterparts to *jauk*. Like solo *Baris, jauk* is often danced independently. *Barong, jauk,* and *telek* characters are accompanied by a single drummer. The *arja* theater, a late nineteenth-century creation modeled on *gambuh* but using local story types and simpler poetic meters, is often accompanied by *kebyar,* though it actually has its own special *gamelan* of *suling, kendang, cengceng,* and bamboo slit-gongs, the *geguntangan.*[20] *Prembon,* a fusion of *arja* and *topeng,* is a mid-twentieth-century innovation.

The women's *rejang* and *gabor* and the men's *mendet* are the root of a special lineage of ceremonial offering dances that have particular significance for *kebyar.* They are performed in the middle or inner courtyard of the temple in simple steps requiring little or no special training, usually by large groups of villagers. Among the oldest dances in Bali, they are known throughout the island and may be accompanied by whatever *gamelan* is available, including sacred seven-tone genres in Aga villages. Their performance is an act of devotion central to religious practice. During this century *gabor* has been developed and cultivated as a more refined form, *Gabor,* largely under the eye of the influential teacher Anak Agung Raka Saba of the royal family in Saba village. He shaped the choreography for formal performance by infusing movement elements from *legong,* and later collaborated on *Panyembrahma,* a condensed updating of his *Gabor* for use as a "welcoming" dance at secular events, with music by Wayan Beratha (Bandem and DeBoer 1995:134; see also fig. 8.2).

Gabor, jauk, legong, and *baris* are the main predecessors to most of the *tari lepas* (free-standing dances) and their predominant influence, an influence that extends beyond dance music and deeply into *tabuh kreasi. Tari lepas* are the forum for pure *kebyar* dance, and represent a concentrated visual embodiment of the music's emblematic capriciousness. They are brief, and while sometimes nominally connected to a historical character or event, they are unencumbered by the literary influence that shapes theater. The few *klasik tari lepas*—*Kebyar Duduk, Teruna Jaya, Oleg Tumulilingan,* among select others—are showpieces in which music and dance are tightly intertwined and in which

---

20. Detailed information on *legong, calonarang, jauk,* and related forms may be found in Wiratini 1991, Bandem and DeBoer 1995, and De Zoete & Spies 1938:86–134, 174–77, and 218–32. *Arja* is covered in depth in Dibia 1992a.

a dancer's performance is judged by the same standards of precision and expression as that of the accompanying musicians.

The recently developed theater forms accompanied by *kebyar* are characterized by a less static and stylized presentation of character and story than their predecessors *gambuh, topeng,* and *arja,* and, as in all *kebyar* aesthetics, a more forward-directed, compressed sense of dramatic time. They are also extraordinarily popular and seemingly deleterious to the survival of the older forms, though these continue to be performed. The spectacular and big-budget *sendratari* presented at the yearly PKB were first developed in the mid-1960s by Wayan Beratha and various collaborators at SMKI. Based on Javanese models, they are usually enactments of *Ramayana* and *Mahabharata* fragments, using enormous casts and crew, and often accompanied by more than one *gamelan.* Among these may be non-*kebyar* genres such as *gong gdé* or *semar pegulingan. Drama gong,* contemporary plays with much spoken dialog and relatively little music, are performed on television and at ceremonies throughout Bali by specialist troupes.[21]

Topic Classes

Progressing to the subcompositional level is like moving into the inner world of perception, where evident forms may be transformed or distorted by composers and listeners. Put differently, historical events, characters, genres, and compositions are more tangible entities than the coded and polysemous symbolism of topics, but they are the cultural basis for interpreting them. Awareness of the various types and modalities of topic gives a significant perspective on the kinds of meanings *kebyar* provides for Balinese listeners. Because they use and transform structural and stylistic conventions to create a persuasive musical utterance, topics may be seen as the music's rhetoric. However, music is not exclusively dependent on external reference to be expressive, and topic is only one component of a deeper approach. The rhetorical discourse of topic has its counterpart in the coherence of the musical language, which carries its own messages about the affective qualities of sound organized in time. In the remainder of the chapter I sketch and link features of both.

Some *kebyar* topics are defined by attributes such as colotomic meter, drum pattern, or elaboration style; others suggest connections to theater or dance. A given musical situation can contain many such kernels, prompting the listener to reference several related genres, affects, or analogous musical moments all at once. In the court-derived subgenres topical discourse is relatively slow and sparse because constraints on musical style limit access to topics originating elsewhere. With the relaxing of these restrictions in twentieth-century music like *tabuh kreasi,* the speed and density of the discourse increased. This is

---

21. See DeBoer 1996 for treatment of these two genres.

because the music may not only draw on the other subgenres within *kebyar*, but also simulate the styles of other Balinese *gamelan*, adding them to the vocabulary. To wit, many Balinese speak of *kebyar*'s versatility and ubiquity in the same breath, citing the former as an explanation for the latter.

Describing this activity is perforce provisional, and we are often reminded not to be tempted by illusions of intellectual closure. In Nattiez's definition, "meaning" is achieved as soon as "an individual places [an] object in relation to areas of his lived experience"; but "for music, it is paramount not to define meaning solely as a reflection of some *linguistic* meaning" (1990:9). Bearing such injunctions in mind, I have grouped *kebyar* topics into four classes, which differ in degree and kind of referentiality.[22] They are *character topic, abstract topic, stylistic topic,* and *quotation topic.* This splitting of musical signification processes into classes is related to the way Leonard Meyer grouped mid-twentieth-century Western composers' accessing of past styles in *Music, the Arts, and Ideas* (Meyer 1967). Meyers's categories (paraphrase, borrowing, simulation, and modeling) do not match mine exactly, but both of our groupings concern the uses of past music in contemporary music. They involve the application of a set of compositional techniques sharing a central feature, described by Meyer as providing

> the basis for all or part of a new work whose spirit and significance are clearly contemporary. Through a reordering of parts or materials, a modification of syntax, a change of inflection or vocabulary, an alternation in manner of representation— or some combination of these—a stylistic modification takes place. (1967:195)

Character Topics

Character topics originate in the family of melodies and their affiliated colotomic meters, melodic elaborations, and drumming that are used to accompany stock characters or character types in dance and theater music. Some character topics may be traced to specific tunes and dances that are widely known and easily identifiable for Balinese, or they may evoke features of a more generalized type, and are best described as being "in the style of" some well-known dance (*Baris* or *Gabor,* for example). Character topic sources usually consist of a single, short *gongan.* They may be free-standing or part of a larger composition. Exactly what it is that shapes the identity of these melodies is a subject to which I shall return later in the chapter, after developing concepts for discussing structure with greater precision.

---

22. There is referential significance obtained by simply introducing an instrument associated with a particular style or genre, but I do not define this as a class of topic because it does not involve the use or transformation of musical materials. The use or omission of such instruments as the *trompong,* or the choice of *kendang* with or without *panggul* and small or large *cengceng,* are important factors shaping a composition's general affect. In particular it is the drums which affect the perception of music as being traceable to either *gong gdé* or *semar pegulingan* lineage. The *trompong* could trace to either one, but in *kebyar* context it generally connotes *gong gdé.*

Character topics point to intertextual pathways between source melody types in court genre dance and theater forms and melodies in new dance forms such as *tari lepas* or *sendratari,* or in instrumental contexts like *tabuh kreasi.* The original dance character and its affect are transmitted by suggesting the original melody type through the use of some of its musical characteristics—colotomic meter, for example, or structural aspects of melody and elaboration. In this way an affect inherent in the original, such as strength, humor, majesty, or grace, may be portrayed, and information about setting may be inferred, placing the music in the realm of the mundane, spiritual, or demonic; or in court or commoner spheres.

A good example of character topic is a melody heard near the beginning of the *tari lepas Oleg Tumulilingan* (see figs. 6.4 and 7.6A). It invokes both *Gabor* (gong punctuation and drumming) and the opening melody of the *condong's* dance in *legong keraton* and *gambuh* (melodic contour; compare fig. 6.3L and O), as well as the elaboration style of *lelambatan* compositions in the form *Tabuh Telu.* These references enrich the character of the dance, which is an energetic and lissome *condong*-like solo depicting a bumblebee flitting among flowers. The *Gabor* allusion overlays an element of worship, one familiar to all who have participated in or observed *gabor* dancing in the temple, while the *lelambatan* element, seemingly incongruous owing to its origin in an instrumental and essentially masculine courtly form, adds a further measure of both regality and gender ambiguity.

Abstract Topics

Abstract topics are in some ways best described as the negative complement to character topics. They are defined by their meter and scope, and to a degree their drumming patterns, but not by the particular contents of their melodies or elaboration. A specific composition with an abstract topic does not project any aspect or mood of its own, is not connected to specific characters, and is indifferent to dance or instrumental origin. Most abstract topics originate in the broad colotomic meters of *pengawak pegongan* and *pegambuhan,* and *as a class* carry an affect described by Balinese with words like *suci* (sacred, pure), *murni* (pure), *agung* (great; imposing), and *luhur* (exalted or sublime).

Like all colotomic meters, those of *pengawak* can function as containers for potentially limitless melodies. But whereas shorter melodies are widely known and many could readily be sung or quoted by nearly anyone, only a few longer ones are familiar in more than a general way to most people.[23] Shorter meters

---

23. Sometimes longer pieces are mastered only by musicians responsible for playing the leading melody, especially for ritual performances. Melodic elaborations are mainly in a simple and predictable style, so *gangsa* and *reyong* players can get by adequately by following the melodic anticipations that the *trompong* or *ugal* provides. *Calung* and *jegogan* can similarly derive their parts. Colotomic instruments and drums need only follow the conventions of the meter and can plausibly "piggyback" without knowing a melody at all. Such forms of extreme dependence on a leading musician are likely to take

support character topics by acquiring a cluster of identifying characteristics from details of their structure, but large-scale meters like *pengawak* are impartial in this regard. *Pegongan pengawak* are by their nature abstract because there is no dance. In *legong* and other *tabuh pegambuhan* dance meters each *pengawak* melody is identified with a specific story, but its choreography is a formalized prelude to the narrative; it does not actually tell the tale. In both *pegongan* and *pegambuhan,* the kinds of drumming and melodic elaboration used are often severely constrained, so that the difference between two *pengawak* in the same colotomic meter may amount to little more than the difference in the progression of *pokok* tones (and the specifics of melodic elaboration strata, which are shaped by the *pokok*).

Pengawak melodies thus stand apart from one another, but all project similar qualities. The affect of an individual *pengawak* is subject to further refinement based on its tessitura or melodic shape, or by its extramusical associations, if any, but these attributes do not carry over to other melodically similar *pengawak*. Put differently, any similarity between two *pengawak* may make them related to one another, but the similarity does not ascribe any expressive attribute to them as a pair other than that carried by the entire class of abstract topics. With character topics two similar melodies *would* share affect as a pair. As an example, consider the most widely known *legong* story, *Lasem*. It tells the famous tale of the eponymous king, who kidnaps a princess and is subsequently slain in battle. Though this story and its characters are very familiar, *Lasem's pengawak* (fig. 6.3X) does not transmit a character topic. Only subsequent parts of the dance, with shorter melodies, do. Consequently, a *pengawak* with a melody similar to *Lasem's* for a new *legong* choreography would not obtain any intertextual associations with the *Lasem* story.

When composers use abstract topics in new compositions, they often stay close to the original musical contexts. *Tabuh pegongan* are used in *kreasi lelambatan* and *tabuh pegambuhan* in new versions of *legong*. There is no distortion of the meaning or significance of the topic here; it is simply a case of a well-known meter used in a conventional way. When *pengawak*-like meters are imported to new contexts, as they occasionally are, striking conflations of their abstract qualities with some of the more overtly expressive aspects of other topic classes result.

Stylistic Topics

Certain formats leave "space" for stylistic tags that do not refer to a particular melody, meter, or theatrical character. Instead they use signature musical

---

place only in less formal performances, such as at a temple ceremony. For concert performances like the *Festival Gong*, nothing of the sort would be tolerated.

Familiarity is also circumscribed by the fact that, save for some prominent exceptions, *sekaha* do not maintain more than a small number of long pieces in their active roster. People hear the same ones repeatedly at ceremonies and performances in their villages throughout their lives. They may recognize these, but not others from neighboring areas.

properties associated with other *gamelan* genres and adapt them to fit the compositional context. The general topography of the source genre's characteristic textural, rhythmic, and melodic devices determines the identity of the topic. Stylistic topics may be imported to individual strata, multiple strata, or applied with broad strokes to compositional design and form. Unlike character topics, they do not use preexisting compositions for material or allusion, but instead involve the application of a *technique* of composition or elaboration.

Stylistic topics are particularly important because they can be drawn from any genre, not only those of the court traditions. *Gamelan* that are not part of *kebyar*'s core repertoire, such as those in the *tua* group and the bamboo *gandrung,* may all be signified in this way. The effectiveness of stylistic topic depends on the listener's ability to recognize the surface features or devices used in these genres, as opposed to specific compositions or formal types within any of them. Or, in the case of noncourt genres, to at least recognize that a contrasting element that points away from the mainstream of the tradition has been introduced. The opening up of *kebyar* to the full range of stylistic topics has had radical consequences, for court and noncourt lineages have contrasting structural bases. In figure 4.1 I showed stylistic topics appearing in melodic elaboration strata, and suggested some relations between the topics' sources and what they express.

Quotation Topics

Quotation topics combine qualities of character and stylistic topics. In quotation, all or most of the strata of a preexisting composition are adapted for *kebyar* presentation, usually as a section of a larger piece. In the process the composition may be modified, but it remains recognizable. This specifically excludes the use of entire pieces, as in *kebyar lelambatan.* While the impulse to relate or translate from the original to *kebyar* style is common to both instances, the modernizing of *lelambatan* is better described as rearrangement or adaptation.

In quotation topic the source must be inserted into a larger context and surrounded by other, more or less contrasting material. The quotation links the new composition both to the specific affect of the source composition and to the general affect of its genre, setting it in relief with the surrounding music. Sometimes the source genre may be *kebyar* itself. It frequently happens that short musical ideas, gestures, or motives enjoy currency and may appear in several new compositions during a brief span of time. Quotations of this sort typically appear in the unstable, noncolotomic opening sections of *tabuh kreasi,* and their sources are usually other *tabuh kreasi.* They are distinguished from other kinds of passages using generic motive-types of *kebyar* style by the degree of precision with which they copy their sources, and the way in which such passages are set off formally from surrounding music. The separation is often accomplished by short fermata-like silences, acting, as it were, as quotation marks.

Sekar Gendot, an instrumental composition of the *gamelan gender wayang,* furnishes an important example of quotation from another repertoire in *tabuh kreasi.* Lotring had contributed pieces called *Sekar Gendot* to *pelegongan* repertoire in the 1920s, though they bore the title without citing the source directly. Later he adopted a version of the *gender wayang* music verbatim for the *sekaha* of *Geladag,* creating a brief, free-standing piece (appendix A). Among the first to quote *Sekar Gendot* within larger pieces was Lotring's student Gusti Madé Putu Griya, who did so in the celebrated *Jaya Warsa,* composed for Geladag's appearance in the 1969 *Festival Gong.*

In the most-quoted portion of *Sekar Gendot, calung* and *jegogan* repeat a two-note ostinato while the *gangsa* create a swirl of elaboration patterns above it (the beginning of figure 8.4B is a typical example). This may be followed, as in *Jaya Warsa,* by an expanded melody of irregular size and shape, elaborated with further intricacy. As in *gender wayang, kebyar* versions use only metallophones, though with the addition of gong strokes at key points. The appeal of quoting the music lies in its complexity and in meeting the challenge of coaxing the same precision and subtlety from a *kebyar gangsa* section as would be expected from a good *gender wayang* quartet. In 1969 many *sekaha* considered the performance challenges of *Sekar Gendot* quotations beyond their reach, but borrowing it and other *gender wayang* compositions became standard in due course. This helped raise the ante on *kebyar* composition to the point where it is no longer possible to say, as it once was, that some other genres are more demanding or complicated. It also further whetted the omnivorous *kebyar*'s appetite for other repertoire, broadening its scope to include—potentially, at least—all Balinese *gamelan* music.

Analytical Interlude: From Topic Class to Structural Class

In the analysis of figure 4.1, I associated the stately *gong gdé*-style interlocking elaboration in *Pelayon* with "regularity" and "following the melody exactly," and the playful, *gandrung*-influenced elaboration of *Wilet Mayura* with "irregularity," "discontinuity," and melodic "independence." Because of the way that they refer to other genres, we have already been able to identify these examples as instances of stylistic topic. But what of the underlying melodic stratum, the common denominator that facilitated the comparison? By according it "neutral" status in that context, I contrived to present it as an entity without any of its own associations, but with the potential to serve as the basis for diverse kinds of elaboration. And indeed, taken on its own, the melody could be applied to many musical contexts. Below the surface of the so-called neutrality, however, are structural properties which bear on issues of character and expressivity, and which also influence the composition of elaborating parts in various ways.

Consider the *pokok* of figure 4.1 once again, for the moment in the *Pelayon* context only. As stated, the melody may be played by the *ugal* in *neliti* style. *Neliti* ordinarily corresponds with the beat *(ketokan* or *maat)* of the *kempli*, so I represented it with quarter notes and will hereafter refer to a single *neliti* duration as one beat. This melody, therefore, is eight beats long. It is a cyclical progression iterated upon the arrival of each gong tone. The gong tone is considered the *final* scale tone of the melody, not the initial one. This concept is an important antidote to the pitfalls of taking the metaphor of circularity in *gamelan* musical form too literally, for along a truly circular progression there are neither ends nor beginnings. Balinese would count the tone coinciding with the gong as the eighth tone of the melody rather than the first, and give it the greatest stress when singing, perhaps by temporarily abandoning the solfège and substituting the gong mnemonic *gir* or *sir*. I adopt this method of counting to be consistent with Balinese (and Javanese) practice, but also because not doing so distorts the syntax of the music and obscures analytical results.[24] Here as in other transcriptions I add an extra beat at the beginning in order to show the gong at the end of the previous *gongan*, setting it apart by placing it in parentheses.

I give the vowel of the scale-tone solfège name (capital letters for the lower octave and lowercase for the upper one) under each *neliti* tone. On the *ugal*'s two-octave range the *Pelayon* gong tone is *dIng*, the lower of the two *dings* available on the instrument, so there are ample keys above and below it to accommodate the ambitus. The midpoint of the melody *(dAng*, fourth beat) receives the second-strongest stress and is reinforced by the *jegogan*, as is the final *dIng*. The melody thus consists of two four-note units, *deng-dong-dIng-dAng* and *dIng-dUng-dAng-dIng*, each metrically stressed at their last note, with the second group weighted more. The *calung* part (the *pokok* proper) falls only on the even-numbered beats *(dong*, second beat; *dAng*, fourth beat; *dUng*, sixth beat; *dIng*, eighth beat), adding moderate stress to the second and sixth tones in addition to the final and midpoint ones.

Calung and *jegogan* parts derived from a *neliti* must be compressed into their single-octave *ding*-to-*dang* span. All melodic contours in the *neliti* must be adjusted accordingly. Adapting an aspect of a term from Western theory, I will call this configuration *pokok order*.[25] To get at the structure of the full melodic shape, however, it is also useful to represent all three parts as direct derivations of the *neliti*, thereby preserving its contour at all levels. This will be termed *neliti order*. In figure 5.3 the *neliti* is arranged into a three-tiered

---

24. McPhee's notations do not reflect this, a fact which disturbs at least some Balinese who are familiar with *Music in Bali*.

25. The original term, "normal order" (Forte: 1973:3), refers to the ordering of a pitch-class set by expanding interval size and ascending pitch, such that the smallest interval is between the first two tones and the largest interval is between the last two. My terms "*neliti* order" and "*pokok* order" distinguish only between the one- or two-octave registral space occupied by a melody, and do not call for reordering the tones.

Figure 5.3. Levels of melodic abstraction in *Pelayon* (CDI/5). All parts shown in *neliti* order.

representation of melodic strata, the second and third staves of which represent the *calung* and *jegogan* parts in *neliti* order. The following additional observations can now be made:

1. The eight *neliti* tones are distributed among five *ugal* keys only, one of each scale tone. These are arranged symmetrically around the gong tone *dIng*, two above (*dong, deng*) and two below (*dUng, dAng*). Three of these tones are used once and only once, while the midpoint tone appears twice and the gong tone appears thrice.

2. The tones in the *jegogan* stratum divide the melody in half and define a simple level of structural melodic movement: statement (*dIng*), downward displacement by one scale tone (*dAng*), and return (*dIng*).

3. The two pairs of tones in the *calung* stratum are inversionally symmetrical with respect to one another, the first descending by two scale tones (*dong-dAng*) to the midpoint and the second ascending by two to the gong tone (*dUng-dIng*). The stepwise moves linking the second note of each pair with the first of the next pair are similarly inverted.

4. The two four-note units of the *neliti* part are *imperfect* inversions of one another; that is, one would have to alter exactly one note in either half to make the symmetry exact. In this case the maverick note is the first in each group. One could, for example, change the first note of the first group (*deng*) to *dAng*, thereby perfecting the inversion. But doing so would undermine the symmetry mentioned in point 1 above and reduce the number of different scale tones used in the passage from five to four. One could also change the first note of the second group (*dAng*) to *dEng*, but this would break the symmetry described in point 5 below.

5. Parsing the eight tones according to recurrences of the scale tone *dIng* reveals a different kind of symmetrical organization. This segments the melody into three units, the first of three notes (*deng-dong-dIng*), the second of two notes (*dang-dIng*), and the last of three (*dUng-dAng-dIng*). Here the outer units are inversions of one another symmetrically arranged in time around the middle unit, and in pitch-space around their common tone, *dIng*. The 3 + 2 + 3 grouping is in conflict with the prevailing meter but its perception is

strongly (I would say irrefutably) supported by the repetition of *dIng* at the end of each segment. Such stepwise motion in small, irregular-length units around a repeating focal pitch produces a *rhythmic* phenomenon of syncopation or cross-rhythm that is characteristic of the music and often evident also in the elaborating parts (such as in the *Wilet Mayura* example) and drumming.

Structural Classes

There is a dialectic between the kinds of symmetry in points 1–4, all of which confirm the meter, and that in point 5, which challenges it. The *Pelayon* interlocking parts contribute to the confirmation of the meter since they match each *calung* scale tone, but in *Wilet Mayura,* where the segment is part of a much longer melody and no gongs are sounded, the elaboration enriches the dialectic by adding on more cross-rhythms and deviating from the *neliti* contour. Looking at the music in terms of these contrasting levels of structural tension, which are evident in some combination in all *kebyar* music, constitutes a relevant approach to analysis. The relevance comes partly from the fact that perceiving this structural tension can lead to elegant ways of hearing, but the tension is not solely music-structural in nature. It is also iconic with respect to historical origins. Balinese *gamelan* uses two classes of structure—symmetrical and asymmetrical—plus their combination, in which this tension is revealed and through which it can be experienced. The symmetrical/asymmetrical duality has many additional facets that form the conceptual underpinning for all of the analysis in the next several chapters. Among these are the term-pairs cyclic/linear, static/kinetic, continuous/discontinuous, stable/active, and conventional/innovative.

Music with Symmetrical Structure

Structural symmetries of the kind evident in the *Pelayon* example are most pronounced in music of court *gamelan* and genres influenced by them, including *kebyar*. Factors affecting the symmetry include the presence of gongs, which overtly proclaim the metric framework against which symmetry is perceptible. The quadripartite periodicity of colotomic meters ensures the temporal and large-scale melodic symmetry of the music around a midpoint axis (point 2 above).

Another significant factor affecting symmetry in court-derived music is the two-octave range of the primary melodic instruments.[26] The wide range increases the possibilities for spatial symmetry in addition to the temporal symmetry that gongs provide. In music of the court ensembles, gong tones do not

---

26. This refers to *ugal* in *kebyar, trompong* in *kebyar, semar pegulingan* and *gong gdé,* and the 13- to 15-key *gender rambat* (played in parallel octaves) of *gamelan pelegongan.* The long *suling* used in *gamelan gambuh* extend into a third octave.

fall at the extremes of the multioctave instruments' range, but always on a tone which can be approached from both above and below. The kinds of symmetry vary with the length of the melody: in shorter ones of 8, 16, or 32 beats the organization is tight, the contours of *neliti* phrases leading to *jegogan* tones tend to be related by inversion or other symmetrical function, and features of the kind noted in point 5 above are common. The longer the tune (64, 128, or 256 beats), the higher the number of *jegogan* arrivals between gong strokes and the greater the temporal distance from gong to the midpoint of the melody and back again. In these compositions the *neliti* register of a *jegogan* tone becomes a matter of considerable significance. In some long melodies, often those especially praised by musicians for their elegant shape, the *neliti* tones stressed by *jegogan* may describe symmetrical arches reaching both higher and lower than the gong tone during the course of the cycle (though the temporal symmetry may not be exact). Sometimes the quarter-way stresses on either side of the midpoint are marked by the same scale tone in different octaves. Or the *neliti* may traverse the tessitura in a more leisurely manner, exploring different registers and providing, through *jegogan* arrivals, a series of contrasts to the gong tone, always touching on scale tones both above and below it. The kinds of melodic elaboration associated with court genres' music tend to reflect the symmetries found in the *neliti* and meters at their own (more rigorous and localized) structural level, and often consist of stylized patterns formulaically worked out from the slower strata.

Music with Asymmetrical Structure

The structure of court-derived and court-influenced *gamelan* may be contrasted with that of the seven-tone *pélog* ensembles *gambang, selunding, caruk,* and *luang,* and the *slendro* ensembles *gender wayang* and *angklung,* all of the *tua* group. Any gong punctuation employed by these *gamelan* was a later, only partially assimilated addition used to mark melody endings or keep a steady beat and not to delineate internal sections. Consequently there is no quadripartite superstructure to which compositions must conform, and melodies are often (though by no means exclusively) of uneven and irregular lengths.[27] There is the strong likelihood that the music of the seven-tone *pélog gamelan,* once used to accompany singing, sprang from the irregular poetic meters used in the song texts.[28] Without going so far as to posit cause-and-effect interrelation between the absence of gongs and musical form, it is nonetheless the case that the repertoire of the *tua* ensembles contains many examples of irregu-

---

27. McPhee's statement that cyclic meter is the "basis for all Balinese instrumental melody" (1966: 83) reinforces the impression of his unquestioning allegiance to the court genres' prestige, even though he implicitly offers contradictory evidence elsewhere in *Music in Bali* simply by discussing the music of precourt genres.

28. McPhee (ibid.: 303) explicitly denied this possibility. For more on this subject see Schlager 1976, Wallis 1979, Schaareman 1986, and Vickers 1986.

larity, asymmetry, and nonquadripartite meters. Gusti Madé Putu Griya put it simply when he told me in 1982 that music of *madya gamelan* such as *gong gdé* and *gambuh* was "even" and that of the various *tua gamelan* was "odd." [29]

Similar contrasts with the court *gamelan* are evident in melody. In *tua gamelan* there is no multioctave expansion of the *pokok* because no instrumental strata cover a range of more than an octave (the special case of *gender wayang* will be addressed in chapter 6). There is no *neliti* order distinct from *pokok* order for these *gamelan*. The possibilities for the kinds of spatial symmetry in a cyclic meter described above in relation to two-octave instruments are extremely limited when melody is thus narrowed, because only some of the scale tones can be approached from more than one direction, and none has the possibility of being realized in more than one register. A melody that ends on the lowest pitch cannot be approached from below, a melody that ends on the highest cannot be approached from above, and only melodies ending in the middle of the scale could be centered in a melodic arch. With multioctave pitch space not an operative factor, the importance of contour as an aspect of melodic structure is diminished. Patterns of interlocking figuration in these *gamelan* are in many cases less formulaic than those in the court ensembles, as if conceived of integrally with the melodies rather than as stylized patterns to be added on to them.

Assimilation in *Kebyar*

Since branching out from court genres early in the century *kebyar* has developed many features of its own in which symmetrical and asymmetrical structural classes combine in a process of diachronic musical change. The court traditions have been transformed in *kebyar* as *tua* music and recent innovations act upon them, moving gradually toward deeper levels of reconciliation. Structural classes thus turn out to be the most generalized kinds of topic classes, because they correlate music and historical periods.

These interactions are not the product of a watershed confluence of independent musical worlds that took place after Bali fell to the Dutch and *kebyar* emerged at the beginning of the century. Throughout the Balinese past artistic genres and the social groups that express themselves through them have been connected in continuously shifting ways, so there is an artificiality to the notion of isolating them from one another for study. [30] The contexts for the various *gamelan* types were never fully independent to begin with, just as court and village culture never truly were, and the processes of musical transformation were complex and interactive, just as the social and historical ones have

---

29. "Tabuh-tabuh pegongan dan pegambuhan adalah genap, sedangkan gending-gending gambang, selunding, gender, dan sebagainya adalah ganjil" (personal communication, October 1982).

30. See Vickers 1986:177–87 for a discussion of the overlapping histories and audiences of musical, literary, and theatrical genres.

been. What did transpire is that composers' access to these genres grew in tandem with the social and technological changes of the twentieth century. *Kebyar,* the ensemble of choice, proved able to assimilate this variety of forms. Now, as a result of its prominence, other *gamelan* exhibit some aspects of this eclecticism, too. It passes directly to other *baru gamelan,* and ricochets back to some *madya* and *tua* genres. But *kebyar* makes use of them most effectively because of the capabilities of the instruments themselves.

Far from being a laboratory hybrid of past styles, many *kebyar* features are the result of composers' innovations. Some of these are melodic, the most characteristic being the kind found in *kebyar* textures (fig. 2.13), a stylistic signature. They often have prominent roles at composition beginnings and endings, and as links between successive cyclic melodies. Other important features such as the faster rates of change in metric context, texture, dynamic, and tempo may additionally be a by-product of the intensive rehearsal process and the level of ensemble virtuosity that has been achieved. These features will be discussed in chapter 8, after the court-based norms of melodic and metric structure have been sufficiently explored.

Inside Melodies

How does a melody "feel"? What makes a note choice aesthetically satisfying? These are difficult questions, but there is both the need and sufficient basis for at least broaching them now. Balinese apply words like *polos* (straightforward, elegant, easy to grasp), *wayah* (complex, mature, challenging), and *nguda* (easy, childlike) to these sensations, but never without reference to a melody's usage and to the larger musical texture surrounding it. When I expressed interest in exploring these qualities in terms of the tones themselves, few Balinese offered anything beyond mild approval or skepticism of my venture. Any attempt to restrict the boundaries of their responses to exclude the affective characters, specific dances, and ritual contexts I have surveyed was counterintuitive from their point of view. Some cautioned that it was unproductive to discuss *neliti* or *pokok* melody separately from the other strata, stressing that the entire musical fabric was what one needed to evaluate, and beyond this the dance movements, story, and so on. Other factors need to be assessed too, such as the tuning, instruments, and the skill of the performers.

Composer Wayan Beratha answered my queries with a discussion of melodic balance (*keseimbangan*), relating the concept as he applied it to music to ideas about multiple dimensions of balance in Balinese philosophy.[31] Practi-

---

31. Balinese concepts of balance are elucidated with reference to numerical divisions of order, ranging from ideas of the world as a unity, through dualism (good/evil, visible/invisible, mountainward/seaward, and so on), three dimensions (upper, middle, and lower worlds, Hindu trinity), and continuing to ten dimensions.

cally speaking, balance in melody for him means judging the proper distribution of the five tones, knowing (especially in longer meters) when to stay around a given tone, when to move, and at what rate. Returning inevitably to character and association in relation to dance music, he prescribed melodies in the upper register for feminine, refined, or sweet characters and those lower down for male strong characters, a differentiation borne out in practice in a general way. Beratha makes a sharp distinction between composing instrumental music in *lelambatan* form, in which the meter governs many choices, and the freer *tabuh kreasi*. In the latter, he explained, there is little established terminology, and the *kawitan-pengawak-pengecet* model cannot be applied with much rigor. In all of his assessments, Beratha invoked personal expression and feeling (*rasa*) as the dominant factor in the act of composing (see also Sadra 1991:110).

My inquiries in this area led me to two related subjects: melodic identity and what I shall call concepts of melodic "quality." Exploring them improved my listening skills, and gave me extra confidence that my observations were sufficiently grounded in the music. Using these concepts is an aurally significant way to refine the symmetry/asymmetry classes and use them to explain topic-structure interaction in a satisfying way. As in the analytical interlude, this preliminary discussion is limited to *neliti* melody. Here and in the rest of part 2 I try to probe some fundamentals of composition: how are melodies and drum patterns shaped, and what sorts of displacement and motion characterize them? Are these factors tied to genre or topic? Which aspects are solely syntagmatic? Though few musicians anywhere consciously ponder this kind of information, those with well-honed listening skills are nonetheless sensitized to these phenomena.

Melodic Identity

Despite the growing importance of the individual composer in this century, it remains inappropriate to speak of an authoritative version of a Balinese composition. In a manner characteristic of many orally transmitted musics, regional variation is the norm in Bali. Such variation takes many forms. Two different *sekaha* may know the same composition but call it by a different name, such as the *calonarang* melody for the dance of the *sisyan,* or witch's disciples, which is called *Ngalap Basé* in *banjar* Binoh and *Ampin Lukun* in Teges. Conversely, the same name may be used for two compositions that are related only marginally, if at all. This is true of the *topeng* melody *Jaran Sirig* as performed in *banjar* Blangsinga and central Denpasar. In the majority of cases the name is the same and all of the major structural features identical, but details such as *angsel* ordering, number of internal repetitions, or tempo may vary. Drumming and elaboration patterns vary from region to region, or even from year to year within the same *sekaha. * Sections of a composition may be reshuffled, omitted, or added depending on musicians' or dancers' changing preferences. Some instrumental compositions clearly stand alone and are known only by one *sekaha* or in a single region, though such compositions routinely borrow or vary material from other ones. There are many more possibilities.

Regional or village tastes tend to assert themselves in the ways noted above; that is, in terms of nomenclature, surface detail, or the ordering and selection of formal components. Two elements, however—*pokok* (or *neliti*) melody and colotomic meter—are much less variable. Within corresponding segments of two variants of the same composition, *pokok* tend to vary only minimally and the meter not at all (though small details of internal gong punctuation may differ from place to place). A well-known melody like *pengecet legong Lasem,* for example (figs. 6.3U and 7.12), is virtually the same everywhere and has the same meter, however much elaboration strata or choreography may vary. Yet a few court genre melodies, notably shorter ones used for dance (the primary sources of character topics), do have recognized variants. Because of the insight it affords into fine-grained details of hearing and distinguishing between two closely related musical objects, this is a significant phenomenon worth isolating for a moment.

The melodies that exist in variant forms are precisely those that are most widely played. Among the short dance melodies in this group are *baris* and *topeng* ostinati, and parts of longer dances like *Gabor* and *legong keraton*. If certain kinds of structural changes are made to one of these melodies, the resultant can be accepted as a variant. Other kinds push it over the edge to where it becomes a different melody altogether, recognizable as being "like" the original but distinct from it. The controlling factors are the same ones that I have stressed as analytically significant thus far (gong tone, other stressed tones, and overall contour).[32] Not all of these identity-bearing elements need to be held constant for identity to be maintained, but the strength (or ambiguity) of topical reference between two melodies varies in proportion with the amount of similarity between these elements.

The first four versions of the *neliti* for the solo *Baris* dance shown in figure 5.4 all share the 8-beat meter *gilak*. In *gilak* either the same large gong or—if

---

32. My judgments on this issue are a distillation of the answers to many questions that I have asked my teachers on the subject. I acknowledge a chicken-and-egg component to the conclusions I have drawn: is a given variant "unacceptable" because of structural changes to an "acceptable" version that are deemed too extreme, or are the structural changes "unacceptable" simply because no such variant (yet) exists? None of my teachers came down squarely on this issue, nor did any fully disallow a melody on the basis of structural factors alone (except for meter) as long as the variant at least had some kind of overt connection to the original. The key word here is "fully." In discussing, for example, the *Baris* melody analyzed below, none said that a given variant "could not" be *Baris*. It could, but neither they nor anyone they knew had ever heard of such a version, and they would not choose to use that melody for *Baris* unless it was for a *kreasi baru* of some kind (in which case the melody would have acquired a character topic reference to the original). It is these preferences—clearly based on what is comfortable and familiar rather than any explicit structural criteria—that I interpret here.

Figure 5.4. Regional variations of *Baris neliti*, and two unacceptable versions. A. Peliatan village. B. Singapadu village. C. Tunjuk village. D. McPhee (1966:414).

the *gamelan* has one—a second, differently tuned large gong, is played at the midpoint of the tune. Two *kempur* strokes, anacrusis to the ending gong, fall in between *calung* tones on beats 5 and 7. In addition, each of the four has the same final gong tone (*dAng*) midpoint tone (*dong*), and nearly the same tessitura, differing only in the details of contour. The fifth, judged unsatisfactory as a variant by those whom I queried, is an exact transposition up one scale tone. The sixth, also rejected, preserves the gong tone but alters the midpoint. Both are suggestive of *Baris* because of what they preserve, though even at the proper tempo, with the addition of appropriate drumming and elaboration, neither could be made to fit the bill. It is not that there is anything compositionally wrong with them: they were not dismissed as poorly composed. Used in a new composition, they could be heard as character topics.

Altering meter brings more drastic results. Any of the first four melodies used with a different gong cycle would offer a very bewildering experience for an accustomed listener, so strong is the association of meter and melody. As the only completely invariant factor determining identity, it is axiomatic that specific melodies are inseparable from their colotomic patterns. The martial associations of the *gilak* meter comprise the single most important component of *Baris*'s affect, and substituting a different gong pattern deprives the melody of any topical power. But meters are not exclusively associated with specific melodies: there are literally hundreds of other *gilak* melodies in the current repertoire and more composed all the time. Most of these do not evoke *Baris* directly. Only those *gilak* melodies ending on *dAng* and bisected by *dong* are "reserved" especially for *Baris* associations. Other changes to the melodic contour are tolerable if they do not disturb these two elements.

There are other similar instances. Melodies with midpoints and endings on *dUng* using the 8-beat *bapang* meter inevitably suggest the *penasar* character in *topeng* plays, while ones with a similar structure beginning on *deng* invoke the magical dragon *Barong*. In some melodies the features held constant and the ones allowed to change are different. Melodies for the stock solos *Topeng Keras* and *Jauk Longgor* have variants in which the entire tune is shifted up or down one scale tone. In these cases no modifications of contour are made at all, as if to compensate for the changed gong tone.

These examples suggest that a specific melody wedded to a specific meter has a particular affect, and that the fixity of the melody's most important structural features delineates an area within which the affect remains in focus. The more these features are distorted, the more the affect loosens and the music becomes susceptible to other moods and associations. Beyond *pokok* and meter, of course, other features (drumming pattern, elaboration, and so on) can also modify the associations. The full range of criteria provide each melody with a much more multidimensional cluster of identity-forming components than has been observed here. But these provisional considerations reconfirm that a melody's contour and the tones stressed within it are fundamental analytical concerns.

Melodic "Quality"

Crediting his teachers Nyoman Rembang and Gusti Madé Putu Griya, Wayan Rai gave me some tools for discussing the "quality" (hereafter removed from quotations) of melodic motion by impressing the importance of the terms *ngubeng* and *majalan* on me. The former, meaning literally to go around and around or to spin one's wheels, connotes something like "static" or "immobile." Rai uses it both neutrally, as to describe a melody that stays on a given tone for a prolonged period, and for critique, as for example in disapproval of a drummer using an inadequate stock of patterns. *Majalan* is *ngubeng*'s complement: to go or progress in a certain direction. To Rai this suggests a consistent rate of scale-tone turnover in melody, or, following the example given for *ngubeng*, fluid and constantly changing drum patterns. Both words may be used as adjectives. Applied to melody they describe rate of movement between scale tones; hence I will call their domain of applicability the kinetic quality of a melody.

Ngubeng and *majalan* become manifest in different ways depending on the length of the melody, and may also take effect in different ways simultaneously: elaboration strata can have a quality of stasis or motion different from that of the *neliti*. Though the terms are value-free and their meanings context-determined when applied to melody in this way, a short melody can be grating if too *ngubeng*, and a long melody fails to succeed without some points of repose. In most situations the two qualities are in dialog, each either rising periodically to predominance or striking a balance. They typically coexist on different levels of structure as well. The *Pelayon neliti,* for instance, is *ngubeng* at a high level, in the sense that it is fast, repeated many times, and each *gongan* is brief. The gong is heard nearly continuously owing to the temporal proximity of successive strokes, and this adds to the music's sense of throbbing immobility.[33] Reiterated, irregular spiraling back to the tone *dIng* makes the surface *ngubeng,* but in another way it is *majalan* because there is melodic change on every beat. The intermediate levels of *jegogan* and *calung* are more *majalan* in character because they contain no repetition at all.

In short melodies *ngubeng* is not usually expressed through literal repetition of successive *neliti* tones, though some few melodies do this. The *jegogan* provide clues. The gong and midpoint are the only *jegogan* stresses in 8-beat *gilak* and *bapang,* and there is only the one coinciding with gong in the tiny 2- or 4-beat *batel* meters. Most *batel neliti* consist of the regular alternation of two tones, one of them stressed by *jegogan.* In *gilak* and *bapang* there is no time for the *neliti* to stray too far, yet it must also have a good shape and not stay on or around a single tone for too long. In most cases a movement in one direction between gong and midpoint will be mirrored in the second half, often tagged with a "kink" in the symmetry (as in the fourth point made about *Pelayon*).

Sixteen-beat melodies can usually be divided into two segments marked by *jegogan.* Thirty-two-beat melodies may have four stresses or eight. In *kebyar* 16-beat melodies are typically marked at 4-beat intervals by the common gong-pattern [(G) . . . P . . . t . . . P . . . G]; or they may be of the shortest *pegongan pengawak*-type, *tabuh telu* (see fig. 7.1). The same principles apply as in *bapang* and *gilak,* but there are more kinds of contours. There is sufficient breadth to expand the tessitura and explore contrasting kinds of melodic motion. Some segments may be literally *ngubeng,* staying on or around one pitch, while others function to usher the melody toward a new stress tone. The tight intertwining of *ngubeng* and *majalan* loosens in extended cycles. Like shifting planes, the areas of stasis and motion come into focus independently and show affinity for particular regions of the meter. Gong punctuations and *jegogan* stresses exert "pull" or "gravity" on melodic motion, causing the regions that lead up to them to be more *majalan* in character. The more important the arrival in relation to the overall meter the more powerful the force exerted. Just after such arrivals the pull is weakest. The melody may then transform instantaneously and become totally static, as if unable to budge from a single tone. As the next arrival gets closer, motion gradually accelerates.

Extra dimension is added to the music when different strata display different kinetic qualities. Shorter melodies, *ngubeng* or not, may be given *ngubeng* interlocking elaboration in which a basic pattern that is two beats long is repeated continuously at the same scale-tone level for the full *gongan.* Or, as in

---

33. Maceda 1986 suggests that such structures constitute a uniquely Southeast Asian model of musical time.

figure 4.1's *Pelayon* example, elaboration may move at the same rate as the *pokok* line. In the *Wilet Mayura* fragment, the elaboration was *more* kinetic than the *neliti* and competed for prominence with it.

Elaboration tends to be simpler and more *ngubeng* in long *pengawak*. This is an aspect of the sense of continuity and "regularity" that I discussed with relation to the *Pelayon* excerpt. *Ngubeng* elaboration deflects attention away from itself and back onto the melody that generated it. The fleshing out of the *trompong* or *ugal* part may contribute to this, too. *Neliti*, it should be remembered, is an idealized form of *pokok* elaboration. In practice, *trompong* or *ugal* melodies are shaped with great care. *Ngubeng* quality in a *pokok* line is inevitably clarified when the *trompong* or *ugal* part suddenly coalesces around a single pitch, heightening the effect of stasis by repeatedly tracing a motive-like design around it. When such a motive breaks, the sense of moving toward *majalan* quality is palpable.

One additional issue of melodic quality should be addressed: I will call it *tonal quality*. Affect and other factors aside, how does the amount of scale-tone melodic displacement between gong tone and midpoint tone (or other significant arrivals) affect quality? Does increasing displacement correspond to a sense of having traveled "farther" or to a more "distant" tonal region? If not, what is an acceptable metaphor for describing the motion? Put in terms of an example, what is the difference in quality between three 8-beat melodies of identical meter, each beginning on *dIng,* one of which has its midpoint also on *dIng,* another displaced up by one scale tone to *dong* (or down to *dAng*), and the third displaced up by two scale tones to *deng* (or down to *dUng*)? The first melody is strongly *ngubeng* because of the absence of melodic contrast at the *jegogan* level. The last two are more *majalan,* but how can we distinguish between their qualities? It seems reasonable that they should be distinguishable, if only because—as I explained in chapter 2—each of the five *pélog* tones comprises a discrete region of tonal color, associated with its own cardinal point, and in many ways discontiguous with the other four. Thought of this way, each kind of scale-tone displacement is a move both literally up or down and *in a different cardinal direction*. The quality of motion is thus affected by the amount of displacement.

All I am really saying is that the specific scale-tone choices in a melody *matter*. That is almost painfully obvious, but there is a hidden aspect to it that may be less clear. How do melodies that a composer invents interact with intransigent structures like the inherited colotomic meters? I will try to provide some clarification with a comparative exercise. In Western tonal music, metaphors of openness, closure, tension, and release are applied to harmonic change. The intensity of these sensations is usually correlated with the structural significance of harmonic arrivals, the precise sequence of which is different for each composition. In cyclical Balinese melodies matters are more predictable. Stress and release are governed by the gongs, which arrive in the same way for each melody in each colotomic meter, indifferent to the scale tones that they support. Applied to Western music, it would be as if there were only a limited number of harmonic progressions and harmonic rhythms, but any member of the collection of scale tones could be used in the soprano voice at each harmonic change. Each such tone would be tonally stable, unaffected by notions of consonance or dissonance, and subject only to local constraints on linear motion. The cycle of gong punctuations interacts with the linear procession of scale tones in such a way. Gongs shape the line by marking it periodically, and the scale tones that are punctuated, in turn, imbue the gongs' tonal anonymity with their "directional" character. The character of each meter is thus affected by each melody composed in it.

As I explained above in reference to *ngubeng* and *majalan,* gongs affect kinetic quality. In Western tonal music form and quality may also be linked, but differently. I can convey some sense of Balinese melodic stasis in long cycles by contrasting the *ngubeng* extension of a single tone after an internal punctuation with the quintessential cadential strategy of Western music, the prolongation of the $^6_4$ chord followed by its resolution to the dominant and the tonic. In the latter case stasis and growing tension are linked prior to the cadence. In *gamelan,* accumulating tension precedes the cadence, but stasis comes after it. When a $^6_4$ chord resolves, it is a sudden release, characteristically leading to some kind of melodic motion in a stable key area. A gong provides comparable release, but melodic motion pauses serenely in the area of stasis. The relaxation of *ngubeng* gradually fades as motion returns, until gong punctuation once again breaks the sense of motion, releasing it anew into an area centered on a single tone.

TAKING stock of the terrain covered in this excursion, I hope that it is now possible to imagine how small changes in a melody (or some other musical element) can affect the way a composition is perceived and the associations it evokes. The impact of certain kinds of alterations can ripple upward, ultimately bearing on the most general categories of historical and social identification that Balinese listeners have. Other kinds do not, but it is important to understand the limits within which one can move if a certain affect is the desired compositional end.

Kebyar composers sift through this Stravinskian universe of possibilities and make choices. By way of summary and review, I have outlined the various aesthetic and compositional factors that they must assess below.

Contextual and stylistic considerations for a composition precede all others:

- where, on which instruments, by whom, and for what occasion the music will be played
- appropriate general style and subgenre based on the above
- choreography, narrative, and/or vocal part, if any

The palette thus constrained, individual materials—encompassing any use of character, abstract, or quotation topics—are then chosen on the basis of:

• appropriate conventions of large-scale form and/or colotomic meter;
• elaboration, drumming, and other features of the composition suggested by the form, meter and context (including the use of stylistic topics);
• details of orchestration, *angsel,* dynamic, and tempo.

Other (most likely implicit) considerations that further affect the way the music is heard and understood:

• symmetrical or asymmetrical features of melodic design
• kinetic quality
• tonal quality

These are the frameworks that now require study, in terms of isolated melodic and drumming components in the next two chapters, and ultimately, by the end of chapter 8, for entire compositions.

6 Melody and Figuration

Gamelan gong gdé, Sulahaan,
1979. Photo: Author.

A melody, classic or contemporary, tends toward regularity, simple repetitions and even symmetry. Hence, it generally reveals distinct phrasing.

Thus it becomes evident that master composers freely introduce irregular or non-symmetrical procedures as demanded by the musical idea or the structure. Often such procedures contribute fluency and spontaneity. But they are neither arbitrary nor casual. On the contrary, a high degree of skill and sensitivity are necessary to achieve the necessary balance and proportion.

Arnold Schoenberg, *Fundamentals of Musical Composition*

THE PRIMARY goal of this chapter is to examine symmetrical class melodies. I first develop analytical tools and apply them to a set of twenty-five transcribed *neliti* and their reductions. The same tools, partly modified, are then applied to elaboration strata.[1] In the concluding third of the chapter

---

1. The terms "figuration" and "elaboration" are used interchangeably throughout.

I survey asymmetrical melodic types and examine representative examples of them.

Comparison between symmetrical melodies reveals the variety that Balinese achieve within syntactic constraints, and clarifies why certain melodies are more typical and why others test the norms. Atypical melodies do not necessarily depart stridently from these norms, but they can distort them in subtly refreshing ways. Each such melody achieves an internal referentiality that calls attention to its own idiosyncrasies. This is a different kind of signification, unlike the external allusions characterizing the four topic classes I have described.

Tonal and kinetic quality play important roles in this regard, because they determine so much about the abstract connections listeners make. These ambiguous, perhaps inchoate, yet real and significant linkages feed into a network of impressions that may or may not be directly musical. To explore this I focus on the metaphors *ngubeng* and *majalan,* using the terms as a springboard to an overarching theoretical approach that extends their conventional usage. In their original senses, the two concepts describe the relations between tones at their most autonomous and abstract. Choosing them as guides in a search for melodic coherence allows me to show how subtle changes in musical structure have manifold affective repercussions. Indeed, my ultimate motivation for this venture arises from an urge to relate music's structural properties to the ineffable sensations it can evoke. This is a creative process in which I endeavor to be faithful to my Balinese teachers, the music, and my intuition.

Analytical Conventions and Preliminaries

In selecting court genre *neliti* for analysis (fig. 6.3 A–Y) I have drawn from a variety of forms and sources in instrumental, theater, and dance music. Because most of the melodies in the selection are pre-twentieth-century in origin they are topic sources rather than tropes. Rather than organize the melodies for discussion by meter, genre of origin, or some strong identity or topic determinant such as gong tone, however, I prioritize kinetic and tonal quality. By removing the melodies from the more conventional categories with which they are usually associated I aim to spotlight the ways in which affect is shaped through structural process.

The progression of figure 6.3 is from short melodies (8 beats), which use the meters *gilak* and *bapang,* to long (256 beats) *pengawak* in *pegongan* and *pegambuhan tabuh.*[2] This layout reflects the gradual disentangling of *ngubeng*

---

2. There are *pegongan tabuh* that are longer still (*tabuh nem,* 384 beats; and *tabuh kutus,* 512 beats; see fig. 7.1B), but aside from this feature they do not differ in essence from their *tabuh empat* cousins, and so have been bypassed here to conserve space.

and *majalan* features that I described at the end of the last chapter. Within each group of melodies of a given length, I use increasing gong-midpoint scale-tone displacement as the ordering criterion. Starting from melodies that have identical gong and midpoint tones, which are *ngubeng* in that sense, I continue to melodies with progressively larger scale-tone distance between gong and midpoint, which are *majalan*. Only one melody in the collection (6.3P) has a midpoint tone a full octave away from the gong tone; to my knowledge none in the repertoire lies farther than that. I reiterate, however, again invoking the metaphor of cardinal directions for scale tones, that increasing scale-tone distance does not necessarily mean more *majalan* quality exclusively. It may also mean *different majalan* quality. Articulating the "feel" of *kebyar*'s five *pélog* tones as discontiguous tonal regions within individual melodies would, however, be a highly speculative challenge that I am not yet prepared to meet. Factors affecting it include the associations that isolated scale tones carry for individual listeners (as a function of the repertoire familiar to each listener), and the tones' dispositions in the tuning of individual *gamelan*. Both issues resist generalization. Though I shall not return to this subject, the very notions of tonal independence and discontinuity as dimensions of melodic quality are enriching, and worth keeping in mind during the ensuing discussion.

Before commencing I need to introduce some theoretical terms and concepts. My purpose in formalizing the discussion is to make it possible to identify and discuss different melodic units with an efficient, generalized vocabulary. The first term, "Axis," connotes the amount of scale-tone displacement between a melody's gong tone and its midpoint tone. "Axis" always precedes an integer specifying this distance; for example, Axis 1 means that the midpoint tone is one scale tone higher than the gong tone, Axis 0 means that the two tones are the same, and Axis –1 means that the midpoint is one tone lower.

A second, more multifaceted term is "contour class," or *CC*.[3] A CC is an ordered, four-member set of integers showing the contour and interval relationships between four consecutive tones in a given stratum. The four tones themselves are referred to as the "CC-group." The last of the four must be a stressed tone. Stressed tones in each stratum are those obtained by beginning at gong and counting backward to every fourth tone (in the examples stressed

---

3. The term "contour class" is adapted from Michael Friedmann's original formulation. He defines it as "[a]n ordered series that indicates what registral position a pitch occupies in a musical unit. If n = the number of pitches in a musical unit, then the highest pitch in that unit is signified in the CC by n – 1. The lowest pitch is signified by 0. For example, the theme of the Finale of Mozart's *Jupiter* Symphony has CC <0–1–3–2>" (1985:246).

Friedmann uses dashes to connect the elements in each CC. In his system all integers are positive and 0 is always the lowest pitch. For clarity, I have substituted commas for the dashes because in my system 0, the final tone, is not necessarily the lowest pitch, and CC elements are represented by negative numbers if they are lower than the final tone.

tones are shown with open noteheads and unstressed tones with black ones).[4] The number of CC-groups in a stratum is thus equal to the number of tones in the stratum divided by four. In each CC the last member is set to 0, making the stressed tone a point of orientation. The first three members are integers measuring the scale-tone distance between each of the first three tones in the CC-group and the final one. Setting each final tone to 0 makes it possible to compare CCs in terms of their contour relationships, regardless of their stratum of origin or specific scale-tone content. It also allows me to speak of scale-tone movement in terms of generalized numbers of scale tones rather than by using scale-tone solmization syllables.[5] Thus, a pair of identical CCs have CC-groups that are either the same or transpositions of one another; and CCs whose corresponding elements all sum to the same number (indicating equivalent scale-tone movement in opposite directions) are inversions.

Temporal distance between CC-group members depends on the host stratum's level of abstraction from the *neliti*. *Neliti* CC-group members are contiguous at the beat (quarter-note) level. The *neliti* of an 8-beat melody has two CC-groups, but in the *calung* stratum, where there are four tones, there is only one CC-group. Its members are 2 beats apart. At the other extreme, a 256-beat melody has 64 *neliti* CC-groups. Reducing to omit all of the odd-numbered notes in such a *neliti* would reveal the *calung* stratum of 128 tones, which in turn has 32 CC-groups. Like the *calung* level in an 8-beat melody, these are also 2 beats apart. And so on down to strata of 64, 32, 16, 8, and 4 tones, which contain, respectively, 16, 8, 4, 2, and 1 CC-groups whose members are 4, 8, 16, 32, and 64 beats apart. Note that these strata may come under analytical discussion *even if they are not explicitly stated* by an instrument in the *gamelan*. In a 256-beat *lelambatan* melody, for example, *calung* generally play 128 times, *jegogan* 32, and there are 8 points of colotomic punctuation; but there are important melodic phenomena to investigate in the 64, 16, and 4-note strata too, so these are included in my transcriptions.

Specific CCs are identified with the notation

$$CCx(y) = \{a,b,c,0\}$$

where x is the total number of tones in the stratum, and y denotes which CC-group in the x stratum is referred to. The maximum for x is equivalent to the number of beats in the *gongan,* and the maximum for y is (x ÷ 4). Shown in curly brackets, a, b, c, and 0 are the four members of the CC. In a 256-beat

---

4. In Java, the term for each four-note segment of the *balungan* ending on a stressed tone is *gatra.* In Bali there is no comparable term. *Gatra,* however, is used only for the *balungan* and theorists do not apply it, as I do with CC, to other strata and levels of density.

5. It should not be inferred from this practice that melodies can be transposed freely without changing their character. Far from it: as I have shown, the specific gong-tone and scale-tone sequence of each melody is central to its identity. But introducing these conventions allows me to compare scale-tone contours between any two melodies, a useful procedure.

First quadrant

Neliti	CC256	(256 tones)	...1	...2	...3	...4	...5	...6	...7	...8	...9	...10	...11	...12	...13	...14	...15 ...16
Calung	CC128	(128 tones)	. . . 1	. . . 2	. . . 3	. . . 4	. . . 5	. . . 6	. . . 7	. . . 8							
	CC64	(64 tones)	. . . 1	. . . 2	. . . 3	. . . 4											
Jegogan	CC32	(32 tones)	. . . 1	. . . 2													
	CC16	(16 tones)	. . . 1														
	CC8	(8 tones)	.														
	CC4	(4 tones)	.														

Second quadrant

	CC256, cont.	...17	...18	...19	...20	...21	...22	...23	...24	...25	...26	...27	...28	...29	...30	...31 ...32
	CC128, cont.	. . . 9	. . . 10	. . . 11	. . . 12	. . . 13	. . . 14	. . . 15	. . . 16							
	CC64, cont.	. . . 5	. . . 6	. . . 7	. . . 8											
	CC32, cont.	. . . 3	. . . 4													
	CC16, cont.	. . . 2														
	CC8, cont.	. . . 1														
	CC4, cont.	.														

Third quadrant

	CC256, cont.	...33	...34	...35	...36	...37	...38	...39	...40	...41	...42	...43	...44	...45	...46	...47 ...48
	CC128, cont.	. . . 17	. . . 18	. . . 19	. . . 20	. . . 21	. . . 22	. . . 23	. . . 24							
	CC64, cont.	. . . 9	. . . 10	. . . 11	. . . 12											
	CC32, cont.	. . . 5	. . . 6													
	CC16, cont.	. . . 3														
	CC8, cont.	.														
	CC4, cont.	.														

Fourth quadrant

	CC256, cont.	...49	...50	...51	...52	...53	...54	...55	...56	...57	...58	...59	...60	...61	...62	...63 ...64
	CC128, cont.	. . . 25	. . . 26	. . . 27	. . . 28	. . . 29	. . . 30	. . . 31	. . . 32							
	CC64, cont.	. . . 13	. . . 14	. . . 15	. . . 16											
	CC32, cont.	. . . 7	. . . 8													
	CC16, cont.	. . . 4														
	CC8, cont.	. . . 2														
	CC4, cont.	1														

Figure 6.1. Positions of CC-groups in a 256-beat melody. Going down the left edge of the table, the total number of tones in each stratum is shown as the x coefficient in CC notation, CCx (y). The numbers in each horizontal row designate that stratum's y coefficients, the points of arrival of metrically stressed tones in the stratum. Dots show the three unstressed tones leading to each stressed tone.

melody such as that schematized in figure 6.1, the designation CC32(8) = {1,0,−1,0} would be understood as follows: 32 refers to the thirty-two-tone *jegogan* stratum, and 8 refers to the final CC-group in that stratum, which includes the 29th through 32nd *jegogan* tones. The first member in the CC indicates that the 29th *jegogan* tone is one scale step above the 32nd, the 30th is the same as the 32nd, and the 31st is one step below the 32nd. (The 32nd tone in a 32-note stratum is also, of course, the gong tone.)

A stratum with four tones has only one CC, that is, CC4(1), or simply CC4. The CC4 shows the intervals between tones at quarter-way points in the *gongan,* partitioning it into what I shall call quadrants. The last member of a

CC4-group is the gong tone and the second one is the melody's Axis tone; all four members coincide with important *jegogan* stresses. This level of abstraction is of particular importance. In an 8-beat melody, the CC4 represents every other tone in the *neliti,* but in a 256-beat one it describes relations between tones 64 beats apart and is much farther in the background. There are, of course, the various intermediate melody lengths to consider as well. Because CC4 tones often coincide with colotomic punctuations they constitute an important musicians' memory aid, especially in long cycles (Brinner 1995:190). For analytical purposes, grasping CC4 similarity or equivalence between pairs of melodies is a valuable aural skill, particularly if the melodies are of different dimensions. This is because the structural relationship thus perceived provides a meaningful starting point for their further comparison.

Since any of the *ugal*'s ten tones may be used in the *neliti,* it would seem to be the case that CC members can have numbers as high as 9 or as low as −9. Consideration of Balinese melodic style allows us to exclude most of these possibilities almost at once, however. Few *neliti* of any length have an ambitus of more than eight tones total. In many cases, such as the by now paradigmatic figure 4.1, there is a balance of tones above and below the gong tone. The following two tendencies, based on a study of the 519 CCs derivable from the melodies in figure 6.3 (and many others not included in the sample), explain constraints on melodic syntax further:[6]

1. The first three members of most CC-groups lie no more than two scale tones above or below the final one. In a fair number of cases one and only one of them may be three tones away. CC with members beyond ±3 are unusual: the sample contains only ten such CCs, distributed among five melodies.[7]

2. The probability that the members of a CC-group will form a conjunct segment when arranged in scalar order is strong at all levels. But at each suc-

---

6. The total number of CCs in a given melody can be expressed as $(x/2) - 1$, where x is the number of beats. Thus an 8-beat melody has three CCs (two in the *neliti* stratum and one in the *calung* stratum), a 16-beat melody has seven CCs (four in the *neliti,* two at the eight-tone level, and one at the quadrant level), and so on. The following shows how the total number of CCs in example 6.3 was calculated.

# of beats in cycle	# of CCs in each	# of examples	Total CCs
8	3	8	24
16	7	8	56
32	15	4	60
64	31	2	62
128	63	1	63
256	127	2	254
Totals		25	519

7. The ten are fig. 6.3K, CC8(2); P, CC8(1), 8(2), and CC4; T, CC16(4); U, CC64(3), 64(5), and 32(6); and Z, 32(6) and 16(3).

4-Tone				3-Tone			2-Tone		1-Tone
			3						
		2	2			2			
	1	1	1		1	1		1	
0	0	0	0	0	0	0	0	0	0
−1	−1	−1		−1	−1		−1		
−2	−2			−2					
−3									
Type									
1	2	3	4	5	6	7	8	9	10

Figure 6.2. CC-group scale-segment types

cessive level of abstraction from the *neliti* the possibility that they will form a disjunct segment is slightly greater.

Figure 6.2 shows the ten conjunct scale segment types from which the great majority of CC-groups are drawn. The ten are displayed on the chart vertically as if on a staff, and so that the ending tone 0 is visible across the middle as a common point of orientation. They are of four sizes: four-tone, three-tone, two-tone, and one-tone. In all ten types the tones may come in any order save for the last, which must of course be 0. Four-tone segments (types 1–4) may use all available tones, or one of the tones may be omitted and replaced by a repetition of one of the other three. In three-tone segment types 5 and 7 the middle tone (−1 or 1) may be omitted, leaving a pair of tones two scale steps apart (see below under 2- and 4-beat *batel* melodies). In type 6 all of the tones are used and one of them must be repeated to form a complete four-element CC-group. Three-tone configurations are characteristic at all levels of structure and in elaborating parts (see especially figs. 6.12–14). Types 8 and 9 must by definition always occur complete. One-tone segments (type 10; four consecutive repeated tones) are common in the *ngubeng* portions of longer *neliti*.

Analytical Commentary on 4-, 8-, and 16-beat Melodies/Character Topic Sources

2- and 4-Beat Melodies

This small family of ostinati is not represented in the sample, but merits passing mention. Only melodies in the *batel pesiat* (fighting music) meter may be this brief. Such tunes often underpin scenes of battle in dance or drama. They are played fast, repeated many times, and inflected over the course of the repetitions, constantly changing drumming and *angsel* to emphasize dance movements and vary the musical texture. Gong finishes each cycle, and *klentong* marks the midpoint. Most *batel pesiat neliti* are simple alternations between

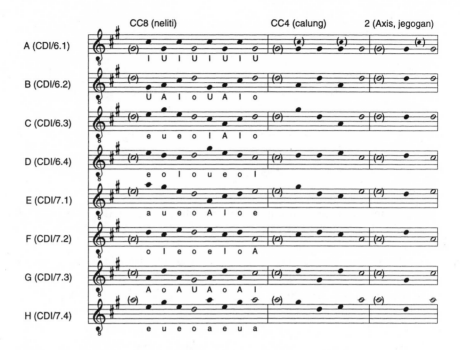

Figure 6.3. Twenty-five melodies in *neliti* reduction. A-H. Eight-beat melodies in *neliti* reduction (CDI/6–7).
Axis 0: A. *Penasar (Bapang Gdé)*. B. *Bapang Jauk Keras*. C. *Gabor*.
Axis 1, –1: D. *Gilak Jagul*. E. *Gegilakan*.
Axis 2, –2: F. *Gilak Baris*. G. *Bapang Garuda*.
Axis –3: H. *Gilak Baris II. (Continued)*

two tones either one or two steps apart. Because there are only two or four tones the only CC reflects the *neliti* itself. A typical *batel pesiat* CC would be {2,0} (for the special case of a 2-beat *neliti*) or {2,0,2,0}. The *ngubeng* quality, rapid tempi, irregularly spaced *angsel,* and overlapping gong stroke decays in *batel pesiat* combine to produce high dramatic intensity.

8-Beat Melodies

Of the eight 8-beat melodies shown (fig. 6.3A-H; CDI/6–7), all but D and E (which come from *lelambatan*) are important character topic sources. All of the melodies reveal characteristic CC shapes at both *neliti* and *calung* (CC4) levels; only the CC4 of H has a member beyond ±2.

A is the melody for the *penasar* clown-attendant of *topeng* masked-dance-drama and B is the melody for the demonic *Jauk Keras*. F and H are from the solo *Baris* dance. These four, like most male dance forms, are ostinati unattached to any larger composition. C comes in the final section of *Gabor,* when a group of female dancers crisscross the performance area dispersing flower petals over the congregants (or audience). G is one of a pair of so-called *garuda* melodies at the end of the *legong Lasem* story, where the *condong* dancer, absent since before the *pengawak*, returns costumed with the wings of a raven sent to foretell King Lasem's demise. C and G are parts of long, complex compositions, typical for female dance forms. The nature of the interaction between structure and character topic in each of these cases can be more fully assessed with reference to elaboration and drumming, but some determinants are present here.

Conflation of *ngubeng* and *majalan* qualities typifies melodies of this length. All of the examples are *majalan* in the sense that there are no successive repeated tones in any of the *neliti*. *Neliti* A is particularly *ngubeng* because of its iterated 2-beat cell, and correspondingly kinesthetic. This fits with the *penasar* routine it underpins, which prefaces the drama. *Penasar* and his sidekick-brother *Kartala* use narrative, comic banter, dance, and elaborate song to set the tone, while the *gamelan*'s minimal vamp continues behind them as if coiled in tension. The parenthesized notes in the *calung* and *jegogan* strata of A are optional tones many *gamelan* use to provide some (unstressed) motion in the lower parts. The *Jauk* melody B, with its iterated 4-note cell, is also *ngubeng*, though less than A.

The contrast between the qualities of C and D is revealing. C is Axis 0, and therefore *ngubeng*, but very *majalan* (and inversionally symmetrical) at the *calung* and *neliti* levels. D is Axis 1, has a repeated note in CC4, and has an imperfectly symmetrical *neliti* (moving the midpoint down two tones would make the two halves transpositionally equivalent). One cannot say which of the two is more kinetic, for both possess different aspects of kinetic quality at different structural levels. E, at Axis −1, is otherwise very closely related to C, while the palindromic F, at Axis 2, is related to D.

G's −2 Axis makes an otherwise repetitive *neliti* come alive, for it takes until the final tone to fill in the contiguous four-tone scale segment implied by the preceding tones. The high-register, Axis −3, imperfect symmetry of H's *neliti* makes it somewhat unusual, and heightens the effectiveness of its contrast with F's lower range and narrower axis. In performance, F is the "main" tune and H supplants it at select moments of highest dance intensity.

It is noteworthy that all of the Axis 0, 8-beat melodies are *bapang*-type meters; the only other *bapang* is G. The remainder (D, E, F, and H) are *gilak*. In *bapang* the midpoint is punctuated with *klentong*, while *gilak* uses a second gong at the midpoint, preferably one of different pitch. This is reflected by the midpoint pitch displacement in *gilak* axes, and gives the melodies a driving tonal quality that goes hand in hand with their martial associations. *Gilak* drive is intensified by the asymmetric *kempur* punctuation on beats 5 and 7.

16-Beat Melodies

In this group (fig. 6.3 I-P; CDI/8–15) five of the eight (I, K, M, O, and P) carry *gong gdé* associations and three (J, L, and N) trace to *gambuh* or *legong*. Char-

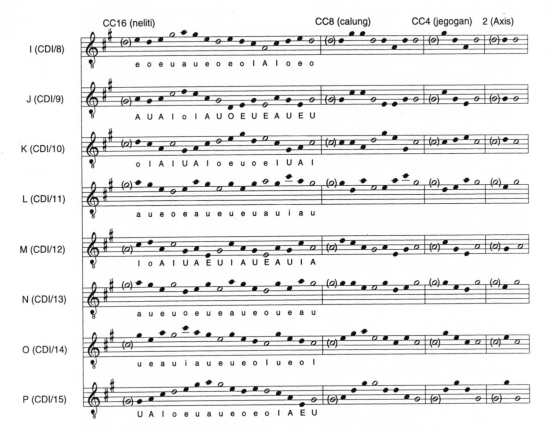

(*Fig. 6.3 continued*) I-P. Sixteen-beat melodies in *neliti* reduction (CDI/8-15).
Axis 0: I. *Pengecet Tabuh Pisan Dong* (STSI Academy). J. *Oleg Tumulilingan* (Peliatan village).
Axis 1, −1: K. *Topeng Keras.* L. *Condong legong.* M. *Pengecet Tabuh Telu* (Pindha village). N. *Perong Condong* (*gamelan gambuh*, Pedungan village).
Axis 2: O. *Pengecet Tabuh Pisan Bangun Anyar.*
Axis 5: P. *Gegilakan* (STSI Academy).

acter topic sources include the *gilak* K, which is the melody for the stock character *Topeng Keras* (masked dance of a strong male), and L and N, the *condong* of
legong keraton and *gambuh* respectively. J is newer, part of the *tari lepas Oleg Tumulilingan* composed in the early 1950s, and notable for its structural similarity
(at CC4 level) to the *Gabor* melody of C. This fits, as I noted in chapter 5, with
Oleg's affect. The remaining melodies (I, M, O, and P) are instrumental. I and M
are both *klasik lelambatan pengecet* and O is from a recent *kreasi lelambatan*. P is
a free-standing *gilak.* (In 16-beat *gilak* the colotomic pattern may be either the
8-beat pattern played twice, in which case a gong falls every four beats and *kempur* at beats 5, 7, 13, and 15, or else the 8-beat pattern augmented to twice its
length, with gong at beats 8 and 16 and kempur at 10 and 14.)

As in 8-beat melodies, *neliti* activity here is *majalan* to the extent that there are no successive repeated tones. At the CC8 level the appearance of repeated tones in all except M demonstrates embedded *ngubeng* quality, though this quality recedes again in most of the CC4. This kind of affinity between the background structure (the CC4) and the *neliti* is especially characteristic of 16-beat melodies. In longer melodies *ngubeng* is increasingly evident in the *neliti,* but background motion tends to remain *majalan,* which suggests a fundamental rate of tonal movement in the sparser strata that is common to melodies of all lengths.

As a consequence of the "kinetic rhythm" provided by the CC4, 16-beat *neliti* readily submit to aural division into quadrants which show a variety of symmetrical relations to one another. In I, CC16(2) and CC16(3) are both {3,2,1,0}; together they span an octave tracing the ambitus of the tune as a whole, though only the lower octave tone is stressed. The outer quadrants CC16(1) and CC16(4) are retrograde inversions of one another. Their more restricted contours keep the region around gong more *ngubeng* and the center of the tune *majalan.* Such dovetailing of tonal qualities before and after gong is a very tactile manifestation of the gong's structural weight, and is common to many of the melodies in this group, as well as those of 32 and 64 beats (see especially V).

Neliti J is a transposition of I for its first half, but traces a different contour starting in the third quadrant. J's *neliti* leaps between beats 8–9 and 12–13, which shifts the symmetry away from the middle of the tune (as in I) and gives it greater urgency at the end. K recalls I in that an octave span is traced by steps beginning at beat 5, but here the upward motion is dramatically retraced by downward leaps. This results in the octave-wide CC8(2) of {3,2,−2,0}. This is striking when compared with the *neliti* CC, which move only within characteristic three- or four-note ranges. The CC4 range is more reflective of the *neliti,* though its initial member, 0, is a repetition of the gong tone, and hence *ngubeng.*

In the serpentine *condong* melody L a narrow range of four tones prevails until *ding* freshens the approach to gong. The CC16(2) and (4) are both {0,2,1,0} and thus transpositionally related, while the first and third quadrants are imperfect inversions (lower the tone at beat 9 two steps to "correct" this). Perfect symmetry is evident in the CC4. The CC16(1) and (2) of the *lelamba-tan* melody M are both {0,1,−1,0}, while CC16(4) is their inversion: {0,−1,1,0}. The symmetry is broken at CC16(3), the effect of which is still noticeable at the CC8 level (take the fifth tone down three steps to "correct"). Perfect symmetry emerges at CC4, as in L.

N, from *gamelan gambuh,* was clearly the source-model for the more recent L, though its four-tone range disallows the latter's surprise fifth scale tone near the end. In N, CC16(1) and (2) are transposed inversions of one another. CC16(3) is identical to CC16(1) save for the last tone, and CC16(4) reshuffles the tones in CC16(1), thus linking the first and last quadrants through common scale-tone content. The restricted ambitus of the melody makes it easy to observe two heretofore unmentioned common traits of typical 8- and 16-beat symmetrical *neliti:* the tendency to follow leaps by a step in the opposite direction, and the frequent preparation of a new tone in an unstressed position before it is reached in a stressed one.[8] Here such a tone is *dong,* the lowest of the four, which is brushed in CC16(2) and then stressed in CC16(3).

The Axis 2 melody O stands out in this group because the last three *neliti* CCs are all {3,2,1,0}, imparting an emphatic rhetorical insistence to the tune. Moreover, the last two are repetitions at the same scale-tone level, making the latter half of the melody more *ngubeng* than any other 16-beat melody in the sample. This quality is evident in all strata. Significantly, the melody is a recent one, composed by Wayan Beratha in 1978 for his prize-winning *Tabuh Pisan Bangun Anyar* (see also fig. 8.1D). It comes at the end of the piece, where the expected dynamism of the affect is heightened by the melody's atypical shape. Though Beratha gave it conventional elaboration and drumming, the idiosyncrasies are evidence of his wish (conscious or not) to distort the inherited affect of the form.

The remarkable Axis 5 trajectory of the *gilak* P makes it unusual in that sense, but the clear palindromic symmetry at CC4 and the predominantly conjunct *neliti* motion mitigate the effect. The kinetic sweep of this example is highly *majalan,* an exaggerated yet consistent version of the tonal motion characteristic of other *gilak.*

Analytical Commentary on 32- and 64-beat Melodies

32-Beat Melodies

Melodies of this length and longer (fig. 6.3Q–T; CDI/16–19) contain too many internal symmetrical patterns of interest to note them all. They also begin to develop longer internal tonal regions, as evidenced by the repeated tones at the CC16 and CC8 strata. Unlike shorter *gongan,* in which the *ugal* (or other leading instrument) may play the *neliti* virtually unadorned, the *neliti* in these examples is often abandoned in favor of a more rhythmically varied and motivic line that enlivens the points of stasis. This technique is used sparingly here and more as melodies lengthen. It is also used in shorter melodies when they are played at slow tempi. I will make some comments about this *payasan* style later in the chapter but have preserved *neliti* notation in melodies Q–Y for the sake of the current analytical focus.

Q is an extended *gilak* underpinned by back-to-back 16-beat cycles. (It is common in many kinds of *gamelan* to have melodies that last for multiple

---

8. These characteristics apply to melodic syntax in other traditions and kinds of music too numerous to mention.

(*Fig. 6.3 continued*) Q-T. Thirty-two-beat melodies in *neliti* reduction (CDI/16-19).
Axis 0: Q. *Gilak Adeng.*
Axis 1: R. *Puspanjali.*
Axis −2: S. *Telek.* T. *Ngalap Basé.*

cycles.) R is part of the *kawitan* for *Puspanjali*, a 1989 *Gabor*-like dance choreographed by Swasthi Bandem with music by Nyoman Windha. S is the *pengecet* of the female masked dance *Telek*, but it has been adapted for *kebyar* and
is also heard in many instrumental *semar pegulingan* compositions. T comprises one of a series of melodies in the composition *Ngalap Basé*, the dance of
the *sisyan* (witch's disciples) in the *calonarang*.

Q's subtitle *adeng* means slow in tempo. Unlike other *gilak* thus far examined it is Axis 0, but this is in keeping with its special regal affect. It is used for
processionals and ceremony rather than dance and is in some ways like an
abstract topic. The decidedly unabstract martial affect of *gilak* meter is partly
subverted here by the combination of the extended length (unusual for *gilak*)
and the *ngubeng* background structure. At CC4 *dang* and *dAng* are seen to be

the goals of the first and third quadrants respectively, defining the background symmetry by scale-tone octave equivalence (compare this with C, where the first and third CC4 tones are equidistant from the midpoint). The same phenomenon is evident, with imperfections, at the CC8 level. The tone deng's appearance in the same register prior to each stressed tone adds a new level of symmetry and tonal quality. This is reflected in the neliti by the fact that the last five tones of each half are the same. In the neliti an octave descent bridging CC32(4) and (5) is mirrored asymmetrically in CC32(7) and (8), the withheld dIng having been supplied in the interim.

Melody R is the most majalan of this group for it is the only one with a CC4 containing four different scale tones. The neliti is more restless overall, and has the tonal qualities of 16-beat gongan. For this reason and others it stands apart from its kin Gabor and other recent gabor-based compositions, which all use Axis 0, shorter melodies in their kawitan and pengecet sections (as in C), though all, including this one, share the same gong tone (dong). Windha remarked that he was trying to make the music bolder than its models by intensifying its kebyar-style aspects. He realized this intention by accelerating the pace of tonal movement in R and throughout the piece, and by using a metrically asymmetrical pengawak and various asymmetrical elaboration patterns. These innovations add up to a distortion of the gabor topic, and an extension of what is normative structure for gabor-style compositions.

Both S and T have iterated, untransposed CC at the beginning of the neliti, a defining structural characteristic common to many pengecet of the pelegongan-pegambuhan lineage. S preserves the same four-note range as N did for twice as long, partly by building up interest in the unstressed upper tone dang in every CC32-group before the midpoint, then abandoning it at CC32(5) and returning to confirm it at CC32(6). The melody also avoids its low tone dong completely until it arrives by surprise at the midpoint. Dong is reconfirmed at CC32(7) with the same downward $\{3,2,1,0\}$ motion. The resultant control exerted by the two axial tones—the gong tone dung for the first half of the tune, and dong for the second half—is quite strong. The melody is thus split between a pair of well-defined tonal regions, the first of which is associated with stasis at the beginning, and the second with more pronounced motion in the second half. This trait, common to pengecet, is a clear manifestation of the intermediate stages of ngubeng and majalan separation.

T is similar to S in that it is controlled by its axial tones deng and dIng, and because of the thrice repeated $\{-1,-2,-1,0\}$ CC-group at the beginning. The three tones in this group are used exclusively through the first half of the neliti. Unlike S, the midpoint tone is prepared repeatedly, subtly changing position in CC32(4), and returning for reconfirmation, as in S, at CC32(7). In the second half new stressed tones are introduced at CC32(5) and (6), as part of an expanding wedge that first confirms the only tone from the first half yet to be stressed (dong), then adds one new tone (dAng), and finally expands to include

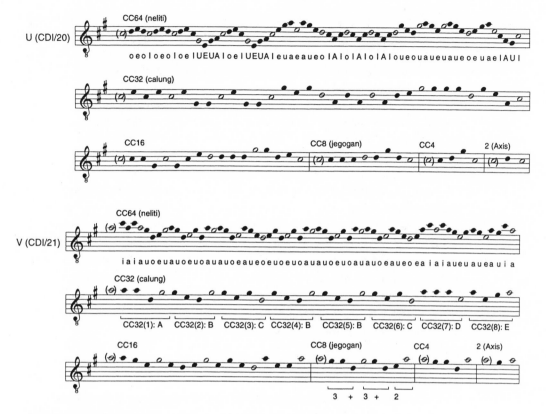

(Fig. 6.3 continued) U–V. Sixty-four-beat melodies in *neliti* reduction (CDI/20-21).
Axis 1: U. *Pengecet legong Lasem.*
Axis –1: V. *Topeng Dalem Arsawijaya.*

dUng and *dung* in CC32(7) and (8), linking them with a stepwise scalar ascent that summarizes the entire tune. I have always felt that this is a particularly haunting melody, vividly communicative of its affect of witchcraft and magic by virtue of its hypnotic repetitions, spiraling contour, and gradually accelerating motion.[9]

64-Beat Melodies

U, the well-known *pengecet* of *legong Lasem,* is a beautifully balanced example of processes I have already described, here within a more expansive architecture (fig. 6.3U–V; CDI/20–21). As in S and T, the second *neliti* CC is an untransposed iteration of the first. Here the shape is {1,2,1,0}, which serves as

---

9. Rai's teacher Gusti Madé Putu Griya told him that if the gong tone [of a melody] is *deng* and the contour of the melody stresses *deng* as well, as is the case in 6.3T, the feeling of the melody would be *aeng,* or frightening. Therefore pitch *deng* is commonly used in *calonarang* (Rai 1996:101 n. 27).

the basis for motivic *ugal* elaboration (for a version of the elaborated *neliti*, see fig. 7.12). In this longer cycle, however, the process is repeated after the midpoint at CC64s (9) through (11) with the inverted shape {−1,−2,−1,0}. Because the melody is Axis 1, this contrast is also between two scale-tone levels (*dIng* and *dong*). CC64s (3) to (8) dramatically expand the ambitus of the tune, in the process touching on the nadir *dEng* and the apex *dang* without stressing either. The range of the stressed tones in the *neliti* reaches exactly an octave, from *dUng* to *dung*. A glance at CC32 and CC16 levels reveals that for all of the *neliti* motion, prior to the midpoint only three scale tones receive stress, none of which is the midpoint tone itself. It is thus fresh when it arrives. The final quadrant *neliti* CC-groups explore the upper register with local iteration around *dung* at CC64(13) and environs; characteristically, this mirrors the low-register tessitura of the second quadrant. Further comparison of strata shows structural economy in that the CC32 stratum uses all five scale tones, the CC16 omits *dang* (with *dung* in both octaves), and CC8 and CC4 omit *deng* as well. It also filters out the complexities of the *neliti* to reveal different kinds of *ngubeng* in each stratum. In the CC4, strong contrast between the halves of the *gongan* is exposed: the gong tone *dIng* is dominant until the midpoint, after which the pace of tonal change doubles en route to gong.

The anomalous V, with its five-note, *dong*-to-*ding* ambitus, is the melody for the highly refined masked dance of king Arsawijaya. Like H, it is one of the few melodies with a gong tone near the extremes of the *ugal* range. *Arsawijaya*'s contour persists in *kebyar* repertoire untransformed from its original shape in *gong gdé* repertoire for *topeng* plays. In this special group of pieces the *trompong* was not used, which limited melodic range to a single octave, as in *tua gamelan*. This accounts for *Arsawijaya*'s unique structure and the unusual intensity of its affect in the *kebyar* context. Unlike H, which also ends on *dang*, V touches on *ding*, though exclusively in the *neliti* CCs immediately preceding and succeeding gong. This characteristic dovetailing of pitch content around the gong was described above for melody I, but here it is magnified by the fact that the *ding* appears nowhere else in the tune and at no other structural level. Only the gong tone and the three tones below the gong tone are used throughout the rest of the cycle. V's CC4 is itself unremarkable, but singular structural characteristics emerge in the CC8 stratum. There, *ngubeng* treatment of the tone *dung* suggests division into 3 + 3 + 2 tones (*dung-dung-dong/dung-dung-dong/deng-dang*) rather than into a pair of conventional CCs. In CC32s this is seen to expand into an asymmetrical dialog between CC groups containing *dung* plus the two tones below it: CC32s (2), (4), and (5) are the same, as are CC32s (3) and (6), while CC32s (1), (7), and (8) are all different. The resulting [A B C B B C D E] layout of CC32s does not map precisely onto the 3 + 3 + 2 CC8 structure. There is an interesting kink in the mapping owing to the fact that A (CC32[1]) has the same final tone as B (CC32[2]), but its own content. *Arsawijaya* is a rare case where structural conflict with the meter persists far below the *neliti* level.

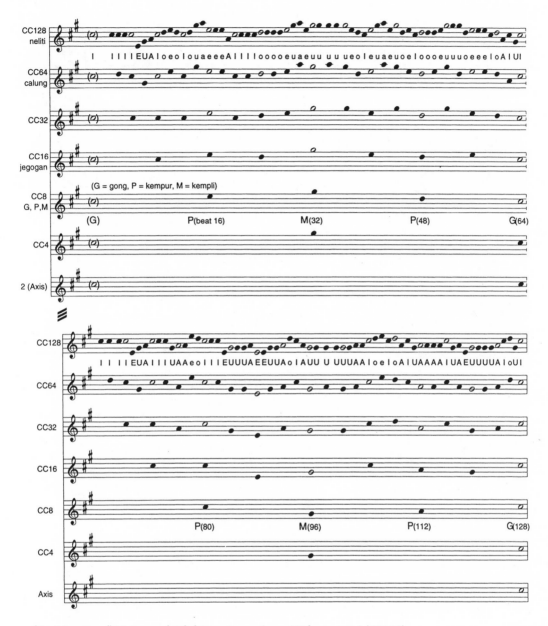

(Fig. 6.3 continued) W. *Pengawak Tabuh Pisan Bangun Anyar,* 128 beats, Axis 0 (CD1/22).

Analytical Commentary on 128- and 256-beat Melodies/Abstract Topics

The topical abstractness of melodies such as the three long *pengawak* (W, X, and Y) in the sample is an aspect of their dimension and function. Structurally, this is reflected by the drastic increase of *ngubeng* quality in the *neliti* and the

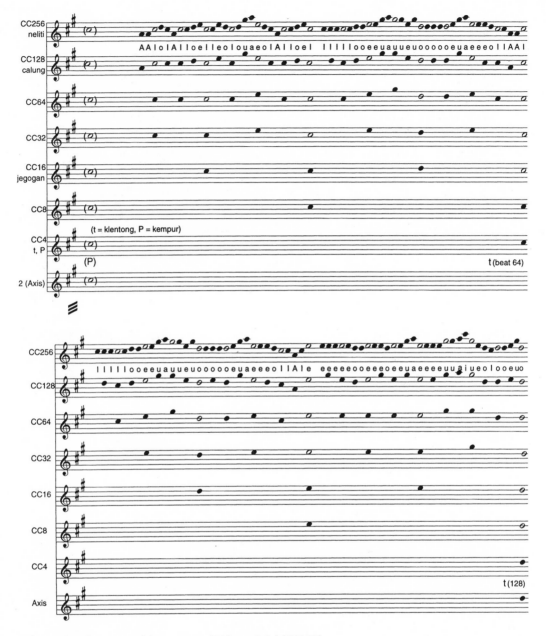

(Fig. 6.3 continued) X. *Pengawak legong Lasem;* 256 beats, Axis 1 (CDI/23).

elaborating parts. These differences are apparent at a glance, for unlike any of the examples examined thus far, there is a high incidence of repeated tones in the *neliti*. When they occur, repeated tones follow points of stress; generally speaking the greater the stress the more the repetitions. It seems that the overt stasis characterizing the *neliti* of long *pengawak* is a direct correlate of the

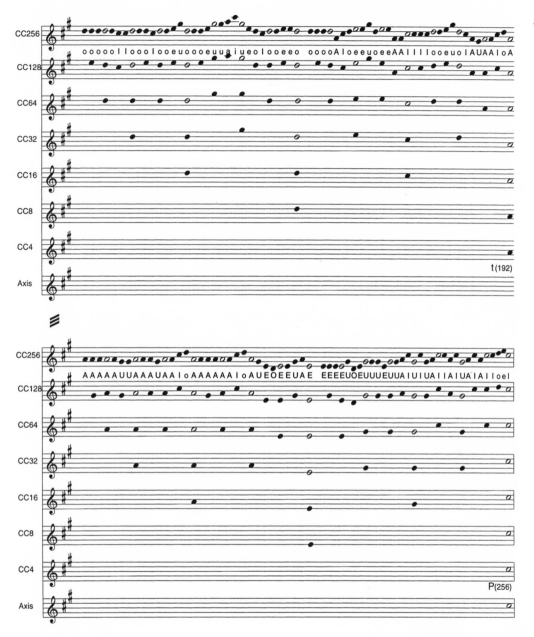

(Fig. 6.3X continued)

affects of sublimity and detachment that define the topic class. If sparser strata in these long melodies are imagined as *neliti* themselves, they bear a closer resemblance to shorter melodies than the actual *neliti* do.

The repeated tones in the *neliti* inspire most *kebyar* groups to substitute scale-tone neighbors in the unstressed positions of the concurrent *calung* line.

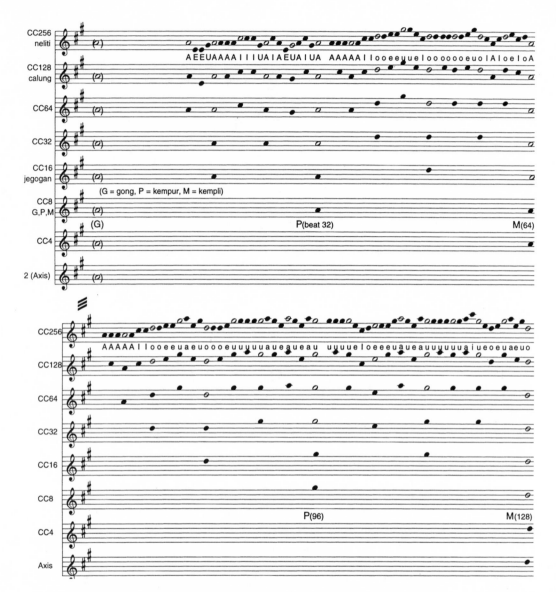

(Fig. 6.3 continued) Y. *Pengawak lelambatan Tabuh Gari;* 256 beats, Axis 2 (CDI/24)

This provides an underlying sense of local motion without subverting the affect. It does cause some unorthodox first-order vertical relations between the two strata, but these are always resolved at *jegogan* stresses. *Gong gdé* and *semar pegulingan gamelan* are more likely to preserve *neliti* repeated tones in the *calung* stratum. I have represented the *kebyar* versions in the examples.

Melody W, *Bangun Anyar,* is the *pengawak* of the 1978 composition by Wayan Beratha that ends with melody O above (CDI/22; also fig. 8.1B and CDII/1, 4:38–7:28 and 9:18–9:57). Though Beratha composed O himself,

(Fig. 6.3Y continued)

W was taken nearly verbatim from the *lelambatan* repertoire of Geladag village. It consists of a single melody spanning two metric periods of 64 beats each. Alterations that he made to the original affect only unstressed tones in the *calung* and *neliti* parts and the rate of change in the interlocking figuration.

The interaction between *ngubeng* and *majalan* in W is revealed by comparison of the CC8 and CC128 strata. In CC8(2), the gong tone *dIng* exerts control over the quadrant following the midpoint gong, but scale tones change steadily elsewhere in the stratum, giving it an overall *majalan* character. Like most longer *neliti,* the CC128 stratum has regions of strong *ngubeng. DIng* is reiterated for the entire CC128(1), then departed from and returned to at the stresses of CC128(2) and (3), and again in (5), extending into (6) before moving to *dong.* A similar process recurs after the midpoint gong as the melody descends into the lower register, and the "pull" exerted is comparably strong. CC128(17) and (18) are identical to (1) and (2), but (18)'s stress extends into (19). CC128(20) returns to *dIng* before (21) gives preconfirmation to *dUng,* the upcoming quadrant tone.

Large-scale symmetry in the melody is powerfully yet flexibly organized. At CC4 the melody's Axis 0 fulcrum is enhanced by quadrant tones an octave apart *(dung, dUng).* I pointed out an identical span between the lowest and highest stressed tones for U, but the relationship receded below *neliti* level. Here, as in the shorter Q, it is a fundamental background characteristic. Richer patterns are evident at the CC64 level, where many CCs in equivalent positions with respect to the midpoint and final gong show close symmetrical relations. CC64s (1) and (9) are identical; (2) and (10) are both {0,–2,1,0}; (6) and (14) are both {3,2,1,0}; and (8) is {–2,–1,1,0}, which is inverted at (16) to {2,1,–1,0}. CC64 (3) and (10) are imperfectly symmetrical, differing only by the direction in which the third tone moves to the last. Comparing all the strata, the inversion of the quadrant tones with respect to the axis at CC4 is seen to become gradually more imperfect moving toward the *neliti.* The CC4's sinusoidal contour is thus audible, but its working out is irregular. These relations, incidentally, are enhanced by Beratha's changes to the original tune.

X and Y are *pengawak* in the meters *tabuh telu pegambuhan* and *tabuh pat pegongan,* respectively (CDI/23–24). Both have 256 beats, though their internal punctuation differs (see fig. 7.1). *Tabuh telu* is the longest *pegambuhan* meter. Longer *pegongan* meters exist, expanding by increments of 64 beats. The only standard ones are those of 384 *(tabuh nem)* and 512 *(tabuh kutus)* beats.[10] Leaping to 256 beats from the 128 of W is a substantial shift in magnitude. While the amount of "information" in melodies of 128 beats and less increases in proportion to length, weakening bonds of melodic attraction and concomitant deceleration of motion at this length retards the increase, spreading out information more thinly. "Pull" between CC4 points is weaker. Each quadrant has substantial interrelations of its own, yet any sense of completion is held in abeyance until gong.

Pengawak of 256 beats or more do not cycle continuously but are interrupted by a brief pause after the final gong. The pause is like a fermata but it

---

10. *Tabuh lima* (320 beats) is rare; one example is the *pengawak* of *Kembang Kuning* from Pindha village. I have never heard a *tabuh pitu* (448 beats), though McPhee notated two of them in appendix 4 of *Music in Bali* (1966:406–7). Wayne Vitale (personal communication) recorded one in Tunjuk village in late 1997. *Tabuh roras,* theoretically of 768 beats, is mentioned by McPhee, but had already "become half legendary" by the 1930s (1966:88ff.).

also has metrical value, extending into and truncating the first quadrant of the next *gongan* (this explains the small gap at the beginning of the transcriptions). The ensuing *gongan* is cued by an introductory passage on *kendang*, *trompong*, or both. Though this section follows the unrivaled structural weight of the previous cycle's final gong, a typical 256-beat melody is not at its most *ngubeng* here. Instead, melody in this part of the cycle is *majalan* up to the entrance of the full *gamelan* halfway through the quadrant. The otherwise steady waves of motion from *ngubeng* to *majalan* resume once the succession of internal punctuations is underway. Motion thereafter is most static after internal gongs, and most directed leading up to the final gong.

To analyze this pair of melodies in depth would require many pages, but I hope to capture their salient features with a few comments. In X, which directly precedes U in performance, the leisurely underlying pace is disclosed by the CC16 stratum. Only three tones—*dIng, dong,* and *deng*—are used until *dAng* arrives at the end of the third quadrant. In the course of the last quadrant's contrasting focus on the low register, CC16(4) introduces *dUng* to complete the five-tone collection. Another perspective on this phenomenon is audible in the CC8 stratum: CC8(1), leading to the Axis 1 midpoint, uses a conjunct ascending scale segment, and CC8(2), leading back, a disjunct descending one. At the CC(64) and CC(32) levels, extended repeated-tone passages demonstrate the degree to which *ngubeng* penetrates the structure. *Ngubeng* in the form of large-scale internal repetitions is revealed in CC64, and is manifest up to the *neliti* level. CC64(3) and (4) are the same as CC64(5) and (6), save for the last tone of the latter. CC64(7) and (8) are repeats, as are (9) and (10), but (7) and (9) are a scale tone apart.

Y is more restless than X. The *neliti* uses all ten available tones, touching on eight of them by CC256(20), judiciously meting out the ninth (*ding*) just before the midpoint, and supplying the tenth (*dOng*) at a parallel point before gong. The above-and-below symmetry of the CC4 {0,2,–2,0} is further expanded in CC8(1) and (2), which surround the midpoint by reaching two tones above it. Unlike the conservative behavior of X's CC64 stratum, Y's explores all five *pélog* tones in its first half. Yet *ngubeng* is nearly as evident in the *neliti* as in X, and at CC16 (like X's CC16), only three scale tones (*dAng, dong, dung*) appear before the end of the third quadrant. The missing ones (*dEng, dIng*) appear between there and gong with characteristic accelerated change.

Conclusion

The variety of CC contours and interrelationships found in the sample demonstrate that there is no fundamental *ur*-contour (or even group of contours) underlying symmetrical melodies. Rather there is an essential *process* informing their structure by which degrees of kinetic and tonal qualities, background symmetry, and small (but potent) internal disruptions in that symmetry are brought into balanced interaction. This balance shifts as the dimensions of the melodies do, and, depending on their individual features, within melodies of a given size. The shifts also affect the melodies' associations and character. Explanations of such connections between topic and structure, where I have endeavored to suggest them above, will remain partial until I augment them with similar considerations applied to further strata, and to the relationships that inhere between strata.

Unfixed *Pokok* Elaboration: *Payasan*

Pokok elaborations are either unfixed or fixed; if fixed, they are either non-interlocking or interlocking. Unfixed elaborations are those played by individual performers on *trompong, ugal, suling,* or *rebab*. These are referred to as *payasan*.[11] The designation unfixed means that *payasan* allow for a limited kind of improvisation. Fixed *pokok* elaboration is played by *pemadé, kantilan,* and/or *reyong,* and is fully worked out in advance. Noninterlocking types will be taken up in the next subsection, before proceeding to interlocking figurational grammar.

Payasan improvisations (I use the term cautiously) are based on the *neliti* and *pokok*. They are strongly constrained by instrumental idiom and by motives accepted as standard in specific cases, such as the kind described above at the beginning of the subsection on 32-beat melodies. I have thus far sedulously avoided the designation "ornamentation," but if the word is applicable anywhere, it is here. *Neliti*, as I have emphasized, are provisional melodies that are routinely departed from in practice. Literal statements of the *neliti* appear compressed into the single octave span of the *penyacah* (when these are used). *Payasan* diverge from the *neliti* in order to ornament it, but they do not add a new structural dimension to the music.[12] At the same time, aesthetically speaking, they are prized more than any other part of the texture for their capacity to enrich the whole through singable, beautiful melody. My remarks below are limited to some comments on *ugal* and *trompong* styles, as these instruments fulfill leadership roles in the *gamelan* and their *payasan* parts are essential to the whole. Though clearly of timbral and aesthetic importance, I will forgo

---

11. Formerly many *gamelan* used two *ugal,* the second following *(nutug)* the first, though as the importance of *ugal* leadership has increased in recent decades, the practice has declined. In *kebyar* only one *trompong* is used, though in *gamelan gong gdé* there is a second one, an octave higher. *Gamelan pelegongan* use two or four *gender* in an equivalent role (if four, two are an octave higher). The leading pair play a fairly fixed part, but even here there is some room for deviation (see McPhee 1966:155–61). *Gamelan* may use multiple *suling* players, each creating its own *payasan*. More than a single *rebab* is a rarity.

12. Bamberger and Ziporyn (1992) provide an interesting perspective on *payasan* improvisation and the cognitive processes involved in learning to do them.

discussion of *suling* and *rebab* to limit the length of the digression away from structural concerns.

Individual *payasan* players are valued for their special skills. For *suling* and *rebab* the emphasis is on sweetness of tone and richness of ornament, and not necessarily on pitch-matching. Indeed, some *sekaha* seek a clash between *suling* and bronze tunings. Individuality on *ugal* and *trompong* is partly expressed through cueing style and performance charisma, particularly because of the leadership roles these instruments play. This is especially so on the *ugal*. The elaborate hand signals and general body language players of these instruments (and the *kendang*) bring to performance, especially in contemporary music, are used to transmit information about *angsel,* tempo, dynamics, and form, but the refinement and continuity of their gestures can edge into the realm of choreography. Such cues may break the melodic line for a moment to allow for a larger physical gesture, such as raising the *panggul* or turning to look at the other players. Technically speaking, however, *payasan* depends on subtly applied rhythmic and melodic variety. The variety helps it cut through the texture and distinguish it from other strata, which are less elastic.

Payasan do not diverge from the *neliti* contour very often, but may at times extend their range slightly or approach a tone from the opposite direction. The stressed tones of the *neliti* are the nominal goal tones, though these may be temporally displaced via syncopation or, rarely, bypassed altogether in favor of an upcoming, more weighted stress. At their sparsest, especially when coinciding with *ngubeng* areas in longer melodies, single *payasan* tones may last four beats or more. At the other extreme they may last for only a quarter or an eighth of a beat (sixteenth and thirty-second notes in the transcriptions); some types of ornaments are best thought of as grace notes (and are so notated).

In older music *payasan* are a combination of preset melodic shapes and stylistic details contributed by the performer. In new music composers may allow performers this leeway, or they may make specific suggestions, compose the *ugal* or *trompong* part outright, or some mixture of these. At slow tempi an *ugal* player may vacillate between independent melody and tracking the *gangsa* or *reyong*. Faster tempi mandate simpler style, both for technical reasons and because it helps keep the ensemble synchronized. In figure 6.4 (CDI/25/1–25.2), from a 16-beat melody near the beginning of *Oleg Tumulilingan,* the two types are compared. The nearly four-fold difference between their tempi is actually eight-fold, because the time-beating gong *kempli* aligns with the *pokok* in the slow version and with the *neliti* in the fast. In the slow version the *ugal* paraphrases the *pokok* with complex figures and articulated damping of the keys. This same technique, simplified somewhat, is used for longer melodies with comparably simple elaboration. In these contexts the *ugal* closely shadows the *gangsa* and *reyong* parts (here shown conflated into interlocking parts on the *gangsa),* often at double or quadruple their density, and interpolates idiomatic embellishments such as *ngoret,* a double grace-note

Figure 6.4. *Ugal payasan* in *Oleg Tumulilingan* at slow and fast tempi (CDI/25.1–25.2)

slide connecting two adjacent scale tones by dipping below (or above) the first of the pair. At the faster tempo playing at the rate of the composite figuration is impossible for the *ugal*. The *payasan* is thus streamlined, in this case moving mainly at the same rate as the *neliti* and adding a few simple alterations to it.

Composers may also indicate a general style category which the performer, familiar with the category's conventions, then translates into music. An example of this is the florid *trompong* style *cerucuk punyah* (drunken *cerucuk,* a kind of bird), so-named because of its dizzy, disorienting syncopation. It is commonly called for in the fast closing sections of *kreasi lelambatan.* In figure 6.5 (CDI/26), laid out over two cycles of *neliti* 6.3D, *payasan* aligns with the *neliti* only on the fourth and sixth beats in the first cycle, and in the second

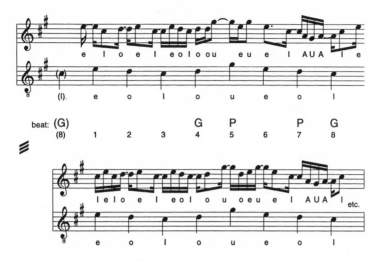

Figure 6.5. *Trompong* in *cerucuk punyah* style, over two cycles of *gilak Jagul neliti* (CDI/26)

cycle not at all. The *trompong* either anticipates, delays, or omits the rest of the *neliti* tones.

McPhee treats *trompong payasan* styles in depth and also deals at length with the gender style of *gamelan pelegongan,* which has many similarities to *kebyar ugal* playing (1966:67–75 and 155–61). He also covers the free-rhythm *trompong* passages called *gineman* (379) and their gender equivalents, sometimes also called *pengrangrang* (185). It would be redundant to recapitulate here the detailed information and transcriptions that he provided, for other than a few negligible points of emphasis that I might shift, his documentation remains complete and up-to-date. In this book there are further examples of *payasan* in figures 2.14–16, 7.12, 8.1A, and 9.3A–B. McPhee's terminology also remains current, though there are many other regional variations. Gusti Madé Putu Griya compiled (and also invented) many terms to describe the function, technique, and playing styles of all *kebyar* instruments (Mustika et al. 1979).

Fixed *Pokok* Elaborations I: Noninterlocking Parts

By virtue of the sheer number of bright-timbred instruments used to play them, fixed *pokok* elaborations dominate the texture of *kebyar* music. To use a Balinese metaphor, fixed elaborations are like the leaves and flowers of a tree, the branches, limbs, trunk, and roots of which are the underlying melodic and colotomic strata. But just as the leaves are the most numerous and finely wrought parts of the tree and cast a partly obscuring shadow over the parts that support them, so do the variety and sheer presence of fixed elaborations tend to eclipse the simpler underlying strata. Many of the strongest textural contrasts in *kebyar* are achieved through the juxtaposition or combination of interlocking and noninterlocking *pokok* elaboration, and the manipulation of these contrasts is a fundamental compositional consideration.

The technical characteristics of fixed noninterlocking elaborations are in some ways the same as those of improvised *payasan*. They also bear the same kinds of close resemblances (including "singability") to the underlying strata. Yet the two types of elaboration have very different affective potential. Because they are fully worked out in advance, fixed elaborations exhibit greater compositional diversity and may adopt any of several distinct vocabularies, making them a site for stylistic topics. In contrast, improvised *payasan* use a strictly court-derived style that does not signify beyond itself.

In fixed elaboration types the *gangsa* (excluding *ugal*) are usually split into two parts: one that tracks the *neliti,* and one that parallels the first at the interval of a *kempyung* above (see also the discussion of interlocking parts below, and fig. 2.12). The first part is called the *polos* (simple, straightforward), and the second is called the *sangsih* (differing, following). In the *gangsa* section there are four *polos* and four *sangsih* players, divided equally between *pemadé* and *kantilan,* and further distributed among the four *pengumbang* and four *pengisep*-tuned instruments such that no single *polos* or *sangsih* part is doubled at precisely the same tuning and register.

The expressive and technical specificity of noninterlocking elaborations often makes it desirable for the *ugal* to abandon improvised *payasan* and play along with the *gangsa polos,* effectively dissolving the distinction between the two strata. Elaborating melodies may match or slightly exceed the *neliti* range, making *gangsa* much more suited for this kind of playing than the *reyong*. Indeed, a common format is to have *gangsa* play in a noninterlocking fashion while the *reyong* interlocks (fig. 2.15). Sometimes *kantilan* and *pemadé* are given separate parts, with interlocking figuration assigned to one and noninterlocking melody to the other. In other cases, such as slow *norot,* the *reyong* and *gangsa* play the same music, with second-order relations added as necessary on the *reyong*. The *reyong* may also play in *ocak-ocakan* format (fig. 2.16) or drop out altogether.

There are four noninterlocking elaboration subtypes that signify court genres.[13] Like underlying strata, each is defined by a unique rhythmic density and proceeds in an unbroken chain of constant rhythmic values. As elaboration, however, each of the four subtypes has an identity as a stylistic topic. In *kekenyongan* (fig. 6.6A, CDI/27, a passage from the *pengecet* of *lelambatan Tabuh Gari* that follows the *pengawak* of 6.3Y) the *gangsa* play at the same rate

---

13. Specialized terms like the four discussed here generally do not enjoy wide usage, but they have long been of interest to specialists or musicians with a theoretical inclination. These particular designations are increasingly well known. I compiled them from my teachers Wayan Rai, Nyoman Rembang, and especially Wayan Sinti. All credited Gusti Madé Putu Griya as an important oral source.

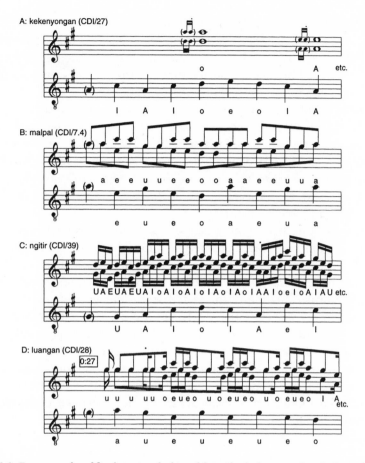

Figure 6.6. Four examples of fixed, noninterlocking elaboration (*polos* stems down), shown above *neliti*

A. *Pengecet lelambatan Tabuh Gari* (CDI/27)

B. *Baris* (CDI/7.4)

C. *Teruna Jaya* (CDI/39)

D. *Puspanjali* (CDI/28)

as the *jegogan,* resulting in a sparseness reminiscent of *gamelan gong gdé* and suggestive of its detached and regal loftiness. In ironic contrast to *gong gdé,* where the style is a norm, *kebyar kekenyongan* passages typically conclude after the dissolution of the affect in a storm of acceleration and crescendo.

In *neliti* figuration, *gangsa* play the *neliti* line verbatim, sometimes adding syncopation and/or *ngoret.* This suggests strong male dance and theater characters, evoking their purposeful stride and sweeping movements. *Neliti* figuration is used over melody 6.3Q, accompanied by interlocking parts on the *reyong. Malpal* figuration (fig. 6.6B, used over the *Baris* melody 6.3H, CDI/7) moves at twice *neliti* rate and maintains its contour, but intensifies its affect. A *gangsa* section playing *malpal* can coax the most concentrated combination of volume, clarity, and rhythmic momentum from their instruments, and can also change to soft and sweet instantaneously. Originally a dance term, *malpal* refers to the quick, high step of a character in an agitated mood. It is typically used at the climax of a dance, or in a drama during battle scenes. In instrumental music too it can play a climactic role, with passages of softer dynamic interpolated to build suspense. *Ngitir* figuration (fig. 6.6C, over a melody from *Teruna Jaya*, CDI/39) has a suggestively sensual affect. Also a dance term, *ngitir* is a wide undulation of the hips brought about by a slow prance-like step common to many female dance styles. The figuration is restricted to slow tempi and moves at a rate of four tones per beat, connecting *neliti* tones with winding passagework. At faster speeds, *ngitir* passages may be separated into interlocking parts (see fig. 7.10).[14]

Noninterlocking figurations based on *tua* genres need not import their structural asymmetry, though in some situations they may. To create stylistic topics they need only modify these genres' rhythmic vocabularies and adapt them for use in symmetrical contexts. The special rhythmic vocabulary of interlocking ornamentation in the sacred seven-tone *gamelan luang* was not often heard in *kebyar* before the 1980s, but it is an important resource now. Known in *luang* music as *sekatian* and in *kebyar* also as *luangan* (fig. 6.6D, CDI/28), it is distinguished by its syncopation, additive rhythms, and repeated tones. Regarding the example, from the *pengawak* of *Puspanjali* (see also fig. 6.3R above), composer Nyoman Windha remarked that he used *luangan* because he wanted "a direct way to capture the atmosphere of temple worship in a secular musical setting."[15]

Fixed *Pokok* Elaborations II: Interlocking Parts

Kotekan, or interlocking parts, are highly developed in *kebyar*, and constitute a complex and clearly differentiated structural layer.[16] Like ametric *kebyar* passages or the *reyong byar*, the variety and abundance of *kotekan* patterns is one of the music's signatures. The use of *kotekan* has expanded throughout this century in tandem with the growth of *kebyar*, so that it is now often a principal focus of the music. It rose to prominence first in *tabuh kreasi*, where long passages are often devoted exclusively to showcasing *kotekan*, but the trend soon spread to other *kebyar* dance and instrumental forms.

Several factors account for the growing prevalence of *kotekan* in *kebyar*.

---

14. When separated into interlocking parts *ngitir* passages may become *nyog cag* or *ubit-ubitan* patterns (see below) or as in this case, a combination of the two.

15. Personal communication, July 1989.

16. See also McPhee 1966:162–66, Schlager 1976 (discussed below), Ornstein 1971a:224–72, Vitale 1990, and Bandem 1993 for analytical treatment of *kotekan*. Bandem introduces many terms for specific pattern combinations, most of which he learned from Gusti Madé Putu Griya (1989, personal communication). Griya probably adapted the terms from the *Prakempa lontar*, which he knew deeply (see Bandem 1986:70).

First, it is a challenge to interlock at high speeds, and mastering patterns is a favorite musicians' activity. Well-executed *kotekan* is sure and dramatic proof of a skillful group, a point not lost on ambitious *sekaha* and individual players in the current musical climate. Second, unlike the slow-speaking *gangsa jongkok* of *gong gdé* or the restricted single-octave range of *gangsa* in *gamelan semar pegulingan* and *pelegongan*, *kebyar gangsa* and *reyong* are built to play at quick tempi, and suited, by virtue of their two-octave range and lightweight *panggul*, for a wider variety of patterns. Third, *kotekan* is richly evocative, and the basis for most stylistic topics. The combination of expressivity, technical aptness, and spur to individual and ensemble precision is a formidable one that has proven increasingly attractive.

The third factor calls for educated speculation about the origins and significance of interlocking on Bali. Melodic interlocking has developed to a higher level of complexity on Bali than it has elsewhere in Southeast Asia, though it is known throughout the region—indeed, throughout the world—in some form. Balinese identify especially strongly with the notion of interlocking as a way to share work. Ernst Schlager suggested that the "work rhythms" (*Arbeitsrhythmus*) of women pounding harvested rice in rhythmic alternation with bamboo poles, an activity known in Bali as *oncang-oncangan*, are a basis for the rhythmic vocabulary of *kotekan*. He showed how the combination and permutation of two basic *oncang-oncangan* rhythms (*tingkadan*, 4 + 4 pulses; and *oncangan*, 3 + 3 + 2 pulses) yield a much larger set of rhythms, which, transformed into melodic patterns, correspond with those in the *gamelan* he studied (1965:319–32, 1976:36–38). The cultivation of an activity designed to make harvest efficient and socially pleasurable in an expressive art such as music is typically reflective of Southeast Asian collectivity.

Schlager's research mainly concerned the *tua gamelan*, which I link to asymmetry. *Kotekan* developed in these ensembles over time, acquiring stylistic idiosyncrasies in each. Yet *gambuh*, progenitor of the court genres, does not use melodic interlocking parts at all. The limited degree to which later *madya* repertoire uses them traces to influence from the *tua* group. How and over what span of time this influence was absorbed is difficult to say, but for at least a century now *kotekan* has been featured in *pelegongan* music and *lelambatan*. For the absorption to take place the *kotekan* styles from *tua* sources had to be simplified to facilitate combination with the colotomic meters and melodic symmetries of *madya gamelan*. *Tua kotekan* may also be simple in this sense, but they may be much more varied and complex too, owing to the genres' often irregular melodies and forms. In *kebyar*, assimilation of more complex *tua kotekan* styles provides important enrichment.

Kotekan Categories and Analytical Preliminaries

Schlager's theory of origins notwithstanding, the explicit role and strongest impulse of interlocking parts in *gamelan* is melodic. In *kebyar kotekan* a composite melody moving at four times (rarely, eight times) the *neliti* rate is formed from the interlocking of *polos* and *sangsih* parts. In general, the *polos* leads by tracking the contour of the *pokok,* and the *sangsih* follows, by interlocking with the *polos*. On the *reyong,* because of the restricted ranges of each position, players routinely switch back and forth between *polos* and *sangsih*-like parts. As a result, the two terms are usually avoided when referring to *reyong,* and the names of the four positions (or some equivalent) are substituted instead.

The three most common categories of *gangsa kotekan* are *norot, nyog cag,* and *ubit-ubitan*. Each *could* be composed for *any* melody, but style and topic regulate which is chosen. We have already encountered *norot*. In *nyog cag,* the *polos* plays only on duple subdivisions aligned with the beat and the *sangsih* fits in between. The parts tend to be melodically disjunct, but they fill in each other's gaps so that the composite is mainly conjunct. The two parts never coincide. In *ubit-ubitan* both *polos* and *sangsih* are syncopated, and they coincide at irregular temporal intervals.

Kotekan strata follow their own definite structural norms, and may be considerably more independent from the melody than noninterlocking elaborations. There are many possible relations between *kotekan* and other melodic strata, both in terms of larger design and at the local level of pattern syntax. Among the larger issues are the effect of combining different *kotekan* types and/or noninterlocking elaboration during a single *gongan,* and the contrast, if any, between the overall kinetic and tonal qualities of the *kotekan* and the melody. These are compositional concerns that will be taken up in chapter 8. The present discussion is limited to local pattern syntax in simpler *kotekan* styles, that is, those associated with *gong gdé* and *pelegongan* repertoire. As with melody, I will turn to asymmetrical patterns at the end of this chapter.

I must first define the analytical object, the pattern unit. For most *kotekan,* in cyclic meters of all dimensions, the normative unit is of two beats' duration, consisting of eight *kotekan* tones (four per *neliti* tone). This length matches that of single tones in the *pokok* stratum, the stratum with which *kotekan* goal tones usually align. Nearly all repeating patterns (see next paragraph) turn over at this rate. (While it is true that *norot* patterns seem to "repeat" every two tones, tones are nonetheless grouped in sets of eight that end aligned with *pokok* tones. As will be described shortly, *majalan norot* patterns show this most clearly. *Ubit-ubitan* units may be of four beats' duration, but such cases are best considered as extended normal units.)

Kinetic quality in *kotekan* is manifest at the pattern unit level, not at the note-to-note level as it was for melody. A *ngubeng kotekan* pattern is one that can be immediately repeated at the same scale-tone level without breaking the rules of syntax anywhere in the resultant set of sixteen tones. Such patterns can be used in repetition to connect successive *ngubeng* tones in underlying strata, or they may be used singly to reinforce tonal stability after a melodic arrival. *Majalan* patterns are those used to connect moving tones in underlying strata. These cannot be immediately repeated at the same scale-tone level without violating syntax over the link.

The analyses that follow use modifications of the tools applied to *neliti*. To encompass the length of the basic unit, *kotekan* CC-groups—hereafter kCC(x)—will have eight members rather than four; the maximum value of x is the number of beats in the *gongan* divided by two. The eight members of each kCC will be separated into two groups of four by a slash to facilitate comparison between the halves (wherein symmetries are revealed). The last tone of each kCC is the stressed tone and is set to 0. As before, the stressed tone is represented with an open note head, though its value is a sixteenth note. The term "Axis" was used earlier to denote the interval between the midpoint tone and the gong tone, encompassing a temporal distance that varied with the length of the melody. Below, *kAxis* refers only to the interval between the fourth and final members of a kCC, which are separated by one beat. I will introduce one further tool under *ubit-ubitan* below.

Analysis of Symmetrical *Kotekan* Patterns

Norot

Norot has already been discussed in chapters 2 and 4 and above, and requires only a few additional comments now. It bears repeating that *norot* is a stylistic topic for *gong gdé,* because its most common and consistent usage is in *lelambatan*.[17] Unlike *ubit-ubitan* and *nyog cag, norot* has only a single melodic and rhythmic shape. The notion of syntax, then, is superfluous. All *ngubeng norot* kCC are {1,0,1,0/1,0,1,0}; and all *majalan* ones end with { . . . ./0,0,1,0}, with the first four members determined by the scale-tone distance between the previous *pokok* tone and the upcoming one. If the melody is moving down one tone, for example (fig. 6.7), the kCC would be {2,1,2,1/0,0,1,0}. If it is moving down two tones, the kCC would be {3,2,3,2/0,0,1,0}; if moving up one tone it would be {0,–1,0,–1/0,0,1,0}, and so on.

At slow speeds *norot* may be played as noninterlocking elaboration, augmented with second-order relations (fig. 6.7A and B), and at faster speeds with characteristic *polos/sangsih* splitting of the composite (6.7C). Once a composer has chosen to use *norot* for a given melody, the only details left to work out are whether to shift position to match every new *pokok* tone, or whether to ignore some, thereby making the *kotekan* more *ngubeng* than the *neliti* at those points.

---

17. While agreeing that *norot*'s strongest association is with *gending pegongan,* Asnawa (personal communication, August 1998) speculated nonetheless that its true origin was in *gamelan semar pegulingan.* He pointed out that while *norot* is omnipresent in *kebyar* presentations of *gong gdé* repertoire, it is not used when the same repertoire is played on actual *gong gdé* instruments. It is used, however, by some *semar pegulingan* ensembles, for example in *banjar* Pagan Kelod.

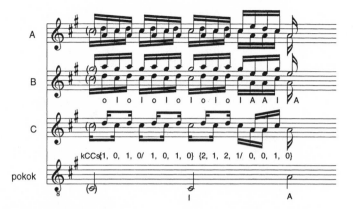

Figure 6.7. *Gangsa* realizations for *norot*
A. Slow tempo, with a combination of unison, *nelu,* and *kempyung* second-order relations played by *sangsih*
B. Slow tempo, with *sangsih kempyung* throughout
C. Fast tempo, with characteristic *polos/sangsih* split

Norot is straightforward on *gangsa,* but on *reyong* it is a test of skill. Players play all of the pattern tones that fall within their ranges, adding second-order tones when appropriate. This becomes difficult at fast tempi. Moreover, as none of the four positions' ranges are the same, the four parts differ. These differences may be exaggerated through the application of a certain amount of variational freedom afforded each part. This is especially true for the *pemetit,* the uppermost part, whose peak tone *dung* cuts sharply through the sound. This *dung* is often used judiciously in what might otherwise be inhospitable tonal situations as a way to boost the prominence of the *reyong* in the texture and add extra cross-rhythmic vitality. The same also holds for the lowermost *deng,* accessible only at *penyorog* position. Figure 6.8 illustrates the twenty-five basic *norot* successions on the *reyong,* from each of the five *pélog* tones to one of the other four, or remaining on the same tone. Since *reyong norot* is unaffected by *ugal* register, the referent here is the single-octave range of the *calung.* Most of the realizations shown are plain, though I have occasionally included *pemetit* variation. Each begins from the initial stressed (*calung*) tone, continues through the goal tone, and stops immediately before what would be a third *calung* tone.

Nyog cag

Though symmetrical-class *neliti* and their reductions all exhibit a mixture of perfect and imperfect symmetries, the analysis of figure 6.3 showed that melodic strata are not structurally interchangeable. Just as CC4 strata behave differently from *neliti,* so are *kotekan* symmetrical in their own ways.

Interestingly, *kotekan* patterns are subject to stricter syntax than melodies. *Norot* is too limited to demonstrate the flexibility within these constraints convincingly, but in *nyog cag* some characteristics begin to emerge.

Nyog cag is particularly suited to the wide range of *kebyar* instruments and appears to have been invented for them in North Bali during the early years of *kebyar* (McPhee 1966:332).[18] (Some *tua gamelan* use *nyog cag*-like patterns, but without the expansiveness and flexibility of *kebyar*.[19]) As a stylistic topic *nyog cag*'s referent is thus *kebyar* itself. Individual *nyog cag* kCC have wide ranges; and a succession of them may touch on the entire range of the *gangsa*. However, *nyog cag* is impossible to play on the *reyong* because the disjunct nature of the parts would cause them to cross repeatedly between players' positions. When *gangsa* play *nyog cag* the *reyong* must do something else; what that is determined to be depends on the desired orchestral texture.

Nyog cag patterns can be played very fast (up to 200 beats per minute), and are often used for exuberant, virtuoso passages. In contrast, they are also standard in *lelambatan pengawak,* where they alternate with *norot* (in such cases, the *reyong* continues to play *norot*). Unlike *norot* and *ubit-ubitan* composites, those of *nyog cag* bear a strong family resemblance to some *neliti:* compare especially shorter ones such as fig. 6.3B, C, and E with fig. 6.9A, C, and D. *Nyog cag* sounds like *neliti* accelerated to quadruple speed with an equivalent increase in intensity. Even when *ngubeng,* the patterns race about by traversing a looping course around the goal tone. The following six rules summarize *nyog cag* syntax:[20]

1. *Nyog cag* kCC-groups have a minimum range of four tones, and a maximum of six.
2. The tones in a *nyog cag* kCC-group should form a conjunct scale segment when reordered. (All tones within the range must occur at least once.)
3. No successive repeated tones are allowed within a kCC-group.
4. Within a kCC-group, tones at the extremes of the range may not be sounded more than twice; inner tones not more than thrice.
5. *Ngubeng nyog cag* kCC-groups are kAxis 0, with the two halves either (1) literal repetitions or (2) perfect inversions of one another.
6. *Majalan nyog cag* kCC-groups may be kAxis 0 or ≠ 0. If kAxis 0, their two halves must not have the properties named in rule 5.

---

18. McPhee calls these patterns *chandetan (sic),* a term now in disuse. At other times he uses *chandetan* to refer to *kotekan* in general, a practice also unknown now, though Ornstein (1971a:225) reported that it persisted in the 1960s.

19. The *gender wayang* composition *Tulang Lindung* comes to mind.

20. Exceptions to the following are unusual, but they may occur if the goal tone is near the extremes of the instrument. In such cases, a tone that lies beyond the highest or lowest key may be called for to complete a standard pattern, thus requiring the substitution of a different tone. This mostly leads to transgressions of rule number 1, causing four-tone groups to be compressed into three-tone ones.

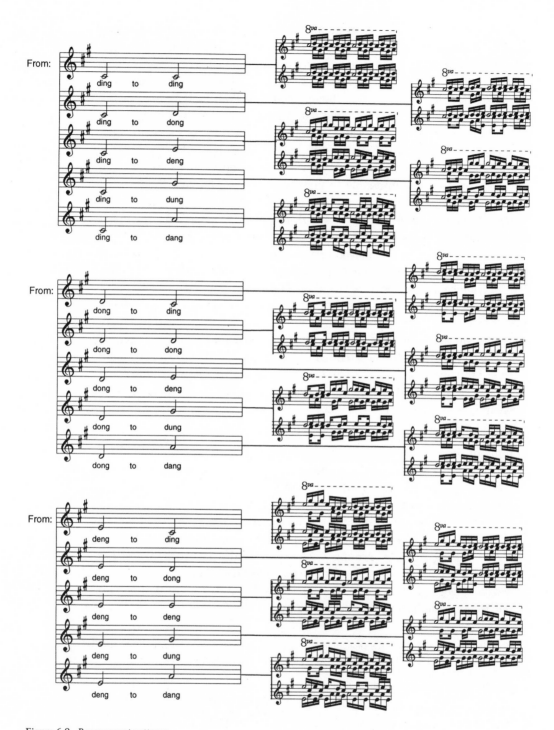

Figure 6.8. *Reyong norot* patterns

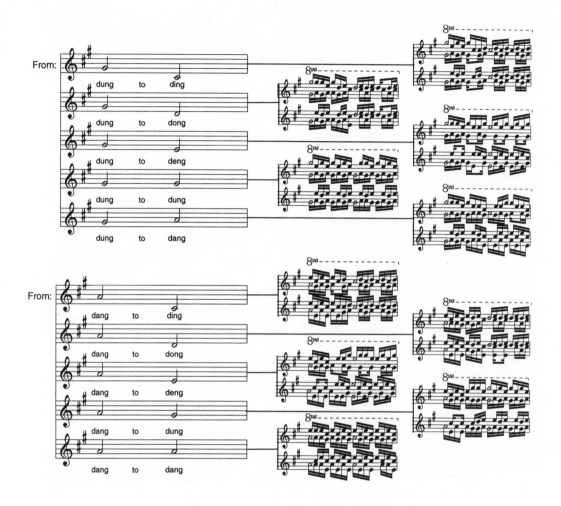

Figure 6.9 shows seven characteristic *nyog cag* kCC-groups (to facilitate comparison, all use the goal tone *dIng*). A and B show the two *ngubeng* subtypes described in number 5 above: the two halves of A are the same and the two halves of B are inversions of one another. C–E show characteristic *majalan* patterns. F and G are common patterns built from four pairs of adjacent steps forming an imperfect palindrome; the two are related to each other as transposed retrograde inversions.

Neliti contour suggests which of the many possible subtypes is appropriate to figure a given segment of melody. B may be used several times in a row at *ngubeng* moments, such as after internal stresses in *lelambatan*. The descending sequential pattern of D may be repeated—shifted down a step each time—to elaborate a sequential *neliti* such as figure 6.3M, CC16(1) and (2). Patterns of kAxis ±1 are often used at the two beats prior to gong or some

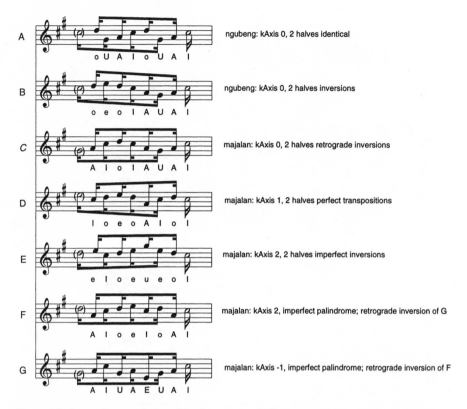

Figure 6.9. Seven subtypes of *nyog cag kotekan* patterns (*polos* is stems down, *sangsih* stems up)

other prominent internal stress, because *neliti* motion is generally by step at such points. Figure 6.10 (CDI/29; see also 6.3K) gives a *nyog cag* elaboration for *Topeng Keras* with the subtypes from fig. 6.9 identified. The *kotekan* here spans eight tones while the *neliti* spans only six. The *ngubeng* pattern 6.9B covers the first quadrant of the tune, centered around *dIng*. A thrice-repeated pattern leading to *deng* (bracketed), made up of the first six elements of 6.9F, begins at the last two notes of kCC(4). During this the *kotekan* aligns with the *neliti* at every beat, while forming a 6:4 cross-rhythm with it. In the process kCC(5) iterates 6.9G, first introduced at kCC(3), then kCC(6) varies it. When the six-note pattern breaks at the end of kCC(6) the *nyog cag deng* is aligned with the *pokok* for the first time.[21]

Ubit-ubitan

The specific histories and uses of *norot* and *nyog cag* make for clear, albeit limited, referentiality. The ensuing discussion of the much broader *ubit-ubitan* category also focuses on symmetrical patterns associated with court genres.

---

21. A rhythmic process analogous to the Western hemiola or Carnatic *mora*.

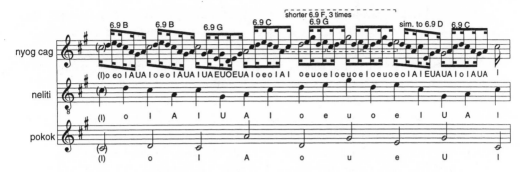

Figure 6.10. *Nyog cag kotekan* above *Topeng Keras neliti* and *pokok* (on the recording the two interlocking parts are heard on separate channels; CDI/29)

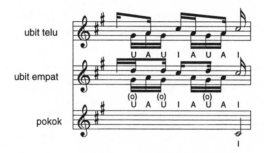

Figure 6.11. *Ubit telu* and *ubit empat* patterns with identical kCC and *polos* parts but differing *sangsih* parts

These follow rigorous syntactic constraints, and provide a basis for later exploration of asymmetrical *ubit-ubitan* types with origins in *tua* genres.

Balinese distinguish two types of *ubit-ubitan* patterns, named for the number of scale tones used in a single pattern unit. In an *ubit telu* (*ubit*-three) pattern unit, *polos* and *sangsih* each use two adjacent *gangsa* tones. Together the two parts span three tones, sharing the middle one. *Ubit empat* (*ubit*-four) patterns build their *polos* in the same way as *ubit telu*, but their *sangsih* take two additional adjacent tones next to the *polos*, sharing none with it. This forms a four-note span. *Ubit telu* patterns coincide on a shared inner tone, but *ubit empat* ones coincide at a *kempyung* formed from the two outer tones. Recurring *kempyung* form cross-rhythms, so that an *ubit telu* and an *ubit empat* pattern sharing the same *polos* and melodic composite have not only different *sangsih* but a different overall sound. Figure 6.11 shows an *ubit telu* and an *ubit empat* pattern that share the same *polos*. The latter's *sangsih* forms a *kempyung* with the lower *polos* tone which gives rise to a cross-rhythm, but both composites give the kCC {−2,−1,−2,0/−1,−2,−1,0}.[22]

_____

22. See also figure 6.13A1 and A1a below.

Through careful alignment of kCC-groups with the *neliti* and *pokok,* the use of a single three-tone scale segment may be extended for as long as the underlying strata remain in the area of those tones. Such prolongation stabilizes a narrow band of pitch and timbre within which special syntactic rules apply. Figure 6.12 shows the eight three-note *ubit-ubitan* positions available on the *gangsa,* and their possible correlations with *neliti* and *pokok* tones. Tones at the extremes *(dOng* and *ding)* may be projected into only one position; those adjacent to the extremes *(dEng* and *dang),* into two positions, and the others into three positions. Only four positions are available on the *reyong* (see fig. 2.10); these are equivalent to *gangsa* positions 2–5.

The special properties of *ubit-ubitan* kCC emerge if we imagine each of the eight positions as a self-contained, "wraparound" system. The three tones in a given position's range (call them 0, 1, and 2 for the moment) can be thought of as lying 120 degrees apart around the surface of a cylinder. Facing the cylinder, up or down movement as on a scale is illusory in a way. One step "higher" than the highest of the three tones wraps around to become the lowest tone again; and in the other direction, one step "lower" than the lowest tone is the highest tone. We do not actually need to think about exceeding the range of each position in practice, but analytically it is important. For example, the untransposed inversion of a stepwise descent from the highest tone to the middle tone (2 to 1) would be a step up from the highest tone (2 to 3)—an inadmissible move because there is no "3" in the system. To encompass this we have to imagine "wrapping around" back to the lowest tone instead. The inversion of the descending step from the highest tone is thus a descending leap (2 to 0).[23]

This is a *mod 3* field. In mod 3 calculations only 0, 1 and 2 may be used; other numbers must be converted by subtracting or adding 3 until the result is 0, 1, or 2 (3 and 4 mod 3 are, respectively, 0 and 1; and −1, −2, −3, and −4 are 2, 1, 0, and 2. These are the only conversions we shall need). To see the symmetrical relationships between the two halves of an *ubit-ubitan* kCC we need a new tool, which I will call *sum3*. To use it, sum corresponding members of the two halves of the kCC and convert the results to mod 3. If the numbers are all the same, the two halves of the pattern are perfect inversions of one another in the wraparound system. Figure 6.11, for example, fits these conditions: adding corresponding members gives the result [−3,−3,−3,0]; in mod 3 this is [0,0,0,0]. The two halves are sum3 inversionally symmetrical.

This seems abstract, but it is completely audible, and provides a rigorous perspective on the music's overall melodic coherence. *Ubit-ubitan* patterns *feel* like full-fledged *neliti* melodies that have been squeezed into a more limited scale-tone field. *Neliti*-type symmetries are distorted by this compression. The

23. See also Kubik's description of the Amadinda *miko* system for melodic transposition, which works in a related way (1994:261).

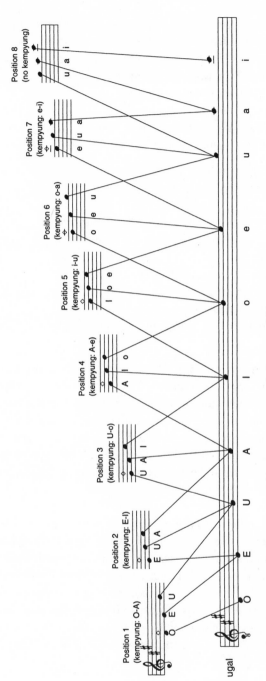

Figure 6.12. Projections of *neliti* tones into *ubit-ubitan* "wraparound" three-tone fields. *Kempyung* tones for *ubit empat* are shown with diamond noteheads.

distortion intensifies the timbre and rhythm of the *kotekan* and produces syncopation, a characteristic feature of Balinese *gamelan*. It is interesting, in fact, to project *ubit-ubitan* patterns back out into a wider range by "decompression": selectively adding or subtracting 3 to members of the kCC to form a *neliti*-like contour. Adding 3 to each of the first four members of the kCC of figure 6.11, for instance, gives {1,2,1,0/–1,–2,–1,0}, a shape that is exactly the same as the *neliti* of figure 6.3C (and also the *nyog cag* of 6.9B).

The following rules of syntax apply to symmetrical *ubit-ubitan*:

1. *Ubit-ubitan* kCC-groups have a range of three adjacent scale tones, exclusive of second-order relations (restricted, in other words, to one of figure 6.12's eight positions).
2. Beginning anywhere in an *ubit-ubitan* kCC-group and taking four consecutive members, all three tones in the range must occur once, and one tone must occur twice.
3. No successive repeated tones are allowed within a kCC-group.[24]
4. The two halves of *ngubeng ubit-ubitan* kCC-groups must be either (1) sum3 inversionally symmetrical or (2) kAxis 0 and identical.
5. *Majalan ubit-ubitan* kCC-groups must not have either of the properties of rule 4.

Rules 1–3 bear on performability. Since keys are sufficiently close together, rule 1 dictates that a player's forearm need not move within a pattern, and that the mallet can be manipulated by wrist and finger muscles alone. By rule 2, neither *polos* nor *sangsih* may play more than three successive kCC-group tones without taking a rest on the fourth, which must lie beyond its range and is filled in by the other part. Rule 3 assures lateral wrist motion between successive mallet strokes. All of these factors promote relaxation and conserve energy, which is especially important at quick tempi.

Ngubeng ubit-ubitan patterns. Twenty-four kCC satisfy the conditions in rules 1–3 and the first part of rule 4. They are shown in figure 6.13 in both their *telu* and *empat* forms. To facilitate comparison, all are notated in position 3 of figure 6.12, though each could occur at any position (save for position 8, which cannot accommodate *ubit empat* patterns). Here and in figure 6.14 the initial noteless stems represent the ends of unspecified previous patterns; as before, the final stressed tones are shown with open noteheads. It is important to recall again that Western notation conflicts with Balinese practice, and that the

---

24. The recently invented *ubit empat* pattern {–2,–2,–1,0/–2,–2,–1,0} is the single exception to this of which I am aware. A *kempyung* on 1 coicides with the repeated –2. It is found in Wayan Beratha's dance composition *Panyembrahma* and his *tabuh kreasi Kosalia Arini* (see figs. 8.2B and 8.4C). Such a pattern would never be found in court repertoire, however, and need not be thought of as a member of the group of *ubit-ubitan* patterns defined here.

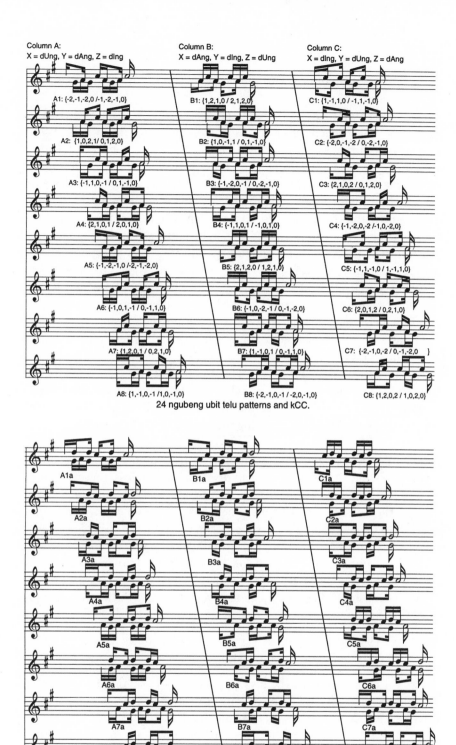

Figure 6.13. Forty-eight *ngubeng ubit-ubitan* patterns (shown at position 3, fig. 6.12)

stressed tones are grouped with the previous seven tones, even though they are not beamed to them.

The patterns in figure 6.13 are rotatable. This means that if a kCC-group is played and immediately repeated, all of the conditions under rules 1–3 and the first part of rule 4 will continue to be met, starting from each tone in the first playing and counting ahead eight tones (across the link). Scanning down the columns in figure 6.13 each successive kCC can be seen to have been formed accordingly, by rotating the kCC above it one tone to the right. Patterns 2–8 are thus easily derived from pattern 1. In fact, as the column superheadings show, the entire set of forty-eight patterns can be reduced to the "master" kCC {XYXZ/YXYZ}: assigning X to *dUng,* Y to *dAng,* and Z to *dIng* gives A1; assigning X to *dAng,* Y to *dIng,* and Z to *dUng* gives B1; and assigning X to *dIng,* Y to *dUng,* and Z to *dAng* gives C1. The rest follow from there.[25] I use the designations A, B, and C for labeling patterns in later analyses, followed by their number and the suffix "a" if they are *ubit empat.*

Of the kCC that satisfy the conditions in rules 1–3, there are only four that also fit the second part of rule 4. They are {−1,−2,−1,0/−1,−2,−1,0}, {−1,1,−1,0/−1,1,−1,0}, {1,−1,1,0/1,−1,1,0}, and {1,2,1,0/1,2,1,0}. Of these only the first is commonly used, and only in a special kind of *ubit empat.* In addition to sharing the tone 0 with the *polos,* the *sangsih* plays the fourth tone of the *ubit empat* span, 1, above the *polos*'s −1, forming the second-order relation *nelu.*

Majalan ubit-ubitan patterns. The number of kCC that satisfy the conditions in rules 1–3 and rule 5 are many and diverse. Nonetheless, there is an archetypal pattern used in court genre music when the *neliti* is *majalan.* In the archetype, the tones in the kCC-group occur as a three-tone conjunct fragment (ascending or descending), which is repeated until the end of the pattern unit. This sets up a 3 + 3 + 2 grouping of the pattern unit's eight subdivisions. Under this grouping the axis tone comes on the first note of a three-tone fragment, and, four subdivisions later, the final (stress) tone comes with the fragment's second tone. The arrangement is as follows, with the three conjunct tones labeled x, y, and z:

Three-tone fragments:	x y z x|y z x y|
Axis and stress (aligned with *neliti*):	A S

The kCC cannot, therefore, be kAxis 0, because the *neliti* tones aligned with the axis and end of the kCC-group must be one step apart (tones x and y above). Hence the inherently *majalan* quality of the patterns.

Seen in contrast to *ngubeng* patterns, *majalan* patterns are structurally asymmetrical and tonally unstable. The set of four identical members obtained

---

25. Not all of these patterns are in common use, but in the interests of completeness I have taken the theoretical framework and extended it as far as it could go.

by applying sum3 to the *ngubeng* kCC in figure 6.13 demonstrated perfect symmetry masked by irregular sequences of tones in kCC-groups. For *majalan* kCC, applying sum3 gives the opposite result: the maximum turnover of members, demonstrating asymmetry masked by a *regular* (though grouped in sets of 3) sequence of tones. Put differently, the *majalan* sum3 results look like the patterns themselves. By way of illustration, consider the *majalan* kCC {1,0,2,1/0,2,1,0}: the sum3 for this pattern is [1,2,0,1].

In court genres the use of these patterns is mostly limited to bridging 2-beat distances between separate areas of tonal stability. However, patterns may be chained together by continuing to repeat the three-tone conjunct fragment over the link, such that a prolonged 3:4 cross-rhythm results. In such cases each successive kCC-group must be a rotation of the previous one, two tones to the "right." When patterns are extended to two units' duration (4 beats), the prolonged instability renders their affect ambiguous. In symmetrical contexts such patterns not only intensify the rhythm and *majalan* quality, but may dislodge the topic, making the music seem inherently more modern. Patterns extended to three units or beyond are never heard in court genre music.

Figure 6.14 shows the basic *majalan* collection, also notated at position 3 of figure 6.12. The master pattern here is {XYZX/YZXY}, with the following two configurations: the ascending succession X = *dUng*, Y = *dAng*, and Z = *dIng*; and its descending inversion X = *dIng*, Y = *dAng*, and Z = *dUng*.[26] Permutations are derived by rotating each of the patterns by one tone for two times (at the third time the conjunct three-note group has already rotated back to its starting position). The two master pattern configurations head columns D and E in the figure, with each rotation further labeled as in figure 6.13. Under each I show a provisional *neliti* line, as indication of the kind of motion that the kCC-group could elaborate.

Ubit-ubitan in standard practice. Pelegongan music and the *kawitan* sections of *lelambatan* employ the *ubit-ubitan* patterns of figures 6.13 and 6.14 nearly exclusively. (The *pengawak* and *pengecet* of *lelambatan* use mainly *norot* and *nyog cag.*) The scope, size, and familiarity of that repertoire established this limited collection of patterns as the standard for *kebyar*. The active vocabulary of patterns in court music is even smaller, however: C2 and its inversion D2 (and their *ubit-empat* equivalents C2a and D2a) are the most characteristic *majalan* kCC; and only a limited group of the *ngubeng* patterns appear with any regularity.

In typical instances, only two kCC (one *ngubeng* and one *majalan*, plus their inversions) are used to elaborate an entire melody. The contour of the *neliti* determines whether and where the selected patterns or their inversions

---

26. Other configurations, such as those assigning X to *dAng,* yield no further patterns. If, for example, X = *dAng,* Y = *dIng,* and Z = *dUng,* applying the master pattern yields pattern D2—already present in figure 6.14.

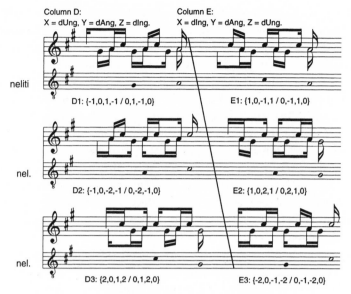

Six majalan ubit telu patterns and kCC.

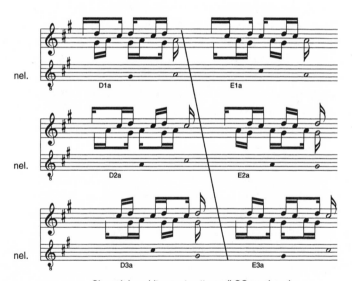

Six majalan ubit empat patterns (kCC as above).

Figure 6.14. Twelve Basic *majalan ubit-ubitan* patterns (shown at position 3, fig. 6.12)

are used. This is illustrated in figure 6.15A (CDI/30), which shows an *ubit telu* realization for the 16-beat melody in the *garuda* section of *legong Lasem* (in the full composition, this melody alternates with that in figure 6.3G).[27]

---

27. This may also be compared with versions given at McPhee 1966:187.

Both C3 and E2, the selected *ngubeng* and *majalan* kCC, feature the descending contour 2,1,0. Their inversions C7 and D2 feature the ascending contour −2,−1,0. The descending kCC are used when the local stressed tone is approached by descent; in this melody the second, third, and fourth *neliti* stresses are so reached. The first *neliti* stress is the melodic apex and is reached by scalar ascent; hence it is elaborated by the inverted kCC. As a result of this design the *ubit-ubitan* never exceeds the range of the melody. For the entire duration of the melody, *majalan* patterns precede *neliti* stressed tones and *ngubeng* ones succeed them, reflecting the characteristic symmetrical-class dialog between motion and stasis. In a short *gongan* such as this, however, the *ngubeng* kCC-groups do not literally repeat, and when they end they no longer align with the *neliti* (cf. beats 2, 6, 10, and 14.) But their sum3 inversional property strengthens the sense of tonal stability whenever they occur.

As I indicated earlier, economy of motion is prized in *ubit-ubitan*. For the first ten beats of the melody the *kotekan* stays in positions 5 and 6 (fig. 6.12) only. At beats 2 and 6 the *polos* leaps between the upper and lower stressed tones (*dung* and *dIng*), while the *sangsih* fills in the *ubit telu* by remaining in between on *dong* and *deng,* tones common to both positions. This basic technique was imaginatively illustrated to me by Wayan Gandera, a musician from Peliatan. Waving his two hands like fishtails and pointing them away from him with the left one parallel to and slightly behind the right, he remarked that *polos* and *sangsih* are like a pair of fish chasing each other through the water. When they swim straight (he moved both hands ahead, keeping them overlapped) one simply follows the other. If the leader decides to change direction, as *polos* often must do to follow the melody (he bent the right wrist to the left until the hand pointed back toward him), the other can respond efficiently by taking the inside bank of the curve (he bent the left hand also to the left). In this way, the *sangsih* remains always close behind the *polos* without, however, traveling as far.

Figures 6.15B and C (CDI/31), alternate versions of a melody from *Oleg Tumulilingan,* illustrate how the kinetic interaction between *neliti* and *kotekan* can be manipulated by compositional choice. In the first version the *kotekan,* uncharacteristically in a higher register than the *neliti,* accentuates the latter's Axis 0 shape through the simple iteration of kCC C7. In the second, exclusively *majalan* patterns are used to trace the {2,0,−1,0} shape of the melody's CC4.

Figure 6.15D (CDI/32) shows a *reyong ubit-ubitan* for a portion of the *pengipuk* (a melody accompanying a flirtation or seduction scene) from *Teruna Jaya.* Economy of motion is a necessity on the *reyong,* which cannot track the registral shifts in the *neliti* line. Here the *reyong* remains fixed in position 3 (fig. 6.12) almost to the end of the excerpt, despite the seven-tone ambitus of the *neliti.* This is possible because the *neliti* tones aligned with kCC-group stresses are limited (with one exception) to *dIng, dUng,* and *dung.* These tones

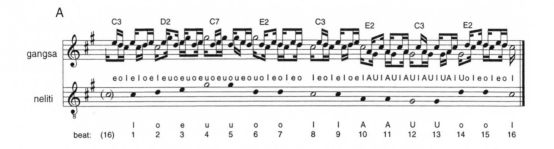

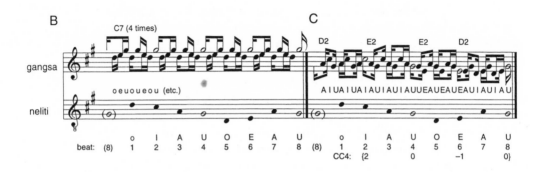

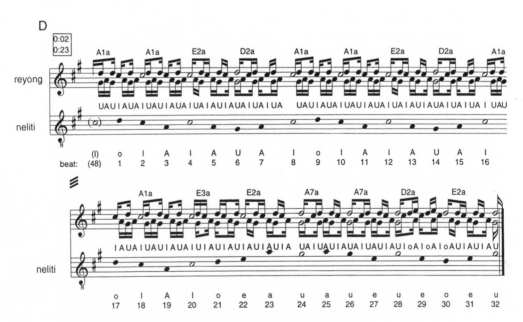

Figure 6.15. *Ubit-ubitan* in standard practice (CDI/30–32)
A: *"Garuda"* melody from *legong Lasem* (CDI/30; interlocking parts heard on separate channels). B and C: Two realizations of a melody from *Oleg Tumulilingan* (CDI/31.1 and 31.2; interlocking parts heard on separate channels). D: Beats 1–32 (of 48) of *pengipuk* melody from *Teruna Jaya* (CDI/32).

can all be covered at position 3 once one reimagines the line in *pokok* order (as it is played on *calung*), thus conflating *dUng* and *dung* to conceptual unison. The exception comes at beat 22, in the middle of the sixth *neliti* CC-group, where the tone *deng* is bypassed in the *kotekan* in favor of a 4-beat long *majalan* pattern leading to *dUng* (*dung* in the *neliti*). The linking of E3a and E2a here is an example of the prolongation of the 3:4 cross-rhythm mentioned earlier. And indeed, its appearance here underscores the youthful intensity of the dance, distancing it from more refined court genre dances. Cross-rhythm is prominent not only at that point, however, but throughout the example, because the frozen scale-tone field and *ubit-empat* texture result in constantly shifting recurrences of the *dUng/dong* vertical interval. Note too the contrary motion at 21–24 between the descending *kotekan* pattern and the ascending *neliti*. Such contrapuntal behavior is unique to the *reyong*.

The first, third, and fifth *neliti* CC-groups in 6.15D are *ngubeng* around *dIng*. All three are elaborated by the iterated kCC A1a. The second and fourth CC-groups are bisected by *dUng*, which is reflected by identical pairs of *majalan* kCC. The first, E2a, descends to the *dUng*; and the second, D2a, ascends back to *dIng*: the two form a little palindrome around *dUng*. The sixth *neliti* CC-group pushes up in register to establish a new, upper-register stress on *dung*; its elaboration was discussed in the previous paragraph. The seventh *neliti* CC-group, *ngubeng* around *dung*, is a transposition of the first, up three steps. But the *reyong*'s elaboration remains in place on *dUng*. As the lowest of the three tones in position 3, the *dUng* suggests a *ngubeng* kCC such as the one selected here, A7a. When the *neliti* dips down to *dong* in the eighth CC-group (a move that parallels the second CC-group), the shift cannot be accommodated by the *reyong* within position 3, so there is a shift up to position 4 (D2a, beats 28–29), once again in contrary motion with the *neliti*.

Asymmetrical Melody and Elaboration

The *tua* ensembles that have most profoundly influenced *kebyar* are the *gamelan gender wayang* and *angklung*, and the sacred seven-tone *gamelan gambang* and *luang* (and very recently, in a limited way, *selunding*). Also important is the *madya*-era *gandrung*, an ensemble with a history of changing and tenuous connections to the courts that contains elements of both court and *tua* music.[28] This is a diverse group ranging widely in sound, repertoire, instrumentation, and size, and often differing within a genre from village to village. None of these ensembles can be assumed to have existed in their present form during the pre-Majapahit era, nor are they known to have remained completely outside the court sphere for their entire histories. But it is in their current manifestations that they have made their impact on *kebyar*, and despite the

---

28. *Gandrung* is also known as *joged, joged pingitan* and *pejogedan* (McPhee 1966: chap. 13).

complexity of their pasts it is the perception that their origins are ancient that shapes the affect their music carries in *kebyar* contexts. The particular histories, contexts, functions, and ritual uses of *tua gamelan* have been explored by others, and, save for essentials, will be omitted from the present discussion to conserve space.[29]

Until the 1980s, *tua* influence on *kebyar* varied regionally, and depended on the kinds of music cultivated in a given area. For example, *gamelan angklung* has long been extremely popular in North Bali. Many villages had (and continue to have) both *angklung* and *kebyar* groups, with considerable overlap in *sekaha* membership. As suggested in chapter 3, this probably resulted in strong *angklung* influence on *tabuh kreasi* right from *kebyar*'s inception. The impact of the more esoteric and specialized music of *gambang* and *gender wayang* came later, largely through the work of individuals such as Lotring and Gusti Madé Putu Griya. Many composers of the current generation, among them Beratha, Sinti, Windha, and Asnawa, have a broader and deeper knowledge of several *tua* repertoires and can apply it in subtler, more pervasive ways than their forebears. Because of conservatory prestige and the cassette industry, their music has a more immediate, homogenous, and substantive island-wide impact than it would have had in the past.

Tua music is not *systematically* asymmetrical (if that were possible); it is simply less consistently symmetrical than court genre music. The court genres' shared ancestry in *gamelan gambuh* accounts for their use of colotomic meters, which was my basis for grouping their repertoires together as a structural class. In *tua* music gongs and drums are (or once were) absent, and quadripartite meter is only one stop along a fluid continuum of possibilities. It occurs often, but there is no sense of transgression or abnormality when it does not.[30] One cannot speak of normative metrical dimensions as one can in court genres, where symmetry is imposed by the gongs.

Most *tua* music has only two strata—*pokok* and *kotekan*—and therefore lacks the layered vertical dimension of court music.[31] *Tua pokok* are thus

---

29. Aside from McPhee, Schlager 1976, Toth 1975, and Schaareman 1980, 1986, and 1992 are the best sources for sacred seven-tone music. Gold (1998) and Vonck (1997) have written dissertations on *gender wayang*. Ornstein's brief article on *angklung* in North Bali (1971b) focuses mainly on the way it has absorbed *kebyar* influence. McPhee's coverage of *angklung, gender wayang,* and *gandrung* remains essential.

30. Formal terms in *tua* genres do not specify metric length, as do the various *tabuh* designations; and musicians do not distinguish between compositions on the basis of meter, as they do in court genres.

31. The *gamelan luang* presents a noteworthy exception in some cases. The ensemble in Ampuan that McPhee wrote about uses many melodic strata, and moreover uses musical forms of quadripartite dimensions. McPhee dubbed its method of orchestration a combination of the seven-tone *gamelan caruk* and *gamelan gong gdé* (1966:282). The *luang* in Tangkas village which Toth studied is a smaller *gamelan* with fewer strata. An ensemble from Kesiut village in Tabanan district recorded for me by Tom Deering in 1982 is similar.

neither abstracted by other instruments nor conceived of as a succession of tones of specific hierarchical weights. The lack of these constraints leads to enrichment of the music's horizontal flow, often resulting in internal rhythmic variety, irregular meters, fractional beats, and the forefronting of melody, elaboration, and surface rhythmic details and contrasts. This combination of features can make segmentation of the music a speculative task yielding ambiguous results. It also forces a reassessment of how tonal and kinetic quality are to be evaluated, for in symmetrical class music degrees of *ngubeng* and *majalan* were closely linked to the "pull" of structural markers.[32] Moreover, these issues cannot be addressed with reference to asymmetrical music as a whole, because *tua gamelan* differ substantially and must be understood separately.

Fortunately, this challenge is eased somewhat in *kebyar* contexts, for when composers transform *tua* styles for new music they need to orchestrate them. In so doing they insert structural markers in the form of *jegogan* and *calung* tones and/or gong punctuations, which segment melodies according to composers' perceptions of what their most important internal stresses are. Using these markers as orientation, it is possible to effectively compare the qualities of symmetrical and asymmetrical music.

Such analytical goals must be pursued flexibly. The relevance and efficacy of theoretical constructs like CC, Axis, and kCC were dependent upon metric hierarchy and quadripartition. All of the discussion that resulted from their application was designed to demonstrate the primacy of symmetry within a closed cyclical unit, and at the same time reveal the variety achievable therein. In strong contrast, the basic impulse of asymmetrical music is not always cyclic, and can approach (or even achieve) linearity. Applying CC, Axis, and kCC in these contexts may not always be revealing, or at least necessitates adapting them on a case-by-case basis. The axis on which a melody turns, if there is one, need not be its actual midpoint, nor must all points of stress be equidistant.

In what follows I look backward from *kebyar,* first by categorizing the kinds of *tua*-based asymmetries that occur in the repertoire, and then by

---

32. My own research, discussions with Balinese and non-Balinese musicians, and published writing shed little light on issues linking affect, formal segmentation, and melodic quality in *tua* genres. This was also the case with *kebyar,* but it is even more so here. As with *kebyar,* musicians prefer considering the music in its larger context, responding to questions by deferring to the concept of *rasa* (feeling). This is particularly true for the seven-tone ensembles, for which all music is tied to ritual. Schlager (1976) and Schaareman (1980) have probed the technical means and ritual function of the music in depth, explaining how figuration interlocks, naming standard forms, rhythms, and patterns and their proper use, and so on, without moving beyond received categories. Wayan Loceng, a specialist in the complex music of the *gamelan gender wayang* and among the most thoughtful musicians and literary scholars in Bali, was clearly spurred by our discussions on this subject, which took place over a period of years. His ultimate reluctance to commit himself on the issue was part of what led me to accept that many of these questions are better answered, even if speculatively, through the music itself.

analyzing samples of each in a *tua* context. The point is to demonstrate the origin of some *kebyar* devices in specific *tua* genres, and also to reveal some of the affinities between *kebyar* and the music of the pre-Majapahit era as a whole. The analyses encompass melody and figuration in *tua* compositions only; analysis of asymmetrical music integrated into the *kebyar* context will come in chapters 8 and 9.

Kinds of *Tua*-based Asymmetry in *Kebyar*

Asymmetrical features like those found in *tua* repertoires appear in *kebyar* compositions in several ways, exerting at times full control over the music, and at times combining with symmetrical procedures. Asymmetry may affect anything from the *pokok* elaboration to the entire structure. When meter is asymmetrical, it is likely that all levels of the structure will be as well. On the other hand, asymmetrical elaboration over a symmetrical *neliti* and gong pattern is also a very characteristic formation.

At present, there are no names or standard sizes for asymmetrical cycles in *kebyar*. When composers decide on *jegogan* or gong stresses to be used in them, they are imposing an interpretation on the melody, not delineating an independent structure. Often, melodies strongly suggest punctuation in 8- or 4-beat units, but sometimes they do not. Without codified metric plans such as the *tabuh pegongan*, however, meter and dimension become synonymous, and can be treated together.

Asymmetrical Melody in Kebyar

Asymmetrical melodies are identified by their overall nonquadripartite dimensions. In *kebyar* they may be presented entirely without colotomic punctuation, with punctuation at irregular intervals, or with only a stroke of the gong at the end. Regardless of which, *calung* and *jegogan* parts indicate which tones are stressed. Such melodies may be one of the following types:

1. A melody can be built up from an odd number of 4- or 8-beat units, or from an even number of such units arranged in odd-numbered subgroups. This results, for example, in melodies of 40 (5 × 8) beats, such as the *pengawak* of Puspanjali (fig. 6.6D). Another case is the *pengipuk* of *Teruna Jaya* (fig. 6.15D), which is 48 beats long, divided 2 × (3 × 8).

2. Melodies may contain predominantly 4- or 8-beat units, but include one or more units of differing length. Such units may be half the prevailing value, as in 4 + 4 + 2, or 8 + 8 + 4, or they may be more irregular, as in the 8 + 5 meter of figure 2.15. The 68-beat *pengawak* of Nyoman Windha's 1990 composition *Jagat Anyar*, with internal divisions of (5 × 8) + 7 + (2 × 8) + 5 beats, is a longer example of this type.

3. Melodies may resemble either of the above kinds, and also include interruptions in the pulse caused by fractional or extended beats. Such a melody,
   consisting of 5½ + 4 + 4 + 4 beats is found in the early-1960s *tabuh kreasi*
   Hujan Mas. A longer example is in the composition *Bima Kroda* from Sawan village (1982), in which the succession of *jegogan* tone lengths is
   (5,5,5,4½,4,4,4,1,4,12½,9,4½,4½,3½,5,5,2), which sums to 82½ beats. See
   also figure 8.5.
4. A melody may consist of a single ostinato-like unit that is other than 4 or 8
   beats long, such as the 5-beat cycle in Wayan Beratha's 1968 *tabuh kreasi*
   Palguna Warsa or the 6-beat one in Gusti Madé Putu Griya's 1969 *Jaya*
   Warsa.

All of the *tua* repertoires influential in *kebyar* contain compositions of the
first and second types. Melodies of the third and fourth types occur in *angklung* and *gender wayang* music.

Asymmetrical Elaborating Parts in Kebyar

Trademark rhythms and contours that shape elaborating parts in *tua* music are
used regularly in *kebyar*. In asymmetrical melodic contexts such as those described above, fixed noninterlocking parts may appear as if over symmetrical
neliti, composed to fit thè particular dimensions of the melody. *Gamelan gambang* may be evoked by using its 5 + 3 rhythm (or various modifications and
extensions of this rhythm that have entered the musical language over the past
few decades). *Gamelan angklung* is suggested by mimicking its restricted four-
note range and some of its characteristic melodic turns. An example of *luangan*
was already provided in figure 6.6D. The potency of the stylistic topic that
these kinds of usage generate is regulated by additional factors, such as placement in the overall form and orchestral texture.

   To my knowledge, *norot* is virtually never used in asymmetrical situations
because of its unshakable court genre topic. Improvised *payasan* of the kind
described earlier is also absent, save for occasional very small ornamental deviations that may be possible, and with allowances made for the cueing styles
of individual performers.

   In asymmetrical *ubit-ubitan* the symmetrical patterns given in figures 6.13
and 6.14 are not abandoned, but they are juxtaposed, transformed, and combined in novel ways. Placed over asymmetrical melodies, a succession of *ubit-
ubitan* pattern units need not adhere to the 2-beat unit length so firmly mandated in symmetrical contexts. Units may shrink to 1½ or extend to 3 or more
beats before a clear stress tone is sounded, in agreement with the often irregular progression of the underlying parts. The norms of syntax and standard
usage can be severely stretched, resulting (especially since the 1980s) in pattern sequences of a complexity unprecedented in any Balinese music. This is

an unmistakably contemporary development, albeit one clearly catalyzed by composers' increased knowledge of *tua* music.

Individual *ubit-ubitan* pattern units can have inherently asymmetrical structures, and may exhibit:

1. more frequent use of second-order relations other than *ngempat* (e.g., *nelu* and *nelima*),
2. the use of a range greater than three tones (excluding second-order tones),
3. *majalan* patterns other than the standard ones of figure 6.14.

Seen in relation to the melodies they elaborate, pattern sequences may contain:

4. first order relations other than scale-tone equivalence at *jegogan* stresses,
5. long sequences of (or the exclusive use of) *majalan* patterns,
6. rapid and repeated switching back and forth between *kotekan* and non-interlocking figuration types.

Asymmetrical *ubit-ubitan* patterns occur in all of the *tua* genres cited, plus the *gamelan gandrung*.

Asymmetry in *Tua* Compositions

The transcriptions in figures 6.16–19, from *gamelan gambang, gender wayang, angklung,* and *gandrung* respectively, represent the sources of the kinds of asymmetry described above.

Gamelan Gambang (CDI/33)

Of the four genres, *gamelan gambang* shows the least variability in texture and composition from piece to piece within its repertoire. The ensemble consists

Figure 6.16. *Pokok* tones from the *pingkalih* (second section) of *gending Panji Marga, gamelan gambang, banjar* Bedhe, Tabanan (CDI/33).

Gamelan gambang, Bebetin, 1982. Photo: Author.

of four wooden *gambang* of fourteen keys (two octaves of seven-tone *pélog*), each with slightly differing range, plus two bronze *saron* of seven keys. In Tatulingga village,[33] a standard *gambang gending* has four sections: an introductory *kawitan*, followed by *pingkalih, pingtiga,* and *pingpat* (meaning, respectively, second, third, and fourth parts), which succeed each other without a break.[34] The only significant change in the continuous staid texture of the music comes at the seam between the *kawitan* and the *pingkalih*. The jagged *kawitan* is played in scale-tone and rhythmic unison by all instruments. In the *pingkalih* and subsequent sections, the *saron* play the *pokok* in the 5 + 3 rhythm or some duple augmentation of it, and the four *gambang* each have their own interlocking parts (usually referred to as *oncang-oncangan,* the same term as the rice-pounding music from which Schlager showed they were derived), executed with a pair of two-pronged, Y-shaped mallets designed to strike pairs of keys separated by an octave. A tempo of approximately mm 74 and a medium dynamic are mostly held constant. Ritual context determines which of fifty-odd compositions in the repertoire is to be used and which of several interlocking figuration types may be applied to the post-*kawitan*

33. This summary is based on Schaareman's 1980 article in *Ethnomusicology*. Tatulingga is a fictitious name for the village where research was carried out, which Schaareman uses in all of his publications.

34. In an expanded type of composition known as *geguron,* two further sections, *taksu* and *kalé,* are added to standard *gending*. Ritual context determines whether *geguron* or *gending* form is used.

sections. The length of individual sections, the five-tone mode, and the sequence of *pokok* tones are the factors that vary from *gending* to *gending*.

The *pokok* for the *pingkalih* of the composition *Panji Marga* (fig. 6.16, from *banjar* Bedhe, Tabanan district) is eighty-eight beats long and consists of twenty-two tone-pairs (forty-four tones).[35] By scanning the melody in anticipation of the longer tone in each pair, *gambang* players create figuration patterns according to formulaic conventions. Within a given performance, these patterns will all be of the same type, and distinguishable from one another only by their melodic goals, not in terms of kinetic quality. The coordination between the figuration and the longer tones establishes the shorter tones as structurally secondary, making it possible to accord "stress" status to the longer ones, but there is no further basis for grouping the *pokok* into larger segments. Seen this way, the tune divides into twenty-two structurally equivalent 4-beat units and is an example of the first kind of melodic asymmetry defined above.

To demonstrate the strength of the contrast between the kind of melodic motion observable here and that in court *neliti,* I have notated the longer tones as a separate stratum. A comparison with the *neliti* and CC16 strata in 32-beat melodies (fig. 6.3Q–T; the closest court genre size) reveals a much more pronounced shaping of tonal regions than is evident here, and far less disjunct motion. Of the twenty-two tones in the hypothetical *gambang* stratum, fourteen are connected by disjunct motion, six by conjunct motion, and two do not move. The two stationary connections could be interpreted as *ngubeng* if there were a larger structural matrix against which to hear them, but since there is not they come across instead as passing horizontal phenomena without vertical girding. Listening for tone patterns and symmetrical relations in either stratum that would support a mid-level segmentation is also difficult because of the 44-beat length. Though many candidates for such a segmentation could be proposed, none is compelling enough to mandate a particular hearing of the tune, and in the absence of strong contrast, none is supported by other structural evidence.

The lack of overtly *ngubeng* elements in the melodic structure is preserved when *gambang*-type melodies are used in *kebyar,* and disjunct connections between *pokok* or *jegogan* tones are often highlighted. Such melodies are in constant motion, which could, as is possible in the staid *gambang,* be perceived simply as a different kind of stasis. In *kebyar,* however, they are arranged with colorful and rapidly shifting contrasts in tempo, dynamic, and orchestration. This provides them with a kinetic propulsion that is unlike either *gambang* or court music. As a consequence, the *gambang* topic acquires a separate identity from its source, merging the old and sacred with the modern and capricious.

---

35. The forty-four is significant because it is the number of syllables in one kind of stanza in the *sekar madya* poetic meters *Mayura* and *Demung.*

Gamelan gender wayang and one of its most respected teachers, Wayan Loceng, 1979. Photo: Author.

Gamelan Gender Wayang (CDI/34)

Gender wayang repertoire, accompaniment to the shadow puppet theater and many other rituals, exhibits much greater textural and affective variety than does *gambang*.[36] Four ten-key *gender* comprise the ensemble, two in a medium range and two an octave above. In the difficult instrumental technique, each is played with a pair of wooden mallets with disc-shaped ends, while keys are damped with the fingertips or the base of the hand. Left and right hands have separate music, usually configured so that the left hand plays melody and the right hand plays *kotekan*. Pairs of players may share identical left-hand parts, dividing *polos* and *sangsih* between the right hands, though it is also common to add second-order relations to the melody, sometimes to the point where it resembles or actually is itself separated into *kotekan*. Some melodies exceed the single-octave range characteristic of *tua* melody in general by extending upward into the second octave of the instrument, if the right-hand part is sufficiently high up to permit it. In still other situations texture is restricted to an entirely noninterlocking single line, shared between the hands, that can extend to the entire ten-key range. There is also a distinctive fluidity of movement between textures, dynamics, and tempi, and in and out of strict pulse.

   Gender wayang compositions are categorized according to their dramatic

---

36. See Zurbuchen 1987 for analysis of textual, linguistic, and vocal conventions in the shadow play.

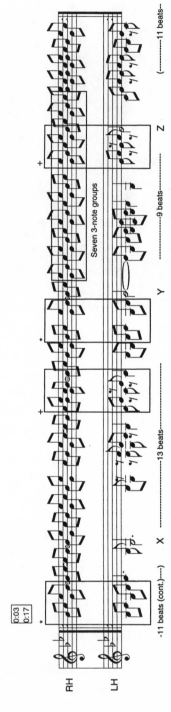

Figure 6.17. Opening section, *Sekar Sungsang*, gamelan gender wayang, Sukawati village (CDI/34). Stems down: first gender (*polos*). Stems up: second gender (*sangsih*). Transcription by Evan Ziporyn.

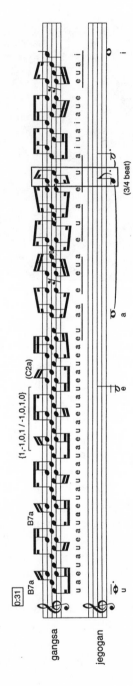

Figure 6.18. *Kempul Ndung*, gamelan angklung (CDI/35). The statement and repetitions of the *deng-dung-dang* sequence are underlined.

affect and whether they underpin the *dalang*'s (puppeteer's) singing, accompany action and dialog, or are one of a body of instrumental pieces used in rituals or rendered before the play begins. A significant portion of the repertoire, including the 4-beat *angkat-angkatan* melodies ("traveling" music for scene changes), is based on quadripartite ostinati, but even these short pieces support a variety of asymmetrical *ubit-ubitan* patterns and numerous idiosyncratic approaches to interpart relations. In nearly all other music form is asymmetrical as well. By way of illustration, consider the opening section of *Sekar Sungsang* (*Hanging Lily;* in the fig. 6.17 transcription the composite left- and right-hand parts are each shown on a single stave). It lies, by Balinese standards, in sharp syntactic opposition to court music.

In this 33-beat melody, three agogic accents formed by long rhythmic values in the left-hand part (labeled X, Y, and Z) are separated by 13, 9, and (bridging back across the repeat) 11 beats. These markers seem to provide the basis for a mid-level segmentation. X, Y, and Z can be seen as roughly analogous to *jegogan* tones, and obtain their connotations of stress. This is so despite the fact that the *kotekan* aligns with X and Y half a beat late and that at Z the two strata are related by a first-order *kempyung*. Though unheard of in court genres, these are both common procedures for aligning melody and elaboration in *gender wayang*.

Overall, the two strata fluctuate between full stratified independence and close coordination as parallel lines, rather than being characterized by strict differences in rhythmic density. The right hands play noninterlocking figuration enriched with *kempyung* and *nelu* second-order relations, and the left hands alternate between that and interlocking. In some places, such as the passage beginning three beats after X, the left-hand part seems to be derived from the right rather than vice versa. At others, such as the extension (seven repetitions) of the archetypal three-note *majalan* group that begins just after Y, the right hand is abstracted from the left to a point of considerable independence.

The repeating *majalan* group continues for 10½ beats, and does not change to a *ngubeng* pattern in acknowledgement of the agogic accent at Z. This is one of several features suggesting that a reevaluation of the analytical decision (taken above) to see the left-hand agogic accents as points of arrival is in order. The stability of X, Y, and Z is also weakened by the presence of repeating and sequential patterns that occur in differing relationship or proximity to them. In one case, the pair of identical 2-beat units marked *, the first of the two ends two beats before X, while the second one leads directly to Y. This truncation (or elision) obfuscates the parallel structural function of X and Y. Another example is the pair of transpositionally related 2-beat units marked + . The first comes some distance before Y while the second, one scale tone higher, proceeds to Z directly. This has the same truncating effect, but the relationship is further complicated by the fact that each + is given different right-hand figuration. The net effect of these "mis"-alignments is generally to loosen things, by suppressing vertical stability in favor of opening the music to conflicting, overlapping linear impulses.

The larger form of *Sekar Sungsang,* which continues far beyond this excerpt, is no less intricately designed. The attention to detail and seeming through-composed construction is characteristic of many pieces in the repertoire. McPhee wrote that *gender wayang* music was "like a prism revolving in sunlight" (1970a:168), an apt metaphor for the kinds of tonal and metrical complexity and ambiguous kinetic quality evident in the example. In *kebyar, gender wayang* topic has been much exploited both through direct quotation and through a more general application of its technical features. Composers doff their hats to the richness of its repertoire, and consider assimilating *gender wayang* influence into their music a worthwhile goal and a mark of erudition. It is not unlike the contrapuntal "learned style" of the Western classic era.

Gamelan Angklung (CDI/35)

The ubiquitous *gamelan angklung* has doubtless undergone many transformations in its long history, but today it is a bronze ensemble consisting of eight to twelve *gangsa,* a pair of *jegogan,* a *reyong, cengceng,* two tiny *kendang* played on one end with small mallets, *kempur,* the small timekeeping gong *tawa-tawa,* and often a *suling.* The four-tone *gamelan angklung,* in which all of the metallophones have a single-octave range of four keys, is the most common. Its two-octave *reyong* is divided among four players, two tones per person. There are also five-, seven-, and eight-keyed *gamelan angklung,* mostly in North Bali, with the fifth tone of the *slendro* scale included. The bamboo *angklung* rattles of former times have been dropped save for occasional revivals. McPhee chronicled his own efforts to reintroduce them (McPhee 1970b).

Angklung music is a versatile component of processions and temple ceremonies, where it is often heard in close proximity to and simultaneously with the more imposing *beleganjur* or *lelambatan.* Balinese have repeatedly called my attention to its bittersweet, plaintive affect, which for them provides an unpretentious and humble antidote to the pomp of larger ensembles. There is an aura of informality around *angklung* that contributes to this, too. Though *topeng* and some *tari lepas* may be adapted for it, *angklung*'s own repertoire is entirely instrumental. The *gamelan* lacks any former court affiliation, has no special prestige, and is taken for granted everywhere as an all-purpose adjunct to the routine schedule of ritual undertakings. Many begin their musical training on *angklung* because the size of the instruments makes them well suited for children. Yet the music is not simple by any means. As if to overcome the restrictions in range, *angklung* pieces use constantly varying *kotekan* and forms that combine symmetry and asymmetry.

This combination of factors makes *angklung*'s impact on *kebyar* seem a natural development, albeit one that few speak of. Possibly this is because of

Gamelan angklung, augmented here with *kebyar*-size drums, Mas, 1992. Photo: Tom Ballinger.

the music's very familiarity. None of those whom I asked discounted its effect, but their acknowledgments came with a shrug. They were unwilling to compare the kind of osmotic influence I posited with an individual's conscious championing of a genre, such as Lotring or Griya's infusions of *gender wayang* into *tabuh kreasi.* I am nonetheless convinced, on the basis of musical evidence, that *angklung* provides an important background for the details of *kebyar* style. The plasticity achieved within the tight four-note range of *angklung* music is prominently reflected in *kebyar,* particularly in the use of complex *ubit-ubitan* and the frequent desirability of freezing *kotekan* position if possible (as in fig. 6.15D). Though these may seem specialized concerns, they are truly the music's bread and butter.

Angklung music has two melodic strata: *pokok* (played by *jegogan* in sparse tones) and *gangsa* elaboration. The pair of *kendang,* often played by a single musician, are assigned brief repeating patterns which do not function as colotomic elaboration. The *kempur* marks endings only. By Rembang's reckoning, drums and gongs are later additions in any case, a credible notion judging by their supplemental roles. McPhee asserted that most *angklung gending* are "completely free in form. Each has its own individual shape, not too different from the others, but organized in its own special way" (1966:252). He noted two main *angklung* composition types, one which features *kotekan* and a steadily moving *pokok,* and the other noninterlocking elaboration and flexible or irregular pulse (1966:246).

In figure 6.18, from *Kempul Ndung,* a composition I learned from Wayan Rai, the two types are combined. (The title means that the *kempur [kempul]* stroke aligns with the scale tone *dung.*) The excerpt is part of a longer cycle consisting of thirteen subsections: ten of 8 beats, one of 6, one of 10, and this one, of 15¾ beats. This subsection is clearly divided into two slightly unequal segments (8 + 7¾ beats) by the combined effect of the *jegogan* arrival (on *dang*) and the change in texture from interlocking with support from a *tawa-tawa* beat to noninterlocking without *tawa-tawa.* The first segment uses standard *ubit-ubitan* patterns. Of these, the first two have been labeled as in figure 6.13. The latter two, paired here as they commonly are in *kebyar* as well, are conjoined to create a 4-beat pattern underpinning an ascending stepwise *pokok.* The one labeled kCC {1,−1,0,1/−1,0,1,0} is *majalan,* though not one of the figure 6.14 archetypes. Pattern C2a, ordinarily *ngubeng,* is heard here as driving to the *jegogan* arrival on *dang.* Overall, these 8 beats comprise a progression from *ngubeng* to *majalan* that is comparable with similar passages in court genre music. In the second segment, the lack of a rhythmically continuous composite line, the absence of additional *jegogan* tones, and the subtle disruption of the pulse all combine to prolong the *ngubeng* stability of the *pokok* arrival on *dang* to the *ding* at end of the segment. The multiple repetition (in changing rhythms) of the *deng-dung-dang* motive that ended the first half, which culminates in an ascent to *ding,* is an additional factor.

Seen in its entirety, the segment illustrates distortion of quadripartite balance, and exemplifies how proximate symmetry and asymmetry may be in certain contexts. *Angklung* music in general, despite its shibboleths, is more structurally compatible with court music than other *tua* genres, which is one more way to explain its pervasive influence. On the other hand, quirky passages like the one in the second half of figure 6.18 are characteristic and distinctive, and intensify the stylistic topic when such passages are used in *kebyar.* But because of the ensemble's village roots, *angklung* topics convey everyday familiarity more than anything else.

Gamelan gandrung (CDI/36)

The *gandrung* dance, formerly performed by young boys, is a subtype of the otherwise female genre *joged.* These solo dances were once associated with providing sexual favors for, or at the behest of, royalty. In the nineteenth century princes kept *joged* dancers at court to fulfill their whims or use them as "diplomatic emissaries" to entertain guests (Bandem and DeBoer 1995:86–92). Because of its illicit affiliations, the music had lower status than other court *gamelan,* though the dance uses a movement vocabulary drawn from the more prestigious (and less overtly suggestive) *legong.* When the courts weakened, *joged* and *gandrung* were among the first *gamelan* to be denied patronage, and by the early Dutch years they were entirely village-based.

Figure 6.19. *Pokok* and *kotekan* fragment from *Gegandrangan, gamelan gandrung, banjar* Ketapian Kelod, Denpasar (CDI/36). *Indicates second-order-relation *nelu.*

Gandrung and *joged* instrumentations have had many configurations and changed substantially over time (Vickers 1985: 164–65, 174). At one time the instruments were primarily of bronze, but the *gandrung* that has been influential in *kebyar* is a five-tone *pélog* ensemble made mainly of bamboo. Once popular in the villages of South Bali, it is now known only in a few places: notably Ketapian, near Denpasar, and Tegenungan, near Kemenuh. The Ketapian ensemble uses four *pemadé* and two *kantilan,* each with fifteen keys that span three octaves. They are constructed from long bamboo slats resonated over tubes and played with two mallets in parallel octaves. The two ten-key *calung* each span only a single octave, with two scales in the same register laid out consecutively. Bamboo's sound is brittle and short, but by "rolling" a pair of mallets between each pair of keys tuned to the same tone, *pokok* on these *calung* can "sustain" almost like their bronze counterparts. There are also *ceng-ceng,* a single *kendang,* and three bamboo "gongs"—*kempli, kempur,* and *kemplung* (equivalent to *klentong*)—each made by suspending a large slat over a wide resonator.

Five of the six pieces in the Ketapian ensemble's surviving repertoire are instrumental and stylistically identical to *gamelan pelegongan* instrumental music. Members of the group report that they were learned in the 1920s from Nyoman Kaler, then a prominent teacher and composer. The single pre-1920s piece, in what I was assured is a more authentic *gandrung* style, is *Gegandrangan,* accompaniment for the dance, which is excerpted in figure 6.19. It exhibits the *kotekan* style already mentioned in reference to fig. 4.1B, with which it may be compared.[37]

In figure 6.19, *polos ubit-ubitan* patterns move among three tones instead of the usual two, and tend to align with the *sangsih* at the second-order-

---

37. Older generation composers, notably Wayan Jebeg of Batubulan, Nyoman Senken of Kesiman, Nyoman Rembang, and others, cited *gandrung* as especially important, noting that because it shares *kebyar*'s five-tone *pélog* scale it is especially easy to adapt *gandrung kotekan* patterns for *tabuh kreasi.* They stressed the tendency of *sangsih* parts to weave both above and below the *polos* within the same unit—a technique more evident in figure 4.1B than here.

Gamelan gandrung and *gandrung* dancer, Tegenungan, 1989. Photo: Tom Ballinger.

relation *nelu* rather than *ngempat. Ngempat* occurs too, providing another level of textural contrast. The composite line spans four tones rather than three, and, in the last two beats, five tones. Though each new *calung* tone achieves stable first-order alignment with the *kotekan,* none of the 2-beat kotekan units are conventionally *ngubeng* or *majalan.* The whole divides into a pair of 4-beat units, a segmentation based on the prominence of the *polos'* low *dong* in the first half and the *sangsih*'s high *ding* in the second. At the same time, the two strata are related by a constant density ratio of 8:1, standard for *pokok* and *kotekan* in court genre music.

Gandrung is of course of the court too, but the winding asymmetry of its *kotekan* style links it to *tua* music. To its onetime royal patrons, perhaps, the way that these complexities strain at the boundaries of symmetrical syntax was in some way emblematic of the music's tawdry and somewhat compromised social status. Today these erotic associations are practically gone, but their aura of excitement lingers. The structural reflection of this is *gandrung*'s audacious complexity, which has inherent appeal for *kebyar* composers.

Conclusion: Asymmetry and Vocal Traditions

The broadest perspective on the history of *kebyar* melody comes from seeing it in the light of vocal traditions, for in all probability *gamelan* instrumental melody is rooted in sung poetry. This relationship has been explored by writers on both Balinese music and Javanese music, though the richness of the connection has been diminished for too long to facilitate accurate reconstruction of its former complexity.[38]

The four main categories of *tembang* (Balinese vocal genres) are *sloka* (Sanskrit intonations of Brahman priests), *kakawin* (Kawi vocalization of Indic and early Javanese epic poems), *kidung* (Balinese language genealogies and poems of the later Hindu-Bali era) and *geguritan* (shorter, topical verses, also in Balinese). Each has a particular vocal style, set of linguistic conventions, and metric organization that strongly evoke their original milieu for Balinese who sing and listen to them. All are founded on the vocal interpretation of a large repertoire of poetic texts written, preserved, and continuously recopied and transformed on *lontar*. In all *tembang* but *sloka,* prescribed patterns of syllabification, numbers of lines in a stanza, and specific vowel endings for each line are codified in a large stock of conventionalized poetic meters. When the poems are sung, rhythm often lacks an underlying pulse, and extended melismata are standard.[39]

It is clear that the irregular poetic meters of *kidung* had a formative influence on the sacred seven-tone *gamelan* repertoire. Indeed, *kidung lontar* often contain notation (called *grantangan*) for a *pokok* melody, intended to be played on *gamelan,* that was once commonly used to accompany the singing of the poems. The *pokok* was at least partly constructed from a mapping of the text's succession of vowel sounds onto *gamelan* tones through the solmization system, a relationship that Schlager (1976) and others have been at pains to demonstrate. (The solmization system itself may well have originated in connection with this practice.) For all of the enticing clues such scholarship has unearthed, however, the relationship is far from consistent.[40] Nonetheless, the dimensions of many *kidung* meters match those of specific seven-tone *gending,* which often bear their names (Wallis 1979:213). This provides a more empirical explanation for asymmetry in this music than the absence of gongs does.

The practice of singing *kidung* poetry to the accompaniment of sacred seven-tone *gamelan,* once thought to have been abandoned, is still extant in some East Bali locations. *Kakawin* is sung to *gender wayang* accompaniment when *Mahabharata* and *Ramayana* stories are enacted in the shadow play, but whatever specific connections may have once existed between the

---

38. Many have contributed to the discussion of these connections. See Wallis 1979:208–25; see also McPhee 1966:165–66, 280–81; Schlager 1976; Vickers 1986:84–85; and Toth 1975. See Sumarsam 1995 for a discussion of the vocal origins of Javanese *gamelan* compositions.

39. Additional kinds of vocal music include children's songs (*dolanan*), trance-inducing songs (*gending sanghyang*), and others.

40. For more on the problems of fleshing out these issues, see Wallis 1979:241–43.

dalang's melodies and the compositions underpinning them are tenuous to-day.[41] Though in general these voice-and-accompaniment connections are less developed than they once were, vocal genres themselves thrive independently and have in fact undergone an impressive renaissance in the past several decades. The performance and interpretation of *kakawin* especially, with its link to pre-Majapahit Indic culture, has been embraced and promulgated by the public at large in the spirit of internal conversion (Geertz 1973:170–89), wherein cultural values are reclaimed and rationalized with a level of conscious awareness unknown before the modern era. Vocal genres communicate the morality and values of all stages of Balinese history, reinforcing their continued relevance. Linked to the poetic meters of *tembang* through the reascendance of asymmetric design, *kebyar* too reclaims this past.

The development of Balinese *gamelan* is a process of gradual reconciliation between the sung poetry of religious, moral, and cultural continuity, the ordered hierarchies of the courts and bronze technology, and the interlocking rhythms of cooperative work. These fundamental cultural practices continue to endure and vitalize Bali, both separately and in the guise of their many transformations.

---

41. See Gold 1992:254, and also note the free relationships, both tonally and metrically, between the vocal and *gender* parts in the transcription of *Alas Harum* in McPhee 1970a:164. Vickers (personal communication, 1993) has researched the history of *wayang* and uncovered evidence that in former times *dalang* sang *kidung* stanzas during performance.

7 Meter and Drumming

Mantra for the *kendang*

Bunut waringin pipituk kubegadang
surup rupe cahyenku
sekali kadih nabi Allah
mapanaku ngaduh senggeger Yusup
jejuluk yut
kabu lindur sejagat.
Beat the drum thrice[1]

(Wood of the beringin tree, be as one with me;
veil my countenance,
unite me with Allah
and child Yusuf, thunderous and noisy,
the clamor, the commotion
darkening, quaking the world.)

Wayan Suweca, *kendang*, 1980. Photo: Rachel Cooper.

Prelude: *Kebyar* Drummers as Leaders and Stylists

LIKE confident drummers everywhere, my teacher Wayan Suweca has some-thing of a penchant for bravado. He used to confide in me that "even among musicians, drumming is a specialist's skill." It was a favorite subject that he returned to time and again during the years that we played together.

> Only drummers are equipped to appreciate it. People are generally aware of what roles drummers play and can speak about them a little bit. They hear a sharp stroke

---

1. Wayan Tembres, Blangsinga Village, November 1982. Tembres received this from his brother-in-law, a *dukun* (healer dealing with forms of magic). It is not really a *mantra*, which would be used by *pedanda* (high priests), but a kind of invocation. The reference to Allah is an acculturation present in many Balinese incantations that signifies an exotic and potent but subjugatable foreign spiritual power (Vickers 1987:44–45; mantra translation (Kawi to Indonesian) by Madé Persib, 1997). Yusuf is a symbol of beauty in Islamic mysticism.

or a rush of accents and understand the way it affects the rest of the *gamelan* or the dancer. But the patterns themselves are buried down below the melody where they are hard to hear, and not even other musicians pay the kind of attention to them that they warrant. Only other drummers can pick them out by listening, memorize them, criticize them, and know how their small details have the power to control the performance. It's much more difficult than melody. Knowing the melodies is easy. (Personal communication, September 1982)

Judged solely on the basis of their tone, there is nothing extraordinary in Suweca's comments, because artistic rivalry has been a high-profile component of *kebyar*'s milieu from the beginning. By spotlighting drummers, however, Suweca singles them out as a uniquely prestigious minority. The artistic higher ground he claims for them trumps the usual kind of sparring about *gamelan* style or ensemble precision by boasting that a good drummer's aesthetic sensibility takes the highest performance standards as a given. Drummers are too busy fulfilling their many responsibilities to be preoccupied with such issues: after all, one of the two drummers (usually the player of the deeper-pitched *wadon*) holds the reins for the group as a whole, acting as director, rehearsal leader, general authority figure, and often composer and choreographer too. In Suweca's view drummers have access both to broader perspectives and levels of subtlety in the music that other players, while skillful in their own domains, are just not equipped to understand.

Suweca molds his self-image after that of his primary teachers, many of whom helped shape *kebyar* style at midcentury by building careers as ambitious musical entrepreneurs. They traveled from village to village, impressing the authority of their knowledge on the independent *sekaha* organizations, acquiring networks of *anak buah* (disciples), and elevating drumming to new levels of complexity and responsibility, in part so that they would be indispensable. As a result many groups would not perform without the presence of these outside specialists (Tenzer 1998:114). Suweca also defines a field within which drummers compete with each other. Who has the best patterns, clearest and most artful cues, best body language, and best technique? These subjects are much discussed among drummers, who, as Suweca points out, are avid connoisseurs of themselves. They form a subculture whose membership often cuts across *banjar,* village, or regional affiliations. Drummers seek out new patterns either by asking to be taught them directly or, more often, by surreptitiously copying them. Only players of the rarefied *gamelan gender wayang* are comparably covetous of each others' styles and techniques.

Aside from Suweca, who was born in 1948, I studied with many older members of this community: Wayan Tembres of Blangsinga, Gdé Manik of Jagaraga, Wayan Beratha of Denpasar, Wayan Pogog of *banjar* Lebah, Denpasar, Ketut Rintig of Geladag, Madé Kuna of Sanur, Anak Agung Raka Sibang of Sibang, Nyoman Senken of Kesiman, Wayan Konolan of Kayumas (Suweca's father), Wayan Suweca (unrelated) of Sanur, Ketut Dibya of Tampaksiring,

Madé Lebah and Madé Demong of Peliatan, Ketut Tutur of Petulu, Ketut Kumpul of Pindha, and Wayan Jebeg of Batubulan, among others, who collectively helped bring *kebyar* drumming to its current state of refinement. Between the late 1970s and mid-1990s many of these players were rapidly becoming weaker or dying, and the influence of those unaffiliated with the academies was diminishing. Some were given honorary teaching appointments at STSI, but usually this amounted to little actual work, and their access to students was, for all intents and purposes, minimal.

At the same time, Suweca and many others of his generation, including Partha, Mustika, Astita, Asnawa, Sukrata, Rai, and Sinti, most conservatory-trained and employed, have studied their elders' styles well and, what is more, can usually articulate the differences between them when asked. Indeed, Suweca could be called nothing less than obsessed with the subject. Overall, my studies uncovered an individuality in drumming styles that surprised my expectations. In part this is because drummers comprise a kind of hidden elite in the world of Balinese musical collectivity: within certain limits, drummers can vary their patterns without impacting the rest of the *gamelan*, and safely assume that only the most astute musicians will even notice the difference. Such changes must necessarily be subtle, and are resistant to meaningful characterization without preparation in the theory and syntax of drumming. I aim to provide this, but anything more than a preliminary approach to the fine distinctions between individual styles is beyond the scope of the book. This prelude is offered as a partial substitute: an homage to these details, so painstakingly worked out by my teachers, but perhaps fully appreciated only by them.

Chapter Overview

In this chapter *kebyar* drumming will be analyzed to discover its structure, and to evaluate its contribution to the ongoing dialog between symmetry and asymmetry in *kebyar*. The goal, parallel to that in the last chapter, is to depict various facets of this dialog through the analysis of a selection of drum patterns. The now-familiar bywords "syntax" and "quality" will remain central, in much the same way as they were for melody. Two further concerns, already implicit in the discussion of melody but explored with new emphasis here, are the notions of stability and disruption. Briefly, the two words may be thought of as congruent to *ngubeng* and *majalan*. Their domain of applicability is not at the note-to-note level, however, or even within cycles, but at the higher level of interactions between cycles. Stability, linked to symmetry and court genres, refers to the controlling influence of colotomic meter and the independence of strata; that is, the default state of the music. Disruption, linked to asymmetry and contemporary compositional process, implies challenges to cyclic structure, and explicit coordination between strata. The impulse guiding disruption is rhythmic, and coordinated by the drums. Such drumming does not lead to the abandonment of court meters, as the influence of the *tua* genres can for melody, but it challenges them, and in so doing suggests alternative hearings of cyclic structure.

What are the sources for disruptive drumming patterns? Unlike melody, *kebyar* drumming is not directly influenced by *tua* repertoire, because drums were a later and mainly inessential addition to *tua gamelan*. Some indirect influence can be said to exist, because *tua* music's asymmetry has been an important resource in the general search for structural alternatives that characterizes *kebyar*. Many of the innovations can be seen as extensions of the idea of *angsel* that has its modern antecedents in the *legong* dance.[2] Another explanation for drumming innovation can be found by recalling the reasons for the search itself: the growth of a context for music as artistic presentation, the pursuit of high artistic standards in the *sekaha* context, and the increasingly personalized contributions of drummer/composers and their collaborations with choreographers. Moreover, drumming is more conspicuous in *kebyar* than in court genres. The patterns are more intricate, the size and tuning of the drums in relation to the *gamelan* make them acoustically more prominent, the technique is more demanding, and the lead drummer takes a more vital role in teaching, composing, directing, and above all interacting with musicians and dancers in performance. Twentieth-century changes in drumming stem from a desire to add intricacy to the patterns as a way of boosting their intrinsic compositional interest, making them more challenging to play, and amplifying the vividness of their interface with other musical strata and the dance.

Depicting the scope of these qualities through musical analysis calls for multiple approaches, which I have set forth below as a set of five areas of inquiry. Some are new to drumming, and others involve reinterpretation of concepts applied to melody. They are presented in the following order:

1. The relationship of drum pattern to meter
2. Drum styles, the vocabulary of drum strokes, syntax, and structure
3. Pattern identity and quality
4. Stable and active drum patterns and the impact of drumming on form
5. Drumming and dance movement

Each area is a separate lens through which to view the complex but outwardly minimally differentiated (even to other musicians, as Suweca would have it) language of Balinese drumming. The selection of patterns is restricted to fixed *kendang matimpal* (*timpal* = companion, friend) patterns for the main body of the discussion. *Matimpal* drumming calls for *wadon* and *lanang* drums

---

2. The term *angsel* is also used in *gambuh* and also many *tua* repertoires, with a variety of meanings. The most common sense of the term in *kebyar* is that of a sharp, transitional dance movement that is reflected with a disruption in the surface rhythm of the music.

to play together in interlocking parts. At the end of the chapter, two kinds of *matimpal* improvised drumming plus samples of solo *kendang tunggal* (*tunggal* = sole, alone) improvised patterns will be taken up separately. Most drumming falls in the fixed category, but the latter comprises an important kind of playing that has never been addressed in the literature.

Before proceeding I must clarify exactly what I mean by "drum pattern." Nearly all Balinese words for drum pattern are meter-specific, save for the umbrella term *kendangan* (drumming). Thus there are *gilak* patterns (*kendangan gilak*), *bapang* patterns (*kendangan bapang*), and so on, but although the linkage of pattern and meter is clear, there is no terminology to indicate whether a pattern lasts for a part or whole cycle, or extends across multiple *gongan*. I will use the term "pattern" to denote the drumming for a single full cycle in any meter, save for the longer *gongan* of *pengawak* in *tabuh pegongan* and *pegambuhan*, which I will refer to as *kendangan*. A second meaning I ascribe to pattern is the large, metrically delineated subdivisions of *kendangan*: in other words, the drumming that comes in between the colotomic markers in longer meters.[3] The *kendangan* for a cycle such as the 256-beat *pengawak legong Lasem* (appendix B), for example, is divided into four patterns of 64 beats each, which end, as I shall explain below in the subtopic on meter, in alignment with the meter's internal punctuations. Two considerations lead me to adopt this dual definition of pattern: first, as is the case with *Lasem*, some patterns within *kendangan* may be near or exact duplicates of one another, and it seems intuitively correct to characterize patterns as through-composed musical objects without extensive internal repetitions (though even short patterns may contain *some* internal repetition). It also seems apt to limit the meaning of "pattern" to shorter segments of music without major internal cadences or subdivisions.

Pattern segments, which I shall call *subpatterns*, are formed by agogic accents and/or timbral contrasts created by shifts from the predominance of one kind of stroke to another.[4] In short meters, subpatterns are to patterns as patterns are to *kendangan* in long meters; that is, they ordinarily end in alignment with metrically stressed points. When they do not (especially in recent music), this may be indicative of disruption and innovation. Decisions about how to segment patterns into subpatterns are taken on a case-by-case basis in the analyses.

---

3. The standard usages of *kendangan* in Bali are somewhat less specific. It may be used in the sense in which I use "pattern," or it may also mean the drumming for an entire composition, encompassing the drumming for a series of cycles used therein. Nyoman Rembang (1984–85a) uses the term *melodi kendang* for drum pattern in his monograph on *pegongan* repertoire, a calque illustrative of the Balinese perception that drum patterns are melodic in nature. I prefer to avoid any confusion that might result from adopting this otherwise attractive locution.

4. Balinese sometimes use the Indonesian word *pola*, meaning pattern, to describe what I am calling subpattern.

Drum Pattern and Balinese Meter

In the last chapter I avoided scrupulous discussion of meter in order to show that in important ways, melodic affect is independent of it. It was not my intent to downplay questions of metric organization, which to the Balinese are un-questionably fundamental to musical structure and expression, but to take them as a given, and to look beyond them when possible. I will persist in this approach to some degree with drumming, but at the same time it is unwieldy to pursue the subject without recourse to the details of meter. This is because drumming has a much closer relationship to colotomic structure than melody does. Composers are continually creating new melodies in existing meters, each with its own inner relationships, but drumming is—at least in prin-ciple—"plugged-in" according to metric conventions, and new drum patterns are composed less often than new melodies.

Meter must be clearly distinguished from form. The latter, explored in the next chapter, is inherently linear in temporal character. It refers to the large-scale organization of *gending*—the succession of melodies, their relationships to one another, and any interruptions, interpolations, or changes in tempo, dynamic, and texture that animate the music and are significant from a large-scale compositional point of view. Balinese colotomic meter, to at last define it explicitly, refers to the sequence of gongs that punctuate *individual* cycles in court and court-derived repertoires, and extends to include any drumming and changes in intensity, dynamic, and tempo that are linked to the meter generically, as opposed to being a feature of a specific composition.[5] Meter invokes topic: shorter meters for character topics and longer ones for abstract topics. I stress the word "individual" in the definition because although most *gongan* repeat, there are many *gending* containing cycles that do not.[6] It is also important to emphasize that this definition of meter involves factors other than simply dimension and stress, all of which contribute to each meter's spe-cial affect. This contrasts with the usual Western understanding of the word as a set of pulses with an overlaid pattern of accents.

The inherited collection of Balinese court meters has now shrunk to the point where only some fifteen are in wide circulation, despite evidence that at one time others, systematically derived from one another via processes of expansion and diminution, were in use. Figures 7.1A (*pegambuhan* and *pegambuhan*-derived meters) and B (*pegongan* and *pegongan*-derived meters) display the extant ones. A comprehensive listing of meters taking regional

---

5. The only colotomic meters that are not court-derived occur when gong punctuation is super-imposed on *tua*-influenced, asymmetrical melodies, as described in the last chapter.

6. Becker (1980:105–47) introduces the idea of repetition right at the outset of her theory of Javanese *gongan* derivations and considers it fundamental to the concept of *gongan,* but I see too many exceptions to this in Bali to carry the idea over.

variants into account would be impractical, so only the most widely known versions are included.[7] In general *pegongan* meters have more overt links with *kebyar* because, like the older *gong gdé*, *kebyar* uses gong at cycle endings. *Pegambuhan*-derived meters include those of *gamelan semar pegulingan*, to which they are essentially identical, and those *of gamelan pelegongan*, which exhibit only minimal transformation from their *gambuh* predecessors. These three genres' meters are treated as a single broad category here and throughout the book. All ended with *kempur* in their original forms, though gong is routinely substituted in *kebyar* contexts.

In the charts meters are listed in order of increasing size. Only six of them—one *tabuh pegambuhan* and five *tabuh pegongan*—are fully systematized (7.1A.7, 7.1B.4–8); in addition there are two more *pegambuhan* meters that came to be fully systematized only in their *pelegongan* transformations (7.1A.5–6). Because their rigorous architechtonics suggest a learned approach that the courts are held to have provided, these meters' abstractions (hence my term "abstract topic") are felt to embody court values in a worthy way. Their proper punctuation is a favorite subject matter of musicians' shoptalk.

In the absence of further specification, musicians consider the dimensions of *tabuh* to mean the dimensions of their *pengawak*, even though a full *gending* will also include at least a *kawitan* before the *pengawak* and a *pengecet* after. In all cases except one (*tabuh telu pegongan*: 7.1B.4; see also below), *pengawak* are at least 128 beats long. The metric schemes of *kawitan* and *pengecet* cycles are less broad than the *pengawak*, and may use its punctuation scheme in diminution. The scheme itself is known as the *jajar pageh* (from *jajar*, lined up or in rows; and *pageh*, fixed or permanent). *Jajar pageh* demarcate the *palet*, 64-beat (32-*pokok*-tone) subsections of the meter that end with some kind of internal punctuation. A *tabuh*'s final *palet* is called the *milpil*; it is here that melodic motion, drumming, and often dynamic and tempo intensify in preparation for the end of the cycle.

Most of the remaining seven (7.1A.1–4, 7.1B.1–3) court meters are not restricted to any single size or shape, but all are 64 beats or less. An unruly bunch in comparison with the others, their flexibility stands in contrast to the latter's rigidity. Their comparative lack of standardization also suggests less court influence, so that while all are part of court repertoire it is likely that their origins lie outside the courts in the village dance traditions. Indeed, the most basic types—*bapang, gegaboran,* and *gilak*—are most closely associated with, respectively, *barong, gabor,* and *baris*-related music. These are all old,

---

7. Variants abound. Here are two examples. In many North Bali renditions, 8-beat *gilak* melodies use an additional *kempur* stroke one beat prior to the gong in the middle of the cycle, and many *sekaha* in Gianyar district insert an additional *kempur* in *tabuh* 4, 6, or 8 *pengawak* four beats prior to the final gong. See also chap. 6, n. 10, on metric types that are rare or in disuse.

Meter name	Punctuation scheme	Dimensions	Comments
	Key: P = *kempur* (gong [G] if *kebyar*) k = *kajar* (*kempli* [M] if *kebyar*) kn = *neruktuk* t = *klentong* (aka *kemong*)	Gong notations carry value of one "."	
1. *Batel*	(P).P or P. . .P(*gambuh*) (P)tP or (P).t.P (*pelegongan*)	2 or 4 beats (. = 1/2 or 1 beat)	k on every beat
2. *Bapang*	(P). . . . . . .P (*gambuh*) (P). . .t. . .P (*pelegongan*) (G).P.t.P.G (*kebyar*)	4 or 8 beats (. = 1/2 or 1 beat) *Longgor* version expands to 16 beats	*Gambuh*: k follows drums *Pelegongan*: k on every beat *Kebyar*: M on every beat
3. *Gegaboran*	(P). . .t. . .P (*pelegongan*) (G).P.t.P.G (*kebyar*)	8 beats (. = 1 beat) *Longgor* version expands to 16 beats	
4. Miscellany (e.g., *kawitan, bebaturan, pemalpal, pengecet, pekaad*)	(P). . . . . . .P (*gambuh*) (P). . .t. . .P (*pelegongan*)	16, 32, or 64 beats (. = 2, 4, or 8 beats)	k follows drums in some cases, keeps beat in others
5. *Tabuh 1 (Besik)*	(P). . .kn(t) <u>. . .P</u>	128 beats (. = 16 beats) (dimensions and proportions may vary in *pegambuhan*)	*Pegambuhan*: k follows drums but inserts *neruktuk* at kn *Pelegongan*: k and kn as in *gambuh*, plus t in addition
6. *Tabuh 2 (Dua)*	(P). . .kn(t) . . .kn(t) <u>. . .P</u>	192 beats (. = 16 beats) (Dimensions and proportions may vary in *pegambuhan*.)	
7. *Tabuh 3 (Telu)*	(P). . .kn(t) . . .kn(t) . . .kn(t) <u>. . .P</u>	256 beats (. = 16 beats) (Fixed dimensions and proportions in both *pegambuhan* and *pelegongan*.)	

Figure 7.1A. *Pegambuhan* and *pegambuhan*-derived meters. In longer *tabuh*, final *palet (milpil)* is underlined. (P) indicates final *kempur* of previous cycle.

Meter name	Punctuation scheme	Dimensions	Comments
	Key: G = gong M = *kempli* t = *klentong* (in *kebyar* only) P = *kempur*	Gong notations carry value of one "."	
1. *Gilak*	(G). . .GP.PG or (G). . . . . . .G.P.M.P.G	8 beats (. = 1 beat) or 16 beats (. = 1 beat)	1. M on every beat 2. Melody may span multiple cycles
2. *Bapang*	(G). . .P. . .G (*gong gdé*) (G).P.t.P.G (*kebyar*)	8 beats (. = 1 beat)	*Kebyar:* M on every beat
3. *Lelonggoran* (e.g., *Gabor Longgor, Bapang Longgor*; general *kebyar* usage)	(G). . .P. . .t. . .P. . .G	16 beats (. = 1 beat)	
4. *Tabuh 3 (Telu)*	(G/M). . .M. . .G/M .P.M. P.G/M	16 beats (. = 1 beat)	1. Typically uses multiple cycles in single melody 2. Midpoint gong omitted in some regions
5. *Tabuh 1 (Pisan)*	(G/M). . .P. . .M . . .P. . .G/M . . .P. . .M . . .P. . .G/M	128 or 64 beats (. = 4 beats in *pengawak* and *pengisep*; 2 in *pengecet*)	*Pengawak* complete only with two 64-beat *gongan* (or multiples of two)
6. *Tabuh 4 (Empat)*	(G/M). . .P. . .M. . .P. . .M . . .P. . .M. . .P. . .G/M	256 or 32 beats (. = 8 beats in *pengawak*; 1 beat in *pengecet*)	1. *Tabuh 4, 6,* and *8* all use *tabuh* 4-size *pengecet* 2. In some regions, an extra *kempur* is added four beats before final gong
7. *Tabuh 6 (Nem)*	(G/M). . .P. . .M. . .P. . .M . . .P. . .M. . .P. . .M . . .P. . .M. . .P. . .G/M	384 beats (. = 8 beats)	
8. *Tabuh 8 (Kutus)*	(G/M). . .P. . .M. . .P. . .M . . .P. . .M. . .P. . .M . . .P. . .M. . .P. . .M . . .P. . .M. . .P. . .G/M	512 beats (. = 8 beats)	

Figure 7.1B. *Pegongan* and *pegongan*-derived meters. In longer *tabuh,* final *palet (milpil)* is underlined. *Tabuh 2, 5,* and 7 forms are documented in McPhee (1966:390-409) but are rare today. When used they follow the basic plan of *Tabuh 4.* (G) or (G/M) indicates final gong or final gong/*kempli* of previous cycle.

probably of pre-Majapahit origin. Their assimilation into court performance genres illustrates how porous court-village boundaries were. The miscellaneous kinds listed in 7.1A.4 are best thought of not as meters, but as melody types used in certain formal or theatrical contexts to which particular kinds of metric punctuation are more or less consistently applied.

In fact, according to Rai, one does not think of this group of meters primarily in terms of a particular dimension; one thinks of the melody (which need not be of a specific length, though it is in effect always quadripartite) and the use to which it will be put first, and then applies an appropriate punctuation scheme. The *bapang* used for *Jauk Keras,* a *pegambuhan*-derived piece, appears in two forms during the course of the *gending:* initially at fast tempo as an 8-beat cycle, and later in slow tempo, expanded to 16-beats. Terminologically speaking both are the same meter; Balinese distinguish the expansions from one another by calling the longer version *longgor,* or in this specific case *bapang longgor.*[8]

Rai's directive also explains why—depending on their melodic style, what they accompany, and on the particular court genre evoked—some *gongan* classified with the same name can have different punctuation; or, conversely, how ones with identical punctuation can be classified separately. *Bapang,* for example, is a meter with both *pegambuhan* and *pegongan* origins (7.1A *and* 7.1B.2). *Bapang* for *jauk* or *barong* dances are finished with *kempur* and bisected by *klentong* when accompanied by *gamelan pelegongan,* but a *bapang* from the *topeng* repertoire could be played on *gamelan gong gdé* and use *kempur* at the midpoint. Yet the same *pelegongan* punctuation used with female dance is likely to be called *gegaboran.* In *kebyar* all of these become the 8-beat [(G).P.t.P.G] (see 7.1A.2, 3 and 7.1B.2).

A 16-beat, *longgor* version of this, that is, a cycle punctuated as [(G) . . . P . . . t . . . P . . . G], is perhaps the most commonplace type in the *kebyar* repertoire, yet it has no widely accepted name. When accompanying a *gabor*-like dance it may be called *gabor longgor,* but it is identical to the expanded *bapang* mentioned above, and in *tabuh kreasi,* where it often appears, there is no standard way to refer to it at all. Among Balinese there is indeed uncertainty about what to name this most ubiquitous of cycle-types. To avoid misleading associations with inappropriate dances or forms I shall adopt the term *lelonggoran,* a generic abstract noun meaning expansion (in this case understood to reflect origins in the 8-beat *gabor* and *bapang* cycle types).

In addition to *kempur* (P), *kajar* (k) gives the main punctuation in

---

8. In Java the term *irama* is used to denote various levels of subdivisional expansion in the performance of a succession of cycles. There is no equivalent Balinese phenomenon or term. The case of the fast expanding to slow *bapang* cited here is not really an *irama* expansion, though when heard it sounds at first as if it might be. In actuality the *bapang longgor* is a different melody created by doubling the number of *neliti* tones in the fast one. This is achieved by interpolating a new tone between each of the original tones, such that the original fast melody is heard in the slow one's *pokok* stratum.

Figure 7.2. *Kajar neruktuk*

pegambuhan and *pelegongan*. In short meters at fast tempi the role of the *kajar* is to keep the beat, but at medium or slow speeds and in longer meters it doubles the drum patterns, striking on the sunken boss for a muted sound that goes with the *lanang tut*, and off the boss about halfway along the radius to match the *wadon dag*. In *pengawak*, the *neruktuk* (or *angsel kajar*, see fig. 7.2), an approximately 2-beat long, logarithmically accelerating series of strokes played on the boss, is begun at *palet* endings. In *tabuh pegambuhan, pengawak* are named for the number of *neruktuk* between *kempur* strokes.

In *pelegongan* the *klentong* (or *kemong*; abbreviated as t) is added to the midpoint in shorter *gongan* and to supplant or reinforce the *neruktuk* in longer ones. Not shown in figure 7.1A is the tiny piercing gong *kelenang*, which plays throughout all *pegambuhan* and *pelegongan* music. In short meters like *batel* it plays on the offbeats, augmenting to coincide with unstressed *neliti* or *pokok* tones in longer meters. A collection of other small metal percussion provide a jangling and continuous background to nearly all *gambuh* music, but these instruments are ordinarily omitted in *pelegongan*. For a description of them see McPhee 1966:119–21.

Pegongan music uses large gong (G) not only at endings, but sometimes at middles. In shorter cycles bisected by gong such as *gilak* and *tabuh telu*, a deep-pitched *gong wadon* and a somewhat higher *gong lanang* may be used in alternation. Internal punctuation in *pegongan* meters comes mainly from alternating strokes of the *kempli* (M) and *kempur*. In *pengawak* of *tabuh* the *kempli* marks *palet* endings, a function parallel to that of the *kajar neruktuk*. The *kempur* marks *palet* midpoints, a point stressed only by *jegogan* in *pelegongan* music and discernable only through close attention to drumming patterns in *pegambuhan*.

The *pengawak* of *tabuh pat* (or *empat*, "four"), *nem* ("six"), and *kutus* ("eight") are named for the total number of *kempur* strokes in between gongs. *Tabuh empat* has four *palet* and thus four such strokes; *tabuh nem* has six, and *tabuh kutus* eight. *Pengawak* for the remaining two *tabuh* in the *pegongan* group—*pisan* ("one") and *telu* ("three")—follow different plans.[9] In these cases the words *telu* and *pisan* are merely numerical labels that do not describe

---

9. McPhee documented a *tabuh telu* composition (*Sekarini*) from Payangan village (1966:393) which takes the form of a three-*palet* cycle punctuated as if a three-quarters-length version of *tabuh empat*, with regular *kempur-kempli* alternation. But to my knowledge compositions like this one are unknown today. The current understanding of *tabuh telu pegongan* corresponds with what McPhee calls *gending gangsaran*.

length or punctuation (Rembang 1984–85a:10). Punctuation for *tabuh pisan* consists of two *kempur* per gong stroke, with a minimum of two gong strokes required to complete a full cycle. Distance between *kempur* and *kempli* strokes is compressed from the 32 beats of *tabuh pat, nem,* and *kutus* to 16. *Tabuh telu pegongan* is even more compressed: a brief 16-beat cycle finished (and often bisected as well) by gong, with *kempli* at the quadrant points and *kempur* on beats 10 and 14. It typically supports melodies lasting three *gongan* (48 beats) or more. *Tabuh telu* meter is related by duple augmentation to 8-beat *gilak*, and both are easily recognizable by the asymmetrical pattern of *kempur* strokes adding emphasis to the approach to the end of the *gongan*.

Tabuh telu pegambuhan (fig. 7.1A.7) and *tabuh telu pegongan* (fig. 7.1B.4) should not be confused with one another. They are two of the most important and oft-encountered meters, but they are entirely distinct. The former has four 64-beat *palet* and is named for its three *neruktuk,* which come at the end of the first three *palet* but not at the end of the cycle. At 256 beats it is the same length as *tabuh pat pegongan.*

Save for *tabuh telu pegongan* and *gilak,* punctuation for all meters is entirely balanced and symmetrical around the midpoint. In a general way, the kinds of enrichment that drumming and melody supply for these closed systems are comparable: each provides musical movement that textures the symmetry by overlaying linear motion, creating a dialog between static and directed. As with melody, drumming intensifies in anticipation of punctuation points and relaxes after them, with the most concentrated movement reserved for the approach to the end of the cycle.

Drumming configuration of meter is simplest to perceive in the *kendangan* for *pengawak* with four or more *palet* (*tabuh 3 pegambuhan* and *tabuh 4, 6,* and *8 pegongan*). In these cases the inner *palet* all use the same pattern, creating large-scale internal drumming repetitions not matched by melodic ones.[10] The opening *palet* pattern is close to but distinct from the inner one(s), and the *milpil* pattern is sharply different. Within *palet* recognizable opening and cadential subpatterns clearly mark the boundaries of the span. *Kempur* marking the midpoints of *pegongan palet* are occasion for further contrasts in subpattern.

In *tabuh telu, gilak,* or shorter meters without fixed lengths, drumming is composed for a given melody by manipulating or varying stock subpatterns affiliated with the metric type. Thus *pelegongan pengecet,* no matter what their length, share similar opening subpatterns and cadence types. Composers commonly say "use *pengecet* drumming here" when teaching a melody of *penegecet*-like character, and expect drummers to tailor the generic *pengecet* subpattern types to it according to their regional norms or personal preferences. The com-

---

10. Indeed, as was pointed out in regard to fig. 6.3X, the melody may have internal repetitions that conflict with the *palet* structure.

poser may also call for the use of special or unusual subpatterns, which the performers may later choose to adjust.

Some *kendangan,* such as that for *tabuh telu pelegongan,* admit only to minor regional variants, but are similar enough throughout Bali so that any pair of drummers can play together passably without prior rehearsal. In the majority of cases mitigating factors—such as regionalism, compositional issues of specific *gending,* the necessity of matching the character of changing dance movements, and the flexible definitions of many of the meters—all combine to complicate the situation. Ask a drummer to play a basic *kendangan (kendangan dasar)* for *tabuh pat pegongan* and he will easily produce a pattern identified with a specific *tabuh pat gending* that he knows. But ask him to play *tabuh pat* drumming in the context of an unfamiliar *gending* and questions arise. What is the melody? Old or new style? From what area? What is the music's character? Simple or complex patterns? Who will my partner be? And so on. There is a justifiable assumption that the pattern he is familiar with is necessary but insufficient information.

In light of this, it can be said that in theory drum patterns and meters in *kebyar* and court repertoires correspond one-to-one, but that in practice this notion is only a starting point for portraying the diversity of the patterns themselves. But what combination of stylistic norms, stroke syntax, and other identifying features determines the shape of individual patterns and subpatterns? These issues will be explored in the next two sections.

Drum Styles, the Vocabulary of Drum Strokes, and Their Syntax and Structure

Three styles of drumming are used in *kebyar,* each an indicator of the repertoire affiliation of the music performed. In chapter 2 the names and method of producing the basic drum strokes for *gupekan* and *cedugan* styles were introduced. *Gupekan* is the standard style for most *kebyar* compositions, including *tabuh kreasi* and *tari lepas.* The thunderous *cedugan* style, played with a mallet in the right hand, is used for all *gong gdé* repertoire, most male dances, and for any new compositions based on *gong gdé* repertoire, such as *kreasi lelambatan.* To these two styles must be added the stroke vocabulary for *krempengan,* light hand drumming usually done on a separate pair of smaller, higher-pitched *kendang. Krempengan* is used in *pegambuhan* and *pelegongan* repertoire, and in the *gamelan geguntangan* that accompanies *arja* theater. In *kebyar* pieces based on *pelegongan* style *gupekan* drums are sometimes substituted, because the deep bass of the *wadon's dag* stroke cuts through the texture more effectively and better supports *kebyar* orchestral techniques that may be employed.

Gupekan, cedugan, and *krempengan* each use a limited collection of from six to eight strokes/timbres, three or four each for the *wadon* and *lanang* respectively. All three styles share the basic right-hand pitched sounds *dag* and *tut* (the latter called *dug* in *cedugan*) and the left-hand unpitched strokes *kap* and *pek*. *Gupekan* also uses the right-hand, partially muted pitched strokes *krum* and *pung,* while in *krempengan* analogous sounds are produced with the fingers of the left hand, and called *kom* and *peng*. There are other strokes particular to each style as well. The distinctions between the styles are many from a performer's point of view, because differences in the size of the drum and the presence or absence of a *panggul* call for different playing techniques. Functionally speaking, however, each stroke is assigned part of a small collection of clearly defined musical roles (providing cues, marking metric arrivals, etc.) shared by all of the styles. Strokes common to more than one style may assume single or multiple roles in each depending on the context. Strokes may also substitute for one another, or be omitted precisely where one would most expect them to fall.

A complete list of strokes is given in figure 7.3A-D, along with preliminary (generic) assessment of the role(s) of each one. Interstyle functional equivalents are given in figure 7.3E. Letter abbreviations for each stroke, as they will be used in notation and discussion, are given after the names. Omitted here and throughout the discussion of *matimpal* drumming is the muted, unpitched right-hand stroke *kep,* which is used to damp successive left-hand strokes and stabilize the rhythm at high speeds, but is insignificant as far as musical function is concerned.[11]

In staff notation, each drum part is represented on a pair of special staves, respectively containing two lines for the left hand and one for the right. As with melodic interlocking parts I shall be speaking almost entirely of composites and not separate components, though this subject offers ample material for further study. For ease of grasping the composite, the *wadon* and *lanang* parts are beamed together and must be reisolated from one another (by the interested reader) to discern their individual contents. Figure 7.4 is a staff notation template that can accommodate all three styles. In the transcriptions, gong punctuation and at least one melodic stratum are shown, and beats are numbered to simplify reference. Stroke abbreviations are given below the staves, as solfège was with melodies. In the text, when strings of strokes are represented by these abbreviations for illustrative purposes, I enclose them in square brackets, with the metric stress at the end. Slashes separate beats, and where a subdivision is not filled by a stroke a dot serves as a rest. As with CC, this convention is used to reflect Balinese ways of hearing rather than Western notational practice. Thus, in [KPDT/DT.D], the T before the slash and the final D fall on the beat.

There is no drumming in which *wadon* and *lanang* rhythms are composed

---

11. McPhee (1966:101) provides a prescriptive transcription as an example of how this technique works. However, like me, he generally prefers descriptive transcription and analysis of musically significant patterns.

A. Strokes common to all drum vocabularies

1. *Dag* (D)   (1) Primary metric stress, (2) placed in opposition to *tut,*
2. *Tut* (T)   (Called *dug* in *cedugan,* but always notated as T) (1) secondary metric stress,
                (2) placed in opposition to *dag,* and (3) cue for *angsel* in *cedugan*

B. Additional *gupekan* strokes

3. *Pek* (P)*   (1) Placed in opposition to *kap,* (2) preparation for *tut,* and (3) cue for *angsel*
4. *Kap* (K)   Placed in opposition to *pek*
5. *Pung* (u)   (1) Placed in opposition to *kum,* and (2) preparation for *tut*
6. *Krum* (r)   Preparation for *pung*
7. *Plak* (Pl) Sharply accented *pek* used to emphasize a sudden dance movement; obtained by slapping both drumheads at once and muting their pitch. Notated as *pek* with an accent.

C. Additional *krempengan* strokes

3. *Peng* (p)   (1) Placed in opposition to *kom,* and (2) preparation for *tut*
4. *Kom* (k)   Placed in opposition to *peng*
5. *Pung* (U)   Cue for *angsel*
6. *Krum* (R)   Preparation for *pung*
7. *Pek* (P)   (1) Preparation for *peng,* and (2) placed in opposition to *kap*
8. *Kap* (K)   Placed in opposition to *pek*

D. Additional *cedugan* strokes

3. *Tek* (e)   Timbrally muffled version of *lanang's dug* obtained by damping the left drumhead while striking the right. Notated with a + over the note.
4. *Tak* (a)   Equivalent of *tek* on the *wadon*
5. *Pek* (P)   (1) Placed in opposition to *kap,* and (2) preparation for *tut*
6. *Kap* (K)   Placed in opposition to *pek*

E. Interstyle functional equivalents

	Gupekan	Cedugan	Krempengan
	D	D	D
	T	T	T
	K	K	k
	P	P	p
	r	—	K
	u	—	P
Angsel cue	P	T	U

* The abbreviation P is also used for the *kempur,* but the two will always be restricted to separate lines in the transcriptions.

Figure 7.3. Drum stroke roles, interstyle equivalents, and abbreviation key

or intended to be heard as separate entities. The two always interlock as if a single part. This is reinforced through the most basic of syntactic norms: a stroke on one drum is normally answered directly by its equivalent on the other, so that the total number of strokes played by each drum during the course of a pattern is roughly equal. The stroke vocabulary thus reduces to—and is best imagined in terms of—sets of balanced *wadon-lanang* (or *lanang-wadon*) pairs: D-T (or T-D), K-P (or P-K), u-r (or r-u), and so on. In many

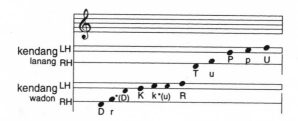

Figure 7.4. Drum notation template.
D = *dag* (or tak in *cedugan* style, with + above).
r = Right-hand *krum* (*gupekan* style).
K = *kap* (all styles).
k = *kom* (*krempengan* style).
R = Left-hand *krum* (*krempengan* style).
T = *tut* (*dug* in *cedugan*, or *tek* with + above).
u = Right-hand *pung* (*gupekan* style).
P = *pek* (all styles; or *plak* [Pl with accent above]).
p = *peng* (*krempengan* style).
U = Left-hand *pung* (*krempengan* style).
*(D) = Left-hand *dag* in *kendang tunggal* playing (figs. 7.15 and 7.16 only).
*(u) = Left-hand *pung* in *kendang tunggal* playing (figs. 7.15 and 7.16 only).
Note: In figs. 7.13, 7.15, and 7.16 filler and damping strokes are notated with headless stems.

shorter cycles, where the drums play at a characteristic density of four strokes per beat, this one-to-one alternation bears a resemblance to the interaction of *polos* and *sangsih* in *nyog cag kotekan,* with the composite pattern filling in every subdivision. Unlike *nyog cag,* however, the order of the succession is not fixed and is often shifted within patterns. This happens when either of the drums plays a pair of consecutive strokes. The effect is to make the *wadon* and *lanang* exchange places with respect to the beat, as in [DTDT/DDTD] or [KPKK/PKPP]. Strings of stroke-pairs accumulate these changing rhythmic relationships, are further marked by timbral contrasts obtained by changing stroke types, and extend to become patterns with distinctive shapes. Many patterns do not fill in every metric subdivision in this way, but as a description of basic syntax these are powerful initial concepts.

D-T interaction at the stroke-to-stroke level is a reflection of similar interactions at the metric level, but here the order of succession is less flexible. *Dag* is the most weighted stroke, and a prominent low pitch. It is normally linked to gong, and can also coincide with some internal punctuations, depending on the colotomic structure. Drum patterns (or subpatterns) often culminate in a *dag* arrival aligned with gong, where the actual stroke is sometimes omitted in deference to the gong's (or internal marker's) preeminence. *Tut* is also metrically weighted, but less so. It is characteristically linked to internal punctuations, and only in very special cases with gong; like *dag,* it may also be withheld. Other strokes can align with internal colotomic stresses, but this tends to occur early in the cycle and may be thought of as preparation for later, more heavily weighted *dag* or *tut*. In *gongan* or parts of *gongan* that end with a D stroke, a local *wadon-lanang* (D-T) succession has a quality of openness or progression, and a *lanang-wadon* succession (T-D) conveys closure. The reverse is true in cases where T is linked to endings.

Strokes so aligned (or implied and withheld) represent the colotomic structure *translated,* as it were, into a skeletal sequence that is filled in at progressively greater densities, ultimately yielding the composite pattern itself. The intermediate densities are analogous to *neliti, pokok,* or *jegogan* strata. In this sense drumming has embedded within itself a kind of hierarchic, stratified behavior that is comparable to that observed in melody. I will call the strokes that comprise implicit, slower-moving strata *structural* strokes and the strata themselves *levels,* to distinguish them from melodic strata. (The crucial difference, of course, is that none of the drumming levels other than the composite pattern is explicitly stated in the texture.) A cycle's succession of structural strokes is an important factor in influencing the timbre, succession, and rhythmic orientation of stroke-pairs that fill in the distances between those points. Two processes are at work: building patterns from the local level up, and elaborating the metric structure from the colotomic level down. A tension is generated where the processes interface, and this is where the patterns' rhythmic interest lies.

Specifically, the tension arises from a basic property of metric hierarchies: what is stressed at the highest (sparsest, closer to the background meter) levels remains so at lower (denser, closer to the surface) levels, but what is subordinate higher up *becomes* stressed lower down. If, for example, D is linked to gong and T to the midpoint, as in [(D)TD], this implies that T-D (weak-strong) ordering will govern activity at lower levels. But at the next level down, dividing the cycle into quadrants, the midpoint acquires greater stress. We would then expect [(D)TDTD], but this midpoint D conflicts with the higher level's T. In order not to contradict the colotomic structure, T must be reinstated. The sequence of strokes at the quadrant level might thus become [(D)DTTD], causing a reversal of stroke-pair orderings. With this configuration D acquires a double function: elaborative at the quadrant level, and structural at the axis level. Other configurations would be possible too, as long as T remains at the midpoint and D at the end. Moving to lower and lower levels, the switches from D-T to T-D ordering and vice-versa generate syncopation.

One analytical method that seeks to account for these multiple roles is to literally abstract a series of levels from a composite pattern in the same way that melodic strata were presented in chapter 6. As with melodies, the number of levels changes with the dimension of the meter. The first of the following pair of analyses illustrates how some patterns behave identically to melodic strata. As the second one will show, however, the number of levels is not necessarily the same as the number of strata, nor is it always possible to separate patterns and subpatterns into CC-like groups that end at points of metric

A

Wadon (w) or lanang (l)	(w)	w l w l w l l w
Level I (composite pattern)	(–)	k p D T D T T –
Level II (quadrant)	(D)	p T T (D)
Level III (axis)	(D)	T (D)
Gongs	(P)	P
Beat	(2)	1 2

B

Wadon (w) or lanang (l)	(w)	w l w l w l w l w l w l w l l w
Level I (composite)	(–)	k p D T k p D T k p D T D T T –
Level II	(D)	p T p T p T T (D)
Level III (quadrant)	(D)	T T T (D)
Level IV (axis)	(D)	T (D)
Gongs	(P)	P
Beat	(4)	1 2 3 4

Figure 7.5. Stroke levels in simple *krempengan* patterns
A. 2-beat *batel* ostinato, *gamelan gambuh,* Batuan village. B. Expansion of 2-beat cycle to 4 beats.

stress. Isolating the content of the levels and determining the identity of structural strokes can be more problematic than it was for melody, but the two examples together show that there is an intermediate rate of stroke activity that fuels the patterns, reconciling the surface with the meter.

In figure 7.5A and B a simple *krempengan* pattern for a short cycle in slow-tempo *batel* meter is compared with its expansion to a pattern twice as long. The *wadon* or *lanang* affiliation of each stroke is shown at the top and the *kempur* (P) punctuations at the bottom. The (D)TD of the 2-beat pattern's level III moves to level IV in the 4-beat one. It expands in the latter's level III to (D)TTTD rather than (D)TDTD, in order to preserve the midpoint T. At level II of 7.5B, the hierarchy of strokes is enriched to include p, which prepares T three separate times until just before the end, where T prepares the implied final D. In both composite patterns, k fills in the spaces before each p, while D reemerges, here in a preparatory role, to set up T. Almost to the end, the members of each stroke pair move from *wadon* (weak metric position) to *lanang* (strong). The persistence of the deep-pitched, acoustically prominent D in these slots produces off-the-beat accent. In the second pattern, the rate of off-the-beat D quickens as the cycle progresses, adding momentum. The absence of k and p near the end reflects the characteristic stronger weighting of the end of the cycle (as in melodies, where beginnings were *ngubeng* and *majalan* quality intensified moving toward gong). In both cycles, closure is achieved by reversing the D-T ordering at the last two strokes. This results in the pair of adjacent Ts directly prior to the *kempur.*

In short patterns such as these, as I indicated earlier, drumming behaves like *kotekan* or other melodic strata with fixed densities. In other short patterns and all longer patterns and *kendangan,* strokes still link up in pairs, but the surface rhythms are much more varied. Such patterns are in some ways akin to melodic *payasan* in character, but without the element of improvisation. While less structurally crucial stroke pairs like K-P and r-u tend to remain rhythmically adjacent to one another in these cases, the duration of successive D and T strokes may be extended to anywhere from two to six subdivisions. Unlike in *payasan,* however, there is no *pokok* or *neliti* "grid" to provide clear information about structure. Many metrically stressed positions are left open, so the criteria for identifying the content of the levels must be reassessed.

In making such determinations, my aim is to locate a stroke sequence that highlights the metric structure and plausibly resembles a comparable sequence in a more rhythmically continuous pattern. One path to these decisions is to compare regional (or historical) variants of the same pattern to discern their similarities and differences and locate an embedded sequence of structural stroke interactions that unites them. Figure 7.6 (CDI/37) compares four versions of a subpattern for an 8-beat segment toward the end of the *kawitan* section of *Tabuh Gari,* a *pegambuhan* composition often played, as it is here, on *semar pegulingan* instruments.[12] (W-Z rather than A-D are used to eliminate confusion with the drum stroke D.) Spanning the distance between two consecutive *jegogan* tones, the subpatterns occur at equivalent points in the metric and melodic frame. Allowing for regional variation in composition and performance style, each subpattern accompanies what is in essence the same melodic material, one version of which—that accompanying 7.6Y—is shown here above the top system. The four subpatterns differ markedly, save for the second halves of X and Y, which are the same, and the first halves of Y and Z, which differ only minimally. Their arrangement in the example reflects increasing complexity: W uses only T and D strokes, with T literally stated at the midpoint. X also uses only T and D, but the midpoint is open. Y introduces k and p, while Z also adds K and P and has the most syncopated second half.

Structurally, the subpatterns retain their distinctiveness but are closely linked. To get at their similarities I have removed all k, p, K, and P strokes in order to place Y and Z on a footing with W and X; and I have also taken away any immediately reduplicated D or T strokes, on the (perhaps arguable) premise that the initial occurrence of a stroke takes structural precedence. This exposes four structural sequences using only D and T, shown to the right of their respective subpatterns. The first three are identically ordered, while the last is slightly intensified in the second half. Each has a series of three "opening" D-T progressions leading to the midpoint followed by their inversion, a

---

12. The *pegambuhan Tabuh Gari* is related to but distinct from the *pegongan* version, the *pengawak* of which was illustrated in figure 6.3Y and is discussed again below in figure 7.14.

Figure 7.6. Subpattern variants in *Tabuh Gari semar pegulingan*.
W. Kamasan village (1991 recording, CDI/37.1)
X. Teges village (1941 recording, CDI/37.2)
Y. Teges village (1972 recording, CDI/37.3)
Z. Binoh village (1990 recording, CDI/37.4)

set of three (four in the last case) "closing" T-D progressions leading to the end of the unit. The insistent reiteration of these stroke-pairs and their reversal of direction after the midpoint confirms the idea that the midpoint and closing metric stresses belong to T and D respectively, though the actual strokes are conspicuously withheld in all cases except at the middle of W. The contrast between the first halves of X and Y, which were recorded in the same village three decades apart, especially demonstrates how a rhythm is elaborated and shifted, resulting in something with the same underlying impulse but a different surface.

Comparing my analyses of figures 7.5 and 7.6 instructively reveals some differing assumptions and a few contradictions. In the former case, because the rhythms were continuous, I identified structural strokes on the basis of whether or not they aligned with the metric grid. In the absence of consistent alignments in figure 7.6, the same decisions were made in a more deductive, ad hoc manner. One contradictory result was that off-the-beat D strokes, considered surface phenomena in the first case, were sometimes elevated to a structural position in the second. Another was that the stroke p was admitted at level II in 7.5 but dismissed as ornamental in 7.6. One could plausibly return now to the first analysis and argue, on the basis of the second, that *all* D-T interaction is structural; or, reassessing the second on the basis of the first, argue that only strokes falling on the beat are structural. Either way the results would be credible.

Within the limited perceptual field delineated by combinations of the small number of strokes in each drumming style's vocabulary, it is undesirable (and, I think, irrelevant) to come down decisively on these matters. In longer patterns especially, the similarity between the behaviors of melody and drumming cannot help but break down, because drumming cannot support the kinds of many-tiered interrelationships that the multioctave tuned gamut can. Drumming levels are conceptually important, but their borders are permeable and their contents open to multiple, conflicting interpretations.

Pattern Identity and Quality

In chapter 5 melodic identity was defined in terms of structural traits that tend not to change from variant to variant, and thus are essential contributors to a melody's affect. The main ones were meter, gong tone or other important tones, and contour. The more traits preserved among variants, the closer the shared affect. An interesting by-product of the analysis of figure 7.6 is to show that drum pattern identity can be assessed in a similar way. Just as in melody, a pattern is first and foremost linked to its meter. Second, levels of activity below the surface can serve to identify variants as structurally the same, even though they may sound different. This is like saying, as in melody, that the gong tone and other stressed tones are indispensable. In figure 7.6, the strokes designated as structural convey that structure in essentially the same ways, so that despite many surface differences, the four subpatterns were—or could be—interchangeable.

The emphasis on meter and structural similarity in figure 7.6 answers part of the identity question for drumming, but there is another side to it, and for me it is a critical one. I have stressed that all patterns in a given meter are conceptually identical but distinctive case-by-case. These distinctions are not solely a matter of regional, historical, or performer preference (aspects addressed in the *Tabuh Gari* analysis) but also depend on the composed-in features of each pattern in each *gending*. The life in these details—a pattern's specific fit with its *gending*—is part of what makes playing and learning *kendang* so much more than an exercise in memorizing and executing stock phrases. A valuable complementary perspective on pattern identity, therefore, comes from seeing just how *unalike* the composition of two patterns in the same meter accompanying *different* melodies can be.

Dissimilarities between patterns, which may be structural as well as surface, endow each pattern in each piece with its own kinetic qualities (*ngubeng/majalan*). Such qualities are more elusive in drumming than melody as a result of two factors: the aforementioned weakness of the stroke vocabulary (as opposed to the tuned gamut) to suggest multidimensional interconnections, and the controlling effect of meter, which mitigates against pattern individuality. I nonetheless feel compelled to isolate analytically what remains after allowing for these factors because of my contention that quality occupies a place so near to the core of the musical impulse.

My teachers provided valuable, if indirect, guidance on this subject. Three interconnected concepts were raised repeatedly when I asked them about what makes a drum pattern well composed: balance, utility, and proper function. These are aesthetic ideals rather than recipes for motion or stasis, but they can be interpreted as providing instructions for the latter. Beratha and Sinti in particular articulated the significance of using all of the strokes in balanced proportion, with the understanding that D and T are inherently more *majalan*. Tembres often stressed the utilitarian importance of simplifying the rhythm and limiting the number of different stroke timbres used if necessary in order to send clear messages about the tempo to the dancer and/or ensemble. Complexity, meaning irregular, syncopated exchanges between the two drums, varying rhythmic density, and frequent changes in prevailing stroke timbre, was for him expressive, witty, personal, and vibrant. On the other hand, both Rembang and Jebeg—only slightly younger than the septuagenarian Tembres—voiced nostalgia for the austere and abstract calm of *kuno* (old-fashioned) and *langah-langah* (sparse) patterns; and chastised the younger generation for favoring too much complexity. All drummers spoke of the functional weight of D-T interaction, and the appropriateness of using it sparingly after gong and more liberally at the approach to gong.

The following list of features that intensify drumming *majalan* quality is distilled from my teachers' comments:

1. greater variety and complexity in *wadon-lanang* interaction
2. shifting from a predominance of one timbre to another
3. changes in rhythmic density
4. increasing D-T interaction nearing gong (or other markers)

Save for the last, which weakly evokes an effect analogous to that felt in the tuned gamut, each of these features is defined by the use of simple contrasts to stimulate motion. Consequently, too much of any single factor tends to negate the *majalan* effect. Changes in timbre that are too predictable or frequent become *ngubeng,* as does excessive timbral prolongation—even if the strokes involved are the inherently *majalan* D and T. Unlike in melody, where literal repetition signifies stasis in any and all contexts, the limited field of relationships in drumming means that the context established in each pattern affects quality. What is *ngubeng* in one case can be *majalan* in another and vice versa.

The following analysis explores these issues plus those of identity and dissimilarity. I will first compare two patterns in the same meter, and then use the results of the comparison to assess the different shades of kinetic quality that each conveys. Figure 7.7A-B (CDI/38–39) illustrates a pair of 16-beat *lelonggoran* patterns (punctuated [(G) . . . P . . . t . . . P . . . G]); the first from *Oleg Tumulilingan* and the second from *Teruna Jaya*, both *tari lepas* repertoire standards. Both cycles are played quietly and at slowish tempi (ranging from mm 40 to 80, depending on *sekaha* preference). A, somewhat slower than B, appears at the beginning of the dance when the coy, idealized feminine character of a bumblebee sipping nectar from flowers first appears. B portrays the reflective, gentle side of an impetuous and androgynous youth (danced by a woman), and is preceded by a *kebyar* introduction and a long passage of fast and aggressive music in *bapang* meter.

Both patterns recall the drumming to 8-beat cycles in *Gabor* (see fig. 7.8, below), despite having been expanded to *lelonggoran* format and developed considerably. I chose them because they represent something close to the extremes of dissimilarity that can occur in *matimpal* drumming in a given meter and dimension. There is less composed-in variety in other short meters and most longer *tabuh*. Scanning the composites for similarities, only the [KPKP/ruru] subpatterns of the first two beats (at x in fig. 7.7A and B) and a series of eleven strokes beginning two beats before gong (y) are seen to be precisely the same. A more general similarity is that both patterns end in a flurry of strokes at double density lasting roughly for the final quadrant of the cycle. There is one more literally shared subpattern lasting four beats (z), but its metric orientation is different in each case: in A it begins two beats before the second *kempur* stroke and extends to two beats before gong, while in B it begins right after the midpoint and squarely occupies the third quadrant. (Small differences between the two z subpatterns, marked *, are spontaneously inserted ornaments that experienced drumming partners can anticipate and leave room for at slow tempi.)

In all other respects the patterns are dissimilar. After the first two beats (x) of A, a varied turnover of stroke timbres prevails until one beat before the midpoint, with K-P, r-u, and D-T exchanges intertwined. A few K-P pairs dot the second half of the pattern, which otherwise features continuous D-T interaction in many configurations. This stands in strong contrast to the varied colors and simpler rhythms of the first half. Pattern B moves directly to D-T exchanges after x until just before the midpoint, which is heralded by a brief K-P interruption. D-T exchange then returns with z. The doubled rhythms of the final quadrant are composed at first of irregular K-P exchanges,

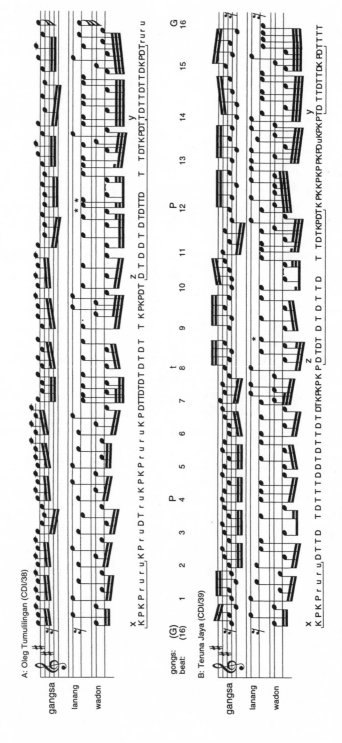

Figure 7.7. Two *lelonggoran* patterns compared. A. *Oleg Tumulilingan* (CDI/38). B. *Teruna Jaya* (CDI/39)

which soon concede to D-T at the final approach to gong. The four successive T strokes at the very end synchronize with light, scuttling dance steps.

Both similarity and contrast are evident, too, when structural strokes are abstracted via the metric grid. Strokes at the first (P), second (u), seventh (T), tenth (T), twelfth (T), and fifteenth (D) beats correspond; of these six only the three even-numbered ones are still present at the next level up (strokes aligned with *pokok* tones). At the quadrant level only the twelfth beat (second *kempur*) T remains in both patterns. That even this should remain would seem to have been precluded by the module-like portability of z, which is shifted by a distance of two beats right in that region of the meter. But since there is a T both at the beginning and the middle of z, T's alignment with the *kempur* is preserved. At this gateway to the last and most *majalan* quadrant of the cycle, the T arrivals are felt to reinforce the meter strongly. At the same time, the misalignment of the two z subpatterns reorients the surfaces.

In sum, contrast between the patterns arises from an intricate combination of surface, background, rhythmic, and timbral details. Though their general rhythmic profiles are comparable, most of the rhythmic specifics of A and B are distinct; and while both depend on timbral contrast, they arrange the timbres in different orders and prolong them for different spans. Studying a larger sample of *gabor*-derived patterns (which space precludes here) would reveal that introductory subpatterns like x are widely used, but that otherwise no other feature is predictably shared. Indeed, when I asked Rai to demonstrate *lelonggoran* drumming for me without referring to a specific *gending*, he unhesitatingly responded with something that included x but was different from either of the patterns discussed here. A reminder of these more complex versions drew from him a calm caution that each musical situation demands its appropriate response. The identity of such patterns then, like other patterns in short meters, hovers ineffably between the specific content of each pattern and the general affect and framework provided by the melody and the colotomic structure.

Assessing the quality of the patterns on the basis of the four features listed above leads to comparable open-endedness. From one point of view, the first half of B is *majalan* in comparison to A because of its focus on D-T and the irregularity of *wadon-lanang* exchanges (after x). In A the drums' continual one-to-one exchanges could be deemed *ngubeng,* but the timbre changes more than B's does during this portion, which is a *majalan* trait. Both patterns are, appropriately, more *majalan* near gong because of the higher rhythmic density, though B exhibits slightly more of this activity than A. Yet the pre-gong subpattern in A is comprised almost exclusively of D-T interaction, while in B it is not. In A this works to sharpen the contrast with the first half, further boosting the sense of *majalan* en route to gong. B, on the other hand, uses K-P exchange at the equivalent spot to achieve the same level of contrast, precisely because D-T had already been prolonged in *its* first half, and to continue with

D-T would have disturbed the vital sense of timbral balance. That B uses K-P to achieve motion there while A uses D-T is indicative of how quality is contextually determined. Both patterns balance stasis and motion, but in different ways.

Such interacting details are embodiments of fragile concepts. A fleeting, particle-and-wave type of duality pervades the inquiry into drumming identity and quality: as with the difficulty of separating them into discrete structural levels, patterns resist being pinned down. Even if these factors are somehow mysterious, however, not being able to map them precisely need not preclude surveying their territory. Cultivating a sensitivity to patterns' ambiguities most assuredly brings us closer to what Suweca claims as drummers' special expertise. Though he and his peers do not articulate the issues in the way that I have, their life-long experience makes them that much more intimate with what makes the patterns tick. Conversance with the rich and subjective texture of this network of interrelationships enhances musicianship, and exploring it is reason enough for the kind of dedication that music can and does inspire.

Stable and Active Patterns and the Impact of Drumming on Form

Having chased these fugitive minutiae, it is time to step back and view drumming in interaction with the rest of the strata and the dance. Now I wish to take first steps toward emphasizing a compositional perspective that accounts for the prominent role of disruption in shaping *kebyar gending*. Disruption sets *kebyar* apart most vividly from inherited court styles, wherein it occurs far less often. In *kebyar* a repeating cycle will not always be restated literally, but will sometimes undergo a series of juxtapositions between two "states," which I will call *stable* and *active*. The music may be said to be in a stable state if all of the strata proceed continuously, independently, and without disruption for the duration of a full cycle or *palet*. It is in an active state if explicit rhythmic coordination between drumming and melodic strata occurs. I refer to such coordination as disruption (or discontinuity) because it weakens the stratified rhythmic independence of drumming and melody that characterizes court genres. Drumming oversees the shifts between stable and active states in ways which I shall describe presently.

I distinguish three pattern types on the basis of how and whether they explicitly interact with melodic strata.[13] *Stable* patterns are played when the

---

13. Becker's (1968) classifications for Southeast Asian colotomic drum patterns—configurative, extended, durational, and metronomic—comprise the only previously published framework for addressing this issue. In her approach, configurative patterns are "hierarchical, binary, 8 or 16 beats long, and cyclical" (178). Extended patterns are much the same but longer, and may contain internal repetitions and cadential patterns. By durational, Becker also means additive, in that these patterns do not easily divide into subunits of equal dimensions and parse more readily according to groupings of shifting size (eg. 3 + 3 + 2). Metronomic patterns are unsyncopated and resemble colotomic punctua-

music is in a stable state, and function as an elaboration of colotomic meter. All patterns analyzed thus far in the chapter have been stable. *Active* patterns are used in cases of discontinuity within metric contexts. The degree of disruption that active patterns generate spans a continuum ranging from minimal, in which a stable pattern is only slightly modified, causing a small melodic detail to erupt at the surface, to radical, in which the disruption lasts for a full cycle or longer. Radical disruption can yield a pattern bearing little if any resemblance to a stable counterpart. *Kebyar* patterns, the final type, are a modern innovation used only in *kebyar* textures and other similar passages in which there is no cyclic meter (see fig. 2.13). These patterns usually contain D and T strokes only, which are assigned to melody tones according to the amount of stress accorded them, and they do not comprise an independent stratum. Stress is felt contextually in the absence of meter. *Kebyar* patterns behave like active patterns intensified to the point where each stroke is exclusively linked to a melodic event, possessing few of the hierarchic multiple meanings that meter accommodates. The absence of colotomic structure means that *kebyar* patterns are strongly asymmetrical.

Stable patterns are the norm in older music where *angsel* and other surface details had yet to play a prominent role. Some, particularly in *klasik* renditions of *tabuh pegongan,* are so simple as to reduce drumming practically to its essential functions of marking colotomic arrivals.[14] Such patterns can still be heard in villages such as Sulahaan and Geladag where *gong gdé* drumming is protected from *kebyar* influence. In many Geladag renditions of *tabuh pat pengawak,* for example, simple K-P interaction prevails until just before the end of each half-*palet,* where a few D-T exchanges signal the upcoming *kempur* or *kempli* punctuation, all done to the unbroken murmur of *gangsa* and *reyong norot. Stable* patterns in *pegambuhan* and *pelegongan pengawak,* on the other hand, are more timbrally and rhythmically varied. In contemporary music active patterns may predominate. Many *tabuh kreasi* and *kreasi lelambatan* use hardly any stable patterns at all, so intense and continuous is the interaction between drumming and melody.

Disruption comes in three ways: via *angsel, ocak-ocakan,* or other *miscellaneous* kinds of composed-in coordination between drumming and melodic instruments. *Angsel,* introduced in chapter 5, are of many types. The most characteristic occur in short meters and use one of many variants of the rhythm ♩♩♩ (in fast tempi) or ♩ ♩ ♩ (in slower ones). The first rhythmic value in the *angsel* is often silent or may represent the end of a preceding musical unit, but the last two are forcefully articulated on the beats just prior to gong.

---

tion patterns, but they stress the end of the cycle more heavily, and are thus "unbalanced," whereas colotomic patterns are "balanced" (187). Balinese drumming can fall under all of these rubrics. Useful as Becker's designations are, however, they do not encompass the formal issues I am addressing in this section.

14. Drums in the seven-tone *gamelan luang* serve precisely this function and no more: they are struck metronomically two or three times prior to cycle endings.

Lasting respectively (1 + 3) and (½ + 1½) beats, these rhythms clash with the quadripartite metric frame, creating asymmetry. *Angsel* rhythm is heralded by a drum cue, typically given one cycle in advance. At the cue or soon after it the entire ensemble suddenly raises the dynamic level *(nguncab)* in preparation for the accented components of the rhythm itself, which are converged on by D-T strokes, *gangsa, cengceng, reyong,* and the choreography. The second type of disruption, *ocak-ocakan,* has already been described (fig. 2.16) as an orchestration technique that links D-T interaction with *cengceng* and the *reyong byar.* The vocabulary of stock *ocak-ocakan* rhythms is related to *angsel* rhythms, in that they play off the meter with insistent syncopation and, in dance music, are directly tied to detailed movements. Composers also invent new ones as frequently as they reuse the old. Miscellaneous types of disruption, not classified with any specific names, may take many forms. They usually involve drum emphasis, or at times strict doubling, of the rhythms of non-interlocking *gangsa* elaboration.

In short meters an active pattern is typically inserted after one or more occurrences of a stable one. The active pattern may then last for a single cycle, or a series of active patterns may be linked in a chain lasting several *gongan.* Once completed, the process may begin again, in the same or different proportion between stable and active, or there may be a shift to a different melody. Such alternation between stable and active states groups *gongan* together into *metacycles.*[15] In dance pieces metacycles correspond with large-scale choreographic patterns. In both dance and instrumental music, they provide an intermediate stage of continuity that bridges the gap between the structure of individual cycles and the succession of meters, melodies, and transitions between them that constitute form.

Figure 7.8 (CDI/40), from the *kawitan* of *Gabor,* shows this process and the interaction between drumming, here in *gupekan* style, and melodic strata. In the example three *gongan,* all using the same *pokok* and 8-beat *gegaboran* meter [(G).P.t.P.G], are joined to create a metacycle. The metric structure and *gangsa* part (in *ngitir* style; see fig. 6.6C), are also shown. The first *gongan* uses a stable pattern; there is no literal connection between dance movement and drum strokes during this cycle. As in figure 7.7A, K-P and r-u interaction predominate for some time until they are replaced by D-T exchanges. The K-P and r-u alternation is precisely one-to-one between the two drums, but the

---

15. No comparable term is in use in Balinese. I rejected *metagongan* for its awkward fusion of languages. Ketut Gdé Asnawa proposed adapting *pupuh,* a word that in the most general sense means something sectioned or delineated (as in a plot of land or planted crop), but also, in poetry and song, is one of several terms referring to metric organization and the number of syllables per lines of text in a stanza. Asnawa felt that *pupuh* could also be used in this context, to designate a group of drum patterns that link together and are "cordoned off," as it were (personal communication, July 1998). Because *pupuh* already has other, more established musical connotations and could therefore be ambiguous here, I opted, at least for the present and with apologies to Asnawa, to retain metacycle.

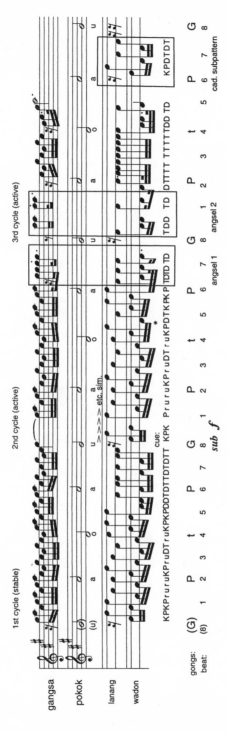

Figure 7.8. Stable and active patterns in *Gabor* (CDI/40)

Mid-level D-T interaction in cycle 1 (stable):	. . . . . . D T .
Mid-level D-T interaction in cycle 3 (active):	. . . . . D . T .
Gongs:	(G) . P . t . P . G
Beat #	(8) 1 2 3 4 5 6 7 8

Figure 7.9. Symmetrical and asymmetrical strokes in *Gabor*

pair of consecutive Ds and two pairs of consecutive Ts add syncopation to the end of the cycle. Reducing this closing exchange to beat-level, D and T are seen to fall on the sixth and seventh beats respectively, while the drums are silent at gong. The sixth-beat D both emphasizes the concurrent second *kempur* stroke (recall, by way of contrast, that T fell with the second *kempur* in the *lelonggoran* cycles 7.7A and B) and prepares the seventh-beat T; and the two strokes together prepare gong. This has the effect of intensifying the colotomic structure in a manner parallel to the symmetry of the meter and commensurate with the increased stress given to cycle endings.

The second and third cycles use active patterns, and are inseparably linked as a compositional and choreographic unit. In the second one, during a brief pause in the *gangsa* part immediately after the previous gong, the soft dynamic is broken by an accented [KPKP] sequence, which acts as a cue. When the *gangsa* resume a beat later they (and the rest of the ensemble) *nguncab,* led by the *ugal* in response to the drums. The drums continue as in the stable pattern until just after the midpoint, where the stroke sequence of the fifth and sixth beats changes from [KPKP/DDTD] to [KPDT/KPKP]. This new sequence contains an anticipatory D (marked *) that leads, at the seventh beat, to the first of a pair of *angsel* on which the *gangsa, kendang,* and (not shown) *cengceng* and *reyong byar* converge. The *gangsa* articulate their part so that a staccato tone aligns with the drums' T. The *angsel* stroke sequence [TDDT/D . . .] reduces, when both Ts and the second D are removed, to the *angsel* rhythm ♩ ♪ ♩, which matches the rhythm of the dancers' upper torso and shoulder movements at those points.

The *angsel* is repeated immediately after gong one scale tone higher. Next, a series of nine consecutive Ts between the second and fourth beats of the third cycle upsets the balanced *wadon-lanang* interaction that has prevailed thus far. This highlights the D stroke arriving on the fifth beat, the first on-the-beat D since the sixth beat of the first cycle. A cadential subpattern closes the cycle, with T preserved on the seventh beat as it was in the stable pattern. In contrast to the stable pattern this structural D-T-gong succession does *not* proceed at the beat-to-beat level, for the sixth beat, where *kempur* arrives, is left empty. This has the effect of intensifying the structure in a manner *not* parallel to the symmetry of the meter, thus creating asymmetry, or structural syncopation, in relation to it. The subtle but crucial contrast between the structural symmetry in the first cycle and the asymmetry in the last one is summarized in figure 7.9.

Throughout the active patterns, drum rhythms and dance are closely co-ordinated, as the dancers match the various D-T combinations with torso movements (particularly forceful and angular at the two *angsel*), hand gestures, and quick steps. Following the third cycle, the dynamic drops (*ngisep*) to where it was, and the stable pattern and *ngitir* figuration of the initial cycle return. The process is then renewed, culminating in a different series of active patterns, which lead to a transition to the *pengawak*.

The *Gabor* example is exemplary of the disrupting influence of *angsel* and its related techniques, and representative of the ways that drumming and composition are linked in fostering asymmetry within metric contexts. Splitting the third *gongan* into 5 + 3 beats (via the fifth-beat D) is typical for active patterns. The rhythmic impulse generated is equivalent to that of the melodic rhythm in *gamelan gambang* and the other seven-tone *tua gamelan* (see fig. 6.16), and most likely homologous with it.[16] Having penetrated modern drumming and composition, this impulse supports a dialog between symmetry and asymmetry in the arena of meter that parallels that in melody.

Figure 7.10 (CDI/41) illustrates a cycle-length *ocak-ocakan* pattern from *Teruna Jaya*. As in all *ocak-ocakan*, *reyong kecekan* (cymbal-like sounds played off-the-boss; shown with x-headed stems) double K and P strokes. Open *byar*-chord types *byong* (°) align with D, and closed ones, *byot* (·), with T. The pattern shares the same melody and forms part of a metacycle with fig. 7.7B, coming after an intervening transitional cycle. The tempo is faster, ca. 104. The subpattern segments demarcate the meter in 7.10, but in a way different from the stable pattern with which the whole is juxtaposed. This is typical for *ocak-ocakan*, which tend to build up in 4- or 8-beat blocks. Here the cycle is overtly bisected, so that the subpattern leading to t is identical with that leading to G. This is simpler than the through-composed, accumulating complexity of the stable 7.7B. The first quadrants of the two *gongan*, however, are nearly the same; with the opening [KPKP/ruru] simplified to [KPKP/KPKP] for the *ocak-ocakan*. (Extended K-P alternation is often used to help stabilize

---

16. Such careful asymmetry is by no means uniquely Balinese. Simha Arom has identified it as a formative organizing principle for Central African music (and it applies as well to other related musics):

One particular form of asymmetry which is very frequently found in Central Africa may be called *rhythmic oddity*. When the number of pulsations in the period involved is divided by two, the result is an *even* number. The figures contained in this period are nevertheless so arranged that the segmentation *closest to the middle* will invariably yield two parts, each composed of an *odd* number of minimal values, wherever the dividing line is placed. These figures are always constructed by the irregular juxtaposition of binary and ternary quantities. The resulting rhythmic combinations are remarkable for both their complexity and their subtlety. They follow a rule which may be expressed as "half − 1/half + 1" . . . The figure with eight minimal values (i.e. containing two binary pulsations) is articulated as follows: $3/3.2 = 3/5 = 4 - 1/4 + 1$. (1991:246)

It is a simple step from there to reverse the order of the 3 + 5 in Arom's example to the 5 + 3 of *angsel* patterns or *gambang* melody.

a new tempo.) The T strokes at *kempur* arrivals are also preserved in both. These similarities direct attention to the strong contrasts at beats 7 and 15, where the stable pattern's Ts are conspicuously altered to D, and followed by T a half beat later. This has the double effect of "resolving" the syncopated D strokes of the three preceding beats and shaping the approach to the colotomic punctuations differently than the stable pattern did. This kind of "rehearing" of the meter is as characteristic of active patterns as the asymmetry shown for *Gabor* in figure 7.8. It offers another perspective on metric elaboration through drumming by demonstrating that even within a piece the quality of a meter is subject to compositional control. Such reinterpretation is rare in the mainly stable context of pre-*kebyar* music.

As an example of the kinds of miscellaneous interaction between strata mentioned earlier, fig. 7.11 (CDI/42) shows three cycles of *tabuh telu* meter in *Kembang Kuning*, a *lelambatan* composition from Pindha village. The first cycle is stable, and the second and third are active. The excerpt is part of a much longer metacycle in which the same *pokok* is repeated for sixteen *gongan*, underpinned by a set of eight related but distinct *cedugan* patterns, which are irregularly ordered to support a lengthy succession of disruptions. In the example, continuous *norot* in the opening cycle is interrupted in the active cycles by coordinated rhythmic breaks, followed, respectively, by silence in the second cycle, and a switch to *malpal*-like figuration (see fig. 6.6B) in the third.

The strict palindromic curve of the *neliti* is offset by asymmetry in the first cycle's stable *kendang* pattern. A [KPKP] subpattern just *after* gong is echoed *preceding* the *kempli* at beat 4, and again *before* the midpoint gong at beat 8. The D-T exchange that covers beats 1–2, [DT.D/TDT.], is repeated en route to the cycle midpoint, expanded through the interpolation of additional strokes at beats 4–6 to become [DT.D/TT.D/TDT.] (interpolated strokes underlined). The second half of the cycle is all D-T interaction, culminating, at beats 14–15, in [TT.D/TDT.]—the same as beats 5–6, but a disorienting nine beats later. Thus, the original subpattern of beats 1–2 appears in multiple transformations and nonanalogous metric alignments.

Drumming in the second and third *gongan* begins just as it did in the first, but branches off just before beat 5. In the second cycle the [KPKP] just prior to the midpoint is truncated to [KP. .], leaving a brief silence which sets off the [DTae] leading to beat 9. The conspicuous *tek* stroke at 9 emphasizes the contrast with the first cycle, where D occupied the equivalent position. While the *gangsa* and *reyong* rest between there and gong, the *kendang* vary the stable pattern's second half by substituting K-P for D-T exchanges at 9–11 and 14–15. In the driving final cycle, the third [KPKP] subpattern comes a full beat early, at beat 6. It prepares the coordinated break at beat 7, where D-T aligns with the figuration strata and *reyong byar*, replacing what had been K-P in the first two cycles. K-P exchanges underpin the *malpal* figuration of the next several beats, interrupted by D-T to support the agogic accent at beat 13.

The figuration at 12–13 is iterated (minus the dotted rhythm) leading to 15 and 16. Gong is left open by the drums as before, but the u stroke at 15 replaces the first cycle's D. This switch, combined with the effect of the agogic accent, isolates the final three beats of the cycle in the same asymmetrical way that the end of figure 7.8 was set off.

Active patterns, then, aside from coordinating changes in orchestral texture and surface activity, interact with structure in two related ways: they support asymmetrical hearings of the meter, and they replace key structural strokes from stable patterns with contrasting substitutions. The most powerful and significant effect of the proliferating variety of active patterns in *kebyar* drumming is to loosen the ultimate authority of cyclic structure. Unlike in older court styles, where a predominance of stable textures insured that a one (or at most a few) patterns were available for each meter, in *kebyar* such formulaic constraints are rejected. Rather than being imposed "from the top down," contemporary music acquires more of its features from the bottom up, as composers and choreographers collectively work to transform structural norms. In this process the court-derived vertical, cyclic approach to musical time progressively accedes to a horizontal, linear one. The result has been the emergence of carefully wrought details and strong individual profiles in each *gending*.

Drumming and Dance Movement

The references to dance in connection with the *Gabor* analysis in figure 7.8 occasion a reminiscence. In 1978 and 1979 I played nightly for many months with the fledgling *pelegongan* group Tirtha Sari in Peliatan village. It had been organized by Anak Agung Gdé Mandera and my teacher Madé Lebah, long-standing patriarchs of music and dance in the area. Late one evening, after a rehearsal during which I was invited to display my nascent *krempengan* technique, Mandera's son Bawa beckoned and escorted me to a quiet corner of the courtyard. There he opined, much in Suweca's vein, that drum patterns were difficult and (here he went beyond Suweca) that as a foreigner I might be able to execute them but would never be able to feel them in a Balinese way. He then played a few slow passages from *legong* on the drum in his lap, reverently caressing each stroke and dreamily singing along all the while, using the drum syllables as lyrics for the melody. Eyes closed and torso subtly evoking the choreography, Bawa's body language insisted that it was the connection between music and movement that mattered: the need for the drummer to understand both and act as a conduit for translating between them.

There is a one-to-one correspondence between movements and strokes in many cases, but there is more at stake than a simple linkage. Drumming also converts movement into musical quality. While Bawa sang he quivered his fingers like the young dancers must, making a graceful segue to playing the

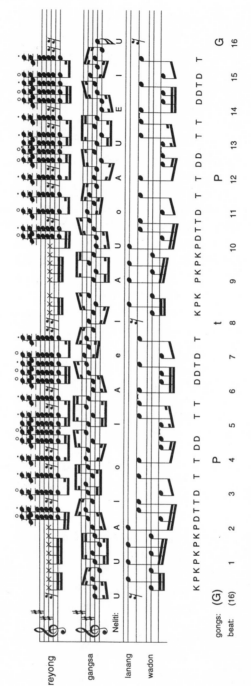

Figure 7.10. *Ocak-ocakan* in *Teruna Jaya* (CDI/41)

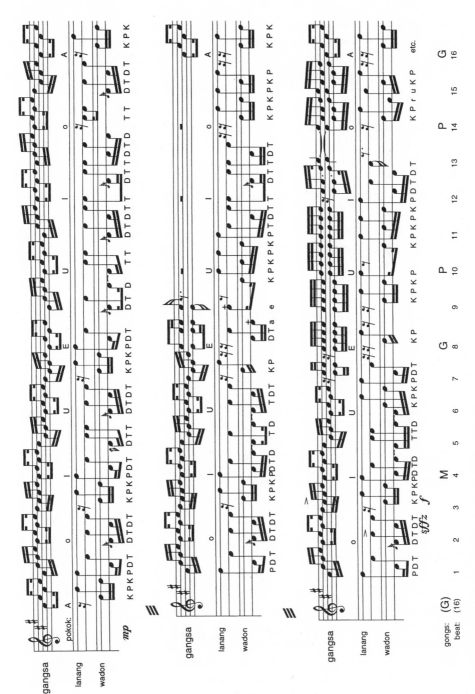

Figure 7.11. Three *tabuh telu* cycles in *Kembang Kuning* (CD1/42)

repeating *pung* strokes before gong. He gently lifted his feet to show the firmly planted steps linked to a strong (but not too aggressive) *tut* stroke, and with his elbows and upper torso depicted the restrained, lithe curves of *pengecet* movements to the accompanying spans of their drum patterns. All of these are as much a part of what constitutes *legong*'s affect of grace and femininity as the melodies. Each pairing marks a point on a spectrum of mood just as it guides choreographic progression or coordinates rhythmic alignment.

Choreography and genre determine movement vocabulary, but cycle length determines the structural aspects of music/dance interaction. In long cycles (abstract topics), nearly all movements are explicitly coordinated with the drums. Pairings are literal, nonreferential, and aim for a pure and transcendent fusion of movement and sound. This is suggested in the following Balinese research report with respect to *legong pengawak* (in *tabuh telu pegambuhan* meter); "points of accent" are precise alignments between strokes and movements.

> The movement vocabulary in *legong kraton* is closely tied to the *wadon dag* and *lanang tut*. The vocabulary of drum strokes may be said to be as one with the movement vocabulary, and the two may be said to have developed hand-in-hand.
>
> *Kendangan* for *pengawak* in *legong kraton* of Sading (village), Binoh and Teges are very simple, as are the dances themselves, especially in their points of accent (*aksentuasinya*). This simplicity defines the style in these places as *klasik*. At KOKAR, where the drummers are mainly very young, *kendangan* have acquired much more complexity, and along with it the dance has as well.
>
> In addition, dancers tend to follow different drum strokes in different regions. In Saba dancers place their accents with *dag*, while in Denpasar *tut* is used; this results in a difference of style. Yet in principle the two are the same, if seen from the perspective of dance vocabulary. (Pandji et al. 1974–75:25)

In the case of short, stable cycles supporting character or stylistic topics the interdependence tends to loosen, as drum/dance interaction contributes to the depiction of a character type, setting, mood, or story. Dance movements in the stable cycle of figure 7.8 portray *Gabor*'s prayerful mood and are continuous rather than sharp and angular, coordinated in a general way with meter. *Angsel* in the active cycles display direct links in which the feet or shoulders literally shift into new positions, as if striking the drum themselves.

Medium-length contexts like *legong pengecet* are intermediate stages in which the above plus other types of relationships are discernable. Figure 7.12 (CDI/20; see also fig. 6.3U) shows the drumming, elaborated melody, and terminology for movements and movement progressions in the melody Bawa demonstrated. *Nyingklak* is a rapid, swishing up-and-down gesture of the forearms before the chest, named for the motions of retrieving stones and bouncing a ball in *cingklak,* a children's game similar to jacks.[17] It occurs at the beginning of each of the first three quadrants and concludes with a slight upward jab of the left elbow, aligned with the D strokes at beats 6, 22, and 38. *Tanjek ngandang* is an important item in *legong* movement vocabulary, a pivoting turn that shifts and releases weight from an off-kilter posture back into standard *agem* (stance). It has a transitional function, here leading back to repetition of *nyingklak,* via *seledet* punctuation. In *seledet* the eyes are flicked to one side in advance of metric accent, and back to center to coincide with it. This takes place at 15–16 and 31–32, as if to mark semicolons at the ends of the first two quadrants.

Angsel in medium and long *pegambuhan*-derived cycles such as this have the pure dance connotation of a break in preestablished pattern; in this usage no explicitly repeating cycle or metacycle is implied. Replacing *tanjek ngandang* at 24–26, *angsel* comprises a forward step and sharp, angled downward thrust of the elbow at the second half of beat 25.

In the third quadrant's *mundur* (move back or retreat), the dancers take two backward steps upstage, preparing and enlarging the choreographic space opened before them. This leads to *milpil,* which, as with the *majalan* musical connotations of this term, is a sweeping, contrasting move preparing the path to gong. The dancers return downstage to complete the quadrant with weight shifted right and left fingers spread before the right hand, which bears the fan each holds close to the right breast. Broader walking movements, covering a larger part of the performance space than had previously been traversed, continue through the climactic *angsel* of 50–52 to the end.

Three levels of music/dance connection are distinguishable among these elements. In the first, most local level, as with *Gabor*'s active cycles or the *pengawak*'s "points of accent," certain accentuated strokes map to movements exactly. Examples are the foot movements coinciding with D on the second half of beat 9 or at 13, the *seledet* coordinated with the second subdivision of beats 15 and 31, and the "point" of the *angsel* at the second half of 25 (all enclosed in boxes in the transcription). At the second, middle level, subpatterns or regions dominated by certain stroke timbres accompany more fluid movement passages. This is the case for *nyingklak,* in which the playful mood of the children's game is depicted by the buoyant, high-pitched, and syncopated interplay of k and p strokes that accompany the arm movements each time they occur. As k and p give way to the timbres of D and T, the *nyingklak*

---

17. The choreography and terms used in this analysis were provided by Gusti Ayu Srinatih (personal communication, August 1998).

Nyingklak is one of many evocatively named dance movements invoking birds, animals, or human activities. Lovric's (1990) perspective on dance terminology, positing semiotic connections between dance movement, ancient healing practices, and the movements of people afflicted with illness and disease, is noteworthy and enriching in this regard.

Figure 7.12. *Pengecet Lasem* drumming and dance movements (CDI/20)

rounds to the concluding elbow motion, which aligns with D at beats 6, 22, and 38. At these two levels, strokes delineate segments or provide accent at points that can be asymmetrical with respect to the meter. *Nyingklak,* for example, is six beats long; and *angsel* accent off-beats.

In contrast, at the third, highest level, the dance is grouped into larger "phrases" that support cyclic structure and the composition of the drumming as a whole. The cycle's 64 beats divide into 16 + 16 + 32, as the first two quadrants have identical drumming but the third, while beginning the same way, diverges after 42 and continues to gong with new material. If seen from the perspective of the embedded structural strokes aligned with quadrant endings, the *gongan* reduces to a [TTTD] progression, with T implied at 16 and 32, stated at 48, and at last deferring to D at gong. The dance mirrors these attributes. The first quadrant's *nyingklak-tanjek ngandang-seledet* progression is repeated in the second, where *angsel* substitutes for *tanjek ngandang.* The syncopated side-to-center eye motion of *seledet* parallels the local D-T succession in both quadrants (15–16 and 31–32), in which the latter stroke is strongly felt but withheld in the actual subpattern. The third quadrant begins with *nyingklak* but diverges, like the drums, from *milpil* onward. T is literally present at the beginning of the final quadrant, but the *milpil* does not arrest the progression as the *seledet* did; instead it drives forward to create the 32-beat, midpoint-to-ending phrase. In the cadential subpattern [KPDT/DT. .] at 62–63, T falls on the cycle's penultimate beat, confirming D's association with gong.

The combined musical effect of the three levels of action is both to reinforce the meter and, in a manner analogous to the examples of disruption discussed earlier, to enrich our perception of its elaboration. And as Bawa impressed upon me, a proper grasp of these relationships is a significant step toward understanding feeling, affect, and expression, which leads in turn toward something of the essence of artistic sensibility. In their variety these relationships form a spectrum ranging from the spiritual and impersonal to the flamboyant and individual:

> In extended metrical forms [e.g., *pengawak legong*] all movement is impelled and controlled by the metric structure, the divisional accents, the inner phrasing of the melody. Here the dance is purely abstract; it tells no story. A mood is created or a character presented as the dancer scans the music with gesture and movement. But as the story emerges the dancer is freed. A new relationship with the music is established. The dancer occupies the foreground, the music recedes. (McPhee 1970c:311–12)
>
>   . . . [In *kebyar*] the dancer is still closely linked with the music; he is still its visual projection; his movements are in traditional style; his facial expression, while no longer immobile, is still colored by the stylistic conventions of the mask. But there is now a strong personal appeal in his performance; individuality begins to

assert itself; the dancer establishes a closer, warmer contact with the audience. It is he himself they are watching, no legendary figure from the past. (Ibid.: 321) [18]

Though Bawa's remarks spurred me to focus on *legong* above, connections can be tracked across this spectrum. Sharp *pek* strokes match mercurial head movements in *baris* and *barong* or hand movements in *jauk*; repeating *dag* strokes exaggerate comic posterior shakes for clown scenes in *topeng* plays; the unstable rhythms of *kebyar* patterns in the *kebyar* proper of *Oleg Tumulilingan*—danced while kneeling—match equally darting movements of the upper body and eyes, and so on. The interaction of drumming and dance is tactile, immediately evident in performance, and, because it mediates between abstractions of sound and movement, of special aesthetic and semiotic significance.

Drum Improvisation and *Kendang Tunggal*

There are three kinds of improvisation in Balinese drumming, one each in *gupekan, krempengan,* and *cedugan* styles. Though improvisational creativity is valued, the main purpose of this drumming is not to showcase drummers. In the first two styles its essential function is to lead the ensemble through *angsel* sequences in particular kinds of repeating cycles, reflecting the mood of the dance (if there is one). In *cedugan* improvisation, a highly constrained rhythmic elaboration is created in various musical spaces where only skeletal fixed patterns are given. Improvisation in *krempengan* and *cedugan* involves both players, one of whom leads the improvising while the other plays a supporting role. *Gupekan* improvisation is played solo. As with melodic *payasan,* I use the term "improvisation" guardedly, for the degree of freedom and the span of the musical segments in which such freedom is allowed are often quite limited. Though drummers describe what they do in these contexts as *bebas* (free), in practice many do not avail themselves of the opportunity to create

---

18. It is often remarked that today there are few dancers of the caliber of Maria, Raka, Kakul, and other major figures of midcentury, all of whom were renowned for their concentration, performance charisma *(taksu),* remarkable rapport with audiences, and their deep knowledge of characterization. Part of the reason may lie in what Herbst (1997: 134–41) has called the "marginalization of presence": the change of performance content and context from the solo dances or small ensemble theatrical performances given in intimate village arenas to the massive dance dramas with amplified sound of the Bali Arts Festival, performed at the Ardha Candra amphitheater before audiences of thousands. The individuality of the soloist is hard to convey there, and most new choreography, in order to be clearly visible to the crowd, is designed for dozens of dancers as a series of tableaux. Soloists' moods are rendered through the amplified singing and dialog provided by a narrator *(dalang),* and dancers' facial and movement expression, in substantial degree, is lost as a function of their miniscule size in comparison to the width of the stage. There is no shortage of fine dancers in Bali today, but many of the best ones dance most frequently in this more impersonal context, thus losing some of the chance to develop their skills in the intimate performance situations of earlier times.

spontaneously at all, but instead recycle well-rehearsed stock phrases. Yet the choice of pattern is open, and better players exploit the chance to exercise their powers of invention and mastery.

Structurally speaking, however, improvised drumming is very different from *payasan*. In chapter 6 I stressed that *payasan* was ornamentation of the *neliti* and therefore did not constitute a separate structural entity. Improvised drumming, like fixed drumming, is not based on a separate stratum comparable to *neliti* or *pokok*. Without that external grid for reference, structural strokes must be located embedded in the pattern. Moreover, given the nature of improvisation, this structure can vary from cycle to cycle even in stable textures. Where fixed drumming patterns recur unchanged in a series of repeating stable *gongan*, the shifting continuity of improvised drumming adds a *majalan* layer of change to a repeating melody. The patterns themselves and the precision and skill of the drummer's sensitivity to dance become focal points for the audience in such cases. For many performers, the chance to take advantage of these moments in the spotlight is extra incentive to hone their improvisation technique. This is especially true for *gupekan* improvisation. In this connection I was told that Gdé Manik, the great *kebyar* drummer from Jagaraga, could play dozens of repetitions of the *gandrung*-based cycle in *Teruna Jaya*—a well-known showcase for improvisation—without once repeating himself. When I sought him out in 1982 Manik was too frail to comply with my entreaties to demonstrate, but he did not deny the feat.

Krempengan improvisation goes by several names, among them *batel* drumming (because this meter is often present when improvisation is called for), and *krumpungan* (because of the prominent role of the *lanang*'s left-hand *krumpung* stroke in cueing *angsel*). *Batel* drumming is also used in *bapang* and *gegaboran* meters, most often at tempi above 90; otherwise fixed drumming is prescribed. *Cedugan* drumming's *batu-batu* improvisation may be employed under certain circumstances in nearly any *pegongan* meter, be it short or long. *Batu* means "stone"; the word is used as a simile for the sparse and syncopated D or T strokes that are "dropped" (with a report, like little explosions; not dropped as in omitted) during the improvisations. *Gupekan* improvisation is called *kendang tunggal*, solo drumming. It is used in the same metric contexts as *batel* drumming, plus others that derive from *gamelan gandrung*, such as the *Teruna Jaya* example mentioned above. Both *batel* and *batu-batu* are used only in strictly prearranged compositions in which the number of *gongan*, sequence of *angsel* (or other disruptions), and the specific length of the segments to be improvised are planned. In contrast, *kendang tunggal* is mostly used for music in which the number of *gongan* and the ordering of *angsel* are open and decided extemporaneously by the dancer, whom the drummer follows. I will discuss *batel* and *batu-batu* briefly before giving fuller consideration to *kendang tunggal*.

Wayan Rai, *kendang,* 1982. Photo: Author.

Wayan Tembres, *kendang,* 1985.
Photo: Author.

Wayan Beratha, *kendang*, 1982.
Photo: Author.

Madé Labah, *kendang*, 1982.
Photo: Author.

Batel Drumming

Gambuh plays, *calonarang* dramas, and *legong* choreographies often open with the energetic introductory music for the *condong* (maidservant) in *gegaboran*-type meters, and by the end of the performance there is ample occasion for swift music in *batel* meter to accompany scenes of battle or confrontation. These are the prime dramatic contexts for *batel* improvisation, which can also appear in instrumental *pelegongan* compositions.[19] In *batel*, as in other *krempengan*, the *lanang* leads. Its improvisation is generally more syncopated than the *wadon*'s and, because of the ringing p and U strokes, acoustically more prominent. *Lanang* drummers aim for a predominance of p, with some T and P, switching emphasis to U for *angsel* cues. The *wadon*'s role is to offset the *lanang* with occasional D emphasis, filling in the intervening spaces with light k and K strokes that need not interlock with the *lanang* precisely, though it is considered better if they do. For *angsel* and their cues, D is cast in interaction with the *lanang* U.

While the notion of simultaneous interlocking and improvisation may seem a contradiction in terms, it is possible to achieve if drummers have long experience together. Such seasoned pairs may share a favorite *pola dasar* (basic pattern), a 2- or 4-beat subpattern on which the improvisation is based.[20] This makes it possible to anticipate which subdivisions of the beat tend to be filled and which remain empty, and to design one's playing accordingly to fill the spaces. Though less-audible strokes (such as the right-hand *kep*) comprise 30–50 percent of the total strokes used, because of the element of improvisation it is inevitable that from time to time the *wadon* and *lanang* play strokes intended to be audible simultaneously. Though this transgresses standard syntax, it is of little concern to the drummers so long as equivalent strokes (k-p, K-P, and particularly D-T) do not clash. K-p and k-P alignments are routine, however.

It is common to reserve the last two or four beats of every stable cycle for a fixed subpattern containing only D-T exchanges as a way of insuring that the approach to gong receives appropriate emphasis. The most common such subpattern is [. . . T/DT.D/TDT.], with gong at the last (open) position. Drummers must abandon their improvisation at these points to deliver the proper strokes. The stroke sequence for *angsel*, with D intensified by simultaneous

---

19. The phrase "*batel* drumming" also refers to the *gamelan gender wayang batel*, a *gender wayang* quartet augmented by gongs, *cengceng*, and *krempengan* drums. This configuration is used to accompany shadow play or *wayang wong* (masked dance drama) depicting *Ramayana* stories. The adjective *batel* is added because of the prevalence of *batel* music in the repertoire of accompanying music for these plays, and their extensive fight scenes.

20. The best *batel* improvisers have experience in the *gamelan geguntangan*, a small ensemble consisting of drums, *suling*, and miscellaneous colotomic instruments used to accompany singing in *arja* plays. *Geguntangan* drummers are known as specialists in working out intricate *pola dasar*, which they can skillfully and continuously vary without clashing or losing the flow of interlocking.

Figure 7.13. Two cycles of *batel*-style improvised *krempengan* drumming (the first stable, the second active) in the *condong* portion of *legong kraton* (CDI/43). This transcription is provisional and, in its details, does not match the recording.

lanang P or p, is similarly prearranged. The general shape of the *angsel* cues is also fixed. Drummers tend to rely on stock ways of providing clear cues, but the best ones know many ways to cue and choose from among them when they play.

Figure 7.13 (CDI/43; see also fig. 6.3L) illustrates two cycles from the *condong* music for *legong,* the first one stable and the second containing an *angsel* and its preceding cue.[21] Since both drums have complex parts that do not always interlock, I have not beamed them together as in previous examples, save for the fixed subpatterns at the end of each cycle. I have also separated the two parts in the letter notation below the system. Less audible filler strokes are

---

21. The transcription is provisional, based on my knowledge of *batel* improvisation technique. I have not based it on an actual performance because of the difficulty of separating the parts from a recording, and also because of the difficulty of finding an actual performance that demonstrates the most salient features of the style in the concentrated way given here.

notated with headless stems, longer ones for the left hand and shorter ones for the right.

The *lanang*'s *pola dasar*, [pPT./p.P.], is two beats long. It appears right after the initial gong and is immediately repeated at beats 2–3 before it is varied. Because it is made up almost entirely of strokes falling on the extreme offbeats, rhythms that occupy the intervening subdivisions predominate in the *wadon* part. In the drums' interaction occasional small clashes occur, such as that between k and p halfway through the sixth beat of the first cycle, but otherwise the two parts interlock. The fixed subpattern sets off the final two beats of the first cycle without challenging the meter, but in the active cycle, the full-beat pause at beat 5 and the D arrival at beat 13 announcing the *angsel* proper segment the *gongan* into a *gambang*-like (5 + 3 + 5 + 3) beats. Thus the precomposed elements (cadential pattern, *angsel*, and general shape of the cue) are precisely those elements that assert the structural contrasts between the stable and active cycles. The restrictions on players' freedom that they impose prevent the improvisations from undermining these contrasts.

Batu-batu Drumming

Windows for *batu-batu* improvisation open just after gong in short meters like *gilak* and *tabuh telu*, and after *kempli* or *kempur* punctuation in *pengawak* in *tabuh* 1, 4, 6, or 8 meters. One drummer is the leader; the *lanang* in some regions of the island and the *wadon* in others.[22] In longer meters the two drums may pass the leadership back and forth. The follower drum provides a brief, repeating left-hand part in which all strokes fall either on the beat or halfway between, such as the simple [.P. ./.P. .] or the 4-beat [.P. ./.P.P/ . . . P/.P. .]. The leader interlocks with this by placing left-hand strokes, judiciously and unpredictably, in some of the intervening subdivisions. This technique ensures that the two left hands always interlock and produce a shifting composite. Against this the leader periodically "drops" the *batu* proper: right-hand D (or T) strokes sparingly meted out, singly or in small subpatterns lasting a beat or two. *Batu* are highly syncopated; one landing on a beat is invariably part of a subpattern that extends until just before the following beat. Here, then, is a unique case in *matimpal* drumming during which, at least for brief segments, D and T strokes do not intertwine but are heard independently and without each other as complement.

Batu-batu improvisations begin at the most *ngubeng* points in *pengawak* melodies, supporting them as they move away from repeating tones to quicker scale-tone turnover. The *batu-batu* leader should reflect this by using right-hand strokes sparingly if at all for the first several beats, gradually adding them as the next colotomic signpost approaches. Just prior to the signpost, as in

---

22. In *kabupaten* Badung the *lanang* usually leads but in Gianyar it is the *wadon*.

Figure 7.14. Half *palet* (from first *kempli* to second *kempur*) of *cedugan* drumming in *lelambatan Tabuh Gari* (*tabuh* 4 meter) showing combination of *batu-batu* improvisation and fixed drumming subpatterns (CDI/24).

batel drumming, the improvisations are interrupted with fixed subpatterns involving both D and T.

Figure 7.14 (CDI/24, 4:17–4:35; see also fig. 6.3Y) shows *batu-batu* improvisation in beats 64–96 of the *pengawak* of *lelambatan Tabuh Gari,* which is in *tabuh* 4.[23] In the letter notation below the system I have separated the drummers' left and right hands into separate composites, so that K-P exchanges are isolated in the upper line, and *batu* strokes in the lower. The excerpt, with drummers Gdé Arya (*lanang*) and Wayan Suweca (*wadon*), stretches a half *palet* from the cycle's first *kempli*, through an intervening *jegogan* stress, to the second *kempur*. The drumming segments this 32-beat span into 16 + 8 + 8 beats by the insertion of three fixed subpatterns.

In the fourteen beats leading to the first fixed subpattern the *wadon* leads the improvisation. The repeating *lanang* left-hand part is the second of the two cited above. There is only one *batu* during the first eight of those beats (just after 69), which reflects the *ngubeng* quality of this portion of the *palet*. Even

---

23. Not to be confused with the *pegambuhan Tabuh Gari* discussed earlier in the chapter.

in the more crowded subsequent six beats only one *batu* falls on the beat (at 75), but the beat is not stressed, even at the *pokok* level. The fixed subpattern at 78–79 anticipates the *jegogan* tone at 80, after which the improvisation resumes with the *lanang* in the lead role. Arya begins by imitating, at 80–81, Suweca's *batu* of 74–75. Now there are no beats "empty" of *batu* comparable to 64–67, for at this point in the *palet* the *majalan* impulse is already fairly strong and growing. It continues to intensify all the way to the *kempur*, but this distance is first bisected by another fixed subpattern, identical to the first. In the final eight beats the *wadon* briefly reassumes the leadership (88–91), but this soon gives way to the third fixed subpattern, double the length of the others. The extended D-T interaction in these final few beats is expressive of the *majalan* quality, which reaches a local apex here but drops back down after the *kempur*.

Kendang Tunggal

Unlike *batel* and *batu-batu*, most *kendang tunggal*[24] accompanies solo dances in which the dancer has the freedom to initiate *angsel* spontaneously. The main dances using it are those in *bapang* meter originating in *pelegongan* repertoire, such as *Jauk Keras, Telek, Jauk Longgor,* and *Barong. Tunggal* drumming contexts are also found in cycles derived from *gamelan gandrung*, such as the *pengipuk* (flirtation or love-scene melodies) of *Teruna Jaya* and *Kebyar Duduk.* In each of these dances, as the melodic and colotomic instruments cycle their parts, the drummer and dancer square off in a kind of contest. Playing a continuous thread of four strokes per beat, the drummer braces to respond to the dancer's *angsel* cues, which must be given at places fixed in relation to the meter. As in *batel* drumming, a good percentage of the subdivisions are given over to light damping strokes intended to stabilize rhythmic continuity.[25] Cues volley from the dancer to the drummer, who then signals the rest of the *gamelan*, which responds with *nguncab* and *angsel*.

In the original *pelegongan* and *gandrung* contexts *tunggal* drumming was done on a medium-sized instrument somewhat larger than *krempengan* drums

---

24. This type of playing is known variously in Bali as *gedig tunggal, kendang tunggal, kendang besik,* and *kendang pereragaan*—which translate respectively as solo pattern, solo drum, one drum, and drum by oneself.

My research on this subject comprises my own study and performance experience plus discussions with and recordings (made between 1982 and 1987) of fifteen drummers playing *kendang tunggal* patterns, accompanied only by a single *gangsa* playing an *ugal*-style *payasan* part, for a set of four *gending* that require improvised drumming (*Jauk Keras, Jauk Longgor, Kebyar Duduk, Teruna Jaya*). The idea of making these recordings was novel to the drummers, but most were so intrigued by the idea of at last being able to isolate and study their colleagues' styles that I fulfilled many requests to provide copies of the tapes.

25. The less audible strokes are also needed because solo drumming tempi are usually fast— above mm 120—and they relieve the drummer of the technical challenges that would be posed by having to execute over 480 audible strokes per minute. Damping strokes also separate the main strokes, shaping them into patterns that are articulate and of manageable information content.

called *kendang babancian* (the latter meaning "androgynous"; i.e., neither *lanang* nor *wadon*). In *kebyar* the *kendang wadon* is used. The drumming for a few dances, notably *Barong* and *Jauk Longgor*, is done with a *panggul* in the right hand, and uses slightly different techniques and patterns than *tunggal* hand drumming. The following discussion and analysis of *tunggal* patterns pertains only to the latter.

In *tunggal* hand drumming the basic stroke vocabulary consists of the right-hand D and u, and the left-hand P. (P and u, normally *lanang* stroke names, are applied to the *wadon* for solo drumming.) Secondary versions of D and u can also be produced on the left skin, enabling the drummer to play strings of identical sounds by alternating hands. Playing in this way, consecutive right-left (or left-right) strokes can simulate the sequence r-u (or u-r) on a single *kendang*. Pairs of consecutive right- or left-hand u are also common. The prolonged bass resonance of two or more consecutive D strokes performed by switching skins in this way is a special timbral and motivic feature of the style. Drummers use it sparingly. T does not appear in *kendang tunggal*, but u can substitute for it.

Musicians agree nearly unanimously on the criteria for assessing solo drumming performances. Explicit and clear response to dancers' cues is paramount, for the viability of the performance is at stake. This is supported by a second widely held view: that patterns should not be so complex as to divert attention from the dance, interfere with its mood, or draw too much attention to the drummer. At the same time, drummers aim to complement the dance with their own movements of the upper body and facial expressions, a display of panache that audiences appreciate.[26] A drummer's technique should be facile, with no evident physical effort expended while playing. The patterns should flow through the hands in a natural way, so that attention can be given over to monitoring the dance and leading the rest of the musicians. All drummers stress the need to have mastered precise cueing much more than they stress developing interesting patterns to use between the cues. Many of those with whom I spoke downplayed the musical value of their favorite pattern-models, which until my investigation had been mostly a private source of satisfaction for them.

My teachers provided a variety of technical tips to aid my learning. Wayan Pogog advised me to "always avoid the beat" when playing, as, he contended, this gave the patterns a particular beauty and added life to the music and

---

26. Though these ideas are almost universally subscribed to, there is interesting contradictory evidence. A performance in which an upstart drummer does abandon normal propriety and engage in a showily competitive face-off with the dancer for control of the flow of the music and rhythmic breaks can create a sensation. During the final melodies of *Teruna Jaya* and *Kebyar Duduk* this excitement has been formalized, as the choreography explicitly calls for the dancer and drummer to engage in an interactive duet. Here not only the drummer's patterns, but also his facial expressions, body language, and hand movements share the spotlight with the dancers' movements.

dance. Pogog also told me that "*tunggal* patterns are meant to be approximations of *matimpal* patterns for the hands of a single performer." This was probably his way of opining that improvisation thrives on its associative connections to fixed forms. Wayan Beratha, consistent with his philosophical approach, advised me to be conscious of "using the main strokes in relatively equal numbers, always keeping a feeling of balance." Komang Astita urged me to "increase the number of *dag* when approaching gong," while Wayan Sinti counseled that it is best to "use *pek* mostly on the second and fourth subdivisions of the beat to keep the music buoyant." Wayan Tembres promulgated the opposite point of view, namely that the unpitched, neutral P should be used mostly on the beat and its third subdivision lest the continuity become too syncopated and threaten the stability of the rhythm.[27] Gdé Manik's only advice, based on his own life history, was to seclude myself, start practicing, and be confident that good patterns would "enter my hands" on their own.

All stressed that the character of the drumming at any given moment should reflect the movements of the dancer in appropriate sonic code. A preponderance of P is called for when the dancer is executing continuous small movements that involve relatively little change of position, especially if the feet are stationary.[28] When the dance is in transition, or if a sudden change to a more *majalan* quality occurs, a good drummer will change the content of the patterns to use more u and D. D, as mentioned, is considered more aggressive, and may be used in greater concentration if specific movements have an especially gregarious or warlike character, or involve traversing a big part of the stage. The more delicate u may be added to underpin small steps, or movements of the arms and upper body that derive from older female dance styles. By altering the patterns in these ways, drummers may either complement the dance being performed, or refer, through the patterns themselves, to styles that are precisely *not* present, but which, through their evocation, enrich the performance.

If asked about the underlying basis for improvisation, many drummers boil *tunggal* patterns down to a skeletal *pola dasar* which, in Lebah's words, is *beneh ken jangkep* (correct and sufficient) for cueing and accompanying *angsel* and maintaining continuity between them, and *could* be used in performance (though few drummers actually do so). Three drummers' *kendang tunggal* styles are shown in figure 7.15 over three *gongan* of *bapang* meter for the dance

---

27. Almost predictably, none of these drummers were true in performance or teaching to their own recommendations with much consistency. Indeed, a lesson in solo drumming might contain such verbalizations, but would otherwise consist of the rote memorization of a teacher's favorite combinations, with instructions to "go home, practice and internalize them, and then create your own"—without any further instructions about how to do so. Happily, these drummers' ability to both follow and disregard their self-imposed constraints has the end result of infusing the language of solo drumming with a greater number of patterns and a seemingly less restricted syntax for them.

28. *Pek* played in a continuous succession of eighth notes is used in a special pattern called *tarik* (to pull) to regulate tempo, most often during accelerandi.

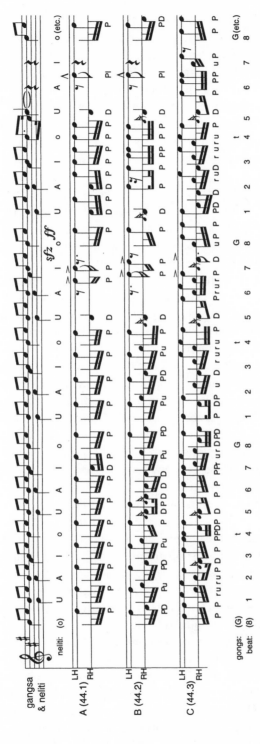

Figure 7.15. Three *kendang tunggal* renditions, each three cycles long, of *Jauk Keras* (one stable cycle, one stable cycle with *angsel* cue, one active cycle with *angsel*)

A. Simple (*dasar kendang tunggal*): Tempo's version (CDI/44.1)

B. Somewhat complex: Tembres's style (CDI/44.2)

C. Complex: Pogog's style (CDI/44.3)

of the demon *Jauk Keras* (CDI/44). The simple, *ngubeng gangsa* figuration used is shown on the top staff, with the *neliti* (see also fig. 6.3B) below it. Wayan Tempo provided the first, most basic pattern. In the initial, stable *gongan,* his drumming consists entirely of P strokes halfway between beats, surrounded by damping and filler strokes, with a single D on the seventh beat to prepare gong. The second cycle begins the same way but is interrupted at beat 5 for the *angsel* cue, which lasts for two beats. The P at beat 7, heard in contrast with the D of the previous cycle, completes the cue. Extra D strokes on the first two beats of the last cycle intensify the link to the *angsel* proper, which falls at beats 5–6.

The spareness of this pattern demonstrates the essential functions of the strokes more clearly than any other pattern examined thus far in the chapter. The fact that u is entirely absent testifies to its generally secondary function. Here P provides continuity, and assumes a structural role only at the *angsel* cue. When all is said and done, the onus of communicating structure falls on D. Comparing this pattern with the two more intricate and improvisatory examples below it offers a fresh perspective on how principles of syntax and structure become distorted in practice. Consider version 7.15 B, Tembres's, which is similar to Tempo's but different in some crucial respects. For the first four beats of the first cycle, Tembres employs P like Tempo does, but he immediately suffixes each with a D or u, used in alternation. These strokes are acoustically prominent, and their syncopation adds rhythmic drive, but they are at a low level of structure. Where Tempo articulated the upcoming gong with D on the seventh beat, Tembres eschews this in favor of a two beat D-based subpattern beginning at beat 5. By placing the structural D stress there he syncopates the pattern's relationship to the meter in the manner of an *angsel.* Tembres's handling of the second two *gongan* is, on the other hand, close to Tempo's, though more syncopated.

7.15 C, Pogog's version, maintains the stress on beat 5 of the first cycle established in Tembres's, but builds more complex patterns around it. Pogog makes P a flexible element of the improvisation, rather than a mainly immobile one, as the others do. Overall his subpatterns are more fluidly composed and less repetitive. He approaches the gong at the end of the first cycle with a delicate [rur.] sequence, only to defy expectations with syncopated, irregular D strokes *after* each of the first three beats of the new cycle (where one would ordinarily expect more *ngubeng* quality). This extra burst of energy propels the drumming to the cue, which is more intricate than either of the other versions, and halves the length of the agogic pause at beat 5. The link to the *angsel* and closing beats of the third cycle are similarly elaborate.

Dancers are sensitive to the way that drumming can affect them in performance, though they rarely have the opportunity to choose the drummers with whom they work. For some, the complexity of a style like Pogog's can enhance their dancing by offering a more rounded, colorful, and even (one might say) urbane approach to improvisation. In Pogog's quickly shifting rhythms and timbral interplay, dancers so predisposed will find inspiration to deepen their character portrayals and magnify their nuances. Others, perhaps more concerned with vigor and incisive, direct expression, might prefer to be paired off with a drummer like Tembres, whose clarity and drive are second to none. Dancers who perform with him speak of the power that he contributes to their performance and their confidence in his leadership. The sharp and regular P strokes in Tembres's style also support the menacing persona of the *Jauk Keras* demon, whereas Pogog's style adds irony and partially undermines (one might say enriches) the demon's personality by emphasizing ornate and studied refinement. These distinctions, it should be noted, are felt, understood, and responded to at the dance's typical, pulse-pounding performance tempo of mm 180 or more.

Pogog and others with comparably florid *tunggal* styles cite *gamelan gandrung* as the source for their overall concept. Whereas the *tunggal* styles developed for dances like *Jauk Keras* are said to be forceful and straightforward, like Tembres's, those taken from *gandrung* are considered more capricious and playful, like Pogog's.[29] *Gandrung* ensembles are scarce today, but just as *gandrung kotekan* appears as a stylistic topic in new *kebyar* compositions (fig. 6.19), so too does *gandrung* drumming live on in *kebyar*. Its evocation of the somewhat disreputable dance it once accompanied provides an important counterbalance to the association of drumming with court repertoire.

Pogog's use of *gandrung* drumming when performing *Jauk Keras* is a topical reference because the drumming style is provocatively mismatched with the meter, dance, and melody; that is why I described the combination of the two as having an element of irony. More compatible contexts for *gandrung* drumming come in longer cycles with direct *gandrung* associations, such as the *pengipuk* of *Kebyar Duduk* and *Teruna Jaya,* which accompany overtly flirtatious dances based on their *gandrung* predecessors. Indeed, the brevity of the *bapang* cycle in *Jauk* constrains the *gandrung* patterns, which find fuller and more elaborate expression in these extended formats.

The longest such format that I know of in the current repertoire is the 48-beat *pengipuk* of *Kebyar Duduk*. One cycle of a recording of Suweca improvising to this melody is given in figure 7.16. (This is heard at the third cycle of CDI/45, 0:45–1:05, with just drum and a single metallophone. CDI/46 features Suweca playing to this melody with full *gamelan*.) The melody's gong punctuation bears scrutiny first, because it is asymmetrical and unlike any court meter: t appears one-third of the way through at beat 16 (at a registral shift to *dung*). The midpoint is left empty, and there is no further punctuation until the *kempur* at 45 and 47, which prepare the upcoming gong in a manner

---

29. While most drummers say that there should be a contrast between *bapang* and *gandrung* styles, only a few demonstrate these distinctions in performance.

Figure 7.16. Wayan Suweca: *kendang tunggal* in *Kebyar Duduk* (CDI/45)
Note: CDI/46 is a recording of Suweca improvising alternate patterns, with full gamelan accompaniment.

reminiscent of *gilak*. *Jegogan* play every eight beats throughout the cycle, dividing it into six equal parts. A CC representing the sequence of *jegogan* tones, which in a cycle of this unusual length could be labeled the CC6, is {0,4,5,5,2,0}. The melody's internal repetition at beats 25–32 and 33–40 make the fourth and fifth sixths of the cycle uncharacteristically *ngubeng*.

Suweca responds to all of these factors in his playing, most pointedly with his cautious and limited use of the D stroke. D appears on the beat only six times (each is circled in the transcription), once and only once between each pair of *jegogan* tones. It falls on beats 5, 13, and 37, dividing the first, second, and fifth sixths of the cycle asymmetrically into the now-familiar (5 + 3) beats. In a carefully executed contrast, he divides the third and fourth sixths of the cycle into metrically supported groups of (6 + 2) beats by shifting D over one beat to 22 and 30. In stabilizing the rhythm at those two points he relaxes the

	First half	Second half	Full cycle
P strokes	32	25	57
u (and r) strokes	25	21	46
D strokes	5	17	21
Total	62	63	125

Figure 7.17. Distribution of stroke types in Suweca's improvisation.

character of the pattern to support the mood of the ensuing internal repetitions in the melody. The final sixth of the cycle is marked early by D at beat 41 in a sudden intensification. Subsequent Ds are all off the beat, but D's role as structural marker is assumed by the *kempur* at 45 and 47. The combination of the D at 41 and the two *kempur* segments the closing eight beats into a driving (1 + 3 + 1 + 2 + 1).

The proportion in which Suweca combines the strokes illuminates D's role from another perspective. With forty-eight beats in the cycle there are 192 (= 48 x 4) subdivisions available to fill; but only 125 audible (i.e., nonfiller) strokes are used in the pattern: this gives an average density of 65 percent. The strokes are apportioned as in figure 7.17. Although the number of strokes is virtually the same in both halves, the dominance of D increases in the second half, displacing some P and u in the process. This reflects a gradual overall shift in timbral weight, which in turn supports a continuous and incremental rise in *majalan* quality. This impulse reaches its payoff at 44–47, where damping and filler strokes are forgone and the density increases to 100 percent (the only such change in the pattern). As the cadential subpattern [DPuP] repeats through these four beats, the insistent and regular exchanges between syncopated D and u combine with on-the-beat P to intensify the gong arrival.

While D shapes the pattern in these ways, P and u/r contribute shifting, motive-like behavior. Compare, for example, 1–4 and 17–20; two segments identically aligned with respect to the *jegogan*. The simple [.ruP] reiterated at beats 1–4 establishes the interaction of these strokes early on in a way that is predictably *ngubeng*. When Suweca brings this unit back after beat 16 the metric position is analogous, but the interaction between the strokes is transformed: with a suffix it becomes [.ruP/uP. .] at 17–18; and prefixed it becomes [PuPP/.ruP] at 19–20. These new combinations both refer back to the opening and give the sense of having traveled some distance from it.

Though the turnover of timbres and rhythms is generally faster in *tunggal* patterns than it is in *matimpal* drumming, the influence of the meter in shaping the basic aspects of structure and quality is the same. With great subtlety, Suweca was able to balance competing structural nuances of symmetry and asymmetry within a single cycle. Quality revolved around the growing prominence of D. In subsequent *gongan* he might again choose to make D the linchpin, or he could alter the process by saturating the beginning of a cycle with D and forcing one of the other strokes to assume the role of providing contrast. Or, he could save strong contrast for the end of every other cycle, linking repetitions of the melody into metacyclic pairs. Here, as in all drumming, the fine points of quality and syntax emerge from the context established in each pattern. Ideally such decisions are made not only with the beauty of the pattern itself in mind, but also in spontaneous reaction to the dancer, whose movements may suggest a focus on certain strokes or elicit a drumming sub-pattern that strives to capture the essence of a movement in sound.

Conclusion

Like symmetrical-class melodies, stable and active drum patterns embody a multilevel dialogue between stasis and motion, carried out in a cyclical frame where energy accrues as the completion of the circle nears. In active patterns this process is magnified through contrasting, often asymmetrical segmentation of the cycle. The succession of stable and active patterns in each *gending* contributes a metacyclic dimension of change, located at a level between meter and form, to repeating melodic contexts. The role of this intermediary structure is both narrative, in that it is modeled after choreography in dance music, and compositional, in that it represents a transformation of inherited meters and repeating melodic materials.

Having opened with his commentary, it is fitting that this chapter should also conclude with Suweca, one of the most technically accomplished, charismatic, and inventive *kebyar* drummers. Throughout the chapter I have marshaled evidence to show how the subtle language of drumming to which he alluded in the prelude is not, finally, an entity with sharply defined and immutable characteristics. It is a fluid field on which the competing influences of meter, syntax, structure, identity, regional style, performer preference, dance, and the occasional added wild card of improvisation all interact. The medium for the interaction is the small vocabulary of available strokes, each of which can acquire different nuances of function and quality in each pattern.

This flexibility is exploited to the music's advantage. The drums use it to translate efficiently between dance and music, art forms that, each in their own way, display deeply ingrained cultural convictions about rhythm in time and movement in space. At the nexus of dance and music the drummers sit, called upon to manipulate the sounds available to them to communicate information ranging from the elusive character of a movement to specific and literal rhythmic instructions. In instrumental music the aura of movement lingers, ghostlike, to hone the compositional impulse. In the next chapter I elaborate on the depictions of these impulses, developed in the last three chapters in relation to both drumming and melody, and apply them to musical form.

8 Form and Composition

Nyoman Windha, *ugal*, leading STSI students and faculty in rehearsal to record the CDs for this book, 1998. Photo: Author.

Form owes its existence to the ability of the listener to remember the music he has heard and to integrate its individual sections while he listens so that after he has heard the composition (no matter how many times) he is [capable] of perceiving it as an idea that, like a painting or a sculpture, exists outside the limits of time . . .

Thus the closed form is a complex phenomenon, for it is based on the concept of a dual role that time can play in a musical composition. The composition evolves in a given period of time, it is true, but once it has been performed it begins an independent existence of its own in the consciousness of the listener due to the facilities of memory and to the ability of the listener to integrate impressions. Unrestricted by time, the composition can be conceived in its entirety in one brief moment.

Witold Lutoslawski[1]

Ké-wah! It is hard! to compose. Sometimes I cannot sleep for nights, thinking of a new piece. It turns round and round in my thoughts. I hear it in my dreams. My hair has grown thin thinking of music.

Wayan Lotring[2]

---

1. Quoted in Stucky (1981:127), from Robert Stephan Hines, ed., *The Orchestral Composer's Point of View: Essays on Twentieth Century Music by Those Who Wrote It,* 133–34 (Norman: University of Oklahoma Press 1970).

2. Quoted by Colin McPhee in *A House in Bali* (McPhee 1946:162).

Prelude: *Kebyar* Composers

SOMETHING that never changed over the years I studied in Bali was my admiration for the awesome fluency with which the better composers I knew produced music. Notwithstanding sly protestations like Lotring's, the sheer volume of their output, their lightning creation of it, and the fluid, efficient, and essentially notationless transmission process (at most the composer would refer sporadically to a sketch of the *pokok*) which brought it to life remain things that I cannot satisfactorily explain to myself even though they took shape before my eyes all the time.

The most prolific and proficient worker is the firebrand Nyoman Windha of the STSI faculty, born in 1956 in *banjar* Kutri, on the road just north of Singapadu. Windha attended KOKAR and STSI (then called ASTI) during the 1970s and early 1980s, and was first known as a performer and leader, especially on the *ugal*. Demand for his music has been high both in Bali and Indonesia at large since he began composing in 1983. Between then and 1998 he completed 50-odd works in disparate genres. Some are of unprecedented scope for Balinese music. The hour-long *Derap Tersada Nusantara*—a narrated "oratorio" portraying the history of Indonesia that was televised nationwide from Jakarta in 1991—is one of the largest; it calls for multiple *gamelan* and singers, both Balinese and Javanese, as well as a Western drum battery to evoke the Dutch forces. Windha's reputation has also brought him opportunities to teach, perform, and compose in the United States and Europe, often in experimental or collaborative situations.[3]

Every June, when contributing a portion of the music for one the Bali Arts Festival dance-dramas, Windha sits before his students at their instruments and with what I can vouch is virtually no forethought generates thirty minutes or more of new music on the spot.[4] Granted much of this is preordained by choreographic exigencies suggesting the use of stock meters in familiar sequence, meaning that most of what Windha does is invent a series of brief dance melodies, or vary existing ones that carry the appropriate affect or character. To these he adds melodic elaboration, *angsel* to fit the dance move-

---

3. See Vitale 1996 for a full listing of Windha's works to 1996. See also Tenzer 1993:405 for a description of Windha's collaboration with American composer Evan Ziporyn (available on New World CD 80432, *American Works for Balinese Gamelan*).

4. The entire *sendratari* score of more than two hours is customarily divided among four composers on the faculty, on the reasonable assumption that their contributions will be stylistically compatible.

ments, and some introductory and transitional passages. The drummers mostly work out their parts themselves on the basis of meter and *angsel,* and the ensemble swiftly comes into focus. Though remarkable and dependent upon vast knowledge of the idiom, this is actually not very challenging work for Windha. It calls for an abundant bag of tricks reflecting a kind of stylistic facility all too rare in my North American academic compositional world, but it is, it has always seemed to me, a bag of tricks nonetheless. Windha does not disagree and shrugs off his creativity in this context.

For what both he and I consider more weighty and creative occasions, such as supplying a *tabuh kreasi* for a *Festival Gong* group, Windha thinks things out more in advance. This is his preferred medium. He invariably claims to have assembled materials only the day before the first rehearsal, but it is likely (and he does not deny it) that he ruminates over interesting new melodies and figuration patterns constantly. The penetrating look and clipped succinctness in his self-presentation make it plausible that he is working out some music, perhaps several different things, in another region of his mind—even as you sit in conversation with him. These ideas accumulate and once he has a specific commission he mentally selects, refines, and arranges those that are ready. Over the course of a few rehearsals he sets them before the musicians with unhesitating panache, then leaves the group to polish the material on its own. Since 1985 his *tabuh kreasi* have grown remarkably lengthy and intricate, and every June news of Windha's latest *Festival Gong* surprises redounds in the musical community.

This is a bag of tricks too, of sorts, but at a higher level of technical preoccupations and compositional concerns that I feel sure is there, though Windha does not say much about it. Like other Balinese composers he embraces the template of *tabuh kreasi* form, but he surely scans his imagination for things to experiment with. He devises quirky melodic and rhythmic approaches to the gong, serpentine *kotekan* that even the best players despair of aurally disentangling, and uses the pitch flexibility of the human voice, the *suling,* and the *rebab* to reintegrate the sixth and seventh tones of *pélog* into *kebyar.* He places meters and elaboration styles into new formal contexts and alters *palet*-lengths asymmetrically. He delights in complexity, lights up in praise of musical *keberanian* ("guts"), but does not value them for their own sakes; he wants to baffle musicians and audiences, but not beyond the point of surprise and beguilement where they are drawn to the music's challenge. Like virtually all Balinese, however, he cares to sustain cultural vitality in any way he can, meaning that certain musical limits are not to be exceeded. Widely used motives, styles, and quotations come up again and again in his music. He does not eschew *kebyar*'s formal conventions; he just extends and distorts what they can bear as much as his sensibility allows. But to me he remains mysterious. "The first thing I think about when I compose is *desa, kala, patra*" Windha told me, invoking a Balinese homily meaning "everything in its proper place, time and context." "My music has to use the right materials at the right moments to speak directly to the audience. I have to give them something new each time using all the resources I have, but the result must sound Balinese." Such remarks left me wanting.

Foremost of an older generation whose achievements are now part of Windha's springboard is a composer whose name I have often had cause to mention in these pages: Wayan Beratha, born in 1924 to Madé Regog, leader of the pioneering *gamelan* of Belaluan. A tall man of imposing seriousness and severity yet thoughtful and gentle in conversation, Beratha is a formidable drummer and widely celebrated as a primary architect of *kebyar* forms. His contributions to the conventions of *kreasi lelambatan, tabuh kreasi,* and *tari lepas* comprise an intimidating edifice, and many of his compositions have canonical status. Like a ruler of a latter-day musical kingdom in the Majapahit tradition Beratha dwells at the center of musical life, where credit for changes and advancements in style clings to him as if magnetically. He did not, of course, design the forms alone but assimilated them from various sources encountered through long experience teaching and performing throughout the island. If the achievements attributed to him are at all exaggerated, part of the explanation lies with the authority and stature he has accrued over a lifetime working among the culturally and politically powerful in and around Denpasar, and because he taught at SMKI and STSI since the earliest days.

Viewing his work in hindsight, Beratha now appeals to tradition more than Windha does to innovation. He is more concerned at his age to preserve what is old than to risk pushing the envelope on musical norms. When asked about his groundbreaking *tabuh kreasi* of the 1960s he is quick to recall how he was *jelap bani* (intentionally daring) when he composed a 5-beat cycle into *Palguna Warsa,* or tried to coax the *kendang* into mimicking sounds of gunfire in *Gesuri* (an acronymic title invoking the revolutionary struggle that expands to <u>Ge</u>nta <u>Su</u>ara <u>Ra</u>kyat <u>I</u>ndonesia, The Resounding Voice of the Indonesian People). But by the 1980s these modernisms seemed *kirang wayah* (immature) to him and he gradually narrowed his focus to composing dignified *gending lelambatan,* explaining his retrenchment on the basis of love for the sacred music and his perception that he must do his part to preserve it. "It would be a shame if those wonderful pieces were ever lost or forgotten," he confided on the way to a rehearsal for his new *Festival Gong lelambatan* in 1982, "so I'm doing what I can to keep them alive." And a moment later, under his breath: "This is the best one I've ever done and the other groups might as well pack it in." When I congratulated him on taking first place a few weeks later over coffee at his home, he smiled and praised the challengers. Inadvertently demonstrating with these works that compositional specifics matter more in *kebyar* than in the court forms, he gradually began to delegate the working out of musical details. By the late 1980s his output slowed and he settled into semiretirement as a tuner and merchant, preparing only *pokok* tones and some drum patterns for his occasional compositions, and allowing students (Windha among them) to fill in the rest and do the actual teaching.

In conversational discourse, Windha and Beratha and their peers tend to emphasize conformity and practical skills over the kind of shoptalk about design and process I was always on the lookout for. In *banjar*, at the conservatories, and on *Festival Gong* juries *gending* are assessed for how well they meet genre requirements and the level of performance they receive, and far less for their individual features.[5] This conservatism quantifies the most measurably "Balinese" aspects of music in accord with the prevalent ideology of cultural preservation, creating a pervasive consciousness that I found it a challenge to transcend. When I noted that someone found a particular composition interesting or valuable and asked why, the answer usually was that the *sekaha* was disciplined and skillful and that the formal structure was *correct*; in other words recognizably similar to others of the genre, or observant of the strict metric plans of court music.

Pressing beyond the dogma was rarely fruitful, so I treasured the few probing remarks about nuts-and-bolts subjects that I actually could elicit. For example, I had asked Rai numerous times about how he composed the *pengawak* for his stunning 1982 *lelambatan Singamurti* and was feeling frustrated with his perfunctory reply that he "made sure the gong structure was right," which struck me as like hearing the overture to *Don Giovanni* defended by its composer in terms of proper voice-leading, or Frank Lloyd Wright enthusing over the well-poured foundation of his Guggenheim museum. I wasn't expecting an analytical sketchbook—I was merely hoping for some morsels to satisfy my curiosity. One night I presumably succeeded in better conveying my interests, and learned that he first chose the gong tone according to what he determined the desired affect to be: for Rai, *dIng,* the one he settled on, was *wibawa* (authoritative) and *kereng* (strong). Next he picked the scale tones coinciding with the *kempur* and *kempli* punctuations, making sure that their succession included a balance of high and low registers with no consecutive ones more

---

5. If asked whether music analysis seems a subject worth developing in the curriculum at STSI, some say that it seems worthwhile and they wish there were more, but they lament their all-encompassing commitments to composing and performing, and the lack of precedent for viewing pieces on individual terms.

A few feel differently. In a June 1991 conversation on the STSI campus, composer Gdé Yudana rued the sameness of most new music and speculated that analysis was a way to change that: "STSI is a factory for *kreasi baru*. Every year at the thesis performances, the Arts Festival, and the *Festival Gong* the output is so predictable, like a weather report. How will the weather be tomorrow? Hot, as always. People are satisfied only as long as their music is just like everyone else's, and who can blame them, really, because they are under pressure to create so much so fast. But how can our music develop if we don't question our assumptions about how we listen and compose?"

Yudana touches a nerve, but his criticisms need to be seen in light of the fact that as in all academic environments, particularly a Balinese one like STSI, there is pressure to conform. He had lived in Europe for a time and had a more individualistic perspective.

than three scale steps apart. Finally he joined these structural points by improvising passages of connective melodic tissue, either in his mind or at an instrument, at the same time envisioning the details of drumming and surface texture that would ultimately put meat on the bones. To be sure, I was neither surprised nor even particularly edified by these remarks, just relieved to gain assurances that a composer was at work behind the facade of cultural propriety.

As I argued in chapter 4 in relation to classic Western music, there exists in *kebyar* a tension, exemplified in these composers' music, between the seemingly sacrosanct conventions of musical forms as they have evolved from court repertoire over the decades of the twentieth century, and the pressure exerted on each *gending* by the composer's contributions. In some ways the form of each piece in the repertoire can be explained with reference to a succession of procedural norms. In other ways, because of its unduplicated specifics and singular interpretation of the norms, each *gending* is also like an expansive and autonomous system in which compositional logic is explored—a world unto itself, inviting our scrutiny.

Chapter Overview

With regard to early Indian music, Lewis Rowell asserted that "the influence of the [poetic] text forms is manifest at the intermediate levels of musical structure, but not at the level of whole compositions" (1992:231), and the same may be said to apply for *kebyar*. There is a difference in kind, not just magnitude, between the sung poetry-influenced syntax of melodies in cycles and the broader succession of elements that constitute form. Intuition accurately tells us that it is one thing to grasp the workings of an isolated cycle and another to make plausible statements about what connections can be made when many cycles are brought together, just as it is some distance to go from understanding the structure of words and sentences to a metanarrative of literature. The possibilities quickly come to seem unlimited, the complexities unmanageable. And yet of course this is a level on which we readily experience music, and on which we may ultimately ascribe to it its most significant attributes of coherence, elegance, beauty, and power. My focus in this chapter is to suggest how these attributes can be experienced at the level of complete *kebyar* compositions, putting the insight in terms of use to those who, like Lutoslawski's listener, wish to think "in" the music.

The remainder divides into three large parts. The first is a survey of compositional tools and techniques, which means naming, classifying, and describing the behaviors of musical elements in various contexts. The descriptions are mostly generalized and restricted to the kinds of things one can find in most any *kebyar* piece, though specific *gending* are continually referenced for demonstration. The second part is a predominantly ethnotheoretical

Reyong and gongs (Komang Astita and Ketut Gdé Asnawa, second and third from left on the *reyong*), 1987. Photo: Ketut Prasetya.

approach to musical form, chronicling the characteristic orderings of melodic and metric units in court and *kebyar* repertoire and the Balinese terms labeling them. In the third I take an opposite stance by emphasizing content over process and form in the nongeneralized and individual worlds of four well-known works.

The *gending* I have chosen to concentrate on are mostly Beratha's. They date from various stages of his career and are included in full on CD II. All are central to the *kebyar* canon, continually performed into the 1990s while *gending* of the same vintage have fallen by the wayside. The number is small to allow for the presentation of longer segments in transcription and facilitate viewing some passages from several angles. Locations in the transcriptions are referred to with their CD timings, which are given periodically in lieu of measure numbers or rehearsal letters. Timings function as well to indicate changing proportions of rhythm and tempo, which are sometimes so flexible as to bring the value of metronome markings into question.

The decision to focus on Beratha was not intentionally exclusionary (the next chapter features other composers), but is due to the encyclopedic presence in his music of most of the materials I need. It is also because I have internalized all four pieces by memorizing, teaching, and performing them over many years. From the *lelambatan* repertoire I selected his 1978 *kebyar* version of *Tabuh Pisan Bangun Anyar* (hereafter simply *Bangun Anyar*, fig. 8.1A-D, CDII/

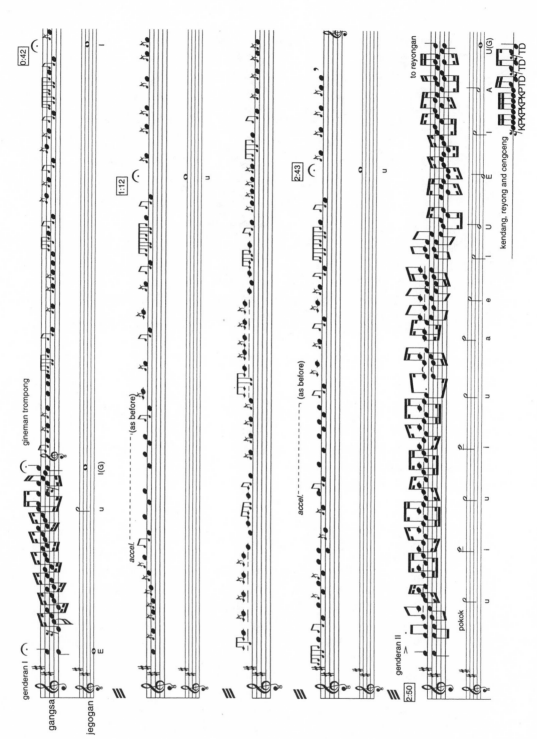

Figure 8.1A. *Bangun Anyar: Genderan I/gineman trompong/genderan II* (CDII/1, 0:00–3:00).

Figure 8.1B. Five versions of the *pengawak* in *Bangun Anyar* (CDII/1, 4:38–730; 9:18–10:08).

(continued)

Figure 8.1B. (*continued*)

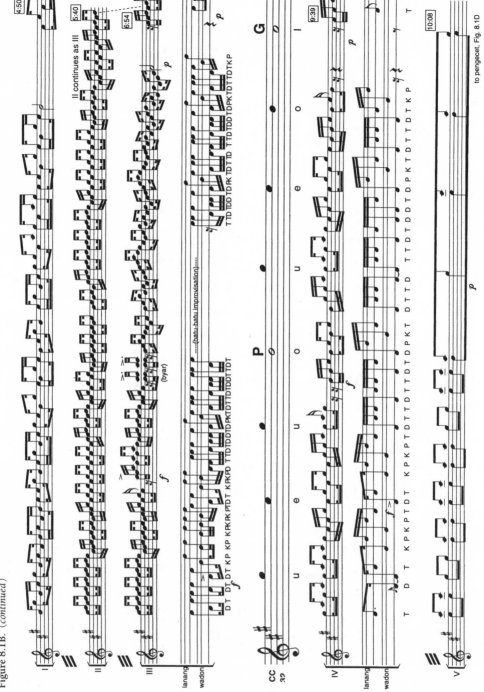

(continued)

Figure 8.1B. *(continued)*

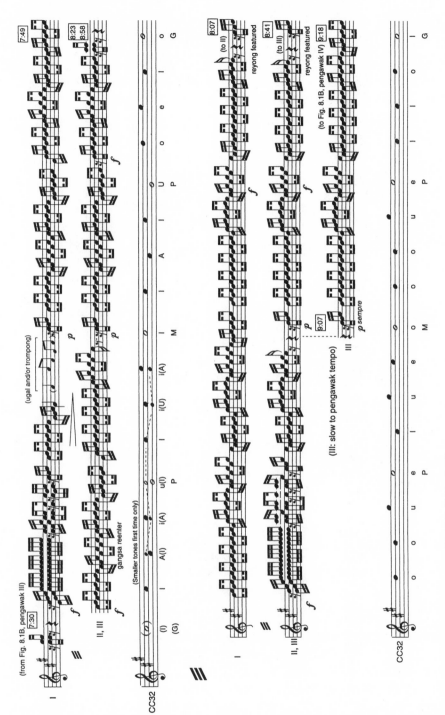

Figure 8.1C. *Bangun Anyar: Pengisep* (CDII/1, 7:30–9:18).

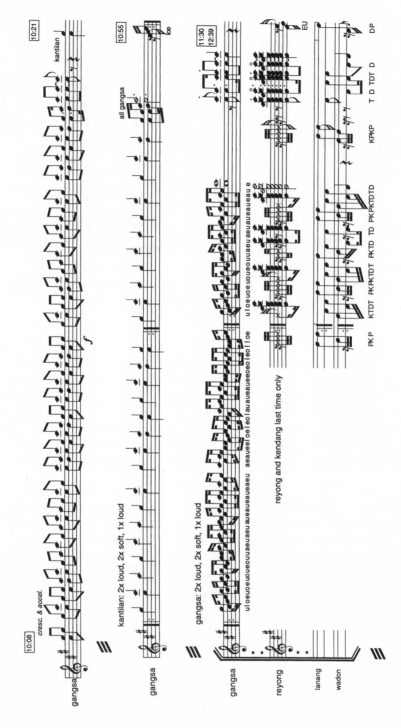

Figure 8.1D. *Bangun Anyar: Pengecet* (CDII/1, 10:08–14:08).

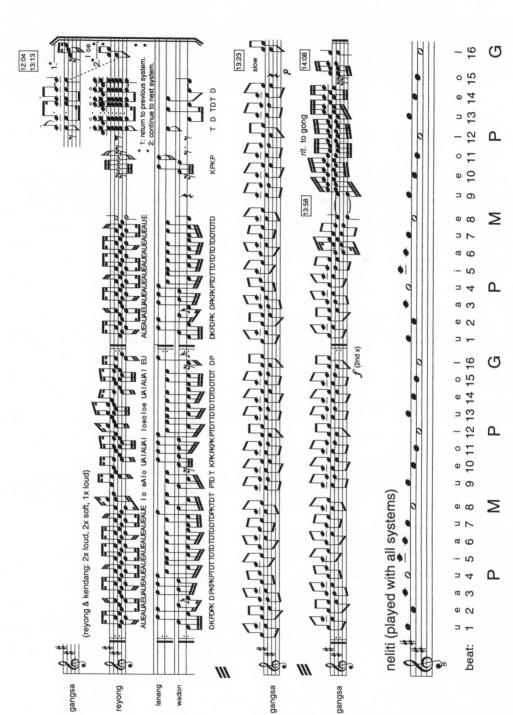

Figure 8.1D. (*Continued*)

Figure 8.2A. *Panyembrahma: Kawitan/Pengawak* (CDII/2, 0:00–2:10).

Figure 8.2B. *Pengecet Panyembrahma* and surrounding transitions (CDII/2, 2:10–3:43; 6:33–6:46).

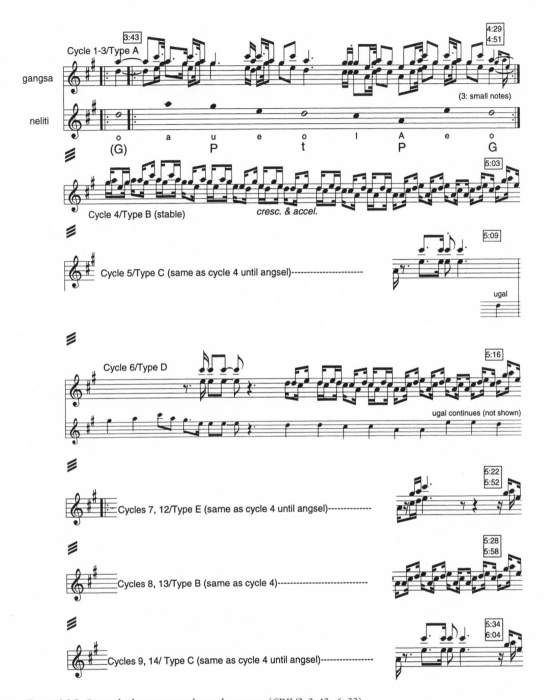

Figure 8.2C. *Panyembrahma* prayer and *angsel* sequence (CDII/2, 3:43–6:33).

Cycles 10,15/ Type F (after 15, skip next system)

End of 15: ugal solo;
gangsa & reyong tacet;
suddenly faster

5:40
6:09

Cycle 11/ Type E
(same as cycle 4 until angsel; return to 5th system)--------------

5:46

Cycle 16/Type G

rit.--------a tempo

6:16

Cycle 17/ Type E (same as cycle 4 until angsel)----------------------

6:22

Cycle 18/ Type B (same as cycle 4)----------------------------------

6:28

Cycle 19/ Type H (same as cycle 4 until angsel); continue to
ending (shown at Transition B, Fig. 8.2B).

6:33

etc.

1; see also fig. 6.30 and W). From the *tari lepas* repertoire I use the 1971 *Panyembrahma* (fig. 8.2A-C, CDII/2), an offering dance based on the temple genres *mendet* and *gabor,* but with new music. The *tabuh kreasi* are the early-kebyar-style *Jaya Semara* of 1964, a Beratha reworking of the composition *Kapi Raja* already familiar to McPhee in the 1930s (fig. 8.3A-B, CDII/3);[6] and *Kosalia Arini* (fig. 8.4A-C, CDII/4; see also figs. 2.16–18) composed for Karangasem's *Festival Gong* group in 1969, which represents the more or less standard *tabuh kreasi* form of the past several decades. Though shorter and simpler than its counterparts of the 1990s (exemplified by Windha's music), *Kosalia Arini* nonetheless has all of their formal features, for it helped set the cast for a model that is still in use. In the next two parts of the chapter I also discuss Windha's *Wahyu Giri Suara* (fig. 8.5; CDII/5) and Ketut Gdé Asnawa's *Sekar Kamuda* (fig. 8.6; CDII/6), both of the 1980s.[7] Relevant transcriptions and analyses from earlier chapters are reintegrated as well.

Elements, Contexts, and Element-Progressions

What kinds of longer-range connections can be appropriately made between the diverse musical components of a *kebyar* form, and what sorts of tools do composers have for shaping them? I choose to answer by determining which *elements* of structure we need to be attentive to, in what *contexts* to listen for them, and what their characteristic *progressions* are.

Elements

By *elements* I refer simply to the three basic elements of the music already explored—texture, melody, and meter/drumming—as well as two so far little-discussed (hence given somewhat more extended treatment here)—dynamics and tempo. Over the course of a *gending* there are discursive continuities and discontinuities to be perceived in the progression of all five of these. It is essential to cultivate awareness of them and their relationships to each other, either as they are heard against the background of the cyclic successions in *lelambatan* like *Bangun Anyar* or in relation to the more ad hoc architectonics of pieces like *Jaya Semara.*

Contexts

By *contexts* I mean metric and other related contexts. Meter provides the grid that suggests a hierarchic experience of musical time, and we use the hierarchy to rank and distinguish among classes of musical events. Two kinds of context

---

6. The Peliatan *gamelan* has performed *Kapi Raja* since at least 1952, when they took it on their world tour. McPhee presents a passage from it on pages 345–48 of *Music in Bali* (only some of which resembles the versions in circulation today), indicating that it was originally imported from North Bali.

7. See Mack 1992:326 for transcription and brief discussion of a different fragment of *Sekar Kamuda.*

Figure 8.3A. *Jaya Semara: Gineman/kebyar* (CDII/3, 0:00–1:59). (*continued*)

Figure 8.3A. (*continued*)

Figure 8.3B. *Jaya Semara: Pengecet* and ending *kebyar* (CDII/3, 2:20–3:56).

Figure 8.4A. *Kosalia Arini: Gineman* (CDII/4, 0:00–2:15).

are already familiar: the cycle or *gongan* and the metacycle. There are also frequent passages that are noncyclic. Some of these are continuous, having reasonably extensive continuity of texture but without circular design, as in *kebyar* texture (fig. 2.13), or in parts of the *genderan* of figure 8.4A (e.g., 1: 14). Others are fragmentary, that is, comparatively brief noncyclic segments interrupted by pauses or sudden texture change (the openings of figure 8.3A and 8.4A). Noncyclic music may have a steady beat, (as in *genderan* texture, fig. 2.17), an elastic and changing pulse (as in *kebyar* texture) or be entirely unpulsed (fig. 8.1A, *gineman trompong*). Finally, there are events that take place over the course of a succession of different contexts or even the *gending* as a whole; I shall refer to these as *gending*-level contexts.

The problem of whether noncyclic contexts can be treated like conventional *gongan* for analytical purposes arises at once. The solution often is a straightforward yes, because the lion's share of such music is governed by the same kinds of stratified and hierarchic first-order vertical relations as cycles are. Noncyclic passages thus behave like *gongan,* though we must bear in mind the significant difference that their melodies may begin and end on different tones (for example in fig. 2.17). But in certain other cases, such as *kebyar* texture, the situation may be less clear-cut. Strata are conflated, the rhythm uneven, and hierarchy less immediately apparent. Rather than expend the considerable effort that would be required to explore this issue from scratch, I shall rely on an analogy to a relevant analysis from the previous chapter. In the analysis of drum pattern syntax in figure 7.6 there was no "grid" with which to align D and T strokes, which were of irregular durations in the sub-patterns under discussion. Structural strokes were identified contextually after discovering embedded and motive-like recurring stroke sequences. Similarly, in these cases we shall be able to rely on certain tones to behave *as if* they received stronger first-order stress than others, via implied or actual *calung* and *jegogan* support, and make contextual assessments of how they can be assigned positions in a hierarchy.

Element-progressions

I propose the following six element-progressions: *structural rhythm, repetition/ metacyclic progression, textural rhythm, dynamic profile, tempo profile,* and *extended melodic relationships;* all of these are further divided into subcategories.[8] The discussion circumscribes the limits of what can ordinarily happen to the musical elements (melody, meter/drumming, texture, tempo, and dynamic) in their contexts (cyclic, metacyclic, noncyclic continuous, noncyclic fragmentary, and *gending*). They describe characteristic musical states, relations between such states, and processes of transforming states one to another, which the composer controls. The composer's role is both passive, in that the

---

8. Much of the terminology for this section was inspired by terms coined in Berry 1987.

Figure 8.4B. *Kosalia Arini: Kotekan, kebyar* transition, and *reyongan* (CDII/4, 2:48–4:03).

Figure 8.4C. *Kosalia Arini:* End of *variasi kendang, peralihan II,* and *gambangan* (CDII4, 6:30–9:45).

After ugal cue play once more, then to link II
Last pass: gangsa/reyong loud/soft alternation

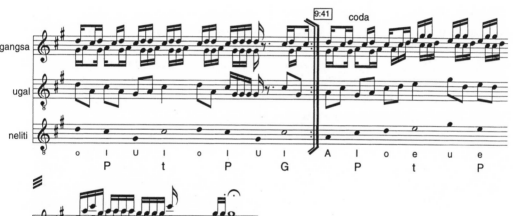

ments may progress according to well-established conventions, and active, in that the conventions are utilized differently in each piece. We may consider the element-progressions symmetrical if they change or progress synchronized with major structural points; asymmetrical if not. Similarly, to invoke other terms used thus far, rapid or irregular changes in element-progression are evidence of *majalan* quality, whereas sparse or regular ones are *ngubeng*.

Structural rhythm. "Structural rhythm" refers first of all to the pacing and density of gong strokes (including all gongs listed under "punctuation scheme" in figure 7.1) and *jegogan* and *calung* tones relative to one another and the beat. *Gong:jegogan:calung density* relationships strongly anchor the music's basic momentum. As shown throughout figure 6.3 and elsewhere, in court genre cycles this can be expressed as a simple ratio. Long cycles generally have the slowest, most *ngubeng* structural rhythm. Shorter cycles have faster ones that conspire with their quicker tempi to effect a change in momentum at points of transition between cycles of different lengths. The *gong:jegogan:calung* relationship in the 128-beat *pengawak* of *Bangun Anyar,* for example—in figure 6.3W, the densities of the gong, *jegogan,* and *calung* strata (CC8, 16, and 64) respectively—reduces to a $1:2:8$ ratio, whereas it is $1:1:2$ (most groups prefer $1:1:4$) in the ensuing 16-beat *pengecet* (6.3O), a marked intensification. This rhythmic conflation of *jegogan* and gong parts is acutely felt in the *pengecet.* It robs them of their stratified independence, streamlining the texture by adding gong, *kempur,* or *kempli* emphasis to every *jegogan* tone. The *change of context,* here between two kinds of cycles (though it could as well involve noncyclic music) is a prominent formal event. Increase in structural rhythm from *pengawak* to *pengecet* is in part prepared by the other types of *majalan* intensifications usually operative at the end of the *pengawak,* such as faster scale-tone turnover, greater D-T emphasis in the drumming, and tempo acceleration. But at the moment of the change there is a palpable sensation of stepped-up drive.

   Structural rhythm does not always conform to the simple ratios of quadripartite symmetry. In cyclic melodies with *tua* influence or otherwise asymmetrical basis, gongs and the melodic stresses provided by *jegogan* tones are often irregularly spaced, or may move between one fixed ratio and another, as in the common situation where a composer alters the pace of the *jegogan* to provide special emphasis to a portion of a tune. This is clear from fig. 8.5, in which the length of *jegogan* tones shrinks from 4 to 3 to ½ beats over the course of the cycle to support the phrasing of the melody. In noncyclic contexts structural rhythm may be unstable, or in varying degrees of flux. *Jegogan* and gong punctuations throughout the noncyclic figures 8.3A and 8.4A shift between regular and irregular stresses in continuous segments, or mark the unpredictable distances between ends of successive fragments.

Figure 8.5. *Wahyu Giri Suara kotekan* (CDII/5)

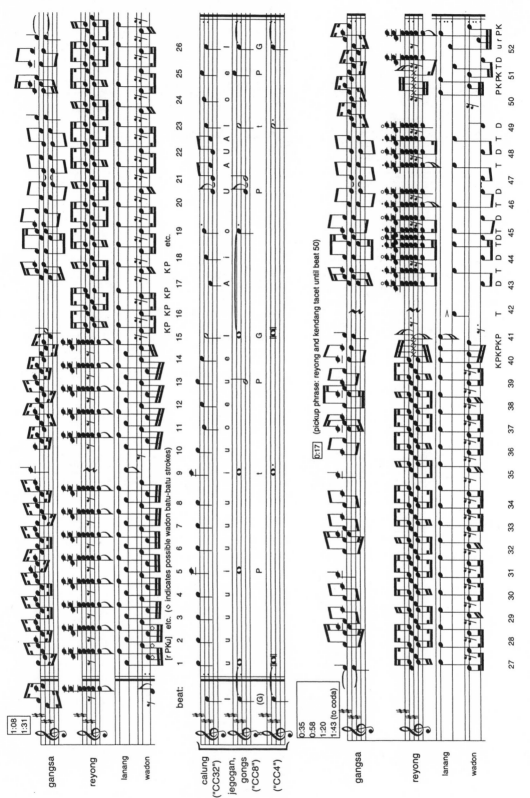

Figure 8.6. *Sekar Kamuda*: Closing section (CDII/6)

A final dimension of structural rhythm, *gong tone change,* involves melody, and has to do with whether the scale tone coinciding with gong changes over the course of a *gending.* Such shifts bring intensification. In most *lelambatan* gong tone remains constant or perhaps changes once during a *gending,* in some cases returning to the original tone and in others remaining on the new one (McPhee 1966:98). Once its restless opening passages are done *dIng* is the gong tone of *Bangun Anyar,* but during the *pengisep* section (8.1C), alternating cycles switch to *dong,* intensifying the tonal quality there.[9] In *kebyar* compositions gong tones change repeatedly, especially where structural rhythm is unstable and gong is used for melodic emphasis as much or more than for structural closure. Rapid and irregular gong tone change is part of *kebyar's* temporal dynamism: within the first two minutes of *Jaya Semara* (8.3A) all five *pélog* tones are allotted gong emphases of varying structural weights. Listening for gong tone change is similar to cultivating awareness of CC4 within a cycle, but at the higher level of *gending* rather than cyclic context.

Repetition and metacyclic progressions. Repetition and metacyclic progressions are fundamental element-progressions, comprising a portion of virtually all pieces in *kebyar* repertoire. Writing of Southeast Asian music generally, Maceda has evocatively referred to rhythmic ostinati and recurring melodic units as kinds of drone: sonic extensions and elaborations of the timbre of the gong itself, with all the same connotations of nature, ritual, trance, magic, and spiritual power (1986:12). But in *kebyar* repetition is rarely untainted by composed-in linear elements. In chapter 7 I showed how stable and active cycles accumulate into metacycles, suggesting that the dance-inspired topography of a series of metacycles shapes form. Each metacycle involves *dynamic change,* sometimes *tempo change,* and includes the *disruption* of *angsel* and/or *ocak-ocakan* rhythm.

In the simplest free-standing types of *gending,* such as the 16-beat dance melody *Topeng Keras* (fig. 6.3K; 6.10), form is wholly determined in this way, reflecting the dancer's spontaneous interpretation of a basic choreography.[10] Some *angsel* are cued and completed within one or two cycles, such as the *angsel bawak* (short, full body pivot), *angsel batis* (foot stamping), or *seledet* (eye flicking). These local events can be concatenated in numerous ways but finally lead to the climactic *angsel lantang* (long), which itself involves at least two separate *angsel bawak* disruptions several cycles apart. Normatively

---

9. This use of the term *pengisep,* denoting a cycle juxtaposed with the *pengawak* that tends (somewhat inconsistently, in practice) to use higher-register melody tones, is analogous to its use in connection with paired tuning. In that context *pengisep* refers to the higher-tuned of a pair of instruments or keys, and is juxtaposed with *pengumbang,* the lower.

10. For a description of metacycle formation in *Baris* see Tenzer 1998:68–71.

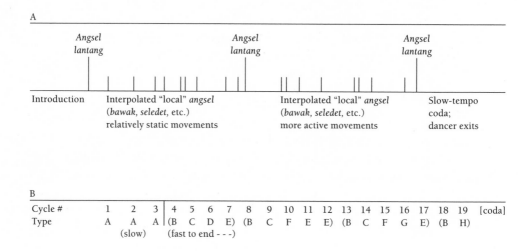

Figure 8.7. A. Form in *Topeng Keras*. B. Metacycles at the end of *Panyembrahma*, based on figure 8.2C.

angsel lantang open the performance (before the dancer emerges), delineate one major structural division in the choreography, and cue the ending. In figure 8.7A's schematization of this essentially two-part form (plus introduction and coda), the horizontal line represents the unbroken continuity of the repeating melody.

In dances with fixed choreography like *Panyembrahma, angsel* ordering is preset and memorized, and the repeating melody only a part of the complete form. Combinations can be both extended and inventively asymmetrical. The nineteen cycles of figure 8.2C comprise three slow and sixteen fast cycles, and reduce to the ordering shown in figure 8.7B. Letters A and B denote the two stable types used. A indicates the slow tempo cycles 1–3, which use non-interlocking figuration, and B designates cycles 4, 8, 13, and 18, which use *ubit telu* and *nyog cag* interlocking. The six active cycle types C-H use most of B's *kotekan,* but each breaks into its own particular *angsel.* The entire fast group, extending from cycles 4 through 19, contains four metacycles, each commencing with B. As set off with parentheses in 8.7B, these are, respectively, four, five, five, and two cycles long: BCDE, BCFEE, BCFGE, and BH (cycles 4–7, 8–12, 13–17, and 18–19). The inner ordering of the first three metacycles is similar, yet their parallelisms all have interesting "kinks." The two five-gongan metacycles differ only in the substitution of type G for type E (cycles 16 and 11, respectively); but G provides such a striking break in texture and tempo that it subverts the similarity. Texturally, G also hearkens back to type D (cycle 6), creating a different kind of metagrouping. The twice-heard succession EBCF at 7–10 and 12–15, though interestingly out of synch with metacycle beginnings, is reflected in the dance by repetition of the same set of movements.

In instrumental *gending* and longer *tari lepas* the number and variety of *angsel* are streamlined and the distance between them regularized. One of a few basic strophe-like formulas may be applied in such situations, for example $A_1A_2A_3 \ldots B \sim X$, in which A_n represents a metacycle culminating in a given *angsel*. To the last A is appended B, a final time through the *gongan*, usually accelerating, that contains a different *angsel* or an *ocak-ocakan* pattern. $\sim$ represents the moment of disjuncture, and X represents the next part of the *gending* or the ending. The disruption in B functions as a signpost preparing the change to X. We can observe this process near the end of *Jaya Semara* (8.3B). At first, a pair of alternating *angsel* shape the repetitions of the melody into metacycles cued by *kendang* in the standard manner. Each metacycle constitutes an "A." At the fourth *angsel* the tempo increases, leading first to an accelerating, cycle-length *ocak-ocakan* at 3:36 ("B"), and then to a break ("$\sim$") into *kebyar* texture ("X") at 3:43.

Pengawak pegongan and other long melodies are usually repeated verbatim a limited number of times and do not form metacycles. When played in temples there is no prescribed limit on *pengawak* repetitions, for the music's role is to reinforce the stasis of ritual time. Pauses between them may last minutes, and the eventual progression to *pengecet* may be put off until the *pengawak* has been played five or six times. But for *kebyar* performance care will always be taken to impose varied patterns of tempo, dynamic, and melodic elaboration on successive repeats, which mold the repetitions into a larger design. Literal repetition is minimized not only in *pengawak,* but elsewhere in the *gending*. The 64-beat *pengisep* of *Bangun Anyar* (8.1C) is played thrice, each time with a modified plan of *angsel* and dynamics; and at the last quadrant of the third time (9:07) at the slower speed of the section to ensue. The composed-in changes distort cyclicity to emphasize linear design.

Textural rhythm. As I have noted, texture change is a prominent compositional element distinguishing *kebyar* from other Balinese *gamelan*. Unlike the Western orchestra's potential for *klangfarbenmelodie,* wherein instrument groups can dovetail, combine, and overlap to provide smoothness or blurring in the shift from one sonic environment to another, in most *kebyar* situations instruments' fixed roles and the restricted collection of ensemble combinations do not permit gradual transformation. Changes mainly occur abruptly and in tandem with other structural discontinuities. The highest level of textural rhythm, *ensemble texture change,* encompasses all situations in which contrasting full and partial orchestral textures are juxtaposed. It is most characteristic and dramatic when it coincides with cycle or section boundaries and is aligned with discontinuities of structural rhythm, tempo, or dynamic. At 4:00 in *Kosalia Arini* (8.4B; the change from *genderan* to *kebyar* texture) the *kempli* drops out and there is a change of *jegogan:calung* ratio, while the beat-length stretches from ♩ to ♩ + ♪. Shadings of texture may also generate variety within the flow of a cycle or metacycle, such as when a softer dynamic is sought to allow *suling* or *rebab* to predominate, or when *gangsa* momentarily drop out to expose *reyong* over unbroken *pokok* support (as in 8.1C at 8:07 and 8:41, the beginnings of the second and third passes through the melody).

A second kind of textural rhythm, *elaboration change,* is shaped by the rate and placement of changes in elaboration style within a cycle or section. Elaboration change has much in common with metacyclic disruption, for both involve a change of surface texture. But whereas disruption originates with a rhythmic process emanating from the drums (and dance), elaboration change is manifest only at the surface. It is a matter of a composer's decision to elaborate a certain passage in a certain style. Elaboration changes occur within a cycle or a section smoothed by the continuity of a steady beat, may or may not involve a change in instrumentation, and may take place either in or out of alignment with metric stresses. They are tantamount to shifts in stylistic topic since elaboration styles are referential. Because such topics are so sharply defined, switches between them are also cleanly drawn, for example as when *gangsa kekenyongan* switches to *ubit telu,* or *ubit telu* to *malpal.*[11] One common elaboration change is between *norot* and *nyog cag;* see, for example, the uppermost stave of figure 6.4, in which *norot* changes to *nyog cag* right after the *kempur* stroke at the boundary of the final quadrant. The faster rate of scale-tone change in *nyog cag* makes it an effective choice to underscore the approach to gong.

A final kind of textural rhythm, *registral change,* also involves elaboration strata, and concerns the rate and degree of movement around the registral space occupied by *gangsa* and *reyong.* Elaboration tenaciously frozen in one registral position can accumulate tension and dispel it upon release, even if the movement is only by one step, as in figure 6.15D. Unlike that example, such a release may also involve a change in elaboration style. In the driving 16 beats between *kempur* and gong in the first half of *Bangun Anyar*'s *pengawak* (8.1B; beginning at 6:45), *nyog cag kotekan* spirals through the entire ten-tone

---

11. In some contexts one can identify hybrids, or closely knit alternations between a pair of elaboration styles, that give the impression of blending into a single entity.

range of the *gangsa*, whereas the *norot* in both the preceding and succeeding 16 beats spans only an octave.

Preliminary comment on dynamics and tempo. Compositionally speaking, dynamics and tempo add to structure in a way different from other elements, in that greater performer input is the norm where they are concerned. In rehearsal, changes are more freely made to them, with or without assent from the composer(s) providing the pitches and rhythms of the "actual" music. This dispersion of creative authority suggests that control of dynamics and tempo must equally be seen as aspects of ensemble virtuosity. The same cannot be said for texture, melody, and drumming. Management of speed and volume is both the most significant contribution a *sekaha* can make to animating a *gending* and a singular mark of agility. Working hand-in-glove with timbre and tuning, dynamic and tempo profiles send concentrated messages about Balinese conceptions of time and acoustical space.

Dynamic profiles of *kebyar* compositions range over an extremely broad field of amplitude owing to both the potentialities of the instruments and *kebyar*'s penchant for extremes. Often occurring parallel to tempo changes, dynamics have enough independent behaviors to merit separate discussion, though common pairings are graphed in tandem in figure 8.8. Here and in the next subsection I treat dynamics and tempo as "fully-formed" elements and element-progressions, forgoing the sorts of chapter-length treatment of syntax granted texture, melody, and drumming. While not a part of the present book, a systematic investigation of manifest dynamic and tempo patternings would be revelatory, for they contribute importantly to structure. This overview introduces Balinese terminology and transmission, types of dynamic change, and contexts for such change.

Musicians rely more on kinesthetic and aural sensitivity for regulating dynamics and tempo than they do on terminology. *Keras* (strong, loud) and *manis* (sweet, soft) describe the two basic dynamic states, with the neutral *sedeng* (average) ranging widely in between them. Movement from one state to another is indicated at rehearsal by terms introduced in chapter 7: *nguncab,* increase, and *ngisep,* its opposite. *Ngeseh* refers to crescendo paired with acceleration. A localized swell is an *ombak* (wave; *ombak-ombakan* is the plural form), a term that also refers to tempo and tuning. Intermediate shadings are worked out and discussed during rehearsal, though eye contact and the body language and cues of dancers, drummers, and *ugal* players provide more nuanced information than verbal instruction. Numerous rehearsal strategies are employed to ensure continuity of acoustic balance when dynamics alter; for example, in adjusting soft passages *gangsa* and *reyong* players know that they have dropped back sufficiently if they can clearly discern *jegogan* tones while playing.

Dynamic change may be *abrupt* or *incremental.* The most characteristic

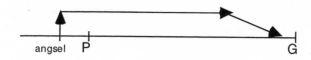

A

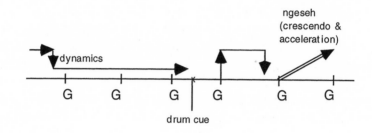

B

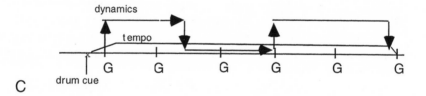

C

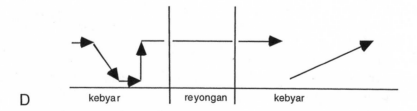

D

Figure 8.8. A. *Pengawak Bangun Anyar:* Dynamics in the approach to gong. B. Dynamics and tempo approaching the end of a metacyclic group. C. Dynamics and tempo in *angsel lantang.* D. Dynamics at the beginning of *Jaya Semara.*

abrupt rises are those provoked by *angsel* cues, which retrench as sharply just after the *angsel*. The quintessential opening gambit, the crashing *byar* chord, is itself intended as a rupture out of ordinary and into musical time; like the *angsel* it cuts to the gist of *kebyar* intensity. *Ngeseh* passages extend through entire *gongan* or more and are used to lead up to major disjunctions. While gravitation toward more aggressive volumes is an essential tendency, a complementary restraint is attended to. Climaxes become murmurs as if submerged. Gradual decrescendi rein in energy preceding or succeeding important gong arrivals and for fade-out endings. When *angsel* capitulate to transparent rebeginnings they expose the current of the softer *pokok* before the elaboration instruments reenter almost imperceptibly, emerging from silence as if from a distance. Terraced dynamics, already mentioned as a strategy for animating metacycles, appear in full textures if one or another instrument group is featured.

In light of these many situations, Balinese associate dynamics with *rasa* (feeling, expression), both in the freely emotive sense and because they enhance structure and allow feeling to speak through it. Dynamics are *systematically* shaped, however, only at cyclic, metacyclic, and noncyclic levels of structure. Tempo profiles, as we shall see, are intrinsic to the conventions of form at *gending*-level, but not dynamic profiles. The range of possible volumes is present and in flux from early on in each piece; there are no *gending* that, for example, build large-scale trajectories toward a single dynamic peak or nadir (as the Hindusthani *alap-jor-jhala* form does).

At the cyclic level, such as in *klasik* long cycles like *tabuh empat,* contrasts in volume are often arranged in staid patterns of antiphonal alternation. In Geladag village renditions, the continuity of soft *norot* elaboration is predictably broken during the 16 beats prior to *palet* midpoints and endings, in the first case by a choir of interlocking *cengceng kopyak,* and in the second by switching to *nyog cag kotekan* (see also McPhee 1966:80–82), both played loudly. In modernized *lelambatan* the alignment of metric structure and dynamic change may shift, in effect making dynamics a separate "stratum." In each half of *Bangun Anyar*'s 128-beat *pengawak,* for example, a drum cue and subsequent sudden rise by the rest of the *gamelan* leads to an *angsel* just *before* the second *kempur;* the high dynamic is sustained until a decrescendo leads to gong 16 beats later (fig. 8.8A; 8.1B, 6:01–6:18 and 6:37–6:54). Though slightly skewed from the gong punctuation, the function of this profile is to highlight the *kempur* by peaking at the preceding *angsel,* and to defer to the gong by dropping back in advance of it. Recession just prior to gong also enriches the *majalan* scale-tone progressions there by adding a complementary dimension of restraint.

The perceived romance and sensuality of longer *pegambuhan* cycles, particularly in their *pelegongan* transformations, accounts for the way they hew to different, more pliant dynamic profiles. These melodies usually begin with a default low dynamic that changes mainly through *ombak-ombakan.* Volume swells to a small crest just before *jegogan* or *klentong* markers, and then pulls back to allow the punctuation to ring through. This shape is not applied at every such arrival, but sporadically at first and more so as the cycle proceeds. In the *milpil* section toward the end the proportions of loud and soft finally reverse, so that the characteristic "sweet" passage immediately prior to gong is felt as a strong contrast.

In both *tabuh kreasi* and older repertoire certain dynamic profiles consistently shape shorter cycles and the metacycles built from them. Cues in a cycle's final quadrant command dynamic increase at the gong, often leading to disruption. Players train to follow the closely, often jaggedly spaced cues and respond with corresponding and extreme group shifts in volume (or *angsel* if that is what is called for). In the last of a series of metacycles, extended *ngeseh* during the final cycle constitutes a typical escape route to a closing *angsel* and subsequent change of structural rhythm (fig. 8.8B, based on 8.3B, 3:36). Another characteristic move is to begin a *gongan* at peak dynamic and retract suddenly a few beats later in anticipation of release at some further point. Such a profile comes between the opening and closing cycles of *angsel lantang,* where the dynamic begins high but dips for a cycle or more before rising again for the concluding portion (fig. 8.8C). In these contexts, so unlike the comparative stillness of lengthy *pengawak,* the expectation of imminent release imbues soft dynamics with tension.

In noncyclic contexts like those in *tabuh kreasi,* dynamics may be specified at the phrase or note-to-note level rather than in relation to meter. The profile of each fragment can be different. This adds a desired element of surprise to the mix and contributes to the move away from court-derived musical process (fig. 8.8D, based on the first system of 8.3A). Miniprofiles such as this are not confined in impact, of course, but gather meaning and momentum in relation to those surrounding them.

Tempo profile. The tempo profile of a *kebyar gending*—the changes in continuity of beat speed as given by *kempli* or other indicators—is never uninflected, and indeed is regularly in flux.[12] The study of tempo encompasses not only beat speed as an absolute factor but also the rate and degree of its change, the process of setting and controlling it, the amount of tolerance for ebb and flow in a "steady" pulse, the proportional relationship between differing tempi at various points in a composition, and other factors. As with dynamics, my

---

12. Berry (1987:305) writes: "Tempo . . . has two aspects: the eventfulness of music (degree to which the temporal continuity and flow are filled with articulate impulses or related silences) and the frequency of pulsation at some given level. We shall refer to these two aspects of tempo as *activity-tempo* and *pulse-tempo.*" My discussion of tempo uses the latter sense. The former sense is partly encompassed by the idea of structural rhythm discussed above; in general, however, activity-tempo as Berry defines it is less variable in *gamelan* than in Western music.

approach to this multifaceted subject considers Balinese tempo terminology, transmission, and types of tempo change; but I shall also touch on tempo and form, and tempo proportions.

Balinese speak of tempo with such words as *enggal* or *gelis* (fast), and *adeng* or *lambat* (slow). As with dynamics, conventions of musical context and sensitivity to leadership provided by *kendang* and *ugal* convey more than words can. These instruments, working closely with the *kempli* in its time-beating role, share responsibility for tempi, and their players constantly check with each other for feedback and confirmation that coordination is in hand. If this interaction is poorly interpreted by the rest of the ensemble at rehearsal, teachers will stop to demonstrate proper tempo and tempo changes on an instrument beside them or by gesturing to the *kempli,* occasionally reminding musicians to play *magelis-gelisan suud gong ané katelu* (faster after the third repetition), to play *cara pengawak kanti mulih* (at *pengawak* speed until gong [lit. until arriving home]), to *jemak adengné penyuwud* (switch to closing tempo), that *kempli mokok* (*kempli* plays at the same rate as *pokok* tones), or some other admonition construed in reference to structure. If faulty interaction impedes tempo coordination in performance, musicians listen first for guidance from the *kempli.*

Tempo change in cyclic, metacyclic, and noncyclic contexts is often tied, as stated above, to dynamic change. We may distinguish four categories: *gradations, increments, abrupt changes,* and *interruptions. Gradations,* or minor modifications, are temporary and subtle departures from an otherwise steady beat, as in figure 8.8C. *Incremental* changes smoothly connect one tempo area with another in a manner like that described for dynamics. Incremental changes in speed may conclude a group of repeating cycles (as in *ngeseh*) or take a new melody in an unexpected direction from the moment it arrives. *Ngeseh* can be a radical and virtuoso device: at one metacycle conclusion in *Teruna Jaya,* the tempo rushes on a smooth curve from mm 56 to 192 over the course of a single 16-beat cycle.[13]

As with dynamics, graded tempo changes are called *ombak-ombakan,* but there is a crucial point of distinction in that these may be paired with abrupt dynamic shifts (whereas gradual dynamic change and abrupt tempo shifts never go together). In metacycles, a tempo *ombak* begins at the initial drum cue, plateaus once the *gamelan* has responded to the cue, and returns to the original tempo after the *angsel,* sometimes spilling over to the beginning of the next metacycle. In dance ostinati like *Topeng Keras* (fig. 8.7A) a local *angsel's* difference in speed from the base rate may be minimally perceptible, as if a by-product of the concurrent sharp dynamic rise. Some *sekaha* are vigilant about keeping the tempo steady through such passages, viewing capitulation to the

---

13. On the CD *Anthologie des Musiques de Bali no. 2* (Buda Musique 92601–2), disc 1, cut 2, beginning at 6:26.

urge to speed up at higher volumes as deficiency in ensemble technique. The climactic *angsel lantang,* on the other hand, are always measurably swifter. In *Gabor* and other female-style dances the crest of the tempo en route to even local *angsel* (in situations such as that depicted in figure 7.8) is higher, the release longer.

In long *pengawak, ombak* effect only slight tempo fluctuation (if any) early on in the *gongan.* In some *tabuh pegongan* the tempo rises almost imperceptibly before internal markers and relaxes after them; in *pegambuhan* these tendencies are stronger. In either case the increase is steeper beginning with the *milpil.* The tempo ultimately retreats to or beyond its original state in the beats prior to gong if the cycle will repeat; otherwise the graded increase becomes an incremental one as the music accelerates on to the faster tempo and denser structural rhythm of the *pengecet.*

Abrupt changes and *interruptions* in tempo, on the other hand, are definitive *kebyar* events, essentially unknown in court repertoires. The former denotes juxtaposition of two markedly different continuities. The music proceeds directly on through the connective seam, with a conventional beat present on at least one side of the fissure. On the "left" side, typically, there is an incremental accelerando leading out of a preceding cycle, as in 8.3B, 3:43, where the *kempli* stops keeping time and yields to *kebyar* texture. Interruptions, while not exactly a kind of tempo change, encompass the silences and breaks that disrupt temporal flow in noncyclic contexts. Successions of many are characteristic in *tabuh kreasi* and can be seen throughout the opening passages of *Jaya Semara* and *Kosalia Arini,* where the pauses intervene in an admixture of continuous and fragmentary segments. Constructing a convincing continuity from a series of phrases separated by interruptions is an ensemble challenge. Depending on whether the ensuing music has full or partial ensemble texture, responsibility for calculating pause length and cueing the reentry is taken by *kendang* (if the texture is full), *ugal* (if *kendang* is absent), or by the *reyong pengenter* player (for *reyongan* textures). If a sustaining *jegogan* tone is exposed when the rest of the *gamelan* stops, as is often the case, the ensemble waits to proceed until its paired tuning has penetrated to the acoustical forefront and had a chance to sustain and decay slightly.

Correlation between tempo and form at *gending*-level is an important trait in court genres. Tempo is crucial to affect and near the top of a list of factors that help orient listeners to where they are in the form. An inverted-arch design in court genre music—vigorous beginning followed by a more stately *pengawak* and a return to quicker tempo for the closing sections—infuses some *kebyar* forms too, which also tend to begin and end quickly and include slow music at least somewhere in between. The inverted arch is distorted in such cases, to be sure, but appears with enough frequency to suggest a cultural affinity for it. Within this framework tempo profile and structural rhythm work together to determine much about compositional balance. In effect short cycles, with their compressed structural rhythms and quicker tempi, are repeated more so as to offset, in real and perceptual time, the slowness and sparseness of long ones.

Tempo relations at *gending* level have a further compositional dimension, in that they are used to reconfigure melodic materials. Systematic density and tempo levels like those known in Java under the *irama* rubric are less well explored in Bali, but in some circumstances a melody will be presented in both fast and slow speeds and densities. This is the case in 8.1B versions III and IV, in which the former is at double the density of the latter. By interpolating new *neliti* tones a melody can be augmented to twice its length in a slow version, and the structural rhythm halved in the process. The inverted-arch tempo scheme in the dance *Jauk Keras* (fig. 6.3B) is constructed precisely this way, with metacycles based on the fast version flanking a slow, *pengawak*-like interior made from the same tune in expansion. In simpler kinds of tempo juxtaposition, a *pokok* such as that used in *Panyembrahma* throughout figure 8.2C is played slowly at first, and then linked through incremental acceleration to metacycles in which it is played much faster and with contrasting elaboration.

Kebyar tempo proportions can be discovered by comparing base-rates (i.e., disregarding gradations or increments) of tempi between sections of a *gending*. The tempo continuum of the style as a whole includes absolute values ranging from the infinitely deliberate mm 20 to top speeds of over 200. Within these limits and in individual *gending*, we may ask, how does "fast" relate to "slow," and how are in-between speeds related to those at extremes? The answer is that base rates are for the most part simply related, but the relationships can be enriched by constant fluctuation of tempo within cycles, and change of both tempo and structural rhythm between formal sections.

Elegant underlying tempo proportions are both fundamental and satisfying. In *Shaping Time* David Epstein argues for human affinity for low-order tempo ratios ($1:2$, $2:3$, $3:4$, and so on) within a piece of music. Ability to understand and manipulate tempo comes from a combination of received knowledge and intuition, both of which rest on biological—hence likely universal—inclination to favor such basic periodicities. In music contrasting tempi are closely related "because proportionally related tempi involve phase synchrony" ($1995:100-101$). At the same time, "although all of us as human beings have neural mechanisms that control time and timing, we are not machines. We can override these mechanisms at will" (362). And with some stress on ability to "override," we can understand *kebyar* tempo proportions in this light. The following two cursory examples hint at what systematic study of tempo proportions might uncover.

Lelambatan display proportional simplicity most consistently. The relationship of fast to slow tempi at *gending*-level in *Bangun Anyar*, for example, is unambiguously $2:1$—passages of steady tempo at the beginning and the end deviate less than 5 percent from a common base rate of approximately mm 170

(8.1A, initial phrase and last system; and 8.1D), while the central *pengawak* (8.1B, III) stays near 85 in a typical performance.[14] Various kinds of change at transitions into and away from these sections, plus *ombak* and other incremental changes within them, make the manifest tempo continuity seem more intricate. Understanding the formal structure, then, makes it possible to grasp which relationships are essential. Such tempo proportions gain further significance when understood in relation to changing structural rhythms and rhythmic stratification of parts.

In a *tabuh kreasi* the greater number of passages where measurable tempo is absent or unstable, plus the presence of abrupt changes and interruptions, make it more challenging to posit structural contrasts between tempo areas. When there is steady beat, the preponderance of faster speeds makes greater deviation from a single basic rate seem more tolerable, and less likely to be felt as structural. The first several fragments of music with steady tempo in *Kosalia Arini,* for example (8.4A at 0:46–1:14) stay close to mm 140. These are followed (1:14–1:33) by a lengthier, more continuous passage at mm 168. This change does not acquire larger significance until later, when the same tempi are iterated but prolonged. The mm 140 returns at the cyclic *kotekan* (8.4B, 2:48–4:00). This soon leads to ensemble textural and abrupt tempo change, but resettles at 168 (4:14–6:37), again for a longer time, thus mirroring the local acceleration from before. It is difficult to say whether the extended mm 120 of the final section (8.4C, following 6:48) represents the arrival of a long-awaited base rate which the previous 140 and 168 have been grotesquely exaggerating, or if the approximately 3:2 ratio between 168 and 120 (actually 2.8:2, a 6.66% difference) is a true structural contrast. Possibly it is the even starker differences between areas with and without steady beat that create the most architecturally significant tempo structures in such music.

Extended melodic relationships. In proposing an element-progression category of extended melodic relationships, I enlarge the concepts of CC and CC-group explored in chapter 6 for individual melodies to encompass higher-level contexts.[15] I have three types of phenomena in mind. The first is a kind of variation akin to passacaglia, in which two separate realizations of identical melodies in the same meter and within the same piece are radically different. The realizations may or may not be contiguous, and their differences may encompass texture, dynamic and tempo, drumming, melodic elaboration, details of *neliti* and *pokok,* and structural rhythm. Because the meter and the essential

---

14. On CDII/1, the central *pengawak* is slightly faster, about 90–95, an acceptable deviation but arguably a performance flaw.

15. In doing so I wish to state clearly that I do not assert the existence of pitch "prolongation" in *kebyar,* whose definition in nontonal contexts has been problematic even in Western theory (Straus 1987).

features of the *pokok* are identical, Balinese would assert that the variations are in essence one and the same melody, and that they have been intentionally composed as such. But for our purposes they are different enough in all other respects to justify analytical comparison.

Variation abounds in *kebyar*, particularly in *lelambatan*. Figure 8.1B's five realizations of the *Bangun Anyar pengawak* are displayed above and below the CC32, the densest stratum with which all versions align. Of these I is the most *majalan* in terms of texture, dynamic, and tempo change. III is the central *"pengawak* proper" and the sparser IV yet another rendition of the same minus *angsel* and texture changes. The others are partial versions: II links I to III, and V connects IV to the *pengecet*. Many musicians refer to quick, dense realizations like that in version I as *periring,* and expanded versions like III and IV as *wilet.* The use of both *periring* and *wilet* variations is standard in most *tabuh* 1, 4, 6, and 8 compositions.

Tabuh kreasi also use variation: while *Sekar Kamuda*'s 26-beat closing melody is repeated in the slower-moving strata (fig. 8.6, center system), the elaboration instruments and *kendang* play an alternating pair of realizations of it (upper and lower systems) that stretch into a single long phrase. The relentless 3-♪ *reyong* and drumming pattern beginning at gong in the middle of the upper system extends through the rebeginning of the *pokok,* obscuring the boundary. The blurring is further supported by the iterating *dIng-dUng-dAng♩ neliti* implied by the *reyong* (seen by taking the *reyong* part's scale tone coinciding with each beat). This starts in rough alignment with the actual *pokok* but is soon at odds with it. The drumming reinforces hearing the full 52 beats as through-composed by withholding T and D strokes until 42 and deploying a lone structurally accented D at 49.

While variation is a kind of progression to be consciously composed and manipulated, the remaining two extended melodic relationships are potentially but not necessarily so; they are revealed by discovering hidden structural connections between pairs of melodies. In *diagonal relations* a melodic stratum in one part of a *gending* resembles a different stratum located in a separate melody elsewhere in the piece. Viewed from the perspective of either one, the two appear in augmentation/diminution relationship. In *Panyembrahma*, the CC4 of figure 8.2C's repeating melody is {2,0,−2,0}, ending on *dong.* Compare this with the sequence of five gong tones of the 40-beat melody (five cycles of 8 beats) embedded in the *neliti* staff of figure 8.2A. Omitting the initial gong to preserve the music's end-accented character, they are, in order, *dAng, dong, dung, deng,* and *dong,* or {−2,0,2,1,0}. Whether one hears the 1 (*deng*) as a nonsystematic, compositionally motivated "excursion" toward the continuity of 8.2C's *pokok* line, or simply as an asymmetrical wrinkle in the underlying structure, both melodies are as if perched on the three-pronged scale-tone region defined by 2, −2, and 0 (*dung, dAng,* and *dong*), a relation perceptible despite contrasting tempi, texture, and strata.

Some extended scale-tone connections derive from *motivic relations* between a pair of melodies. One restricted example of this can be seen in a comparison of the *gilak* shown in figure 6.3F and H, which alternate with one another in *Baris*. The former has an Axis-2 up-down contour while the latter is Axis 3 with an accordingly inverted curvature. Inverting one for comparison with the other reveals a mixture of direct correspondences and melodic reversal-pairs that help to both unify and distinguish the two melodies. Just as relevant is the fact that the two share the same gong and midpoint tones (*dAng* and *dong*) and overall ambitus (four tones), and that they use a comparable mixture of conjunct, disjunct, ascending, and descending motion.

The relationships explored above are summarized in figure 8.9, with all categories of context, element, and element-progression included therein and cross-referenced. Observing them in the foregoing has provided a sense of the available palette of compositional tools applied to *gending* at a level higher than that of the internal syntax of cyclic melodies and drum patterns, which was the focus of chapters 6 and 7. Next we need to survey the formal canvases to which the palette is applied.

The Shape of the *Gending:* Balinese Categories of Musical Form

Ideas about form and formal function in music must be flexible and schematic enough to cope with the diversity of compositions they purport to illuminate. Western theorists assume that individual works manifest sufficient uniqueness to justify analysis and that the value of the analysis is self-evident. Analytical concepts for tonal music like Schenker's *ursatz* or formal plans like the tripartite structure of sonata-allegro form describe a common structural framework, but the significance of the frameworks is that they offer a basis for knowing pieces in terms of their unique surface and middleground features. A rapprochement is sought between the general and the specific.

There is only one widely accepted framework that Balinese use to describe larger forms in court genres and *kebyar*. I introduced it during chapter 5's scan of the repertoire: the *kawitan-pengawak-pengecet* tripartition (introduction, slow-tempo main body, and faster conclusion) originally applied to *lelambatan* in *pegongan* and *pegambuhan* repertoires; hereafter abbreviated as *KPP*. This concept evolved during the golden age of court culture and was handed down orally and through propagation in compositional practice. Like sonata-allegro, *KPP* is mainly associated with a restricted "classical" repertoire. But sonata-allegro architecture is founded on tonic/dominant polarity, which, understood analytically via the *ursatz,* is thought of as kin to a genetic code reflected in diminution at every level of structure. I do not perceive the same kind of organicism in *KPP*. It is too general to tell us very much about a specific piece on its own, though when the identifying mechanism of the operative *tabuh* meter (the *jajar pageh*) is considered, we know a little more. Where the West-

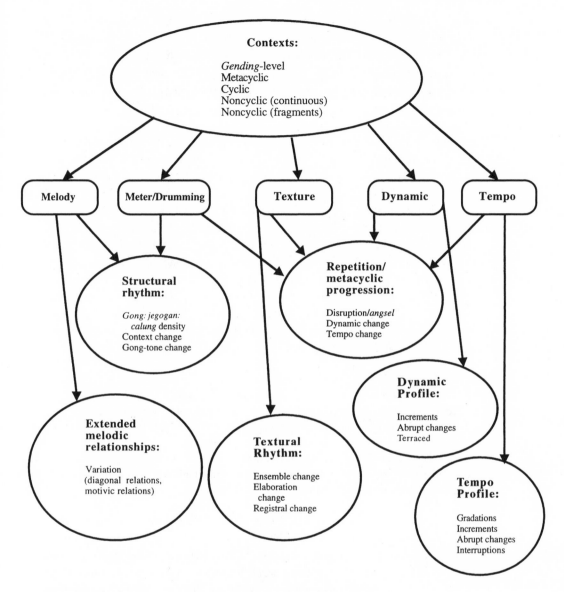

Figure 8.9. The elements, contexts, and element-progressions of *kebyar* forms

ern concepts specify tonal relationships, *KPP* does not address scale tone or melody in the music at all; instead it sketches an ordering of cycle types and points only to their dimensions, tempi, and, implicitly, their affect.

The *KPP*'s durability as a beginning-middle-ending formal archetype is attributable to its religious, philosophical, and aesthetic moorings, and to its association with *lelambatan*. Because they are the longest, weightiest, and most prestigious *gending,* "people feel that *lelambatan* emanate a sacred essence, perhaps because they were inspired by and created within a religious context. Hearing *lelambatan* makes one feel as if transported to a sacred ritual" (Rembang 1984–85a:xi). The *KPP*'s three-part structure habitually prompts the drawing of analogies with the concept of *tri-angga* (an anthropomorphism referring to the head, torso, and legs), the three courtyards of the Balinese temple (*jeroan, jaba tengah* and *jaba),* the *tri-murti* (the Hindu deific trinity of Brahma, Vishnu, and Siva), the *tri-loka* (upper, middle, and lower worlds of existence), and numerous other culturally valued dimensions of "threeness."

As an archetype the *KPP* is a narrative framework; a strategy for "drawing on deep-seated cultural impulses . . . one might say, by resorting to local habits of storytelling" (Rowell 1992:231). In this narrative sacred time in the *pengawak* is flanked by the preparatory gateway of the *kawitan* and the more human manifestations of that sacred time in the *pengecet.* "Lelambatan are for the gods," Lebah told me, "but the *pengawak* has the most godly feeling. In the *pengecet* we bring more of our own feelings to the music." Overlaying imagery of creation and growth, many refer to the *kawitan* as an *inti* (kernel) or *sumber* (source) out of which the full composition emerges. In progressing through the *gending* one follows a path from uncertain beginnings and initial exploration in the *kawitan* to the abstract grandeur and spiritual repose of the *pengawak* and ultimately to the control, power, speed, and release of the *pengecet.* McPhee says it this way:

> While the *pengawak* is essentially static in form and mood, the *pengecet* is dynamically progressive, passing through successive phases of rising rhythmic tension . . . What with the successive diminutions of the meter, the regulated contraction of gong accents, and the corresponding increase in tempo and force of the drumming, the effect of the *gending* from start to finish is one of slow awakening, a gradual gathering of momentum in a series of transitions that build to a peak of maximum power and excitement. (1966:83)

McPhee also implies that strictly speaking, virtually no *lelambatan* are actually constructed from precisely the three units of the *KPP* in order. In practice the *kawitan* and *pengecet* are often extended entities. Alternatively, *kawitan* may be quite brief, comprising barely a melodic "pick-up." In terms of the idealized *KPP, kawitan* and *pengecet* serve more than anything else as *regions* surrounding the central *pengawak,* the only component that is metrically well defined. And the *pengawak* itself need not be a single unit, but may consist of two or more melodies sharing the same meter. Thus most *lelambatan* have in fact more than three parts. Additions can be affixed to each of the root components, forming *kawitan-, pengawak-,* and *pengecet-* groups. The *pengawak* itself, while the conceptual anchor of the whole, may comprise only a small percentage of the total length.

The *KPP* originally applied only to *lelambatan,* but Balinese also map it onto *tari lepas* and *tabuh kreasi.* Doing so can focus the cultural lens through which the music is viewed, but also mask the distinctiveness of form in newer music (though perhaps only in a different way than its use evidently does in the genres of origin). To survey this in practice, and to give a sense of the scope of the forms in a diversity of individual *gending,* I will look at some sample formal plans in each of the genres, including the four *gending* by Beratha. But a brief digression into the *legong kraton* dance repertoire must come first, for its meters and forms are an important basis for *tari lepas* and even a glance at them can facilitate comparison between the two. Many formal plans conforming to the *KPP* framework are named for the meters of their *pengawak;* hereafter reference to forms is capitalized to distinguish them from the meters, which remain lowercased.

Gending pegambuhan. In *kebyar* the *lelambatan* meters of *pegambuhan* are mainly represented via *legong kraton* dances, which are in *KPP* and use the 256-beat *tabuh telu pegambuhan* (see fig. 7.1A) for their *pengawak.* Like other *lelambatan,* complete *legong* are so expanded as to bear little resemblance to a three-part form. Plans for the choreographies *Lasem, Jobog,* and *Kuntul* were given by McPhee and are reproduced in figure 8.10. I prefix them with *Tari Condong* (dance of the court attendant), which serves as a common prelude.

During her lengthy presentation (ca. 15 minutes) the *condong* at first dances alone, then presents a pair of fans to the two *legong,* finally withdrawing before the *legong* proper begins.[16] Metacyclic groups built from repeating 16-beat melodies arranged in rondo-like alternation (here labeled *condong* I, II, and III) and an 8-beat *bapang* are the basis for the *condong's* music. In each of the ensuing choreographies the *kawitan* proper comprises no more than a brief melodic introduction, sometimes drawn from the final *palet* of the *pengawak,* and urged on to *kempur* cadence by the subsequent entrance of *kendang.* The *pengawak* are single cycles but followed by *pengecet* groups consisting of up to ten additional units. Of these *batel, pangkat,* and *garuda* are music for fight scenes, mainly in short cycles that employ intricate *angsel* sequences.[17] The *pengipuk* are repeating 16- or 32-beat melodies used for love scenes. *Pengetog* and *penarik* are linking passages: in the former several repetitions of a *neliti*-texture melody begin slowly and then dramatically accelerate to a quick tempo; in the latter a single tone sustained in a repeated-note tremolo culminates in a *kempur* stroke. *Gineman* has several meanings, about which more under *tabuh pegongan* and *tabuh kreasi,* but here connotes an

---

16. Curiously, McPhee omits this even though it was clearly part of the performance during the 1930s (see DeZoete and Spies 1937:219).

Nowadays, in response to demands for succinct tourist performances, it is more and more the case that Balinese feel no compunction about deleting virtually any of the formal sections of *legong kraton* in order to shorten the performance. The edited results are often presented for Balinese audiences as well, despite a resurgent awareness that the complete versions are preferable.

17. The *garuda* melody of figure 6.3G is used in alternation with the longer one of 6.15A.

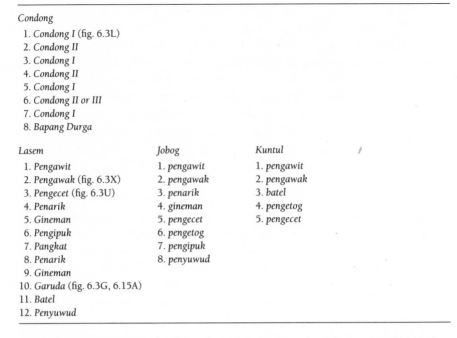

Condong

1. *Condong I* (fig. 6.3L)
2. *Condong II*
3. *Condong I*
4. *Condong II*
5. *Condong I*
6. *Condong II or III*
7. *Condong I*
8. *Bapang Durga*

Lasem	*Jobog*	*Kuntul*
1. Pengawit	1. pengawit	1. pengawit
2. Pengawak (fig. 6.3X)	2. pengawak	2. pengawak
3. Pengecet (fig. 6.3U)	3. penarik	3. batel
4. Penarik	4. gineman	4. pengetog
5. Gineman	5. pengecet	5. pengecet
6. Pengipuk	6. pengetog	
7. Pangkat	7. pengipuk	
8. Penarik	8. penyuwud	
9. Gineman		
10. Garuda (fig. 6.3G, 6.15A)		
11. Batel		
12. Penyuwud		

Figure 8.10. Form in *gending pelegongan* and *pegongan*. A. Form in *legong keraton* (based on McPhee 1966:190). The term *pengawit* is equivalent to *kawitan* and comes from the same root.

unpulsed, noncyclic melody played by *gangsa* (in the *gamelan pelegongan* version, by four *gender*) punctuated by *jegogan* tones. *Penyuwud* (from *su[w]ud*, end) are 16- or 32-beat closing melodies in slow tempo. A complete performance of *Lasem*, from *condong* to *penyuwud*, lasts nearly forty-five minutes.

Smaller *pegambuhan gending* types include *Bapang* and *Bebaturan* forms.[18] *Pengawak* in the former use slow *bapang* meter, and those in the latter employ *tabuh besik* or *tabuh dua*. These are three-part forms close to the *KPP* ideal, but pared to an ABA structure in which the single *kawitan* melody is reprised verbatim in lieu of an independent *pengecet*. Any of the three parts of the form may be repeated before proceeding. *Bapang* form was discussed in relation to *Jauk Keras* in chapter 7; *Bebaturan* compositions include items originating in *pegambuhan* repertoire such as *Godeg Miring* and *Jaran Sirig*.

Gending pegongan. *Lelambatan* in *pegongan* repertoire are instrumental compositions with a purely musical story to tell. As with their meters, the forms come in three main *gending*-types: those "in" *Tabuh Empat* (and its expansions *Nem* and *Kutus*) are one, while *Tabuh Pisan* and *Tabuh Telu* each comprise another.

18. See also Zurbuchen 1987:165–66 for discussion of the term *bebaturan* in relation to vocal melodies in the shadow play and other meanings.

I. *Tabuh Empat Pegongan* (*pengawak, pengisep* cycle = 256 beats; *pengecet* cycle = 32 beats):

Gending name	Banda Sura	Berare	Semarandhana
1. *Kawitan*	48 (3 × 16) beats	96	64
Pengawak-group			
2. *Pengawak*	standard	standard	standard
Penyalit begins at:	last 16 beats	2nd P	4th P
3. *Pengisep*	standard	standard	standard
Penyalit begins at:	last 16 beats	none	last 16 beats
Pengecet-group			
4. *Pengecet ngawit*	2 cycles	2 cycles	1 cycle
5. *Pengecet bebaturan*	1 "	1 "	—
6. *Pengecet ngembat*	4 "	4 "	4 "
7. *Tabuh Telu ngawit*	2 "	3 "	1 "
8. *Tabuh Telu pengisep*	1 "	2 "	—
9. *Tabuh Telu ngembat*	3 "	6 "	6 "
(aka *tabuh telu pengawak*)			

II. *Tabuh Pisan Pegongan* (*pengawak, pengiba, pengisep* cycle = 64 beats; *pengecet* cycle = 16 beats):

Gending name	Bebarongan	Pisang Bali
1. *Kawitan*	(64 beats)	(64 beats)
Pengawak-group		
2. *Pengiba*	1 cycle(s)	1 cycle(s)
3. *Pengawak*	2 "	2 "
5. *Penyalit* I	1 "	1 "
6. *Pengisep*	2 "	2 "
7. *Penyalit* II	4 "	8 "
8. *Pengawak*	2 "	2 "
9. *Pengiba*	1 "	1 "
Pengecet-group		
10. *Pengecet*	1 "	1 "

III. *Tabuh Telu Pegongan* (all cycles = 16 beats)

Gending name	Lempung Gunung	Lilit
1. *Kawitan*	—	2 cycles
2. *Pengawak*	9 cycles	4 cycles
3. *Penyalit*	—	1 cycle (after *pengawak* 2nd cycle)
4. *Pengecet*	—	1 cycle

Figure 8.10B. Form in selected *Tabuh Empat*, *Tabuh Pisan*, and *Tabuh Telu* (based on Rembang 1984–85a; see also McPhee 1966:107-12 for further examples of *Tabuh Telu*).

Gineman/Kawitan group		Timing	Length
1. *Genderan* (fig. 8.1A)		0:00	3:47
2. *Gineman trompong* (8.1A)		0:06	
3. *Genderan* (8.1A)		2:50	
4. *Reyongan*		3:00	
5. *Genderan*		3:26	
6. *Reyongan*		3:37	
7. *Kawitan* (drum intro + 4 cycles of 16 beats)		3:47	0:51
Pengawak group (fig. 8.1B; no. 10 is in 8.1C)			
8. *Pengawak* variations	I	4:38	2:52
	II	5:08	
(changes to III at midpoint, 5:44)			
9. *Pengawak* variation	III	6:18	
10. *Pengisep* in repetition (8. 1C)		7:30	1:48
		8:07	
		8:41	
11. *Pengawak* versions	IV	9:18	0:50
	V (partial)	9:57	
Pengecet (total 37 repetitions; fig. 8.1D):			
12a. Initial unison melody	(2x)	10:08	4:00
12b. *Pengecet* metacycles: *neliti* alone	(6x)	10:21	
Gangsa kotekan	(6x)	10:55	
Reyong/kendang	(6x)	11:30	
Gangsa kotekan	(6x)	12:04	
Reyong/kendang	(6x)	12:39	
12c. transition (2x) and slow coda (3x)		13:13	
End		14:08	

Figure 8.10C. Form in *Tabuh Pisan Bangun Anyar* (CDII/1; fig. 8.1A-D)

The foremost Balinese scholar of *lelambatan pegongan* is Nyoman Rembang (Rembang 1984–85a), whose authoritative monograph on the repertoire in Geladag I draw on in figure 8.10A and B; reference to meters can be correlated with fig. 7.1B.[19] The Geladag pieces are performed in the comparatively un-nuanced *klasik* style close to that of the original *gong gdé,* while composers of their contemporary *kebyar* updates, like Beratha, are at pains to develop subtler and more intricate arrangements of these revered *gending.*

In *klasik* style, most *kawitan* are prefixed by *gineman trompong* (8.1A is characteristic) forming a *kawitan*-group. Here as in *pegambuhan, gineman* connotes a melody rendered in unpulsed rhythm, but the term can have the additional connotation of something prefacing the *kawitan* (felt to be the "true" beginning). Led by the *trompong* player and closely followed in loose doubling

---

19. Much of the Geladag repertoire of *gending lelambatan* is available on Bali Stereo cassettes B637–642, recorded a year after Rembang's publication was issued. In the recordings *gineman trompong* were omitted to shorten the pieces. Rembang notates forty-three compositions in his book, including five *Tabuh Pisan,* seven *Tabuh Telu,* twenty-two *Tabuh Empat,* four *Tabuh Nem,* and five *Tabuh Kutus* (Rembang 1984–85a).

by *suling* and *rebab, gineman trompong* always perform this function in *lelambatan*. McPhee described them as "freely performed, quasi-recitative" introductions (1966:68; transcribed on 379). Balinese consider them introspective and best done by older players seasoned enough to eschew the inessential. They present three or four prolonged and hovering phrases, each containing chains of a few tentative ornamental approaches to single tones or small melodic cells, and brought to cadences with a *jegogan* stress. Like Indian *alap*, *gineman trompong* are unmeasured and proceed from an elemental exploration of the tones of the scale, at first only one and then gradually expanding to encompass more. They also set a comparable contemplative mood through "a process of playful exploration and clear projection of the underlying emotion" (Rowell 1992:239).

By comparison the ensuing *kawitan* proper is resolute, beginning at full dynamic in a medium tempo. In *Tabuh Empat* and *Telu* types it is heralded by a protracted pause during which the *jegogan* slowly fades, the subsequent resumption of the *trompong*, and finally the *kendang* and full *gamelan*. (In *Tabuh Pisan* the drums precede the reentrance of the *trompong*.) In *Tabuh Empat* and *Pisan, kawitan* are composed in multiples of 16 beats and played once only en route to the *pengawak*. Their meter is not considered to be related to that of the *pengawak*, but gongs punctuate the melody with a recurring [PMPG] pattern at distances of 2, 4, or 8 beats. In *Tabuh Telu* compositions the entire *KPP* is set in 16-beat *tabuh telu* meter.

Pengawak melodies in *Tabuh Empat* types fill a single cycle, while in *Tabuh Pisan* the melody extends to two or three concatenated *gongan* (*Bangun Anyar* uses two). In *Tabuh Telu* compositions it may extend to as many as nine, though since each *gongan* is 16 beats this totals only 144 beats, or just more than half the length of one in *Tabuh Empat*. Unlike the others, however, in *Tabuh Telu pengawak* the numerous gong strokes combine with many changes in gong tone to add a colorful dimension of intensified structural rhythm.

Pengawak are often immediately followed (or in the cases of *Tabuh Telu* and *Tabuh Pisan*, sometimes preceded as well) by another melody, known variously as *pengisep, pengiwan,* or *pengiba*, with the same metric plan but different drumming, and sometimes a different gong tone. *Pengawak* and *pengisep* in *Tabuh Empat* types are frequently linked via a *penyalit*, a substitute for a latter portion of the *pengawak* inserted prior to the *pengisep*. If the *pengisep* has a new gong tone, the *penyalit* will cause the final repetition of the *pengawak* to end on it. In *Tabuh Pisan* and *Tabuh Telu, penyalit* are separate and last a full cycle or more; in *Tabuh Pisan* further *penyalit* may also lead back to a subsequent repeat of the *pengawak*.

Tabuh Empat pengecet-groups are extended like those in *legong*. Two or three different melodies in a 32-beat contraction of the *pengawak* meter may be used, beginning with an internal *ngawit* (a kind of *kawitan* to the *pengecet*), and subsequent others featuring *ngembat* (*trompong* played in octaves) or *kendang batu-batu*. After this there is a lengthy section in *tabuh telu* meter, with its own internal demarcations. In some cases this contracts further to a *gilak* near the conclusion. *Pengecet* in *Tabuh Pisan* are simpler, comprising but a single 16-beat melody; and many *Tabuh Telu*, perhaps because of the form's unchanging cycle length, dispense with the designation *pengecet* entirely.

The behavior of the six element-progressions in *klasik lelambatan* as played in Geladag comprise a good basis for comparison with *kebyar* repertoire and can be summarized as follows:

1. Structural rhythm is a function of cyclic meter. *Gong:jegogan:calung* density is sparsest in the *pengawak*-group. The exception is *Tabuh Telu*, where density is constant throughout, but the stasis is compensated for by gong tone change and more variety in drumming.

2. Repetition occurs in *pengawak* and, especially, in *pengecet*-groups, encompassing dynamic and tempo changes. *Angsel* and *ocak-ocakan* are mostly absent.

3. Ensemble texture is virtually a constant. Exceptions are *gineman trompong* and *trompong* or *kendang* links between *gongan*. *Norot* elaboration predominates, with some use of *nyog cag*, *kekenyongan* and *malpal*.

4. In the *pengawak*-group, dynamics change in alignment with metrical markers. Terraced dynamics among instrument groups is common, though the entire ensemble plays continuously. Abrupt dynamic contrasts increase in the *pengecet*-group.

5. Incremental tempo changes take place at *pengawak*-group cycle beginnings and endings, as the music settles into or moves out of the default slow speed. The *pengecet*-group as a whole is much faster and passes through stages of further increase until a final slow cycle ends the *gending*.

6. Melodic variation occurs in repeating cycles in conjunction with the few points of elaboration change.

Geladag's reputation rests on faithfulness to the *gong gdé* source. In many other *sekaha* some of the more active element-progressions characteristic of *kebyar* have long been incorporated into the *lelambatan* repertoire.

In comparison with the two *Tabuh Pisan* shown in figure 8.10B, the *KPP*-portions of *Bangun Anyar* (fig. 8.10C) are modest in scope. Beratha, however, is largely responsible for transplanting the extended *kebyar*-style *gineman* (a hallmark opening strategy in *tabuh kreasi*, about which more below) to *kreasi lelambatan*, as a way of updating older *gending* for festival performance. After the opening phrase, the stillness of the *gineman trompong* fades into the effulgent flow of the *gineman*'s partial ensemble textures and noncyclic phrases. A brief *kendang* fanfare heralds the *KPP* proper, within which subtler changes are made. The *pengawak* is two cycles long, but repeated in a total of five different guises of melodic variation (8.1B). There is no *penyalit*, but structural rhythm intensifies in the *pengisep* because Beratha halves its length to two cycles of 32 beats, with a corresponding increase in *gong:jegogan:calung* ratio to 1:2:4 (8.1C). Also, as mentioned earlier, in the *pengisep*, *dIng* and *dong* alternate as gong tones, the only such change from the *kawitan* onward. The gong tone settles back to *dIng* for the reprise of the *pengawak*. Throughout, and especially in the virtuoso *pengecet* (8.1D), *angsel* and other kinds of *kendang*-based disruptions vary what would have been a static textural facade in a *klasik* rendition.

Tari Lepas

In this first category of *gending* actually composed for *kebyar*, the *modus operandi* is to attach various short, dance-appropriate melodies end-to-end as in *legong kraton*. But in *tari lepas*, *legong*'s longer court-derived meters have mostly given way to the still older and briefer village and temple ones, and their *kebyar* expansions. Those predominating are *bapang*, *gegaboran*, and *lelonggoran*, the first representing strong affect, the second more refined, and the latter, most characteristic in these contexts, capable of both. Form depends on the continuity these meters provide and the contrasts obtained by filling them with a variety of melodies and metacyclic progressions, all ordered according to the choreographic needs of the moment. Large sectional divisions are articulated, and the *gending* as a whole given a modern persona through the insertion of *kebyar* passages at beginnings, transitions, or endings.

Figure 8.11A outlines the plans for two icons of the repertoire, plus, for comparison's sake, *Gabor*, the classically inspired midcentury version of sacred temple dances. All *bapang* shown are 8-beat; both they and the 16-beat *lelonggoran* use [PtPG] punctuation at the quadrant points. *Pengecet* in *Oleg* and *Teruna* (to use their familiar names) have the same dimensions and punctuation as *lelonggoran* but use a distinct *kendang* pattern commonly known as *kendang pengecet kebyar* (see the top system of fig. 8.3B for a version of this). All melodies are presented with *angsel* and *ocak-ocakan* in metacyclic repetition. *Bapang* are intense and aggressive, while *lelonggoran* wax and wane through a number of moods and tempi ranging from restrained to swift. To highlight the contrast between the two types, I have glossed their *tempi* as simply fast or slow in the plans.

KPP clearly regulates *Gabor* because of the structural weight of the lengthy, slow, and centrally situated *pengawak*. As there are no *kebyar* interruptions, the *gending* unfolds continuously, the *pengawak* and *pengecet* in sustained *norot* texture. The piece begins with the gong tone *dung* but soon moves to *dong* for the *pengawak*, which is also the final tone for each of the remaining sections. *Lelambatan* context-indicators like tempo and *gong:jegogan:calung* density reveal where one is located in the form. In contrast these markers are absent in *Oleg* and *Teruna*, making their forms unlike *KPP* in the sense that both lack the extended, slow-tempo inner *gongan* that secures its perception. Neither dance is without slow passages, but these are of smaller dimensions, very un-*pengawak*-like, and soon give way to faster speeds in acquiescence to

Oleg Tumulilingan	Teruna Jaya	Gabor
1. *Kawitan* (ugal intro)	1. *Kebyar* I (Long)/	1. *Kawitan* (ugal intro)
2. *Lelonggoran* I (slow)*	2. *Genderan*	2. *Gegaboran* I (slow, fast, slow)
3. *Lelonggoran* I (fast, slow)/	3. *Bapang* I (fast)	3. *Pengawak* (slow; 64 beats)
4. *Kebyar* I (long)/	4. *Bapang* II (fast)*	4. *Pengecet* (3 x 24 beats)
5. *Bapang* (fast)	5. *Bapang* I	5. *Gegaboran* I (slow;
6. *Lelonggoran* II (slow, fast)	6. *Lelonggoran* I (slow, fast)	transposed, augmented)
7. *Pengecet* I (fast)	7. *Bapang* I	6. *Gegaboran* III, IV (fast,
8. *Kebyar* II (coda)/	8. *Bapang* III (fast)	alternating)
9. *Lelonggoran* III (slow)	9. *Bapang* I	
10. *Lelonggoran* IV, V	10. *Bapang* IV (fast)/	
(alternating, slow, fast)	11. *Lelonggoran* II (slow, fast)	
11. *Pengecet* II (fast)	12. *Bapang* I	
12. *Kebyar* III (coda)	13. *Pengecet* (fast)	
	14. *Kebyar* II (short)/	
	15. *Pejogedan* (slow; 64 beats)	
	16. *Bapang* I (transposed)	
	17. *Pengipuk pejogedan* (fast; 48 beats)	
	18. *Bapang* I (transposed)	
*Dancer(s) enter		

8.11. Form in *gending tari lepas*. A. Formal plans in selected *tari lepas*. Slashes (/) represent pauses coinciding with formal divisions.

the music's normative high-energy state. A measure of context-predictability analogous to that of *KPP* does inhere owing to the nearly exclusive use of *bapang* and *lelonggoran* meters; in each new melody one can safely assume that it will be one or the other.

Despite dissimilarities to *KPP*, *Oleg* and *Teruna* nonetheless divide into three large sections (In *Oleg*: 1–3 [+ 4], 5–8, and 9–12; in *Teruna*: [1 +] 2–10, 11–14, 15–17) separated from one another in most cases by a *kebyar* interruption.[20] The *pengecet* of *Oleg* (7 and 11) and *Teruna* (13) are much faster than their *legong* predecessors at near mm 160. They also lead to formal procedures of their own that carry the music to closure: the brief *kebyar* following each of the three *pengecet* emerges directly from its final *angsel*, proceeding always to a new gong tone. This either remains in place for the subsequent section of the piece or is the ending tone itself (the end of 8.3B also works this way).[21]

Beratha's *Panyembrahma* (fig. 8.11B), a welcoming dance mainly for official (tourist or state) occasions, is, like Windha's 1989 *Puspanjali* (figs. 6.3R, 6.6D) a streamlined successor to *Gabor*. It never departs from its [PtPG]

20. The exception is after *Teruna* 10, which stops abruptly with the withholding of the final gong, followed by a pause and an *ugal* introduction to 11; all of which amount to an equally radical *kebyar*-like disjuncture.

21. Ornstein calls this kind of ending or transition passage *ngucek* (1971a:170), and the term is also mentioned in Aryasa 1984–85:92; but among musicians I have found that these passages are simply called *kebyar*.

	Timing	Length
1. *Kawitan/Pengawak* (Fig. 8.2A)	0:00	2:10
2. Transition-*pengecet*-transition (Fig. 8.2B)	2:10	1:33
3. *Gegaboran longgor* I (slow, prayer; Fig. 8.2C)	3:43	1:08
4. *Gegaboran longgor* I (fast metacycles; 8.2C)	4:51	1:56
End	6:47	

Figure 8.11B. Form in *Panyembrahma* (CDII/2; fig. 8.2A-C).

gegaboran punctuation, but displays the variety of moods characteristic of longer *tari lepas*. However, noncyclic passages play no part. The opening melody (8.2A) stands for both the *kawitan* and *pengawak* (an unusual hybridization I will consider later in the chapter), while the *pengecet* employs more innately *kebyar*-style elaborations and disruptions. The concluding melody (8.2C, 8.7B), preceded by a single transitional cycle, is at first presented slowly while the dancers mime prayer, then quickly as they scatter flower petals over the audience, moving in synchrony with the *angsel*. The transition used to introduce this melody returns as a closing cycle.

Tabuh Kreasi

Tabuh kreasi compositions have gone through two evolutionary stages and are entering a third. In the first, generated in North Bali and characteristic until the revival of the *Festival Gong* in the late 1960s, form was freely cast, experimental, and most definitely uncodified. Among the earliest such pieces was *Kebyar Ding*, mentioned in chapter 3; after independence some of the better-known were *Hujan Mas* (Golden Rain) and *Kebyar Susun—susun* aptly meaning assembled from diverse ingredients. Since the major innovation on display was the eruptive *kebyar* texture, many early pieces forefront this and other noncyclic kernels to the extreme, extending such passages to outrageous lengths until at last, with the freedom-intoxicated composer as if not knowing how else to proceed, a conventional cycle appears seemingly from the blue; this then repeats many times until inevitable crescendo and acceleration overtake it, after which the process may begin anew. In time Balinese adapted the term *gineman* to designate the noncyclic sections preceding the first repeating *gongan* in a *tabuh kreasi*, thus suggesting a parallel to the relation between *gineman trompong* and *kawitan* in *pegongan* repertoire. Understood this way *gineman* may refer to music played in any combination of solo, partial, and full textures; and it may involve music both continuous and fragmentary, pulsed and unpulsed.[22]

---

22. Asnawa opined to me that the term *gineman* derives from *guneman*, which itself has roots in the verb *guna*, meaning life-energy or magic, but also, more plainly, to use or make use of. *Guneman* comprise part of the opening sequence of the shadow play, during which the puppet master (*dalang*)

	Timing	Length
Gineman/kebyar group (fig. 8.3A)		
1. *Kebyar*	0:00	2:20
2. *Reyongan*	0:08	
3. *Kebyar* 2 more phrases, interrupted by *kendangan*	0:10	
4. *Reyongan*	0:30	
5. *Kebyar*	0:32	
6. *Reyongan*	0:34	
7. *Kebyar*	0:47	
8. *Genderan*	0:52	
9. *Kebyar*	0:55	
10. *Genderan*	0:58	
11. *Kendangan; byar*	1:03	
13. *Reyongan*	1:06	
14. *Kebyar*	1:20	
15. *Reyongan*	1:22	
16. *Kendangan, cengceng* interjections	1:28	
17. *Norot* and *malpal*	1:37	
18. *Calung* and *jegogan*	1:46	
19. *Malpal*	1:52	
20. *Kendangan*	1:59	
Pengecet group (fig. 8.3B)		
21. *Pengecet* metacycles (total 13 repetitions)		
gangsa I *kotekan* to *angsel* (3 cycles)	2:20	1:36
gangsa alt. *kotekan* to *angsel* (3 cycles)	2:39	
gangsa I *kotekan* to *angsel* (3 cycles)	2:58	
gangsa alt. *kotekan* to *angsel* (3 cycles)	3:16	
concluding cycle	3:36	
22. *Kebyar* with genderan interruption	3:43	
End	3:56	

Figure 8.12A. *Tabuh kreasi* form in *Jaya Semara* (CDII/3; fig. 8.3A-B)

The early *tabuh kreasi* style is represented here by the concentrated *Jaya Semara* (shown in chart form in figure 8.12A), in which the progression from noncyclic to cyclic structure happens only once. Its opening *gineman* (sometimes also called a *kebyar* because of its initial texture), highly unstable and asymmetrical, is eventually succeeded by a 16-beat *pengecet* cycle of the kind described for *Oleg* and *Teruna*. The *gineman's* vigorous fragments zigzag between textures, fast and slow tempi, loud and suppressed dynamics, all a far cry from the tranquil entry provided by *gineman trompong* and another world from the sedate *lelambatan* cycles they lead to. *Jaya Semara's* structural weight

removes, one by one, all of the puppets from their box and places them together for a few moments before the screen, thus asserting control over their magic and ritually preparing for the actual beginning of the story. *Gineman,* in *kebyar,* has the related connotation of "overture": a preparatory sequence in which musical materials are briefly introduced before moving on to the body of the piece, though perhaps without the explicit connotation of thematic foreshadowing that the Western understanding of overture implies. As in *Jaya Semara* and other compositions, *gineman* expand to fulfill more than an introductory role and introduce material that ordinarily does not return later on.

	Timing	Length
Part I		
Gineman group (fig. 8.4A)		
1. 7 noninterlocking fragments	0:00	2:15
2. Continuous, accelerating *kotekan*	0:35	
3. 3 *kotekan* fragments	0:46	
4. Continuous *kotekan*	1:04	
5. Longer continuous *kotekan*	1:14	
6. 3 noninterlocking fragments	1:33	
7. *Kebyar* fragment	1:43	
8. Noninterlocking fragment	1:49	
9. *Kantilan/pemadé/calung/jegogan/gong*	1:55	
10. Continuous *kotekan*	2:07	
11. *Suling* solo	2:15	0:33
12. Noninterlocking continuous	2:40	
Cycle I (fig. 8.4B):		
13. *Kotekan* (39 4-beat cycles)		
10 cycles *dong* (9 + trans. up)	2:48	1:12
10 cycles *deng* (9 + trans. down)	3:06	
10 cycles *dong* (9 + trans. up)	3:24	
9 cycles *deng* (8 + trans. down)	3:43	
Part II		
Peralihan I		
14. *Kebyar* fragment	4:00	2:37
15. *Reyongan* (fig. 2.18)	4:03	
Cycle II		
16. *Bapang/variasi kendang*	4:14	
Part III (fig. 8.4C)		
Peralihan II		
17. *Genderan*	6:37	3:08
Cycle III		
18. *Gambangan* (41 8-beat cycles + Coda; Links last 2 cycles)		
3 cycles (1 + link I)	6:48	
6 cycles (4 + link II)	7:00	
6 cycles *dIng* (4 + link I)	7:23	
6 cycles *dang* (4 + link II)	7:46	
6 cycles *dIng* (4 + link I)	8:10	
8 cycles *dang* (6 + link II)	8:34	
6 cycles *dIng*	9:05	
Coda (12 beats)	9:41	
End	9:45	

Figure 8.12B. *Tabuh kreasi* form in *Kosalia Arini* (CDII/4; fig. 8.4 A-C; figs. 2.16–2.18)

ultimately tips toward the *pengecet,* which, when it finally arrives, repeats until it takes up 40 percent of the *gending*'s total length. But even with the symmetrical stability of familiar metacycles the *pengecet* is hard-pressed to counterbalance the energy accumulated earlier on.

Since the *Festival Gong* was institutionalized in the late 1960s, every year a

Sekar Kamuda (Pindha village, composed by Ketut Gdé Asnawa)

Part I: *Gineman* and *kotekan*

      1. *Genderan,* fragment
      2. *Kebyar,* fragments
      3. *Genderan,* fragments
      4. *Genderan,* continuous, to *kebyar* cadence
      5. *Kebyar,* followed by *reyongan,* return to *kebyar*
      6. *Suling,* "*gineman trompong*" style
      7. *Genderan kawitan,* continuous, to 8
      8. *Kotekan* cycle A: 32 beats, repeated
      9. *Kotekan* cycle B: 20, then (67 beats, repeated)

Part II: *Peralihan* and *bapang*

     10. *Kebyar,* fragment
     11. *Reyongan,* continuous
     12. *Bapang;* alternation between 16-beat cycle featuring *genderan,* and 8-beat cycle featuring *reyongan/kendangan*

Part III: *Peralihan* and *gambangan*

     13. *Genderan* "*kawitan*" to 14; fragments, then continuous
     14. *Gambangan:* repeating 26-beat cycle (fig. 8.6).

Figure 8.12C. *Tabuh kreasi* form in *Sekar Kamuda*

new *tabuh kreasi* is prepared by each competing group. These compositions soon came to resemble one another closely in form and style, though over time the style has continued to develop rapidly. In this second phase, exemplified by *Kosalia Arini* and *Sekar Kamuda* (outlined in fig. 8.12B-C), metacyclic oases emerge to articulate a more conventional three-part structure that distantly echoes *KPP*. Like *Jaya Semara* in full, each part begins noncyclically and ends cyclically, but there are always three such parts, and the cyclic goal of each has a distinct character and function.

The opening *gineman* sets forth with fragments as in *Jaya Semara,* but, in an enhancement of continuity, with fewer texture changes. In between fragments longer pauses permit focus on their concluding *jegogan* tones, as if to suggest a special dimension of prominence for these pulsating bass tones alone. Major texture change is not freely meted out but saved for maximum impact, sometimes quite far into the piece (at 1:43 in 8.4A). The overall direction is from shorter to longer phrases as fragments evolve into full-fledged melodies with steady beat and multiple internal phrases. This process can be traced through the *genderan* that opens *Kosalia Arini* (8.4A up to 1:33, the first gong stroke), and especially seen by juxtaposing the opening three-note fragment and the 37-beat *kotekan* that ends with gong.

Usually the first cyclic port of call features *genderan* texture with ear-catching and athletic *kotekan,* using many *tua*-influenced kCC distanced from the conventional *ngubeng* ones of figure 6.13. The melody underpinning the *kotekan* is characteristically also not court-derived. Clear internal contours and phrases and rhythmic variety distinguish it from the comparatively featureless expanse of court *neliti*. *Gending* like *Kosalia Arini,* from the early days of this model, use brief cycles (top system of 8.4B), but in Windha's latest music they stretch into the hundreds of beats. Often one or more phrases are extended by sequential repetition up a scale step, a technique rare in court genres but common in *gamelan gender wayang.* Indeed, *gender wayang, gandrung,* and other *tua gamelan* constitute important models here, and the focus on melody and *kotekan* makes this portion of the piece a locus for stylistic and quotation topics like the *Sekar Gendot* type described in chapter 5. In 8.4B, the melody supporting the *kotekan* quotes the *gender wayang* ostinato *angkat-angkatan* ("traveling music," used to shift between story locales in the shadow play) in full, which is based on just such a melodic sequence.

Wahyu Giri Suara's 49.5-beat cycle (fig. 8.5) uses several transpositional sequences and motivic variants, bracketed over the *ugal* staff. With the repeating 8-beat unit at the beginning, the melody is asymmetrically divided into (8 × 2) + 8 + (6 × 3) + 7.5 beats. *Jegogan* stresses emphasize local alternation between *dong* and *deng* at first, expanding to include *dAng* at the twenty-fourth beat and *dIng* as the structural rhythm contracts to 3 beats; the fifth tone *dung* is withheld until just before gong in an intensification reminiscent of court cycles. Windha's stated interest in "finding satisfying new ways to get to gong" is reflected in the surprise of the extended beat on that tone. In other ways the melody is conventional. The initial *dAng* is the first-order stress closest to the arithmetic midpoint, which nominally gives the cycle a background structure and Axis -2 spine not unlike those of its near-relatives in figure 6.3, the 32-beat melodies S and T. In the *kotekan* stratum the first stylistic topic, at beats 1–8, evokes *gamelan gender wayang.* A fleeting but unmistakable suggestion of the wooden *gambang's* special style of interlocking (known as *oncang-oncangan* in the *gamelan gambang*) is heard in the repeated tones at beats 25, 28, and 31; and a distortion of *gamelan gandrung* patterns into 3-beat sequential units is found from beat 24 onward.

Often ushered in by acceleration in the final *kotekan* cycle, the second sections of *tabuh kreasi* return to the noncyclic character of *gineman* en route to the next cyclic stopping place. Since they are no longer situated at the actual beginning, it is imprecise to call such passages *gineman;* the only alternative is *peralihan* (or *pengalihan,* from *alih,* to seek) a word with no particular musical pedigree that is nonetheless often used and means, in this case, transition. If the piece thus far has underemployed *reyongan* texture, this is the point at which it will come to prominence, as it does in both *Kosalia Arini* and *Sekar Kamuda. Reyongan* are usually unaccompanied but can imply a steady beat, and, for at least part of their duration, a clear cycle, as suggested by the internal repetition of an 8-beat *kotekan* (see 8.3A, following 0:34 and 1:06).

The trajectory of this *peralihan* is toward a hard-driving up-tempo cycle recognizable by its position in the form and certain invariant features: *calung* playing *neliti* rhythm, *majalan* melodies that are never Axis 0, and an intense *gong:jegogan:calung* ratio of 1:1:4. In early pieces to use this, like *Kosalia Arini* (4:14 with gongs alone, *calung* enter at 4:32), the cycle was only 8 beats. By the 1980s (*Sekar Kamuda;* also *Dharma Putra:* fig. 2.19 [CDI/4]) the length had doubled and the melody was sometimes introduced with *kantilan* doubling the *calung,* a textural innovation leaving a Stravinskyesque gap where the *pemadé* would be. The punctuation was the ubiquitous [PtPG] type. By the late 1980s the melody extended to two such 16-beat cycles, and the *kantilan* were given a syncopated *neliti* variant, but the other traits did not change. In all cases a context is created for vigorous interlocking, presented antiphonally with either *reyong* in opposition to *kendang (Kosalia Arini),* or *gangsa to kendang/reyong (Sekar Kamuda).* Arranged in metacycles, the conversation between instrument groups is articulated by cycle-length interjections, either from the *gangsa* (in *Kosalia Arini* at 4:36, 5:33, and 6:32) or *ocak-ocakan (Sekar Kamuda).* In the 1990s composers have gone further, interpolating additional melodies between metacycle groups.

Musicians call these sections either *variasi kendang* or *ocak-ocakan* owing to the likely prominence of this instrument and texture; or *bapang* because of the punctuation, though the music does not carry *bapang* character topic connotations. None of these terms seems satisfactory, a fact which all acknowledge, especially given the music's striking impact and design. It emerges in the heart of *tabuh kreasi* form in a position analogous to *pengawak,* and carries the most symmetrical and, in a sense, rigorous construction, yet it is also the site for the most bravura displays of virtuosity, *gaya,* and sheer pleasure in speed and complexity. After twice through the metacyclic group, *variasi kendang* commonly end with a sudden stop just before gong and a withholding of the final cycle's gong stroke (fig. 8.4C, end of first system), an audacious maneuver both in terms of ensemble technique and equally so because of its guillotine incompleteness. Firmament is yanked away, and though audiences know what to expect next they relish the *maut* (deadly) swiftness of the transformation.

A second *peralihan* follows, brief and intended to slow things down. This leads to the *gambangan,* so-called because it usually features this ensemble texture, often with fast shifting variants in elaboration (figs. 2.15, 8.4C, and 8.6). After the intensity of *variasi kendang* the payoff of the *gambangan* is sunnier and several notches down in energy. *Kosalia Arini*'s is short and regular, but in *Sekar Kamuda* and its contemporaries and successors length and asymmetry prevail. The ascendant status of orchestral color and the emphasis on composed melody instead of rhythmically undifferentiated *pokok* allow the music to unfold freely over longer spans in confident disregard for metric constraint. Seemingly through-composed at first because of their fluid textural and metric course, *gambangan* ultimately return to their beginnings and repeat at least once before the *gending* concludes, either with a declamatory final *byar,* a slow fade, a short coda, or a combination.

Tabuh kreasi have been described in terms of *lelambatan KPP* by STSI faculty (Astita 1990) by matching up the three parts of each. This seems in many respects inadvisable, given their obvious differences. While the classical forms articulate an ordered succession of cycles and meters, *tabuh kreasi* revel in disorder and discontinuity, embracing cyclic meter only at times, and, it increasingly seems, more as a goal than a fundamental state. Yet in the most general understanding of *KPP* as beginning, middle, and end the designation has value. With the *variasi kendang* acting as ersatz *pengawak*, there is a notable analogy in the presence of the most metrically stable music (though hardly stately as in *lelambatan*) in the "middle" position. *Gambangan* are similarly comparable to *pengecet* and in early-style pieces like *Jaya Semara* explicitly labeled so. In still another sense the formal conventions of *tabuh kreasi* are so recognizable that their very succession is culturally ingrained and ordained, just as the original *KPP* was for court repertoire. The *KPP* seal of approval secures proof of authenticity.

Tabuh kreasi have grown longer over the decades: Windha's recent ones approach twenty minutes. In *Kosalia Arini* and *Sekar Kamuda* reliance on fragments in the *gineman* and *peralihan* exposes the seams between sections, giving these portions a jolting quality that is in fundamental contrast to the flow of cycles. Form in the compositions of the 1960s to the early 1980s relies on the juxtapositions between these states which, in a *gending*-level analogy to the terms I developed for drumming, can be thought of as stable (cyclic) and active (noncyclic or linear). An important formal process in *tabuh kreasi*, then, is the stabilizing movement from active to stable regions. One of the achievements of Windha's generation has been to refine this distinction and blur the contrast. Less dependence on fragments combined with extension of noncyclic continuous passages and subtle tempo gradations unify the form. Always changing orchestral color is used not so much to create disjuncture, but to hide it by changing so often that the instant of structural shift is concealed. New levels of *sekaha* virtuosity and musicians' ease amid difficult musical details enable the pieces to shoot structural vines and tendrils. These factors support the illusion, revolutionary in some respects, that newer *tabuh kreasi* have a predominantly linear thrust. Repetition and cyclicity remain the norm, but they are often as if hidden from view. Active and stable states are in such constant interaction that neither has the upper hand. Only the composer does.

Since 1995 composers Gdé Yudana, Madé Subandi, and a few others now in their twenties or early thirties have achieved a self-conscious and fundamental break with the *tabuh kreasi* form of the recent past. Their music is bold and exploratory, and parts ways more overtly than have Windha and his cohorts with the norms of cyclicity, first-order relations, formal plan, tempo, and orchestration. Musically, these developments are intriguing and promising, though as of this writing it is too soon to evaluate their significance. Among the compositions in this newest phase are Yudana's *Lebur Seketi* (1995), and Subandi's *Bajramusti* (1997). Windha, too, in his 1998 *Candra Baskara,* has tested this new style.

Inside *Gending* Looking Out

We have gone some distance toward laying out the range of procedural conventions in *kebyar* repertoires and are in a position to make sense of the recordings and transcriptions of Beratha's *gending* more comprehensively, as complete pieces. But the number and variety of elements, progressions, and formal categories presented thus far may seem so copious as to be diffuse, and therefore require an alternative, consolidating perspective. One of the aims of the following four analytical commentaries, restricted to considering Beratha's music at *gending*-level, is to refocus the discussion by looking at composition from within the *gending* facing out, rather than, as in the foregoing, as a set of techniques to be applied to templates. In this way the individuated *gending* emerges more fully, and while creating this was perhaps not Beratha's consciously articulated goal, it nonetheless exists for the perceiver. That this is so does not, of course, diminish the importance of the stylistic coherence and convention on which the tradition relies, but it gives what Balinese recognize as four distinctive and extraordinary products of the tradition due individual attention. And finally, reaching the end of the analytical core of the book, this is an appropriate moment for me to offer my interpretation—for that is what analysis must ultimately be—of *gamelan* compositions as entireties.

To think about the music at *gending*-level I appeal to our ability, identified by Lutoslawski in the chapter epigraph, to mentally parse and condense musical events that take place over a long span of time. Without having rehearsed these pieces so many ways in my mind I would have little to say here; likewise I urge readers to return to the recordings and transcriptions often, compare their own conclusions with mine, and add to the creative imaginings. To commit the music to memory, of course, as *kebyar* performers must, leads to irreproducibly fecund conditions for contemplation. At this point in my own listening, no doubt in large part as a result of my background, I have a strong predilection for experiencing progressions of continuity in layered tension with those of discontinuity, and for listening among elements for contributors to this dialogue.

I should first stipulate how I identify the components of this tension. How is continuity sustained? Not to belabor the obvious, but one factor is the very limitations inherent in the scale structure, instruments, and orchestrational conventions of the *gamelan,* which create its signature timbral world and stratified texture. Beyond this I see it as axiomatic that a symbiosis between formal context and the element of melody/scale tone is the primary arbiter of continuity. Formal category-successions such as *KPP* enable reasonably accurate prediction of what metric context to expect at a given point in a piece. The successions are conventions subject to some manipulation as we have seen, but knowledge of them serves deeper sensitivity to scale-tone structure by clarifying which melodic arrivals are candidates for *gending*-level significance. Significant melodic arrivals such as gong and axis tones (or *jegogan* in noncyclic contexts) must be tracked according to structural rhythm in each part of a *gending*. One must wait 128 beats for the axis tone in a *Tabuh Empat pengawak*, whereas in its concluding 16-beat *tabuh telu* cycles gong itself comes eight times more often. The changing time span separating significant *gending*-level tones elasticizes the music's overall temporality

Melody is singled out as it lends itself so readily to multitiered relationships, a quality underscored in *gamelan* by the simple duple density relations between strata in court cycles. To hear scale-tone connections across contexts is to expand the application of CC and CC-group concepts, as I indicated under extended melodic relations earlier in the chapter. While successive melodies may or may not have any apparent motivic similarity, following the sparser strata through a piece produces the impression of a *gending*-level melodic backbone.[23] Building on the habits acquired listening to *gongan* locally this can be imagined as one stratum of a hypothetical "melody" that spans the full composition. As in discrete *gongan* there is no *ur*-shape to consider, for the contour of each such backbone differs. Accordingly, in each commentary I identify the gCC (*gending*-level CC), a distinctively shaped progression of structural tones drawn from across the entire *gending*. The upper staves of the reductions in figure 8.13A-D present gong, axis, and important *jegogan* tones grouped by formal category while the lower staves further strip this down to an essentialized contour, the gCC proper.

As for discontinuity, throughout I have associated it with linearity and *kebyar*'s innate radicalisms: texture change, noncyclic and asymmetrical cyclic contexts, abrupt dynamic and tempo changes, *angsel, ocak-ocakan,* and so on. Discontinuity acts against and enriches the connections between gCC-group members since these are drawn from varied musical environments. When mentally juxtaposed the environments collapse into a montage of dramatic change. This must be factored in to understand *kebyar*'s impact during its formative decades, and for current purposes is an appropriate perspective to work from. One must also bear in mind, however, that by now this montage has been displayed many times and its characteristic successions enshrined to the

---

23. The metaphor of backbone is inspired by the Balinese *tulang* (spine or bone). Balinese apply this word to music to indicate an essence of something unchanged despite external transformation. *Kreasi lelambatan* are considered fundamentally equivalent to *klasik* renditions despite how different they sound, for example, because their *tulang* are the same.

A: Bangun Anyar (Fig. 8.1, 8.10C)

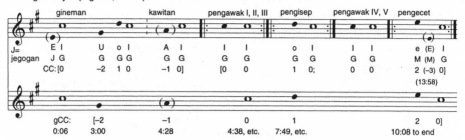

B: Panyembrahma (Fig. 8.2, 8.11B)

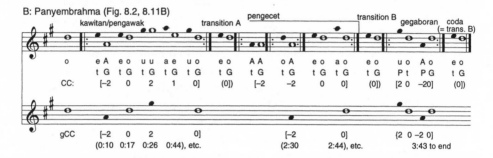

C: Jaya Semara (8.3, 8.12A)

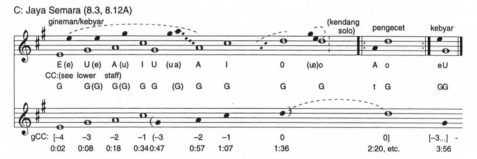

D: Kosalia Arini (Fig. 8.4, 8.12B)

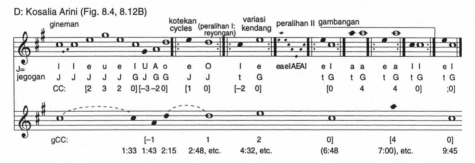

Figure 8.13. *Gending*-level CC

extent that their shock value is more stylized than actual. This in turn reillu-minates the felt necessity for the project of 1980s and 1990s composers: the energy of the fragmentary style of the 1960s and 1970s has been depleted, and regeneration is sought in the expanded, less repetitive structures of recent music.

There is one last detail to iron out, that of the convenient but troublesome spatial metaphors "cyclic" and "linear." Though favored by scholars interna-tionally and by Balinese themselves for transmission purposes, the circle anal-ogy is problematic when considering full compositions analytically in a more than cursory way.[24] Assuming congruence between shapes and temporal con-tinua is enriching for certain kinds of description, but we have completed those. To deny the directional motion of cyclic melody through time so as to assert the primacy of repetition or posit a nondirectional "stasis" is to under-value the details that distort "circles" into progressions that cannot be fully grasped under the glare of a geometric gaze. More usefully we can now take the step of discarding the spatial imagery—while retaining the terms "linear" and "cyclic" with their newly refined meanings—and simply consider quadri-partite court cycles and repetition *normative,* hence promoters of continuity. Noncyclic passages and asymmetrical cycles have the opposite effect. All are perceived to coexist in the same temporal flow and so are not as fundamentally opposed as the flat images line and circle would suggest. On now to the *gending*.

Bangun Anyar

A compelling premise on which to build an experience of *Bangun Anyar* is to imagine the *pengawak* as its "exemplary center," to use Geertz's felicitous term for the position of the Majapahit kings in their realms (1980:11). Making this association with the courtly lineage that nurtured the style is beneficial

---

24. This correspondence has developed throughout the book, but seen in the light of some West-ern music theory it involves an ironic realignment. For some Western writers—Kramer 1988 is char-acteristic (see especially p. 24 for reference to Bali; see also the discussion in chapter 9 below)—the presumption is that directed linearity, as in tonal forms, implies continuity, while cyclicity (in the "non-Western" sense used in these pages, not the nineteenth-century European senses of song cycle or de-veloping variation) is equated not with discontinuity but with stasis. It is then inferred that this stasis reflects non-Western modes of perception. It is seen not as relative but absolute, at least metaphori-cally: time stands still. The linkage is an orientalism: another trope on the "timeless" East, recalling also Geertz's characterization of Balinese time as a "vectorless now" (1973:404).

From within the *gamelan* tradition it is evident that conditions are very much otherwise, as the relative character of the term for static, *ngubeng*, illustrates. Of course from a Western music perspec-tive ideas like Kramer's have long been significant, and have exerted a powerful (by now virtually prosaic) impact on composers throughout the century. See also Hasty 1990 for a critique of the linear/cyclic bifurcation.

By way of contrast, in my analyses cycles are continuous in the sense of unchanged from their normative state, or undisturbed. Linearity alters this condition, hence its discontinuity.

for a *gending* of this stature, though I am wary of resurrecting the circle right after its demise at my own hands. Do not take this meaning; think instead of the center as a physicist's singularity (a space-time fusion well matched to music), attracting the energy of surrounding musical matter, with the extremes of the piece least susceptible to its pull. The *gending*-level tension of *Bangun Anyar* dwells in the specific nature of the equilibrium among its forceful, fragmentary beginning, its dense and powerful core, and an ending that synthesizes the two.

The *gineman* has six textural/melodic components, listed in 8.10C. As in other *gineman* one is drawn to the seeming entropy of textures, phrase lengths, and structural tones without necessarily being aware, even after many encounters, of the thoughtful tonal framework in preparation. The opening *genderan* bridges from the initial *dEng* (the only *jegogan* stress given this scale tone in this register until the end) to *dIng*. The *gineman trompong* wafts gently to *dUng*, followed by two *genderan-reyongan* pairs, ending on *dUng/dong* and *dong/dIng*. I include the *genderan dUng* (3:00) in the lower staff of 8.13A because it is prepared by an arresting full ensemble cadence. The gong on *dUng* is unique in the piece and forms a symmetrical pair, with the *pengecet's deng,* of both formal and registral "parentheses" around the *dIng,* which emanates outward from the *pengawak* core to control the final gong of each section (as shown on the upper staff of 8.13A). In confirmation of the *KPP*-based notion that the *kawitan* is a kernel of the full *gending,* the {−2,0,2,0} *dUng/dIng/deng/dIng* fulcrum is projected to the elaboration strata as a diagonal relation at the beginning of the *kawitan,* a shape preserved in the gCC. In the *kawitan* the {−2,0,2,0} contour is heard twice in succession in the *pokok* stratum: at 4:00, with *kekenyongan* elaboration, and at 4:10, with *norot.*

The *pengawak* is played three times before the *pengisep* (I–III in fig. 8.1B; 4:38–7:30). At 128 beats, III is by far the broadest gesture in the piece. Its Axis 0 insistence on *dIng* is fleshed out by the curving CC4 connecting the gong strokes with quadrant tones *dung* and *dUng* and the distortion of this shape in the upper strata, as analyzed for fig. 6.3W. But discontinuities of density, texture, and tempo shroud this before III, the true core, is unveiled.

In I the melody is presented in diminution, halved in length to 64 beats. *Malpal* texture and acceleration at the beginning of I continue from similar music at the end of the *kawitan,* which softens the effect of the *angsel* articulating their mutual boundary. Next, *ubit telu kotekan* starting at the first M stroke continues past the axial gong to the next M (4:44–4:55), filling I's central quadrants and forcing the texture one quadrant out of alignment with the meter. In the last quadrant the texture reverts to noninterlocking elaboration. The tempo slows and recedes through the *norot* figuration at the beginning of II. This is an inversion of the tempo profile at the beginning of I, which supports the textural discontinuity by isolating the "misaligned" *ubit telu* on a tempo plateau.

After the first P of II doubled density, lighter texture featuring the *trom-pong*, and a halving of the *kempli* rate to every two beats highlight an entrance to the initial stage of the core at the first M stroke. (In *Bangun Anyar* as in other *kreasi lelambatan* two *kempli* are used—one to keep time and the other, M, for punctuation.) In II the core's characteristic *angsel* and *nyog cag* elaboration is withheld (see also fig. 8.8A), but upon reaching the axial gong II defers to III to complete that cycle plus one more before the *pengisep* begins.

The *pengisep* (8.1C), condensed to 64 beats, uses the axial gong tone *dong*. This commences an ascent above *dIng* in the gCC. It does not loosen *dIng's* grip but it shifts the tonal quality of the music with regard to it: where the *pengawak* axis was static, the *pengisep* injects background motion at each axis and final gong, which now come twice as often as they did in the *pengawak*. As is characteristic of all *gending Tabuh Pisan*, the *pengawak* subsequently re-turns. In *Bangun Anyar* its restatement, further varied (8.1B, versions IV and V), interrupts the incipient structural scalar ascent, which later resumes and terminates at *deng* in the *pengecet* (8.1D).

The innovative and much imitated ending, which both upholds and up-dates the *KPP*, is one of Beratha's major contributions. In it the driving meta-cycles of *variasi kendang* from *tabuh kreasi* form are transplanted to *lelambatan pengecet* position, a rejuvenating conflation of affects. A full thirty-seven repe-titions of this intense 16-beat melody magnifies the prominence of the *deng/dIng* axis, liquidating the expansiveness of earlier sections to achieve a cyclic recapturing of the *gineman's* rough energy. Consequently I elevate *deng* to *gending*-level despite the fact that, unlike comparable points in the *pengawak* and *pengisep*, it receives only M stress. At the close (8.1D, 8 beats before the end of the final *gangsa* system) *deng* transforms to *dEng*, recalling the opening.

Bangun Anyar's discontinuity unfolds on the basis of the particular entan-glements of texture, tempo, metacycle, and melodic variation to which the *KPP* is subjected, as set forth here and in piecemeal discussions earlier in the chapter. Its continuity ultimately rests on the *KPP* and a clear ranking of the five scale tones. *DIng* is in consummate control throughout, followed in order by *dong*, the *dUng/deng* pair, and finally the negligibly present *dAng*, whose fleeting alignment with gong near the end of the *kawitan* (4:28) is its sole instant in the structural spotlight. I have nonetheless carried it over to the gCC. One reason is that its appearance as a gong tone in the *kawitan* grants a perfection of symmetry and completeness to the analysis, but that is not all. Like all of the factors mentioned, it affects the supple dialogue of foreground and background asymmetry, symmetry, balance, and imbalance animating the *gending* as a whole.

Panyembrahma

In the original temple genres *gabor* and *mendet,* dancers young and old, trained and untrained, dance in simple costumes for the gods at rituals, snaking in

Panyembrahma dancers, Pengosekan, 1998. Photo: Author.

long rows around the *balé gamelan* and shrines laden with offerings. *Panyembrahma,* though usually performed only by girls of student age, aspires to the same admixture of the quotidian, the sacred, and the dignified. Musically, it does this first of all by borrowing the gong tone *dong* from its more recent precursor *Gabor* and sustaining it throughout, as with *dIng* in *Bangun Anyar.* In the absence of a full-fledged *pengawak* the piece inevitably has a lighter mood than *Gabor,* but Beratha packs dense activity into its brief frame.

The first section uses a mode of discontinuity I have not encountered elsewhere in *kebyar:* a nonduple ratio—in this case 5:4—of melody length to elaboration and drumming phrases.[25] The 8-beat [.P.t.P.G] *gongan* is overlaid with both a 40-beat (5 *gongan*) melody and a 32-beat (4 *gongan*) phrase of *norot* elaboration, *kendang,* and *angsel,* with which the dance is synchronized. In figure 8.2A these two out-of-phase beat-counts are numbered separately below the systems; CD timings are provided each time one of the counts ends. Because of the 5:4 relationship, the *neliti's* alignment with the elaboration strata and drumming is always changing. Moreover, the first *norot* group, including the initial *ugal* solo, is introductory and composed differently from the following three. Entering during the introduction, the dancers perform the same set of movements thrice to the remaining 32-beat groups: first to one

---

25. None of the Balinese whom I asked were aware of this relationship.

This melody can be compared with *Arsawijaya,* fig. 6.3V, in which the sparser strata of a quadripartite cycle are segmented asymmetrically.

side, then the other, then center. The music is not permitted to continue to the 20-cycle mark at which the entire musical action would repeat to reveal the process openly, so the aural impression is that of a continuously unfolding single melody phrased by a regular pattern of disruption. (The two phrases indeed appear to end together, but it should be remembered that at the beginning the *neliti*'s entrance was delayed for 8 beats.) In this striking way the shorter units characteristic of *kawitan* are fused with *pengawak* abstraction.

A 40-beat unit length persists in the *pengecet* (8.2B) but now with an 8-beat internal repetition (beats 9–16/17–24), thus reducing to a squarer 32 beats. Structure and surface are conventionally aligned to grant the music clarity and growing momentum appropriate to a *pengecet,* a process catalyzed in several ways. In an elaboration change, *norot* is abandoned for shifting patterns of *ubit telu, ubit empat,* and *nyog cag,* some symmetrical and some not. The rate of movement among registers intensifies, owing to the elaboration's sweeping contour at beats 1–24 and its subsequent rise through the upper range. The changing role of the *reyong* brightens the ensemble texture, beginning with *kecekan* (on the rim), gradually adding melodic doublings of the *gangsa,* and ending with *ocak-ocakan.* These progressions carry the intensity beyond where a court *pengecet* would go to give *Panyembrahma* contemporary character.

Part of figure 8.2C's concluding *gegaboran* section's interest lies in the tempo change and irregular *angsel* ordering, as described for fig. 8.7B. The unpredictable metacycles recall the opening of the *gending,* with its melody-to-surface misalignment, while its contour and scale-tone content reflect the registral sweep of the *pengecet* and summarize the melodic continuity of the whole. The upper staff of figure 8.13B demonstrates a remarkably clear scale-tone hierarchy in which the preeminent *dong* is framed by *dAng* and *dung,* a contour mirrored in the *gegaboran*'s CC4. *Deng*'s smaller role is in the *kawitan/pengawak* and as the axial tone of transition passages, while *dIng* is eschewed entirely. In the gCC the spare and articulate curve of the music's foundation could not be more apparent.

Jaya Semara

The analyses of *Bangun Anyar* and *Panyembrahma* suggest that Balinese linkage of KPP to the Hindu *tri-angga* ("threeness" of head, body, and legs) and my notion of the gCC as a backbone combine harmoniously to support a conception of the *gending* as organic and "alive." By this reckoning, *Jaya Semara,* no less vital, is evidence of mutation and evolutionary diversification. Signs of the KPP are evanescent and must be mentally exaggerated to make sense; and in the gCC hierarchy is supplanted by saturation. The thrashing and bucking opening minutes in compositions of this type prompted a disheartened McPhee to call *kebyar* "the negation of all that is classical" (1938:56). To view *Jaya Semara* as less than completely realized, however, either because of these seemingly undisciplined discontinuities or owing to its transitional position in the history of *kebyar* composition (just as C. P. E. Bach's *Sonatas* and *Fantasias* were marginalized for so long) is to miss its particular coherence, which is bold and sui generis.

Jaya Semara illuminates a comment Rai once made to me to the effect that one can always hear continuous melody in Beratha's music even when it is not actually there; in other words, despite partial textures and other interruptions. In figure 8.3A, tones in the lowest staff show my understanding of this encoded surface continuity. Circled groupings in this staff are conjoined by lines to demonstrate motivic relations among events heard across and through juxtapositions of texture and elaboration. Solid lines link partial motives that together constitute one grouping and dotted ones link iterations of the same or similar groupings in contrasting realizations. These relations are manifold and it would have overcrowded the transcription to show more, but the motivic pathway thus exposed amply demonstrates the compositional sensibility of which Rai spoke. The many ensemble texture changes are labeled and marked by extended barlines.

The path extends in other directions as well. One way to trace them is to begin with the multiple functions of the opening *kebyar* fragment, the disjunct scale-tone grouping *dEng, dAng, deng, dUng*. In the first place this establishes both *dEng* (as instantly projected to *deng*) and *dUng* as structurally significant—both receive gong stress and are included in the gCC—as well the source of many surface motivic unities. One of these follows directly, binding the ensuing *reyongan* and *kebyar* textures to one another as well as to the opening; another is a diagonal relation to the coup de grace of the ending *kebyar* (8.3B; 3:43), in which the *jegogan* stratum retraces the *deng-dUng* interval as if to suggest a *gending*-level cyclic return. Others are identifiable in between. The *dAng* is not abandoned, however, merely put on hold; for it twice receives gong stress in the second system. Additionally, in the same opening phrase the *dEng-deng* interval instantiates a compound line tracing the structural *dEng-dUng-dAng* contour in the upper octave. Shown in reduction by the black noteheads in the upper staff of 8.13C, it persists on-and-off all the way to the drum solo that separates the *gineman/kebyar* from the *pengecet*.

Stemmed notes in 8.3A's *jegogan* staff become the gCC of 8.13C. Having thus disentangled the compound line, only tones in the lower register are included there. Once *dAng* is established the next member of the gCC-group is *dIng* at 0:34, a port in the storm owing to the 8-beat repetition beginning there (the only repeating unit in 8.3A), and because the pattern used is a prevalent one associated with *gilak* meter that momentarily suggests its familiar presence. *DIng* thus confirmed, the upward progress of the gCC is interrupted to return to *dUng* (0:47) and *dAng* (1:03), and again to *dIng*, with the same repeating quasi-*gilak* (following 1:06). The locally stable arrivals of *dIng* at 0:34 and 1:06 segment the entire *gineman/kebyar* roughly into thirds. The apex of the gCC, however, is *dong*, reached at 1:37 and essentially immobile through the *pengecet*. Beginning after 1:37 a glimmer of slow-tempo *norot* texture fleetingly suggests a *pengawak*, but in a parody of *lelambatan* style the music accelerates directly and dissolves into more new textures: the martial *malpal* and a solo turn for the *calung* and *jegogan*. *Dung* is given play here but soon returns to *dong*. The passage leading to the drum solo at 1:59 has an unexpected, repeating [PtPG] underpinning. It has the affect and structure necessary for formal closure, but the last gong is withheld as if to maroon the music, waiting for the resolution of the *pengecet*.

The gCC comprises an ascending scale from *dEng* to *dong* in which each tone is represented but none exerts pervasive control as did the gong tones of *Bangun Anyar* and *Panyembrahma*. *Dong* persists for considerable time, it is true, but it is conspicuously absent at the beginning, and once it has arrived, background progression halts. A conservatively defined problem of formal analysis for *Jaya Semara* is whether in fact the stable *pengecet* compensates for the tonal and textural restlessness of what precedes it. For if it does not, then the form must be somehow askew, hence flawed. This is not an unreasonable conclusion to weigh, especially in such an experimental genre. In this case it is equally tempting, however, to set aside doctrines of unity and equilibrium to celebrate this concentrated and compact piece for its rough edges and insolence, which in themselves communicate meaningfully about the dynamism of *kebyar*'s early life and times and the daring of those who composed and played it.

Kosalia Arini

Kosalia Arini seems deliberate and rational compared *to Jaya Semara*, as though when composing it Beratha was impelled to strip away some of *kebyar*'s excesses and reconfront the fundamentals. A freshly evident concern for transparency and functional precision is unmistakable, even if its working out is in some ways inchoate and restricted to the basics. Most of the music is modest and foursquare save for the *gineman*, where a long string of asymmetrically phrased fragments is made easy to follow by unchanging *genderan* texture. Thus limited, however, the music can equally be described as whiplike: taut, strict, and demanding, with sharp corners. The lucid construction of each component maps an efficient route through the piece, but the onus is on the performers to build and sustain the intensity that simplicity demands.

Kosalia's *gineman* is more than preparatory; it is, along with the *suling* solo/ *kotekan*, the *variasi kendang*, and the *gambangan*, one of four balanced formal components. The first part of the upper staff of 8.13D shows the *gineman*'s skeletal structure. *DIng* is anchor from the outset as the final tone of a series of fragments, each with the goal of a *jegogan* stress. Arching for a local detour through stresses on *deng* and *dung* (third and fourth systems of 8.4A), the interlocking parts in this passage—an erudite *gender wayang* stylistic topic—

are registrally frozen but internally supple in moving among these tones. The release of elaboration and registral changes for the phrase at 1:14 leads to reinstatement of *DIng* at the first gong stroke, at last conferring closure on what in retrospect coheres as a continuum stretching back to the beginning. Compare this with *Jaya Semara*'s opening, where within seconds three tones receive gong stress. This stability bestows substantive structural importance on the passage, so that it takes several phrases, including the *kebyar* interruption preceding the gong stroke at 1:44, to shift the controlling scale tone to *dAng* and give the recapitulated "stuttering" figure at 1:49 its own stability in this new tonal region. *DAng* nonetheless proves transitory, a preparation for the *dong* tying the final *genderan* phrase to what follows.

This turns out to be a series of five textures—*suling* solo, *kotekan*, *kebyar* interruption, *reyongan*, and *variasi kendang*—that play multiple roles. They advance the form through its first two cyclic oases and leave it poised at the second *peralihan*. They speed up the ensemble textural rhythm, sending the piece lurching through a tour of rudimentary and uninflected orchestral combinations. The *suling* melody is oddly unflorid, the *kotekan* cycle an insistent 4 beats long and extended only through transpositional sequence, the *kebyar* peremptory, and the *reyongan* shorter than comparable passages in other pieces. The *variasi kendang* is so spare that for the initial metacycle even the melody is withheld, and only left-hand unpitched strokes are used in most of the drums' patterns. The primary colors in these block-like passages have an abstract expressionist quality. Tonally their net effect is even more forthright: despite sequential alternation between *dong* and *deng* in the *kotekan*, *dong* as structural tone persists to the *reyongan*. Here at last the gong tone shifts up to *deng* and remains there throughout the *variasi kendang*.

The *gambangan* uses the satisfyingly familiar Balinese rhetoric of a single cycle varied through dynamic and tempo changes, *ocak-ocakan* disruptions, and transposition to a new gong tone.[26] The unorthodox contour here, involving exchange between the primary gong tone *dIng* and the seldom used *dang* is foreshadowed by the section's prefix, the second *peralihan*. In its sweeping line (systems 2–3 of 8.4C and partially quoted in small noteheads on the up-

---

26. The *gambangan*'s repeating components have an interesting interrelationship. Both have the midpoint *deng*, while the first (8.4C, between repeats on the third system) has the gong tone *dIng* and the second (between repeats on the fifth system) has *dang*. For three beats following the midpoint of each the *kotekan* is the same, marking the identical midpoint tones. And for the remaining beats the *kotekan* is also the same though transposed by four scale steps between *dIng* and *dang*, reflecting the two gong tones. In the *ugal* and *neliti*, however, an intriguing difference can be seen. The one is a half-cycle *rotation* of the other, in this case transposed only by two steps, since the midpoint lies exactly that distance from each of the two gong tones. The CC4 of the first of the two, [0,2,2,0], reveals why this is possible. In both inversion and rotation the result is [0,–2,–2,0], the CC4 of the second. This –2/0 interval is further transformed and reflected in the kCC of the midpoint *kotekan* pattern: [–2,–2,–1,0/–2,–2,–1,0].

per staff of 8.13D), there is an inkling of earlier *kebyar*'s abandon. It is some-how alien to this piece, yet hints at what the composer has withheld.

Kosalia Arini partakes of a trio of clichés that were ubiquitous in 1970s and 1980s *tabuh kreasi*. One is the stuttering repeated-note gangsa figure on a structural tone finished with a *jegogan* sustain, heard twice in the *gineman* (8.4A at 0:27 and 1:49), which has a freeze-frame effect. The second is four or more units of the rhythm ♩♩ ♪ applied to an upper or lower neighbor-note figure. Characteristically flanked (as in 8.4B) by contrasting textures, it is, to continue the cinematic analogy, the equivalent of a swish-pan between scenes. Also common was the *nyog cag kotekan* riff leading to the sudden "blackout" of the *variasi kendang* melody (8.4C, beginning 3 beats prior to the rests at the end of the first system). Still larger portions of *Kosalia Arini* are not irrefutably Beratha's but were obviously "in the air" that year, for they appeared elsewhere. Sizable chunks of the *gineman* and almost the entire *gambangan* are literally the same as those of *Jaya Warsa*, a more intricate and less popular work attrib-uted to Gusti Madé Putu Griya and performed by the Geladag group at the same festival. The two pieces are esteemed for different reasons, their shared components no cause for admirers' alarm.

Kosalia's gCC shows the outer sections' primary and secondary allegiances to *dIng* and *dAng* (*dang* in the *gambangan*) respectively, and the inner ones' *dong* to *deng* progression. *Dung* plays no role at this level. Given *dAng/dang*'s lesser function, the piece can credibly be reduced to a stepwise ascent, *dIng-dong-deng*, with a return to *dIng* for the ending, since these three tones are each so clearly isolated in their formal and textural environments. The trajec-tory of the *gineman* line can therefore be said to extend through the following sections and reach a climax at the abrupt, gongless ending of the *variasi ken-dang*. The idea, at this background level, of a single, *incomplete* "cycle" lasting this long is a *gending*-level force of unification, a directional arrow transcend-ing discontinuities and accumulating a musical energy not fully spent until the *gambangan* concludes.

Is *Kosalia Arini* economical or impoverished, sleek or plain? Viewed from the present it is all of these, though by the standards of its day its chief asset was probably novelty. The progenitor of decades of music, it represents the *tabuh kreasi* template itself pared, as Dibia likes to say, to its *bantang* (scaffold-ing). As such it furnishes proof of the idiom's vitality. More than any other product of twentieth-century Balinese music, the *tabuh kreasi* form is truly innovatory, an unprecedented and by now undeniably durable sonic formula. *Kosalia Arini* crystallized this at what turned out to be precisely the right juncture, during the political and cultural resurgence following 1965. Perhaps its clarity spoke encouragingly to Balinese about their circumstances and just what it meant to be coming of age at that time, and as a result innocently triggered a historical process in which Beratha's contribution became a beacon for the work of others.

Conclusion: Form and Composition

The title of this chapter couples form, an essential state of being, and composition, an activity, on the assumption that the former is a result of the latter. It has been a useful and valid but admittedly partial premise. I wish to suggest in conclusion that what I have perhaps accomplished is to give a compositional *perspective* on form, which is hardly the same thing as knowing either of the two independently; that is, if such subjects can actually be known at all without constraining them as I have. It goes without saying that form is manifold and also perceptible in philosophical, numinous, literary, and linguistic ways—the list is extendible—and that possessing the compositional craft I describe is only one, arguably insufficient, prerequisite for embarking on the project of creating new music. Yet if form is ultimately ineffable, what more suitable terrain to glimpse it from than that of the composer's imagination?

Throughout part 2, I have stressed the simultaneous and multidimensional apprehension of dualities (cyclic/linear, symmetrical/asymmetrical, static/kinetic, continuous/discontinuous, stable/active, and conventional/ innovative) as a way of responding to the qualities of form as well as conjuring a trace of the intangibles that composers weigh. Clearly, the intent was not to reduce the music to oppositions, but to let the cumulative force of numerous specialized perspectives hint at a less knowable reality. Indeed "form is not what one should desire to understand; one should know the knower of form."[27] At this late hour it is almost immaterial where the intricacy of these means has brought us, for opening the door to them has led to a room without walls.

---

27. *Kausitaki Upanisad* 3.8, from Hume, *Thirteen Principal Upanishads* (1931:327), quoted in Rowell 1992:225.

Kebyar in Bali and Abroad

3

9 Fantasy on *Wilet Mayura*

Nyoman Rembang (l.) and Wayan Sinti, 1982. Photo: Author.

What we appreciate about *kebyar* is that our whole culture is in there, and we can use it to say whatever we need to say.

Komang Astita, March 1994

All of us are caught in modernity's inescapable momentum. Something similar occurs whenever marginal peoples come into a historical or ethnographic space that has been defined by the Western imagination. "Entering the modern world," their distinct histories quickly vanish.

James Clifford, *The Predicament of Culture*

I consider that music, by its very nature, is essentially powerless to *express* anything at all, whether a feeling, an attitude of mind, a psychological mood, a phenomena of nature, etc . . . *Expression* has never been an inherent property of music. That is by no means the purpose of its existence. If, as is nearly always the case, music appears to express something, this is only an illusion and not a reality. It is simply an additional attribute which, by tacit and inveterate agreement, we have lent it, thrust upon it, as a label, a convention—in short, an aspect which, unconsciously or by force of habit, we have often come to confuse with its essential being.

Igor Stravinsky, *Chronicle of My Life*

THROUGHOUT my study in Bali I sought ways to view *kebyar* and Western music, particularly new music, as interrelated.[1] I perused scores and tapes of chamber and orchestral music at night, imagining connections to the music I was learning daily in the equatorial heat. Unlike McPhee, who during

---

1. An early version of this chapter was read as a paper at the joint AMS/SEM/SMT meeting in Oakland, California, in 1990, and subsequently at several university colloquia.

an interlude in Paris found the sounds of the Western concert hall "torpid and mechanized" (1946:77), and wanted nothing more than to return to Bali and dissolve further into the landscape, I was impelled to work toward an internal reconciliation of the two worlds. In this chapter I try to evoke some of this process, in two stages. The first presents in some detail the 1982 *kebyar* composition *Wilet Mayura*, analyzing its discourse of topics and syntax with an eye toward considering the music's resonance for Balinese audiences. The second stage engages the piece in a dialogue with music of Western composers W. A. Mozart, Charles Ives, and Witold Lutoslawski, and jazz musicians Jaki Byard and George Tucker. In making the bridge to the West I deliberately exclude composers of the post-Debussy lineage with overt connections to *gamelan* (McPhee, Harrison, Reich, Cage, etc.); instead I elect to locate, in these decidedly uninfluenced examples, the fortuitous deployment of procedures such as orchestral stratification and stylistic quotation that are familiar from *kebyar*.[2] This eliminates any question of intentional similarity and enables a comparison alive to the differing impacts of related musical practices.

Setting this course is not an assertion that twentieth-century Balinese and Western composition are comparable in geographical reach, diversity, international impact, or most any other scale of measurement. As much as is possible, however, I shall keep such issues of hegemony and politics separate from the qualitative, essentially private musical experiences of composer and listener. Accordingly I choose different points of departure. The first of these is simply a conviction that composers (indeed all concerned musicians) anywhere may understandably seek affinities with their counterparts elsewhere. In the case of Bali and the West there exists significant common ground by virtue of the fact that composers create detailed and complex music for large ensembles in both contexts. Finally and most explicitly, there is an aesthetic parallel: for most of the century *kebyar* and Western music have shared a stance valorizing innovation alongside reinterpretation of the past.

This is what the West calls modernism, but it would be thoughtless (though hardly unheard of, as Clifford implies above) to draw a non-Western realm like Bali into this conceptual frame. Modernism is not a Balinese category, and to underscore this we need only note the chasm between the characteristic Balinese assessment of new music's purpose, articulated in the epigraph by Astita, and Stravinsky's influential pronouncement. The goal here is also not to depict clashes between Balinese and Western discourses of the modern and the imbalances in power relations they connote (something

---

2. *Gamelan*-influenced Western works by composers who have acknowledged interest in or even learned to perform music of Java and Bali are too easy to pigeonhole. They have been misused by journalists as fodder to sustain orientalist clichés about the nature of *gamelan* music (Holland 1996). In the same breath such works have also been unfairly reduced to the status of dependency on Javanese and Balinese musical ideas for justification, and I do not wish to fan these flames by claiming them as brethren in a book on *gamelan*.

already effectively achieved: see Vickers 1996), but to observe the two value systems imbedded in the materials of their respective new musics, and to show how they result in various kinds of expression and communication. I launch the comparison from *Wilet Mayura*.

Background and Reception

Between April and June of 1982 I attended rehearsals of *Wilet Mayura* at the *balé banjar* of *banjar* Dalem in Angantaka village, a northern suburb of Denpasar. The *sekaha*, called Genta Budaya, was preparing it for the upcoming *Festival Gong*. The piece's primary composer, Wayan Sinti (b. 1942), is a *gamelan* polymath of the SMKI faculty, notably in the realms of pre-*kebyar* and vocal genres, with extensive experience teaching and studying in the United States. The respected musician-scholar Nyoman Rembang (b. 1930) also contributed a crucial passage of *kotekan* in the middle of the piece. Sinti is from Binoh and Rembang from Sesetan Tengah; both are *banjar* located in areas (to the northwest and south of Denpasar respectively) with high concentrations of court and pre-*kebyar* ensembles. *Wilet Mayura* is of the *kebyar* subgenre *gegitaan* (composition with singing): a setting of *kidung* poetry for solo singer, small mixed chorus, and *gong kebyar*. This was a new kind of composition, tried previously only in the 1978 festival. *Wilet Mayura* is in *kreasi lelambatan* form (*gineman* followed by *KPP*), modified with a few additions and interpolations such as Rembang's *kotekan,* which follows the *pengawak. Mayura* is the name of the *kidung* source text, itself a part of the larger *Malat.*[3] Sinti set one *pada* (stanza) of it in the *pengawak,* while the *pengisep* and the *pengecet*-group, of lesser importance for the present chapter, use his own text on national development.

Sinti and Rembang's collaboration grew out of workshops and study sessions they had recently organized at SMKI with teachers of the sacred seven-tone genres *gambang* and *selunding,* both of which once accompanied *kidung* singing. Informed by this practical experience, *Wilet Mayura*'s music blends structural innovation and stylistic reference, conflates linear and cyclical designs, and harmonizes old and new. It was widely held to be a cut above its peers and a summation of sorts, and Genta Budaya took first prize in the festival. While preparing the piece the musicians projected a serene sense of having something special on their hands, and once the air of secrecy surrounding the festival preparations had dissipated I often encountered small groups of them teaching the music to rapt friends at impromptu sessions around Denpasar. With rare nonpartisan generosity Wayan Dibia, who had composed and choreographed for the Singapadu group that lost to Angantaka, said after the performances that "I was moved by *Wilet Mayura.* So much was there: *kebyar,*

---

3. *Wilet,* as in Java, means "variation or elaboration"; *Mayura* means "peacock."

classical beauty, the mood of ceremonies, an encyclopedia of *gamelan* styles, *kidung* singing, and the excitement of new music." Seven years later, when I commissioned a recording of the piece, the session was attended by Wayan Beratha and a roster of other well-known musicians who traveled to *banjar* Dalem, uncharacteristically without a formal invitation, for a chance to hear it again.

My choice to focus on *Wilet Mayura* here rather than on one of the outwardly more adventuresome recent *tabuh kreasi* (by Windha, Asnawa, or their students) is due to its thoughtful integration of the *KPP* form with the full range of new compositional resources available. The composers' learned sensibility gives the music an uncommon and distinguished scope and weight. Its virtually polyphonic, heightened differentiation of strata and wealth of topics suggested a Mahlerian canvas—a deceptively simple use of familiar materials in a new context to revivify an established form.

The inclusion of *gegitaan* in the festival requirements that year was ancillary to a larger revival of poetry and literature underway for over a decade. Voicing these texts had been an important part of cultural life early in the century (recall that *kakawin* recitation was instrumental at the birth of *kebyar*), but between the Japanese occupation and the tragedies of 1965 there was a serious decline. The post-1965 revival of *sekaha pepaosan* (*kakawin* clubs) was managed and generously funded by the government arts council LISTIBIYA, which took license to link oral literature to *Pancasila* by explaining them both as formative of Indonesian culture and character (Rubinstein 1992:109). Otherwise singing with *kebyar* was new territory, but since the founding of national centers for cultural dissemination like the conservatories and radio stations, there had been new Balinese awareness of the prominent role of singing in central Javanese *gamelan* and a desire to experiment with it. Sinti, a self-appointed missionary for older music, was also cognizant of McPhee's research into the virtually extinct tradition of performing *kidung* with sacred *gamelan*, and, like McPhee, bemoaned its loss. With this piece and his *gegitaan Gita Swadita* of 1978, he aimed for a more compositionally integrated synthesis of song and instruments than had been achieved in other twentieth-century genres like *arja*, where the small *gamelan* of *suling* and percussion provides merely a structurally incidental accompaniment to the singing.

Kidung singing is melismatic, unmeasured, and extremely slow-paced. It requires a strong throat vibrato, and careful attention to microtonal melodic and timbral fluctuations.[4] Hence it is most effectively performed solo. Though text fragments are sung informally by groups at rituals, its proper execution is considered a matter for trained specialists. Ultimately this was seen as a hindrance to the government's goal of making participation in the festival an

---

4. Sinti certainly believes that were more known about the connection between *kidung* and seven-tone genres it would become apparent that instrumental tunings evolved from vocal melodic practices.

activity open to as broad a cross-section of the community as possible. Despite *Wilet Mayura*'s enthusiastic reception, *gegitaan* were destined for a brief life span in the competition. In 1984 Governor Mantera mandated replacing them with a newer genre, *sandhya gita* (harmonized, accompanied song), which called for simpler, newly composed melodies to be sung by large mixed choruses drawn from the youth organizations in participating villages. Without departing from *pélog,* the melodies were to include, when possible, harmonizations in parallel lines and overlapping polyphonic entrances in the manner of Indonesian Christian church choirs. But with mostly untrained singers, problems of tuning and intonation—particularly those of blending unison voices and paired *gamelan* tunings—have been left unaddressed.[5]

The Text and Singing

Wilet Mayura's *pengawak* uses *kidung* poetry of a type known as *lelungid,* which combines descriptions of natural beauty with erotic and mystical allusion. (Text and translations for the full *gending* are given in figure 9.1; timings refer to CDII/7.) Like nearly all *kidung* it is composed in Middle Javanese (Kawi) and originated at the sixteenth and seventeenth-century courts. Sinti chose to set it for the primarily musical reasons to be set forth presently, and not for an exercise in word painting (though he told me that its mournfulness appealed to him). The very use of *kidung* was sufficient for him as an emblem of reconnection to older musical and cultural values, which he—like others—felt deserved greater attention in the midst of *kebyar*'s thirst for the new. In selecting this text he also could be confident that listeners would attach personal associations to it. Adrian Vickers, who has explored *kidung*'s intertextuality with theater, painting, and other genres, observes that "listeners combine their experience of the song with their memory of past performances, and locate the small section sung within a narrative known through other types of experiences of the text" (1992:239). *Kidung* songs carry a strong affect of the noble past and the potential to interact with it in the present, through ritual or even in secular contexts such as the *Festival Gong.*

The second text, like many other contemporary texts such as those used in *sandhya gita* compositions, short stories and novels, *drama gong* story lines,

---

5. Matters of intonation and tuning present compositional problems when composing for voice and Balinese *gamelan.* According to Sinti, a soloist works more harmoniously than a chorus with *kebyar* because a single singer can freely and effectively oscillate between the *pengumbang* (lower) and *pengisep* (higher) halves of the paired tuning. Whether or not this can actually be said to occur in practice, it is certainly the case that the complex melismata of *kidung* vocal style enable the melody to wend in and around the fixed tunings and the subdivisions of the beat, rendering precise pitch and temporal alignments both transitory and infrequent. A chorus cannot coordinate on such matters, but Sinti nevertheless opted for one in *Wilet Mayura* to accentuate selected parts of the text and provide antiphonal contrast. The chorus does not strive for sharp coordination, but emulates the relaxed rhythm and staggered entrances of an a cappella group *kidung* performance of the type heard at rituals.

*Pengawak (2:57-6:51)*_____

Om . . .

Tuhanku sangasawang hyang Smara wadu
Mapa marmanta gong wiro sarira wenesakusut
Yaya medapa kalahron
Embeh ayunta sang anom
        Om . . .
        My lady, you are like Goddess *Smara* [Goddess of Love]
        Why is your face scarlet, your body so pale and thin?
        You are like a *gadung* flower in the dry season
        Your beauty is gone, my lady.

*Pengisep (7:55-10:02)*_____

Tiang prayowana,
Truna truni jagat Badung
ngerajegang
jagat guru wisesa
Ngemargiang wewangunan
Kedasarin Pancasila dan
        undang undang dasar empat lima
Lintang luwih mautama (2X)
Ngamolihang tatujone nepituwe
Kerta raharja jagat Indonesia
Pepek antuk sandang pangan dan wisma
Rencanane sami anut
        Young men and women of *[kabupaten]* Badung
        Let us improve our country together with the government
        Carry out development
        Based on *Pancasila* and the ordinances of 1945
        It is glorious, it is noble [2X]
        To achieve our true goal
        An Indonesia safe and prosperous
        Enough necessities for our homes
        All our plans going smoothly

*Pengecet (10:03-11:45)*_____

Nincapang kotaman guru, guru pengajian ring asrama
Mangda sida pikayune ngamolihang tetujone (2X)
ngerajegang karahayuan gumi
Ngiring mangkin sareng sami
Jemetang, telebang, ulati
Jagate kerta raharja
Ngiring mangkin makinkinan
Truna truni sareng sami
Om . . .
        Advancing our education, education at school
        To achieve our goal [2X],
            achieve the ideal of a prosperous nation
        Let us strive together
        Diligent, persevering, with modesty
        For a safe and prosperous country
        Let us begin
        Young people together
        Om . . .

Figure 9.1. *Wilet Mayura* text and translation (CDII/7)

and teleplays, is a Sukarnoist paean to collectivity and nation-building. Written in contemporary high (polite) Balinese, it is at first sung by the soloist in a florid *kidung*-like style, but toward the end presentation is given over to the chorus and the prosody becomes entirely syllabic. The path linking classical poetry in the *pengawak* to a free imitation of the same in the *pengisep* to contemporary choral song in the *pengecet* is reflective of LISTIBIYA-promoted cultural ideology and metaphoric on several other levels as well. For the moment it is sufficient to point out that musical time in it can be seen as iconic with post-Majapahit history, moving diachronically from the perceived former glories of the *negara* to the objectives of Indonesian nationalism.

Despite its *KPP*-based form, *Wilet Mayura* is completely through-composed and contains only one small internal repetition in the *gineman*. None of the *pengecet*-group melodies repeats, itself a fact sufficient to set the piece apart from its contemporaries. The incantation of *om* at the beginning and end encloses the whole in a frame of cosmological time, sanctioning both past and present under the umbrella of religious belief. It also suggests that, in concept, the entirety is a single cycle. Indeed no other *gending* takes the concept of cyclicity quite so far as to follow a completely linear trajectory only to end as it began. Sinti relished this feature of his piece for its economical embrace of both ancient Balinese practice and, paradoxically, cross-cultural influence. "This OM is first for the gods, second for concentration, and third," he said, "to use an idea from outside Balinese music—in this case, from Western music the idea of harmony [i.e., beginning and ending on a tonic], and from Indian music, the drone" (Diamond 1985:8).

But Sinti's central concern was to find a technique by which *kidung* could be introduced into new music. Understanding how he achieved this calls first for a sketch of *kidung* poetry's elusive structures and their relationships to *gamelan*.

Kidung poetic meters belong to a group known by the Javanese term *sekar madya* ("middle" meter; in between the *sekar alit* [small] of *geguritan* poetry and the *sekar ageng* [large, great] of *kakawin*). Wallis explains the basic unit of *sekar madya* as "two double stanzas, one longer than the other. Only the final vowel sound in each half stanza is prescribed. There is no regular internal phrase division" (1979:177). *Rara Kadiri,* an example he discusses (176), is said to contain two parallel stanzas of eighty syllables, each ending with the vowel *a,* followed by two of thirty-three syllables, each ending with *i.* Such definitions turn out to be provisional, though, for various reasons. One is that consecutive stanza-groups within a manuscript may vary in syllable count. Consistency of syllable counts and vowel endings has also proved difficult to find among various *lontar* sources, as even Balinese court scribes who copied the texts conceded (Vickers 1986:81, 354; 1992:226). *Wilet Mayura*'s *kidung* stanza is drawn from the introductory canto (known, like its instrumental counterparts, as the *kawitan*) of the full text and conforms to the meter *ma-yura*.[6] It has forty-four syllables with final vowel *o*. Sinti interprets it as divid-ing into four subphrases of twelve, sixteen, eight, and eight syllables, as may be seen by referring to fig. 9.1.

As for performance, a "correct" manner of voicing *kidung* stanzas is not generally agreed upon. There is a melody associated with the texts that repeats from stanza to stanza, but singers have broad freedom to extend syllables, elaborate the basic contour, and inflect the pitches. They may opt to stress this or that syllable, word, clause, or subphrase. Regional and individual styles of vocalizing the texts are profuse, a variety in part inculcated by the fact that the poems and melodies are learned by rote from older practitioners, who usually do not verbalize about them. For scholars a challenge has been to relate sing-ing practice to performance context to text sources in a consistent way. (Figure 9.3B's transcription of soloist Ketut Suryatini singing with the Angantaka *ga-melan* makes only minimal attempt to render her abundant glissandi, shakes, and microtonal bendings of five-tone *pélog*. Including them would raise more technical and stylistic issues than space permits considering.)

Since McPhee's lament of the 1930s, Balinese investigators like Rembang and Sinti as well as foreigners Schlager, Wallis, Schaareman, Vickers, and Hinzler have tried to reconstruct the vocal/instrumental relationship that once thrived between *kidung* and the sacred seven-tone ensembles *luang, gambang, caruk,* and *selunding.* One way has been to examine the shorthand notation (*grantangan*) of solfège vowels inscribed in the *lontar* below syllables in the poetry, which seem at one time to have functioned either as a kind of *gamelan* "lead sheet," or, conversely, as a reminder to the singers of the instrumental melody they needed to follow. There is some (albeit scattered and inconsis-tent) correspondence between the vowels used in the poetry itself and the accompaniment's solfège vowels.[7] Wallis found that with some exceptions "only at the beginnings of stanzas and near the ends do any *kidung* poems . . . seem to obey this type of patterning" (1979:200), and Vickers adds that "the relationship between the sung verses and the accompanying music is a very flexible one, which can be imagined as two different contours going off on their own patterns and coming together at key vowel points" (1986:86).

Sinti sought a creative use for his beloved poetic songs, not a definitive answer to these riddles. But he also had a scholarly curiosity about their rela-tion to *gamelan*. The ideas had been simmering for years:

> I learned *kidung* poetry and singing when I was young from Pekak [grandfather, old man] Kelamu in Wangaya [north of Denpasar]. I didn't know enough then to

---

6. In this case the poem and its meter have the same name, but there is other poetry also using *mayura* metrics.

7. It may well be that the solfège naming system has this specific linguistic origin.

ask questions about the poems and the melodies. All that my *guru* told me about *Mayura* was that it could be sung at weddings! As an adult I studied *gamelan gambang* in Sempidi and on my own noticed correspondences between the melody of *kidung mayura* that I had learned when I was young and the *gending gambang* called *Manukaba*. I had no *lontar* that explicitly linked the two and the linkages weren't perfect, but I was struck by them. I puzzled over these connections for a long time and this ultimately led to composing the *gegitaan*. (Personal communication, March 1994)

Among the challenges facing Sinti were to work out the relationships between *Mayura* and *Manukaba,* to compose an appropriate cyclic vessel for the *kidung* poetic meter, and to make the free-floating *kidung* melody and rhythm conform credibly to the melodic conventions of a gong cycle. Simply orchestrating the *kidung* or *Manukaba* melody would have been decidedly unidiomatic and ill-suited to *kebyar*'s eclectic 1980s vernacular. Yet many of the decisions to be made were actually predetermined, for to achieve his expressive ends Sinti could hardly have considered doing without some sort of *KPP* form, the only framework both immediately comprehensible to the audience and suitably prestigious for the poetry. The amalgam of the *kidung* and *Manukaba* melodies thus yielded, through Sinti's imagination, an entirely distinct *lelambatan* melody that aligns with one or both of them at key points but has its own integral structure, in this case based closely on *tabuh telu pegambuhan* meter (fig. 7.1A.7). The *Manukaba* melody is actually present only as a kind of phantom, anchoring the *kidung* melody to the *gamelan*'s.

The nature of this combination as well as Sinti's and Rembang's choices for the material to precede, succeed, and coincide with it are the focus of the analysis to follow. The gist of the argument is that *Wilet Mayura*'s particular modernity results from its artful distortion of traditional forms and near-saturation with topical allusions to changing historical and cultural contexts. But *kebyar*'s emphasis of form over content, rooted in music's role as a cultural emblem, sets important constraints on how far the distortions can go and how the stylistic allusions are used. This has consequences for musical meaning, and is the point from which the comparison to the West can begin to unfold.

Locating Innovation and Expression

Though no two are precisely alike, *KPP* forms are indeed sacrosanct. In *Wilet Mayura*'s case, injecting the numinous *kidung* catalyzes a different sort of malleability that a Balinese listener comfortable with *KPP*'s conventions would not perceive as disorienting or inappropriate, but as leading to intensified expression. The form is recognizable but distorted, and layers of the texture coalesce into a thick stream of multiple concurrent topical references.

From a Balinese perspective this constitutes worthwhile enrichment of the

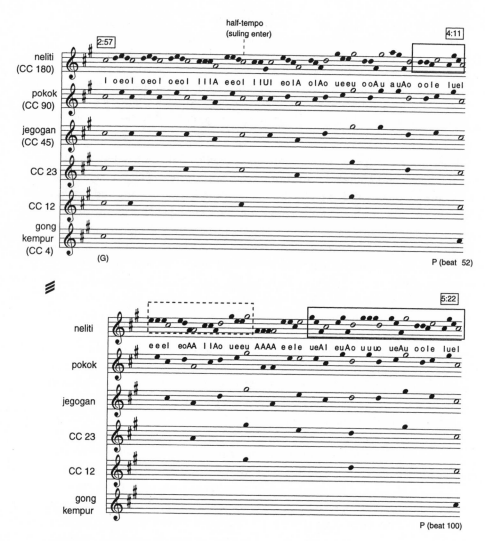

Figure 9.2. *Wilet Mayura pengawak* strata (CDII/7, 2:57-6:51)

language and acceptable innovation because the agreed-upon identities of the music's syntactic and referential signs are unchallenged. Seen from the West, the same distortions seem modest and the possibilities restricted, which raises the question of limits. What defines the limits binding Balinese composers to their own and their audience's expectations? What is the point beyond which they are unlikely to stretch? If Western composers operate with dissimilar premises, how does the dissolution of limits alter expectation and understanding? *Wilet Mayura*'s particular structure affords insight into these fundamentally social issues. The analysis considers first the *pengawak*, via reduction of the *neliti* melody (fig. 9.2, using the kinds of reductions shown in fig. 6.3);

second, the relationship between the *kidung* melody, the *gambang Manukaba* melody, and the *jegogan* stratum (fig. 9.4); and third, the location and significance of the topics used (fig. 9.5). Figure 9.3A-C comprises a full score of the piece to 7:46, the end of the *kotekan* interlude.

The *Pengawak* Melody

In the *pengawak*'s modified *tabuh telu pegambuhan* cycle, the conventional four *palet* of 64 beats each are altered asymmetrically to 52, 48, 48, and 32 beats respectively, a total of 180. Because of the heavier sound of *kebyar*, Sinti substitutes *kempur* for *gambuh*'s *kajar neruktuk* at the end of each of the first

Figure 9.3A. *Wilet Mayura gineman* and *kawitan* (CDII/7, 0:00-2:57).

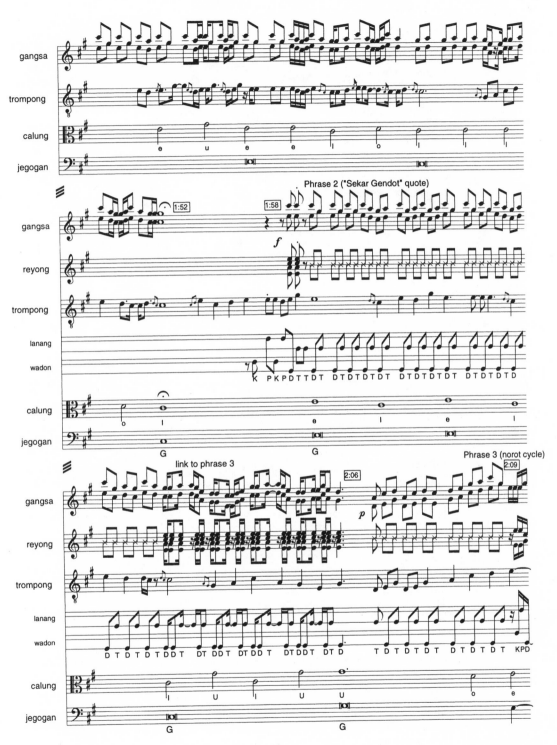

(*continued*)

Figure 9.3A. (*continued*)

three *palet,* and gong supplants what would have been a final *kempur.* Other than being compressed, the two central *palet* behave conventionally. Of the outer *palet,* the extended initial one commences with a full ensemble unison passage, moves to a reduced texture featuring the vocal soloist and the *trompong,* and finally settles into a slow tempo and soft dynamic (at beat 20 via a quasi-Javanese density shift) with the crowded texture that continues for the

remainder of the cycle. The shortened final *palet* telescopes an acceleration and crescendo to the gong. Ordinary *tabuh telu pegambuhan* drumming is stretched and edited where necessary to fit into this altered container. Merely reconfiguring the size of this staid and abstract classical meter involved considerable internal deliberation for Sinti, "but," he stressed, "the feeling of the text demanded changes in the music."

Figure 9.3B. *Wilet Mayura pengawak* (CDII/7, 2:57-6:51).

(continued)

Figure 9.3B. (*continued*)

(continued)

Figure 9.3B. (*continued*)

Getting at this innovatory feeling and Sinti's response to it requires perceiving astute and subtly applied compositional touches. The bottom stave of
figure 9.2 reveals that *dIng* is the final tone of each *palet,* giving a CC4 of
{0,0,0,0}. Such utter background stasis intensifies the mood of abstraction to
a point where the melodic quality of the cycle as a whole is like no other in the
repertoire. At the surface, however, *neliti* shape both counteracts and reinforces the stasis. It counteracts because its engaging motives and consistent
high rate of scale-tone turnover and registral change keep the melody in constant motion; it reinforces because each *kempur* stroke is approached identically, even though overall each *palet* is different. The solid-border boxes in
the *neliti* staff of 9.2 show that the unchanging passage stretches backward for
8 beats from first *palet*'s *kempur* but is greatly extended in the other three. The
dotted-border boxes show additional recurring elements; all of the foregoing
are transcribed in full at corresponding places in the *gangsa, reyong,* and *trompong* staves of 9.3B. What is noteworthy is that the conventional ebb and flow
of stasis and motion, symmetry and asymmetry in cyclic meters is undermined
by the top-down compositional process of motivic development and varied
repetition.

Figure 9.3C. C. *Wilet Mayura kotekan* (CDII/7, 6:52-7:46; CDII/8).

(continued)

Figure 9.3C. (*continued*)

The *Kidung/Gambang/Kebyar* Interface

The *pengawak* melody's unconventional shape is due to the different kind of order imposed by the *kidung* and implicit *gambang Manukaba* melodies. In our conversations Sinti sang first the *kidung* in a familiar *kebyar*-style five-tone *pélog*, and then the *Manukaba* with its strict 5 + 3 syncopation and entirely different *gambang*-type *pélog* intervallic structure. But since he himself did not know precisely how they mapped onto one another I was left to probe beyond the general similarity in contour that he remarked on. Figure 9.4 graphs some of the correspondences, which I admit are often speculative, using the skeletal *kidung* tones (those receiving agogic stress: refer to 9.3B), *Manukaba* (which I have "transposed" to *kebyar* tuning), and *Wilet Mayura*'s *jegogan* tones.[8] I have

---

8. The lack of correspondence between vowel sounds in the *kidung* poetry and the *kebyar* ding-dong-deng-dung-dang system is not a problem here, for the *gamelan gambang* uses a different sequence of vowels in its solfège and one would have to examine that set of mappings.

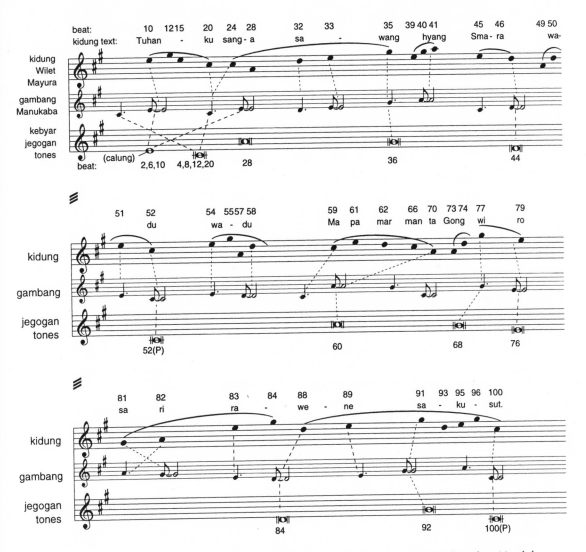

Figure 9.4. First 2 Palet/100 beats of *Wilet Mayura kidung* (skeletal) and *jegogan* strata aligned with *gambang Manukaba* melody

had to bend time a little, allowing connections between disparate trios such as the *jegogan* at beat 60, the *gambang* tone that appears to align with it, and the sung syllable *ta* ten beats later. Others are more straightforward, like the cadences to *dIng* at *palet* endings or the opening *deng-dIng* interval. At the same time I was unable to avoid interspersing clashes throughout. But while the various relationships probably cannot be deciphered definitively, it is clear that their ambiguity informs *Wilet Mayura* beneficially. In preserving the free-floating *kidung* performance style for the *pengawak* Sinti generated a polyphonic tension resulting from the *kidung*'s complex temporal displacement from the other parts, the framework of a foreign cyclic structure, and the conceptual difficulty of composing-out a *kebyar* melody with only the fuzzy *kidung-gambang* parallelisms as a basis. The result is interesting, as is imagining Sinti's internal dialogue while he tried to bring about the melodies' rapprochement.

Topics and Narrative

In the serene world of *lelambatan pengawak* the net effect of these changes in syntax seems anything but sensational; instead they are considered, deliberate, and refined, comprising the repositioning of elements in an existing universe rather than an attempt to break free. In a compatible way, the layers of stylistic topic coursing along with this mixture all refer to sacred repertoires, both of the post-Majapahit courts and earlier, in a simultaneous, vertical embodiment of *kebyar*'s hallmark reconciliation of musical pasts. The *gambuh* drumming, in 1982 still a novel incongruity in *kebyar,* provides one such focal point, with its easily identifiable subpatterns (such as the [T/.T. ./T. .(P)] cadence at the end of each *palet*) and alternating simple and complex rhythms. The *gangsa* and *reyong* figuration provide another by playing in *luangan* style (fig. 6.6D), with its particular contours and syncopations. Ordinarily in such a context one would expect the standard interlocking patterns of court-derived repertoire such as *norot* or members of the symmetrical *ubit-ubitan* collection (figs. 6.13 and 6.14). The *trompong* carries the lead melody as it would in *gamelan gong gdé* or *semar pegulingan.* The vocal line, a topic in its own right, has the most hallowed connotation of all. This totals four strands, each evoking a different aspect of historical awareness and religious experience, and all aptly placed in the segment of the composition that triggers an expectation for sacred music in the audience.

Synchronic and stable in the *pengawak, Wilet Mayura*'s progression of topics extends into what comes before and after, coalescing into a narrative spanning the whole. In the *gineman/kawitan* portion (9.3A), after the introductory *om,* the story opens in the present with a pair of sudden and succinct, but quickly dwindling phrases identically decimated by the crashing "surprise" (as Sinti put it, flinging open two closed fists) of a single *byar* chord (0:29, 1:15). Having dispensed the *byar* as a bow to convention, Sinti composes the *trompong* melody that remains after the dust has settled to lead elegantly to a series of four phrases. These are at once more structurally and topically focused than those in comparable *gineman.* The first two, slow and fast (1:32, 1:57), use a quotation adapted from Wayan Lotring's *gamelan pelegongan* instrumental composition *Sekar Gendot.*[9] Sinti acknowledges this

---

9. Named after, but structually only a cousin to the *gamelan gender wayang* composition of the same name mentioned in chapter 5 as a popular source for quotation topics.

homage and feels a profound artistic debt to Lotring, for in the 1920s Lotring taught in his *banjar* and composed a repertoire that has been maintained up to the present, and which Sinti grew up performing.[10] The repeating third phrase (2:09, 2:16), in *norot* texture at *pengecet*-like tempo, emerges directly out of an *ocak-ocakan* link from the second. It constitutes the major "arrival" area of the *gineman* because the music settles here for the only time into a cyclic meter, before continuing slightly beyond it to cadence (2:25). Last comes the *kawitan* itself (2:36), orchestrated precisely like the *pengawak*, minus the singing.

Each of the four phrases (labeled phrases 1–3 and *kawitan* in 9.3A) is distinguished from the others by its configuration of element-progressions structural rhythm, cyclic repetition, texture, tempo, and dynamic; what unites them is a common background melodic trajectory beginning on *deng* and falling two scale steps to *dIng*. This shared fulcrum balances and rationalizes the gradual unfolding of Sinti's erudite structural plan, which coaxes the listener by stages from the arresting opening gestures to the *pengawak*'s austerity. It is as if the music travels backward in historical time by reinterpreting a simple melodic pathway at each stage of the journey.

Subsequent to the *pengawak*, Rembang's exuberant *kotekan* (6:52–7:46)[11] reverses the direction of travel in preparation for the secular verses to follow, which are set in a mixture of *pelegongan* and *kebyar* styles analogous to that of the opening. The background structure of the *kotekan* is simple, comprising a unison introduction followed by a series of paired 8-beat phrases, interrupted only once by an extra half-beat during a brief unison segment in the second half (7:26). But the very intrusion of the entire passage (smoothly interwoven as it is) into the center of the KPP form is the most overt disjuncture of the piece. At the time of its composition this *kotekan* was of cutting-edge intricacy, length (surpassed in the years since), and eclecticism for *kebyar*, notably in its close juxtaposition of models based on the three asymmetrical source genres *gandrung*, *gender wayang*, and *gambang*. In figure 9.3C these are identified where they occur; of the three the first two are pre-Majapahit in historical association and the last is a bridge between court and secular arts (see also figs. 6.16, 6.17, and 6.19 for discussion of the styles in their source contexts). One pairing that extends for a good portion of the interlude is the alignment of the 5 + 3 *gambang* rhythm in the *jegogan* with *gangsa* figuration modeled on *gandrung*. The effect is similar to the vertical combination of topics in the *pengawak*, but is more jarring and emphatic in this context. These features demarcate the sacred/secular juncture in two ways: in the temporal plane, because the *kotekan* splits the KPP form by intervening between the two text settings;

For this segment Sinti also mentions the stylistic influence of the *gamelan angklung*, referring to the four-tone ambitus (*dIng, dong, deng, dung*) that applies to most of the two phrases.

10. A recording of the Lotring repertoire from Sinti's *banjar* (Binoh), including *Sekar Gendot*, is available on King Records CD KICC 5155, *Gamelan Semar Pegulingan of Binoh Village*.

11. In CDII/8 this passage, fig. 9.3C, is isolated and played thrice at slower tempo.

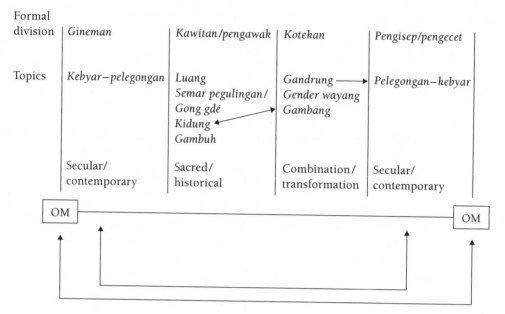

Figure 9.5. Narrative of topics in *Wilet Mayura*

and on the vertical, orchestral stratification axis, because the sacred associations of the bass line are used to underpin the secular disposition of the interlocking figuration.

The *pengisep* (7:55) and the *pengecet* group set the second text to a series of melodies that regularly contract in length as they quicken in pulse. The first of the two *pengecet* (10:02) is closely modeled on counterparts in the *legong* dance repertoire (compare its phrasing to *pengecet Lasem*, CDI/20), while the second (10:45), also the closing melody, returns finally to a *kebyar* affect. Figure 9.5 graphs the topic and formal plan for the entire piece, showing as well the "round-trip" narrative progression plotted by the nine different genres evoked.

Topics in *Wilet Mayura* are integrated with form, acting to modify it. As Agawu stresses,

> Even those listeners who are sympathetic to the referential implications of topical material will agree that the individual gestures derive their importance less from their paradigmatic or associative properties than from their syntagmatic or temporal ones. In other words, it is [a matter of] . . . how their conjunction is logically executed in [the] movement. For [it is] the relationship between phenomena [that] determines their nature, not any intrinsic aspect of the phenomena themselves. (1987:37)

In Sinti and Rembang's music the references are likewise significant not for simply appearing but for their grounding in melodic details, orchestral stratification, the *KPP* structure, and the small and circumscribed but expressively potent innovations applied to all of these by the composers.

Balinese and Western Temporalities in Context

Wilet Mayura's diverse topics make the music inimitably contemporary for the Balinese by exploiting the audience's ability to identify the references and draw connections between genres that are ordinarily distinct. Its effectiveness lies with its success in organizing these connections in a way that is technically sophisticated and aesthetically pleasing, and, especially, through its narrative presentation of the current intermingling of sacred and secular worlds.

Both the historical chronology suggested by the text and the path between sacred and secular traced by the topics symbolically depict Balinese cultural self-image. Additional, spatial dimensions can be grafted onto these programs with the inclusion of other identifiable Balinese metaphorical journeys from sacred to secular places. Like the "intermediary" region suggested by 9.3C's *kotekan*, these often progress via interim zones ideally suited for human activity. One is the direction from the holy inland mountains to the menacing spiritual disorder of the surrounding ocean, in which the densely populated "neutral" lowlands lying in between are designated uniquely suitable for human activity. Another is the centrifugal action of going from the inner to peripheral courtyards of a temple, and beyond them to the village graveyard. Balinese are famously and acutely aware of the *kaja/kelod* (mountainward/ seaward) axis (and its complement 90° clockwise, *kangin/kauh*), and use these directionals to signify all aspects of orientation in physical space. People routinely describe movement ranging from that between villages to that between *gangsa* keys not to the left or right but in terms of these axes.[12] Continuing similarly, we quickly accumulate a bundle of compatible metaphors, all reflective of the traditional iconicity of macro- and microcosmos and very much in current use in Bali.

A search for musical meanings must naturally take this marvelously homogenous set of epistemologies into account without necessarily stopping there, just as Balinists in other disciplines have sought the suppressed histories and overlooked viewpoints drowned out by such irresistible demonstrations of "official" cultural coherence (Picard 1990, Robinson 1995). But one looks in vain for anything going against the grain in *Wilet Mayura*, for the music's culturally based rhetoric is so closely fused to its structure.[13] It fits the estab-

---

12. See further Belo 1970:90–93.

13. External to the music itself, "going against the grain" may not appear as such; changes in social behavior related to music gradually reconcile with general social attitudes. Suryatini, the singer on the recording, was one of the first women to graduate, in 1979, with a music degree from STSI. Performing with Genta Budaya as a singer was novel but not extraordinary in 1982, but in subsequent years she composed new works (*Irama Hidup*, 1983), taught and performed with all-female *sekaha* (from 1985

lished pattern perfectly. With the exception of the *kidung,* all of the topics are woven into the warp and weft of cyclic syntax and stratified instrument functions. Even the plan for integrating the *kidung* ultimately amounts to a way of forcing it into this grid, too. At no point is there irony or a suggestion that these precepts could conceivably be violated. To undo the tight fabric would be to relinquish control and render the music culturally incoherent, for Balinese composers a radical notion. This conservative side of contemporary music, tinged with current politics, contrasts with the revolutionary swagger of pieces like *Jaya Semara* from *kebyar*'s early years.

Inevitably these considerations take us back once more to the characters of Balinese cyclic and linear time—the former standing for continuity, the latter its opposite. The inference stressed now is that continuity refers not only to music but to culture. At *gending*-level, the expectation-generating conditions permitting cyclic repetition in *Wilet Mayura* remain even though repetition itself is denied. There is no precedent for imagining that the KPP will be challenged any more than this. Vertical relations and stratification remain intact. Their limits of extendibility, while never tested, are clear. Despite the music's innovatory touches and through-composed trajectory its temporality remains cyclic, its message decodable, its comprehensibility and relevance secure. Though this is an unusually rich example, every year the *Festival Gong* sends similar messages to its constituency, even as the small innovations wrought in each new piece sustain *kebyar*'s overall pace of change and development. Put simply, the relationship between temporality and context in *kebyar* is that cyclic time and orchestral stratification promote a shared sense of cultural uniformity and permanence.

Temporality is both a facet of cultural knowledge that composers bring to bear when composing as well as a way of knowing time and experience through musical performance and appreciation. It is a phenomenon that composers objectively create through their application of compositional techniques (colotomic meters, for example, or harmonic progressions), and also a subjective experience shaped by the listening environment and the mood and perceptual predilections of the listener. What unites these and provides the conduit for communication is composers' and listeners' shared background and expectations.[14]

Writers on Western temporality use the word "linear" with a meaning that differs from my application of it as discontinuous, or the opposite of cyclical. For many observers, Western music's normative temporality is the linearity

---

onward), and in 1997 was one of five female performing members of a mixed-gender *sekaha* that toured Canada and the United States, and the only one playing in the *gangsa* section (the others played simpler *calung* and *jegogan* parts). Strictly speaking, however, there is nothing subversive about her roles so long as they are acceptable to others, which they now very much are.

14. Kramer writes further about the notion of expectation (see the succeeding paragraphs), and the standard work on the subject is Meyer 1956.

best exemplified by and most deeply rooted in music of the tonal common-practice. To Jonathan Kramer, leading theorist of these issues, the "golden age" of tonal linearity "coincides with the height of linear thinking in Western culture" (1988:23), which encompasses humanism, Newtonian physics, Adam Smith, Darwinism, and the rest, spanning nearly a half millennium prior to World War I (an era coterminous with the Majapahit-influenced epoch during which the norms of Balinese temporal cyclicity were enshrined). He defines linearity in Western music as "the temporal continuum created by a succession of events in which earlier events imply later ones and later ones are consequences of earlier ones." Against this he posits that *nonlinearity* "results from principles permanently governing a section or piece" (20). He is careful to stress that these definitions are but rough guidelines, and that most any piece of music involves the interpenetration of the two conditions. It is nonetheless instructive to accept his definitions at face value for the moment—not to critique him, but to underscore how fragile concepts of temporality are in the face of the richness of musical experience.

At first blush Kramer's linearity seems the negative/complement to Balinese cyclicity (and indeed it is to him, for he goes on to characterize Balinese music as nonlinear [24]).[15] Kramer's linearity is a powerful concept for hearings of tonal music in which events follow a dramatic curve that ends up on a predictable harmony, but, at least at the middle and surface levels of structure, by unpredictable means. By contrast, all strata in a Balinese cycle move dependably toward gong according to predetermined metrical units and the special constraints of vertical relations.

Yet experiencing the opposite is quite possible. By relying on the normative unit of the four-bar phrase with its characteristic harmonic underpinnings, much common-practice tonality—at least of the classic era—can be heard as if cyclically, its smaller metric units expanding into larger hypermetric groups exhibiting large-scale regularity, the dramatic instabilities but a diversion from the drive to the tonic. In a Balinese cycle, on the other hand, the working-out of symmetries and the placement of *angsel* and other discontinuities is the realm of perception to which the skilled listener will be drawn, wherein the dependable metric structure allows for maximal play among changing patterns and tonal qualities. Such perceptions can be even stronger when one accounts for the growing prominence of noncyclic and fragmentary elements in *kebyar*. I do not understand *kebyar* as a linear experience in the same way that I or Kramer would understand Beethoven's Opus 132, but I will hold that it is *not* a *nonlinear* one. Regardless of how one in fact hears it, it is fair to state that

---

15. Kramer reaches his conclusions about *gamelan* by drawing on McPhee's (1970c:311) somewhat orientalist descriptions of "stasis" and "lack of climax" in the music. Kramer later opines that "the dramatic curve is peculiar to Western art. It is not a universal of mankind, as much Eastern music readily demonstrates" (1988:217).

like Balinese cyclicity, tonal linearity reinforces the values of those conditioned to the culture that engendered it.

(Always caught among these changeable modes of perception, after decades of listening to both Balinese *gamelan* and tonal music I cannot concede any fundamental opposition between their temporalities. Although this can never be more than a debate over impressions, one's perspective is shaped by how one listens; those better attuned to one or the other music will succumb to the tendency to categorize the unfamiliar as static and the known as temporally dynamic.[16] I digress, but shall apply these thoughts to the analyses later in the chapter.)

Moving into the sphere of twentieth-century music, one-to-one comparisons among styles or genres such as the foregoing become difficult to circumscribe, because Western stylistic pluralism has generated multiple temporalities (nonlinear, vertical, moment, and others, in Kramer's terminologies) reflecting multiple meanings, cultural identities, and experiences. Since serial composition's influence waned in the 1970s, most observers no longer trace the origin of Western musical modernity to Schoenberg's abandonment of tonality and formulation of the twelve-tone system. The revisionist view of his venture is that it was a failed attempt to sustain tonal-style linearity as a predominant music/cultural feature. Instead the roots of modernity are now seen as marked by Debussy's watershed exposure to the Javanese musicians and dancers at the 1889 Paris Universal Exposition. Though far from the first encounter of its kind, his articulate response to the experience has come to stand for the genesis of stylistic freedom and the realization that musical language is not an inevitability but a choice. Over a century later, it appears that lack of a common syntax, cross-cultural interaction, and temporal multiplicity are the preeminent features of post-tonal music.

Since this variety reflects a shattering of the notion of Western cultural coherence, no comparison of a twentieth-century Western work with *Wilet Mayura* can generate results applicable to anything more than a fictitious "West." (And *Wilet Mayura*—allowed to stand for a unified Balinese perspective in the foregoing—represents not an actual Bali but a particular, albeit widely shared, construction of it.) A given Western work may reflect broad currents of experience or thought, but can only be seen as reflective of a "Western" culture when combined with other, different works and seen in conjunction with them. Indeed Western temporality and musical structure are now so open as to be hospitable to anything. In the process of absorption newly

---

16. Most of my Balinese friends were inexperienced with eighteenth- and nineteenth-century Western art music, and when I played it for them their reactions were only faintly approving. Upon further probing most admitted hearing it as muddled and directionless. McPhee got the same response (1946:45). Ironically, my teacher Tembres's rejoinder to Steve Reich's *Drumming* (1971), which has much to do with its composer's perceptions of stasis in African and Balinese music, was to ask with disdain why it never seemed to *go* anywhere.

assimilated elements relinquish whatever more restricted meanings they may have had in their earlier incarnations and assume new roles as components of an omnivorous, all-inclusive cultural project. Hence the anonymity of modernism intimated by Clifford in the epigraph.[17] Stravinsky's words, positioned there as a response, indicate an extreme and characteristic consequence: a situation in which music is a blank slate on which individuals write their own meanings.

Approaching a twentieth-century Western work one must presume an open temporality that could move in any number of directions simultaneously and is incapable of shielding the meanings of its materials from transformation. Recontextualized, they will always be understood as a step removed from their former meanings by the time the piece ends. For Balinese compositions like *Wilet Mayura* the materials are similarly borrowed and remade—indeed this process has been at the center of my interpretation of *kebyar* throughout—but the temporality remains a bounded system. Rewarded by audience acceptance and unwilling to abandon the *lingua franca,* Balinese composers know that forsaking cyclicity would overstep the agreed-upon limits to that most fundamental of human sensibilities—the experience of time—and bring them unwanted, excessive freedom.

Focusing on musical specifics tends to blur rather than reinforce such distinctions. The ensuing brief comparisons between *Wilet Mayura* and envoys from jazz and Western music complement and illustrate this discussion, but rather than iterate the starkness of the contrasts made above, they reveal how delicate and paradoxical they can be in light of particular situations. Instead of straining for conclusions, my hope is to create optimal conditions for these musics to enjoy their newfound companionship and illuminate one another.

Wilet Mayura in Cross-Cultural Perspective

In bringing together this assortment, I rein in the discussion's potentially limitless directions and outcomes by keeping *Wilet Mayura* as a common denominator and staying close to the issues raised in its analysis. It must be stressed that the majority of the connections I propose are conceptual or structural and not based on literal similarities in actual sound or surface design. These would tend to concretize the discussion in stylistic terms whereas I am interested in the more abstract parameter of compositional sensibility. The first comparison, with a Mozart string quartet, investigates the juncture of topic, form, and syntax. The second, with a blues composition by Jaki Byard

---

17. Clifford continues on from the epigraph quotation to promise a "different historical vision" for his book in which "distinct ways of life once destined to merge into 'the modern world' reasserted their difference in novel ways" (1988:5–6). Thus even though the excerpt I chose does not encapsulate his concerns, it nonetheless contains an important truth that aids in understanding the process of cultural absorption in Western music.

and George Tucker, examines quotation, cyclicity, and meaning. The third, with the opening moments of Lutoslawski's Third Symphony, looks at the interweaving of stratification and structure; and the last, with the first movement of Ives's Fourth Symphony, considers how multiple textures, temporalities, and references coexist.

The ordering of the comparisons situates the pieces along two continua, with *Wilet Mayura* at a different end of each. The first of these traces a path from limits to freedom in musical language. Mozart and Sinti sit together at one extreme, united in their restrictive allegiance to a unifying common practice; Ives, with his multiple syntaxes and all-inclusive openness, is at the remote end. Byard/Tucker and Lutoslawski, strange bedfellows, form a middle region in their contrasting blends of improvisation and preset structure. The other continuum has to do with strata and texture. In this regard there is a striking visceral similarity between the Ives movement and the *pengawak* of *Wilet Mayura,* each with its many layers and integration of the singing voice. Progressing by decreasing ensemble size and textural variety leads back to Mozart, for his quartet occupies the narrowest and most timbrally focused band of acoustical space. Still and all, the character of the comparisons is consistent with the chapter title, and should be understood that way.

Mozart: String Quartet in A Major, K. 464

Mozart String Quartet in A Major, K. 464, First movement, measures 1–36; fig. 9.6 (with Wilet Mayura, *last three phrases of* gineman *and transition to* kawitan *[fig. 9.3A, 1:32–2:36]).*

Analogies between Western classic music and *kebyar* have been a presence in these pages since chapter 4, so it is worthwhile in the current context to introduce a representative classic work before proceeding to music of the twentieth century. The conventions of *Wilet Mayura's KPP* and the sonata allegro form in the quartet accommodate similarities of thought that are considered here, though it would also be of interest to explore other features such as quality of motion or the construction of cadences.

The distinct textures and characteristically succinct periods in the first theme-group of Mozart's exposition suggest several points of affinity with the series of noncyclic continuous phrases in *Wilet Mayura* at the end of figure 9.3A (referred to and labeled, as for the earlier analysis, as phrases 1–3 and *kawitan*). The quartet's opening theme is a sixteen-bar period in which the initial balanced pair of four-bar units presents the basic melodic idea first with tonic, then dominant harmony. The subsequent pair provides appropriate symmetrical balance, melodic and registral change, and harmonic completion; they abandon the opening melody's details but retain its characteristic upbeat phrasing. Following the perfect authentic cadence at measure 16 there is a switch to the parallel minor which initiates the modulatory transition to the second theme. This is coordinated with the transformation of the first theme's lyric *singing style* topic into an austere fugato in *learned style,* and subsequently to a bucolic *musette* with pedal point (at measure 25, now in the relative major of the tonic minor). The *musette* marks the end of the fugato and abandonment of the basic melody; its cadential function is clarified when the C-major harmony is transformed into an augmented sixth chord (measure 32) that prepares for the full stop on V[V] at measure 36.

In sum, the quartet's thematic continuity is coupled with discontinuities in topic, textural density, and range; even the unifying basic melody is dropped when approaching cadences. Sinti also applies changes of texture, mood, and color to a common melodic element, and makes similar departures from it. I noted earlier how the final three phrases of the *gineman* and the *kawitan* each rest on a melodic curve that begins at *deng* and ultimately descends to a cadence at *dIng;* this may be imagined as congruent to Mozart's application of the first theme's melody in the transition. In *Wilet Mayura* the transformation takes place through the *deng-dIng*'s varied composing-out in the upper strata and through changes in tempo, dynamic, and ensemble texture; in the Mozart the transformation is a matter of changing mode, harmony, and texture. As at measure 9 or the *musette,* Sinti abandons the *deng/dIng* focus to strengthen an upcoming cadence, for example at the detour through a gong on *dUng* during the link to phrase 3 (2:06).

There are further correspondences in the way texture and topic are manipulated. In both pieces these two elements transform in synchrony following cadences, and are thus both entwined with syntax. Like the genteel and balanced opening theme of the Mozart, the three 8-beat subphrases of the first *Sekar Gendot* quotation (1:32) are sweetly rendered, parallel in construction, and lead to a clear cadence (on *dIng*). Embarking on the second quotation there is a pronounced intensification of mood and texture, as in measures 16–17 of the quartet. Another example, comparable to the same moment in the Mozart, can be heard during the passage connecting the end of phrase 3 to the *kawitan,* where the *kebyar* and *pelegongan* styles give way to the weightier, multiple flow of sacred topics in the *kawitan* (identical to those in the *pengawak*). Mozart likewise uses the formal cornerstone of the authentic cadence to change from the effervescent, basically homophonic singing style to the ensuing imitative counterpoint.

What the compositions share is a shifting balance among phrase lengths, between textural similarities and dissimilarities, and between shades of mood and affect. The composers worked with a conception of melodic coherence sufficient to support the numerous discontinuities in other realms. This plus the tendency toward quadripartite metric groupings preserves, despite the near-absence of literal repetition, a persistent cyclicity (or, perhaps, nonlinearity) in both pieces, while the discontinuities keep the music moving forward.

Figure 9.6. Mozart, String Quartet K. 464, I, m. 1-38

Jaki Byard and George Tucker: "Bass-ment Blues"

Jaki Byard and George Tucker, "Bass-ment Blues," second chorus, bars 1–7; [fig. 9.7] (with Wilet Mayura, gineman Sekar Gendot quotations [fig. 9.3A, 1:32–1:58] and pengawak [fig. 9.3B]).

Most jazz forms are entirely cyclic, especially in a standard twelve-bar blues like this one. But although the cycle's length and harmonic progression are a constant, players' improvisations unfold over them with continuous change.[18] The character of this sharply layered contrast between cyclicity and

18. Yet writers on jazz never refer to it as static. Instead a metaphor of dynamism is preferred, inspired perhaps by the prominence of improvisation and the individual personalities that shape the music. Indeed musics of Africa and the African diaspora are all far more rigidly periodic than *gamelan*, but their metric cycles are usually accorded a status of background support for a continually developing surface progression, whereas in *gamelan* cycles are considered to be the actual substance of the music. Granted, in *gamelan* there is more literal melodic repetition. But there remains even so a tendency to exoticize *gamelan* and overlook its many anticyclic elements.

Figure 9.7. From the second chorus of "Bass-ment Blues," Jaki Byard and George Tucker (*The Jaki Byard Quartet Live!* vol. 2. Prestige PR-7477. Recorded West Peabody, Mass., April 15, 1965). Transcription by Ingrid Monson (1996:144–45, reformatted with permission; Alan Dawson, drums, omitted).

linearity is among jazz's many African-derived features. This aspect is far more pronounced than in Western tonality, where harmony is sufficiently independent to distort cyclicity. In jazz it can only be a fixed (though decorable) and inseparable component of cyclic structure. In a blues the fundamental tonic, subdominant, and dominant harmonies color the regions of the cycle in a way that makes them analogous to the characters of the various subregions (*palet,* for long cycles) in a Balinese *gongan;* and the quality of harmonic intensification in the "turnaround" chords of a blues' final two bars is akin to the *majalan* melodic drive to gong in a midsized (32- or 64-beat) cycle.

When a jazz improviser integrates a quotation from one tune in the harmonic context of another, an experienced listener delights in recognizing it in a way that is probably similar to a Balinese noting references in *Wilet Mayura.* The dimensions of this enjoyment are several, for there is pleasure in knowing what has been preserved as well as what has been changed, shifted, or omitted.

In "Bass-ment Blues" pianist Byard quotes verbatim the first four bars of the melody of Charles Mingus's "Fables of Faubus" between the fifth and eighth measures of the second chorus, which are controlled by subdominant harmony. Like *Wilet Mayura*'s *kidung* and the *Manukaba* melody, Byard suggests a phantom third element, in this case the chords and key that underpinned the quotation in its original setting. Mingus composed the tune in B♭ minor, where its changes were B♭$^{-7}$ for bars 1–2 and D♭$^{7\sharp 11}$ for bars 3–4. To move it into the fifth measure of "Bass-ment Blues's" key of G, Byard transposed it up a whole step from the original so it lay comfortably with the region's C^7 harmony. More subtly, he also reinterpreted the melody's original tonic quality as a subdominant one and allowed for its shift in position (and hence syntactic character) from being an antecedent/opening gesture to being a consequent/continuation. These changes are related to the ones Sinti made when he forced the *kidung* into the *pengawak*'s metric and melodic frame.

Here again, as with Mozart, melodic recognizability is a compass to orient the listener's understanding of features that are changed. The relative proportions of familiar and new in these situations can exhibit a broad range, and numerous aspects of genre and style play a part in determining what the minimal and sufficient resemblances need to be between a quotation in its new and its source contexts. In the cases just compared these proportions were more or less alike, but consider, for instance, that when Sinti quoted *Sekar Gendot* in the *gineman*, very little was changed save for the context; he could not have transposed it or altered its metric layout. To do so, as I explained when discussing melodic identity in chapter 5, would have shattered its intervallic relationships and structure, making it an unattributable quotation. In jazz cohesion is not hanging in the balance in the same way, and a great deal more distortion is tolerable.

Quotations can add to the interaction among jazz performers and thus contribute to the linear aspects of the form extemporaneously being constructed. Monson argues that an allusion like Byard's gives the music the "functional equivalent of a past tense, and . . . this indexical, intermusical capacity is crucial to thinking about the constitution of social meaning through music" (1996:188), an idea compatible with what I have been saying about *Wilet Mayura*. But the way the meaning is constructed is very different. In jazz it takes shape in part by being channeled through an African American–derived outsider sensibility that often critiques or "signifies" on the dominant culture. It is achieved conversationally among musicians in performance through an alchemy of technical proficiency and knowledge, improvisational spontaneity, and the cooperation of individual personalities. In *Wilet Mayura* meaning is something less contested and volatile: rather than spontaneous, it is embedded in a composer's preplanned composition, reproduced faithfully in a demonstration of social and musical conformity by a large group of players, and obedient to cultural precepts of the Balinese mainstream.

Figure 9.8. From Symphony no. 3, by Witold Lutoslawski, opening. Reprinted by permission of G. Schirmer, Inc., on behalf of Chester Music Ltd.

Witold Lutoslawski: Third Symphony

Witold Lutoslawski Third Symphony, opening; [fig. 9.8] (with Wilet Mayura, pengawak [fig. 9.3B, 2:57–6:51]).

Lutoslawski here stands alone as representative of a particular current of late-twentieth-century European musical modernity typified by sonoric and syntactic individuality and abstraction. Although he at one time (in the 1954 Concerto for Orchestra and many earlier works) used folksong-derived materials, he eventually eschewed them and developed instead, over many years, a heuristic harmonic and melodic technique capable of fleshing out large-scale symphonic architectonics. Like much late-nineteenth and early-twentieth-century Western music, development is continuous and the sense of cycle or periodicity virtually extinguished. A further aspect of his mature work of the 1960s and later was a concern with the manipulation of textural masses in the orchestra. Like his equally prominent contemporaries in this venture, György Ligeti and Krzysztof Penderecki, Lutoslawski had been influenced by the recent advent of electronic music composition, and like it his work is also a part of the Western tradition's search for the expressive potential inherent in sound itself.

In all of these ways Lutoslawski's Third Symphony of 1983 is the antithesis of *Wilet Mayura.* I nonetheless find in *kebyar* and Lutoslawski's music certain compositional parallels. Among these are scrupulous attention to the distinctiveness of orchestral colors, which are often arranged in strata that are maximally differentiated through the use of various techniques (two of which are described below); another is that both are large ensemble musics with forward-driving, *nontonal* syntaxes. Put differently, a relationship between the two musics emerges especially prominently when one hears them, as a contemporary Western-trained musician can easily do, against the background of a common-practice Western tonality considered as normative. When one views the music of a composer like Sinti as a particular kind of alternative answer to issues of large-scale compositional coherence posed by tonality, Lutoslawski can be heard in a related way as still another. (Many other nontonal composers also provide such alternatives, but when the element of orchestral stratification in Lutoslawski is factored in, critical mass for comparison to *gamelan* is attained. On the other hand, a composer such as Edgard Varèse could also fit this bill.) This strictly musical perspective takes into consideration sound and syntax only; cultural differences play no role.

At the opening of the symphony, a *byar*-like fanfare of four multioctave Es instantiates a pedal point for the string section over which three strata enter in succession. These are distinguished by instrumental color, but also by additional idiosyncratic means. One is Lutoslawski's technique of limited aleatorics, in which individual players within instrument groups are each given similar but distinctive patterns to repeat ad libitum until a cue from the conductor instructs them to stop or continue to something else. This ensures a sound mass that never sounds the same way twice but is yet finely differentiated internally. The strata are further distinguished by rhythm and register, and especially by pitch content. One of Lutoslawski's favored strategies is to divide the full chromatic into complementary tri- or tetrachords and distribute them among instruments or groups. Here, the eleven pitches other than the pedal E are apportioned to the two flutes and piccolo (F, Ab B, C), three oboes (F#, A, C#, D), and four French horns (Bb, Eb, G). When all have entered, pitch-class space is saturated but the instrument groups are articulately separate. Such a combination of upper parts with varying ranges and rhythmic values set against a sustained lower one is, of course, familiar from *gamelan*. The pitch-complimentarity of Lutoslawski's strata is something of a conceptual inversion of *gamelan*'s vertical relations and an interesting substitute for them.

The less one knows about Bali, the more natural and complete this analogy could seem. But when one begins to hear *Wilet Mayura*'s strata as an insider, their referentiality injects the rich ingredients of specific context and meaning, which are absent in Lutoslawski's abstractions. At the same time this is a good moment to recall that at the beginning of chapter 2 the expert drummer Suweca was quoted as saying that he mainly feels "enveloped by the fierce and sharp sounds of the music and instruments" when he plays. His words are a reminder that the ideal of the unimpeded perception of sound in process should always remain central to musical experience.

Charles Ives: Fourth Symphony

Charles Ives, Fourth Symphony, First Movement; [fig. 9.9] (with Wilet Mayura, pengawak *[fig. 9.3B, 2:57–6:51]).*

The Fourth Symphony of 1911–15 is in many ways the apotheosis of Ives's voluminous and varied output. Though it does not encompass all of his proficiencies as a composer, it brings together most of the technical and expressive concerns that led to the retrospective view of his music as visionary. The symphony's extensive use of collage, quotation, and allusion, attention to the spatial and temporal aspects of sound, employment of multiple orchestral strata, and adherence to more than one musical language (sometimes several at once) are typical of Ives's interests and among the many features of his music that by the 1970s, some fifty years after he ceased composing, came to be recognized as crucial to the project of twentieth-century music. Many of Ives's compositional goals were pointedly different than those of his contemporaries. While modernists (Lutoslawski being a characteristic latter-day example) were preoccupied with "finding a way of reconciling new compositional 'content' with traditional form, what Ives attempted was to develop a new kind of form for traditional musical content" (Morgan 1973:9). An Emersonian transcendentalist raised in late- nineteenth-century New England, Ives aimed to portray in his compositions the specific sonic memories of his own

4

Figure 9.9. From Symphony no. 4, by Charles Ives, I, entrance of voices. © 1965 (Renewed) by Associated Music Publishers, Inc. (BMI) International copyright secured. All rights reserved. Reprinted by permission.

past, including brass band marches, church choirs, ragtime, minstrelsy and much more, as well as suggest their universal aspects—not by reconciling them to uniformity, but by juxtaposing them in all of their contradictions and letting them be.

Through stratification and allusion the first movement of the symphony, like *Wilet Mayura*, suggests many dimensions of faith and experience simultaneously. In it, the musical spaces above, below, preceding, and following the central setting of the hymn "Watchman Tell Us of the Night" are suffused with disparate religious references set in unusual tonalities that evoke a familiar but transformed American spirituality of Ives's day. Additional hymn allusions or quotations include "Bethany" in harp and muted violins and "In the Sweet Bye and Bye" for solo cello, plus many others heard fleetingly. The polymetric combination of harp/muted violins, piano and string section at rehearsal number 2 gently propels the music into a rich world of manifold inner sensations, soon to be augmented with additional lines from the flute, celesta, and soft timpani. By rehearsal 4, when a "distant choir" begins singing the main text, at least ten distinct musical parts are engaged. The layers are not grounded to a single source stratum as they would be in *gamelan* but are allowed to float, seemingly untroubled by their independence from what surrounds them. The stunning consequence is that through "the illusion of visionary space, the fluidity of motion between thoughts, and these strong religious images, this movement recreates an inner, mystical, ultimately unnamable experience" (Burkholder 1995:392).

When this movement is directly superimposed on the *pengawak* of *Wilet Mayura* striking additional parallelisms are revealed, particularly in the opening minute or so of each. Consider the following uncanny correspondences, more specific than the general ones suggested above:

1. The opening fortissimo piano and string declamations in the Ives mirror Sinti's strong *tutti* melody at beats 1–8 of 9.3B.
2. The solo cello at rehearsal 2 and *Wilet Mayura*'s *trompong* at beat 9 are similarly forefronted against the other strata, and relinquish this role as other instruments accumulate.
3. The entrance of the flute and celesta seven measures later is like that of the *suling, gangsa,* and *reyong* at beat 20.
4. These layers all anticipate the vocals, which enter 5 measures later in the Ives and 4 beats later in the Sinti. From these points the musics continue for some time in a stable and continuous state.
5. Both composers alter the received version of their vocal line to adapt it to its new surroundings.

Subsequently the pieces diverge. *Wilet Mayura* gravitates without disruption to gong, a foregone conclusion in a *lelambatan pengawak*. The Ives, after several interruptions and continuations of the textural flow, concludes questioningly on subdominant harmony, echoed briefly by a tonally indistinct, disembodied whisper in the harp and muted violins.

The Ives ending, while satisfying in the context of his music, is a solution as arbitrary and provisional as the final outcome of *Wilet Mayura*'s *pengawak* is inevitable. This contrast highlights the fact that *Wilet Mayura* aspires to represent and address a more orderly world than the symphony does; one that in this special sense makes it comparable to Mozart. Yet although their syntactic procedures are at odds, in their atmospherics and evocation of the composers' lived experience the resemblance between the two pieces is impressive. This correspondence is perhaps not so difficult to grasp if one considers that the clashing sounds of multiple brass bands marching from different directions toward the central square of Ives's boyhood town—a memory he loved to recount—are none other than an American version of the copious, cacophonous mix of multiple *gamelan* playing concurrently in the open air of a Balinese temple ceremony, an experience as familiar to Sinti as it is to any Balinese. The inspirational quality of these and related recollections may have nurtured the composers' imaginations in a like manner. That Sinti and Rembang's response is more public and culturally sanctioned than Ives's extraordinarily individualistic one does not detract from the fact of the resulting music's multiplicity. The cross-cultural, cross-temporal dialogue between these composers underscores the twentieth-century quality of their aesthetics.

Playing in All Registers

Today we know all kinds of music and expect them to hybridize unpredictably: certainly in the real world, perhaps even more so in our inner ones. The dilemma is one of how to best understand and contribute to the proliferation ourselves. Ives's expanding and horizonless soundscape is a metaphor for our condition. But insofar as we may (perhaps nostalgically) wish for a situation in which the opposite prevails, namely the keener perceptions and shared sensibilities of a unified and bounded language, so too is Sinti and Rembang's.

In a characteristically provocative essay, Karlheinz Stockhausen describes what is for composers (presumably the chief referent of "earthling," below) and indeed for musical humankind, the problem and challenge of having access to music of all times and places:

> Although there have been universalists now and then in the course of European history—among artists as well—there remained predominantly, nevertheless, out of the limited perspective of a culture or even of a specific region within it, the striving to have a personal style, to express oneself and perhaps, too, the vital consciousness of the group of people among whom one lived. When, however, an earthling for the first time can literally embrace the earth and becomes aware of the simultaneity of all stages of culture and the fantastic manifoldness of musical forms of expression and ceremonies, the narrow field of musical specialization is under-

mined. With the danger of not yet being capable of mastering the instrument of all human vibrations and now and then plucking the wrong strings, the most creative spirits from now on will try to play in all registers. (1979:8–9)

But the resulting extended reach and supersaturation of possibilities has its ominous side:

> And therein, naturally, lies the great danger of moving about constantly in all registers, thereby losing all the strength which was once based on the tremendous concentration and one-sidedness of certain musical cultures and certain forms of these cultures. When one can produce in a very limited instrument only very specific tones, this very limitation is a guarantee that one is making a very original music which is strongly differentiated from that music which one might produce with other instruments of quite other potentialities . . . For it was always an unwritten law that precisely within limitations the real master is revealed. (9)

On the one hand there is the likes of Ives, the transcendentalist/universalist, one of the century's "most creative spirits," plucking right and wrong strings on the "instrument of all human vibrations." We recognize in him a striving to "play in all registers" and see in it a virtual reversal of Sinti and Rembang's tight "concentration and one-sidedness." Ives's temporality is unrestricted, reflecting the many unresolved and conflicting aspirations of his intelligence. Unbound from conventions, he persuades with the power of his personal vision, which radiates outward from his imagination. For Sinti and Rembang the constraints of language, instruments, and a closed temporal system project the music inward with equal force. The wonder is that they share so much. To know such opposites and still discern their commonalties, as I have tried to do here, is the reward of living as a musician in our time.

10 Epilogue: *Kebyar* and Ideas of New Music

We need to note that attachment to our regional traditions often impedes our creative work.

Wayan Sadra, Balinese composer living in Java[1]

Just to beat gongs and utilize a *gamelan* orchestra signifies nothing.

. . . What is of lasting value is that the enrichment yielded by any study of the various musical languages is positive in so far as it has the power to exert a fructifying influence and is transcended.

Pierre Boulez, "Traditional Music: A Lost Paradise?" 1967[2]

EARLY on in *Studies in African Music,* A. M. Jones dryly cautioned that "anyone who hopes for an easy passage through this book had better put it down" (1959:10). Feeling less brazen, I was not tempted to utter a similar warning in my own *invitation au voyage,* but might well paraphrase Jones now to the effect that anyone still holding the book will doubtless have found the passage to this point difficult at times. This is of course as it should be for any challenging subject, especially one so famously reluctant to share its secrets as music. And like most ethnomusicologists, neither Jones nor I had the luxury of assuming, as a writer on (for example) Viennese classic music might safely have done, that our readership comes to the book already engaged with the repertoire under discussion, or at least committed to studying it in depth. The transcriptions and CDs enable the partial bridging of this gap, but surely for any new *kebyar* audiences drawn in through these pages it will take time to reap what has been sown. For the benefit of those remaining in my companionship at this stage it is well to ask not what questions have been answered, but what, given the illusory closure endings supply, we may have achieved thus far.

Charting a course toward a richer hearing of *kebyar* and understanding of its settings is the obvious response, but there is more. Thinking deeply about any music inoculates against the allure of facile meanings ascribed to it by vested constituencies. Such meanings are not a priori objectionable. But

---

1. In Suka Harjana, ed. 1986:426.

2. Extracts from "Traditional Music: A Lost Paradise?" (Boulez 1967: 6, 10). The article is a fragmentary compilation of interview material, so I have not felt compunctions about juxtaposing remarks from separate pages.

because *kebyar* and Bali are so famous they are also especially susceptible to hype (a chicken-and-egg scenario); and the hard-to-dislodge, orientalist clichés about them commodify and impoverish, even as they bring renown and prosperity to Bali and its promoters. Whenever tourist brochures summarily describe Bali as a "timeless paradise," or *gamelan* is reduced to something "static and nonprogressive," there is a regrettable ascendancy of convenience over complexity. It is not at all a matter of resisting these juggernauts, but of understanding them; and not just for Bali, of course, but wherever similar patterns occur.

Western culture invented these representations, and it has also responded to and reproduced them in diverse ways, thus reinforcing them. We can trace this in twentieth-century Western music through the work of radically different composers involved with Bali: their musical responses vary, but what the place signifies, particularly to listeners, remains constant. Compare, briefly, these factors relative to members of proximate generations: Colin McPhee and Benjamin Britten on the one hand, and Steve Reich on the other. McPhee's and Britten's orchestral works contain uncannily true simulations of *gamelan* that reflect the composers' fascination with the Bali idyll. Their inclination to replicate the music as received, as though shielding it from corruption, reveals a familiar midcentury yearning for the sensual, exotic, and "original" in world cultures. McPhee may have seen his compositions as "purely personal," as he wrote in the score of *Tabuh-Tabuhan,* but this sentiment is cast in a provisional light in view of what we know about McPhee's sentiments about Bali generally, and the fact that the piece is actually a compendium of *gamelan* quotations and stylistic topics. Precise *gamelan* scoring also accompanies scenes of an enchanted world in Britten's ballet *Prince of the Pagodas.* These composers wished to depict Bali realistically, but what came across to audiences was a picturesque fantasy world, enlivened by novel sound. In Britten's *Death and Venice,* a more transformed and assimilated *gamelan* sound symbolizes the protagonist Aschenbach's inner obsession with the boy Tadzio's innocence and allure; but this is an overtly psychological, even more revealing trope on the Bali image.

For Reich, such evocations were tantamount to chinoiserie. His aim, following the postwar musical zeitgeist, was to extract from *gamelan* (and Ghanaian drumming, his other main non-Western interest) a structural essence. The surface sound of these musics was of little or no conscious concern; instead features such as the structural role of percussion, interlocking parts, and cyclic formations were there "in the thinking, but not in the sound" (Reich 1974: 40). Like McPhee's, however, Reich's assessment of his own music was only accurate in part, for the music does in fact capture aspects of *gamelan* sound— albeit limited ones shaped by Reich's particular interest in repeated short cycles and restricted tonal materials. The motoric pulsation and harmonic inactivity of his early works, among minimalism's cornerstones, were heard against the grain of the dominant, total serial composition of the time. Audiences and critics understood them as signifying the "non-Western," and they were labeled accordingly as trancelike, static, and to use Kramer's term, in "vertical time." Seen from within the West, Reich's music is completely unlike McPhee's and Britten's, but for all three the link to Bali gave rise to similar associations and meanings.[3] It is noteworthy too that these filtered understandings obtain cross-epistemologically, in that they are consistent with the writings of contemporary intellectuals like Gregory Bateson and Clifford Geertz.

As one of the West's preeminent icons of difference, Bali has been a test case for experimentation with alternative ways of knowing time and experience. These clearly say more about the West than about Bali. For a book like this one, naturally, setting aside the stereotypes was prerequisite. By stressing close listening and sensitivity to the inner dynamics of phrase and gesture, I hope to have effectively argued not for the elimination of the stereotypes, but for their reintegration as perspectives rather than essences. Yet to my readers, a concept like the static nature of cyclic time may not carry orientalist connotations, but rather be one of numerous qualities of true difference to be celebrated. And while I have tried to create a refined interpretation of these qualities, I naturally do not deny their distinctiveness. Balinese music's originality is mainly what draws outsiders to it in the first place. But its features are not monolithic in this regard, and the deeper one's immersion in them, the more they dissolve into a more satisfying ambiguity.

The politics of irreducible difference continues to color our perspectives so long as we view music as the product of fundamentally cultural beings. But at the risk of seeming to adhere to an outmoded anthropological structuralism, it is precisely at the level of musical cell and synapse that it is difficult to sustain categorical difference—no matter how adept, like DNA, these components are at carrying meanings specific to the organism. To show this I was at pains, for example, to thoroughly dissect *neliti* melody in chapter 6. *Neliti* behave according to a Balinese grammar, but the grammatical structure reflects a need to balance motion and stasis, cadence and progression, symmetry and asymmetry, and the other factors I have identified, a phenomenon that is *not* culturally unique. Musically, it is hard to experience this ultimate absence of difference without training a microscope on it, though even at much higher structural levels, such as that of the gCC tones presented in chapter 8, congruent processes are at work. (These, however, require grounding in the lower-level processes before they can be felt.) I doubt that ideas of this sort—and the metaphor of organic structure framing them—are controversial; and they certainly are not new. In the sense that they can be used to emphasize similarity

---

3. For further discussion of this subject, see Oja 1990, Cooke 1987, Reich 1974, and Tenzer 1993.

rather than difference they nevertheless seem to me underappreciated, particularly by those dealing with music interculturally.

Consider also a related, though pointedly not analogous, Balinese perspective on cultural interaction. What use have Balinese made of Western musical ideas? One might first look to find a Balinese counterpart to McPhee, Britten, or Reich, but the island has had virtually no exposure to Western art music traditions. To understand this in light of centuries of worldwide Western musical imperialism, one must first factor in *kebyar*'s vitality, and that of the society as a whole, which have buffered against such exposure or influence. Of course we have seen the Western influences on *kebyar,* but these did not derive from music per se. Christianity and its hymns made only modest inroads in Bali. The Dutch conquest came too late for their military bands to have the kind of impact at court that they did in Java, and the Dutch policy of indirect rule limited introduction of foreign music generally. Indonesian public school curricula currently include only the most basic and rigid explanations of *musik diatonis.* At STSI there is indeed desire to learn about world music traditions but little expertise for teaching them, though international performers and teachers often visit the campus or the Bali Arts Festival and provide direct, if fleeting, exposure. In Java and Sumatra sustained interest in Western music and its exponents is somewhat keener, but neighboring countries like the Philippines are immeasurably more active in this regard than either Bali or Indonesia as a whole.

There is, however, another stream in which Balinese and Western musical values do interact: indirectly but tellingly, and perhaps more potentially than actually. This is the emergence in Java, Bali, and Sumatra, beginning in the 1970s (but with precedents earlier) of *musik kontemporer. Kontemporer*'s thrust is urban, nationalistic, and in a larger sense, pan-Asia-Pacific, in that it runs parallel to movements in Japan, Korea, Taiwan, the Philippines, Thailand, Australia, New Zealand, and elsewhere that have already marked art music composition at a global level. The musical history of each Asian country determines whether, as in Japan and Korea, Western instruments and composition techniques predominate, or, as in Thailand and Indonesia, local ones do. All, however, valorize self-consciously innovative and individual composition and the conviction that the aesthetics, techniques, and materials of local music traditions are an important basis for international new music. Works are conceived not for use in a "traditional" setting, but more universally, for broad-based intercultural appreciation. An organization such as the Asian Composers League, with composer-members from throughout the Asia-Pacific, ecumenically recognizes little professional distinction between the contemporary *gamelan* musician from Java and the digital synthesist from New Zealand.[4]

---

4. See Ryker 1990 on the Asian Composers League.

Shared interest in Western new music composition initially brought this diverse community together in the early 1970s. The conception has gradually evolved to view Asian traditions and contemporary music as part of an artistic continuum, not distinct spheres.[5] This perspective is due in part to the vision of prominent composers such as Toru Takemitsu (Japan), Isang Yun (Korea), José Maceda (Philippines), and Chou Wen-chung (China).[6] Indonesia, it should be stressed, has only a minor, though growing, role in this, and within that niche Bali's involvement is modest. The reasons are already familiar: Balinese are preoccupied with the vitality of their arts and religion, they have showcased the "authenticity" of their culture more for a tourist audience than a regional one, and so on. The production of *kontemporer* works at the conservatories is nevertheless part of a regional consciousness linking Bali to Asian new music.[7]

Indonesian *kontemporer* is a heterogeneous mix characterized by composers' self-conscious experimentation with new resources, most in some way related to *gamelan* or other traditions of the archipelago. Among these are mass instrument groupings, extended playing techniques, interensemble and inter-tradition blends, use of electronics, mixed media, conceptual/performance art, and structured improvisations (with composition-specific rules, not necessarily those of Javanese *gamelan* or other local traditions). *Kontemporer*'s presence is small but vital at institutions such as the national art center Taman Ismail Mazurki (TIM) in Jakarta, and at the various conservatory campuses. Like new music in the West the activity is considered important, but institutional and audience support is scant. The *Pekan Komponis Muda* (Young Composers' Fair), held at TIM yearly from 1979 to 1985, brought composers from Bali, Sumatra, and Java together to perform and discuss their work, giving it

5. This contrasts with the North American/European situation in which Asian musical traditions retain foreigner status except in immigrant communities or until they have been assimilated by composers.

6. Feliciano profiles these four composers and concludes: "These composers are participants in that process of interaction whereby different cultures meet; they are "actors" in the confrontation between Oriental and Occidental cultures. They are part of the throng of Asian composers who have looked Westward in their desire to be equipped with 'Western' compositional techniques. . . . In receiving these outside influences, these composers used them only as stimulae to intensify their own particular ways of life" (1983:130–31).

7. This is not to suggest that Westerners bypass this music in Bali or elsewhere in Indonesia. To the contrary, Western members of the international *gamelan* community claim *kontemporer* composers as brethren. Jody Diamond (1990) is among several who have written about it; and she and Larry Polansky have released CDs of *kontemporer* compositions. A 1991 North American tour of *kontemporer* composers billed as *New Music Indonesia,* part of that year's Festival of Indonesia, generated considerable interest. The Indonesians' new music was seen as compatible with the stream of American and Canadian *gamelan* composition spearheaded since the early 1970s by composers like Lou Harrison and enduring ensembles such as New York's *Son of Lion* and Toronto's *Evergreen Club,* the inspiration for which in part traces to the early works of Harrison and Cage and the invented instruments of Harry Partch. In Europe, Netherlander Ton De Leeuw's 1960s and 1970s interest in *gamelan* was influential. *Gamelan* performance and new music composition has also taken root in Britain, Switzerland, Germany, France, Norway, and elsewhere.

national credibility and creating, for the first time, the sense of a pan-Indonesian composition community. The works presented ranged from Rahayu Supanggah's *Gambuh,* a work for Javanese *gamelan,* to Harry Rusli's *Untitled,* a theatrical and aleatoric piece for mixed Asian and Western instruments (Harjana 1986).

Compositions by Balinese were well received at the fair. Perhaps inevitably, their composers thematized traditional culture, whereas Rusli, Supanggah, and others had more abstract conceptions. Komang Astita's *Eka Dasa Rudra* (1979), Rai's *Trompong Beruk* (1982), Windha's *Sangkep* (1983) and Asnawa's *Kosong* (1984; excerpted in CDII/9) all had theatrical components inspired by Hindu-Balinese ceremony. In the exuberant *Kosong* (empty, or nil) ten musicians sat in a circle holding rocks, whisk brooms, bamboo stamping tubes, and *cengceng kopyak* ("crash" cymbals). Using these they moved, sang, and played all manner and timbre of Balinese-style interlocking parts to reenact the outdoor noisemaking done each year on the eve of the holiday *Nyepi.*[8] *Kosong* integrated the playful ritual of the *Nyepi* ceremony with witty, novel extended techniques. Pairs of palm-sized, smooth, flat rocks were struck together on their edges and on their broad surfaces, and rubbed against one another, producing distinctive percussive colors (heard in close succession at 3:20); and the *cengceng kopyak* (from 3:36) were played conventionally, with mallets, on the ground, and between players in a kind of clapping game.

These works were impressive both because and in spite of their insistent "Balineseness." Like his colleagues, Asnawa made deliberate choices about which Balinese ideas to use. *Kotekan* and brief cyclic structures were retained for their energy and directness of expression, but formal procedures like KPP, laden with solemn cultural associations and more challenging for listeners, were eschewed. This nonetheless resulted in a music literally affirming tradition, not the more distilled and cosmopolitan music that a cultivated cultural distance could have produced. At present, at least, such a venture might necessitate leaving Bali: Wayan Sadra's quotation in the epigraph is a terse summary of the dilemma.

This may change; what is important for now is that experience in *kontemporer* begins to equip *kebyar* composers for work beyond Bali. It reinforces the idea that their musical language is not a necessity but a choice, and at the same time promotes the inclusion of Balinese musical devices in the vocabulary of techniques composers elsewhere know or know about. It gives Balinese calling cards as Asian composers and prepares them to collaborate with other Indonesian and international musicians, directors, and choreographers. This takes place regionally, within the worldwide *gamelan* community, and through the

---

8. The idea of this ritual is to entice unwelcome spirits—who are drawn to the clatter—to the roads, temples, and *banjar.* On *Nyepi* morning Balinese stay in their homes, hoodwinking the forces into thinking that people have abandoned the island and there is no point causing trouble there.

kinds of broadly conceived cross-cultural, multimedia collaborative artistic projects (such as the UCLA Center for Intercultural Performance or the Hong Kong Arts Festival) that are the emerging preference of arts funders, and are bound for increasing prominence at major cultural centers and festivals during the early twenty-first century. Indeed, Astita's latest *kontemporer* work (1997; with co-composer Kadek Suardana) involved the sampling and MIDI-processing of *gamelan* sounds for a full ballet score on the *Mahabharata* excerpt *Bima Kroda*, which was choreographed by Swedish dancer Ulf Gaade and given a major production in Stockholm.

Traditionalisms aside, Balinese *kontemporer* is not *kebyar* by any means, though it is informed by the latter's collectivity, secular role, cultural self-awareness, and the importance it grants to the composer. Seen this way *kebyar* compositions, like those of Western modernism, stand for the end of an era when discrete cultures developed as if in isolation, with inner engines of tremendous originality and power. Correspondingly, although a work like *Kosong* is not the kind of new music that, say, Takemitsu's *Arc* for piano and orchestra is, the two can still be understood as belonging to the same extended family of (for want of a better description) Asian contemporary musics. Pairing these extreme cases under one and the same banner in some respects diminishes the very idea of musical category; but in terms of their common function the linkage is important.

From a Western composer's perspective, a McPhee-style work composed today would seem a pointless anachronism now that the concept of new music encompasses such aesthetic and geographic breadth. For a Balinese composer, *kebyar* remains relevant—but now that broader possibilities have revealed themselves, it can only be seen as the closing stage of a long process of internal musical growth. Both outlooks reflect a characteristic fin de siècle departure, or, perhaps, estrangement, from what recently was a less ambiguous cultural identity.

In these contexts, and in the contexts described throughout the book, *kebyar* is a touchstone: for the Balinese, for myself, and for my readers. My musical autobiography, that of a North American composer who found compelling alternatives stepping through a looking-glass half a world away has gradually come to seem a comparatively common kind of adventure rather than the novel one it felt like when I set out. If one's goal is to create new music, the notion of importing a haul of exotic discoveries from a distant pocket of the planet is by now clichéd, the impact of each such import diffused in an omnibus chorus of others. As Boulez correctly asserted, such borrowings are of use only to the extent that they can be transcended; and however ubiquitous they are, borrowings are no prerequisite for transcendence.

Amid the prismatic cultural and social passages of the late twentieth century that have confirmed this perception, *kebyar* itself as a point of orientation has remained. Behind the icon and its promotion the inner idea of it I hope to have imparted is that of a music of compositional rigor; patterned complexity; imposing architecture; expressive, intellectual, and sensual provocation; sonic power; historical and spiritual depth; contemporary relevance; careful preparation; virtuoso performance; and tight social interaction; in short, a recipe for imagination and challenge. This book grew from all of these things that fascinated me about *kebyar,* but the themes of this epilogue are designed to fortify the provisional soil nourishing the roots of my own authority and particular perspectives, so that the ending leaves conditions optimal for the next planting.

Saturated with the accumulated wealth of the musical past, *kebyar* became for Balinese the pinnacle of a century of radical development and their gateway to cultural interaction with the world. My aspiration has been to assist in this process by transferring ideas about *kebyar* to the imagination of my readership; and to demonstrate its richness and international relevance as systematic musical thought. The most persuasive advocate for this is of course *kebyar* itself, a more formidable force than any individual's efforts on its behalf.

Appendixes

Appendix A: *Sekar Gendot,* arr. Wayan Lotring

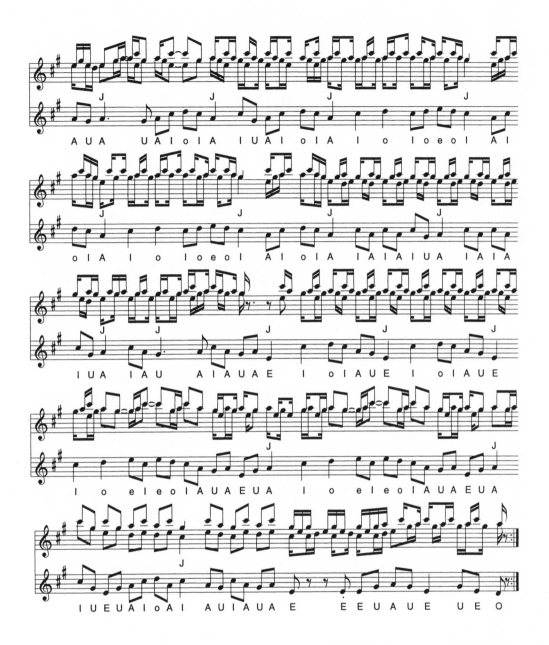

Appendix B: *Kendangan tabuh telu pelegongan*, with *neliti* of *pengawak legong Lasem* (CDI/23)

Glossary of Frequently Used Terms

The following includes only significant Indonesian, Balinese, or English analytical terms that occur in more than one part of the book. The index provides a complete listing of terms, with the page number on which each is defined shown in boldface type.

abstract topic. Segment of music, usually an extended gong cycle at slow tempo, that carries especially sacred or sublime affect.

active pattern. Drum pattern cueing or containing disruption of the stable flow of the music, in the form of *angsel* or related types of explicit coordination between drumming and melodic strata.

anak jaba. Outsider, commoner caste (see *jaba, sudra*).

anak jero. Insider, upper caste (see *jero, triwangsa*).

angklung, gamelan. *Slendro*-tuned ritual bronze *gamelan* ensemble of the *tua* group, often with only four tones.

angsel. Strongly articulated dance movement and/or musical rhythm, cued and coordinated by an active drumming pattern.

Axis. Scale-tone distance, measured in positive or negative integers, between the final tone of a melody and its midpoint tone.

bale banjar. Community meeting hall of a *banjar*; storage and rehearsal area for *gamelan*.

banjar. Ward or hamlet; small to moderate-sized civic community whose members share various obligatory collective tasks.

bapang. Group of 8- or 16-beat meters based, in *kebyar,* on the punctuation (G).P.t.P.G (see also fig. 7.1).

baris. Genre of solo and group warrior dances in *gilak* meter. Also the shortened name of *Baris Melampahan,* the most common, usually solo, type of *baris*.

baru, gamelan. New type of *gamelan,* among those developed in the twentieth century (see fig. 5.1).

byar. Characteristic, accented *kebyar* sonority comprised of a "chord" containing tones 1, 3, 4, 6, 7, 9, 10, and 12 on the *reyong,* scale-tone unison on the remainder of the instruments, the *kendang's dag* and (usually) gong.

calung. Five-key (single-octave), mid-register metallophone that usually plays the *pokok* (also called *jublag*).

CC. Contour class. Ordered group of four positive or negative integers measuring interval (scale-tone distance) between four consecutive tones in a melodic stratum. The last one aligns with a metric stress and is set to 0.

CC4. CC measuring intervals between scale-tones at quarter-way points in a cycle.

CC-group. The succession of four tones from which a CC is derived.

cedugan. Drumming style requiring the use of a mallet in the right hand.

cengceng kecek. Small set of cymbals, some mounted on wood and played with a hand-held pair.

cengceng kopyak. Crash cymbals, handheld and played in pairs.

character topic. Cyclic melody, usually brief, reminiscent of related music for a well-known dance or stock theatrical character.

calonarang. Sixteenth-century tale of witchcraft and exorcism popularly enacted as theater and ritual.

colotomic. Punctuated, as in a cyclic melody, by a recurring pattern of gongs (term coined by Jaap Kunst).

condong. Maidservant; stock character in *pegambuhan* and *pelegongan*-derived theater and dance forms.

dag (D). Open, pitched, right-hand stroke on the *kendang wadon.*

ding, dong, deng, dung, dang. Solfège names for the five *kebyar* scale-tones.

disruption. Explicit rhythmic coordination between drumming and melodic strata.

dug (T). The drum stroke *tut* when played with a mallet, in *cedugan* drumming.

Festival Gong (Kebyar). Yearly Bali-wide government-sponsored competition between *gong kebyar* groups, one male (and until recently, one female) group representing each *kabupaten.*

first-order vertical relations. Simultaneities between parts or strata, ordinarily scale-tone equivalent at metric stresses.

gabor. With *rejang* and *mendet,* one of a group of ancient temple offering dances. Also *Gabor,* the name of a particular twentieth-century choreography based on these.

gambang, gamelan. One of the sacred seven-tone *pélog gamelan tua;* source of *oncang-oncangan* figuration and the 5 + 3 pulse *gambangan* melodic style.

gambangan. (1) The concluding section of a *tabuh kreasi* composition and the multipart texture characteristic of such sections. (2) The characteristic 5 + 3 pulse melodic rhythm of *gamelan gambang.*

gambuh, gamelan. Madya court ensemble used to accompany theater of legendary noble romance and battle, comprised of large *suling* plus *rebab* (considered to play in *saih pitu* scale), *kendang,* and miscellaneous percussion.

gamelan. Balinese and Javanese largely percussive sets of instruments, constructed and tuned to be played together as an inseparable unit.

gandrung, gamelan. Madya bamboo ensemble tuned to *saih lima;* accompaniment to flirtatious solo *gandrung* dance.

gangsa. Any of the group of two-octave metallophones in the *kebyar* instrumentarium, normally including one or two *ugal,* four *pemadé,* and four *kantilan;* or the group as a whole. In everyday use the term can exclude *ugal,* leaving the instruments that play *kotekan* and other fixed melodic elaboration.

gCC. Gending contour class: set of intervallic relationships between key structural tones spaced across an entire *gending.*

geguntangan, gamelan. Ensemble of *krempengan* drums, bamboo slit gongs (*guntang*), *suling,* and other small percussion, used to accompany dialogue and song in the *arja* theater.

gender wayang, gamelan. Tua ensemble comprising a quartet of ten-keyed, *slendro*-tuned *gender,* used primarily to accompany *wayang kulit* (shadow play).

gender. (1) Most generically: any instrument with keys suspended over bamboo resonators, but also variously used to designate (2) any *gender*-type instrument played with a pair of mallets with disc-shaped ends, (3) the *gamelan pelegongan's gender rambat* of 13–15 keys, played with such mallets, (4) an instrument in the *gamelan gender wayang,* and, confusingly, (5) any keyed instrument of a *gong kebyar* (which are not played with such mallets.)

genderan. Texture or passage excluding *reyong, cengceng,* and *kendang.*

gending. Musical composition.

gilak. 8- or 16-beat meter based on (G) . . . GP.PG punctuation (see fig. 7.1B).

gineman. (1) In *pegambuhan* and *pegongan,* a sparsely accompanied, unpulsed, noncyclic melody preceding a composition proper. (2) In *kebyar,* a succession of diverse, irregular, and fragmented musical segments used to open a *kreasi lelambatan* or *tabuh kreasi.*

gong (G). (1) Largest hanging, pitched gong or gongs (see *lanang* and *wadon*). (2) Final tone of a cyclic melody.

gong gdé, gamelan. Immense *madya* bronze ensemble tuned to deep *saih lima;* used at court for state occasions, and in temple for ritual compositions (*lelambatan*).

gong tone. Final scale-tone of a cyclic melody (coinciding with the gong stroke).

gongan. Period spanning one full statement of a cyclic melody.

gupekan. *Kebyar* hand drumming.

jaba. Outside; outer, as of temple courtyards or palace abodes.

jauk. Family of masked demonic or spirit-possessed dance and theater characters.

jegogan. Five-key (single-octave), lowest-register metallophone.

jero(an). Inside; inner, as of temple courtyards or palace abodes.

kabupaten. Regency; one of nine administrative districts subdividing the *propinsi* (province) of Bali, each headed by an appointed *bupati.*

kakawin. Balinese and Javanese Kawi-language poetry in *sekar ageng* (great flower) poetic meters, first composed in the ninth century. *Kakawin* are sung and translated into the vernacular in reading clubs, *sekaha pepaosan.*

kantilan. Ten-key (two-octave), highest register instrument of the *gangsa* section.

kap (K). Unpitched, left-hand stroke on the *kendang wadon.*

kawitan. Origin, beginning. (1) Introduction to a *gending.* (2) First part of the tripartite KPP form of *lelambatan,* followed by *pengawak* and *pengecet.*

kawitan-pengawak-pengecet. See KPP.

kAxis. Scale-tone distance, measured in positive or negative integers, between the final tone of a kCC-group and its midpoint tone.

kCC. *Kotekan* contour class. Ordered group of eight positive or negative integers measuring the interval (scale-tone distance) between eight consecutive tones in the *kotekan* stratum. The last one normally aligns with the *pokok* and is set to 0.

kCC-group. The succession of eight tones from which a kCC is derived.

kebyar. To flare up or burst open. (1) *Gamelan gong kebyar.* (2) *Kebyar* musical style. (3) Passage in *kebyar* texture and rhythm (characterized by minimal independence of strata and irregular, non-metric/additive rhythms).

kecekan. Percussive *reyong* sound obtained by playing off the boss of the gong.

kempli (M). Mounted small gong used for marking the beat in *kebyar* repertoire, and *palet* or other melodic subsection endings in *pegongan* repertoire.

kempur (P). Medium-sized hanging gong used to mark cycle endings in *pegambuhan* and *pelegongan* repertoire, and for punctuation within the cycle in *pegongan* and *kebyar* repertoire (also called *kempul*).

kempyung. See *ngempat.*

kendang batel. See *krumpungan.*

kendang batu-batu. Type of *cedugan* in which one drummer improvises a part to interlock with a simple fixed pattern played by the other.

kendang tunggal. Solo improvised drumming.

kendang. Drum; see also *wadon* and *lanang.*

kendangan. (1) Drumming. (2) (Specific to this book) drumming for extended *pengawak* cycles. (3) Orchestral texture featuring *kendang.*

kep. Soft, unpitched, right-hand drum stroke used for filler and damping.

kidung. Javanese and Balinese language poetry in *sekar madya* ("medium" flower) poetic meters, composed mainly on Bali during the Gelgel period and later. Sung in florid style and formerly accompanied, in some form, by sacred seven-tone *pélog gamelan.*

kinetic quality. Degree of stasis or motion (of a melodic stratum, drum pattern level, etc.).

klasik. Classic. Describes a version, style, or rendition of a composition perceived to embody enduring cultural and musical values.

klentong (t). Small, high-pitched hanging gong used to mark midpoints or *palet* endings (for longer cycles) in *kebyar* and *pelegongan* (also called *kemong*).

kotekan. Melodic interlocking parts, especially as played by *kantilan* and *pemadé;* their composite rhythm characteristically subdivides the beat into four parts (see *norot, nyog cag,* and *ubit-ubitan*).

KPP. Basic tripartite form of *lelambatan* (*kawitan-pengawak-pengecet*).

kreasi baru. New (artistic) creation.

kreasi lelambatan. *Lelambatan* composition arranged or composed in *kebyar* style, usually prefixed with *gineman.*

krempengan. Drumming using small drums and featuring the high-pitched left-hand sound *peng,* used in *pegambuhan, pelegongan,* and *arja* repertoires. Often synonymous with *krumpungan.*

krum (r). (1) Partially damped, pitched right-hand stroke used on the *kendang wadon* in *gupekan* style (also called *kum*). (2) In *krumpungan,* left-hand *wadon* stroke obtained by striking with the base of the fingers near the rim.

krumpungan. Improvisatory *krempengan* drumming, also called *kendang batel,* in which the *lanang's* prominent *krumpung* stroke is responsible for cueing *angsel* (see also *krempengan*).

lanang. (Male.) Higher-pitched of an otherwise matched pair of instruments, especially gong or *kendang* (see *wadon*).

legong keraton. Family of nineteenth-century court dances, originally danced by a pair of young girls and accompanied by *gamelan pelegongan.*

lelambatan. (Lit., slow music.) Composition in *pegambuhan* or *pegongan* repertoire, using one of the longer *tabuh* meters for its *pengawak;* or a similarly constructed new composition (see *kreasi lelambatan*).

lontar. Leaves of the *borassus* palm inscribed with literature, music notation, etc.

luang, gamelan. One of the sacred seven-tone *pélog gamelan tua;* source of *luangan* figuration.

madya, gamelan. "Middle-era" (type of) *gamelan,* among those developed in the post-Majapahit Balinese courts (see fig. 5.1).

majalan. Kinetic, as in motion of a melodic stratum, drum pattern level, etc. (antonym for *ngubeng*).

Majapahit. Powerful east-Javanese dynasty whose nobility emigrated in large numbers to Bali in the fourteenth and fifteenth centuries.

metacycle. Series of repeating cycles grouped together by progression from stable to active states, culminating in *angsel* or other type of disruption.

neliti. (Correct, precise.) Melodic stratum characterized by two-octave range and movement at the even rate of one tone per beat (twice the density of *pokok*).

neliti order. Ordering of the tones of a melodic stratum to preserve the two-octave range of the *neliti* (as played by *ugal*).

nelu. Second-order vertical interval of three tones, inclusive of the sounding tones.

ngembat. (From *embat,* to reach or extend.) To play in parallel octaves on the *trompong.*

ngempat. Second-order vertical interval of four tones, inclusive of the sounding tones.

ngubeng. Static, as in motion of a melodic stratum, drum pattern level, etc. (antonym for *majalan*).

nguncab: Sudden, *tutti* dynamic increase.

norot. *Kotekan* style featuring one-to-one melodic alternation between the prevailing *pokok* tone and its scalar upper neighbor.

nyog cag. *Kotekan* style in which *polos* plays duple subdivisions coinciding with the beat, and *sangsih* fits precisely in between.

ocak-ocakan. Pattern of rhythms played together by *kendang, cengceng,* and *reyong* (the latter using *kecekan* and the *byar* chord).

ombak. (Wave.) (1) Acoustical beating achieved through intentional slight detuning of pairs of instruments. (2) Graded tempo fluctuation. (3) Graded dynamic fluctuation.

orde baru. New (post-Sukarno) order; the policies and goals of the Suharto administration and its national development program.

panggul. Mallet.

payasan. (1) Melodic elaboration (general term). (2) Unfixed *pokok* elaboration, such as that performed by *ugal, trompong, suling,* or *rebab.*

pegambuhan. Of or relating to the repertoire and practice of the *gamelan gambuh.*

pegongan. Of or relating to the repertoire and practice of the *gamelan gong gdé.*

pek (P). Unpitched, left-hand stroke on the *kendang lanang;* primary cueing stroke for *angsel* in *gupekan.*

pelegongan, gamelan. *Madya* bronze court and village ensemble, derivative of *gambuh* and *semar pegulingan,* tuned to relatively high (sweet) *saih lima;* accompaniment for *legong kraton, calonarang,* and related genres.

pélog. Javanese name (familiar in Bali) for the widely used seven-tone *pélog* scale of unequal intervals, or its five-tone derivatives (see *saih pitu* and *saih lima*).

pemadé. Ten-key (two-octave), mid-register instrument of the *gangsa* section.

pemetit. The highest of the four playing positions on the *reyong.*

pengawak. (From *awak,* body.) Central and most significant portion of a composition, particularly in *lelambatan,* with the broadest metric period and slowest tempo.

pengecet. (From *ngecet,* trot.) Post-*pengawak* section of a composition, particularly in *lelambatan,* with shorter metric periods and brisker tempo.

pengisep. (1) Higher of the tones in a pair tuned to achieve *ombak.* (2) Optional cyclic melody in some KPP forms inserted after the *pengawak.*

pengumbang. Lower of the tones in a pair tuned to achieve *ombak.*

penyacah. Five-keyed metallophone, one octave above *calung,* that normally plays at the one-tone-per-beat rate of the *neliti.* Not always present in *kebyar* ensembles.

pokok. (Basis, trunk.) Slow-moving core melody, typically played by *calung* at the even rate of one tone per two beats (half the density of *neliti*).

pokok order. Ordering of the tones of a melodic stratum to preserve the single-octave range of the *pokok* (as played by *calung*).

pola dasar. Basic pattern.

polos. (Simple, direct, basic.) Of the two complementary elaboration parts, the one that most closely follows the underlying melody (compare *sangsih*).

pung (u or U). (1) Partially damped, pitched right-hand stroke used on the *kendang lanang* in *gupekan* style (u). (2) In *krumpungan,* left-hand *lanang* stroke used to cue *angsel,* obtained by striking with the base of the fingers near the rim (U).

quotation topic. Portion of a *gending* quoting directly from or strongly reminiscent of another composition.

rebab. Two-stringed bowed spike lute of Bali and Java.

reyong. Set of twelve mounted small gongs tuned to an ascending scale and played by four musicians.

reyongan. Texture or passage featuring *reyong.*

saih pitu. Seven-tone scale system (see *pélog*) used in *gamelan gambang, selunding, luang, gambuh, semar pegulingan,* and others.

saih lima. One of various five-tone derivatives of *saih pitu,* such as those used in *gamelan gong kebyar, pelegongan, gong gdé,* or *gandrung.*

sangsih. (Different, complementary.) Of the two complementary elaboration parts, the one that adds second-order vertical relations to, and/or interlocks with, the *polos.*

second-order vertical relations. Simultaneities within parts or strata, ordinarily at the interval *ngempat.*

sekaha. Club or organization, especially ones based at *banjar,* for which membership is voluntary.

sekaha gong. *Gamelan* club, ordinarily administered under *banjar* auspices.

selunding, gamelan. One of the sacred seven-tone *pélog gamelan tua,* made with iron keys.

semar pegulingan, gamelan. *Madya* bronze court ensemble, tuned to *saih pitu,* with *pegambuhan* repertoire.

slendro. Javanese name (familiar in Bali) for the widely-used five-tone scale of intervals in the 200–300 cent range.

SMKI (KOKAR). *Sekolah Menengah Karawitan Indonesia (Konservatori Karawitan)* High School of *Gamelan* and *Gamelan*-Related Musical Arts.

stable pattern. Drum pattern lasting for a full cycle in which no disruption occurs (Cf. active pattern).

STSI (formerly ASTI). Sekolah Tinggi Seni Indonesia (Akademi Seni Tari Indonesia) Academy of Indonesian Arts (formerly Academy of Indonesian Dance).

stylistic topic. Use of characteristic and identifiable musical traits of a different *gamelan* genre in a *kebyar* composition.

sudra. See *anak jaba.*

suling. End-blown bamboo flute.

tabuh kreasi (baru). *Kebyar* instrumental composition.

tabuh pegambuhan. (1) Composition in or based on the repertoire of the *gamelan gambuh.* (2) One of the *pengawak*-types in *lelambatan* of *pegambuhan* repertoire (see fig. 7.1A5–7).

tabuh pegongan. (1) Composition in or based on the repertoire of the *gamelan gong gdé.* (2) One of the *pengawak*-types in *lelambatan* of *pegongan* repertoire (see fig. 7.1B4–8).

tabuh. (1) Composition; synonym for *gending.* (2) Group of *pegongan* and *pegambuhan pengawak*-types used in *lelambatan.* (3) As a verb, *menabuh;* to play *gamelan.* (4) Synonym for *panggul.* See also *tabuh kreasi baru, tabuh pegambuhan,* and *tabuh pegongan.*

tak (a). The drum stroke *dag* played with a *panggul* and muted by pressing on the left drumhead.

tari lepas. Free-standing dances portraying a character or brief narrative, unconnected to a larger theatrical presentation.

tek (e). The stroke *dug* muted by pressing on the left drumhead.

tonal quality. Structural quality measured by the amount of displacement between a gong tone and other significant melodic arrivals in a cycle.

topeng. Masked dance; masked dance theater.

topic. Subject for musical discourse (Ratner 1980:9); musical texture, type, or style carrying an affect recognizable by practiced listeners.

triwangsa. Insider, upper caste (see *jero, anak jero*).

trompong. Set of ten mounted small gongs played by a single musician.

tua, gamelan. Old (type of) *gamelan,* originally without drums or gongs, among those developed mostly prior to the Majapahit influx to Bali (see fig. 5.1).

tut (T). Pitched right-hand stroke on the *kendang lanang.*

ubit empat. *Ubit-ubitan* in which *polos* and *sangsih* together span a range of four tones per pattern unit, coinciding on a *kempyung* formed by the two outer tones.

ubit telu. *Ubit-ubitan* in which *polos* and *sangsih* together span a range of three tones per pattern unit, sharing the middle one.

ubit-ubitan. *Kotekan* type in which *polos* and *sangsih* are syncopated and coincide at irregular temporal intervals (see *ubit telu* and *ubit empat*).

ugal. Ten-key (two-octave), lowest-register instrument, and leader, of the *gangsa* section (also called *giying*).

wadon. (Female.) Lower-pitched of an otherwise matched pair of instruments, especially gong or *kendang* (see *lanang*).

CD Contents and Notes

Gamelan Gong Kebyar: The Art of Twentieth Century Balinese Music © 2000 Michael Tenzer

The CDs were designed to match the transcriptions closely. They do not provide a comprehensive or even representative sample of *kebyar* compositions, instruments, *sekaha*, or performances, since sufficient material is available commercially for that.

These recordings are of two types: (1) renderings of analytical transcriptions and other brief excerpts, matched to figures in the book, and (2) complete compositions, major portions of which are transcribed in chapters 8 and 9. The latter comprise CDII tracks 1–4 and 7. The former encompass everything else. Some tracks in this category aurally demonstrate my analyses by modifying the music as it is properly played. The selections keyed to figure 6.3, for example, would not be heard in the stripped-down form presented here, nor would the drums be isolated or amplified the way they have been for some of the chapter 7 selections.

Of the fifty-five tracks, forty-two were recorded at a session on August 3, 1998, in a courtyard of the STSI Denpasar campus, using the school's *kebyar* instruments. The musicians, drawn from faculty and students (some of whom played different instruments on different selections), and the technicians were:

Nyoman Windha (*ugal, trompong, kendang,* and coleader); Pandé Gdé Mustika (gong and coleader); Ketut Gdé Asnawa (*kendang* and coproducer); Wayan Suweca (*kendang* and *gender pelegongan*); Gdé Arya (*reyong, kendang*); Nyoman Sudiana (*pemadé*); Ida Bagus Nyoman Mas (*pemadé, ugal*); Nyoman Sudirga (*pemadé*); Nyoman Pasek (*calung*); Gdé Yudarta (*reyong*); Wayan Suharta (*pemadé*); Wayan Beratha (*reyong*); Gusti Ketut Sudana (*suling*); Ketut Garwa (*kendang, reyong*); Madé Gdé Mawan (*kantilan*); Nyoman Sukarwa (*kempli*); Wayan Suwena (*calung*); Madé Gdé Mandra (*kempur, kemong*); Gusti Ngurah Suastika (*jegogan*); Wayan Semantara (*kantilan*); Anak Agung Dalem Kardinata (*reyong*); Madé Adi (*kantilan*); Pandé Sunarta (second *ugal*); Ketut Bawa (*kantilan*); Nyoman Aryawan (*cengceng*); Wayan Gdé Suradaya (*rebab*); Wayan Karjana (*suling*); Ngurah Widiana (*jegogan*); Michael Tenzer (*kendang* and coproducer). Yong Sagita (recording engineer); Ida Bagus Alit Yudana (technical support); Madé Lila (technical support).

The remaining thirteen tracks were excerpted from other recordings. Information on their sources is footnoted. Permission to use his complete recording of STSI musicians playing *Kosalia Arini* (CDII/4) was kindly granted by Ricky Yulianto of Bali Stereo. I was keen to include one of Yulianto's recordings because the special quality of Bali Stereo productions has shaped Balinese aural experience of *kebyar* since the 1960s. The performance is also especially fine in this case.

CD I (total time 54:17)

Track	Figure	Page(s)	Timing	Composition	Performers and recording	Additional comments
1	2.13	61–63	0:38	*Oleg Tumulilingan*	STSI, August 3, 1998 (hereafter, STSI).	
2	2.14	63–65	0:30	*Baris*	STSI, 1989 [1]	Transcribed portion: 0:07–0:25
3	2.15	65–66	0:41	*Dharma Putra*	*Sekaha Gong* Dharma Kusuma, Pindha, 1985 [2]	Transcribed portion: 0:03–0:10

Figs.2.16–18 are heard in CD II/4 (see figures for timings).

Track	Figure	Page(s)	Timing	Composition	Performers and recording	Additional comments
4	2.19	68	1:14	*Dharma Putra*	See track 3	Transcribed portion: 0:39–1:05
5	4.1A, 5.3	138–40, 168–71	1:02	*Pelayon*	*Gamelan* from Sanur, live at the 1983 *Festival Gong* [3]	Transcribed portion: 0:21–0:25 and 0:49–0:53

Fig. 4.1B is heard in CDII/7 at 7:01, and in CDII/8 at 0:12, 1:08, and 2:03

Track	Figure	Page(s)	Timing	Composition	Performers and recording	Additional comments
6.1 to 6.4	6.3A-D	190–91	1:22	1. *Bapang Gdé* 2. *Jauk Keras* 3. *Gabor* 4. *Gilak Jagul*	STSI	For fig. 6.3 A-P, each *neliti* is played for two *gongan,* then twice more in conventional full *gamelan* format.
7.1 to 7.4	6.3E-H	190–91 (7.4: see also 211–12)	1:14	1. *Gegilakan* 2. *Gilak Baris* 3. *Bapang Garuda* 4. *Baris II*	STSI	
8	6.3I	191–94	0:33	*Pengecet Tabuh Pisan Dong*	STSI	
9	6.3J	191–94	0:31	*Oleg Tumulilingan*	STSI	
10	6.3K	191–94	0:34	*Topeng Keras*	STSI	
11	6.3L	191–94	0:32	*Condong Legong*	STSI	
12	6.3M	191–94	0:36	*Pengecet Tabuh Telu*	STSI	
13	6.3N	191–94	1:01	*Perong Condong*	STSI	
14	6.3O	191–94	0:30	*Pengecet Bangun Anyar*	STSI	
15	6.3P	191–94	0:34	*Gegilakan*	STSI	
16	6.3Q	194–97	1:16	*Gilak Adeng*	STSI	For fig. 6.3 Q-Y (except U and W) each *neliti* is played once, then once in conventional format

continued on following page

1. Personal field recording, July 1989.
2. Field recording in Pindha by Wayne Vitale and Dieter Mack, December 1985. Used with permission.
3. Field recording at the Bali Arts Festival by Wayne Vitale, June 1983. Used with permission.

CD I (*continued*)

Track	Figure	Page(s)	Timing	Composition	Performers and recording	Additional comments
17	6.3R	194–97	0:33	*Puspanjali*	STSI	
18	6.3S	194–97	0:43	*Telek*	STSI	
19	6.3T	194–97	0:53	*Ngalap Basé*	STSI	
20	6.3U, 7.12	197–98 284–88	2:01	*Pengecet Legong Lasem* (*ugal* is replaced by *gender pelegongan*)	STSI	Played three ways: (1) *neliti*, (2) elaborated melody and *kendang*, (3) full *gamelan*
21	6.3V	197–98	2:30	*Arsawijaya*	STSI	
22	6.3W	199–204	1:56	*Pengawak Bangun Anyar*	STSI	*Neliti* only, with *reyong* added for continuity; for complete *pengawak* refer to CDII/1.
23	6.3X App. B	200–201; 204-5; 444–47	8:03	*Pengawak Legong Lasem*	STSI	*Kendang* added for continuity during *neliti* version
24	6.3Y	202–5; 294–96	6:14	*Pengawak Tabuh Gari*	STSI	*Reyong* added for continuity during *neliti* version
25.1 and 25.2	6.4	207–8	0:51	*Oleg Tumulilingan*	STSI	Slow version followed directly by fast version; *ugal* volume boosted
26	6.5	208–9	0:30	*Jagul*	STSI	
27	6.6A	210–11	0:45	*Pengecet Tabuh Gari*	STSI	

Fig.6.6B is heard in CDI/7.4.
Fig.6.6C is heard in CDI/39.

Track	Figure	Page(s)	Timing	Composition	Performers and recording	Additional comments
28	6.6D	212	0:52	*Puspanjali*	STSI	
29	6.10	220–21	0:38	*Topeng Keras*	STSI	Fig. 6.10 and 6.15 A-C: *Polos* and *sangsih* heard on separate channels
30	6.15A	228–30	0:38	*Garuda*	STSI	
31.1 and 31.2	6.15B and C	229–30	0:28	*Oleg Tumulilingan*	STSI	
32	6.15D	229–31	0:49	*Teruna Jaya*	STSI	
33	6.16	236–38	2:26	*Panji Marga*	*banjar* Bedhe, Tabanan (date unknown)[4]	*Gamelan gambang;* transcription begins at 1:19; 2:12
34	6.17	240–42	0:38	*Sekar Sungsang*	*banjar* Babakan, Sukawati, 1982[5]	*Gamelan gender wayang;* transcription begins at 0:03; 0:17

continued on following page

CD I (*continued*)

Track	Figure	Page(s)	Timing	Composition	Performers and recording	Additional comments
35	6.18	240; 244	1:01	*Kempul Ndung*	STSI	*Gamelan angklung;* transcribed portion: 0:31–0:48
36	6.19	245–46	0:34	*Gegandrangan*	*banjar* Ketapian Kelod, 1982 [6]	*Gamelan gandrung;* transcription begins at 0:03
37.1 to 37.4	7.6W-Z	267–69	1:11	*Tabuh Gari Pegambuhan*	1. Kamasan,[7] 1991 2. Teges,[8] 1941 3. Teges,[9] 1972 4. Binoh,[10] 1990	
38	7.7A	271–74	0:34	*Oleg Tumulilingan*	STSI	Figs. 7.7–7.11: Drum volume boosted
39	7.7B	212; 271–74	0:29	*Teruna Jaya*	STSI	
40	7.8, 7.9	276–79	0:41	*Gabor*	STSI	
41	7.10	279–80; 282	0:20	*Teruna Jaya*	STSI	
42	7.11	280–81; 283	0:33	*Kembang Kuning*	STSI	

Fig 7.12 is heard in CDI/20.

Track	Figure	Page(s)	Timing	Composition	Performers and recording	Additional comments
43	7.13	292–94	0:19	*Condong Legong*	STSI	Drum volume boosted

Fig. 7.14 is heard in CDI/24, beginning at 4:17.

Track	Figure	Page(s)	Timing	Composition	Performers and recording	Additional comments
44.1 to 44.3	7.15 A-C	298–301	0:54	*Jauk Keras*	STSI	The 3 versions are heard consecutively.
45	7.16	301–4	1:18	*Kebyar Duduk*	Wayan Suweca, *kendang,* 1982 [11]	Transcribed portion: 0:45–1:05
46	7.16	301–4	1:33	*Kebyar Duduk*	STSI	Same melody as above, but played by full *gamelan.* Drumming untranscribed.

continued on following page

4. Excerpted from *Gamelan Gambang, Banjar Bedhe, Tabanan* (Aneka Cassette 410).

5. Excerpted courtesy of King Records Co., Ltd., Japan, from *Gender Wayang of Sukawati Village* (King Records KICC 5156).

6. Personal field recording at *banjar* Ketapian Kelod, September 1982.

7. Excerpted courtesy of Kurt Renker and CMP records from *Gamelan Semar Pegulingan Saih Pitu: The Heavenly Orchestra of Bali* (CMP CD 3008).

8. Excerpted from *Music for the Gods: The Fahnestock South Sea Expedition: Indonesia* (Rykodisc 10315) Courtesy of American Folklife Center, Rykodisc and 360° Productions

9. Excerpted courtesy of Nonesuch Records by arrangement with Warner Special Products from *Gamelan Semar Pegulingan: Gamelan of the Love God* (Nonesuch LP H-72046). Recorded by Robert E. Brown.

10. Excerpted courtesy of King Records Co., Ltd., Japan, from *Gamelan Semar Pegulingan of Binoh Village* (King Records KICC 5155).

11. Personal field recording at Suweca's home, September 1982.

CD II (total time 61:53)

Track	Figure	Page(s)	Timing	Composition	Performers and recording	Additional comments
1	6.3O 6.3W 8.1A-D 8.8A 8.10C 8.13A	311–19; 360; 375–77	14:21	*Tabuh Pisan Bangun Anyar* (Wayan Beratha)	STSI	The main page references for tracks 1–6 are shown, but all are discussed throughout chapter 8.
2	8.2A-C 8.7B 8.11B 8.13B	320–26; 365; 377–79	7:12	*Panyembrahma* (Wayan Beratha)	STSI	
3	8.3A-B 8.8D 8.12A 8.13C	326–31; 366; 379–81	4:17	*Jaya Semara* (Wayan Beratha)	STSI	
4	2.16–18 8.4A-C 8.12B 8.13D	66–68; 326; 332–37; 367; 381–83	9:50	*Kosalia Arini* (Wayan Beratha)	STSI, 1982 [12]	
5	8.5	326; 329; 338; 369	1:48	*Wahyu Giri Suara* (Nyoman Windha)	STSI	
6	8.6	326; 330; 353; 368	2:17	*Sekar Kamuda* (Ketut Gdé Asnawa)	See CDI, track 3	
7	9.1 to 9.5 4.1B	138–40, and all of Ch. 9	12:00	*Wilet Mayura* (Wayan Sinti and Nyoman Rembang)	*Sekaha* Gong Genta Budaya, *banjar* Dalem Angantaka, 4/25/89 [13]	
8	9.3C	See track 7	3:15	*Wilet Mayura*	See track 7	*Kotekan* section only, played thrice at slower tempo
9	Ch. 10	448	6:48	*Kosong* (Ketut Gdé Asnawa)	STSI, July 17, 1985 [14]	

12. From *Kreasi Gong Kebyar, ASTI-Denpasar Vol. 4* (Bali Stereo Cassette 551), courtesy of Ricky Yulianto and Bali Stereo Recordings.
13. Personal field recording in Angantaka, April 1989, engineered by Andrew Toth using Nagra reel-to-reel recorder borrowed from STSI.
14. Personal field recording at the Bali Arts Festival, June 1985.

Sources Cited

Agawu, Kofi. 1991. *Playing with Signs: A Semiotic Interpretation of Classic Music*. Princeton: Princeton University Press.

———. 1987. "The First Movement of Beethoven's Opus 132 and the Classic Style." *College Music Symposium* 27:30–45.

Anderson, Benedict. 1972. "The Idea of Power in Javanese Culture." In Holt, Claire, ed., *Culture and Politics in Indonesia*, 1–70. Ithaca: Cornell University Press.

Arom, Simha. 1991. *African Polyphony and Polyrhythm: Musical Structure and Methodology*. Cambridge: Cambridge University Press.

Arthanegara, G. B., et al. 1980. *Riwayat Hidup Seniman dan Organisasi Kesenian Bali*. Denpasar: Proyek Penggalian/Pembinaan Seni Budaya Klasik (Traditional) dan Baru.

Aryasa, I Wayan et al. 1984–85. *Pengetahuan Karawitan Bali*. Denpasar: Proyek Pengembangan Kesenian Bali, Departemen Pendidikan dan Kebudayaan.

Asnawa, Ketut Gdé. 1991. "The *Kendang Gambuh* in Balinese Music." M.A. thesis: University of Maryland, Baltimore County.

Astita, Komang. 1990. "Tabuh Kreasi Gong Kebyar dan Permasalahannya." Seminar paper, ASTI Denpasar.

Bakan, Michael. 1998. "From Oxymoron to Reality: Agendas of Gender and the Rise of Balinese Women's *Gamelan Beleganjur* in Bali, Indonesia." *Asian Music* 29(1): 37–86.

Bamberger, Jeanne, and Evan Ziporyn. 1992. "Getting It Wrong." *World of Music* 34(3): 22–56.

Bandem, Made. 1993. "Ubit Ubitan: Sebuah Teknik Permainan Gamelan Bali." *Mudra: Jurnal Seni Budaya*: 59–91.

———. 1987. "*Topeng* in Contemporary Bali." In *International Symposium on the Conservation and Restoration of Cultural Property: Masked Performances in Asia*, 191–208. Tokyo: National Research Institute of Cultural Properties.

———. 1980. "*Wayang Wong* in Contemporary Bali." Ph.D. diss., Wesleyan University.

Bandem, Made, ed. and trans. 1986. *Prakempa: Sebuah Lontar Gambelan Bali*. Denpasar: Akademi Seni Tari Indonesia.

Bandem, Made, and Fredrik E. DeBoer. 1995 [1981]. *Balinese Dance in Transition: Kaja and Kelod*. New York: Oxford University Press.

———. 1978. "*Gambuh:* A Classical Balinese Dance Drama." *Asian Music* 10(1): 115–27.

Bateson, Gregory. 1949. "Bali: The Value System of a Steady State." In Fortes, M., ed., *Social Structure: Studies Presented to A. R. Radcliffe Brown*. Oxford: Clarendon Press. (Reprinted in Belo 1970:384–401.)

Becker, Judith. 1993. "Southeast Asia." In Myers, Helen, ed., *Ethnomusicology: Historical and Regional Studies*, 377–91. New York: W. W. Norton.

———. 1988. "Earth Fire, *Sakti*, and the Javanese *Gamelan*." *Ethnomusicology* 32(3): 385–91.

———. 1980. *Traditional Music in Modern Java*. Honolulu: University of Hawaii Press.

———. 1968. "Percussive Patterns in the Music of Mainland Southeast Asia." *Ethnomusicology* 12:173–91.

Becker, Judith, and Alton Becker. 1981. "A Musical Icon: Power and Meaning in Javanese

Gamelan Music." In Steiner, W. ed., *The Sign in Music and Literature,* 203–25. Austin: University of Texas Press.

———. 1979. "A Grammar of the Genre *Srepegan*." *Journal of Music Theory* 24(1): 1–43.

Becker, Judith, and Alan Feinstein, eds. 1984, 1987, 1988. *Karawitan: Source Readings in Javanese Gamelan and Vocal Music.* Vols. 1–3. Ann Arbor: Center for Southeast Asian Studies, University of Michigan.

Belo, Jane. 1970. "The Balinese Temper." In Belo, Jane, ed., *Traditional Balinese Culture,* 85–110. New York: Columbia University Press.

———. 1953. *Bali: Temple Festival.* Locust Valley, N.Y.: Monographs of the American Ethnological Society, 22.

Belo, Jane, ed. 1970. *Traditional Balinese Culture.* New York: Columbia University Press.

Berry, Wallace. 1987. *Structural Functions in Music.* New York: Dover Editions.

Bloch, Maurice. 1977. "The Past and the Present in the Present." *Man* 12:278–92.

Boon, James A. 1977. *The Anthropological Romance of Bali, 1597–1972: Dynamic Perspectives in Marriage and Caste, Politics and Religion.* Cambridge: Cambridge University Press.

Boulez, Pierre. 1967. "Traditional Music: A Lost Paradise?" *World of Music* 9(2): 3–10.

Brinner, Benjamin. 1995. *Knowing Music, Making Music: Javanese Gamelan and the Theory of Musical Competence and Interaction.* Chicago: University of Chicago Press.

Brown, Robert E., prod. 1972. *Gamelan Semar Pegulingan: Gamelan of the Love God.* Nonesuch Records Explorer Series H–72046. Notes by Robert E. Brown and Philip Yampolsky. Ensemble Gunung Jati from Teges Kanginan.

Burkholder, Peter. 1995. *All Made of Tunes: Charles Ives and the Uses of Musical Borrowings.* New Haven: Yale University Press.

Clifford, James. 1988. *The Predicament of Culture.* Cambridge: Harvard University Press.

Coast, John. 1953. *Dancers of Bali.* New York: Putnam.

Coedes, George. 1968 [1944]. *The Indianized States of Southeast Asia.* Trans. S. B. Cowing. Honolulu: East-West Center Press.

Cogan, Robert. 1984. *New Images of Musical Sound.* Cambridge: Harvard University Press.

Cooke, Mervyn. 1987. "Britten and Bali." *Journal of Musicological Research* 7:307–39.

Covarrubias, Miguel. 1937. *Island of Bali.* New York: A. A. Knopf.

Craft, Robert. 1991. "Bali H'ai." *New York Review of Books,* Oct. 24, 1991:56–59.

Crapanzano, Vincent. 1986. "Hermes' Dilemma: The Masking of Subversion in Ethnographic Description." In Clifford, James, and George Marcus, eds., *Writing Culture: The Poetics and Politics of Ethnography,* 51–76. Berkeley: University of California Press.

Dananjaya, James. 1985. *Upacara-upacara lingkaran hidup di Trunyan, Bali* (Life-cycle ceremonies in Trunyan, Bali). Jakarta: Balai Pustaka.

De Zoete, Beryl, and Walter Spies. 1938. *Dance and Drama in Bali.* London: Faber & Faber.

DeBoer, Fredrik. 1996. "Two Modern Balinese Theater Genres: *Sendratari* and *Drama Gong.*" In Vickers, A., ed., *Being Modern in Bali: Image and Change,* 158–78. New Haven: Yale Southeast Asia Studies Monograph 43.

DeVale, Sue Carole, and Wayan Dibia. 1991. "*Sekar Anyar:* An Exploration of Meaning in Balinese *Gamelan.*" *World of Music* 33(1): 5–51.

Diamond, Jody. 1990. "There Is No They There." *Musicworks* 47 (Summer): 12–23.

———. 1985. "Interview with I Wayan Sinti: Combining the Old with the New." *Balungan* 1(3): 5–10.

Dibia, Wayan. 1996. *Kecak: The Vocal Chant of Bali.* Bali: Hartanto Art Books.

———. 1994. "Berkesenian di Antara Dua Dunia." *Wreta Cita* 1 (STSI Campus Magazine): 30–31.

———. 1992a. "*Arja:* A Sung Dance-Drama of Bali; A Study of Change and Transformation." Ph.D. diss., University of California at Los Angeles.

———. 1992b. "The *Arja* Theater: Vocal and Instrumental." In Schaareman, D., ed., *Balinese Music in Context: A Sixty-fifth Birthday Tribute to Hans Oesch*, 277–96. Winterthur: Amadeus Verlag, Forum Ethnomusicologicum 4.

Dunn, Deborah. 1983. "Topeng Pajegan." Ph.D. diss., Union Graduate School.

Epstein, David. 1995. *Shaping Time: Music, the Brain, and Performance*. New York: Schirmer.

Feld, Steven. 1982, *Sound and Sentiment: Birds, Weeping, Poetics, and Song in Kaluli Expression*. Philadelphia: University of Pennsylvania Press.

Feliciano, Francisco. 1983. *Four Contemporary Asian Composers*. Quezon City: New Day.

Forte, Allen. 1973. *The Structure of Atonal Music*. New Haven: Yale University Press.

Friedmann, Michael. 1985. "A Methodology for the Discussion of Contour: Its Application to Schoenberg's Music." *Journal of Music Theory* 29(2): 223–48.

Geertz, Clifford. 1980. *Negara: The Theater State in Nineteenth Century Bali*. Princeton: Princeton University Press.

———. 1973. *The Interpretation of Cultures*. New York: Basic Books.

———. 1960. *The Religion of Java*. Chicago: University of Chicago Press.

———. 1957. "Form and Variation in Balinese Village Structure." *American Anthropologist* 61:991–1012.

Geertz, Hildred. 1994. *Images of Power: Balinese Paintings Made for Gregory Bateson and Margaret Mead*. Honolulu: University of Hawaii Press.

Geertz, Hildred, and Clifford Geertz. 1975. *Kinship in Bali*. Chicago: University of Chicago Press.

Geriya, Wayan, et al. 1984. *Upacara Tradisionil Daerah Bali*. Jakarta: Proyek Inventariasi dan Dokumentasi Kebudayaan Daerah, Departemen Pendidikan dan Kebudayaan.

Gold, Lisa. 1998. "The *Gender Wayang* Repertoire in Theater and Ritual: A Study of Balinese Musical Meaning." Ph.D. diss., University of California at Berkeley

———. 1992. "Musical Expression in the *Wayang* Repertoire: A Bridge between Narrative and Ritual." In Schaareman, D., ed., *Balinese Music in Context: A Sixty-fifth Birthday Tribute to Hans Oesch*, 245–76. Winterthur: Amadeus Verlag, Forum Ethnomusicologicum 4.

Goris, Roelof. 1960. "The Temple System." In *Bali: Studies in Life, Thought, and Ritual*. The Hague: W. van Hoeve.

———. 1954. *Prasasti Bali: Inscripties Vóór Anak Wungçu*. 2 vols. Bandung: N. V. Masa Baru.

———. 1952. *Bali: Atlas Kebudajaan*. Indonesia: Departemen Pendidikan dan Kebudajaan.

Gould, Stephen Jay. 1991. "Genesis and Geology." In *Bully for Brontosaurus*, 402–15. New York: Norton.

Hanna, Willard. 1976. *Bali Profile: People, Events, Circumstances, 1001–1976*. New York: American Universities Field Staff.

Harjana, Suka. 1986. *Enam Tahun Pekan Komponis Muda (1979–1985): Sebuah Alternatif*. Jakarta: Dewan Kesenian Jakarta.

Harnish, David. 1997. "*I Madé Lebah* (1905?–1996)." *Ethnomusicology* 41(2): 261–64.

Hasty, Christopher. 1990. "The Myth of Linearity: Concepts of Time in Post-War Music." Conference paper, Joint Meeting of the American Musicological Society, the Society for Ethnomusicology, and the Society for Music Theory. Nov. 7–11, Oakland, Calif.

Heins, Ernst. 1990. *Music in Java: Current Bibliography, 1973–1989*. 2nd, enl. ed. Amsterdam: Institute of Musicology, Ethnomusicology Center "Jaap Kunst," University of Amsterdam, The Netherlands.

———. 1976. "On Jaap Kunst's 'Music in Java.'" (Letter to the editor) *Ethnomusicology* 20(1): 97–102.

Helmholtz, Heinrich. 1954 [1877]. *On The Sensations of Tone*. New York: Dover Editions.

Herbst, Edward. 1997. *Voices in Bali: Energies and Perceptions in Vocal Music and Dance Theater*. Hanover: University Press of New England.

Hobart, Mark. 1978. "The Path of the Soul: The Legitimacy of Nature in Balinese Conceptions of Space." In Miller, G. B., ed., *Natural Symbols in Southeast Asia*, 5–28. London: School of Oriental and African Studies, University of London.

Holland, Bernard. 1996. "All About 'Orientalism,' By Way of Brooklyn." *New York Times*, Feb. 20, C13.

Hood, Mantle. 1990. *"Balinese Gamelan Semar Pegulingan Saih Pitu*: The Modal System." *Progress Reports in Ethnomusicology* 3(2).

———. 1971. *The Ethnomusicologist*. New York: McGraw-Hill.

———. 1966. *"Slendro* and *Pelog* Redefined." *UCLA Selected Reports* 1: 28–48.

———. 1954. *The Nuclear Theme as a Determinant of Pathet in Javanese Music*. Groningen: J. B. Walters.

Hooykaas, C. 1964. *Agama Tirtha: Five Studies in Hindu-Balinese Religion*. Verhandelingen der Koninklijke Nederlandse Akademia van Wetenschappen, Afd. Letterkunde. Nieuwe Reeks 70(4).

———. 1966. *Suryasevana: The Way to God of a Balinese Siva Priest*. Verhandelingen der Koninklijke Nederlandse Akademia van Wetenschappen, Afd. Letterkunde. Nieuwe Reeks 72(3).

———. 1971. *Stuti and Stava*. Verhandelingen der Koninklijke Nederlandse Akademia van Wetenschappen, Afd. Letterkunde. Nieuwe Reeks 76.

Hume, Robert Ernest, trans. 1931. *The Thirteen Principal Upanishads*. 2nd rev. ed. London: Oxford University Press.

Illing, Kai-Torsten. 1990. *Das Joged Bumbung: Unterhaltungsmusik und -tanze auf Bali*. Teil I–II. Hamburg: Karl Dieter Wagner Verlag der Musikalienhandlung.

Jones, A. M. 1959. *Studies in African Music*. London: Oxford University Press.

Kartomi, Margaret. 1990. *On Concepts and Classifications of Musical Instruments*. Chicago: University of Chicago Press.

Keeler, Ward. 1975. "Musical Encounter in Java and Bali." *Indonesia* 19:85–126.

Kirk, Donald. 1966. "Bali Exorcises an Evil Spirit." *Reporter*, Dec. 15:42–43.

Korn, V. E. 1960 [1933]. "The Village Republic of Tenganan Pegeringsingan." In *Bali: Studies in Life, Thought, and Ritual*. The Hague: W. van Hoeve.

Kramer, Jonathan. 1988. *The Time of Music*. New York: Schirmer.

Kramer, Lawrence. 1993. "Music Criticism and the Postmodernist Turn: In Contrary Motion with Gary Tomlinson." *Current Musicology* 53:25–40.

Kubik, Gerhard. 1994. *Theory of African Music*, vol. 1. Wilhelmshaven: Florian Noetzel Verlag, Intercultural Music Studies 7.

Kunst, Jaap. 1968 [1927]. *Hindu-Javanese Musical Instruments*. 2nd ed. The Hague: Nijhoff; KITLV.

———. 1949. *Music in Java*. 2nd ed. 2 vols. The Hague: Martinus Nijhoff.

Kunst, Jaap, and C. J. A. Kunst-van Wely. 1925. *De Toonkunst van Bali*. Weltevreden: Koninklijk Bataviaasch Genootschaap.

Lansing, J. Stephen. 1995. *The Balinese*. Fort Worth: Harcourt Brace Case Studies in Cultural Anthropology.

———. 1983. *The Three Worlds of Bali*. Westport: Praeger/Greenwood Press.

Lerdahl, Fred, and Ray Jackendoff. 1983. *A Generative Theory of Tonal Music*. Cambridge: MIT Press.

Levin, Theodore. 1996. *The Hundred Thousand Fools of God: Musical Travels in Central Asia (and Queens, New York)*. Bloomington: Indiana University Press.

Lewiston, David, prod. 1967. *Golden Rain: Balinese Gamelan Music/Ketjak*. Nonesuch Records Explorer Series H–72028. Notes by Ruby Ornstein. *Kebyar* ensemble Gunung Sari from Peliatan and unidentified *kecak* group.

Lindsay, Jennifer. 1985. "Klasik, Kitsch, or Contemporary: A Study of the Javanese Performing Arts." Ph.D. diss., University of Sydney.

———. 1977. *Javanese Gamelan: Traditional Orchestra of Indonesia.* Singapore: Oxford University Press.

Lovric, Barbara. 1990. "Medical Semiology and the Semiotics of Dance." *Review of Indonesian and Malaysian Affairs,* 24:136–94.

Maceda, José. 1986. "A Concept of Time in a Music of Southeast Asia (A Preliminary Account)." *Ethnomusicology* 30(1): 11–53.

———. 1979. "A Search for an Old and a New Music in Southeast Asia." *Acta Musicologica* 51(1): 160–68.

Mack, Dieter. 1992."The *Gong Kebyar* Style of Pinda, Gianyar." In Schaareman, D., ed., *Balinese Music in Context: A Sixty-fifth Birthday Tribute to Hans Oesch,* 313–32. Winterthur: Amadeus Verlag, Forum Ethnomusicologicum 4.

Manuel, Peter. 1993. *Cassette Culture: Popular Music and Technology in North India.* Chicago: University of Chicago Press.

Martopangrawit, R. Ng. 1984 [1975]. "Catatan-catatan Pengetahuan Karawitan." Trans. Martin F. Hatch. In Becker, Judith, and Alan Feinstein, eds., *Karawitan,* 1:1–244. Ann Arbor: Center for Southeast Asian Studies, University of Michigan.

McPhee, Colin. 1970a. "The Balinese *Wayang Kulit* and Its Music." In Belo, Jane, ed., *Traditional Balinese Culture,* 146–97. New York: Columbia University Press.

———. 1970b. "Children and Music in Bali." In Belo, Jane, ed., *Traditional Balinese Culture,* 212–39. New York: Columbia University Press.

———. 1970c. "Dance in Bali." In Belo, Jane, ed., *Traditional Balinese Culture,* 290–321. New York: Columbia University Press.

———. 1966. *Music in Bali: A Study in Form and Instrumental Organization in Balinese Orchestral Music.* New Haven: Yale University Press.

———. 1946. *A House in Bali.* New York: John Day Co.

———. 1938. "A Musician Listens to Balinese Music." *Djawa* 18:50–57.

Mershon, Katharine. 1970. "Five Great Elementals: *Panca Mata Bhuta.*" In Belo, Jane, ed., *Traditional Balinese Culture,* 57–67. New York: Columbia University Press.

Meyer, Leonard. 1998. "A Universe of Universals." *Journal of Musicology* 16(1): 3–25.

———. 1967. *Music, The Arts, and Ideas.* Chicago: University of Chicago Press. [2nd ed., 1994]

———. 1956. *Emotion and Meaning in Music.* Chicago: University of Chicago Press.

Monson, Ingrid. 1996. *Saying Something: Jazz Improvisation and Interaction.* Chicago: University of Chicago Press.

Morgan, Robert. 1973. "Rewriting Music History: Second Thoughts on Ives and Varèse." *Musical Newsletter* 3(1): 3–12 (pt. 1); 3(2): 15–28 (pt. 2).

Mustika, Pandé, et al. 1979. *Menegenal Beberapa Jenis Sikap dan Pukulan Dalam Gong Kebyar.* Denpasar: Proyek Normalisasi Kehidupan Kampus Jakarta, Sub-Proyek ASTI Denpasar.

Nakamura, Kiyoshi. 1992. "Articulating Rituals: The Use of Ritual Music in Selat (Karangasem)." In Schaareman, D., ed., *Balinese Music in Context: A Sixty-fifth Birthday Tribute to Hans Oesch,* 151–72. Winterthur: Amadeus Verlag, Forum Ethnomusicologicum 4.

Nattiez, Jean-Jaques. 1993. "Simha Arom and the Return of Analysis to Ethnomusicology." *Music Analysis* 12(2): 241–65.

———. 1990. *Music and Discourse: Toward a Semiology of Music.* Translated by Carolyn Abbate. Princeton: Princeton University Press.

Oja, Carol. 1990. *Colin McPhee: A Composer in Two Worlds*. Washington, D.C.: Smithsonian Press.

Ornstein, Ruby Sue. 1971a. "Gamelan Gong Kebyar: The Development of a Balinese Musical Tradition." Ph.D. diss., University of California, Los Angeles.

———. 1971b. "The Five-Tone *Gamelan Angklung* of North Bali." *Ethnomusicology* 15(1): 71–80.

Palisca, Claude. 1980. "Theory, Theorists." In Sadie, Stanley, ed., *The New Grove's Dictionary of Music and Musicians,* 18:741–62. London: Macmillan.

Pandji, G. B. N., et al. 1974–75. *Perkembangan Legong Keraton Sebagai Seni Pertunjukan.* Denpasar: Proyek Pengembangan Sarana Wisata Budaya.

———. 1978. *Riwayat Hidup Seniman-Seniwati-Sekaha Terkemuka Daerah Bali.* Denpasar: Departemen Pendidikan and Kebudayaan Propinsi Bali.

Perlman, Marc. 1997. "Conflicting Interpretations: Indigenous Analysis and Historical Change in Central Javanese Music." *Asian Music* 28(1): 115–40.

———. 1993. "Unplayed Melodies: Music Theory in Postcolonial Java." Ph.D. diss., Wesleyan University.

Picard, Michel. 1996. "Dance and Drama in Bali: The Making of an Indonesian Art Form." In Vickers, A., ed., *Being Modern in Bali: Image and Change,* 115–57. New Haven: Yale Southeast Asia Studies Monograph 43.

———. 1990. "'Cultural Tourism' in Bali: Cultural Performances as Tourist Attraction." *Indonesia* 49:37–74.

Polansky, Larry. 1993. Review of Oja 1990 in *Ethnomusicology* 37(3): 437–41.

Powers, Harold. 1980a. "Mode." In Sadie, Stanley, ed., *The New Grove's Dictionary of Music and Musicians,* 12:376–450. London: Macmillan.

———. 1980b. "Language Models and Musical Analysis." *Ethnomusicology* 24(1): 1–60.

Proust, Marcel. 1970 [1928]. *Swann's Way.* Trans. C. K. Scott Moncrieff. New York: Vintage Books.

Rai, Wayan. 1996. "Balinese *Gambelan Semar Pegulingan Saih Pitu:* The Modal System." Ph.D. diss., University of Maryland, Baltimore County.

Rai, Wayan, Ketut Gdé Asnawa, and Ketut Warsa. 1978–79. *Mengenal Beberapa Sikap atau Gerak Dalam Tari Bali.* Denpasar: Proyek Normalisasi Kehidupan Kampus Jakarta, Sub-Proyek ASTI Denpasar.

Ramseyer, Urs. 1992. "The Voice of *Batara Bagus Selonding:* Music and Rituals of Tenganan Pageringsingan." In Schaareman, D., ed., *Balinese Music in Context: A Sixty-fifth Birthday Tribute to Hans Oesch,* 115–50. Winterthur: Amadeus Verlag, Forum Ethnomusicologicum 4.

———. 1977. *The Art and Culture of Bali.* Oxford: Oxford University Press.

Ramstedt, Martin. 1992. "Indonesian Cultural Policy in Relation to the Development of the Balinese Performing Arts." In Schaareman, D., ed., *Balinese Music in Context: A Sixty-fifth Birthday Tribute to Hans Oesch,* 59–84. Winterthur: Amadeus Verlag, Forum Ethnomusicologicum 4.

Ratner, Leonard. 1980. *Classic Music: Expression, Form, and Style.* New York: Schirmer.

Reich, Steve. 1974. *Writings about Music.* New York: New York University Press.

Reid, Anthony. 1993. *Southeast Asia in the Age of Commerce.* Vol. 2, *Expansion and Crisis.* New Haven: Yale University Press.

———. 1988. *Southeast Asia in the Age of Commerce.* Vol. 1, *The Land Below the Winds.* New Haven: Yale University Press.

Rembang, Nyoman. 1984–85a. *Hasil Pendokumentasian Notasi Gending-Gending Lelambatan Klasik Pegongan Daerah Bali.* Denpasar: Proyek Pengembangan Kesenian Bali, Departemen Pendidikan dan Kebudayaan.

————. 1984–85b. *Sekelumit Cara-cara Pembuatan Gamelan Bali*. Denpasar: Proyek Pengembangan Kesenian Bali, Departemen Pendidikan dan Kebudayaan.

————. 1973. *Gambelan Gambuh dan Gambelan-gambelan Lainnya di Bali*. Denpasar: Kertas Kerja pada Workshop Gambuh, 25 Agustus s/d 1 September.

Rembang, Nyoman, and Madé Bandem. 1976. *Perkembangan Topeng Sebagai Seni Pertunjukan*. Denpasar: Proyek Penggalian, Pembinaan, Pengembangan Seni Klasik/Traditional dan Kesenian Baru, Pemerintah Daerah Tingkat I Bali.

Rendha, Wayan, et al. 1992. *Penelitian dan Pemetaan Potensi Kebudayaan Daerah Bali*. Denpasar: Bappeda Tingkat I Bali/Universitas Udayana.

Richter, Karl. 1992. "*Slendro-Pelog* and the Conceptualisation of Balinese Music: Remarks on the *Gambuh* Tone System." In Schaareman, D., ed., *Balinese Music in Context: A Sixty-fifth Birthday Tribute to Hans Oesch*, 195–220. Winterthur: Amadeus Verlag, Forum Ethnomusicologicum 4.

Robinson, Geoffrey. 1995. *The Dark Side of Paradise: Political Violence in Bali*. Ithaca: Cornell University Press.

Rosen, Charles. 1971. *The Classical Style*. New York: Viking Press.

Rowell, Lewis. 1992. *Music and Musical Thought in Early India*. Chicago: University of Chicago Press.

Rubinstein, Raechelle. 1992. "*Pepaosan*: Challenges and Change." In Schaareman, D., ed., *Balinese Music in Context: A Sixty-fifth Birthday Tribute to Hans Oesch*, 85–114. Winterthur: Amadeus Verlag, Forum Ethnomusicologicum 4.

Ryker, Harrison. 1990. *New Music in the Orient*. Buren: Frits Knuf.

Sadra, Wayan. 1991. *I Wayan Berata [sic]: Proses Perjalanannya Menjadi Empu Karawitan*. Surakarta: Sekolah Tinggi Seni Indonesia.

Sanger, Annette. 1992. "Status Relationships in the Performing Arts of Bali." In Schaareman, D., ed., *Balinese Music in Context: A Sixty-fifth Birthday Tribute to Hans Oesch*, 15–28. Winterthur: Amadeus Verlag, Forum Ethnomusicologicum 4.

Schaareman, Danker. 1992. "The Shining of the Deity: *Selunding* Music of Tatulingga (Karangasem) and Its Ritual Use." In Schaareman, D., ed., *Balinese Music in Context: A Sixty-fifth Birthday Tribute to Hans Oesch*, 173–94. Winterthur: Amadeus Verlag, Forum Ethnomusicologicum 4.

————. 1986. *Tatulingga: Tradition and Continuity; An Investigation in Ritual and Social Organization in Bali*. Basel: Wepf & Co. Verlag.

————. 1980. "The *Gamelan Gambang* of Tatulingga, Bali." *Ethnomusicology* 24(3): 465–82.

Schlager, Ernst. 1976. *Rituelle Siebenton-Musik auf Bali*. Winterthur: Amadeus Verlag, Forum Ethnomusicologicum 1.

————. 1965. "Von Arbeitsrhythmus zur Bali." In *Festschrift Alfred Buhler/hrsg. von Carl A. Schmitz, Robert Wildhaber*. Basel: Pharos Verlag Hansrudolf Schwabe.

Schoenberg, Arnold. 1976. *Fundamentals of Music Composition*. Ed. Gerald Strang and Leonard Stein. New York: St. Martin's Press.

Seebass, Tilman. 1996. "Changes in Balinese Musical Life: *Kebyar* in the 1920s and 1930s." In Vickers, A., ed., *Being Modern in Bali: Image and Change*, 71–91. New Haven: Yale Southeast Asia Studies Monograph 43.

————. 1986. "A Note on *Kebyar* in Modern Bali." *Orbis Musicae* 9:103–21.

Seebass, Tilman, I. G. B. N Panji, Nyoman Rembang, and I Poedijono. 1976. *The Music of Lombok: A First Survey*. Bern: Forum Ethnomusicologicum 2.

Simpen, Wayan. 1979. "Sejarah Perkembangan Gong Gedé." Manuscript.

Stock, Jonathan. 1993. "The Application of Schenkerian Analysis to Ethnomusicology: Problems and Possibilities." *Music Analysis* 12(2): 215–40.

Stockhausen, Karlheinz. 1978. "World Music." *The World of Music* 21(1): 3–14.

Straus, Joseph. 1987. "The Problem of Prolongation in Posttonal Music." *Journal of Music Theory* 31:1–21.

Stravinsky, Igor. 1936. *Chronicle of My Life*. London: Victor Gollancz.

Stuart-Fox, David. 1992. *Bibliography of Bali: 1920–1990*. Leiden: KITLV Press.

Stucky, Stephen. 1981. *The Music of Witold Lutoslawski*. Cambridge: Cambridge University Press.

Sumarsam. 1995. *Gamelan: Cultural Interaction and Musical Development in Central Java*. Chicago: University of Chicago Press.

———. 1984a. "Inner Melody in Javanese *Gamelan*." In Becker, Judith, and Alan Feinstein, eds., *Karawitan*, 1:245–304. Ann Arbor: Center for Southeast Asian Studies, University of Michigan.

———. 1984b. "*Gamelan* Music and the Javanese *Wayang Kulit*." In Morgan, S., and L. J. Sears, eds., *Aesthetic Tradition and Cultural Transition in Java and Bali*, 105–16. Center for Southeast Asian Studies Monograph 2. Madison: University of Wisconsin Press.

Sumarsam and Vincent McDermott. 1975. "Inner Melody in Javanese *Gamelan*." *Asian Music* 7:3–13.

Sutton, R. Anderson. 1991. *Traditions of Gamelan Music in Java: Musical Pluralism and Regional Identity*. Cambridge: Cambridge University Press.

Tenzer, Michael. 1998 [1991]. *Balinese Music*. Berkeley: Periplus Editions.

———. 1997. "The Life in *Gendhing*: Approaches to Javanese *Gamelan*." *Indonesia* 63: 169–86.

———. 1993. "Western Music in the Context of World Music." In Morgan, R., ed., *Man and Music IX: Modern Times*, 388–411. London: Macmillan.

Toth, Andrew. 1993. "Selera Yang Selaras: Pepatutan Gong Ditinjau Dari Segi Akustika dan Estetika." *Mudra: Jurnal Seni Budaya*. Edisi Khusus, 92–117.

———. 1980. *Recordings of the Traditional Music of Bali and Lombok*. Bloomington: Society for Ethnomusicology Special Series no. 4.

———. 1975. "The *Gamelan Luang* of Tangkas, Bali." *Selected Reports in Ethnomusicology* 2(2): 65–79.

Vickers, Adrian. 1996. "Modernity and Being *Moderen*: An Introduction." In Vickers, A., ed., *Being Modern in Bali: Image and Change*, 1–37. New Haven: Yale Southeast Asia Studies Monograph 43.

———. 1992. "*Kidung* Meters and the Interpretation of the *Malat*." In Schaareman, D., ed., *Balinese Music in Context: A Sixty-fifth Birthday Tribute to Hans Oesch*, 221–44. Winterthur: Amadeus Verlag, Forum Ethnomusicologicum 4.

———. 1991. "Ritual Written: The Song of the *Ligya*, or the Killing of the Rhinoceros." In Geertz, H., ed., *State and Society in Bali: Historical, Textual, and Anthropological Approaches*, 85–136. Leiden: KITLV Press.

———. 1989. *Bali: A Paradise Created*. Berkeley: Periplus Editions.

———. 1987. "Hinduism and Islam in Indonesia: Bali and the *Pasisir* World." *Indonesia* 44: 30–58.

———. 1986. "The Desiring Prince: A Study of the Kidung Malat as Text." Ph.D. diss., University of Sydney.

———. 1985. "The Realm of the Senses: Images of the Court Music of Pre-Colonial Bali." *Imago Musicae* 2:143–77.

Vitale, Wayne. 1996. CD Notes. *Music of the Gamelan Gong Kebyar*, vol. 2. Vital Records 402.

———. 1990. "*Kotekan*: The Technique of Interlocking Parts in Balinese Music." *Balungan* 4(2): 2–15.

Vonck, Henrice M. 1997. "*Manis* and *Keras* in Image, Word, and Music of *Wayang Kulit* in Tejakula, North-Bali." Accompanied by CD-ROM and audio CD. University of Amsterdam. Print: Bureau Grafische Produkties, UvA.

Wallis, Richard. 1979. "The Voice as a Mode of Cultural Expression in Bali." Ph.D. diss., University of Michigan, Ann Arbor.

Wenten, Nyoman. 1992. *"Gamelan Semar Pegulingan:* Court Music in Transition." In Schaareman, D., ed., *Balinese Music in Context: A Sixty-fifth Birthday Tribute to Hans Oesch,* 297–312. Winterthur: Amadeus Verlag, Forum Ethnomusicologicum 4.

Wiratini, Madé. 1991. *Condong and Its Roles in Balinese Dance Drama.* M.A. thesis: University of California at Los Angeles.

Witzleben, Lawrence. 1997. "Whose Ethnomusicology? Western Ethnomusicology and the Study of Asian Music." *Ethnomusicology* 41(2): 220–42.

Yampolsky, Philip. 1995. "Forces for Change in the Regional Performing Arts of Indonesia." *Bijdragen tot de Taal-, Land- en Volkenkunde* 151(4): 700–725.

———. 1987. *Lokananta: A Discography of the National Recording Company of Indonesia, 1957–1985.* Bibliography Series no. 10. Madison: University of Wisconsin, Center for Southeast Asian Studies.

Zaslaw, Neal. 1989. *Mozart's Symphonies: Context, Performance, Practice, Reception.* Oxford: Oxford University Press.

Zoetmulder, P. J. 1974. *Kalangwan: A Survey of Old Javanese Literature.* The Hague: Martinus Nijhoff.

Zurbuchen, Mary. 1987. *The Language of Balinese Shadow Theater.* Princeton: Princeton University Press.

Index (including Index-Glossary of Indonesian and Balinese Terms)

Numbers in boldface direct the reader to definitions for most Indonesian and Balinese terms (but not titles or proper names) appearing more than once in the book. Many English technical terms are also indicated in this way. The designations *n, f,* and *ph* refer to footnote, figure, and photograph.